W9-BQV-284

Gift from Laura, isTmas 2008

1st visit w/ Mike & Ted, 9/30/09-10/5/09

INSIDERS' GUIDE® TO

PITTSBURGH

FOURTH EDITION

JENN PHILLIPS, LORIANN HOFF OBERLIN, AND EVAN M. PATTAK
REVISED BY MICHELE MARGITTAI

INSIDERS' GUIDE®

GUILFORD, CONNECTICUT
AN IMPRINT OF THE GLOBE PEQUOT PRESS

The prices and rates in this guidebook were confirmed at press time. We recommend, however, that you call establishments before traveling to obtain current information.

INSIDERS' GUIDE®

Text design by LeAnna Weller Smith
Maps by XNR Productions, Inc. © Morris Book Publishing, LLC

ISSN 1546-3133
ISBN 978-0-7627-4796-2

Printed in the United States of America
10 9 8 7 6 5 4 3 2 1

CONTENTS

Directory of Maps

VENANGO COUNTY

MERCER COUNTY

CLARION COUNTY

OHIO

New Castle

LAWRENCE COUNTY

BUTLER COUNTY

PENNSYLVANIA

Area of Detail

Butler

ARMSTRONG COUNTY

Kittanning

BEAVER COUNTY

Beaver

Ohio River

ALLEGHENY COUNTY

Allegheny River

INDIANA COUNTY

Sewickley
Coraopolis

McCandless

New Kensington

Penn Hills

Moon

Pittsburgh

Monroeville

McKeesport

Greensburg

Latrobe

WASHINGTON COUNTY

WESTMORELAND COUNTY

Washington

GREENE COUNTY

Monongahela River

FAYETTE COUNTY

Uniontown

SOMERSET COUNTY

WEST VIRGINIA

MARYLAND

N

0   10   20 km
0   10   20 mi.

Western Pennsylvania

Greater Pittsburgh

Downtown Pittsburgh

PREFACE

When you arrive in Pittsburgh, what sort of folks will you find here? Southwestern Pennsylvania is diverse enough that generalization about our residents can be tricky. Nevertheless, most people tote around an obsolete image of Pittsburghers that was forged in the furnaces of our steel mills. They envision us as a rough-hewn breed, square-shouldered, lantern-jawed men toughened by backbreaking labor in sweltering mills and subterranean mines.

This hardly dovetails with the reality of modern Pittsburgh, which you'll discover to be a sophisticated, diverse city with an economy driven by service and software industries and, to a lesser extent, manufacturing. Nor does this dated image allow for the increasingly important roles of women and minorities in the local economy and society. It's true that the "old boys" network that ran the mills and mines was a tad slow to provide opportunities for women and minorities. The dominance of steel and coal, however, is part of our history, fuller participation of women and minorities is a thing of the present.

Shopworn as that traditional image of our residents may be, as most stereotypes, it still can tell us revealing things about Pittsburghers. First, it speaks of our friendliness, probably our defining characteristic. We are, after all, a people who built America's greatest industrial center, watched it collapse, then rolled up our sleeves and constructed a new, multifaceted economy. In accomplishing all that, we were a cradle of the American labor movement. We're veterans of collective action and the cooperative spirit it requires.

Thus, Pittsburghers are, above all, a friendly, unpretentious people. It doesn't matter who you are or where you're from. Yinz—our peculiar version of the second person plural—will be accepted here. Nor is there a limit to our friendliness. The spirit of volunteerism is alive and well in Southwestern Pennsylvania, among individuals and corporations. We've developed a far-reaching network of civic and charitable organizations to keep our residents from falling through the cracks. We'll give you the shirts off our backs—skin, too, if that would help.

This uncommon friendliness, however, has its downside—a relentless focus on neighborhoods and the local scene. Our neighborhoods are charming, some even unique, and a considerable strength of our region. We are devoted to them. Allegheny County alone boasts 130 municipalities, while the region is carved into 100 school districts. Think of the duplicative costs for elections, for garbage collection, for street maintenance, for a hundred other services. Whatever its costs, we cherish our parochialism. Pity the poor politician who runs on a platform of municipal consolidation. He'll be tarred with the dreaded "M" word—Metropolitanism—and hooted back to the murky obscurity that produced him.

Those who relocate to this region become keenly sensitive to this duality. They are overwhelmed with Welcome Wagons of friendliness but never quite accepted as natives. Michelle Madoff, a native Canadian who for years was a Pittsburgh city councilwoman and one of our most prominent and high-profile public officials, never ceased to wonder at our attitude. "I've been here for 35 years," she was wont to say, "and I'm still not a Pittsburgher."

Can't be helped, Councilwoman. If you're not from this city, you're not of this city.

This engaging friendliness coupled with a tendency toward the insular marks our culture as well. We are a region of stunning and diverse cultural opportunities. These include Carnegie Museums of Pittsburgh, the Andy Warhol Museum, the Pittsburgh Symphony—world-class institutions each. Our Downtown boasts five halls for the performing arts, including two glittering temples, Heinz Hall and the Benedum Center for the Performing Arts. Our colleges and universities offer community theater, and we boast highly regarded opera and ballet companies. The region is rich in art galleries, well-spaced through many communities.

Nevertheless, the arts community has to put a great deal of effort into reminding us Pittsburghers of the presence of these riches. That's because we're likely to set ourselves on a particular track—one that often involves a path between neighborhood, workplace, and favorite shopping mecca—and forget all else.

Finally, while the typical image of Pittsburghers is accurate in some regard, off the mark in others, perhaps the most glaring omission is that it doesn't begin to acknowledge our rich and ready sense of humor. Yes, we tend to be traditional; our focus tends to be local. We know it, though, and we're comfortable with it. If you want to poke fun at our parochialism and odd turns of phrase, go right ahead—we'll laugh along with you.

—Jenn Phillips

ACKNOWLEDGMENTS

It's been a pleasure to have the opportunity to work on the *Insiders' Guide to Pittsburgh*, and I want to thank my editors. I love Pittsburgh, and authoring this guidebook has served to reinforce all the reasons why.

In the early spring in Pittsburgh, especially when we have some unseasonably warm days in February or March, it's common to find the doors of shops and homes propped open and a lot of people standing around outside smiling broadly. Authoring this book involves a significant amount of research, and what I've found in this case—and in my other work as a writer in the Greater Pittsburgh area—is that office doors and hearts here are typically just as open as those we fling wide in early spring.

I would especially like to thank Beth Geisler at the Greater Pittsburgh Convention and Visitors Bureau, as well as Ellen Roth, Ph.D., president of Getting to the Point, a relocation services company. Beth made it very easy for me to feel confident that I'd included all the best attractions in our area, through her comprehensive knowledge of the region and the copious literature she provided. I encourage all visitors to get to the center of downtown. The GPCVB really knows its stuff!

Ellen, who was honored by the governor as one the 50 top women in business in the state, was simply delightful to talk with, and she generously spent time on the phone with me, which gave me a very good feel for what it means to relocate to Pittsburgh, especially if one is doing so as a "trailing spouse," without the ready-made community and commitments a new job provides. This new understanding proved very helpful to me as I added material to the book for newcomers to our area.

From another standpoint, I owe thanks and acknowledgment to coauthors on the first edition of this book, Loriann Hoff Oberlin and Evan Pattak. No matter whose names appear on the cover of this book in coming years, the Insiders' Guide will always owe much to them. So much of the original research here is theirs—and finely done it is.

On the second edition, my good friend and colleague Tanya Reyes assisted me by making the thousands of phone calls involved in fact checking. And during some difficult life circumstances that occurred while I was completing the book, my colleague David Doorley stepped in with great efficaciousness and helped me add good, new entries to several chapters. Thank you, thank you, David!

I was also fortunate to be able to call on another local writer, Michael Dongilli, to write the sidebar in Spectator Sports on our new stadiums, because only a true, blue (or should that be gold?) sports fan could do these terrific new facilities justice.

And finally, I'd like to thank all the people—friends, family, business associates, folks I've just run into—who've expressed enthusiasm about the *Insiders' Guide to Pittsburgh* and my completion of the book you now hold in your hands.

—Jenn Phillips

First and foremost, thanks to the authors of the previous editions of this book, Jenn Phillips, Loriann Hoff Oberlin, and Evan M. Pattak. Though we haven't met, I could sense the love and pride they feel for Pittsburgh in their writings, and appreciated their attention to detail when compiling the many entries in this guide. I would also like to thank my editors for their guidance and help, and the publisher for the opportunity to work on this edition.

Heartfelt thanks to Lynne Glover, a college friend who referred this project to me. Lynne and I talked about this book soon after seeing each other at one of my favorite Pittsburgh events, the WYEP Summer Music Festival. There, along with hundreds of others, we sat on the North Shore and looked over the bandstand and across the river to the nearby downtown skyline. While enjoying great music, Lynne and I talked about how we love living in Pittsburgh and how much has changed here since our college days. Only a week or so later, she called about the opportunity to revise this guide. I couldn't believe my luck—working on a book that showcases a region that often is overlooked, but is absolutely, in my opinion, one of this country's best places to live.

Lynne, who works for VisitPittsburgh, was also a valuable source for suggestions about new attractions and regional destinations. Kudos to the entire staff at VisitPittsburgh and Beverly Morrow-Jones, the Executive Director of Marketing and Communications. They provide tremendous resources for residents and visitors who want to learn more about the region. I strongly urge a trip to their office or a visit to their Web site!

I would also like to thank Lisa Starr, an architecture student and friend, who assisted with updating the Architecture and Nightlife chapters. She did a great job, even recruiting her mom to spend a day with her touring the downtown while using the Architecture chapter as her guide. They both discovered new places in their hometown!

To my wonderful husband Peter—thank you—for your support and advice during this project. Neither Peter nor I are Pittsburgh natives, but we share a great love for this city, our adopted home. One of our first dates was a three-hour walking tour through downtown Pittsburgh, each pointing out favorite buildings and spaces to the other. Now, almost a dozen years later, we continue to explore—eating at new restaurants with friends, visiting attractions with our two young children, Sophia and Nico, and finding ways to give back to our community. Working on this book offered us opportunities to reminisce about those places and events, and to discover new destinations and experiences yet to be enjoyed.

Finally, a thank you to all of the Pittsburghers I have met while revising this guide. From an impromptu coffee shop conversation with four gentlemen who offered a long list of restaurant recommendations, to the many emails from friends and colleagues listing their favorite attractions, I was overwhelmed by the enthusiasm and pride Pittsburghers feel for their hometown. I hope, after reading this book, you, too, will share our excitement and enjoy your own explorations of the Pittsburgh region.

—Michele Margittai

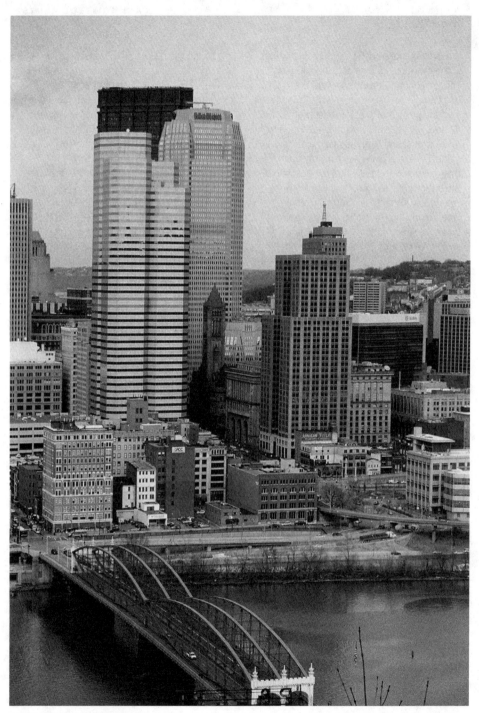

The Smithfield Street Bridge. JENNIFER QUINT

HOW TO USE THIS BOOK ?

Many city guides languish on living-room tables. It is our fondest hope that the *Insiders' Guide to Pittsburgh* isn't one of them.

Rather, our purpose in producing this book is to provide you with the most complete, most dependable resource about Pittsburgh. We hope that you consult it often, that it will become your best source of information about the city, its people, and its amenities. While our guide does not strive to be exhaustive—it does not include every restaurant or hotel in the region, for example—we've tried to provide the best and the brightest of Pittsburgh.

We've researched and organized the guide so that it will serve as a valuable resource about Pittsburgh for those newly relocating to the city as well as for tourists and visitors. But we also believe that even longtime residents will find this an indispensable tool. If you're one of those veteran Pittsburghers, don't be embarrassed to refer to this book again and again. As we found out as we wrote this book, there is much more to this town than even natives could know.

This guide includes useful information about restaurants, accommodations, shopping, nightlife, festivals, spectator sports, recreation, attractions, and day trips. We also have compiled key information that should help you navigate the daily course of life. We've included a chapter about elementary and secondary schools, as well as a chapter about Pittsburgh's colleges, universities, and trade schools. A chapter details many of Pittsburgh's most interesting neighborhoods, while others outline services and opportunities for kids and senior citizens.

You'll also find chapters about art, architecture, health care, transportation, golf,

media, and worship. In some cases, a Pittsburgh amenity or feature fits comfortably in more than one chapter. For example, a description of the Pittsburgh Zoo & PPG Aquarium would be at home in both the Kidstuff and Attractions chapters. In such cases, a full write-up is provided in one chapter, with a shorter description—as well as a reference to the primary coverage—in the second chapter.

Any definition of Pittsburgh is bound to be somewhat arbitrary. Most would agree that Pittsburgh does not end with the city's limits, but just what should be included? This guide goes beyond the city and Allegheny County to include Armstrong and Butler Counties to the north, Westmoreland County to the east, parts of Washington County to the south, and Beaver County to the west.

In determining our geographic definition of Pittsburgh, we imagined you asking the question, "What shall we do today?" By including the additional counties, we've tried to provide as many answers to that question as possible.

To help you locate information quickly, we've followed a specific geographic rotation—Downtown, North, East, South, West—in all chapters where such organization is appropriate. In other chapters, material is organized in ways that make the most sense for readers. Where we've strayed from the geographic breakdown, we'll tell you in the chapter introduction.

In the Day Trips chapter, for example, we've transcended the boundaries of Pittsburgh to include destinations within a three-hour drive of the city. In researching Senior Scene, we noticed that many municipal services are restricted to residents of the offering municipalities. Therefore, we have presented

Pittsburgh as seen from the West End. ALAN AND BARBARA VENTO

those services by county and reverted to standard organization for unrestricted services and opportunities.

In all cases, you can quickly determine if an entity or service is included by checking the comprehensive index in the back of the book.

You'll find several special features that have been developed for your convenience and enjoyment. Frequently called phone numbers and sources of additional information are highlighted in gray boxes. New to town and need a physician? You'll find the phone numbers for physician referral agencies in the Health Care chapter.

We've captured many interesting quick-hitters about Pittsburgh; these "Insiders' Tips" (indicated by ℹ are spaced throughout the book. You'll also find "Close-ups"—feature stories about the city, its residents, characteristics, and peculiarities. Both the "Tips" and "Close-ups" will pique your interest in Pittsburgh.

In the Restaurants and Accommodations chapters, each entry includes from one to four dollar signs to give you some idea of the price of a meal or an overnight stay. Prices represent comparisons within the Pittsburgh market only. Thus, a restaurant listed with "$$$$" would be among Pittsburgh's more expensive establishments, but the price should not be compared to those of restaurants in other cities.

Finally, a word about area codes. The Pittsburgh region has two area codes: 412 and 724. Remember that if you're dialing anywhere outside your area code—even if it's only across town—you'll need to dial 1 and the appropriate area code before the seven-digit phone number.

We hope you enjoy the *Insiders' Guide to Pittsburgh* and use it often. One of the recurring themes of the guide is the helpfulness and neighborliness of Pittsburgh residents. Being neighborly Pittsburgh residents ourselves, we may drop in on you one day. It's okay if we find this guide on your coffee table . . . so long as the book is well-thumbed.

AREA OVERVIEW

Carved out of hilltops, nestled into valleys, and separated by rivers, the Pittsburgh region is a place people eagerly discover. In years gone by, if you told friends of an upcoming visit to Pittsburgh, they might have offered their immediate condolences. Images of the "Steel City" translated into perceptions of smoke, soot, grime, and grunge.

The industrial age, sparked by the War of 1812, saw Pittsburgh capitalize on its bituminous coal resources. Mining, coupled with iron, steel, and glass production, flourished, with three convenient rivers to distribute the finished products to the rest of the country. With all that industry, it's no wonder Pittsburgh was called the Smoky City.

Early morning streets were darkened, and building exteriors were blanketed with the filthy remnants of heavy industry. In 1941 Pittsburgh had a higher rate of pneumonia than any other U.S. city. Pittsburgh pride and partnership took exception to the notion that it was simply a dirty city, knowing that if outsiders peered beneath the surface, they'd find a region with deep roots, bursting with life, strong traditions, positive aesthetic properties, and so much potential that it's still being tapped today. Determination to transform the old Pittsburgh into the new paid off in ways even the best urban planners could not have predicted.

The city's first renaissance was initiated in the 1950s, shortly after World War II, as then-mayor David L. Lawrence began a campaign called "Smoke Must Go." Railroad and shipping companies converted from coal-fired to diesel engines, and the steel and coal industries responded in kind with better technologies for eliminating airborne pollutants. Residents even switched from coal furnaces to much cleaner oil, electric, or natural gas.

That was just the first transformation. Renaissance II followed in the 1980s, under the tenure of the late Mayor Richard S. Caliguiri. Old buildings were razed and more modern towering structures were welcomed to the city skyline. This reformation occurred not only in Pittsburgh and in Allegheny County, but also in outlying towns where mills and factories had forged the foundation of many Western Pennsylvania communities. Areas such as Beaver, Butler, Armstrong, Westmoreland, and Washington Counties had their share of coal mines, steel mills, and industrial sites.

When the wrecking ball demolished the last two blast furnaces at the Jones & Laughlin steel mill in the early 1980s, much of the region's industrial strength crumbled with them, as did thousands of jobs. Workers who knew everything about blast furnaces and organized labor knew little of service industries, reengineering, and how their lives would be affected by Pittsburgh's continuing renaissance.

One thing, however, sets Pittsburgh apart from its counterpart cities—the people who call it home. They are strong, proud, and particularly friendly, even amid adversity.

PITTSBURGH'S PERSONALITY

Pittsburghers stay put. It's not that we think there is no other comfortable place to live, it's just that we value our roots and traditions, our familiar routines, and even our minor frustrations. The occasional complaints about bridge repairs or tunnel traffic along the parkways are understandable, but take away the gorgeous view as we exit the Fort Pitt Tunnel entering the city, and we'd really have something to complain about. Sure, some neighborhoods have more parking problems than others, particularly in the winter, but as for the seasons, we revel in all four.

The Pittsburgh climate is not particularly harsh. Some winters we've been hard hit by snow, and summers have occasionally been real scorchers, but by national standards, the region doesn't stand out weather-wise. A Pittsburgher's only concern might be springtime flooding and a few too many rainy or overcast days. Such is our weather.

If it's a chilly day, you might see us skating in Schenley Park, and on a cold winter's eve it's a hockey night in Pittsburgh with fans packing the Mellon Arena to watch our Penguins. Spring urges us out among friends, visiting neighborhood parks, taking easy day trips, and heading to the stadium to root for the Bucs. In summer the big amusement parks open—Kennywood, Idlewild, and Sandcastle. Office workers take their lunches outdoors and enjoy the Three Rivers Arts Festival in conjunction with their meals. And who could forget Fourth of July fireworks at the Point or the Three Rivers Regatta each July? (See our Annual Events chapter for more detailed descriptions of these popular events.)

As the leaves turn color, it's once again time for those glorious weekend getaways. We'll drive a distance just to pick our own pumpkin out of a patch on an outlying farm. In autumn, we're often back to school, cheering on our Steelers, taking in the fall flower show at Phipps Conservatory and Botanical Gardens, and revisiting and enjoying a vast array of other indoor attractions.

Having such splendid seasons adds to Pittsburgh's appeal. It's no wonder that our pleasant city has often served as the on-screen double for much larger New York City. Film crews have camped out at Pittsburgh landmarks throughout the decades to make

i In 2005 the Pennsylvania Department of Transportation listed Mt. Washington as a State Scenic Byway because of its beautiful views of the rivers and downtown. For a unique Pittsburgh experience, travel to the top via the Duquesne Incline, (412) 381-1665.

such films as *Flashdance* and *Hoffa,* as well as cinema picks such as *Diabolique, Silence of the Lambs, The Mothman Prophecies,* and *Wonder Boys.*

IT'S A 'BURGH THING

Just as the South has its drawl and New England its Yankee accent, Pittsburgh has its own dialect (see this chapter's Close-up). Beyond the spoken word, many other items foster familiarity among the locals. You haven't eaten deli fare unless you've actually experienced the fries and slaw *inside* the sandwich, with Heinz ketchup of course. People all over the world enjoy ham sandwiches, but ours are chipped-chopped. Pittsburghers do take their food seriously. While many ethnic groups enjoy special cuisines and dishes, there's a certain kind of preparation that goes into native pierogies, kielbasa, stuffed cabbages, and Iron City Beer. Ice cream is standard, but Klondike Bars can't be beat. This, friends, is only a sampling of what's on the menu (see the Restaurants chapter to whet your appetite even more).

FAMOUS FACES

If you feel you've already experienced Pittsburgh's personality, it could be a direct result of a famous Pittsburgher. Indeed, this city has served as hometown for more than just Andrew Carnegie and H. J. Heinz, names easily associated with Pittsburgh. Did you know that Arnold Palmer grew up in Latrobe, not far from the origin of Mister Rogers? The famous golfer still has a car dealership in Westmoreland County.

Other natives include actress Shirley Jones, artist Andy Warhol (whose surname was originally Warhola), playwright August Wilson, composer Stephen Foster, and actor Michael Keaton, who has returned home to make box-office hits such as *Gung Ho.*

Television producer Steven Bochco attended Carnegie Mellon University, and novelist Michael Chabon hit it big with *Mysteries of Pittsburgh,* inspired during his stint as an

Downtown Pittsburgh viewed from Grandview. MICHAEL D. REED

undergraduate student at the University of Pittsburgh. Chabon went on to write *Wonder Boys,* the movie version of which was filmed here as well.

Although it's technically outside our coverage area, we must point out that Jimmy Stewart was born and raised in Indiana, Pennsylvania, where his father held on to the family hardware store just in case Jimmy's film career didn't pan out. Well, Jimmy didn't need that contingency plan!

Jim Delligatti, a McDonald's franchisee in Western Pennsylvania, introduced the ingredients from his special sauce to a sesame seed bun, creating a sandwich better known today as the Big Mac. Other drive-through chains served double-decker burgers, and Delligatti wanted his creation to be big, so in 1967 the Big Mac was introduced for 49 cents. It took several improvements and lots of fun promotions to get to the Big Mac as we know it today.

In a town known for the industrial strength of men, women have made their marks. Among them are Nellie Bly, the famous newspaper reporter; Rachel Carson, a local biologist whose book *Silent Spring* helped set the environmental movement in motion; and Mary Cassatt, an artist who later found fame in France as the leading female impressionist painter.

Finally, just as appreciated is Mr. Yuk. That's right; the widely recognized safety symbol used to warn children away from dangerous substances was created at Children's Hospital of Pittsburgh.

ECONOMIC INDICATORS

As we've already mentioned, Pittsburgh's economic infrastructure has been transformed. Today over 70 companies with at least one billion dollars in revenues maintain headquarters

Pittsburgh Vital Statistics

Founded: 1758
Incorporated: 1816
Size: 55.5 square miles
Elevation: 1,223 feet
Population:
   City of Pittsburgh (2006): 312,819
   Allegheny County (2006): 1,223,411
Pittsburgh mayor: Luke Ravenstahl
Pennsylvania governor: Ed Rendell
Airport: Pittsburgh International Airport
Average temperatures:
   July: 82.5° F
   January: 20.8° F
Average yearly precipitation: 37.3 inches
Colleges and universities: 33 in Western Pennsylvania, including the University of Pittsburgh, Duquesne University, Carnegie Mellon University, Robert Morris University
Daily newspapers: *Pittsburgh Post-Gazette, Pittsburgh Tribune-Review*
Radio stations: 18 AM, 25 FM
Television stations: 11
Driving laws: Unrestricted driver's license at age 18; junior driver's license (restricted) at 16; maximum speed limit 65 mph; seat belts mandatory for driver and all front-seat passengers.
Famous Pittsburghers: Christina Aguilera, Andrew Carnegie, Rachel Carson, Mary Cassatt, Perry Como, Annie Dillard, Scott Glenn, Jeff Goldblum, Martha Graham, Lena Horne, Shirley Jones, Michael Keaton, Gene Kelly, Oscar Levant, Rob Marshall, David McCullough, Dennis Miller, Joe Namath, Arnold Palmer, William Powell, Fred Rogers, Gertrude Stein, Andy Warhol, August Wilson.

Important dates in history:
1754: Captain William Trent begins construction of Fort Prince George for Virginia. French soldiers and Indians capture the fort soon thereafter.
1758: Brig. Gen. John Forbes in charge of an expedition to reclaim the fort, now known as Fort Duquesne. The French desert the fort, and Forbes names his conquest "Pittsburgh" in honor of British leader William Pitt.
1787: Pennsylvania charters the Pittsburgh Academy, later to become the University of Pittsburgh.
1790: The first U.S. Census shows Pittsburgh with a population of 376, while Allegheny County has 10,309 citizens.
1816: Pittsburgh is incorporated as a city.
1845: The Great Fire destroys 56 acres and 1,000 buildings in the heart of the city. Among the landmarks burned: Monongahela House, Bank of Pittsburgh, Western University, and the Monongahela Bridge.

1848: Andrew Carnegie, age 13, arrives from Scotland.

1856: Pittsburgh hosts the first Republican National Convention.

1858: The Sons of Vulcan, an association of iron puddlers and boilers and a predecessor to labor unions, is formed in Pittsburgh.

1859: Edwin I. Drake strikes oil in Titusville, an hour and a half northeast of Pittsburgh, marking the beginning of the U.S. petroleum industry.

1869: The first H. J. Heinz plant opens in Sharpsburg, just north of Pittsburgh.

1870: Mellon and Sons opens its banking business on Smithfield Street. Also, Monongahela Incline opens.

1880: Immigrants from southeastern Europe begin arriving in large numbers.

1886: George Westinghouse forms the Westinghouse Electric Co. Also formed in Pittsburgh is the Pittsburgh Reduction Co., later to become the Aluminum Company of America or Alcoa.

1892: Pittsburgh's National League baseball team becomes known as the Pirates for stealing a player from the Brooklyn Dodgers.

1905: The world's first all–motion picture theater, the Nickelodeon, opens in Pittsburgh.

1910: Robert L. Vann publishes the *Pittsburgh Courier*, one of the nation's finest black newspapers.

1950s: Renaissance I helps Pittsburgh begin its transformation into a modern city. Among the changes: reclamation of the Point downtown.

1953: Jonas Salk announces success with the first polio vaccine.

1974: Point State Park is officially dedicated with the completion of the fountain.

1980s: Renaissance II revitalizes downtown yet again, with a new subway, convention center, and several prominent buildings on the city's skyline.

1997: LTV Steel, Pittsburgh's remaining link to its once dominant steel industry, permanently closes its Hazelwood coke plant.

1998: Allegheny County voters narrowly approve Home Rule Charter, which changes county government to a single executive and a 15-member county council.

2001: Three Rivers Stadium replaced by two new stadiums, Heinz Field and PNC Park.

2008: Pittsburgh celebrates its 250th anniversary.

VisitPittsburgh:

Regional Enterprise Tower, 30th Floor
425 Sixth Avenue, Pittsburgh, PA 15219
Tourism information line: (800) 359-0758

ℹ️ In 2007 Pittsburgh was named Top City for Geeks by *Wired* magazine. The region ranked seventh and received high marks on such "geek-friendly" measures as its proximity to top-ranked engineering schools and the number of comic book stores and Circuit City stores per capita.

in Pittsburgh. In 2006 Pittsburgh was home to more Fortune 500 companies than cities like Boston, Denver, Seattle, and Los Angeles.

Some companies and conglomerates, including Mellon Bank, PNC, PPG Industries, the University of Pittsburgh, and the University of Pittsburgh Medical Center (to name only a few)—the powerhouses of the local economy in decades past—continue to provide jobs for area residents.

Westinghouse, which had its financial struggles throughout the '80s and '90s, is now expanding in the area. In 2007 the company broke ground on a new 775,000-square-foot campus in Cranberry, just outside Pittsburgh. Moving from its Monroeville location, Westinghouse plans to hire thousands of new engineers.

The region's world-class medical and research institutions continue to attract companies like Google and Rand, and Pittsburgh has established itself as a leader in technological innovation, particularly in information technology, biotech, robotics, and advanced manufacturing.

Small business and entrepreneurship abound here as well. One key word describing the area's employment and economic future would be diversification, as this region continues to be developed to its full potential.

Already a convenient airport from which business travelers can reach most other U.S. cities with only a two-hour flight, Pittsburgh International is built to accommodate more air carriers adding even more routes, destinations, and accessibility. The newly expanded David L. Lawrence Convention Center opened in fall 2003; 2001 saw the opening of Heinz Field, the city's new football stadium, as well as the opening of PNC Park, which replaced Three Rivers Stadium as the home of the Pittsburgh Pirates. American Eagle Outfitters recently opened its new headquarters in South Side Works.

NAVIGATING NEIGHBORHOODS

Within the city limits, our neighborhoods have names you'll hear on newscasts and in conversation. Some are easily definable, like Polish Hill, founded by Polish immigrants. From imbibing various beers and tasting the sauerbraten and schnitzel, you'd rightly guess that the influences at the Priory and nearby Penn Brewery on the city's North Side were of German descent. The Mexican War Streets neighborhood, however, doesn't get its name from Mexican Americans who live there—in fact, few do. The streets were named after Mexican battles and generals.

You'll soon associate Squirrel Hill with the foundations of Pittsburgh's Jewish community, the Hill District with the African-American community, and Shadyside with either old money or the new and trendy. The South Side (along the Flats and Slopes) maintains much of its Eastern European heritage, while Bloomfield revels in its Italian traditions. Nearby Lawrenceville is a blend of Italian, Irish, and Polish pride. You'll quickly come to associate Oakland with top universities, but others know it as home.

As you'll read in our History chapter, many German families still reside on the city's North Side. And as Pittsburgh has attracted very learned engineers, doctors, and other professionals, many of the surrounding suburbs have become much more multicultural than they were half a century ago.

Despite neighborhoods that are composed of a certain folk, there's a good racial and ethnic mix in many areas. While you will find wealthy communities, the per capita income in 2005 (the most current year reported) was $36,530, slightly above the national average of $25,288. And according to the U.S. Census Report, the median family income as of 2000 was $38,795.

Allegheny County is the most populated of the Western Pennsylvania counties. It's interesting to note that this territory, which includes the city of Pittsburgh, encompasses the gamut of urban settings, as well as hundreds of outlying farms, many golf courses, and smaller neighborhoods that seem like little villages. That diversity, coupled with easy accessibility to the city's business district and sporting and cultural events, is the charm of living here. When families decide to live in Allegheny County, they realize their property taxes will be slightly higher than those in surrounding counties. It's a trade-off many people are willing to make for the conveniences, including a greater selection of school districts, hospitals, churches and synagogues, and social services; access to many colleges and universities; and much more.

Don't let the neighborhood names in the region's outskirts confuse you. If you hear Carolina or Indiana mentioned, don't automatically assume we mean "off in another state," for these are towns in Western Pennsylvania. Little Washington certainly isn't near the Pacific or our nation's capital. It's Washington, Pennsylvania, to the southwest of Pittsburgh. Indeed, Allegheny County is much more populated than Beaver, Butler, Armstrong, Westmoreland, or Washington Counties (those we've defined as our coverage area for this book). As a result, most of the attractions, restaurants, and shopping emanate from this area.

COUNTY LINES

Beyond Allegheny there's Beaver County, just a few miles from Pittsburgh International Airport. Towns such as Ambridge (another old steel town) sit along the Ohio River. You might want to visit Old Economy Village, where the Harmonists, a German sect, built their final homestead (see the Attractions chapter). It is beautifully decorated in the traditional German style during the holidays. Beaver is the

i Pittsburgh has been ranked among the top 10 World's Cleanest Cities by *Forbes* magazine. The magazine recognized the city's transformation from a mainly industrial-based economy to a diversified one with health care, education, robotics, and others.

county seat, and Beaver Falls sits at the northern end.

The Beaver River spills into the Ohio, and marinas abound in Beaver County river communities such as New Brighton and Bridgewater. Parks are prevalent. You can visit Raccoon State Park, and the county parks of Brush Creek, Economy, and Brady's Run.

Butler County offers more history in Harmony, where German immigrants first settled in the early 1800s. The city of Butler is the seat of county government, but areas just north of suburban Pittsburgh such as Cranberry Township have seen tremendous growth in recent years. On a leisurely summer weekend, people often drive north to Lake Arthur and Moraine State Park, the state's fourth largest park. Cultural opportunities include the Butler County Symphony Orchestra, which celebrated its 50th season in 1998. (See the Arts chapter.)

In Armstrong County, the Allegheny River runs southward. Towns here include Apollo, Kittanning, Freeport, and Ford City, where the first successful plate-glass manufacturing venture in the United States operated as Pittsburgh Plate Glass Company, now named PPG Industries.

Greensburg is the center of action in Westmoreland County. There, you'll find the Westmoreland County Museum of American

i In 2007 Pittsburgh was ranked as the #1 Most Livable City in America by *Places Rated Almanac*. The region topped 379 other metro areas in the survey of housing affordability, cost of living, transportation, jobs, education, climate, crime, health care, recreation, and ambience.

Close-up

Talkin' Pittsburgh

While traveling, you've probably heard many unique versions of the English language. But if you had a college roommate from Western Pennsylvania, or if you've spent some time here yourself, then you know the version of English to which we refer. For the uninitiated, we call it Pittsburghese.

Indeed, not all inhabitants reflect their Pittsburgh origin when they speak. Many disdain the dialect. Others, however, embrace the vernacular.

Take the following fictitious conversation, for example:

"Jeet jet?"

"Nah, yunz gonna worsh yer hans?"

"Sure. I was just aht at the Jynt Igl. Brought us some jumbo, chipped-chopped ham, a couple of Klondikes—oh, and I stopped Dahntahn for an Arn."

"Then we better redd up this table. The Stillers game starts at one. Ats what the PG says."

And so it is—Pittsburghese. In our own defense, it's not that we Pittsburghers lack the knowledge of correct speech. It's merely that we're so excited, we can't wait to share what we have to say!

Slurred speech and shortened words aside, Pittsburghese bonds many of us. Above all else, we've learned to laugh at our native dialect. Witness the gift books created: Sam McCool's *New Pittsburghese*, Eric Schuman's *Are You a Real Pittsburgher?*, and *The Tongue-in-Cheek Guide to Pittsburgh*—written as much for our own entertainment as an out-of-towner's guide.

Here's a sampling of what's in store:

Ahia	state to the west of Pennsylvania that others spell with an O and an o
aht	out
Arn	short for Iron City Beer
chipped-chopped ham	our form of lunchmeat or deli ham
crick	creek, as in a small body of water
Cleveland	the butt of many a Pittsburgher's jokes
Dahntahn	Downtown
dill	not a pickle, but a deal

Art, the Westmoreland Symphony, and the Laurel Ballet. Fort Ligonier Days are popular for outings, as are the Mountain Craft Days and the Arts & Heritage Festival. Children can't wait each year for the opening of Idlewild Park and SoakZone, with its family setting in the wooded Laurel Highlands and the memorable trolley ride through Mister Rogers' Neighborhood of Make-Believe (check out the Attractions and Kidstuff chapters).

In Washington County, just off Interstates 79 and 70, The Meadows brings out the equestrian enthusiasts who enjoy clubhouse dining and harness horse racing. Burgettstown's Post-Gazette Pavilion is the site of many summer concerts, with performers

dittent	did not
gumbans	elastic fasteners like rubber bands
high hills	a description of women's' footwear
in regards to a	wordy expression that sounds a whole lot more impressive than it ever is
jeet jet?	an interrogatory meaning "Did you eat yet?"
Jynt Igl	Giant Eagle, as in a local supermarket, not a bird
jumbo	bologna
Klondike	popular ice-cream treats savored over the decades
Mon	short for Monongahela (hey, would you want to remember that spelling?)
needs	shortened form of "needs to be"
parkway	trust us, this isn't where you park (unless you're driving at rush hour!)
PG	nickname of the *Pittsburgh Post-Gazette*
The Point	Point State Park (you know, where the fountain flows)
pop	carbonated beverage most of America calls "soda"
Presby	Presbyterian University Hospital
redd up	to clean, tidy, or make better than it is
Sahside	South Side
'Sliberty	East Liberty
spicket	what the tap water flows from
The Strip	not exactly a turn on, unless it's a Saturday morning and you're after fresh produce
Super Mario	our hockey hero who saved the team once by performance, again by ownership
The T	the subway
whole 'nother	another whole item
worsh	to wash
Yock	the Youghiogheny river (try spelling that one, too!)
yunz	all of you or, more literally, "you ones"

Dave Matthews, Jimmy Buffett, Toby Keith, and the Allman Brothers appearing here.

The Pittsburgh Penguins hockey team, now under the ownership of former player and hero Mario Lemieux, practices at the Iceoplex in Southpointe, Washington County. Meadowcroft Village in Avella is a landmark in itself—a 200-acre facility offering a trip into the history of Native Americans, frontier settlers, farmers, coal miners, and conservationists. The Pennsylvania Trolley Museum offers a

i Allegheny County has more than 1,700 bridges, with 720 inside the city limits and 15 major bridges crossing waterways in downtown Pittsburgh alone.

For the best, most current information about attractions and events in the Pittsburgh area, call VisitPittsburgh, (412) 281-0482, or visit www.visitpittsburgh.com. You can also stop by one of two Welcome Centers—Pittsburgh International Airport's Landside Terminal (near the baggage claim) or on Liberty Avenue adjacent to Gateway Center.

chance to climb aboard a streetcar and experience the sights and sounds of an earlier era when these vintage cars were the mainstay of transportation throughout Western Pennsylvania. Don't leave Washington County without photographing a few of the covered bridges you'll find in your travels.

Speaking of travels, some day trips and sights make it worth driving into counties outside our coverage area. A trip to see Frank Lloyd Wright's Fallingwater is one of them. This masterpiece was constructed in Fayette County south of Pittsburgh in the 1930s for the Edgar Kaufmann family. Today it's maintained by the Western Pennsylvania Conservancy, which conducts guided tours of the house on the waterfall.

Shoppers also make several obligatory trips to Lawrence and Mercer Counties (northwest of the city) for the Prime Outlets in Grove City, where more merchants than you can imagine are congregated in one spot. If your Mercer County day trip becomes a weekend getaway, make Tara, a country inn, your romantic hideaway.

Finally, did you know that Indiana, Pennsylvania, bills itself as the Christmas tree capital of the world? Shipping, sightseeing, rekindling romance, and, yes, even chopping down our own Christmas trees are just a few of the reasons we Pittsburghers venture beyond our own communities. (See both the Day Trips and Weekend Getaways and the Shopping chapters for further adventurous ideas.)

PITTSBURGH TODAY

We call the period from 1980 to the present the Post-Industrial Era—and it's still evolving. Corporations continue the diversification of our economy begun in the late 1970s, furthering an infrastructure of finance, research and scientific concerns, high technology, healthcare advances, and educational excellence.

Beyond all the accolades, a city is its people. Pittsburgh will remain prominent because it offers a high quality of life for the people who call it home. It maintains a relatively low crime rate, wonderful recreation, championship sports teams, a thriving cultural community, and tremendous warmth tied to its sense of family, ethnic heritages, and traditions. You'll enjoy it here. We just know it!

GETTING HERE, GETTING AROUND

Pittsburgh has a glorious transportation history, reaching back to its days as the "Gateway to the West" with bustling river and railway traffic. While the riverboats are gone and passenger trains have dwindled to a few, Southwestern Pennsylvania remains a busy inland region, within 500 miles of more than half the U.S. population. Because of its proximity to so many vital destinations, US Airways has designated Pittsburgh a hub, assuring a heavy volume of air traffic.

The region has developed a colorful and diversified transportation system to meet the demand. Pittsburgh International Airport is a sparkling facility with impressive room for expansion. Public transportation can take you just about anywhere you want to go, and the system features a variety of shared-ride services targeted to senior citizens and disabled patrons. As you move out from Pittsburgh and population density thins, public transportation options thin as well.

Highway travel is not always as gratifying, thanks to the double whammy of topography and weather. The region is hilly, the city itself squeezed between three rivers. These factors have contributed to the development of narrow urban streets; if you're looking for a town with broad, sweeping boulevards, you've probably come to the wrong place. Moreover, many of the older highways around town, once high-speed routes to and from the city, have seen neighborhoods and business districts spring up around them. As a result, some are ill equipped to handle the unanticipated influx of traffic. Transportation planners labor to catch up, making highway development a dynamic, ongoing process here. Nevertheless, if you're from Washington, D.C., or New York, you'll think traffic during our rush hour is just breezing along. However, you will want to take note of two 'Burgh things to avoid a potential pileup: Pittsburghers slow down in tunnels, and at lights they often let the person turning left have the right-of-way. That means some people turning left now *take* the right-of-way, so watch out.

Note also that weather does take its toll; winter's freeze-thaw cycles often lead to an annual spring fling of potholes. The good news about winter weather is that it seldom immobilizes the region.

The review of transportation in Southwestern Pennsylvania has been divided into two major segments—travel to and from Pittsburgh, and travel in Pittsburgh, with particular attention paid to three key areas of travel: Pittsburgh International Airport, public transportation, and parking in Pittsburgh's downtown and Oakland neighborhoods. One way or another, developments here likely will affect you just about every day.

TRAVEL TO AND FROM PITTSBURGH

Air Travel

Pittsburgh International Airport
(412) 472-3525
www.pitairport.com
Pittsburgh International Airport is a marvel. It spans more than 9,000 acres, making it one of the largest airport complexes in the United States. To give you a better sense of its size, consider that Atlanta's Hartfield-Jackson International Airport and Chicago's O'Hare Airport—together—would fit comfortably within Pittsburgh International's borders. The airport routinely handles nearly 11 million passengers annually, and by tapping unutilized acreage, it could accommodate more than twice that many.

i Since opening, the Pittsburgh International Airport continues to receive high marks in national surveys. In 2006 *Condé Nast Traveler* magazine ranked PIT in the Top 5 of all U.S. airports. *Airport Revenue News* also recently ranked the airport's Airmall as #1 in retail and concessions.

One reason for its popularity is the airport's proximity to so many important locales. It's within one hour's flying time of such cities as New York, Detroit, and Washington, D.C., and within 90 minutes' flying time of 20 states and much of Canada. Yet another reason Pittsburgh International ranks so highly with travelers is the scope of its amenities and services. Although the facility debuted in 1992 following an $800 million construction project, you'd swear that its grand opening was yesterday. That's how new and inviting it looks.

You'll find the Pittsburgh International Airport in Findlay Township, about 16 miles west of downtown Pittsburgh. Let's take a tour through Pittsburgh International Airport. We'll call it PIT, as they do in air traffic controller circles, to get a real feel for the place.

Design

PIT features two main buildings: the Landside Terminal and the Airside Terminal, which is shaped like a giant X. When you arrive at the Landside Terminal, you'll be shuttled through a half-mile tunnel to the Airside Terminal by PIT's people mover system. You can't get from Landside to Airside except via the people mover, but don't worry about lengthy waits. No matter when you arrive, the people mover will be at your service in less than two minutes. Once you're at the Airside Terminal, you'll be at the center of the giant X, with the four concourses spoking off in each diagonal direction.

Because PIT is so large, it can be quite a hike from the most remote of the airport's 75 gates to the baggage claim area. PIT helps make it a more comfortable trip by providing moving walkways that will take you part of the way through each concourse. In addition, people with physical challenges can receive assistance by contacting their air carrier.

Airlines

PIT offers 240 nonstop flights per day to 64 locations. (That's 236,000 landings and take-offs each year.) In addition to US Airways, major carriers like Continental Airlines, Delta, and Northwest offer flights from the airport. A growing number of low-cost carriers also service PIT, including Southwest, JetBlue, and AirTran. For the most up-to-date listing of air carriers, visit the airport's Web site at www.pit airport.com.

Baggage

PIT likes to claim that its $32 million automated baggage handling system is reliable 98.9 percent of the time, and travelers seem to agree. Among airlines that serve PIT, US Airways is the only authorized user of the automated system. That shouldn't hold you up if you're flying with another carrier—once US Airways passenger luggage is out of the equation, other carriers have relatively few bags to move.

You'll find the baggage claim area on the ground floor of the Landside Terminal, a pretty fair piece from some of the more remote jet gates. In many cases, since the automated system sorts 400 bags per minute, once you've walked and people-movered from your gate, you'll find your luggage waiting for you. Overhead neon signs will tell you which carousel has your bags.

Ground Transportation

You'll find many ways to get from PIT to your ultimate Southwestern Pennsylvania destination. One of the most economical is the Port

i For a nominal fee, the Traveler's Aid Society, located near the baggage claim, offers a car seat loan program for passengers arriving at the airport with an infant or child. Call (412) 281-5474 for details.

Authority Transit's express bus service called the Airport Flyer. Nearly 40,000 customers take advantage of the Airport Flyer each week. The Airport Flyer links PIT, downtown Pittsburgh, and the Oakland university-medical complex with buses that run every 20 minutes between 5:30 a.m. and 12:30 a.m. The bus makes several other stops along its route, including Robinson Town Centre, Crafton, and Ingram. Perhaps the most attractive feature of the Airport Flyer is its price: $2.25 one way.

A number of shuttles service PIT. Airlines Transportation Company, (412) 472-3180, leaves every half hour from the airport, taking guests to downtown Pittsburgh hotels. Rates are $20 one way, $35 round-trip. If you are traveling in a group, you may opt for one of the vans offered by Three Rivers Limousine Service, Inc., (412) 221-2006. The cost to transport 10 people to downtown is approximately $125 plus gratuity. Looking for a car service? Travel from the airport to downtown in one of Star Limousine's Lincoln Town Cars for about $50 plus gratuity. Call (412) 437-1333 to make reservations.

Eight car rental agencies operate at PIT—all rental counters are located in the Landside Terminal. See this chapter's gray box for their names and phone numbers.

Be advised that if you're outside the terminal waiting for pickup, you must be on the correct side of the terminal, since one side is dedicated exclusively to commercial ground transportation. If you look up and don't see a parking garage, head back through the terminal to the other side.

Parking

PIT's tagline when promoting its services is "You Can't Park Any Closer." It would be hard to argue with that, as the airport offers a variety of parking options that can accommodate more than 13,000 vehicles. You'll find a lot and an indoor garage with 2,100 spaces for short-term parking at $1 for the first hour, and $3 for each additional hour. For long-term parking, PIT maintains an outdoor lot with

3,100 spaces. Rates are $1.50 per hour to a $9.75 daily maximum. Both the short-term and long-term facilities provide access to an indoor moving walkway to facilitate your trip to the terminals.

For extended parking, PIT provides an 8,000-space lot, with a rate of $6.75 per day. Because these spaces are more distant from the terminals, PIT offers continuous shuttle service to and from the extended lot. Running late? PIT offers valet parking. Follow the signs to the rental car lot across from the Landside Terminal. Rates are $24.99 for the first day and $19.99 for each additional day. No matter which option you choose, the parking areas are patrolled by Allegheny County Police. You'll enjoy complimentary emergency car-starting service, and you can pay for your parking with a credit card.

Convenient as airport parking may be, there are other options. A number of private carriers offer spacious parking lots and shuttle service to the airport. The shuttle services are easy to contact when you're at PIT—all their phone numbers are grouped on phones that enable you to access them by pushing a single button.

Prices for these services tend to be market driven; in considering them, be aware of the potential trade-offs involved. For example, if you're paying more at the airport, is the convenience and security provided by the patrolling county police worth the extra price to you? Each traveler will answer that question differently. The shuttle services typically offer a number of discount programs, such as reduced prices for AAA West Penn/West Virginia members.

Amenities

The Airmall, a shopping mall contained within PIT, is so vast and attractive that if you're shopping there, you may have a hard time remembering to make your flight. It's described more fully in our Shopping chapter. While we're here, however, we should at least mention that all the shops and restaurants at PIT are required to charge the same prices

By Phone

When you're traveling to or from the region via Pittsburgh International Airport, here's a directory of key phone numbers that can help things go more quickly. For additional information, go to www.pitairport.com.

Airlines
Air Canada, (888) 247-2262
AirTran Airways, (800) 247-8726
American Airlines, (800) 433-7300
   *American Eagle
British Airways, (800) 247-9297
Continental Airlines, (800) 523-3273
   *Continental Express
Delta Airlines, (800) 221-1212
   *Atlantic Southeast, Comair
Express 1, (800) 225-2525
JetBlue, (800) 538-2583
Midwest Airlines, (800) 452-2022
Myrtle Beach Direct, (877) 432-3473
Northwest, (800) 225-2525
   * Mesaba, Pinnacle
Southwest Airlines, (800) 435-9792
United Airlines, (800) 241-6522
   * Mesa, Shuttle America,
   United Express
US Airways, (800) 428-4322
   * US Airways Express
USA3000, (877) 872-3000

Car Rentals
Alamo, (800) 327-9633
Avis, (800) 331-1212
Budget, (800) 527-0700
Dollar, (800) 800-4000
Enterprise, (800) 261-7331
Hertz Corporation, (800) 654-3131
National Car Rental, (800) 227-7368
Thrifty, (800) 847-4389

Other Useful Numbers
Airport Information, (412) 472-5526
Airport Lost and Found, (412) 472–3500
Airport Parking Information,
   (412) 472-5050
Travelers Aid, (412) 281-5474
Police—General Information,
   (412) 472-5510
Weather, (412) 936-1212

inside the airport that they charge at other locations. You won't be paying $6 for a travel-size bottle of aspirin here.

You'll find a food court with emporiums offering everything from pizza to deli fare, from baked goods to frozen yogurt. You also may enjoy several full-service restaurants, and you'll find food purveyors and lounges along the concourses as well as at the food court. You won't lack for nourishment here, but there's occasional congestion in the food court's limited seating area.

If you're traveling with young children, you'll love Kidsport, a multifaceted children's-play area designed to resemble a miniature amphitheater complete with tiered seating, padded floors, and ramps. When PIT's predecessor facility launched Kidsport in 1983, it was the first of its kind in the nation.

Kidsport also offers continuously running videos of vintage *Mister Rogers' Neighborhood* television shows, a map of the United States designed into the floor, and a ticket counter designed to stimulate imaginative play. You'll find a baby-changing station and a gallery and seating area for sleeping children or nursing mothers. Kidsport is in Concourse C in the Airside Terminal, allowing convenient access to the food court and Airmall. Note: Kidsport is an unsupervised play area.

Other Airports

Allegheny County Airport
12 Allegheny County Airport, West Mifflin
(412) 461-4300
This airport, situated on a 432-acre plateau, once served as the region's chief commercial airport and continues to serve as a vital general aviation airport. Dozens of corporate and private aircraft are based at the facility, which functions as a gateway to the Mon Valley. It features three runways, a 23,500-square-foot terminal building, parking for 500 cars, and a range of aviation services. These include fueling, aircraft sales, rental and maintenance, parts and supplies, storage and tie-down services, and flight and mechanical instruction.

Beaver County Airport
15 Airport Drive, Beaver Falls
(724) 847-4662
Since 1950 the Beaver County Airport has functioned as a general aviation facility, used primarily for business, training, and recreational flights. The facility is designated a "reliever" airport for Pittsburgh International Airport to provide additional capacity during times of congestion. Air Heritage of Western Pennsylvania, a working museum that restores aircraft of historical interest, is located on the premises.

Butler County Airport
475 Airport Road, Butler
(724) 586-6665
Both corporate and private plane owners utilize Butler County Airport, which features an asphalt runway; The Runway restaurant; and a full-service, fixed-base operator that provides fueling, maintenance, training, and charter service. The facility is a designated "reliever" for Pittsburgh International Airport.

Washington County Airport
205A Airport Road, Washington
(724) 228-5151
This facility offers a 5,000-foot runway used by corporate and private aircraft, as well as a fixed-base aeronational operator to handle fueling and maintenance needs.

Arnold Palmer Regional Airport
148 Aviation Lane, Latrobe
(724) 539-8100
www.palmerairport.com
Ground transportation from Pittsburgh International Airport to parts of Westmoreland County can be an exhausting three-hour journey. Another option is to land at Arnold Palmer Regional Airport, a convenient spot if your destination is Greensburg or points east. Northwest Airlines services the airport through Detroit. At the airport you'll find charter flights to Atlantic City and Orlando. Denunzio's Italian Chophouse, a full-service restaurant, is on-site. Flight training is also available.

Train Travel

Amtrak
1100 Liberty Avenue
(412) 471-6171, (800) 872-7245
www.amtrak.com
Amtrak's Pittsburgh station is located at the eastern edge of downtown, near the Liberty Center. It's also convenient to many Port Authority of Allegheny County bus lines. Amtrak offers an automated reservation system that will provide you with schedules and fare information. You can also get that information by visiting Amtrak's Web site: www.amtrak.com.

Two, reservations-only trains service the station. The Capitol Limited runs daily between Washington, D.C., and Chicago. Reserved coach seats and Sleeper Service accommodations are available. The train also features a Sightseer Lounge. The Pennsylvanian travels daily between New York City and

New in town? Look out for the "Pittsburgh Left." If you're driving, watch the car horizontally across from you at the intersection. When the light turns green, the driver is likely to quickly make a left rather than yielding. It's a 'Burgh thing!

Pittsburgh. One highlight of this trip is the famous Horseshoe Curve near Altoona.

Bus Travel

Greyhound Bus Lines
990 Second Avenue
(800) 231-2222
254 Monroeville Mall, Monroeville
www.greyhound.com
Greyhound offers two area terminals, on 2nd Avenue in Pittsburgh and in the eastern suburb of Monroeville. (It should be noted that the 2nd Avenue station is temporary and is not located in the heart of downtown Pittsburgh. A new Greyhound Lines station is scheduled to open upon completion of the Grant Street Transportation Center, a project of the Pittsburgh Parking Authority. Located at Liberty Avenue and 11th Street, the center will more than triple the size of the Greyhound building that was demolished for the project. The center is scheduled to open in 2008. For more information, please contact the Pittsburgh Parking Authority at (412-566-5500.)

Greyhound travels to 1,400 different destinations, and you can reach most of them from Pittsburgh, although some involve bus changeovers. You'll find discount programs for advance bookings and kids, as well as a "companion fare" program offering reduced rates. While the company's national fleet numbers about 1,250 buses, not all are wheelchair accessible. To find out if a bus can accommodate your needs, it's best to call in advance.

Car Travel—Interstate Highways

The interstate highway system can make car travel to and from Pittsburgh a pretty easy and comfortable mission, although there is one unusual feature of interstate highway travel here. The Pennsylvania Department of Transportation (PennDOT) reports that while trucks typically account for about 10 percent of all traffic on interstate highways, the percentage in our region is about 50 percent higher, or 15 percent of all vehicles on the road. Note the variability in speed limits from 55 to 65 mph throughout the region; if you're not paying attention, you could easily cross into a 55 mph zone while doing 65.

Interstate 76

This is the Pennsylvania Turnpike, which covers 530 miles and crosses the Commonwealth, linking the cities of Pittsburgh, Harrisburg, and Philadelphia and connecting with the Ohio and New Jersey Turnpikes. The turnpike also features a Northeast Extension that will take you to Scranton and other Northeastern Pennsylvania locations. Locally you'll find access to the turnpike at Monroeville, Harmarville, Warrandale, Butler, and Beaver Valley.

The highway is administered by the Pennsylvania Turnpike Commission, which charges 5.9 cents per mile for passenger cars. You must pay your tolls in cash upon leaving the highway. If you will be traveling the turnpike frequently, consider the E-ZPass, the turnpike's electronic toll-collection program. (Go to www.paturnpike.com for details.) PennDOT maintains a Welcome Center along the turnpike near Beaver Falls. One caution about turnpike driving: Exits can be as far as 30 miles apart, so you don't want to miss yours. Also, make sure to check your interchange numbers. The Turnpike Commission converted its exit numbers several years ago. New exit numbers are based on milepost locations.

Interstate 376

I-376, known locally as the Parkway East, connects the Pennsylvania Turnpike with downtown Pittsburgh and is the principal link between the city and its eastern suburbs. It's heavily traveled, carrying 115,000 vehicles each weekday, and you can expect routine rush-hour delays that can make the road look like a genuine parkway, but pileups usually don't last long. If you travel I-376, you'll course through the Squirrel Hill Tunnels at the city of Pittsburgh's eastern edge. Watch out for delays here—many Pittsburgh drivers slow down as they drive through tunnels.

Interstate 79

This major north-south highway goes from Erie all the way to southern West Virginia. It also intersects Interstate 70 in Washington County. PennDOT maintains a Welcome Center along I-79 in Greene County.

Interstate 279

I-279 is a loop off I-79 and serves as a vital connection between the heavily populated North Hills, the city of Pittsburgh, and Pittsburgh International Airport. Local residents call I-279 either the Parkway West or the Parkway North, depending on which section they're talking about. The highway exits downtown Pittsburgh across the Fort Pitt Bridge and through the Fort Pitt Tunnels; here it becomes the state's most heavily traveled highway, handling 125,000 vehicles per day. Rush-hour traffic jams are common.

An important feature of I-279 is the region's only high occupancy vehicle (HOV) lane, which during morning and evening rush hour is restricted to vehicles with a minimum of two occupants. At all other times, the HOV lane functions as an express lane and is open to all drivers. You'll find the HOV lane between the North Side of Pittsburgh and the city's northern suburbs.

Interstate 70

I-70 is an important highway in Washington and Westmoreland Counties, taking you through the Mon Valley or west into West Virginia, Ohio, and beyond. PennDOT maintains a Welcome Center along I-70 in Washington County.

Interstate 80

It's slightly north of our principal coverage area, but I-80—sometimes called the "Keystone Shortway"—is a road you should know about. It's a good route to central and eastern Pennsylvania points, and it will deposit you

Help for Travelers

Several organizations in the region are dedicated to helping travelers. If you've ever needed emergency road service on a dark and lonely road, you well know the value of the American Automobile Association. (AAA) The AAA member service center in Southwestern Pennsylvania is AAA West Penn/West Virginia, (412) 363-5100, located at 5900 Baum Boulevard in Pittsburgh's East Liberty neighborhood. AAA operates more than 50 branch offices in the tristate area, offering a variety of services that go well beyond emergency help.

Services include worldwide air, cruise, and rail tickets; hotel and rental-car reservations; American Express travelers checks at no service fee; credit cards, maps, and individually tailored routings, otherwise known as the much-loved Triptiks. AAA also operates travel and insurance agencies. There is an annual membership fee.

Also available for wayward wayfarers is Travelers Aid Society of Pittsburgh, a nonprofit agency that helps travelers throughout the country. The agency assists people stranded here through no fault of their own and without the means of reaching home or another destination.

You'll find two Travelers Aid Society locations in Southwestern Pennsylvania—Pittsburgh International Airport, (412) 472-3599, and the Greyhound Bus Terminal.

directly in New Jersey going east or Ohio going west. To reach I-80, take I-79 north to New Castle in Lawrence County.

TRAVEL IN PITTSBURGH

Because public transportation in Southwestern Pennsylvania tends to be organized and administered by county, we'll begin our look at public transportation in the same way. That doesn't mean you can't get from, say, Westmoreland County to Allegheny County. You can, although the options are limited; county boundaries tend to shape the contours of the region's public transportation. That will be important to keep in mind if you're a public transportation user.

Allegheny County

In Allegheny County, public transportation is the domain of the Port Authority of Allegheny County, or PAT as it's popularly known. It's a massive job, as PAT provides service to 240,000 riders per weekday along 213 bus and rail routes. It accomplishes this by deploying about 1,000 buses each day along with several nifty features—inclines and the "T" light-rail and subway system—which is described below.

The bus system also features a number of exclusive bus lanes that serve most of the county and cut much of the time from your trip. These include the South Busway, the Martin Luther King Jr. East Busway, and the West Busway. PAT also operates the 25-mile rail system that includes the downtown's subway. PAT's Stage II Light Rail Transit Project, opened in 2004, included the purchase of 28 new light-rail vehicles, reconstruction of parts of the lines, and new signaling and communications systems.

All PAT bus and rail vehicles are Americans with Disabilities Act (ADA) compliant.

i Here's a handy tip that can help you avoid a moment of embarrassment when riding a Port Authority of Allegheny County bus. On buses heading to downtown, you pay your fare when you board. On outbound buses, pay as you exit. You'll need the exact fare; PAT drivers don't carry any change.

Buslifts—equipment designed to assist persons using wheelchairs or walkers—can be found on most PAT buses. PAT's low-floor buses are equipped with ADA-compliant ramps. In addition, PAT sponsors and administers ACCESS, a door-to-door, advanced-reservation, shared-ride transportation service targeted primarily to senior citizens and those with disabilities. For information about ACCESS, call PAT at (412) 562-5353.

The fare for a ride on a PAT bus depends on how far you need to go. Fares range from free (within the downtown "Free Zone") to $2.75 for a three-zone trip. If you're a frequent rider, PAT offers a number of discount opportunities, including books of 10 discounted tickets; weekly, monthly, and annual subscription passes; a Weekend Day Pass; and a Summer Ride Pass.

Anyone 12 or older pays full fare. Children ages 6 to 11 years old pay half fare. Children under 6 years old ride for free. Individuals with disabilities presenting a Commonwealth of Pennsylvania Reduced Transit Fare card or Medicare card at the time of fare payment can ride for half fare. Seniors presenting a Commonwealth of Pennsylvania Senior Citizen Identification Card or Medicare card at the time of fare payment can ride PAT for free at all times. For certification to either program, call PAT at (412) 442-2000 or stop by the PATransit Downtown Service Center, 534 Smithfield Street. Applications for Senior Citizen Transit Cards also are available at senior centers throughout the county.

PAT modifies its routes and schedules several times per year to respond to changing conditions and customer needs. You can keep up with all routes, schedules, and changes by visiting PAT's Web site, www.portauthority.org, or by calling PAT's customer service department, (412) 442-2000.

Inclines

Imagine a subway car rolling along a track. Now imagine the car and track tilted at about a 35-degree angle to carry you up a mountainside. You now have a mental picture of an

The Duquesne Incline entrance. ALAN AND BARBARA VENTO

unusual transportation mode known as an incline. In Pittsburgh you don't have to imagine it—the city is served by two inclines that function both as tourist attractions and as important daily conveyances for downtown commuters.

Between 1870 and 1901, transportation pioneers in the city erected and operated 15 "inclined planes," as they were formally known, to carry folks up and down Pittsburgh's steep hills. Although most were passenger conveyances, at least one served as a freight incline to haul horses, buggies, furniture, and coal. As the city's roadway and public transportation systems improved, incline ridership declined. Today only two inclines survive.

Both the Monongahela Incline and the Duquesne Incline link the Mt. Washington and Duquesne Heights neighborhoods to the South Side, more than 600 feet below. The cars traverse Mt. Washington at 6 miles per hour. They're popular with tourists, as a ride on the incline can be combined with a stop at the observation decks atop Mt. Washington,

providing breathtaking views of the city and its three rivers. Mt. Washington and Duquesne Heights residents use them to reach the South Side; from there, a walk across the Smithfield Street Bridge gets them to work. Their total commuting costs: $1.75 one way for the incline ride. To save money on a round-trip, ask for a transfer for an additional 50 cents.

The Monongahela Incline ("The Mon Incline") operates from 5:30 a.m. to 12:45 a.m. Monday through Saturday and 8:45 a.m. to midnight on Sunday and holidays. The lower station is across Carson Street from Station Square. The Duquesne Incline operates from 5:30 a.m. to 12:45 a.m. Monday through Saturday and 7:00 a.m. to 12:45 a.m. on Sunday and holidays. There is free parking across the street from the lower station and a number of restaurants located near the upper station. Both inclines run on demand; that means, after waiting only a few minutes, ostensibly you could have the thing to yourself. For information about the Mon Incline, contact the Port Authority of Allegheny County, (412) 442-

2000. The Duquesne Incline is operated by a nonprofit group called the Society for the Preservation of the Duquesne Heights Incline. You can reach them at (412) 381-1665, or go to www.incline.pghfree.net.

Parking

Downtown Pittsburgh offers approximately 20,000 parking spaces, including metered onstreet parking and downtown fringe lots and garages. That may seem like a pretty generous number, but if you consider that 125,000 vehicles whiz past downtown each day on I-279, it's pretty easy to see the peril there. If downtown is the destination for too many of those drivers, there won't be enough parking to go around.

Of course it seldom is as bad as that. Many of those drivers aren't coming downtown, and those who do aren't necessarily parking all day, so there is some turnover. If you arrive early or late enough in the workday, chances are you'll find the space you desire, or one pretty close to it. You will encounter a crunch virtually every midday, when the all-day parkers have yet to depart and downtown crowds are swollen by noontime shoppers and diners.

Downtown won't pose the only parking challenges for you in the city. The Oakland neighborhood, with its phalanx of important hospitals and universities, is notoriously crowded when the colleges are in session. In a few of Pittsburgh's residential neighborhoods, parking is at such a premium that the city has taken to providing permits to local residents for onstreet parking during certain time periods: no permit, no park.

Public transportation and carpooling may be your most reliable alternatives. If you must drive, however, we'll try to give you a wheel up by profiling the largest parking garages in downtown and Oakland, providing some information about PAT's "Park and Ride" program, and offering some insight into Pittsburgh's homegrown parking solution—a chair strategically placed in "your" parking space.

Parking—Downtown

Downtown proper offers about 20,000 parking spaces. With a little ingenuity and luck, you can find one. You may need to walk a little farther than you had planned or grab the "T" to reach your destination, but with persistence you'll find your space.

For each facility, the minimum and maximum hourly rates—in other words, what you'd pay to park from 0 to 30 minutes and the maximum that you'd pay to park all day—are provided. Included within the range is what you'd pay to park on a weekend or weeknight; the cost is often a lower hourly rate or flat fee then. If different pricing applies during special events, it is noted. Phone numbers listed are those of garage operators and may ring at corporate offices rather than onsite. Unless otherwise noted, all garages and lots offer security guards, wheelchair-reserved spaces, and discounted evening rates. Downtown garages also provide escort service upon request. Where valet parking is offered, that usually means a charge and/or a tip over and above the standard hourly rate. The entries below are not comprehensive—you'll find many other surface lots and indoor garages—but these are the largest parking sites, where open spaces are most likely.

Stanwix Street Garage
11 Stanwix Street
(412) 323-4455
When other downtown garages are full, you may find a space here. Perhaps the disappearance of Westinghouse from Pittsburgh's corporate scene has freed up space in the lot. Whatever the reason, this garage is always worth a shot. Rates for its 341 spaces range from $6 to $17. Monthly leases are available starting at $310.

Fort Duquesne and Sixth Street Garage
126 Sixth Street
(412) 391-3380
You'll find this a convenient garage for events in the Cultural District. Rates for the 920

spaces range from $3.75 to $10.00, and you'll receive a discount when you patronize certain downtown establishments. Monthly lease rate is $220 by day, $100 by night. Weekend rate is $5 per day.

Liberty Center Garage
10th Street and Liberty Avenue
(412) 261-6655
You'll be beneath Liberty Center and the Westin Hotel when you park here. The garage offers 500 spaces; the rate is $17 per day. You also may take advantage of valet parking at $22 per day.

The Manor Complex Garage
564 Forbes Avenue
(412) 323-4455
This garage is part of the Manor Building and a quick walk from Grant Street, the hub of the city's legal and political activity. Rates for the 750 spaces range from $6 to $11, with monthly leases available for $185.

Mellon Square Garage
Mellon Square
(412) 255-6138
One of the most popular garages because of its central location, Mellon Square Garage offers 1,100 spaces at rates ranging from $5 to $18. Monthly lease rate is $275, with a discounted monthly lease night rate available.

Mon Wharf Parking
Mon Wharf
(412) 456-2770
If you plan to park on the Mon Wharf, you will enjoy a favorable rate—$8 no matter how long you stay—but you need to be aware of certain things. First, this surface lot is only a few paces from the Monongahela River, meaning you will have a bit of a walk to central downtown locations. Perhaps more important, the lot typically floods several times each year when the Mon rises, so you need to be aware of river conditions before you park here. The lot offers 700 spaces and security from 1:00 to 9:00 p.m. but no monthly leases.

Ninth and Penn Garage
136 Ninth Street
(412) 560-7250
When you're planning to enjoy a play or performance in Pittsburgh's Cultural District, you'll find this lot a short walk from your venue. It features 581 spaces and rates ranging from $3.75 to $10.00. Monthly leases are available for $220, and monthly night leases are priced at $100. Your hourly rate will be discounted with a purchase from participating downtown merchants.

One Oxford Centre Garage
Smithfield Street and Third Avenue
(412) 263-2180
If you're planning a shopping expedition at trendy Oxford Centre, you can't beat the convenience of this 850-space garage. Rates range from $5 to $15, with discounts when you patronize certain shops in Oxford Centre. Cost for monthly leases is $310—slightly less for Oxford Centre tenants. The garage is connected by a series of bridges to both the Forbes Avenue Garage and the Boulevard of the Allies Garage.

PPG Place Garage
311 Market Street
(412) 323-4455
As the name suggests, this garage is part of the six-building PPG Place complex, headquarters to many important Pittsburgh companies and adjacent to Market Square. Rates for the 673 spaces range from $5 to $16, with monthly leases ranging from $280.53 for open parking to $326.33 for a reserved space.

i The Pittsburgh Downtown Partnership, www.downtownpittsburgh .com, provides a map on its Web site of all downtown parking facilities. Here you can also take advantage of its Reserved Parking Program. If you're coming into town anytime from 10:00 a.m. until 2:00 p.m., Monday through Friday, you can reserve a space in a local garage. Call (412) 566-4190.

Sixth and Penn Garage
526 Penn Avenue
(412) 323-4455

On many nights there's a palpable excitement around this garage—it's the closest parking garage to Heinz Hall, home of the Pittsburgh Symphony Orchestra and many touring troupes and plays. The garage offers 500 spaces, with rates ranging from $3 to $12 and monthly leases for $210.

Smithfield Street and Liberty Avenue
629 Smithfield Street
(412) 391-1952

An indoor tunnel connects this 616-space garage to the Duquesne Club, making it a convenient parking site when you're dining at the club. Rates range from $5 to $14 with monthly leases priced at $275.

Third Avenue Garage
238 Fourth Avenue
(412) 323-4455

This centrally located garage offers 550 spaces, with rates ranging from $3.75 to $13.00. Monthly leases start at $250.

USX Tower Garage
600 Grant Street
(412) 263-0440

When you have an appointment at USX Tower, one of the city's most important headquarters facilities, you can't beat the convenience of this 720-space garage. Rates range from $11 to $22, with monthly leases available for $384 and valet parking offered. You can park from 5:00 p.m. until 5:00 a.m. for just $6.

Wood-Allies Garage
228 Boulevard of the Allies
(412) 560-2504

This 541-space garage is convenient to PPG Place and Market Square, both just a few paces across the Boulevard of the Allies. Rates range from $3.75 to $10.00, with monthly leases priced at $220 by day, $100 by night.

Downtown Fringe

Many commuters avoid high downtown parking rates by parking in lots that dot the fringes of downtown. These are among the largest parking sites in the city, offering about 16,000 spaces. From some sites you'll need to walk a bit to reach your ultimate destination, while others provide complimentary shuttle-bus service. Commuters on a budget put the fringe on top.

Allegheny Center Parking Garage
100 South Commons
(412) 323-4455

You'll find 2,500 indoor parking spaces at this garage, which is just across the Seventh Street Bridge from downtown. Rates range from $4 to $10, with monthly leases priced at $115.

Chatham Center Garage
54 Chatham Center
(412) 261-0809

Located in the uptown section near the Mellon Arena, Chatham Center offers 2,281 indoor spaces. The garage is about a five-minute walk from Grant Street in downtown. Rates range from $2.50 to $10.25, with monthly leases priced at $214. You can get a discounted "early bird" monthly lease, good Monday through Friday from 5:30 a.m. to 6:30 p.m., for $192.

Fifteenth and Smallman Lot
15th and Smallman Streets
(412) 323-4455
www.alcoparking.com

This 1,500-space surface lot is in the Strip District, a short walk from the David L. Lawrence Convention Center and Liberty Center. Monday through Friday, the lot provides complimentary shuttle service to and from several downtown locations. You'll pay by day-part. For example, you can park from 5:00 a.m. to 4:00 p.m. for $5 and 4:00 p.m. to close for $5 Monday through Friday. All day Saturday or Sunday is $5.

Mellon Arena Lots
Center Avenue
(412) 642-4284

Washington Place, Bedford Avenue, Lemieux Place, and Crawford Street

You'll find 2,500 spaces to welcome you in the arena area—unless an event at the Mellon Arena causes a jam. The regular daily rates range from $5.75 to $7.75, 5:00 a.m. to 6:00 p.m. Monday through Friday. During Mellon Arena events, which usually take place on the weekends, rates are higher, varying with different events.

Expect to walk no longer than 10 minutes to reach downtown; the most distant Mellon Arena lot is only 4 blocks from Grant Street. If you work in USX Tower, park in the Mellon Arena lot nearby and sprint to work in five minutes or less; you may even be able to look down on your car from your office window.

The Melody Tent lot offers a shuttle bus that operates on weekdays from 6:00 to 10:00 a.m. and 3:00 to 6:30 p.m.

Second Avenue Parking Plaza
Second Avenue
(412) 323-4455

This surface lot in the Uptown neighborhood offers 768 parking spaces for a daily rate of $5, monthly leases for $100, and free shuttle service to downtown points.

Station Square Parking
One Station Square
(412) 261-1993

This popular shopping/office complex features two surface lots and a garage providing a total of 3,500 parking spaces.

You will need to walk across the Smithfield Street Bridge to reach town. Indoor rates range from $3 to $16 with outdoor rates in the East lot ranging from $1 to $14. You also may park for a $5 daily fare in the West lot. During Steelers and Pirates games, expect a rate hike—up to almost twice the price for the day. Monthly lease rates are $105 to $145.

Parking—Oakland

As the hub of the region's higher-education and medical sectors, Oakland frequently has more would-be parkers than it can comfortably accommodate. You'll find plenty of metered onstreet parking, but you can't use most of those spaces during morning and evening rush hours. You'll also find plenty of garages, only to be frustrated by the "Permit Parking Only" warnings, indicating that the garages are reserved—often for University of Pittsburgh personnel. When classes are in session, there's no real remedy for the parking crunch. Here are some garages and lots that can help.

Forbes Semple Garage
410 Meyran Avenue
(412) 621-5922

This 450-space garage is part of Oakland's commercial district. Rates range from $3 to $9, with monthly leases priced at $190 by day, $100 by night.

University Parking
3915 O'Hara Street
(412) 624-4034

O'Hara Garage provides a convenient location between the University of Pittsburgh's lower and upper campuses. From here you're within walking distance of most of Oakland's hospitals and medical offices. Rates for the 455 spaces range from $4 to $10, with discounts for Pitt personnel and students. Leases are

i You'll find one of America's shortest interstate highways in Pittsburgh. Interstate 579, all 0.5 mile of it, connects the Liberty Bridge and I-376 (via the Boulevard of the Allies) to the Veterans Bridge across the Allegheny River and I-279. This mighty little highway often goes by an alternate name: the Crosstown Expressway.

available through the university for its faculty and staff only.

Webster Hall Garage
101 North Dithridge Street
(412) 621-6751

This garage provides 250 spaces at rates ranging from $5 to $17, with a discount for purchases at participating merchants. It also offers valet parking and monthly leases priced from $130 to $150—you also must provide a $50 security deposit for a lease. Webster Hall is a former elegant hotel now serving as an office and apartment building.

Park and Ride Lots

One way of avoiding downtown parking expenses is to utilize the Port Authority of Allegheny's Park and Ride lots. These 64 lots offer more than 14,850 parking spaces, most free or with a nominal charge. They're all located adjacent to public transportation routes, so you can park cheaply and ride the bus or "T" to town. You can print a Park and Ride map from www.portauthority.org, or call PAT at (412) 442-2000 to request a free map.

Pittsburgh Neighborhoods

As you tool through Pittsburgh's residential and commercial neighborhoods, you'll notice a chair standing unattended before the curb. Then another. Then another. These are not the products of some mass sheriff's evictions. Rather, Pittsburghers use chairs to stake their claims to parking spaces in front of their homes or businesses. They're especially prevalent on snowy days, when residents who have shoveled out their parking spaces feel particularly protective about them. The chairs are a colorful facet of Pittsburgh residential life, but don't take them lightly. Although you aren't technically breaking any laws, Pittsburghers take great offense if you shove aside a chair and trespass on a reserved parking space.

The need for such a homegrown strategy stems from the tightness of parking spaces in some city neighborhoods. Many Pittsburgh streets are narrow and can't accommodate parking on both sides of the street. In addition, neighborhoods with institutions such as hospitals draw many visitors in search of onstreet parking to beat the prices of lots, garages, and meters.

The city has implemented a more rational approach to the problem through its Residential Parking Permit Program. Through RPPP, residents of 26 residential areas—including Beechview, Bloomfield, The Bluff, Garfield, Lawrenceville, Lower Hill district, Mt. Washington, North Squirrel Hill, North Side, Oakland, and Shadyside—enjoy exclusive onstreet parking rights during certain time periods each day. To acquire a permit that admits you into the program, you'll need to provide proof of residency and car ownership, a driver's license, and an annual fee of $20 per vehicle. You'll also be entitled to one guest car per household for an annual fee of $10 or a visitor pass for $1 a day. For more information or an application, contact the Pittsburgh Department of City Planning, (412) 560-2500.

If you don't live in an eligible neighborhood, we advise that you pick up a couple of folding chairs.

Subway

Pittsburgh's subway system, known as the "T," is an unusual blend of subterranean and aboveground features. When it courses through the city's South Hills, the "T" is largely an aboveground conveyance that resembles a trolley line, although it's officially called a "light-rail system." When it reaches downtown, the "T" dives beneath the surface to provide riders with an unobstructed trip below city streets. Three downtown stops—Gateway Center, Wood Street, and Steel Plaza—are underground; the "T" stops at First Avenue Station, Penn Station, and Station Square which are aboveground. By combining these features, the "T" serves as both a convenient means of downtown-only travel and a key component of the region's commuting infrastructure.

For downtown travel, it would be hard to beat the price of the "T"—there's no charge for travel between the three underground stations. For longer "T" rides for which there is a charge, PAT encourages riders to purchase tickets and passes by imposing a surcharge, ranging from $1.25 to $1.75, on cash payments. For more information call (412) 442-2000.

Armstrong County

In Armstrong County, the Mid-County Transit Authority, (724) 548-8696, provides three bus programs. The first features fixed-route service in the county's central communities—Applewold, Ford Cliff, Ford City, Kittanning, Manorville, Manor Township, and West Kittanning. The buses run about once every hour, Monday through Saturday, at a base fare of $1.00 to $1.50. As a bonus, MCTA provides service to hospitals and shopping malls in East Franklin.

The second service, Armstrong Rural Public Transit, is a shared-ride program available to all Monday through Friday. You must reserve your transportation at least two days in advance. The buses are primarily, though not exclusively, wheelchair accessible. Service normally runs from 6:00 a.m. to 3:00 p.m. Call (724) 548-8696 for fares.

Beaver County

The Beaver County Transit Authority, (724) 728-8600, manages public bus transportation throughout the county. You'll find routes that operate exclusively within Beaver County, as well as express and local routes between Beaver County and the city of Pittsburgh. Your fare will depend on the number of zones traversed; a one-way fare from Pittsburgh ranges from $2.75 to $3.00. Exact fare is required, unless you pay by tickets purchased at the BCTA Transportation Center in Rochester. Transfers are free. Note: BCTA buses do not operate on major holidays.

Senior citizens may ride BCTA's Beaver County routes free of charge during off-peak hours and all day Saturday. To get your senior

In 1985 the Port Authority of Allegheny County selected the name "T" for its subway light-rail system through a public contest. Losing submissions included "The Unda Grunda Wonda," "The Gazunder," and "YGDT" (Yunz Goin'd Dathn-Tahn?). Now you know why they chose "T."

citizen transit card, call BCTA at (724) 728-8600 or visit the transportation center. For riders who use wheelchairs, most routes are accessible. You may want to check with BCTA to determine which routes might be right for you. The county also provides a shared-ride service called Demand and Response Transit (DART) for people with disabilities. Call DART at (724) 728-4200 for more information or to schedule a ride.

The county maintains several Park 'n Ride lots in close proximity to BCTA stops throughout the county. In addition, you'll find a convenience lot just outside the transportation center where you can park while conducting any short-term activity at the center. Beaver County officials call these lots "Kiss 'n Ride," but these activities are not mandatory when visiting the transportation center . . . at least we don't think they are.

Butler County

Bus service in Butler County is something of a mix-and-match affair. In the city of Butler and environs, bus service is provided by Butler Transit Authority, (412) 283-0445.

Bus routes serve Butler City, Butler Township, and a small portion of Centre Township from 7:00 a.m. to 9:45 p.m. Monday through Saturday and 10:40 a.m. to 4:15 p.m. on Sunday. Fare is $1. Seniors (over 65 years old) ride free.

On weekdays, Myers Coach Line, (877) 733-1045, operates a commuter service to and from downtown Pittsburgh, via Route 8.

Washington County

You'll have several options for bus service in Washington County, depending on your needs. For Pittsburgh or locations in or near the city of Washington, GG&C Bus Lines, (724) 222-2320, provides express service from Washington County to downtown Pittsburgh, connecting with the "T" at South Hills Village Station, as well as local service throughout the city of Washington.

For service in the Mon Valley and along the Route 88 corridor, Mid-Mon Valley Transit Authority, (724) 489-0880, provides local service as well as commuter service to downtown Pittsburgh. Go to www.mmvta.com for fare information.

Westmoreland County

Westmoreland County Transit Authority operates a far-reaching bus system that includes 19 routes and features service throughout the county as well as buses to Pittsburgh. For schedules call WCTA at (724) 834-9282 or (800) 221-9282, or visit them at the Westmoreland Transit Center, 41 Bell Way, Greensburg. Please note that WCTA buses do not operate on major holidays.

As with many municipal transportation systems in the region, fares are based on the number of zones traversed. For travel within Westmoreland County, expect your fare to range from $1.20 to $4.00. Transfers are free when needed to complete one-way travel, but you must use your transfer within one hour from the time it's issued. While exact fare is not required, drivers will change $1 bills only. You can avoid the need for cash by purchasing "Ten Trip Tickets" that offer a 10 percent discount off the total ticket price. Drivers carry the ticket books for your convenience.

Senior citizens age 65 and older ride free during off-peak hours on weekdays and on Saturday and holidays. Patrons with disabilities ride for half fare at all times. Seniors should apply for their eligibility cards at the transit center; persons with disabilities may apply by calling the center at (800) 221-9282. If you're a wheelchair user, WCTA asks that you call them at (800) 221-9282 two days to one week before you need their service.

For disabled persons unable to utilize public transportation, the county operates a paratransit service in association with several local taxi companies. The paratransit service operates in the same communities, and during the same hours, as WCTA's bus routes. Fares, however, are twice the amount charged for a similar bus trip. To apply, call WCTA at (800) 221-9282.

Taxicabs

The first thing you must appreciate about travel by cab in Southwestern Pennsylvania—if you wave your arm for a cab here, you're likely to get a tired arm. Typically, you won't find cabs cruising city streets. The demand is relatively small for standard cab service, and companies size their fleets to match that demand. In fact, most of the cab companies here also provide paratransit and shared-ride service to complement their cab fleets.

You will find cabs aplenty at Pittsburgh International Airport and downtown Pittsburgh's major hotels. If you're anywhere near the airport or a hotel, the best way to get a cab is to call and book one. All companies profiled here offer round-the-clock service every day of the year.

A word about jitneys: You'll find these private operators, who transport customers at negotiated fees, in several Pittsburgh neighborhoods. Residents contend that because licensed cab companies seldom ventured into these neighborhoods in years past, jitneys arose and thrived to meet a pressing need. Jitneys are unlicensed by the state and have no official standing, so you'll have very little recourse should something go awry. Patronize them at your discretion. Frequent jitney users often know their drivers.

Checker Cab
4001 Clairton Road
(412) 664-5600
These distinctive cabs, with their green checkerboard patterns accented by gold striping, operate in downtown Pittsburgh and the city's western suburbs. You'll find cabs at major hotels that are authorized to transport you to and from Pittsburgh International Airport.

Peoples Cab Company
4001 Clairton Road
(412) 466-8300
To reserve your white-and-burgundy Peoples
Cab, you must call ahead. They can provide
you with service to—but not from—Pittsburgh International Airport, where Yellow Cab
operates an exclusive contract.

The Yellow Cab Company of Pittsburgh
1101 Beaver Avenue
(412) 321-8100
www.pghyellowcab.com
By far the largest provider in the region, Yellow Cab offers a fleet of more than 300 vehicles. It serves corporate accounts and stands
at major hotels. As a special service, Yellow
Cab offers several regional phone numbers to
spare residents of those areas toll calls. If you
live in the South Hills, call the company day or
night at (412) 344-TAXI. In Monroeville the
number is (412) 374-TAXI.

Local Driving

Driving in and around Pittsburgh can be at
once rewarding and frustrating. When you
drive here, you'll travel along roads that take
you through charming towns with attractive
river views. The hills and mountains provide
breathtaking vistas that attract international
tourists. Those same hills, however, can
become treacherous in bad weather. Even
more maddening is the way many streets in
the region are named.

Take the city of Pittsburgh, for example.
In downtown Pittsburgh you'll find avenues
numbered from 1 to 7. At the same time,
you'll encounter numbered streets that begin
with 6 and go all the way to the 50s in the
city's Lawrenceville neighborhood. If that
weren't confusing enough, South Side cross
streets begin at 1 and go into the 20s. Got it?
Now, when someone says to meet him on
Sixth, what on earth do you do?

You'll get used to it soon enough, and the
charm of Pittsburgh's streets will prevail. The
following is a look at some of the principal

i City, county, and state government
all have responsibility for highway
maintenance in Southwestern Pennsylvania.

state routes, city streets, and bridges with
which you'll become familiar.

U.S. and State Routes
The primary U.S. and state routes in the region
are similar in a number of key respects. They
pass through residential and commercial districts, offering only the occasional high-speed
sections. They're great for local travel, but
you'll probably prefer the interstate network
for longer hauls.

Allegheny County also offers a beltway
of five concentric rings—designated blue,
green, yellow, orange, and red—with the city
of Pittsburgh at the center. These were developed many years ago as alternatives to driving through the city. They may have been
effective at one time, but with the growth of
commercial and residential districts along the
belts, and the concomitant increase in traffic
and traffic signals, you frequently won't make
good time on the belts. When you get to
know them well—if you're one of the few
who does—you'll find the belts can help you
detour around local traffic snarls.

ROUTE 8
This is an important connector between the
city of Pittsburgh and Butler County, passing
through the city's northern suburbs en route.

U.S. ROUTE 19
US 19 spans both the North Hills and the
South Hills of Pittsburgh, reaching all the way
to Washington County. The highway offers
separate truck spurs in both the North Hills
and South Hills.

U.S. ROUTE 22
A major route from Pittsburgh to the east, US
22 provides access to such communities as
Indiana and Johnstown. Many folks traveling
to Penn State University travel US 22 to State
College.

i You can rent a variety of styles of bicycles and even a "bike trailer," to seat two toddlers, from Golden Triangle Bike-N-Blade (412) 600-0675. Under new ownership, the rental store is located at 600 First Avenue, near the entrance to the Eliza Furnace Trail.

ROUTE 28

Route 28 reaches from the city of Pittsburgh north to Kittanning in Armstrong County, pretty much paralleling the Allegheny River, which is intermittently visible along the way. You can follow Route 28 well into Northwestern Pennsylvania, though with the development of I-79, few would do that.

U.S. ROUTE 30

This highway takes you east, through Westmoreland County and into the Laurel Highlands region. US 30 is linked to US 22 by a 14-mile high-speed highway called the Amos K. Hutchinson Bypass. It's a toll road maintained by the Pennsylvania Turnpike Commission.

ROUTE 51

You can travel Route 51 from Pittsburgh southeast to Uniontown, passing through some of the South Hills and the Mon Valley along the way.

ROUTE 60

Route 60 links most of Beaver County's major towns and extends north all the way to I-80. A 17-mile stretch of the road between Beaver Falls and New Castle is a high-speed toll road, maintained by the Pennsylvania Turnpike Commission, called the Beaver Valley Expressway.

ROUTE 65

Route 65 offers a scenic drive along the Ohio River as it carries you from Pittsburgh west to Beaver County.

U.S. ROUTE 422

This Butler County road links Route 28 with I-79. It's an important highway for residents of Armstrong and Butler Counties.

Pittsburgh Streets

Two of the city's most important streets are Fifth and Forbes Avenues, which run roughly parallel from downtown about 6 miles to the city's eastern neighborhoods. Forbes is one-way outbound through Oakland, while Fifth is one-way inbound from Oakland. When you drive these streets, you'll pass by five colleges or universities—Duquesne University, Carlow University, the University of Pittsburgh, Carnegie Mellon University, and Chatham University. You'll find it positively enlightening.

When you're looking to avoid traffic jams on the Parkway East, Second Avenue and the Boulevard of the Allies might help. The Boulevard of the Allies reaches from downtown to the Squirrel Hill neighborhood, providing a pleasant drive through Schenley Park. The Second Avenue trip also is interesting, paralleling the Monongahela River and passing the gleaming Pittsburgh Technology Center as it takes you to Hazelwood.

Penn and Liberty Avenues also are important routes to and from town, connecting the central business district and eastern neighborhoods. Penn is one-way inbound near downtown. Two steep streets, Perrysville Avenue and Mt. Troy Road, will take you from the Allegheny River to the city's northern neighborhoods.

One of the city's most interesting streets is Carson Street—it's East Carson Street or West Carson Street, depending on which side of the Fort Pitt Bridge you find yourself. The street provides you with views of the city's West End and the town of McKees Rocks, passes through the vital South Side and its brace of trendy restaurants and galleries, and continues through to West Homestead in the Mon Valley, offering glimpses of former industrial sites now being recycled as residential, office, and entertainment complexes. Not a bad tour of the city . . . and you never have to leave Carson Street.

Pittsburgh Wayfinder System

With its steep hillsides, serpentine streets, and many bridges and tunnels, Pittsburgh can sometimes be difficult to navigate. To give some direction, Pittsburgh installed the Wayfinder system, designed by Informing Design, throughout the city in 1995 and 1996. The Wayfinder system is based on a simple map that shows the city as five distinct sections and assigns each a color: North Side (light blue), South Side (green), Downtown/Triangle (purple), Strip District (greenish-brown), and East End (orange).

The Wayfinder System includes two types of signs—directional and destination. Directional signs guide travelers to their destination, say, a museum, park, or local attraction. The Wayfinder map appears at the top of each directional sign, and the background color of the sign helps you to figure out where you are in the city. See a white star on the sign? You've reached your destination. By the way, signs with a "P" or an "H" can help you to locate the nearest parking lot and hospital, respectively.

Bridges

If you like bridges, you'll love Pittsburgh. In Allegheny, Beaver, and Lawrence Counties alone, you'll find an estimated 167 bridges, many of them beautiful and distinctive, sporting ornate metalwork and a vast variety of architectural approaches. Since you'll be using them every day, you'll probably think of them more as convenience than art, but it's nice to appreciate their design every so often.

You'll become familiar with such Allegheny River bridges as the Fort Duquesne Bridge, Veterans Bridge, Sixth Street Bridge, Seventh Street Bridge, Ninth Street Bridge,

i Located in Southwestern Pennsylvania, Pittsburgh is about halfway between Chicago and New York City. It's within a two-hour flight or a day's drive of more than 70 percent of the U.S. population and 50 percent of the Canadian population, according to VisitPittsburgh.

16th Street Bridge, 31st Street Bridge, 40th Street Bridge, 62nd Street Bridge, Highland Park Bridge, and Hulton Bridge, with its lavender superstructure.

Across the Monongahela you'll find the Fort Pitt Bridge (although it could be argued that this bridge is above the Point and therefore crosses all three rivers) and the Liberty Bridge, a major artery—along with the companion Liberty Tunnels (aka Liberty Tubes)—between Pittsburgh and the South Hills. Other Monongahela River crossings include the 10th Street Bridge (remember what we told you about street numbering here?), Birmingham Bridge, and Rankin Bridge.

Near Pittsburgh you'll cross the Ohio River at the West End Bridge, McKees Rocks Bridge, and Sewickley Bridge.

The McKees Rocks Bridge is the longest at better than 1.5 miles, while Veterans Bridge covers the most deck area with its six lanes. Clearly we've presented only a selection of the region's bridges, those that are most heavily used.

One warning about the region's bridges—some bridges have two names. For instance, the Sixth Street Bridge in downtown is also known as the Roberto Clemente Bridge, and the Seventh Street Bridge is also the Andy Warhol Bridge. When giving directions, many locals still use the older names, which can sometimes be confusing.

HISTORY

When the first hardy 18th-century traders gazed upon the land that would come to be known as Pittsburgh, they saw a valley of verdant hillsides cut by a triangle of rivers, with majestic, unspoiled forests rising as sentinels above. The strengths they viewed were formidable. The flatter land between and along the rivers would serve for trading posts, forts, and settlements. The rivers would provide convenient and economical transport routes—both to the settled cities of the East and the unexplored domains of the West—while the virgin woods would offer game as well as timber for building.

It's impossible, of course, to know what really went through the minds of those intrepid early traders as they surveyed for the first time the site of the future Pittsburgh. But it is clear that the assets they saw—and those that they couldn't see, such as abundant coal beneath the soil—would form the foundation of a city that would become the industrial giant of America, as well as a home to generations of immigrants. The story of Pittsburgh is a story of boom, bust, and rebirth—the rise and decline of a great manufacturing center recreated as a thriving, progressive metropolis based on economic and social diversity.

All who observed this land recognized its commercial and strategic importance as the Gateway to the West. Even before 1750, the French had successfully navigated the river network all the way from the Point, where the Allegheny and Monongahela Rivers merge to form the Ohio River, to the Mississippi River. In fact, well before Pittsburgh was officially founded or named, the French and the British, each allied with different Indian nations of the region, extended their European battle for dominance to what was then known as the Ohio Country. The struggle was protracted and bloody, the outcome far from certain.

In 1754 the French held dominion over the Ohio Country from Fort Duquesne, the redoubt constructed at the point. It was in that year that a young major named George Washington led a group of Virginians against the French, only to meet ignominious defeat. A 1755 expedition against the fort, this one led by Gen. Edward Braddock, suffered even worse consequences. Braddock and many of his officers were killed; Washington miraculously defied death in the Ohio Country for the second time in two years.

It was only in 1758, as Britain began to gain the upper hand all across the New World, that the French occupation of the Ohio Country ended. On November 24, as the British army prepared for its final assault on the fort, a scouting party delivered the news: The French had abandoned Fort Duquesne. Three days later, Gen. John Forbes, the British commander, solemnly renamed the fort in honor of British prime minister William Pitt.

The prolonged struggle for control of the Ohio Country may have been over, but the growth of the settlement continued at a measured pace. This was, after all, the wilderness. Beautiful as the land was, life remained harsh. Home very often was little more than a hut along the rivers that could be swept away by the fury of a spring flood. In 1760, two years after the final conquest of the French, the settlement that surrounded Fort Pitt numbered 151 people. Even at the close of the Revolutionary War, the population still numbered in the hundreds.

Slow though growth may have been, the late 18th century brought several important

> **i** At the Forks of the Ohio in 1753, George Washington was thrown into the half-frozen Allegheny River from his raft, where he named the site for a fort.

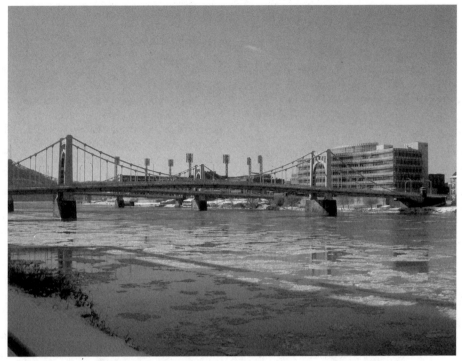

One of the many bridges that span the Allegheny River in Pittsburgh. LINDSEY KEOGH

developments. The year 1787 marked the founding of the Pittsburgh Academy, forerunner of today's University of Pittsburgh. On April 22, 1794, the city became a borough and staged its first elections.

THE RIVERBOAT ERA

As the century closed, the city began to fulfill its promise as the Gateway to the West. With the young nation expanding, Pittsburgh became an excellent launching point for traffic that could navigate the inland waterways all the way to New Orleans.

From the turn of the 19th century, Pittsburgh served as a significant center for flatboat traffic. The craft not only transported cargo but were also a primary transportation mode for immigrants seeking to settle the West. Since Pittsburgh merchants often loaded flatboats with goods for sale at ports of call along the way, the colorful craft resembled nothing so much as floating department stores. Lacking a way to float the boats upstream, the owners typically disassembled the craft and sold them for their lumber at journey's end.

Upstream traffic required a different kind of vessel—the keelboat, long and narrow, pointed at the ends, and propelled by human rowers, or polers. The upstream journey was tedious and arduous for passengers, as the trip from Louisville to Pittsburgh might last a month. More difficult still was the work of the polers, a hard-drinking, hard-living breed.

The riverboat era produced one of the most colorful characters in Pittsburgh history—Mike Fink, self-proclaimed King of the Boatmen, whose brawls and benders took on mythic proportions.

Pittsburgh even became an early hub of shipbuilding, a natural given the volume of its river traffic. With the development of steampowered vessels, however, shipbuilding died

i Pittsburgh marks its 250th anniversary in 2008, and Pittsburghers
will be celebrating throughout the year.
Signature projects, like the completion
of the Great Allegheny Passage, and
celebrations, including homecomings
and reunions, are planned. Go to
www.imaginepittsburgh.com for details.

out in Pittsburgh, and the era of flatboats and
keelboats lasted no more than a few decades.
Mike Fink, frustrated by the advent of steampowered vessels, took off for the badlands
of the Rockies and departed Pittsburgh's history forever.

The city's future would not lie in shipbuilding. But the riverboat era proved conclusively
that Pittsburgh and its waterways could serve
the nation well as a transport center, a role the
city would continue to play throughout the
period of America's industrialization.

FROM EUROPE THEY CAME...
AND CAME...AND CAME

During the 19th century and the first part of
the 20th century, Pittsburgh developed its
modern identity as a melting pot for dozens
of nationalities and cultures, and as the most
important steel-manufacturing center in
America.

Blessed with the natural elements used
for manufacturing, the city needed only the
human component to complete the equation.
In the 19th century, seemingly endless waves
of immigration satisfied that need.

Early in the century, a steady stream of
uprooted Europeans settled in Pittsburgh,
drawn to the city for a number of reasons.
Among that early group were Irish fleeing
famine in their homeland and finding work in
Pittsburgh's mining industry; Scots-Irish,
Scots, Welsh, and Dutch who were among the
earliest settlers; and skilled Belgians who
answered a call for help from a fledgling Pittsburgh glass manufacturer. Still others came as
indentured servants or criminals, working off

their contracts or sentences in the New World.

In the 1840s the trickle of immigration
grew to a flood, with the influx of new Pittsburghers primarily from Germany and Ireland.
Yet another wave, in the 1890s, brought immigrants from Central and Southeastern Europe.

The contributions of these new resident
cannot be overestimated. The immigrants
tended to settle with their fellow displaced
countrymen in neighborhoods ringing the burgeoning downtown that reflected their distinct
cultures and religions. Many Italians, for example, settled in Bloomfield, a few miles east of
downtown Pittsburgh. Even today, Italian can
be heard spoken on Bloomfield's streets.

The Irish gathered in downtown itself
before fanning out to neighborhoods such as
Garfield. Many German immigrants found new
homes in the hilly area north of downtown
that would become known as Troy Hill. European Jews congregated in the Hill District;
later this neighborhood adjacent to downtown would become the city's most important
African-American community with the 19th-
century wave of migration from the American
South. Polish immigrants settled in a number
of new neighborhoods, including
Lawrenceville along the Allegheny and South
Side along the Monongahela.

Even relatively small immigrant groups
made an impact. Scandinavians, for example,
never settled in Pittsburgh in large numbers.
Yet Swedish immigrants who came for work in
the steel mills gathered in the working-class
suburb of McKeesport, where they erected
churches that conducted services in their
native tongue well into the 20th century.
Finnish immigrants clustered in the Monongahela River towns of Glassport and Monessen,
building schools, churches, and fraternal
organizations.

These distinctive neighborhoods, insular
in their way but steeped in the traditions and
culture of the Old World, would provide Pittsburgh with a foundation of ethnicity that, to
this day, is a defining characteristic of the city.
Pittsburgh became the very embodiment of
the "melting pot," and the effects continue to

be profound. A mid-20th-century study found that, years after the principal waves of European immigration had ended, 42 percent of the population of Allegheny County (of which Pittsburgh is the seat) were foreign born or children of those born outside America.

THE HEART OF STEEL

With all the components in place, manufacturing in Pittsburgh was set for takeoff. As early as the 1820s, Pittsburgh boasted eight rolling mills driven by steam power. Between that period and the Civil War, several developments facilitated the transformation of the fledgling steel industry to a growing giant.

One such development was the discovery that bituminous coal, so plentiful in the region, could be used to create coke, an abundant and relatively cheap fuel, to power the mills. A second was the almost simultaneous development, by England's Henry Bessemer and Pittsburgh's William Kelly, of air-cooling the molten iron to strengthen and purify the product. With these refinements in the production process, and others that would follow, such as the creation of the open-hearth process in the early 20th century, Pittsburgh was poised to become the steelmaking heart of America.

It had the economic muscle, through such financiers as the Mellon family. It had the natural resources necessary for steel production and the river and railroad networks to ship products anywhere. It had a willing and skilled labor force. And it had the entrepreneurial talent.

Many of the giants of industrialism grew in Pittsburgh along with the city's manufacturing base. In 1881 a Scottish immigrant named Andrew Carnegie joined with his six brothers in a venture that later would become Carnegie Steel Company, itself a predecessor of the giant U.S. Steel Corp. (today known as USX). In one of those ironies of history, Carnegie located his first major mill, the Edgar Thomson Works, on the site where the ill-fated General Braddock fell to the French.

Other early steel and coal magnates included Henry Phipps, an early Carnegie partner; Henry W. Oliver; and Henry Clay Frick. Nor was entrepreneurship limited to the steel industry. In 1869 George Westinghouse invented the air brake in Pittsburgh, a development that advanced the continuing growth of the railroad industry. A protean figure, Westinghouse helped found or operate an estimated 60 companies, including the business that would become a 20th-century giant—Pittsburgh-based Westinghouse Electric Corp.

These titans of industry left an indelible mark on the region, in a number of ways. Their impact on the area's economy, of course, was profound. But so, too, was their perpetuation—if not downright origination—of the concept of philanthropy. The Carnegie Museums of Pittsburgh, the Carnegie Library (a thriving institution in so many western Pennsylvania towns), the Frick Art & Historical Center, Phipps Conservatory and Botanical Gardens, Mellon Park, Mellon Square—all remain vital features of contemporary Pittsburgh, and all are living testament to the philanthropy of Pittsburgh's leading industrialists.

Aided by such corporate largesse as well as the traditions that the transplanted Europeans brought with them, culture and education in Pittsburgh flourished in this period. These years marked the founding of such foundation arts institutions as the Pittsburgh Symphony in 1895 and the Pittsburgh Opera in 1938.

In education, Carnegie Tech University—later to become Carnegie Mellon University with an infusion of Mellon family money—was founded in 1900, Duquesne University in 1878. The development of the University of Pittsburgh speaks volumes about the community partnership that was at the heart of Pittsburgh's growth.

To finance its landmark 42-story Cathedral of Learning, the University of Pittsburgh asked residents to participate by "buying" bricks for the edifice at a dime apiece. In the 11 years between 1926 and the Cathedral's completion

Preserving the History of Big Steel

Rivers of Steel National Heritage Area
(412) 464-4020
www.riversofsteel.com

From 1875 to 1980, southwestern Pennsylvania was the Steel Making Capital of the World, producing the steel for some of America's greatest icons, such as the Brooklyn Bridge and the Empire State Building. During World Wars I and II, this region's steelworkers carried a nation's defense on their backs, producing more steel, armor, and armaments in a single year than entire countries. While many of the region's legendary mill sites have been dismantled and it has been decades since the mills belched fire and smoke over Pittsburgh's skyline, the enormity of the region's steelmaking contributions and its historical significance to the nation demand its story be told and its sites be preserved.

Created by Congress in 1996, the Rivers of Steel National Heritage Area is committed to preserving, interpreting, and managing the historic, cultural, and natural resources related to Big Steel and its related industries. Encompassing 5,000 square miles in the seven counties of Allegheny, Armstrong, Beaver, Westmoreland, Greene, Fayette, and Washington, Rivers of Steel is building on this area's remarkable transition from heavy industry to high technology and diversified services, as well as bolstering the new regional economy by promoting tourism and economic development based on this region's historic industrial saga.

A multifaceted program, the Rivers of Steel National Heritage Area's mission includes historic preservation, cultural conservation, education, recreation, and resource development. Currently, the Heritage Area has bills in Congress to create the Homestead Works National Park. The proposed park would be located on 38 acres surrounding the Carrie Furnaces, the last of the giant blast furnaces from the Homestead Works, and the Pump House, site of the bloody 1892 Homestead Steel Strike.

—With thanks to Rivers of Steel

---

in 1937, the university "sold" bricks to 114,000 people. The Cathedral of Learning still towers over the city as a symbol of Pittsburgh's commitment to education and to the cohesiveness and community spirit of Pittsburghers.

THE RISE OF LABOR

The impact of the leading industrialists of the 20th century was evident in yet another way—the rise of organized labor. As more and more men went to work in the mines and mills, they realized they would need representation to assure them of fair wages and safe working conditions. The nascent labor movement would not be readily accepted by the same men who had dotted the community with the libraries and museums that spoke of their generosity.

In 1858, as recorded by Arthur C. Bining in *Pennsylvania's Iron and Steel Industry*, a group of steelworkers formed a secret organization called the Iron City Forge of the Sons of Vulcan, the first permanent labor association in the iron industry. In 1876 the Sons of Vulcan merged with three other newly formed organizations to create the national Amalgamated Association of Iron and Steel Workers.

Forming a union was one thing; persuading management to recognize it was another. The growth of steel in Pittsburgh was marked by regular confrontations between management and labor, none more infamous or bloody than the Homestead strike of 1892. In a dispute over wages and the right to organize, workers at U.S. Steel's Homestead plant along the city's southeastern border seized the factory and captured 300 Pinkerton detectives sent in to quell the strike. The situation degenerated into a series of pitched battles along the Monongahela River and a failed assassination attempt against U.S. Steel board chairman Henry Clay Frick. By the time the Pennsylvania Militia restored order, 10 were dead.

Far from hastening management-labor accord, the Homestead strike served only to polarize the parties. It was 45 years after the strike that U.S. Steel officially recognized the steelworkers' union, breaking the impasse in the industry. Finally, with labor and management at relative peace, the boom could roll on.

Pittsburgh's role as the industrial heart of America reached its full flower during World War II, when the Commonwealth of Pennsylvania produced one-sixth of the world's iron and steel.

The city's reputation reached international proportions. On his historic visit to the United States during the height of the cold war, Soviet premier Nikita S. Krushchev included Pittsburgh on his itinerary. While in the city, he was heard to remark that if the Soviets really wanted to cripple America, they would drop a bomb on the Duquesne Club, where Pittsburgh's leading industrialists gathered for lunch and hosted their guests overnight. It was thought to be a joke, but Khrushchev, perhaps mindful of his own words, chose to spend the night at the Carlton House.

A RENAISSANCE DRAMA, IN TWO ACTS

The city in the Golden Triangle, as the land near the Point was called, was a stunning success. Yet as America settled into postwar normalcy, Pittsburgh was in danger of choking on that very success. The problems were twofold.

i Pittsburgh lost the "h" in its spelling in 1891. Twenty years later, bowing to popular pressure, the U.S. Board on Geographic Names approved restoration of the "h."

First, the same plants that were the city's lifeblood also were spewing smoke into the air, creating deadly dark clouds that, at their worst, literally blocked the rays of the sun and created virtual 24-hour-a-day nights. Ask Pittsburghers of a certain age about that era, and what they remember most is the smoke, the gasping for air, the clothes that would turn pitch-black when hung on the line to dry.

The second problem was the helter-skelter pattern of development that had left the Golden Triangle an unattractive warren of dirty warehouses and untended tracks to nowhere. If Pittsburgh were to continue its growth, both problems would have to be addressed.

Pittsburgh Mayor David L. Lawrence and leading industrialist and financier Richard K. Mellon had, independently, reached that conclusion. Lawrence was more than the city's top official and the future governor of Pennsylvania; he controlled the Democratic Party, which in the labor-dominated city was the only party that mattered. Mellon was perhaps the city's most powerful industrialist, one who could lead others in important new directions. They joined forces in a new entity called the Allegheny Conference on Community Development, an organization that, more than 50 years later, continues to play an important role in Pittsburgh's growth.

Their collaboration was historic, as government to that point had played little role in the city's development. John P. Robin, who worked for the Allegheny Conference and

i If you'd like to read an in-depth account of regional history, complete with hundreds of photographs, get a copy of the comprehensive coffee-table book *Pittsburgh: Story of an American City* by Stefan Lorant, now in its fifth edition.

would be a pivotal player in Pittsburgh's growth for five decades, described that historic collaboration in a 1997 oral history.

"It was really a different climate than had existed," Robin said. "There was excitement and willingness. There never was a precise plan for development. The appetite, I usually say, grew with the eating. There was a contagion, a belief that nothing was impossible and we ought to try it."

The result was an unprecedented redevelopment that became known as the Renaissance. The partnership set out to improve their city on both key fronts. On smoke control, the city passed a series of abatement measures that, with the blessing of Mellon and other corporate leaders, industry implemented without complaint.

On the land use front, the partnership in 1947 persuaded the Pennsylvania Legislature to enact a new body, the Urban Redevelopment Authority of Pittsburgh, which would have sweeping powers to acquire and assemble land. With those new powers the city went to work on its Golden Triangle. At the very point where the Allegheny and Monongahela Rivers converge to form the Ohio River, the city and the Commonwealth of Pennsylvania created Point State Park, a 36-acre urban oasis with riverfront benches, a majestic fountain, and the Fort Pitt Blockhouse, the sole surviving section of the old Fort Pitt.

Adjacent to Point State Park, the partnership demolished the rat's nest of tracks and warehouses and created Gateway Center, a six-building office cluster that became a prestigious downtown address. It remains so today, with entities such as the United Steelworkers of America headquartered there.

Uptown from the Golden Triangle, the URA acquired properties and assembled them in a tract that in 1961 became the home of the Mellon Arena (formerly known as the Civic Arena), a pioneering sports and entertainment complex that features a retractable silver dome.

This period of ongoing prosperity also marked the suburbanization of Pittsburgh.

Decades of success had provided thousands of Pittsburghers with the wherewithal to seek larger homes in more pastoral settings. Not all abandoned the inner city, of course, as Pittsburgh's distinctive neighborhoods remain a compelling feature of the city. But people relocated in sufficient numbers that a new term— Greater Pittsburgh—entered the local lexicon. In 1960 the Greater Pittsburgh population soared to nearly 2.4 million.

With the city scrubbed clean of deadly smoke and the public-private development partnership both secure and experienced, Pittsburgh entered the second phase of its Renaissance in the 1970s and 1980s.

As visitors drive through the Fort Pitt Tunnel to enter the city for the first time, they typically are stunned by the unexpected beauty of Pittsburgh's skyline, defined by towering skyscrapers so architecturally and functionally diverse that, in aggregate, they defy quick or easy description. The most common response is a sharp intake of breath and a determination to explore them all.

Even more remarkable is that most of these signature buildings were created during Renaissance II. Their import is so great that they deserve to be mentioned at some length, and an entire chapter of this book (Architecture) is devoted to doing just that.

During Renaissance II these multiple downtown building projects generated about $2 billion in private and public investment while creating more than $21 million annually in new local tax revenues. While the redevelopment efforts of cities are difficult to quantify, let alone compare, it seems fair to say that few cities have accomplished so much over such a short period. Between the first and last of these developments, only about 15 years elapsed.

Once again the world took notice of Pittsburgh's remarkable achievements. It was during this period that the city reaped a number of prestigious honors. *Places Rated Almanac* judged Pittsburgh "America's Most Livable City" in 1985. *Health* magazine ranked Pittsburgh in its top 10 American cities. *Savvy*

He wrote "My Old Kentucky Home," but Stephen Collins Foster was a Pittsburgh native. The Stephen C. Foster Memorial stands at the University of Pittsburgh.

called the city the sixth best in the nation for raising kids. *Fortune* cited Pittsburgh on two fronts: It had the eighth best business climate and was the third Most-Conducive-to-Marriage City.

The two phases of Pittsburgh's Renaissance extended the unbroken record of prosperity in Pittsburgh and promised even more for the future. That promise, however, would not be fulfilled, at least not at once.

DECLINE, THEN DIVERSIFICATION

At first it was just a few troubling signs. In 1984 Chevron acquired Gulf Oil, a bulwark of Pittsburgh's economy, and relocated its functions and employees to California. By 1986 only seven Gulf staff remained in Pittsburgh. In 1989 Pittsburgh's Rockwell Manufacturing fell victim to a similar fate—acquisition and relocation to California.

A casual observer might have viewed these defections as aberrations, blips on an otherwise prosperous economic map. But such optimism would not survive the collapse of Big Steel.

The decline was precipitous. In the 1980s Greater Pittsburgh lost an estimated 127,500 jobs in steel and related manufacturing industries. All the support industries that had grown up around steel also felt the blow.

Analysts differ in their assessment of steel's collapse. In his book *And the Wolf Finally Came,* labor writer and historian John Hoerr points to such factors as incursions by foreign manufacturers and "mini-mills," which could produce steel at lower cost. He also fingers the inability of Big Steel to adequately respond due to a cumbersome organizational structure and the age-old credibility gulf between management and labor.

Whatever the reasons, the impact on the region was severe. Without a healthy manufacturing industry to provide jobs for its young, the region—for the first time in its history—experienced significant out-migration. By 1990 the population of the city proper had plunged to just under 370,000, its lowest mark since 1900. The total for Greater Pittsburgh dipped below 2 million. During its economic heyday, Pittsburgh ranked as America's third-largest headquarters city, behind only New York and Chicago. Between 1984 and 1994, nine Fortune 500 companies left Pittsburgh or vanished from the rankings.

Throughout its history, the hearty folk who had settled Pittsburgh proved themselves a can-do people; now, more than ever, they needed to do it again. With desperate determination, the city, led by the administration of mayor Tom Murphy, in concert with the Commonwealth of Pennsylvania, the private sector, foundations, and neighborhood-based development organizations, unveiled a two-pronged approach to revitalization. First, the partnership would reclaim abandoned industrial sites and develop in their wake a more diversified economy. Just as important, the partnership would exploit the city's rivers, just as Pittsburgh's original settlers had, with exciting new developments that would contribute to the region's emerging economic diversity.

In short order, the city and its partners made significant progress on both fronts. Along the Monongahela, the partnership constructed 300 attractive housing units, with as many as 1,000 more homes to follow. Along the Allegheny, the partnership developed 230 luxury apartments at a site adjacent to new headquarters for Alcoa, the giant aluminum company that renewed its commitment to the city.

In building economic diversity, the region had considerable help from its two largest

Over 800,000 gallons of water are recirculated to create the 150-foot-high fountain at Point State Park, where the Allegheny, Monongahela, and Ohio Rivers meet.

i Pittsburgh's KDKA-AM delivered the nation's first regularly scheduled radio broadcast in 1920, coverage of the Harding-Cox presidential election. Because of their role as radio pioneers, KDKA and Pittsburgh's KQV-AM are among the three radio stations east of the Mississippi River permitted to begin their call letters with "K." (Philadelphia's KYW is the third.)

research universities, University of Pittsburgh and Carnegie Mellon, sources for dozens of technology-based spin-off companies. Today the city ranks sixth in the nation in software sector employment, while the broader technology sector employs more than 100,000.

Encouraged by Pittsburgh's emergence as a fertile bed for the growth of technology-based industries, the National Aeronautics and Space Administration in 1996 committed $50 million to help launch a national robotics consortium along the banks of the Allegheny, to be operated in conjunction with Carnegie Mellon. That development has pushed Pittsburgh to the forefront of robotics.

So complete was Pittsburgh's transformation that in 1996, manufacturing, mining, and construction accounted for only 17.5 percent of Pittsburgh's jobs.

THE NEW PITTSBURGH

Throughout the city there are compelling symbols of the region's transformation. Washington's Landing, an Allegheny River island 2 miles north of downtown, had long been used for industrial operations, including the rendering of animal byproducts. When industrial companies abandoned the island, they left a legacy of contaminated soil. In the 1990s Pittsburgh's public-private development team entombed the tainted soil and readied the land for redevelopment. Today Washington's Landing is the site for light manufacturing, office buildings, a marina, townhomes, and recreation.

In Hays, in the city's southeast corner, the U.S. Army Ammunition Plant had once been

an important cog in the nation's military machine but had been vacant since the Vietnam War. The city's Urban Redevelopment Authority acquired the site from the Army for $1 and prepared it for new uses. Now it is the home of GalvTech, a technology-based company that zinc coats steel coils.

Perhaps the most persuasive symbol of the region's rebirth is the Pittsburgh Technology Center, a gleaming complex along the Monongahela near the Oakland cluster of universities and hospitals. The site just east of downtown was once home to J&L Steel's Hot Strip Mill; it glowed round the clock as one of the brightest lights of steelmaking.

When the site was abandoned in 1983, the city acquired it and began its conversion to a technology center. The complex currently is home to the University of Pittsburgh Center for Biotechnology and Bioengineering, the Carnegie Mellon Research Institute, Union Switch & Signal (a company founded by the ubiquitous Mr. Westinghouse), and a brace of support organizations of technology-based companies.

To stand on the campus of the Pittsburgh Technology Center is to see the city's history encapsulated. Gaze to the west and you see the gleaming skyscrapers that have defined the downtown since Renaissance II. Look toward the east and you notice the hot metal bridge spanning the Monongahela, still connecting the site to the mill's former coking operations across the river. And all of it wrapped by a latticework of highways, as if bound and determined to enclose and preserve the contrast for posterity.

In its roughly 250 years of settlement, Pittsburgh has experienced the booms and busts of an economic roller coaster, rising through most of its years to a position of prominence among the world's manufactur-

i Washington's Landing—an Allegheny River island that's home to manufacturing, office buildings, recreation, and residence life—is so named because George Washington found refuge there during a 1753 storm.

ing centers, feeling the sting when that manufacturing declined, and emerging as a region of multiple strengths.

Its impressive downtown, inviting suburbs, and distinctive, close-knit neighborhoods are appealing for residents and visitors alike. It offers a rich mix of cultural and entertainment amenities, a reflection of the diverse heritage of its residents.

Above all, it retains the two most important characteristics of its spectacular, sometimes surprising development. Pittsburgh remains within 500 miles of more than half of America's population, making it a preferred site for business and residential location. By land, by water, by air, you can get there from Pittsburgh.

And it continues to boast a population imbued with the work ethic brought to America by its forebears, a population that epitomizes the ideals of America's melting pot, a population ready to roll up its sleeves and get the job done together.

ACCOMMODATIONS

Looking to overnight in Pittsburgh? Well, options for you abound. You can stay in a large, happening hotel in the heart of the city; repair to the suburbs for the quiet of a country inn; luxuriate in an all-seasons resort; or grab a room near the airport so you'll be sure to catch that early flight. All are attractive options in Pittsburgh and environs.

Accommodations in Pittsburgh are, in a word, accommodating. You'll find a setting, style, and price range to suit you. Note that one popular category of accommodation—the bed-and-breakfast inn—has its own chapter.

With so many options in Greater Pittsburgh, you might think that dropping in and finding the room of your choice would be no problem. In most cases that's true. Keep in mind, though, that the city is a business center and a popular site for conventions. If we're hosting a major convention, or even several medium-size gatherings, accommodations in the city are snapped up, forcing visitors to more distant sites. Even there, availability during these occasional crunch times is no guarantee.

Therefore, the wise traveler plans ahead when coming to Pittsburgh. Take the time to make a few phone calls and reservations where appropriate. You'll find the effort rewarded with a guaranteed room you're sure to like.

Most of the time, though, there's more than enough capacity, resulting in sometimes-keen competition for business. This has brought some important benefits to customers. For example, virtually all places of

lodging in Pittsburgh offer both smoking and nonsmoking rooms; any exceptions are noted in the individual write-ups below.

Policies on pets have changed as well. It was not too many years ago that if you wanted to bring Bowser along with you, you needed to hide him in your picnic basket. With the boom in rooms, many hotels are accommodating pets as an added attraction for guests. You'll find pet policies detailed in the individual write-ups.

Accessibility for the disabled is another area of growing concern, for both operators and customers. Rare is the establishment in Pittsburgh that doesn't consider itself wheelchair accessible. As anyone who requires such facilities knows, however, there can be quite a difference between compliance with the letter of the law and convenience and comfort for you. When you're making those phone calls, be sure to ask specific questions about facilities and amenities for disabled guests as well as guests with other special needs.

Most establishments offer discount programs, such as those available through AAA or AARP. Many also maintain frequent-traveler programs that help you reduce the cost of your stay. Make sure you inquire about these as well as special packages and offers for which you may be eligible. In Allegheny County be prepared to pay a 7 percent room tax; elsewhere the room tax varies from county to county. All establishments described below accept major credit cards.

In many instances the write-ups describe facilities that are part of well-known national chains, of which many have a strong presence in our area. While the chains are so prominent that you know pretty much what to expect when you stay with them, such facilities are included where their locations make them potentially important to you.

i Need help locating a hotel? Try VisitPittsburgh, (412) 281-7711 or (800) 359-0785, for information about hotels, Pittsburgh attractions, and travel packages.

For example, most hotels and motels near Pittsburgh International Airport are included for the convenience of those traveling here by air. All hotels and motels in the Oakland neighborhood's university-medical complex, which attracts many visitors in need of convenient lodging, are described. For those occasions when downtown's finest are booked, a number of facilities on the perimeter of downtown that are good sites for overflow traffic are featured.

After the section on Hotels & Motels, look for listings for Extended-stay Accommodations, Resorts, and Hotels. We tried hard to include something for everyone.

Exploring Pittsburgh's lodgings will be a joy for you. Whatever your choice, you'll find your enjoyment enhanced by the legendary hospitality of Pittsburghers. If you don't mind our saying so, we'll make any room you choose seem like your home away from home.

PRICE CODE

The area of rates is not easily summarized. It might not appear so on the surface, but Pittsburgh is a community with peak seasons. The summer season is heaviest, fueled in part by convention business. Traveling in Pittsburgh also spikes around holidays and the skiing season. In light of all this, most operators maintain a range of rates rather than a set charge. Asked about her typical rates, one operator replied, "It depends on the day."

That kind of variability makes reporting on rates difficult. With each description, we've indicated rate categories with from one to four dollar signs. The rates are for standard rooms, double occupancy. Here's the key:

$ ....$30 to $65
$$ ....$66 to $100
$$$ ....$101 to $135
$$$$ ....$136 and over

Remember that when capacity is tight, your rate may be appreciably higher than the standard charge.

HOTELS & MOTELS
Downtown

Doubletree Hotel & Suites
Pittsburgh City Center $$$
One Bigelow Square
(412) 281-5800
www.doubletree.hilton.com
Located near USX Tower and Mellon Financial Corporation and recently renovated, the Doubletree offers 188 guest rooms and 120 one- and two-bedroom suites. This hotel touts that it has the largest hotel guest rooms in the city. Each guest room features a coffeemaker, iron and ironing board, hair dryer, a 27-inch flat-screen television with complimentary HBO and pay-per-view movies, and high-speed Internet access. A complimentary *USA Today* is delivered each weekday morning to your room, and a 24-hour business center is available. The hotel also offers its Sweet Dreams® bedding package (plus-top mattresses, luxurious linens, down comforter, and jumbo pillows).

Hotel guest have free access to the largest health club in the city, located in the building. This 13,000-square-foot facility includes a fitness room, jogging and walking track, and indoor pool. Don't forget to dine at the award-winning Bigelow Grille and visit the Golden Spoon Spa, both on-site.

Marriott Pittsburgh City Center $$$
112 Washington Place
(412) 471-4000, (888) 456-6600
www.marriotthotels.com
While some urban hotels struggle to find space for exercise equipment, Pittsburgh Marriott City Center has no such problem. It offers a 40-foot indoor pool, a health club, and a sauna. Parking, another possible headache for urban hotels, also is hardly a problem here, as hotel guests have access to an adjacent 2,100-space indoor garage. Parking ranges from $4.25 to $16.50. Valet service is available for $23 each day with in-and-out privileges.

The hotel offers 402 guest rooms as well as 5 parlor suites and the deluxe Presidential Suite, complete with Jacuzzi and wet bar.

When you're ready to eat, you'll find fare that will match your mood. You'll want to try the Steelhead Grill, the on-premises seafood restaurant that has won national awards. While the hotel is only a few blocks from the center of downtown, it offers complimentary shuttle transportation to key downtown points.

The Omni William Penn $$$
530 William Penn Place
(412) 281-7100
www.omniwilliampenn.com

Relaxing in the Palm Court lobby of the Omni William Penn is one of the city's most civilized experiences. While you enjoy a beverage and bask beneath the ornate chandeliers, you can laugh with friends and watch the swells stroll through the lobby. It's such a comfortable experience that you might not want to leave.

Once you manage to get past the lobby, you'll find 603 guest rooms offering mahogany furnishings, plush carpeting, and marble baths. The hotel welcomes your pets. Ask about the special amenities at the select guest level.

In 1998 the hotel finished a three-year, $25 million renovation that gave face-lifts to meeting rooms on the conference level, including new names that reflect Pittsburgh's industrial history—names such as Frick, Heinz, Oliver, Phipps, and Vandergrift. Many of the luxury suites have also been updated. Each boasts multiple bedrooms, living and dining rooms, sitting areas, and full kitchens. Electronics throughout the hotel were improved as well, so guests now enjoy two phone lines and voice mail.

The hotel features more than 52,000 square feet of meeting space, capped by the two-story Grand Ballroom. For your dining pleasure, you'll choose from several restaurants, including the Terrace Room, one of the city's most popular spots for breakfast meet-

ings, and the Tap Room, a small pub tucked away near the Grant Street entrance. The Palm Court lobby is a grand space flanked by seven arches on each side.

The Omni William Penn sits in the center of the city, within walking distance of all the cultural amenities as well as Grant Street political happenings. Turn to the Architecture chapter, where this hotel, commissioned by Henry Clay Frick, appears as part of the walking tour of downtown Pittsburgh. Don't miss afternoon tea in the Palm Court lobby, a simply splendid tradition (albeit borrowed from the British).

Pittsburgh Hilton and Towers $$$$
600 Commonwealth Place
Gateway Center
(412) 391-4600, (800) 445-8667
www.hilton.com

If you arrive at the Hilton and wonder about that attractive greenery across the street, wonder no longer. That's Point State Park, the unusual urban park that's the site for many entertainment and cultural events, including the annual Three Rivers Arts Festival (see the Annual Events chapter). Stay at the Hilton and the park and its attractions will be at your doorstep—literally.

The hotel is the city's most capacious, offering 713 guest rooms that include a complement of concierge-class rooms. In your room you'll enjoy two phone lines with voice mail, writing desk, in-room movies, a coffeemaker, and an iron set. Each guest room boasts a river or city view.

If business beckons, the Hilton is well equipped to meet your needs. Its Executive Center is sequestered in a quiet corner of the first floor and offers boardrooms, computers, and secretarial service. If it's a meeting that you're planning, consider the Hilton's 18,200-square-foot ballroom, said to be the largest between New York and Chicago.

The health center includes Universal weights, treadmills, Stairmasters, rowing machines, and stationary bicycles. You'll enjoy

i Even children can partake of afternoon tea at the Omni William Penn hotel. Ask for the Mad Hatters Tea, a selection of tasty cookies and confections kids will love!

both casual and more elegant dining in the hotel's two restaurants and two lounges.

The Hilton will allow small pets with management's prior approval.

Renaissance Pittsburgh Hotel $$$$
107 Sixth Street
(412) 562-1200, (866) 454-4400
www.renaissancepittsburgh.com

The Renaissance, the city's only four-diamond hotel, is located right in the Cultural District downtown. A historic 1906 building that once housed offices and later—in one metamorphosis—became a dance club in the waning disco days, the Renaissance has been restored to its former glory. It's resplendent with a granite, brick, and copper exterior and an interior that showcases a spectacular lobby done in mosaic tile, with a grand marble staircase that winds upward. The building itself is notable for its three-story rotunda and roof of leaded glass and copper. In fact, the three-year renovation of the Renaissance became the largest copper restoration project in the United States since the restoration of the Statue of Liberty.

This luxurious hotel offers 286 guest rooms and 9 luxury suites. There is on-site and valet parking. Amenities include high-speed Internet access, voice mail, Web TV, an exercise room and whirlpool, plus an adjacent fitness center. Off the lobby, the fashionable restaurant, Opus has garnered rave reviews for its Mediterranean cuisine, as well as its wine bar.

Overlooking the Allegheny River, the Renaissance is within walking distance of theaters, restaurants, nightclubs, and the convention center. It's also less than a 10-minute stroll across the Roberto Clemente Bridge to the Andy Warhol Museum, PNC Park, and Heinz Field.

Sheraton Station Square Hotel $$$
300 West Station Square Drive
(412) 261-2000, (800) 255-7488
www.sheraton.com

Station Square is a vibrant urban riverfront shopping center with 30 shops, restaurants, and nightclubs. It's actually situated on the city's South Side, but it's so close to Downtown (right across the Smithfield Street Bridge) we decided to include it here. Stay at the Sheraton Station Square and you'll be only a few excited paces from all that activity.

The hotel offers 396 guest rooms as well as a club level on the 15th floor for Sheraton Platinum Members. Many rooms provide dramatic views of Pittsburgh's rivers and skyline, while all guest rooms offer cable television, in-room movies, hair dryers, irons and ironing boards, and coffee service. You'll enjoy an indoor pool, whirlpool, sauna, steam room, and fitness center. Consider making an appointment with one of the massage therapists who are on call. Meeting and banquet facilities can accommodate up to 1,500 people.

The atrium lobby is a must-stop, whether you're staying at the hotel or dropping by for refreshments. There you'll see great views of the rivers, Point State Park, and downtown. Those views and the great food make Pittsburgh Rare restaurant and lounge a particularly great choice for dinner.

The Sheraton is just across the Smithfield Street Bridge (see our Architecture chapter for more details and the start of a walking tour). The hotel welcomes pets.

Westin Convention Center Pittsburgh $$$$
1000 Penn Avenue
(412) 281-3700
www.westin.com/pittsburgh

This is definitely one of the deluxe hotels in town, and very convenient to the David L. Lawrence Convention Center across the street. With 616 rooms, including 42 suites, guests who want a little luxury while on business in the downtown area may opt to stay here. The banquet room seats approximately 960 people, and there are 19 meeting rooms. Guests enjoy two-line dataports with speakerphones and ironing supplies in each room. There are four restaurants, including the Original Fish Market. Parking is convenient underneath the hotel, but because parking is at a premium in downtown, it's $20 a day for guests. Valet parking is available at $22 per day.

North

Butler Days Inn $
139 Pittsburgh Road, Butler
(724) 287-6761, (800) 329-7466
www.daysinn.com

Conferences are popular at Days Inn, which offers meeting and banquet space for up to 1,200 people. That's far from the only attraction, though. The 140 guest rooms feature cable television, and you can also enjoy the pool, Jacuzzi, Brentwood Café, and Frisco's Bar & Grill. Bring your pet, but be prepared to pay a $35 nonrefundable pet fee.

The facility offers specially priced golf packages that allow you to test as many as four Butler-area courses. The Days Inn is located along Route 8.

Clarion Hotel $$
300 Tarentum Bridge Road, New Kensington
(724) 335-9171, (877) 424-6423
www.choicehotels.com

Looking to hold a banquet or meeting in the New Kensington area? This may be your place, with facilities that can accommodate up to 900 and complete audiovisual equipment offered on-site.

Stay in one of the 115 guest rooms and you'll have access to an outdoor pool. If you're willing to sign for responsibility for any cleanup or damages, you're welcome to bring your pets.

Conley Resort $$
740 Pittsburgh Road, Butler
(724) 586-7711, (800) 344-7303
www.conleyresort.com

While the designation "resort" may be a little highfalutin', Conley Resort does offer a number of attractive amenities. It features an 18-hole golf course, a putting green, and an indoor pool. If the kids are along, dare them to try either the 100-foot waterslide or the speed slide. Pets are not permitted.

When you stay in one of the 56 guest rooms, you'll receive complimentary breakfast. Knickers Tavern, a full-service restaurant and bar, is on-site. Ask about specially priced golf packages. Conley Resort is located along Route 8, a major state highway that connects Pittsburgh and Butler.

Fairfield Inn & Suites Butler $$
200 Fairfield Lane, Butler
(724) 283-0009

Operated by Marriott, Fairfield Inn & Suites offers complimentary continental breakfast, in-room work areas, an indoor pool, a whirlpool, and an exercise room. Feel free to use the hotel's fax service. Pets are not permitted in the 75 guest rooms.

While Fairfield Inn is about 30 miles from Pittsburgh, it is convenient to the VA Medical Center and many attractions of Butler, including Butler Memorial Hospital and the fairgrounds, host to the annual Big Butler County Fair in early July (see the Annual Events chapter).

Holiday Inn Express—North $$
10 Landings Drive
(412) 828-9300
www.hiexpress.com

Located in Harmarville, one of the principal attractions of this hotel is a host of unusual entertainment opportunities nearby. Within a few minutes' walk are Blade Runners Ice Complex, featuring two regular ice-skating surfaces, and Ladbrokes, an off-track wagering facility where you can watch and wager on as many as 25 horse-racing tracks per day.

Located just off exit 48 (old exit 5) of the Pennsylvania Turnpike, the hotel offers four suites in addition to its 59 standard rooms, as well as a small indoor pool.

Holiday Inn Hotel & Suites Valley—RIDC Park $$$
180 Gamma Drive, O'Hara
(412) 963-0600
www.holiday-inn.com

The hotel offers 40 apartment-style suites with kitchen facilities and patios. You can take advantage of short- and long-term rates. "RIDC" is short for Regional Industrial Development Corporation, which developed the business park in which the hotel is located. Many who are in town on business in the park take advantage of this Holiday Inn's long-term rates.

Guests can relax in the fitness room, the Cabana Club bar (in the warmer months), and Franco's Restaurant and Nitescape Lounge. Meeting space can accommodate up to 600 people. The hotel welcomes your pets.

Holiday Inn North Hills—Pittsburgh $$$
4859 McKnight Road
(412) 366-5200
www.holiday-inn.com
Stay at this Holiday Inn and you'll hear the "Call of the Mall." It's located in the suburban North Hills on McKnight Road, an active strip of malls sure to satisfy your every shopping need.

The hotel offers 146 standard-issue guest rooms with cable television, computer access, voice mail, coffeemakers, and iron sets. Dine at the Hilltop Bar & Grill.

The Priory Hotel $$$
614 Pressley Street
(412) 231-3338
www.thepriory.com
In the late 19th century, Benedictine priests and brothers traveling through Pittsburgh would take respite at The Priory. Current owners have restored the facility with Victorian-style furnishings in its 24 guest rooms. If you need an office-away-from-the-office, this probably isn't the place. If you're looking for an Old World experience in elegant surroundings, you'll find it at The Priory.

The inn is unobtrusive, located on a North Side residential street, but the appointments are splendid. You'll enjoy complimentary breakfast and evening wine around the fireplace. You can walk in the garden courtyard or to any of the city's nearby attractions, including PNC Park, the Andy Warhol Museum, and the National Aviary.

On weekday mornings you can use complimentary limousine service for the half-mile trip across the Ninth Street Bridge into downtown Pittsburgh. Or you can sip your wine, gaze across the Allegheny River at the hustle

The David L. Lawrence Convention Center

Opened in 2003, the David L. Lawrence Convention Center brings an elegant, functional, and environmentally intelligent facility to Pittsburgh's riverfront. The facility is the first certified "green" convention center in the United States, using features such as natural ventilation, natural daylight, water conservation, and energy efficiency. Stunning, spacious, and unique, the convention center triples Pittsburgh's capacity for meetings, conventions, and exhibitors.

The convention center, designed by Rafael Vinoly Architects, P.C., is operated by the Sports and Exhibition Authority and contains a main hall, a secondary hall, meeting rooms, two lecture halls, 330,000 square feet of exhibition space, a 33,000-square-foot ballroom, and a 700-space parking garage.

and bustle of downtown, and contemplate how good life can be. Pets are not permitted. Parking is complimentary.

Rodeway Inn $
RD 6, U.S. Highway 422 East, Kittanning
(724) 543-1100
www.rodewayinnmotel.com
Here's a quaint establishment with only 20 rooms; what it lacks in volume it makes up in dedicated customer service and its delicious, complimentary breakfast. Each guest room features cable television, microwave, refrigerator, DVD player, coffeemaker, and Internet access. DVDs are available for rent on-site. Bring your pet, but you will be charged a $5 per night fee. This Rodeway Inn is in Armstrong County, about 30 miles north of Pittsburgh.

Sheraton Inn Pittsburgh North $$$
910 Sheraton Drive, Mars
(724) 776-6900
www.sheraton.com

Don't worry about being on Mars. This community is part of Pittsburgh's growing suburban North Hills, which means you'll be close to many attractions.

This Sheraton Inn offers 189 rooms with a number of compelling views. You can request a room with a balcony or one that faces the hotel's atrium. All rooms offer cable television, computer access, coffeemakers, hair dryers, and iron sets. You'll also have access to fax and copier service.

For a workout, try the on-site health club, indoor/outdoor pool, and Jacuzzi. You can slake the thirst you work up at the on-premises lounge, Legends Pub. Sheraton Inn does not permit pets.

East

Comfort Inn Conference Center $$
699 Rodi Road
(412) 244-1600, (877) 424-6423
www.choicehotels.com

Travel up the long winding road that's the driveway, and you'll reach a scenic view of Pittsburgh's eastern communities. You'll also find such amenities as indoor and outdoor pools, saunas, a whirlpool, and lighted tennis courts. This hotel was newly remodeled in 1999.

Free wireless Internet is available, and you may utilize the hotel's fax services. Showtime is available in all rooms. The hotel offers complimentary buffet breakfast, and the onsite restaurant and lounge, Inndigo Blue, takes pride in its wine list. Pets are permitted.

This Comfort Inn is accessible from the Pennsylvania Turnpike (by only a few miles) and I-376 (the Parkway East).

i Pittsburgh's most elegant hotel during the 19th century was the Monongahela House, which stood next to the Monongahela Wharf. Six presidents, including Abraham Lincoln, stayed there during Pittsburgh's heyday as a river port.

Days Inn—New Stanton $
127 West Byers Avenue, New Stanton
(724) 925-3591
www.daysinnnewstanton.com

If you're traveling the Pennsylvania Turnpike, Days Inn will be a welcome stop—it's close to the New Stanton exit (exit 75), where the turnpike meets Interstate 76. You'll find 135 guest rooms with many attractive features, including cable television, computer access, voice mail, hair dryers, and iron/ironing board. There are also laundry facilities.

When you're ready to relax, try the outdoor pool and the weight room. B.T. Spitzers, an on-site restaurant and lounge, features karaoke and a DJ on Saturday night. Days Inn does permit pets.

Four Points Hotel by Sheraton $$
Route 30 East 100 Sheraton Drive
Greensburg
(724) 836-6060
www.fourpoints.com

The Four Points offers 146 rooms—the deluxe rooms and bridal suites have Jacuzzis—that feature cable television, in-room movies, and computer access. You'll enjoy the indoor pool, but if you need a more vigorous workout, you can hit the weights at a nearby fitness center for a fee. Relax at the Prospect Lounge and the Vista Plateau, both on-site. Four Points does permit pets if you're willing to pay an additional $10.

Hampton Inn Greensburg $$
1000 Towne Square Drive, Greensburg
(724) 838-8800, (800) 426-7866
www.hamptoninn.com

This Hampton Inn is much like any other location, only with a few differences. There's an outdoor pool, exercise facility, and 69 guest rooms at this location. You'll find restaurants within 2 miles, and the hotel is not far from the Westmoreland Mall. No pets are allowed here. The hotel offers an outdoor pool, exercise room, and business center for guests' use. Guest rooms have televisions with cable and wireless Internet access. All Hampton

Inns feature complimentary continental breakfast and free local telephone calls.

Hampton Inn Monroeville $$
3000 Mosside Boulevard, Monroeville
(412) 380-4000, (800) 426-7866
www.hamptoninnpittsburghmonroeville.com
The Hampton Inn is strategically located just off the Pennsylvania Turnpike's exit 57, the Parkway East, and Route 22. There are 140 guest rooms and one meeting room for business or conferences. Enjoy the indoor pool, fitness room, and complimentary continental breakfast. Guests can also enjoy the Outback Steakhouse attached to the Hampton Inn. Situated in Monroeville, you're close to shopping with the Miracle Mile Shopping Center right up the road and Monroeville Mall five minutes away. Just drive down Business Route 22 and you're never at a loss for a gas station or store! Boyce Park is approximately 10 minutes away in nearby Plum Borough. And that's a good thing—pets under 20 pounds are allowed at this Hampton Inn location.

Holiday Inn Parkway East $$$
915 Brinton Road, Wilkinsburg
(412) 247-2700
www.holiday-inn.com/pit-east
This hotel offers 177 guest rooms, with suites also available. You'll enjoy the indoor pool as well as privileges at a local fitness center that offers tennis and racquetball courts. For on-site dining try the 915 Cafe. The Grand Ballroom can accommodate up to 300 for banquets and meetings. The hotel welcomes small pets.

Holiday Inn Pittsburgh-Monroeville $$$
2750 Mosside Boulevard, Monroeville
(412) 372-1022
www.holiday-inn.com/monroeville
All 187 guest rooms at the hotel offer satellite television, wireless Internet access, hair dryers, iron sets, and coffeemakers. Pets are not permitted. Amenities include an outdoor swimming pool and an on-premises restaurant called Madison's, which serves breakfast, lunch, and dinner, plus a Sunday brunch.

Meeting and banquet facilities can accommodate up to 300 people. The hotel is a quarter mile from exit 57 of the Pennsylvania Turnpike.

Holiday Inn Select Pittsburgh at University Center $$$
100 Lytton Avenue
(412) 682-6200
www.hiselect.com/pitt-univctr
When you stay here, you'll be smack-dab in the middle of the University of Pittsburgh campus. The historic Cathedral of Learning is several hundred yards away, and you'll enjoy the compelling sight of students on their way to class. You can reach all of Oakland's hospitals by walking or a short bus ride.

All 251 guest rooms feature cable television, in-room movies, coffeemakers, hair dryers, iron sets, and high-speed Internet access. Business travelers might prefer Executive Edition rooms, with refrigerators and a daily complimentary buffet.

Recreational opportunities include an indoor pool, a sauna, and exercise equipment. For dining, try the on-premises Bridge's Restaurant.

The hotel offers 7,500 square feet of meeting and banquet space. While you're here, treat yourself to a tour of the Cathedral of Learning's impressive Nationality Rooms. For more on those, see the Attractions chapter.

Mountain View Hotel and Conference Center $$
121 Village Drive, Greensburg
(724) 834-5300, (800) 537-8709
www.mountainviewinn.com
Built in 1924, the Mountain View has remained under continuous ownership of the Booher family since 1940. They have maintained the Early American setting, with guest rooms featuring antique furnishings as well as brass or canopied beds. You can opt for a suite or schedule a meeting for your group in the facility's spacious banquet rooms.

You'll enjoy the outdoor pool and boccie courts and take special pleasure in dining at the Mountain View, acclaimed for its decor and excellent food. If you're looking for understated elegance, you'll find it at Mountain View.

This hotel also makes for the perfect romantic getaway, with some suites featuring small fireplaces, spacious Jacuzzis, and the lavish touch of fresh, made-to-order floral arrangements.

Quality Inn University Center $
3401 Boulevard of the Allies
(412) 683-6100, (800) 424-6423
www.choicehotels.com

Stay at the Quality Inn and you'll be at the doorstep of Magee Woman's Hospital and the other health-care providers that constitute Pittsburgh's most important medical center. The hotel provides free shuttle service throughout the Oakland university-medical area. Pick up your shuttle schedule at the front desk.

The 117 guest rooms include cable television and private balconies, and you'll have access to fax service, meeting space, and an on-site restaurant. You also can request an executive room and enjoy such amenities as a hair dryer, coffeemaker, and wireless Internet access.

Radisson Hotel Pittsburgh $$
101 Mall Boulevard, Monroeville
(412) 373-7300
www.radisson.com/monroevillepa

A compelling attraction of the Radisson is its proximity to Pittsburgh ExpoMart, a popular venue for a wide variety of exhibits and trade shows. If you're participating in or visiting one of those events, you won't beat Radisson's convenience.

You can select from 322 guest rooms or penthouse suites. All guests can swim in the pool, relax in the Jacuzzi, or drink and dine in the Iron City Grille and the Oxford Dining Room. You also will enjoy privileges at the nearby Club 4 Life, a full-service fitness center.

If that doesn't tire you out, the 160-shop Monroeville Mall, Barnes & Noble, and many restaurants are a quick walk from the hotel,

which is accessible from both the Pennsylvania Turnpike's exit 57 and Interstate 376 (the Parkway East). The hotel does not permit pets.

Ramada Inn at Historic Ligonier $$
216 West Loyalhanna Street, Ligonier
(724) 238-9545
www.ramadainnligonier.com

You'll find 73 guest rooms with wireless Internet access, as well as deluxe rooms that feature a large work and sitting area. In addition, there are seven suites with Jacuzzis and minikitchens. All rooms have access to fax and copier service, and all guests can enjoy the Bistro, located on-site. In season you can splash in the outdoor pool. The hotel does not permit pets.

At the Ramada you'll be in the scenic Laurel Highlands recreation area, close to many attractions. Make sure you inquire about special guest packages featuring the Seven Springs Mountain Resort and Idlewild Park and SoakZone, a popular amusement park (see the Kidstuff chapter for details).

South

Days Inn Pittsburgh $
1150 Banksville Road
(412) 531-8900, (800) 325-2525
www.daysinn.com

This is a serviceable hotel with 70 rooms, an outdoor swimming pool, and banquet facilities that can seat up to 150 people. You also can request a room with a Jacuzzi. Fax service is available, and all rooms offer cable television and Internet access.

The most important feature of this facility, however, is its central location, less than 2 miles from downtown Pittsburgh. When convention or holiday traffic causes congestion at downtown hotels, many travelers look to Days

i   When Prince Charles visited Pittsburgh for the 1988 "Remaking Cities" conference, he overnighted at the Vista Hotel, now the Westin Convention Center.

Inn as a convenient alternative. The hotel does not permit pets.

EconoLodge $
1385 West Chestnut Street, Washington
(724) 222-6500
If you're looking for economical, serviceable lodgings in Washington, this might be the place. The 62 rooms offer cable television, and guests enjoy complimentary continental breakfast. Pets are not permitted. Find this motor inn at exit 39 off Interstate 70.

Holiday Inn Meadowlands $$$
340 Racetrack Road, Meadowlands
(724) 222-6200
www.holiday-inn.com
If horse racing is in your blood, then this Holiday Inn is in your future. It's about a furlong from Ladbroke at the Meadows, a harness-racing facility that features both live and simulcast racing (see the Spectator Sports chapter).

The hotel has 138 guest rooms and a pool. A lounge and restaurant are on the premises, and you can repair to your room to watch cable television or use the wireless Internet access. You also may take advantage of golf privileges at a nearby club.

Because Racetrack Road is an important connector between Interstate 79 and U.S. Route 19, the hotel is a popular and convenient site for banquets.

West

Best Western Parkway Center Inn $$
875 Greentree Road, Green Tree
(412) 922-7070
www.bestwestern.com
Location is an important plus for this hotel. It's 2 miles west of downtown Pittsburgh along the Interstate 279 corridor. That means it's only a 15-minute drive or ride to Pittsburgh International Airport, and you can utilize the hotel's airport shuttle service. The hotel is adjacent to the 85-store Parkway Center Mall, which will provide you with such amenities as shopping, dining, a post office, a travel agency, and automobile rentals.

The hotel offers 138 rooms, a complimentary breakfast buffet, and complimentary cocktails from 5:00 p.m. until 7:00 p.m.—enjoy them around the indoor pool. You can take advantage of the fitness center. Pets are not permitted.

Comfort Inn Pittsburgh Airport $$
7011 Old Steubenville Pike, Oakdale
(412) 787-2600
www.comfortinn.com
Owned by the same family for the past three generations, this Comfort Inn used to be known as The Tonidale. Today it features 66 guest rooms, such business services as a fax and a copier, a fitness center, and courtesy transportation to Pittsburgh International Airport, which is about 7 miles away. Don't forget to stop by the Six Flames Restaurant, adjacent to the hotel.

Courtyard by Marriott $$$
450 Cherrington Parkway, Coraopolis
(412) 264-5000, (800) 321-2211
www.courtyard.com
At Courtyard by Marriott, you can relax while you work, or work while you relax. Either way, you'll find accommodating facilities here.

The 148 guest rooms offer large working areas as well as high-speed Internet access, coffeemakers, and cable television. When you're ready for a break, try the minigym, indoor pool, and whirlpool. Later you can enjoy eating at the Courtyard Café, the on-site restaurant.

The facility can provide meeting rooms for up to 60 participants as well as fax and copier service. The establishment does not permit pets.

Crowne Plaza Hotel $$
1160 Thorn Run Road, Coraopolis
(412) 262-2400
www.cppittsburgh.com
The 193 guest rooms at the Crowne Plaza offer in-room work areas, telephones, and wireless Internet access. For a special treat, try the Concierge Level, where you'll enjoy

ℹ️ More than 10 million people visit the Pittsburgh region annually. Travel here is a $3 billion industry that provides more than 50,000 full-time equivalent jobs just in Allegheny County alone!

complimentary breakfast and cocktails, or swim in the outdoor pool. There is a restaurant and lounge on property.

No matter which room you choose, feel free to bring your pets. The hotel's meeting space can accommodate up to 550 people. You also can access courtesy transportation to and from Pittsburgh International Airport, which is about 6 miles away. The shuttle operates every half hour from 4:00 a.m. until 1:00 a.m.

Embassy Suites Hotel $$$$
550 Cherrington Parkway, Coraopolis
(412) 269-9070, (800) 362-2779
www.embassy-suites.com

As the name suggests, you'll find well-appointed suites here, each with a refrigerator, microwave, coffeemaker, voice mail, and computer access. Take advantage of the pull-out sofa and meeting area within each suite. You'll enjoy cable television and in-room movies.

The hotel offers a health club and swimming pool as well as the Foggy Bottom Restaurant on-site. You won't go hungry here in the morning as you feast on a cooked-to-order breakfast.

Pets are welcome, but you will be charged a $50 nonrefundable fee. Embassy Suites offers a free 24-hour shuttle to and from the Pittsburgh International Airport.

Fort Pitt Motel $
7750 Steubenville Pike, Oakdale
(412) 788-9960

Fort Pitt Motel is an unusual little budget-type establishment with only 21 rooms. The story here is the surprising amenities. Seven rooms offer heart-shaped whirlpools, while a number of rooms feature balconies, patios, and working fireplaces. It's pretty spartan other-

wise, but the unusual features and location about 10 miles from Pittsburgh International Airport make this one worth checking out.

Hampton Inn Greentree $$
555 Trumbull Drive, Green Tree
(412) 922-0100, (800) 426-7866
www.hamptoninn.com

The Hampton Inn is among a cluster of three hotels in the Pittsburgh suburb of Green Tree. All offer great locations, only 3 miles from downtown Pittsburgh and just a 15-minute ride from Pittsburgh International Airport. The hotel offers free airport shuttle service.

Its 132 rooms offer worktables and telecommunication ports. If you're getting in a little work during your visit, feel free to use the copier and fax machine as well as the hotel's meeting rooms. These can accommodate up to 35 people.

If you have a pet under 50 pounds, bring it along, but be aware of the additional $25 cleaning fee. Of course you must sign a pet policy for any potential damages.

Hampton Inn Pittsburgh–Airport $$
8514 University Boulevard, Moon Township
(412) 264-0020, (800) 426-7866
www.hamptoninn.com

Hampton Inn offers complimentary shuttle service to and from Pittsburgh International Airport, which is a convenient 7 miles away. If you're visiting Robert Morris University, the hotel is only a mile from campus. Bring your pets along for the visit—they're welcome here.

Accommodations include 127 guest rooms featuring cable television, a complimentary breakfast buffet, and a fitness center. This Hampton Inn also offers meeting rooms. With Robinson Town Centre and the Pointe at North Fayette about five minutes east (toward the city), you'll have plenty of shopping and restaurants to keep you entertained and fed.

Holiday Inn Beaver Falls $$
7195 Eastwood Road, Beaver Falls
(724) 846-3700
www.holiday-inn.com

The fitness buffs in your party will love the

hotel's Holidome, which features a pool, a whirlpool, a video arcade, billiards, and a jungle gym. When you're ready to eat and drink after your workout, you'll find Casey's Lounge on the premises.

The hotel offers 156 rooms with cable television, wireless Internet access, hair dryers, and iron sets, and it welcomes your pets as long as you're willing to pay the $35 nonrefundable fee. You can reach Holiday Inn easily—it's just off exit 13 (old exit 2) of the Pennsylvania Turnpike.

Holiday Inn Pittsburgh Airport $$$
8256 University Boulevard, Coraopolis
(412) 262-3600, (800) 333-4835
www.hipittsburgh.com

You can almost see Pittsburgh International Airport from the Holiday Inn, and the courtesy transportation the hotel provides will get you to the airport in a few moments. The hotels' 255 rooms include work areas and in-room movies; you also can opt for an executive room with a king-size bed and a sofa bed. Stuck with work on your trip? The hotel's computer ports, fax, copier, and secretarial assistance will help you get it done more quickly.

The highlight of the hotel's recreational facilities is the indoor "aquacade," featuring a pool and whirlpool. You can dine at the on-site Bridges Bar & Grill or choose from the many restaurants along University Boulevard. For meetings and banquets, the hotel offers almost 11,000 square feet of conference space.

Your pets are welcome here.

Holiday Inn Pittsburgh Central/Greentree $$$
401 Holiday Drive, Green Tree
(412) 922-8100
www.holiday-inn.com

The Holiday Inn is part of the Green Tree cluster of hotels, with that great location convenient to both downtown Pittsburgh and Pittsburgh International Airport.

The hotel's 200 rooms offer wireless Internet access, work areas, and balconies, so you can work a little and relax a little. If you're

looking for a workout, try the outdoor pool or fitness center. Afterwards you can repair to the Greenery Restaurant and Lounge, the in-house restaurant that stages a daily lunch buffet that's popular with hotel guests and others in search of a good meal. Bring your pets—they're welcome here.

For banquets, the hotel's Grand Ballroom can seat up to 1,000 guests. You can employ the dozen breakout rooms as well.

Hyatt Regency Pittsburgh International Airport $$–$$$
1111 Airport Boulevard
(724) 899-1234, (800) 233–1234
www.pittsburgh.hyatt.com

After touching down at the Pittsburgh International Airport, what could be easier than walking to your accommodations? Directly connected to the enclosed moving walkway, this full-service hotel offers 336 comfortable guest rooms and 11 suites, plus meeting and banquet space in its conference center. Amenities include high-speed Internet access through T-Mobile.

Approximately 20 minutes from downtown Pittsburgh, the hotel is a surprisingly tranquil spot in the airport complex amid flight departures and arrivals. And nothing reduces the stress of modern travel like the Hyatt's 1,000-square-foot fitness center, with its whirlpool and 50-foot heated lap pool.

Its Olive Press restaurant serves Mediterranean cuisine in stylish surroundings; a coffee bar delivers the prerequisite caffeine jolt needed to catch your next flight. If you want to shop, you have direct access to the Airmall's shops until 7:00 p.m. (For security purposes, you will have to obtain an identification card to go to the Airmall, which is located in the Airside Terminal.)

La Quinta Inn $$
8507 University Boulevard, Moon Township
(412) 269-0400, (800) 642-4271
www.lq.com

Stay at La Quinta and you'll be treated to complimentary continental breakfast and enjoy in-ℹ️ While in Pittsburgh with his orchestra in the 1940s, Lawrence Welk "discovered" his trademark bubble machine at the Omni (formerly the Westin) William Penn. The original machine, devised by a staff chef, remains on the premises.

room movies and complimentary airport transportation.

For business purposes, each of the 128 rooms and three suites features dataport phones and access to voice mail and fax service. The hotel permits small dogs in rooms.

Pittsburgh Airport Marriott $$$
777 Aten Road, Coraopolis
(412) 788-8800, (800) 328-9297
www.marriott.com
There are quite a few hotels in the Pittsburgh International Airport corridor, but the Pittsburgh Airport Marriott physically stands out, rising like a pastel palace off the Parkway West. Its lobby, grand and inviting, extends the palatial theme.

The hotel offers 319 guest rooms as well as a Concierge Level and 5 minisuites. Your pets are welcome here. On-site recreational opportunities include an indoor pool, an exercise room, a whirlpool, and a sauna. Try Meritage Grill for dining and drinking pleasure.

The hotel offers 12,000 square feet of meeting space (16 rooms) and free airport transportation.

Radisson Hotel Pittsburgh Green Tree $$$
101 Radisson Drive, Green Tree
(412) 922-8400, (800) 333-3333
www.radisson.com
The hotel is conveniently located in the airport Parkway West corridor and only 3 miles from downtown Pittsburgh.

The Radisson offers 465 guest rooms, 8 suites, and 9 parlors (meeting rooms with a Murphy bed). In your room you'll find cable television, in-room movies, and voice mail. For a workout, try the health club, indoor pool, outdoor pool, sauna, and gym. You can relax

in the lounge and two restaurants, all located on-site. One restaurant is full-service; the other is a small deli. The hotel features 30,000 square feet of meeting and banquet space, highlighted by the Grand Ballroom.

Bring your pets along—they're welcome here.

Sewickley Country Inn $$
801 Ohio River Boulevard, Sewickley
(412) 741-4300
www.sewickleyinn.com
For an experience that will take you back to a kinder, gentler era, try the Sewickley Country Inn. You'll be situated right along a scenic section of the Ohio River; the view alone will relax you.

The innkeepers have not ignored modern amenities. The 147 guest rooms feature cable television, and you'll have access to an outdoor swimming pool in the summertime as well as a dining room and a lounge on premises. The inn is about equidistant from downtown Pittsburgh and Pittsburgh International Airport. Meeting space can accommodate up to 250 people.

As you might expect in an establishment of such old-fashioned charm, small pets are welcome for a $10 fee. Sewickley Country Inn does weddings, meetings, showers, and dinners.

SpringHill Suites by Marriott— Pittsburgh Airport $$$–$$$$
239 Summit Park Drive
(412) 494-9446
www.springhillsuitespittsburghairport.com
SpringHill Suites has 102 guest rooms, a whirlpool, and an indoor pool. Guests enjoy the continental breakfast provided. Each suite offers a microwave, refrigerator, in-room coffeemaker, and hair dryer. See the Shopping chapter for more information about all that's offered at the Pointe—there is much shopping and many restaurants to choose from. This property is also along the airport corridor, so you're not far from catching your flight.

EXTENDED-STAY AND TEMPORARY ACCOMMODATIONS

One product of Pittsburgh's rich corporate history is a tradition of company teams traveling to headquarters here for extended assignments. While massive corporations no longer are the rule in Pittsburgh, they remain sufficiently numerous to provide a basis for a strong extended-stay and temporary accommodations sector.

Even as many corporations have downsized, the booming film production business has brought many actors, technicians, and executives to town. They, too, require temporary accommodations, enhancing the presence of this hospitality sector.

If you're seeking such accommodations, keep some key questions in mind: Do prospective providers offer accommodations in a variety of locations so you can select one that's convenient for you? Can they provide for your family? Do their rate schedules dovetail with the projected length of your stay? If you get the right answers, you'll know you've found the right temporary digs.

Rather than list these places geographically, we've included the whole region in one listing and present your options in alphabetical order.

AmeriSuites Pittsburgh/Airport
6011 Campbells Run Road
(412) 494-0202, (888) 774-6467

AmeriSuites Pittsburgh/Cranberry
136 Emeryville Drive, Cranberry
(724) 779-7900
www.amerisuites.com
Billed as America's all-suite hotels, guests enjoy separate living and sleeping areas, a refrigerator, microwave, wet bar, and a coffeemaker with complimentary coffee in every suite. There is also 26-inch cable TV, ironing supplies, voice mail, and dataport telephones in each suite. Do partake of the bountiful breakfast buffet, the indoor heated pool, the fitness center, and the MBE Business Express Center. If you need to do laundry, there are both valet service and laundry facilities available. With a free *USA Today* thrown in, it's just like being at home—well, almost.

Bridgestreet Accommodations
1501 Reedsdale Street
(412) 322-3999
www.bridgestreet.com
You'll find a diverse selection here, as Bridgestreet offers 150 units at 11 locations. You can take a virtual tour of each location on the Web. All units are in Allegheny and lower Butler Counties. You'll enjoy cable television, a complete kitchen, a washer and dryer, and housekeeping services. If you've been forced from your home for any reason, you'll find temporary housing options at Bridgestreet.

Daily rates range from $71 to $106; the range for monthly rates is $1,980 to $2,550.

Corporate Accommodations
15 Chestnut Street, Carnegie
(412) 429-5165, (800) 899-5456
www.corpaccom.com
Corporate Accommodations offers a broad selection of units—175 units in 13 complexes, primarily in Allegheny County, but fast-growing Butler County also is represented. Your apartment will feature cable television, high-speed Internet access, housekeeping and linen service, and a furnished kitchen.

To assure that their rooms meet your needs, customer service personnel inspect the preparations of the housekeeping staff before turning the unit over to you. Corporate Accommodations also provides short-term housing options for those forced from their homes by catastrophes.

ℹ️ For a complete listing of extended-stay options, pick up a copy of *Apartment Finder, Apartments for Rent,* and *Apartment Rental Guide* at local supermarkets. These publications also offer searchable Web sites: www.apartmentfinder .com, www.ForRent.com, and www.rental guidepittsburgh.com.

Daily rates range from approximately $79 to $112; the range for monthly rates is $2,370 to $3,360. There are lower rates for longer stays.

Extended StayAmerica
520 North Bell Avenue, Carnegie
(412) 278-4001

3851 Northern Pike, Monroeville
(412) 856-8400
www.extendedstayhotels.com
Extended StayAmerica offers both daily rates, starting at $69, and weekly rates ranging from $239 to $299. As appropriate for an extended stay, you'll find your room equipped with a refrigerator, stove top, and microwave oven, and you can utilize the on-site laundry.

The Carnegie facility is located in the Pittsburgh International Airport corridor and is convenient to both downtown Pittsburgh and the airport. Your pets are welcome here.

MainStay Suites
1000 Park Lane Drive
(412) 490-7343
www.choicehotels.com
Newly renovated, the MainStay Suites is an all-suite, extended-stay property located just minutes from the Pittsburgh International Airport. The spacious suites offer oversized workstations and full kitchens with refrigerators and microwaves. Wheelchair-accessible and nonsmoking rooms are available. Your pets are welcome, although there is an additional charge based on the length of your stay. Rates are based on how long you will be staying at the hotel, starting at $104.99 per night for a studio. Stay longer and that rate goes down.

Shadyside Inn Suites
5405 Fifth Avenue
(412) 441-4444, (800) 767-8483
www.shadysideinn.com
You're more than welcome to stay at Shadyside Inn for one night only, but the facility also can meet your temporary housing needs for weeks or months. All accommodations are suites featuring cable television and a VCR/DVD player, a telephone-answering machine, wireless Internet access, and an equipped kitchen. You also may utilize the on-site laundry and a complimentary pass to a local fitness center. For business needs, optional amenities include fax, copier, and secretarial service. There are 100 guest suites here.

Daily rates range from $99 to $160; the range for weekly rates is $560 to $850. If you prefer the monthly rate, the range is $1,800 to $2,700.

Once here you're within walking distance of the popular Shadyside shopping and dining district, and you're a short bus ride from Oakland's university-medical complex, making this an attractive option for those visiting Pittsburgh's colleges or hospitals for an extended period.

Bring your pets if they're under 25 pounds, but expect to pay a one-time fee of $95 for the privilege.

RESORTS

When you start to discuss resort communities, Pittsburgh may not be the town that springs to your lips. Think about it, though. We have warm, beautiful summers that are just the ticket for golf. We have plenty of inland waterways, the ideal setting for a variety of water sports. We have mountains and snow; last time we checked, those were a couple of the key ingredients in skiing. So who needs a beach and boiling temperatures?

With all these elements, Pittsburgh offers a number of resorts that take full advantage of the four seasons to vary their offerings and assure year-round attractions. While the resorts are a bit outside this guide's five-county geographic coverage area, they're included here rather than in the Day Trips chapter because each is no more than a 90-minute trip from Pittsburgh.

While we've adhered to the rate code for the following resorts, remember that seasonal swings in rates may be severe. Unless otherwise noted, the resorts offer smoking and nonsmoking rooms but do not permit pets.

East

Hidden Valley Four Seasons Resort $$$$
One Craighead Drive, Hidden Valley
(814) 443-8000
www.myhiddenvalleyresort.com

Place a gorgeous community in the heart of the Laurel Highlands, sprinkle with beautiful fall foliage, crisp air, and pure snow, and you have the recipe for Hidden Valley Resort. Located about 60 miles east of Pittsburgh in the Laurel Highlands, the resort is primarily a community of homes. You're welcome to stay for a night or weekend, however, as owners often rent out their homes. That means a treat for you.

You'll enjoy a golf course, tennis courts, four swimming pools, and a playground with basketball and volleyball. The resort stocks its freshwater lake seasonally with trout and bass, and you'll also enjoy canoeing, paddleboating, kayaking, and sailboating. The sports club in the conference-center complex features racquetball courts and exercise equipment, as well as a whirlpool, sauna, suntan bed, massage room, hair salon, and video arcade.

Skiing is particularly popular at the resort (see the Recreation and Golf chapters for fuller descriptions of these features), as are hiking and biking. You'll find more than 30 miles of trails, and you'll enjoy complimentary use of the resort's mountain bikes and helmets.

Hidden Valley offers more than a half dozen restaurants and lounges; it's hard to imagine staying hungry very long. With so many attractions, it's no wonder that so many permanent residents became familiar with the resort as weekend guests.

It should be noted that Hidden Valley is now under new ownership. The resort reopened on December 15, 2007. The new owners have started a three-year improvement plan that will include new snowmaking systems, groomers, chairs for chairlifts, ski rental equipment. Significant improvements are also planned for the lodge and recreational amenities at Hidden Valley. New residential and commercial developments are also in the works. Visit the Web site for an overview of the upcoming improvements.

Seven Springs Mountain Resort $$$$
777 Waterwheel Drive, Champion
(814) 352-7777, (800) 452-2223
www.7springs.com

Seven Springs is justifiably known for its excellent skiing—more about that in the Recreation chapter. The resort offers so much more that it's become one of the region's premier sites for conferences. If you're looking for a romantic getaway, you'll find that here as well.

The resort can accommodate 5,000 overnight guests in its lodges, 10-story highrise, chalets, condominiums, and cabins. They need every bit of that capacity—each year Seven Springs hosts more than 700 conferences and meetings that take advantage of exhibit and festival halls and the many indoor and outdoor recreational activities.

If a fresh snowfall calls to you, try the snow-tubing park or the alpine slide. Indoors you'll enjoy a swimming pool, massage, an exercise room with a whirlpool, a universal gym and a sauna, miniature golf, bowling, racquetball, roller-skating, and a variety of video games. Also, Seven Springs offers a climbing wall, Euro-bungy, and gravity mountain bike trail.

Outdoor activities include golf, tennis, hiking, horseback riding, and volleyball.

You'll work up an appetite with such active participation; Seven Springs is prepared to satisfy the heartiest of appetites with 10 restaurants and 6 lounges, some of which feature live entertainment. Be sure to check out Helen's, the original home of the resort's founders that now serves as a slopeside restaurant serving intercontinental cuisines.

Seven Springs is about 50 miles east of Pittsburgh, reachable from both exit 91 and exit 110 of the Pennsylvania Turnpike.

Downtown Pittsburgh offers more than 3,000 "committable" hotel rooms. Hoteliers save a few beyond that for emergencies and their own needs.

South

Linden Hall $$
432 Linden Hall Road, Dawson
(724) 529-7543 (800) 944-3238
www.lindenhallpa.com

This splendid mansion derives its name from the linden trees imported from Berlin by the original owner, Sarah Cochran, widow of coke and coal pioneer Philip Cochran. The estate has been transformed by its current owners, United Steelworkers of America, into a crackerjack resort and conference center with 74 guest rooms.

Recreation is a key theme at Linden Hall. You'll enjoy golf, biking along the scenic Yough River Trails, and fishing in a 25-acre lake. The picnic pavilion features sand volleyball and boccie courts, softball and soccer fields, and a children's playground.

You can relax in the sports pub and the charming country restaurant. The Great Hall can host your reception, while the outdoor gazebo provides a splendid backdrop for photographs. Make sure you inspect the Great Hall's Aeolian pipe organ, said to be one of only three in the world.

The resort is near Uniontown, 37 miles from Pittsburgh via Route 51 south. Linden Hall is closed from November 1 through mid-April; the golf course remains open year-round, weather permitting.

Nemacolin Woodlands Resort & Spa $$$$
1001 LaFayette Drive, Farmington
(724) 329-8555, (800) 422-2736
www.nemacolin.com

Nemacolin was named for a Native American chief. His name does not translate even loosely into "lap of luxury." Perhaps it should, because when you arrive at Nemacolin, you'll think you've fallen there. The $45 million artwork collection alone is indicative of the ambience of this award-winning resort. You'll encounter pieces by Tiffany, Audubon, Calder, and Remington, just to name a few.

Your experience in this 3,000-acre jewel begins with your accommodations. The Lodge, an English Tudor–style hotel, is the original hotel to the resort. Chateau LaFayette, modeled after the Ritz in Paris, features spacious rooms and suites with vaulted ceilings, crown molding, crystal chandeliers, and marble baths with jetted soaking tubs. Last but certainly not least, there is Falling Rock, Nemacolin's AAA Five Diamond hotel. This 42-room boutique hotel includes 4 suites and 24-hour butler service for all rooms. Guests can even choose from a 19-option Pillow Menu!

Nemacolin's list of activities is long and impressive. Of course they offer a fitness center, tennis courts and programs, rock-climbing wall, and squash courts. They also offer a ropes course with zip line and a gymnasium with a wide range of tumbling and gymnastic equipment.

During your Nemacolin stay, you can play two golf courses, including the Pete Dye–designed Mystic Rock. Or enjoy the six swimming pools, two of which are indoor and one just for families with children. For the equestrian, Nemacolin also features trail rides, surrey rides, and sleigh rides in winter. Or try the Shooting Academy (spring clays facility), the Off-Road Driving Academy (featuring Hummer® H1 and H2 vehicles and Toyota FJ Cruisers, or the paintball target and full-adventure courses. Looking for some quieter activities? There is fly fishing in the nearby streams and lakes, nature hikes, and The Marina @ Paige's Beach where you can use canoes, kayaks, pedal boats, and small sailboats.

Families staying at Nemacolin particularly enjoy the family-dedicated swimming pool, miniature golf course, and the Wildlife Academy and special wildlife habitats featuring black bears, zebras, elk, emus, buffalo, and moose.

Since Nemacolin is located in the heart of the Allegheny Mountains, guests can enjoy the area's winter sports—including downhill skiing, snowboarding, snow tubing, snowshoeing, cross-country skiing, and dogsledding.

All of those activities are bound to make you hungry. Don't worry, Nemacolin offers several dining options, from the casual American fare in the Tavern, the authentic Italian in Autumn, to French fine dining in Lautrec, plus others choices that are open seasonally. When it is time to relax, try Nemacolin's Woodlands Spa, which offers 100 treatments and a full-service salon. Or visit the many retail shops located at the resort and in nearby Uniontown.

Nemacolin is accessible from the Pennsylvania Turnpike, about 60 miles from Pittsburgh. If you'd really like to make a grand entrance, taxi up the resort's 4,000-foot private airstrip. Everything else about Nemacolin says class—why shouldn't your arrival?

The R&R Station Family Restaurant and Inn $
19 West Main Street, Mt. Pleasant
(724) 547-7545
www.therandrstation.com

Located in the same large building as the restaurant (featured in our Restaurants chapter), the R&R Station Family Inn offers 17 rooms decorated in railroad themes. You'll find rooms honoring the Baltimore–Ohio (B&O) Railroad, the Union Pacific, and the Santa Fe, as well as legendary railroad engineer Casey Jones. All rooms have private baths and full amenities, including air-conditioning, telephones, cable television, and wireless Internet access.

The delicious home-cooked food available at the restaurant downstairs will complete that cozy, well-cared-for feeling you'll cultivate here. The R&R Station Family Restaurant and Inn is nestled in the foothills of the Laurel Highlands, and you'll be only 30 minutes or so from major attractions such as Seven Springs ski resort, Frank Lloyd Wright's Fallingwater, whitewater rafting at Ohiopyle, and Fort Necessity in Uniontown. Right in Mt. Pleasant, there's the West Overton Museum, a 19th-century rural industrial village.

Children will especially enjoy nearby attractions such as Idlewild and SoakZone and Living Treasures Animal Park. Each September there's an annual glass festival (this used to be the home of the Lennox factory) and an

i Where do celebrities stay when in Pittsburgh? Jodie Foster stopped at the Shadyside Inn, while Gregory Peck opted for the Duquesne Club. Jack Nicholson chose the Vista (predecessor of the Westin Convention Center Hotel, which was formerly the Doubletree Hotel) and had television coverage of his beloved Los Angeles Lakers piped in via special arrangement.

annual coke and coal festival five minutes away in Scottdale. The R&R Station Family Restaurant and Inn is 30 to 40 minutes southeast of Pittsburgh. You'll find this family-owned gem on the east end of town in Mt. Pleasant, near Cook's Lumber.

West

Oglebay Resort and Conference Center $$$$
Route 88 North, Wheeling, West Virginia
(304) 243-4000, (800) 624-6988
www.oglebay-resort.com

This 1,700-acre resort was once the elegant summer estate of Cleveland industrialist Col. Earl W. Oglebay but now is operated by the city of Wheeling, West Virginia. Oglebay is so fun filled that it will take you several days just to sample it all.

It features four golf courses, including two championship courses at the Speidel Championship Golf Course. (For more on Oglebay's golf delights, see the Golf chapter.) You'll enjoy miles of jogging trails that crisscross the estate, as well as Bissonnette Gardens, which glow with such seasonal flowers as tulips, daffodils, and mums. Wedding parties travel for miles to Bissonnette Gardens to stage their nuptial pictures.

The Good Zoo showcases bears, otters, bison, and rare red wolves in natural settings. The Crispin Center offers outdoor swimming and tennis courts, and you'll find a number of venues for shopping.

You'll work up quite an appetite with all that activity, and you'll satisfy it just as surely in the Ihlenfield Dining Room in Wilson Lodge.

Recently updated and expanded as part of a $15 million renovation, the Wilson Lodge offers 265 deluxe rooms with wireless Internet access and telephones. Some rooms have fireplaces. If you'd like to get a little more rustic than the lodge, Oglebay offers 50 cottages where you can snuggle by the fireplace—the resort provides the firewood, you provide the rest. Pets are permitted only in cottages.

The highlight of the year at Oglebay is the Winter Festival of Lights, featuring more than one million lights. Travelers come from miles

i A brothel once flourished near the Priory when that city inn was a home for Benedictine monks in the 1880s. When the bishop discovered the house of ill repute, he ordered the front curtains closed and relocated the priests to the back room.

around to enjoy the 6-mile driving tour. You can reach Oglebay from Pittsburgh by taking I-79 south, then I-70 west.

BED-AND-BREAKFAST INNS

From lodgings at working farms in the country-side to quaint European-style inns tucked away in the city's neighborhoods, the Pittsburgh region offers a variety of bed-and-breakfast choices. Many of these accommodations are first-class—some of them downright luxurious. And their owners are usually ambassadors of the region—wanting to tell you about why their hometown is a wonderful place to visit, offering you their own "insider" ideas on where to dine, shop, and tour.

Although there are some exceptions, most bed-and-breakfast inns typically offer no more than five or six guest rooms. In addition, as small-business owners, proprietors of bed-and-breakfast inns may take off for vacation or suspend their services for long periods of time for other reasons. Some accommodate guests by reservation only. Under these circumstances, it makes a lot of sense for you to reserve your room, rather than dropping by and hoping for the best.

Planning is also important in the area of amenities; some bed-and-breakfasts do not offer the conveniences we take for granted in hotels and motels, such as in-room baths, telephones, television, air-conditioning, and computer accessibility. Some establishments welcome children, a few permit pets, and only a handful allow indoor smoking. The write-ups will indicate policies on pets and children. Unless otherwise indicated, smoking is permitted only outdoors. If a particular amenity is important to you, check with the proprietors when you call to make your reservation.

In summary, it's important that you consider all your needs—even those you customarily take for granted—in selecting a bed-and-breakfast. Pick the right one and you'll have the ideal opportunity for a memorable experience. You might even make a new friend or two.

PRICE CODE

We've included with our listings a rate guide to help you pick the establishment that best fits your budget. With each write-up, you'll see from one to five dollar signs to help you place the inns within these categories.

$	$45 to $70
$$	$71 to $90
$$$	$91 to $135
$$$$	$136 to $210
$$$$$	$211 to $275

Rates represent average charges for double occupancy. Keep in mind that rates will vary with season and availability, and that many establishments maintain discount programs through such organizations as AAA, AARP, or their own frequent guest programs. The room tax in Allegheny County is 7 percent; elsewhere it varies from county to county. Except as noted, all bed-and-breakfast inns profiled here accept at least one major credit card.

NORTH

Armstrong Farms Bed and Breakfast $$–$$$
1020 Ekastown Road, Saxonburg
(724) 352-2858
www.armstrongfarms.com
Armstrong Farms Bed and Breakfast is a 200-year-old farm/inn, still operating a large, pure-bred cattle herd on 1,000 unspoiled acres of Pennsylvania farmland. Located only 45 min-

utes from Pittsburgh in southeast Butler County, Armstrong is only minutes away from the National Historic District of downtown Saxonburg, where guests can enjoy fine dining, antiques and gift shopping, and walking tours of the town. Guests can stay in Drake's Guest House, the Love Cottage at Westminster Preserve, the Bonnie House, and the Alyson Anne Cottage, for a total of 20 rooms, some with working fireplaces. High-definition television and telephone can be enjoyed in a common room. A hearty country breakfast is served in the private dining room at the main farmhouse, which was built in 1816. Miles of farmland offer safe, gorgeous terrain for outdoor activities such as hiking, horseback riding (stalls available), biking, cross-country skiing, snowshoeing, fishing, bird-watching, wildflower conservation, and still-life painting.

This bed-and-breakfast has received numerous awards, including *Arrington's Bed & Breakfast Journal*'s Best Horse Lovers Inn in 2001 and the National Cattlemen's Beef Association 2002 Environmental Stewardship Award. It has also been featured in *Range Country* magazine. Special packages are available for several holidays; for parties, such as weddings; and for small, corporate retreats. From June 1 to November, "chuck wagon" retreats are offered, with a unique emphasis on farm life. Children are welcome at Armstrong, and so is one housebroken pet per party, with the innkeeper's preapproval.

Ber-Nita Acres Bed & Breakfast $
RD 2, 151 Bennett Drive, Ellwood City
(724) 752-1455, (888) 297-5396
www.pafarmstay.com/bernita

Ber-Nita Acres, a 92-acre working farm, offers three guest rooms in the owners' large home. Private baths are accessible to, but not adjoining, all of the rooms. A phone is available in the large living room, where there's also a television, VCR/DVD player, and an abundance of family-oriented movies on videotape and DVD. You'll be treated to a full country breakfast in the morning.

Your children are welcome to help feed the sheep, cows, and ostriches! From March to September they'll also be able to watch baby ostriches hatch from eggs in the incubator. For adults and children alike, there are two fishing lakes and a paddleboat, and you won't have to worry about bringing along your fishing poles or lifejackets—it'll all be there waiting for you, just like at grandma's house.

Smoke under the stars, but not in the house or in any of the outbuildings, and please leave the pets at home.

Heather Hill Bed & Breakfast $$–$$$
268 Rader School Road, Renfrew
(724) 789-7911
bedandb.isrv.com/

Heather Hill offers seven air-conditioned guest rooms—five with private baths, two with wood-burning stoves. The bed-and-breakfast sits on a secluded 175-acre farm about 30 miles from Pittsburgh in Butler County. You can enjoy hiking trails, swimming, a round of boccie, and watching the farm animals. There's also a game room with a pool table and air hockey table.

If you plan to bring children or pets, you'll need to review that with management. You'll also want to remember there's a large hall here, convenient for receptions, business meetings, and retreats. Credit cards are not accepted.

An Inn on Grandview $$–$$$$
119 East Grandview Avenue, Zelienople
(724) 473-8310

This 1892 home's accommodations include one bedroom and a studio apartment with a full bath, kitchen, and sitting area. Well-behaved children are welcome, but pets are not.

An Inn on Grandview is just a few miles from both the Pennsylvania Turnpike and Interstate 79. That places it in the heart of some splendid outdoor recreation country. Opportunities for golf, tennis, boating, and antiquing will beckon when you stay here. Enjoy a full breakfast at the inn before setting out to enjoy your activities.

The Inn on the Mexican War Streets $$$–$$$$
604 West North Avenue
(412) 231-6544
www.innonthemexicanwarstreets.com
Locals in the know are still surprised that more out-of-towners than actual Pittsburghers know—and enthusiastically praise—this gem on the North Side. A registered historical building more than a century old, the Russell H. Boggs mansion was renovated several years ago to become the Inn on the Mexican War Streets, which offers eight attractively furnished suites, each with a private bath, television, DVD player, and wireless Internet access. There are also two suites available that include kitchens and offices.

With exterior walls of quarry-faced stone and an arched Romanesque front porch, the inn is impressive. Innkeepers Jeff and Karl have recently converted the stone carriage stable behind the mansion into the Acanthus, a fine-dining, country French restaurant featuring a seven course prix-fixe menu.

In a city neighborhood in transition, the Inn on the Mexican War Streets is ideally located across from a public park and within walking distance of many major attractions on the North Side—the Andy Warhol Museum, the Mattress Factory, Heinz Field, and PNC Park—and a leisurely stroll across the Allegheny River to the Cultural District downtown.

Maggie West Bed & Breakfast $
605 Pittsburgh Street, Springdale
(724) 274-8906
This 1857 mansion, only a few blocks away from the Allegheny River, is within walking distance of small, local shops and restaurants in the heart of Springdale. Of the 20 rooms in the house, 4 are rented to guests. All rooms, decorated in Victorian style appropriate to the house, feature access to a parlor and tearoom; one offers a private bath.

All members of the Western Pennsylvania Bed & Breakfast Association subscribe to the organization's code of ethics.

If you need to make a call, use the inn's portable phone. There are televisions in all the rooms. Children are welcome, but pets are not. Maggie West Bed & Breakfast is about 20 minutes from Pittsburgh when the traffic along Route 28 is light.

Credit cards are not accepted.

Step Back in Time $–$$
224 North Washington Street, Butler
(724) 283-7509
www.geocities.com/sbitpa
This charming colonial-style home offers three guest rooms furnished with Victorian-period antiques. All of the rooms have private baths, telephones, and satellite televisions, so even as you soak in the claw-foot tub and dream of yesteryear you'll rest assured, knowing that all the modern amenities are at your fingertips. Step Back in Time is conveniently located in the heart of downtown Butler, within easy walking distance of offices, shops, restaurants, and area churches.

The facility is an hour from Pittsburgh, 30 minutes from I-79, and quite near Moraine State Park. Just imagine waking up the morning, taking a hike through the park, then feasting on scones, clotted cream, raspberry jam, and warm hospitality—that's what you'll find at Step Back in Time.

Your children are welcome here. Smoking, pets, and alcohol are not allowed.

Sun and Cricket Bed and Breakfast $$$
1 Tara Lane, Gibsonia
(724) 444-6300
www.sunandcricket.com
You'll be struck by the appealing blend of old and modern on this 35-acre country estate about 15 miles north of Pittsburgh. There are two spacious guest cottages. The Log Cabin sleeps up to four and adjoins the main house; the Carriage House sleeps up to three and is

Finding a Bed-and-Breakfast

Bed-and-breakfast inns tend to limit their advertising, so it can be tough to find out where they are and what they offer. In Pittsburgh you can get current information from a trade group, the Western Pennsylvania Bed & Breakfast Association. You can reach them at (888) 400-6380. Their Web site is www.westernpabandb.com.

For information specific to Pittsburgh and the surrounding six counties, visit the Web site for the Pittsburgh Bed & Breakfast Association, www.pittsburghbnb.com.

about 500 feet from the main house. (Children are welcome to stay with their family in the Log Cabin.) Each is enhanced by antique furnishings and handmade quilts. On the modern side, you'll enjoy private baths, color television, a VCR/DVD player, a refrigerator, a coffeemaker, and air-conditioning. The cozy log cabin offers a telephone and accommodations for children that offer their parents some privacy. Each cottage has a separate entrance and porch, so you can relax alone while you enjoy the view of the woods surrounding you. (You won't even be able to see the road from where you're sitting!) You'll enjoy a full gourmet breakfast served in your own private sitting area.

Besides the on-site pool, the owner notes that at least 12 golf courses are within a 5-mile radius, including the acclaimed Deer Run. (See the Golf chapter for more information.) While other pets are not permitted, Sun and Cricket will board your horse in a pasture you can view from your window.

EAST

Doone's Inn Bed and Breakfast $$$–$$$$
300 Route 909, Verona
(412) 828-0410

Under new ownership, the emphasis at this Federal-style inn is on charming surroundings and gracious service. The facility features nine rooms with private baths; two of the rooms also offer a fireplace. All of them are furnished with antiques. A special feature in each room is a sleep machine that lulls you off to dreamland with the sounds of tropical rain or the Hawaiian surf.

You'll have a phone and wireless Internet access in your room and use of the house fax machine, as well as access to an in-house fitness center and massage services. Children are permitted, but leave the pets at home.

One of the chief attractions of the inn is its accessibility to the city. It's a short hop from the Pennsylvania Turnpike and about 20 minutes from downtown Pittsburgh along Route 28. When you stay here, enjoy this picturesque town with its quaint, notable shops, such as the Mystery Lovers Bookstore. You'll also find a public golf course right across the street from the inn.

The Inn on Negley $$$$–$$$$$
703 South Negley Avenue
(412) 661-0631
www.innonnegley.com

Looking at the intricately designed decorative ceilings and exquisite fireplaces, you'll think you stepped back into the 1880s when you stay at the Inn on Negley. Yet there are some reminders of the amenities of modern life in the newly renovated rooms. Each of the eight rooms features Egyptian cotton sheets, imported down comforters, and wireless Internet access. Some of them also feature a Jacuzzi. Breakfast is offered daily and prepared on premise by the inn's professionally trained chef. Guests also may enjoy complimentary homemade pastries from 3:00 until 6:00 p.m. and complimentary wine from 5:00 until 9:00 p.m.

The inn is especially popular with corporate travelers because of its location only five minutes from downtown and even closer to the medical/university complex in Oakland, the neighborhood on Shadyside's border.

Ask about the special facilities and discounts available for corporate meetings and events for up to 40 people. The inn is also a luxurious spot for weddings, receptions, and other types of celebrations.

The inn is just 1 block from Walnut Street and Ellsworth Avenue, which offer some of the finest shopping, dining, and entertainment experiences in Pittsburgh.

SOUTH

Campbell House Bed & Breakfast $$–$$$$
305 East Main Street, Ligonier
(724) 238-9812
www.cambellbnb.com
Amenities abound at Campbell House, where the four guest rooms and two suites are what owner Patti Campbell describes as "eclectic" in decor. Whichever room you choose, you'll find a private bath, air-conditioning, cable television, a VCR or DVD player, and complimentary snacks and beverages. You also can utilize the phone and fax machine and receive e-mail messages on the computer located in the common area. Pets and children are not permitted.

Campbell is the owner of a large assortment of Campbell's Soup collectibles—her license plate reads "Soup Kid." At breakfast, make sure you sample one of her "Campbell's Babies," large pancakes with fruit, powdered sugar, and optional chocolate. Mmmmm, mmmmm good.

Champion Lakes Bed & Breakfast $$–$$$
4743 Route 711 North, Bolivar
(724) 238-5440
www.pagolf.com
This facility is located on the grounds of Champion Lakes Golf Course, right next to Champion Lakes Restaurant. (See the Golf chapter for more information about the course.) Owned by two retired Pittsburgh Pirates, Dick Groat and Jerry Lynch, the bed-and-breakfast has nine rooms. (Get it? Like nine innings?)

Each room has a private bath, phone, television with HBO, and heating and air-conditioning system with its own controls. All of the rooms are named after baseball players, and each room has its namesake's autographed uniform and picture on the wall. You'll choose your breakfast, which is included in the price of your room, from the menu at the restaurant next door.

A new five bedroom guest house is located on the fairway and available for group rental. This home features four bathrooms, a deck, grill, and big-screen television. Call for rates and reservations, and don't forget to ask about special golf getaway packages. Your children are welcome; however, your pets are not.

Foggy Mountain Lodge $$–$$$
190 Old Distillery Road, Stahlstown
(724) 593-1000
www.foggymt.com
Foggy Mountain Lodge offers 12 rooms and is set on 120 lush acres dotted with wooded trails, fields, and a lake. The air-conditioned rooms offer private baths, televisions, and phones, and you'll enjoy the game room, which features a pool table and darts. When you're ready to relax, try the outdoor hot tub and Bootlegger's Bar & Grill. Proprietors Rena and Jeff Stumpf think of Foggy Mountain primarily as a couples retreat, but if you want to bring your children and discuss it with them, they'll probably approve it. Pets are not permitted. Note: The rooms are spread over two buildings, a lodge, and a guesthouse; the nightly rate is higher for the lodge.

Foggy Mountain Lodge is near Ligonier in Westmoreland County, 1.3 miles from Route 711.

The Inne at Watson's Choice $$$–$$$$$
234 Balsinger Road, Balsinger
(724) 437-4999, (888) 820-5380
www.watsonschoice.com
Serenity and relaxation is a significant draw at this early-19th-century brick farmhouse in the

Laurel Highlands, 60 miles from Pittsburgh. Situated on a land-grant farm from the 1820s, the Inne at Watson's Choice surveys a 45-acre working farm. Before you go inside, sit on the wraparound porch and gaze at the picturesque hay fields and wooded hills.

While the charm is 19th century, the amenities are 21st. Innkeepers Bill and Nancy Ross have decorated the four guest rooms and one suite individually according to themes, such as bluebirds or a particular flower, with distinct colors and matching fabrics—in fact, when guests make reservations they've already made their selection from the Web site. Each room has queen- or king-size beds; a modern private bath, some with a whirlpool tub; a private phone; and Internet access. All rooms are air-conditioned.

The country breakfast is served in the rustic dining room. The red oak floors and all doors are original. The great room is impressive, with its huge, working fireplace and exposed wooden beams from a local barn. The recently added Harvest House, which was authentically reproduced, has a gathering room, four guest rooms, and one suite. Children over 12 years old are welcome, but pets are not permitted. The inn is a smoke-free facility.

You may be tempted not to stray from the Inne at Watson's Choice, but a short drive away you can visit Frank Lloyd Wright's Fallingwater and Kentuck Knob; Fort Necessity, George Washington's first battleground; antiques shops; and Touchstone Center for the Arts. More demanding activities include whitewater rafting on Youghiogheny River, biking, horseback riding, golf, hunting, fishing, and cross-country and downhill skiing.

The John Butler House $–$$
800 Rock Run Road, Elizabeth
(412) 751-6670
www.butlersgolf.com
About 40 minutes from downtown Pittsburgh, this facility is located by both the Monongahela and Youghiogheny Rivers on the 18th green of Butler's Golf Course. (See the Golf

chapter for more information on the course.) A deck on the house overlooks the course, and you'll be only a mile from the Youghiogheny Trail.

The four guest rooms offer private baths; a television and phone are available in the common living room and kitchen, respectively. You'll be served a full breakfast at the adjacent restaurant, the Rock Run Inn. You'll also enjoy games in the sunroom . . . and the opportunity to learn the correct spelling of Monongahela and Youghiogheny once and for all.

Children are permitted; pets are not. If you have a large party, you may rent all four guest rooms. Check with management for the appropriate fee.

Lady of the Lake Bed & Breakfast $$$
157 U.S. Route 30 East, Ligonier
(724) 238-6955
www.ladyofthelakebandb.com
There is indeed a lake at Lady of the Lake—a 25-acre lake, to be specific. A seasonal home for swans and Canada geese, it's a picturesque element at this lovely Westmoreland County inn. There are four rooms in the main house and one cottage. The rates for these lodging modes vary quite a bit. The listing of $$$ applies to the main house, while a night under the stars would be $ or less. The rooms offer private baths and television—you're welcome to use the office phone. Lady of the Lake is available for company picnics, and it offers a tennis court, in-ground pool, and rowboats and canoes for use at the lake. Lady of the Lake welcomes children—a useful feature, since the inn is adjacent to Idlewild Park and SoakZone and Storybook Forest, both popular attractions for kids. You'll find more about them in the Kidstuff chapter. Lady of the Lake welcomes small pets only.

Lesley's Mountain View Country Inn $$$$
327 Mountain View Road, Donegal
(724) 593-6349, (800) 392-7773
www.shol.com/mtview
Mountain View offers spectacular views of the surrounding Laurel Highlands from each of

the seven rooms in this restored 1850s farmhouse. These are furnished with period American furniture, including tall-poster beds, and feature televisions, phones, and private baths. The inn permits children but does not allow pets or smoking. Don't forget to enjoy fine dining at Lesley's, the restaurant within the inn that also is operated by inn owners Lesley and Gerard O'Leary. For more on Lesley's, see the Restaurants chapter.

The inn is about 1 mile east of the Donegal exit of the Pennsylvania Turnpike. By the way, don't confuse this inn with Mountain View Inn in Greensburg, a separate Westmoreland County establishment. You can read about Mountain View Inn in the Accommodations and Restaurants chapters.

Ligonier Country Inn $$–$$$
1376 Route 30 East, Laughlintown
(724) 238-3651
www.ligoniercountryinn.com

This inn may be the region's most capacious and diverse—it offers 26 rooms and 3 cottages. Each room is furnished differently; here you'll find a brass bed, there a four-poster. All rooms feature private baths, air-conditioning, televisions, and telephones. There is wireless Internet access in the common areas. The cottages also are different from one another. The family-oriented Kids Cottage sleeps up to five and has toys, a television, and even bunk beds. The Getaway Cottage, which offers a working fireplace, sleeps two and is known informally as the "romance cottage." Both cottages sport porches that overlook Mill Creek. The third cottage, Grandma Naugles, sleeps six and has a back porch and large yard that borders a park.

Guests are invited to enjoy the outdoor pool and the adjacent restaurant, also known as Ligonier Country Inn. (For more on that, see the Restaurants chapter.) You're welcome to use the office fax and copying services, and the good proprietors even schedule massage services for you. Discounts are available for stays of at least two nights. Children are welcome in certain rooms only. If you're stay-ing in the cottages, you may bring your dog but no cats, please. (There is a $250 animal deposit.) Ligonier Country Inn is located about 3 miles from Ligonier in eastern Westmoreland County.

Morning Glory Inn $$$$
2119 Sarah Street
(412) 431-1707
www.morningglorybedandbreakfast.com

Morning Glory Inn is a restored 1862 brick Italianate-Victorian home on Pittsburgh's South Side. Not only will you enjoy gracious appointments but you'll also be in the perfect position to experience one of Pittsburgh's most captivating and "hot" neighborhoods. South Side is an unusual blend of professional offices; trendy restaurants and clubs; art galleries; and unusual shops, such as the Bead Mine, where you can string your own necklaces from gem or glass beads. From the Morning Glory you'll also be able to stroll through the friendly streets to the City Theatre, which offers innovative, New York–quality performances.

The Morning Glory Inn offers five well-appointed guest rooms in the main house, each with a private bath, television, wireless Internet connection, and speakerphone with digital answering machine, as well as Swedish pressure-relieving mattress for extra comfort. The Margaret Jackson suite offers a queen-size canopy bed, a desk and several chairs, and a sitting-room bathroom complete with chaise lounge.

Sixteen feet behind the inn are what once were three 140-year-old, two-story row houses. They have been transformed into a first-floor ultraluxury suite that is accessed off the courtyard. Often used as the wedding suite, the suite is described as cozy cottage comfort with love seats, cherry-wood paneling, and French doors. There is also a bathroom with a whirlpool tub, and a fireplace.

You'll enjoy a walk in the Victorian garden after relaxing on the Spanish porch or in the guest parlors, one of which features a restored 1890 grand piano.

Smoking areas are available on the porch or in the garden. A corporate discount is offered, and you may use the office fax machine and copier. You can also hold your business meeting or special event at the Morning Glory Inn. For children's and pet's accommodations, discuss your circumstances with Nancy and Dave, the innkeepers. They pledge to be as flexible as they can.

Oak Noggin $$$
209 Waterman Road, Jefferson Hills
(412) 714-3571
www.oaknoggin.com

Oak Noggin is the only bed-and-breakfast in the South Hills area of Pittsburgh, and a fine one it is. Stay here in a separate, log-hewn guesthouse that is an accurate representation of an early American home—except for the modern amenities of course. The oak logs used to build the home are from two small 18th-century settler's cabins, the earliest recorded houses built in the Jefferson Hills area, which is approximately 45 minutes from downtown Pittsburgh.

Oak Noggin boasts two working fireplaces, including one especially large in the "keeping room," or living area, that would have been used for cooking during settlers' times. Don't worry if you're not familiar with frontier culinary artistry, however: You'll enjoy your own modern kitchen, and a full breakfast will be delivered to your door. There are two bedrooms and a bath, and the large bed has a twin trundle that slides out from underneath, ideal for accommodating children. A crib can also be provided. No pets or smoking, please!

Quiet House Bed & Breakfast $$$–$$$$
667 Elliotsville Road, Farmington
(724) 329-4606, (800) 784-8187
www.quiethousebnb.com

You probably won't find a more romantic stay than at Quiet House, which offers a champagne dinner at an award-winning French country inn followed by the "pure seclusion" that a guesthouse on 234 acres of woodland provides. It's one of the many package deals

Quiet House arranges throughout the year. In fact, owners Marty and Judy Anker will help you create your own special package from a surprisingly large number of options, such as massages, bouquets of roses, and wine tasting at a local winery.

Open year-round, Quiet House is a pre–Civil War Georgian farmhouse with seven guest rooms with private baths. For even more solitude, Quiet House offers the Carriage House Loft or Spring House, Cozy Cottage, or John's Cottage, some of which have wraparound decks and fireplaces. All units are air-conditioned. A full gourmet breakfast is delivered to your cottage, and as one satisfied customer from Wales noted, "It was worth crossing the Atlantic just for Grandma Judy's breakfast."

There is a stocked trout lake on the property and even a small chapel, since Marty is a minister who performs wedding ceremonies. An easy walk uphill awards you with a panoramic view of the entire valley.

Only 60 miles from Pittsburgh, your stay in the Laurel Highlands is a short drive to Frank Lloyd Wright's Fallingwater and Kentuck Knob, Ohiopyle State Park, and Laurel Caverns.

Children ages 14 and older are welcome, but your pets will have to find other accommodations. Smoking is not permitted.

Sunnyledge Boutique Hotel $$$$–$$$$$
5124 Fifth Avenue
(412) 683-5014
www.sunnyledge.com

With eight rooms, intimate enough to be a bed-and-breakfast, Sunnyledge is Pittsburgh's only boutique hotel—and a sumptuous one it is. All suites have Jacuzzis, and they all boast marble baths, wet bars and minibars, fluffy bathrobes, king-size beds made up with Egyptian cotton linens, two-line speakerphones, wireless Internet access, and cable television. The decor is contemporary with eclectic touches, similar to what you might find in a Ritz Carlton or Four Seasons.

You'll find a restaurant and martini lounge in this restored mansion; room service is available. Continental breakfast is included, but you may want to skip the free food and pay for the hotel's delicious Sunday brunch, with such tempting entrees as lobster club sandwiches, spinach-and-feta strudel, and banana rum French toast. Sunnyledge is within walking distance of Shadyside, Carnegie Mellon University, and the Oakland medical complex; it's a 10-minute car or bus ride from downtown.

Weatherbury Farm Vacation $$$–$$$$
1061 Sugar Run Road, Avella
(724) 587-3763
www.weatherburyfarm.com

If a vision of more than 100 acres of rolling meadows, gardens, fields, and valleys appeals to you, then you're the ideal guest for Weatherbury Farm. Your kids will like it too—they're welcome here. In fact, Weatherbury Farms caters to families with special children's programs focused on farm life. This is a working farm with cows, sheep, chickens, goats, ducks, and geese.You are cordially invited to help with the farm's chores after you eat your hearty and filling breakfast.

The three guest rooms feature private baths but no phone or television, in keeping with the agrarian theme. Three suites are also available; each one sleeps up to seven people and includes a living room, bathroom, and deck. Feel free to take a dip in the outdoor swimming pool while the kids enjoy the small playground. (If it rains, there is a Kid's Korner indoors, complete with games, puzzles, and toys.)

WEST

Country Road Bed & Breakfast $$$
199 Moody Road, Clinton
(724) 899-2528
www.pittsburghbnb.com

This country estate near Pittsburgh International Airport offers an appealing 200-year-old log cabin with a fireplace. It is equipped with a small kitchen, private bath, television, and

VCR. Children are permitted, but management needs to review your plans for pets.

You'll enjoy a fully stocked fishing pond and an outdoor pool, and you can take advantage of complimentary airport transportation.

Credit cards are not accepted.

The Inn on College Hill Bed & Breakfast $
3233 Sixth Avenue, Beaver Falls
(724) 843-6048
www.innoncollegehill.com

The mission oak–style inn draws its name from its location near Geneva College, about 3 miles south of the Pennsylvania Turnpike. Guest lecturers and performers at Geneva College often stay here, and you'll love conversing with them.

The facility offers four air-conditioned guest rooms furnished mostly with antiques; two have private baths. A telephone and television are available in a common area. Review your plans for bringing children age 12 and older with the management. Neither pets nor smoking are allowed.

When you wake up well rested, you'll be ready to feast on the country continental breakfast, with fresh-baked goods and great conversation. Note that you'll need to make a reservation to stay here; the inn can't accommodate drop-ins.

Credit cards are not accepted.

The Whistlestop Bed and Breakfast $
195 Broad Street, Leetsdale
(724) 251-0852
www.pittsburghbnb.com

This 1888 brick Victorian about 12 miles west of Pittsburgh was constructed by the Harmonists, an order that founded several western Pennsylvania towns. It features three guest suites with private baths, Two of the suites have kitchens. The Whistlestop is only 2 miles from Sewickley, a charming Ohio River town with many galleries and antiques shops for you to explore. It's also very near the popular historic site Old Economy Village, where the Harmonists once lived. Children are welcome, pets are not.

RESTAURANTS

If you thumb through this chapter, you'll notice that it's a very large one. Pittsburgh and the surrounding areas boast everything from the traditional meat-and-potatoes, old-style restaurants you'd expect to Cambodian, Indian, and Middle Eastern restaurants. On Pittsburgh's trendy South Side, there's even an all vegetarian/vegan restaurant, art gallery, and antiques store combination—the Zenith.

As in most places, the diversity of Pittsburgh's ethnic restaurants is largely dependent on the diversity of its immigrant population. One of the largest populations of immigrants, historically, is Italian. Thus you might expect that one of the largest categories of ethnic restaurants is Italian. Another factor in Pittsburgh's restaurant scene is the large college crowd. Some students seek out traditional America youth fare—hot dogs and fries, likely to be found at the Original Hot Dog Shop, or "The O," as it's known by insiders. Other, more health-conscious types seek organic or vegetarian fare, easily found at the Co-op Café at East-End Food Co-op, at Zenith, or at most ethnic restaurants.

As you travel outside the city of Pittsburgh into the six-county surrounding areas, you'll find less ethnic diversity and more good home-cooking, as in Butler, where Morgan's Diner has been a local fixture for decades. Don't even say "soup starter kit" while you're at Morgan's; it would be like hitting a wrong note with a master pianist in the audience.

In short, if you're in our area you're likely to have access to almost any kind of food you've got a craving for. Now what we can't promise is that it will be right next door, unless you're inside the city proper. Suppose you just want to wander around an area and choose a restaurant with the shortest wait list or the most delicious-sounding specials posted on the menu outside its door. Then we suggest you head for Downtown, Shadyside, or Atwood or Craig Street in Oakland.

To find the area where you'd like to dine, take note of where it is in relation to Downtown: north, south, east, or west of it. To check out the restaurants serving the type of food you're looking for, see the descriptive headings in each of those sections. For instance, if you want to eat Chinese or Japanese in Shadyside, find the East section, then the respective headings within it.

Now get out there and go to dinner, or lunch, or breakfast, or tea…and don't be afraid to venture into a place we just didn't have room to include. If it looks good to you, it probably is. We hope you'll enjoy dining in the Pittsburgh area—we sure do.

PRICE CODE

In addition to aiming to include representative, good restaurants of every flavor, we've also aimed to include places for every pocketbook and occasion. You'll find economical lunch spots as well as places where you'd want to propose or close that most important business deal. Here's how we've indicated the price range at each establishment.

$ . . . . $1 to $16
$$ . . . . $17 to $28
$$$ . . . . $29 to $62
$$$$ . . . . $63 to $100

In this town of business travelers and independent-minded individuals, we're not assuming you'll be dining with anyone else, so each price range is based upon the range of entree costs, from lowest to highest for one person. For instance, when we checked at the Red Bull Inn in Robinson, the lowest price for an entree was $12 and the highest, $20; thus, we've characterized the price range of entrees there as $–$$. Get it?

DOWNTOWN

American

The Carlton $$–$$$
One Mellon Bank Center
500 Grant Street
(412) 391-4152
www.thecarltonrestaurant.com
You're in for an elegant dining experience at the Carlton, which is located in One Mellon Bank Center. It would be hard to cite the restaurant's specialties, because the menu changes each day to keep the dining experience fresh. You can always count on veal and fresh seafood. Lunch and dinner specials might include seafood Wellington, veal portabella, sesame-seared mahimahi, or crab potato cake with citrus ponzu and wasabi aioli.

The wine list is extraordinary. It includes 500 selections, with each selection priced just $10 above cost, per the philosophy of proprietor Kevin Joyce, named Pittsburgh Restaurateur of the Year four years in a row. The wine list also won the city's *Wine Spectator* award six years straight. Reservations are recommended, and the Carlton accepts major credit cards. While the restaurant does not offer banquet facilities as such, it can accommodate private parties of up to 150 people. The Carlton is open Monday through Saturday but does not serve lunch on Saturday.

The Common Plea $$$$
310 Ross Street
(412) 697-3100
www.commonplea-restaurant.com
You are summoned to an important duty at the Common Plea, to wit: "The Bearer is summoned to savor a selection from the following menu and to adjudicate the value thereof." That's what the menu, in the form of a legal summons, advises patrons. As you can see, the restaurant gets plenty of mileage from its location in the city's legal and political district. As for its food, service, and atmosphere, the verdict is in, and it's thumbs up.

The Common Plea serves its food in a seemingly endless succession of courses, so bring a hearty appetite. Entrees include pasta, seafood, veal, beef, and lamb selections, many of them priced daily with the market. The lounge provides an intriguing selection of single-malt Scotch whiskeys as well as such specialty cocktails as Chocolata, a martini concocted with vodka and white crème de cacao. The wine list is extensive. If you're of a mind, you can pamper yourself with a five-liter bottle of 1993 Robert Mondavi "reserve" Pinot Noir—for $600.

The restaurant offers banquet facilities for up to 70 people. It serves dinner Tuesday through Saturday, lunch Tuesday through Friday. The Common Plea closes from 2:30 to 5:00 p.m. though the lounge remains open during those hours. Smoking and nonsmoking sections are available during lunch and dinner.

DeLuca's $
2015 Penn Avenue (Strip District)
(412) 566-2195
Go where the locals go for breakfast—DeLuca's in the Strip. One of Pittsburgh's "no frills" diners, DeLuca's offers traditional breakfast choices, and also some variations like pumpkin pancakes and Italian raisin bread French toast. Ready for dessert? DeLuca's offers several hotcake sundaes on their menu—that's right—ice cream and all the fixins loaded on top of hotcakes. DeLuca's is open every day from 7:30 a.m. until 4:00 p.m.

Eleven $$$$
1150 Smallman Street
(412) 201-5656
www.bigburrito.com

Eleven is the eleventh restaurant of the locally owned Big Burrito restaurant group. Located at the edge of downtown and the Strip, this upscale urban restaurant offers contemporary cuisine. The menu changes often, but expect to find entrees featuring local and seasonal ingredients. Favorites include Elysian Fields farm lamb, smoked Scottish salmon, and lobster and beef short rib. Vegetarian entrees are also available.

For a special treat, make reservations to sit at the Chef's Table, built in the custom-designed kitchen. Here you can watch the masters at work while sampling from the tasting menu. The table seats six and reservations are required.

Eleven is open during weekdays for lunch and dinner, and on Saturday and Sunday for dinner, beginning at 5:00 p.m.

Franktuary $
325 Oliver Avenue
(412) 288-0322
www.franktuary.com
Franktuary, "where the meat shall inherit the earth," is a quirky little restaurant located in the basement of Trinity Episcopal Cathedral, one of Pittsburgh's historic churches. Here you can find 100 percent beef franks, bratwurst, kielbasa, and knockwurst served with a variety of toppings. Franktuary also offers soups, salads, wraps, ice cream, and fruit shakes. A portion of Franktuary's profits support Three Nails, a local church. Franktuary is open Monday through Friday from 8:30 a.m. until 5:00 p.m. All major credit cards are accepted.

The Garden Cafe $$
600 Penn Avenue and Sixth Street
(412) 392-4879
You'll enjoy this outdoor cafe at Heinz Hall, the glittering performing-arts hall. The cafe is set in the courtyard and features a fountain and a waterfall, creating an inviting, relaxing atmosphere. The Fluted Mushroom, a prominent Pittsburgh caterer and Heinz Hall's concessionaire, provides sandwiches and salads, and the cafe can accommodate up to 250 for outdoor events. The cafe serves alcohol, although it does not offer a bar or wine list. It accepts reservations for parties of six or more. As the dining area is outdoors, smoking is permitted anywhere. The Garden Cafe serves lunch Monday through Friday from May through September—weather permitting, of course.

The Grille on Seventh $-$$
130 Seventh Street, Suite 110
(412) 391-1004
www.thegrilleonseventh.com
A favorite of business workers for lunch, The Grille on Seventh might fool you. At first glance, this place looks like a bar with some seating in the back, but if you venture downstairs, you will find a full-service restaurant. Chef Eric Hall offers American/Continental cuisine featuring seafood and steaks. Also, on Sundays, don't forget to order their Steeler Victory Chili. The Grille opens at 11:30 a.m. daily, serving lunch and dinner. Reservations are accepted.

Klavon's Ice Cream Parlor $
2801 Penn Avenue
(412) 434-0451
www.klavonsicecream.com
Step back in time when you visit Klavon's, an authentic 1920s ice cream parlor located in the Strip District. The parlor, opened in 1923 by James and Mary Klavon, is still owned and operated by the Klavon family. Here you can sit on one of the Coca-Cola bottle cap stools at the fountain and select from a wide variety of treats made from Reinhold's Ice Cream. Try the Tin Ceiling Sundae, Strip District Split, "New York" Egg Cream, or the Pittsburgh Pecan Ball, a local favorite. Or, have some lunch in one of the mahogany wood booths; Klavon's offers a simple menu of lunch sandwiches and drinks. Kids enjoy the penny candy section, old telephone booths, and the antique scale. While there, ask to hear about the story of the flood in 1936 that almost reached the ceiling of the

store. Klavon's has summer and winter hours, so it's best to call before a visit.

Morton's of Chicago $$$-$$$$
625 Liberty Avenue
(412) 261-7141
www.mortons.com

You'll know pretty early in your experience at Morton's that you're in a classy restaurant. As you enter you'll spy the private liquor lockers where such celebs as Mario Lemieux keep their supplies for entertaining guests. Even if you don't achieve that status, you'll enjoy the attentions of a staff that won *Pittsburgh Magazine*'s award for excellence in service. That award also cited Morton's steaks, for which the restaurant is known. The menu also offers such entrees as Sicilian veal chops, domestic rib lamb chops, and seafood selections that include shrimp Alexander and broiled Brock Island swordfish steak. When you're ready for libations, Morton's offers a full-service bar and wine list that has won mention in *Wine Spectator* magazine. You can smoke in a small section of the dining room and in the bar, and also buy your cigars here. Morton's serves dinner Monday through Saturday, and it can accommodate banquets of up to 80 people—it also entertains private parties for lunch. Reservations are recommended. You'll find Morton's on the ground level of CNG Tower.

Nine on Nine Restaurant $$$-$$$$
900 Penn Avenue
(412) 338-6463
www.nineonnine.com

Featuring French-inspired American dishes, Nine on Nine is a contemporary restaurant and bistro located in the heart of The Cultural District of downtown Pittsburgh. Start with one of the bistro's many appetizers–ostrich carpaccio, tartare, or tuna and salmon sashimi. Signature entrees feature Maine lobster, rack of lamb and Amish roasted chicken.

Nine on Nine is open for dinner Tuesday through Saturday. Reservations are recommended.

Opus, the Renaissance Hotel $$
107 Sixth Street
(412) 992-2005
www.dineatopus.com

The last time we were at Opus, the party at the table next to us was toasting Pittsburgh. I'll drink to that—and to the restaurant itself, we might add. The food, the wine list, the atmosphere, and the service are all lovely here, as befits the hotel. Opus isn't just another hotel restaurant; it's a place to add to your favorites list.

Some representative entrees include grilled Alaskan halibut, served with black rice and fruit chutney; seared ahi tuna, with mashed potatoes and pickled ginger relish; and New York strip steak, with sautéed leeks and onions and béarnaise butter. Two particularly wonderful appetizers are fried calamari with saffron aioli (perfectly done, and the portion was enormous) and field greens served with buffalo mozzarella, beefsteak tomatoes, red onions, and red wine vinaigrette. By the way, the quality of the seafood here is great and the presentation beautiful, so enjoy.

The wine list is truly extensive, with more than 60—in a range of varieties and moderate prices. By the bottle and glass, there are wines, for example, from vineyards in France, Italy, Spain, the United States, Chile, New Zealand, Australia, and the Russian River Valley. There's also a small, good selection of champagne, sparkling wines, and dessert wines and ports, too. In fact, Opus has been granted an Award of Excellence by *Wine Spectator*.

In addition to the regular menu, you'll find the restaurant offering two specials each evening during the week and more on the weekends. Opus is open for lunch and dinner daily, and there's also a Sunday brunch—particularly bountiful on Steelers Sundays.

Original Fish Market $$$
1001 Liberty Avenue
(412) 227-3657
www.originalfishmarketpgh.com

ℹ️ The Strip District, just east of downtown Pittsburgh, is the city's most vital food marketplace, offering fresh produce, meat, and seafood brought in daily. Many of the region's restaurateurs shop there every day. You'll find it a lively, exciting venue for your own fresh food shopping.

Seafood is the principal theme here, with a seemingly endless variety of tasty variations. Watch for items such as Chilean sea bass, Florida black grouper, Maine wolf-fish, and Alaskan halibut under "Today's Catch." The extensive wine list offers a taste guide to help you distinguish those that are dry, for example, from those that are sweet. You also can select from several varieties of bottled beer, beer on tap, and sparkling water. Original Fish Market is located adjacent to the Westin Convention Center Hotel. Open daily.

The Original Oyster House $
20 Market Square
(412) 566-7925
www.originaloysterhousepittsburgh.com
Since 1870 the Original Oyster House has been delighting downtown patrons with its variety of seafood—crab cakes, fish sandwiches, clams, shrimp, and, of course, its signature oysters. This is a lively, informal spot, with many patrons preferring to sit or stand at the bar/counter while they eat. Booths are available, and around them you'll see one of the oddest collections of photographs you're ever likely to find in a restaurant. Staring at you, with toothy smiles each, will be Miss America contestants in group photos representing many years of the pageant. These have been preserved from the collection of the restaurant's original owner, a Miss America buff. Each time he attended the pageant, he returned with a group photo. The Original Oyster House is open from 9:00 a.m. to 11:00 p.m. Monday through Saturday. It's closed on Sunday. Credit cards and reservations are not accepted.

Palomino's $$-$$$$
Four Gateway Center, Suite 100
(412) 642-7711
www.palomino.com
Featuring European-inspired regional American cuisine, Palomino is an upbeat city restaurant and bar. Palomino serves lunch Monday through Friday from 11:00 a.m. until 4:00 p.m., and dinner Monday through Sunday, starting at 4:00 p.m.

Ruth's Chris Steak House $$$
6 PPG Place
(412) 391-4800
www.ruthchris.com
If you've visited a Ruth's Chris Steak House in other cities, you'll be familiar with the menu and high quality of service at this restaurant. Steaks, of course, are the specialty, but the restaurant also offers an appealing selection of fresh fish that varies daily with the catch. You usually can find fresh lobster and grilled salmon on the menu, as well as coconut shrimp with a honey mustard sauce that makes an unusual appetizer.

The restaurant offers a full-service bar and a 14-page wine list, with prices up to $500 a bottle. Reservations are suggested for both lunch and dinner. While the restaurant is open seven days a week, lunch is served Monday through Friday only. The dinner menu is available all day.

Sammy's Famous Corned Beef $
219 Ninth Street
(412) 765-224
Sammy's is a locally based chain. The signature sandwich is a Reuben, featuring perfectly sliced corned beef, Russian dressing, Swiss cheese, slaw, and sauerkraut.

Seviche $$$-$$$$
930 Penn Avenue
(412) 697-3120
www.seviche.com
Sights and sounds abound upon entering Seviche, located in The Culture District. Latin tunes, Cuban artwork, and South Miami

décor create an upbeat and hip atmosphere that has made it a downtown favorite. Before dinner, sip a South American classic like a mojito, taste an exotic island favorite frozen drink, or choose from one of their many Spanish beers or wines. For dinner, Seviche offers tapas made from authentic Latin American recipes. Salmon Fire and Ice, Pork Empanada and Mebrillo Glazed Finger Lamb Chops are popular picks. For first-time visitors, we suggest that you select the Chef's Table, seven courses of assorted tapas. As they say, "No deciding, just eating."

Seviche is open Monday to Saturday from 5:00 p.m. until 1:00 a.m. Reservations are accepted for large parties only and valet parking is available.

Six Penn Kitchen $$$
146 Sixth Street
(412) 566-7366
www.sixpennkitchen.com
Six Penn Kitchen, a favorite of theater-goers, is an American bistro located in the heart of The Culture District. The menu, which changes often, features unique and tasty offerings like cracklin' pork shank, lobster mac'n cheese, and rotisserie organic deconstructed "chicken and biscuits." Or, stop by for brunch and try one of their hearty offerings--breakfast pizza, cheesecake stuffed brioche French toast, or blue crab and corn quiche.

Six Penn is open Monday through Friday for lunch and dinner. Saturday for late lunches and dinner. Brunch is served from 10:30 a.m. until 2:00 p.m.

Sonoma Grille $$$
947 Penn Avenue
(412) 697-1336
www.thesonomagrille.com
Yves Carreau, Executive Chef and Owner of Sonoma Grille, was raised in Lyon, France, apprenticed in the French West Indies, and established himself as a chef in Los Angeles, California before moving to Pittsburgh. These

travels are one of the reasons for Sonoma Grille's unique dishes, "international cuisine with a California twist."

Here you will find seafood, vegetarian, and mixed grille entrees. Have a big appetite? Try a large size entrée: 16-ounce rib eye steak, double cut pork chop or rack of lamb, or a 12-ounce filet. If you can't decide, consider ordering Chef Yves Table. For $85, you will receive four courses and four wines, selected by the chef.

Sonoma offers more than 100 wines available by the glass. The Russian River Room, a private dining room, can be reserved for groups of 36 guests.

Located near the David L. Lawrence Convention Center, Sonoma Grille is open daily for lunch from 11:00 a.m. until 3:00 p.m. and dinner from 5:00 p.m. until 11:00 p.m. Valet parking is available. Reservations are recommended.

The Terrace Room $$-$$$
530 William Penn Place
(412) 553-5235
Sitting in the lobby of the Omni William Penn Hotel is one of our town's most enjoyable experiences., When you dine at the hotel's restaurant, known as the Terrace, you'll enhance that experience. The Terrace offers breakfast, lunch, and dinner Monday through Saturday, brunch only on Sunday. Each meal has a distinct personality, and power breakfasts are popular here.

[handwritten annotations: 9/30/09 w/m, Tony & Ted okay - pretty room - Camel clientele, not busy, next time check out bar food in lobby]

Dinner is a more leisurely affair. Wheeling and dealing gives way to lingering dinners over such entrees as seared duck breast, roast lamb rack, curry roasted cod, and bronze-skin salmon. The Terrace offers two full-service bars, a wine list, and banquet facilities for up to 150 people.

Cambodian

The Lemon Grass Cafe $$-$$$
124 Sixth Street
(412) 765-2222
Restaurateurs are a colorful breed with engaging tales to tell. Spend some time, however, with the Lemon Grass Cafe owners Kim

Hong and her son, Bophanara "Bo" Meng, and if the mood is just right, you'll hear stories shocking in their cruelty and nearly incredible with their examples of commonplace heroism. It's the story of native Cambodians Kim and Bo, of course, who in 1979 escaped Khmer Rouge "killing fields" and reeducation camps that claimed the lives of 21 members of their immediate family. After enduring four years of reeducation, they escaped to Thailand as the first part of their journey to Pittsburgh.

The menu at the cafe offers a variety of Cambodian dishes, including red and green curry; spicy mussels; and fried rice with sausage, eggs, carrots, peas, and scallions. For many of the entrees you have the option of chicken, beef, or shrimp as the base. You'll also enjoy the green papaya salad and the signature lemongrass soup. The cafe does not use butter or cheese in any of its dishes.

The cafe serves lunch and dinner Monday through Saturday, dinner only on Sunday. It does not serve alcohol. Reservations are accepted. The cafe does not designate smoking or nonsmoking sections. It can accommodate banquets of up to 80 people.

When you're here, take a minute to shake hands with Kim and Bo. If the mood is just right, they might have some tales to tell you.

Caribbean

Kaya $$$
2000 Smallman Street
(412) 261-6565
www.bigburrito.com/kaya
The Caribbean food and decor in this casual Strip District restaurant attracts a noisy, younger crowd. Great hot and cold tropas (like Spanish tapas) and vegetarian selections complement a collection of microbrews. In summer sit outside and watch the nightclubbers pass by. Open daily for lunch and dinner. Kaya went smoke free in 2008. Most major credit cards are accepted.

Chinese

Chinatown Inn $$
520 Third Avenue
(412) 261-1292
www.chinatowninn.net
The Yee family has operated Chinatown Inn for three generations, serving Cantonese, Szechuan, and Hunan selections.

It's located near Grant Street, the center of city and Allegheny County political and legal activity, so you'll be rubbing shoulders with politicos when you dine here. The lunch and dinner menus include beef, seafood, and poultry entrees as well as limited vegetarian menu. Chinatown Inn offers a full-service bar and a wine list, as well as banquet facilities for up to 100 people. Lunch and dinner reservations are accepted, as are major credit cards.

Mandarin Gourmet $–$$
305 Wood Street
(412) 261-6151
www.mandaringourmet.com
Mandarin Gourmet serves lunch and dinner Monday through Saturday. You'll find a broad selection of pork, beef, poultry, seafood, and pasta items as well as vegetarian selections. Check out the "Chef's Suggestions" section for a number of interesting combinations, like Sizzling Two Delicacies, featuring beef and scallops, and Dragon and Phoenix, with lobster and General Tso's chicken. Hot and spicy items are marked with a red star. Mandarin Gourmet offers a full-service bar, and it accepts reservations. It offers banquet facilities for up to 300 people.

Continental

Café Euro $$
600 Grant Street
(412) 434-0800
www.cafeeuropittsburgh.com
Café Euro, located in the lower level of U.S. Steel Tower, offers a casual atmosphere where you can enjoy Mediterranean and Continental cuisine featuring steaks, seafood and

pasta entrees. Open 11:30 a.m. Monday through Friday for lunch and dinner, Café Euro also hosts daily Happy Hours with live music. Closed on Saturday and Sunday, except for private parties for up to 200 guests.

French

| Palate | $$-$$$ |

212 Sixth Street
(412) 434-1422
www.palatebistro.com

Opened by John Valentine, a longtime professional restaurant manager who has worked in New York, Toronto, and Florida, Palate is one of Pittsburgh's newest restaurants, and the only downtown bistro featuring French fusion delights. Fine food entrees featuring duck, steak tartare, and fish are served in this upscale and sophisticated spot. Palate is located directly across the street from Heinz Hall in the Cultural District, and offers a fixed-price theater menu for pre-theater dining. They also feature a wine list, with mostly French wines, and allow guests to bring their own wine ($15 corkage fee). Open Monday through Friday, 11:00 a.m. to 2:00 p.m. for lunch and Monday through Saturday from 5:00 to 11:00 p.m. Reservations and major credit cards are accepted.

Greek

| Christos | $-$$ |

130 Sixth Street
(412) 261-6442

For three years, Christos Malacrinos served as a chef for Jackie Onassis aboard the yacht *Christina*. Now he's bringing the benefits of that experience to Downtown Pittsburgh diners. Christos serves lunch and dinner daily, offering such entrees as spanakopita, lamb kabob, chicken kabob oreganato, and moussaka—you can complement them all with Greek Easter bread. But the real star of the menu is a dessert called *ekmek*, which Malacrinos says he developed and prepared especially for Onassis. It's a white cake

topped with honey syrup, custard, cinnamon, and whipped cream, and you can order a version with a chocolate cake base as well.

Christos offers an outdoor dining area and banquet facilities for up to 55 people. It does not serve alcohol—you're invited to bring your own—and it does not designate smoking and nonsmoking sections. Christos normally does not accept reservations, but it will take lunch reservations for parties of six or more on days when the nearby theaters are staging performances. Open 11:00 a.m. to 3:00 p.m. Monday through Thursday, 11:00 a.m. to midnight Friday and Saturday, and 11:00 a.m. to 8:30 p.m. Sunday. Credit cards are not accepted.

Italian

| Bravo Franco Ristorante | $$$ |

613 Penn Avenue
(412) 642-6677
www.bravofranco.com

Located in the heart of the Cultural District, Bravo Franco offers both indoor dining in an intimate room and dining al fresco on its sidewalk patio. The menu features chicken, seafood, pasta, and beef selections, with the steaks cut thick. A popular selection is the bowtie and salmon pasta, served with a light tomato cream sauce. Bravo Franco offers a full-service bar, and extensive wine list and banquet facilities for up to 100 people. Reservations are strongly suggested (one week in advance is recommended). Bravo Franco does not designate smoking and nonsmoking sections, but it tries to accommodate patrons of each persuasion. The restaurant offers lunch and dinner Monday through Saturday. It's open on Sunday only when the nearby theaters are staging performances. Call ahead to check the Sunday schedule.

| Caffé Amante | $$ |

120 Fifth Avenue
(412) 391-1226

Caffé Amante is the principal restaurant in Fifth Avenue Place, the retail and office com-ℹ️ If you're having one of those days when you just don't feel like leaving the house to eat, order your meal from Wheel Deliver. The service will deliver your order from any of more than 30 restaurants, primarily but not exclusively in the city's eastern neighborhoods. You'll pay restaurant prices plus a 15 percent delivery charge, with minimum and maximum orders. Wheel Deliver accepts credit cards, cash, and checks. It's available for dinners daily, for lunches Monday through Friday. The delivery territory is limited. Call (412) 421-9346, or go online at www.wheeldeliver.net.

plex that features distinctive needle-type ornamenting. Caffé Amante specializes in continental and Northern Italian fare, with seafood, veal, chicken, and pasta entrees. The restaurant offers a full-service bar and an extensive wine list, and it can accommodate banquets. Reservations are suggested. Caffé Amante serves lunch and dinner Monday through Saturday. It's closed on Sunday.

F. Tambellini Seventh Street $–$$
139 Seventh Street
(412) 391-1091
www.eatzucchini.com

F. Tambellini offers a wide variety of lunch and dinner selections, including beef, veal (osso buco or veal shank), seafood, and pasta selections. The common denominator among longtime patrons, however, is considerable affection for the restaurant's fried zucchini—a must when you dine here. The restaurant offers a full-service bar and an extensive wine list, and it accepts reservations for parties of eight or more. The Puccini room hosts banquets for up to 100 people. F. Tambellini is open Monday through Saturday. With its location in downtown's theater district, it also opens on Sunday show nights. It's best to call to determine F. Tambellini's status on any Sunday.

Lidia's $$$
1400 Smallman and 15th Streets
(412) 522-0150
http://pittsburgh.lidiasitaly.com

Lidia's serves Northern Italian cuisine in a grand setting. For a set price you can sample from three pastas of the day, such as homemade ravioli with thyme butter or fettuccine with beef, and it's all-you-can-eat. The price also includes a Caesar salad and tiramisu. The quail with cherry-balsamic sauce melts in your mouth. An extensive all-Italian wine list with almost half the bottles around $20 helped earn Lidia's *Wine Spectator*'s Award of Excellence.

Named for Lidia Bastianich, the TV cooking personality and cookbook author, the restaurant opened with a built-in fan base. Balcony seating increased the capacity for this always busy restaurant, and there's often a bargain selection of wines by the glass and appetizers during happy hour at the long bar facing the kitchen. Open Tuesday through Saturday for lunch and dinner, Lidia's offers brunch on Sunday. Reservations are suggested for larger groups.

Korean

Sushi Kim $$
1241 Penn Avenue
(412) 281-9956
www.sushikim.com

Consistently voted one of the best sushi restaurants in Pittsburgh, Sushi Kim is a local favorite of Pittsburghers who love sushi and traditional Korean dishes. This no frills restaurant recently opened a new second floor where you can find a Korean specialty barbeque buffet featuring an assortment of raw beef, chicken, pork, and seafood that you cook at your table.

Sushi Kim is open Tuesday through Sunday for lunch and dinner. Monday night, they only offer sushi (the kitchen is closed) from 5:00 until 9:00 p.m. The barbeque buffet is available on Friday and Saturday from 5:00 until 10:00 p.m., and Sunday from 4:00 until 8:30 p.m.

Pizza

Monte Cello's Italian Restaurant & Pizza $
Seventh and Liberty Avenues
(412) 261-2080
www.montecellos.com/pittsburgh.html
When you have time for a quick lunch only
but still want to get away from the office,
hurry on down to Monte Cello's. You can
avoid the lines at the counter by helping
yourself to pizza by the slice and sandwiches
at the express lunch buffet—and enjoy your
meal in the dining area. Monte Cello's offers
such unusual pizza toppings as steak and
onions, and chicken and broccoli. You also
can choose from a limited number of
entrees, soups, and salads. Monte Cello's
does not serve alcohol. It accepts reservations for parties of 10 or more, and it offers
catering and delivery services. Monte Cello's
serves lunch and dinner Monday through
Saturday.

Villa Reale $
628 Smithfield Street
(412) 391-3963
Villa Reale calls its pizza "perfect." That may
be an exaggeration, but only a slight one—
downtown shoppers and workers have been
enjoying the restaurant's pizza since 1976.
You can order yours with such unusual toppings as roasted red peppers or pineapple.
Villa Reale also features a limited selection of
entrees—pasta with broccoli and pasta with
ricotta cheese are among patrons' favorites—
and plenty of sandwiches and salads. The
restaurant offers a lounge and a limited wine
list, as well as banquet facilities for up to 50
people. It serves lunch and dinner Monday
through Sunday.

Steelhead Brasserie & Wine Bar $$$
112 Washington Place
(412) 394-3474
www.thesteelhead.com
When the Steelhead opened in 1997, it was
named by *Esquire* magazine as one of Amer-
ica's top 10 new restaurants. It's operated by

Myriad Restaurant Group, the force behind
such restaurants as Montrachet, TriBeCa
Grill, Layla, and Nobu in New York, and Rubi-
con in San Francisco. As you would expect,
Steelhead boasts all the features—excellent
food, classy environment, attentive serv-
ice—that you would expect in a restaurant
that attracts national attention. Specialties
include grilled steelhead salmon and tuna
seared rare with soba noodles and a mush-
room broth. You'll also find beef, chicken,
and pasta entrees, as well as a vegetarian
"plate of the day."

Steelhead offers a lounge, an extensive
wine list, and banquet facilities for up to 50
people. It serves breakfast, lunch, and dinner
Monday through Friday and a breakfast buf-
fet on Saturday and Sunday. While Steelhead
closes each Monday through Friday from
2:00 to 5:00 p.m., the lounge remains open
for eating and drinking during those hours.
Reservations are recommended for dinner
and lunch. When you call for reservations,
remember that the phone number above
spells FYI–FISH. The principal dining area is
nonsmoking, but smoking is permitted in the
lounge.

Steelhead Brasserie & Wine Bar is located
in the Pittsburgh Marriott City Center near the
Mellon Arena. For more on the hotel and its
banquet facilities, see the Accommodations
chapter.

Wholey's Sushi Bar $-$$
1711 Penn Avenue
(412) 391-3737
www.wholey.com
Though there is no seating and a distinct
fish market scent, the freshly made sushi
available just inside Wholey's Fish Market in
The Strip District is said to be some of the
best in the city.

Chef Andy is known for making unique
and delicious combinations on the spot, while
the customer watches. Unsure of what to
choose? Ask the chef for a suggestion. You
won't be disappointed. Open daily.

NORTH
American

Clark Bar & Grill $–$$
503 Martindale Street
(412) 231-5720

Although this building housed the original Clark Bar production facility, you won't find any of those chocolate bars here, as the candy company now is based in Pittsburgh's northern suburbs. You will find a restaurant that serves lunch and dinner Monday through Friday and on weekends that bring an event to Three Rivers Stadium. The menu is limited but trendy, offering ribs, steak, grilled crab cakes, sandwiches, and dinner salads. The wine list is limited, but the bar is exceptionally well stocked, offering 12 brands of vodka and 10 types of single-malt Scotch whiskey, among other delights. The restaurant accepts reservations. The restaurant designates smoking and nonsmoking sections. It's a long field goal from the stadium on the city's' North Side.

Crow's Nest $$
19th Street and River Road, Sharpsburg
(412) 782-3701

When you dine at Crow's Nest, the Allegheny River will be your cheerful companion. The restaurant takes full advantage of its riverfront location by offering a nautical decor, outdoor dining with a view of the river and the dam at Highland Park, and bands performing on a barge in the river each weekend throughout the warm weather months. (Sorry, there's no food available on the barge.)

The lunch and dinner menus offer primarily lighter fare as well as daily specials. But you will find such dinner entrees as shrimp scampi, filet mignon, and pan-fried Maryland crab cakes. You'll enjoy a full-service bar with a broad selection of beers as well as a limited wine list. The restaurant offers banquet facilities for up to 150 people. It accepts reservations for parties of six or more.

Crow's Nest is a few miles north of Downtown. It's open Tuesday through Friday in the summer, Tuesday through Saturday at other times.

Ford City Steak & Seafood Company $$
418 Third Avenue, Ford City
(724) 763-2901

The Ford City Steak & Seafood Company serves dinner only from Tuesday through Sunday. The menu offers diverse American fare, with beef, poultry, and veal selections as well as sandwiches and daily pasta and seafood specials. It offers a full-service bar and a wine list, and it can accommodate up to 120 people for banquets.

Hardwood Cafe $–$$
646 Pittsburgh Road, Butler
(724) 586-5353

On those cold Southwestern Pennsylvania nights, you'll enjoy dining by the fire at Hardwood Cafe, which features a two-story fireplace. You'll also enjoy a diverse menu that offers pasta and chicken dishes as well as pizza and burgers. You can opt for lunch and dinner specials each day except Sunday, when you'll still be able to choose from the wide variety of selections on Hardwood's menu. Reservations are needed on weekends and accepted on weekdays. The Hardwood Cafe offers banquet facilities for up to 50 people. The restaurant is conveniently located on Route 8. Like the entrees available, prices at the cafe encompass a broad range.

J-Barn Country Inn $–$$
495 Monroe Road, Sarver
(724) 353-3300

This Butler County restaurant is a pleasant country inn that offers such appealing country-style fare as ribs, ham, seafood, steak marinated on the premises, marshmallow fruit salad, fried mushrooms, and homemade banana bread and apple butter. Outdoor grilling is one of their specialties. If you like what you're eating, you can stop at the inn's country store and pick up J-Barn baked goods and other branded foods. The store also features crafts fashioned by local artisans. J-Barn is open Wednesday through Sunday for dinner, with lunch served on Sunday only. Reservations are recommended for Saturday, accepted at other times.

Kaufman House $–$$
105 South Main Street, Zelienople
(724) 452-8900

You can have a memorable dining experience here, as each month brings wild-game specials that include such dishes as elk, ostrich, and wild-boar sausage. The less adventurous will enjoy the prime rib and fried chicken selections from the regular menu.

The restaurant offers a bar, a wine list, and banquet facilities for up to 50 people. You'll need reservations on Friday, Saturday, and Sunday. Kaufman House serves breakfast, lunch, and dinner daily Monday through Saturday; lunch and dinner on Sunday.

Luma $$
8 Brilliant Avenue, Aspinwall
(412) 781-0355
www.lumapgh.com

This popular neighborhood restaurant on a quiet tree-lined street in Aspinwall made a welcome replacement for the dark burger joint previously located there. Now a light airy bistro offering American cuisine with an emphasis on fresh seafood, poultry, and beef, Luma does not stint when it comes to large entrees and accompanying side dishes. Their wine list offers sufficient selections with a 20-for-20 section of reasonably priced wines at $20 a bottle. Save room for dessert, like warm chocolate mousse cake by Tallulah's Catering. Dining inside can be noisy; out on the patio it's delightful, with evenings extended through the fall by tall outdoor heaters. Making reservations on weekends is a wise decision. Open daily.

The 1901 Tavern & Grill $$$
143 North Main Street, Butler
(724) 431-0440

Owners Greg and Laura Walter traveled throughout the world when Greg served in the Air Force, sampling exotic fare. They've brought a touch of that exotic flavor to The 1901 in downtown Butler. In addition to the standard steak, seafood, pasta, and chicken dishes served for lunch and dinner, you can sample such unusual dishes as elk, caribou, black bear, rattlesnake, and wild boar—or whatever else chef Don Potter has bagged that day. Alligator is a staple of the appetizer menu, and you'll enjoy the raw bar each Friday.

The 1901 offers more than 100 microbrews and 17 varieties of beer on tap. If you want to enjoy a post-alligator cigar, you'll find a humidor on the premises. Reservations are accepted for lunch and dinner.

Tata's Family Restaurant $$
51 Lyn-Mar Plaza, Lyndora
(724) 287-7359

Since 1971 the Milasincic family has operated Tata's—you pronounce it *TUH Tuh's*, by the way—and it has the feel of an old-time family restaurant. Located just outside the city of Butler, Tata's offers daily lunch and dinner specials; all entrees include visits to the food bar, a buffet of salads and hot foods. You'll also find specially priced seniors' and children's menus. Reservations aren't required, but Tata's will accept them for larger parties. The restaurant offers banquet facilities for up to 110 people. Entrees are priced at the lower end of $$. Smoking is not permitted in the restaurant.

W. Ricks Taproom & Grill $–$$
269 Meridian Road, Butler
(724) 482-2970

Located just outside the city of Butler, W. Ricks offers a diverse menu that includes steak, seafood, and lamb selections regularly; prime rib is available after 4:00 p.m. on Wednesday, Friday, and Saturday. You'll find daily lunch and dinner specials and a children's menu. W. Ricks offers a full-service bar and a wine list. Reservations are accepted but not required.

Asian

Tai Pei Chinese Restaurant $–$$
1124 Freeport Road, Fox Chapel
(412) 781-4131

When you choose Tai Pei for lunch or dinner, you can select from a limited wine list or enjoy the full-service bar. The extensive menu offers plenty of beef, lamb, chicken, pork, and seafood selections, ranging from such traditional favorites as General Tso's chicken (the General's shrimp is available as well) and Peking duck to more daring entrees, such as crispy prawn, Szechuan style. You'll know if you're ordering a "hot and spicy" selection—these are highlighted in red on the menu.

Tai Pei offers a limited selection of "Dieter Gourmet" entrees as well as specially priced family dinners; entree selection for family dinners is limited. The restaurant accepts major credit cards and reservations for lunch and dinner, and provides free lunch delivery for take-out orders. The Fox Chapel location is about 10 miles north of Pittsburgh and only 1 mile south of Sichuan House, while you'll find its sister restaurant in Pittsburgh's Shadyside neighborhood.

French

Acanthus $$$$
604 West North Avenue
(412) 231-6544
www.innonthemexicanwarstreets.com/
acanthus.html

Located behind the Inn on the Mexican War Streets, Acanthus is a 48-seat restaurant set in a historic renovated carriage house. During warm weather, enjoy your meal in the outdoor courtyard, a perfect setting for a romantic evening. Inspired by classical French techniques, Acanthus offers both a prix fixe and an a la carte menu. One of the chef's favorite dishes to make is filet of beef with wild-mushroom bread pudding and wild-mushroom stew.

The restaurant is available for private parties. Acanthus serves dinner Thursday through Saturday from 5:00 until 9:00 p.m.

German

Max's Allegheny Tavern $–$$
537 Suismon Street
(412) 231-1899
www.maxsalleghenytavern.com

If it's sausages, schnitzel, and other German delights you hunger for, you'll find them at Max's Allegheny Tavern on the city's North Side. The restaurant offers daily lunch and dinner specials. If you can't settle on just one German entree, try Max's Sampler Platter—you'll get three entrees with your platter. The restaurant also offers beef and seafood selections prepared with a German touch. You'll find a full-service bar and a wine list, as well as banquet facilities for up to 80 people. Max's accepts reservations for parties of five or more. It's open daily for lunch and dinner and features brunch each Sunday.

Penn Brewery Restaurant $$
800 Vinial Street
(412) 237-9402
www.pennbrew.com

Gemutlich! That's how you'll describe Penn Brewery after you visit this bright, informal restaurant on Pittsburgh's North Side. Tom and Mary Beth Pastorius operate both the restaurant and the adjoining microbrewery, which produces Penn Pilsner and a variety of other beers. There's more than a touch of authenticity here, as Tom Pastorius traces his lineage to Franz Daniel Pastorius, who is credited with establishing the first German settlement in America in 1683.

The menu features such German fare as schnitzel, sauerbraten, schweinbraten, and potato pancakes, as well as dinner salads and beef, chicken, and seafood entrees. You'll find lunch and dinner specials, a full bar, a limited wine list, and banquet facilities for up to 200 on Sunday, up to 100 on other days. If you're planning to hold a birthday party here, you can bring in your own cake, but be sure to ask about the restaurant's "cutting fee," which applies even if the staff doesn't actually cut the cake; this cost can be on the prohibitive side.

You'll be entertained on Wednesday evenings by a strolling accordion player, on Friday and Saturday evenings by a live band. Special events also are fun here. These range from Oktoberfest and Caribbean Night to the annual Pennsylvania Microbrewery Fest, when patrons can sample the wares of more than 30 brewers. But for Oktoberfest, these events are irregularly scheduled, so it's best to call for details about them.

The restaurant accepts reservations for parties of eight or more. Penn Brewery serves lunch and dinner Monday through Saturday.

Indian

Taj Mahal $$
7795 McKnight Road
(412) 364-1760
www.tajmahalinc.com
Taj Mahal serves Mughlai, North Indian, South Indian, and authentic regional Indian cuisine. In 2003 it was awarded *Pittsburgh Magazine*'s Gold Medal award for "Excellence in Serving Indian Food," as well as the magazine's Gold Medal award for "Best Overall Sunday Brunch." The restaurant also offers full-service catering.

Some of our favorite items from the daily, plentiful lunch buffet are the delicious *vegetable pakora* (vegetable fritters), *tikki* (small potato pancakes), special lemon rice, vegetable korma, palak paneer, and the creamy mango dessert. One of the nice things about the buffet is that often many unusual items are also offered.

Taj Mahal's full menu is one of the most extensive of any Indian restaurant in the area. The restaurant is particularly well known for the fresh naans, kebabs, and dosas prepared there. Overall, dining at Taj Mahal retains a quality of true "home-cooked" Indian food, and the environment is gracious.

Irish

Blarney Stone Restaurant
and Catering Service $$$
30 Grant Avenue, Etna
(412) 781-1666

When proprietor Tom O'Donoghue came to Pittsburgh from County Kerry in 1974, he brought a piece of the "oulde sod" with him. It's preserved in a glass-topped square on Blarney Stone's ceramic floor. When you enter Blarney Stone you have the opportunity to set foot on Irish soil.

Be that as it may, the good folks at Blarney Stone asked us to advise you that they serve American as well as Irish dishes. Consider yourself advised. You'll find such Ireland-inspired selections as County Cork Salad, Channon Chef Salad, and Irish smoked salmon, as well as American entrees that include Maryland crab cakes, prime rib, duck breast, and lamb chops. The restaurant serves dinner Tuesday through Sunday, lunch Tuesday through Friday, and a Sunday brunch. It's closed on Monday. Blarney Stone offers a full-service bar, a wine list, and banquet facilities for up to 700 people—it's a popular spot for corporate functions. Reservations are accepted. Smoking and nonsmoking sections are designated for lunch, but the dining room is nonsmoking for dinner.

It's in the area of entertainment that Blarney Stone shows its Irish. It celebrates St. Patrick's Day with a week of lunch and dinner shows as well as an Irish buffet. During November it hosts Irish singing groups. And there's swing dancing on Friday.

Italian

10/1/09

Bona Terra $$$
908 Main Street, Sharpsburg
(412) 781-8210
The menu changes daily, but will always include three entrees from the earth and three from the sea. Bona Terra also offers a selection of appetizers including two soups, and a cheese course after your meal. The most requested entree is the Maple Leaf Farms roasted duck breast, which is often on the menu.

Bona Terra serves dinner Tuesday through Saturday. With seating for only 45, reservations are strongly recommended.

Bravo! Italian Kitchen $$
4976 McKnight Road, Ross
(412) 366-3556

This is a family restaurant that understands families, passing out crayons, coloring books, and pizza dough to each youngster who visits. While your kids are occupied with those pursuits, you get a chance to enjoy the signature Pasta Bravo—rigatoni with wood-grilled chicken and button mushrooms in a roasted red pepper sauce. Chicken scaloppini Romano also is popular here. Located in the North Hills, Bravo! serves lunch and dinner daily. It offers a full-service bar and a wine list. Reservations are not accepted, but you may call ahead for priority seating.

Falsetti's Villa $$
Route 128, North Buffalo
(724) 763-2266

This Armstrong County restaurant specializes in Italian food and seafood selections. Among the most popular items are the Italian platter, which includes spaghetti, lasagna, rigatoni, ravioli and a meatball, and scrod Villa. The restaurant offers a full-service bar and a wine list. Reservations are accepted Sunday through Thursday. Located near the county seat of Kittanning, Falsetti's Villa serves lunch and dinner daily. Credit cards are not accepted.

Mama Rosa's Restaurant & Lounge $-$$
263 Old Plank Road, Butler
(724) 287-7315
www.butlersmamarosas.com

Yes, Virginia, there is a Mama Rosa—Mama Rosa Fusca, who founded this restaurant with her family. Mama Rosa no longer is active in the business, but she still drops in to watch as the staff prepares the handmade pasta that is the restaurant's signature. In addition to pasta you can select from steak, seafood, chicken, and veal dishes. The restaurant offers daily lunch and dinner specials as well as a wine list. Mama Rosa's offers catering services as well banquet facilities for up to 50 people.

Michael's Lake Arthur
Restaurant & Motel $-$$
970 New Castle Road, Butler
(724) 865-9564

Michael's sits on U.S. Route 422, about 7 miles from Moraine State Park. If you've enjoyed an active day at Moraine, you'll also enjoy repairing to Michael's to sample the rock shrimp linguini, chicken parmigiana, and barbecued ribs. Michael's serves lunch and dinner, offers a full-service bar and wine list, and can accommodate up to 65 people in its banquet facilities. Reservations are available. The number of rooms at the motel is limited.

Natili Restaurant & Lounge $$
104 West Wayne Street, Butler
(724) 287-5033
www.natilirestaurant.com

Natili Restaurant & Lounge is a familiar sight at the corner of Wayne and Main in downtown Butler; it's been operated continuously by the same family since 1939. It features what owner Vince Tavolario describes as traditional dishes from the Abuzzi region of Italy, including many selections based on Natili's homemade pasta. The restaurant, which is closed on Sunday, offers lunch and dinner specials as well as a full-service bar and wine list. Reservations are accepted. The restaurant's banquet facilities can accommodate up to 75 people.

Live bands, fronted by such noted Pittsburgh performers as trombonist Harold Betters, are featured each Friday and Saturday evening. Twice each month, a guest pianist sits in. It's none other than Vince Tavolario, who dazzles his dinner guests with an eclectic repertoire that features jazz, rock, and standards. Tavolario and his family also operate the nearby Natili North.

Serventi's $-$$
438 South Chestnut Street, Butler
(724) 287-4474

Serventi's is an institution in downtown Butler—it's been serving its popular Italian-

American fare there since 1973. You'll find a broad selection of steak, seafood, chicken, and veal dishes, as well as daily lunch and dinner specials. Serventi's offers a full-service bar, a wine list, and banquet facilities for up to 30 people. Reservations are accepted but not required.

Mexican

Mad Mex $–$$
7905 McKnight Road, Ross
(412) 366–5656

370 Atwood Street
(412) 681–5656
www. madmex.com

You'll find Mad Mex in both the North Hills and near the University of Pittsburgh campus in Oakland. We're not sure what Mex is mad about—it's certainly not the menu, which is varied and entertaining. You'll find a broad selection of dishes that the restaurants consider "California-Mexican." These include such interesting variations as Heavy Duty Judy's Curry Chicken Burrito, with marinated chicken, white rice, pineapple, and raisins topped with a curry sauce, and grilled chicken chick pea chili burrito, packing a lot of tastes into one burrito. The restaurants offer a generous selection of microbrews as well as "Big Ass Margaritas," which probably don't require further explanation, and happy-hour specials. Each location serves lunch and dinner daily, and the Atwood Street restaurant is open until 2:00 a.m. each day. Reservations are not accepted.

This is a fun place with good food, but take it from an Insider—don't expect a quiet rendezvous here. Mad Mex is for an evening when you feel like good background music and loud conversation.

EAST

American

Baldonieri's Mill Creek Restaurant $$
Springer Road, Ligonier
(724) 238-3636

You'll dine in style here in a restored 18th-century barn furnished in wormy chestnut and boasting a working fireplace and a 2½-story cathedral ceiling. The diverse menu is particularly strong on seafood selections, such as lobster ravioli and Po River catfish. *Choucroute,* a traditional Alsacian dish featuring braised pork loin, sausage, and sauerkraut, also is popular. Baldonieri's offers a full-service bar, a wine list, and banquet facilities for up to 350 in the barn's loft. That's also the scene of entertainment—acoustic guitarists on Saturday nights. Baldonieri's serves dinner only Wednesday through Sunday. It's closed on Monday and Tuesday. Reservations are accepted.

The Bistro $$$
216 West Loyalhanna Street, Ligonier
(724) 238-9545

You'll find the Bistro at the Ramada Inn Historic Ligonier. Specialties include crab cakes, pasta dishes, grilled steak, salads, and sandwiches. You also can dine more informally at Cappy's Deli, which features the same wine list and much of the same menu as the Bistro.

The Bistro serves breakfast, lunch, and dinner—including a buffet—each day but Sunday and Monday. There is no breakfast on Monday, and brunch is offered on Sunday. The Bistro does not designate smoking or nonsmoking sections. The hotel offers banquet facilities for up to 80 people. The restaurant offers occasional special events, such as theater nights; these are irregularly scheduled, so you'll need to call for details. The Bistro is closed from 1:30 to 4:30 p.m. daily.

Buffalo Blues $–$$
216 South Highland Avenue
(412) 362-5837
www.b2restaurants.com/buffaloblues

This Shadyside restaurant specializes in wings, barbecued foods, and blues. The wings come topped with your choice of 12 different sauces, ranging from "Who Do

Voodoo" to "Hotter 'an Hell." The barbecue menu includes ribs, chicken, and seafood, and you can pick from three different sauces. Fresh fish, jambalaya, and fajitas round out the menu. Buffalo Blues offers a full-service bar and a limited wine list. It offers both catering services and banquet facilities for up to 50 people.

On Friday and Saturday evenings, you'll enjoy the restaurant's signature live blues performances. There's often a cover charge for national acts but none for local groups. By the way, the restaurant's phone number is easy to remember—36–BLUES. The most expensive entrees are priced at the lower end of $$.

Cappy's Cafe $
5431 Walnut Street
(412) 621-1188

If you're trying to keep your diet free of fried foods but still love to eat out, try this Shadyside restaurant. Cappy's does not fry any of its foods, preparing them instead on the grill or in a high-heat convection oven. The restaurant offers a diverse selection of burgers, sandwiches, and salads. Cappy's features a full-service bar but does not designate smoking and nonsmoking sections. Reservations are not accepted. Cappy's serves lunch and dinner daily, breakfast on Saturday and Sunday. Late breakfasts are available on weekdays.

Chelsea Grille $–$$
515–519 Allegheny Avenue, Oakmont
(412) 828-0570

Chelsea Grille is part of Oakmont's one-two culinary punch operated by brothers Danny and Tommy Monaco. It serves dinner daily, lunch Monday through Saturday. The menu covers a lot of ground, offering beef, seafood, and chicken entrees, fajitas, barbecued ribs, pasta and Italian selections, and dinner salads. Chelsea Grille offers a full-service bar, a wine list, and facilities that accommodate up to 60 people for banquets. Reservations are accepted.

The Elbow Room $–$$
5744½ Ellsworth Avenue
(412) 441-5222
www.b2restaurants.com/theelbowroom

The Elbow Room has been a fixture in the city's Shadyside neighborhood for more than 40 years, offering a diverse lunch and dinner menu that's particularly strong on salads. Steak salads may be the most popular selections, but you'll also find portabella, grilled eggplant, grilled chicken, spinach, and many other dinner salads. You also may choose from an extensive sandwich selection and a more limited entree list.

The restaurant offers a Sunday brunch, a full-service bar, and a limited wine list. It accepts reservations and provides banquet facilities for up to 100 people. In fair weather you'll enjoy dining on the patio, which is especially nice as it boasts a large Tree in the center and is surrounded by vine-covered garden walls. The Elbow Room is next door to Club Havana, which features Latin dance classes and other evening entertainment, so you can make a night of it at these side-by-side establishments. For more on Club Havana, see the Nightlife chapter.

Gullifty's $
1922 Murray Avenue
(412) 521-8222
www.gulliftyrestaurant.com

Gullifty's won *Pittsburgh Magazine*'s award for the best desserts in town year after year. When you're ready to indulge your sweet tooth, you can sample the restaurant's peanut butter truffle pie, its macadamia truffle torte, or its chocolate intemperance. The pièce de résistance is the "Killer Cookie," featuring a chocolate chip and walnut cookie topped with vanilla ice cream, bananas, chocolate syrup, and whipped cream. It's so loaded with taste that Gullifty's requires 15 minutes to prepare it.

The restaurant's menu features soups, dinner salads, sandwiches, burgers, Mexican fare, pasta, and a limited entree list. Gullifty's offers a significant number of meatless dishes; these are so noted on the menu. Among the most popular sandwiches is Gullifty's Meshugna, grilled corned beef served open-face with coleslaw and Russian dressing on two potato pancakes. Gullifty's offers a full-service bar, a limited wine and beer list, and banquet facilities for up to 40 people. It does not accept reservations. It serves lunch and dinner daily as well as Saturday and Sunday brunches. You'll find Gullifty's in the center of the Squirrel Hill business district.

Hemingway's Cafe $
3911 Forbes Avenue
(412) 621-4100

The spirit of Papa Hemingway comes alive each Tuesday evening when this restaurant on the University of Pittsburgh campus hosts poetry readings. Some readers are scheduled, while other Tuesdays feature open sessions. If the hunger for literature makes you literally hungry, you can select from a varied menu including sandwiches; salads; pasta dishes; and some poultry, seafood, and beef dishes. Hemingway's offers a full-service bar, wine and beer lists, and banquet facilities for up to 60 people. The cafe serves lunch and dinner daily, and it accepts reservations.

Hoffstot's Cafe Monaco
Restaurant & Lounge $$$
533 Allegheny Avenue, Oakmont
(412) 828-8555
www.hoffstots.com

Hoffstot's is a pleasant restaurant near the Allegheny River and the Hulton Bridge. Along with the neighboring Chelsea Grille—the restaurants are operated by brothers Danny and Tom Monaco—it gives Oakmont an attractive dining tandem. Hoffstot's offers a diverse menu with beef, seafood, veal, and Italian selections, as well as dinner salads. Steaks are popular, as is the shrimp Monaco— shrimp and jumbo lump crabmeat baked in butter, garlic, lemon, white wine, and oregano—and sea scallops Palermo. You'll find a lounge and a wine list that includes 11 "reserve" or premier wines. Hoffstot's offers

Only restaurants with Sunday licenses can serve liquor on Sunday and on election day when the polls are open. If you're not sure if your favorite restaurant has this license, don't hesitate to ask.

weekday banquet facilities for up to 50 people. It serves lunch and dinner daily; make it a late lunch on Sunday, when the restaurant opens at 1:00 p.m. Reservations are accepted.

Jaden's $
4727 William Penn Highway, Monroeville
(412) 373-8575

Jaden's is a family restaurant that's open daily for breakfast, lunch, and dinner, with daily specials offered for each meal. If you're hankering for a hearty breakfast, try Jaden's Ultimate, featuring two hot cakes topped with your choice of strawberries, blueberries, or cherries; two eggs; potatoes; and a side of bacon, sausage, or ham. Dinner entrees include beef, chicken, pasta, and seafood selections. Save room of a slice of homemade pie or the waffle sundae. As a family restaurant, Jaden's doesn't serve alcohol.

John Harvard's Brew House $–$$
400 Penn Center Boulevard, Wilkins
(412) 824-9440
www.johnharvards.com

John Harvard's serves lunch and dinner daily. Among the most popular entrees are chicken potpie, meat loaf, and fish-and-chips, and you'll also find beef, seafood, and pasta entrees as well as daily specials. You'll find a full-service bar and a wine list; as befitting a brew house, John Harvard's also offers an extensive selection of ales and lagers. Other features include a humidor and cigar list and a retail area for merchandise imprinted with John Harvard's logo. The restaurant offers banquet facilities for up to 35 people. Reservations are recommended on weekends and are for eight people or more. John Harvard's is located on U.S. Business Route 22.

Kazansky's Restaurant and Delicatessen $
2201 Murray Avenue
(412) 521-4555

Kazansky's has been pleasing Squirrel Hill patrons for decades. It features Jewish-style specialties, including homemade soups, dinner salads, a limited entree list, and a broad selection of sandwiches. These include the Yoy (pronounced oi-ee), the Double Yoy, and the Triple Yoy, all built around corned beef and based on a characteristic exclamation of Pittsburgh Steelers commentator Myron Cope, as in "Another penalty? Yoy." You'll also find the Marv Albert—beef tongue and Swiss cheese on pumpernickel. "Sink your teeth into this one," the menu advises. Hey, we don't endorse 'em, we just report 'em.

Kazansky's offers a retail section and a take-out counter, which is one of the region's busiest places on Christmas Eve, when patrons line up to purchase meat and dairy trays for their guests. Kazansky's serves beer but no other alcohol, and it does not accept reservations. Kazansky's serves breakfast, lunch, and dinner daily and is now a smoke-free establishment.

The Lamplighter Cafe $$
330 U.S. Route 22, Delmont
(724) 468-4545

For more than 40 years the Lamplighter has been a hub for dining and entertainment in Westmoreland County. In fact, the restaurant offers so many activities and specials—such as a daily early-bird menu, a full-course weekly special, and dance bands each weekend—that you're advised to pick up your monthly activities calendar in the lobby. Prime rib and fresh seafood are the menu headliners, and you'll also enjoy the Monday-to-Friday lunch buffet and the Sunday breakfast and dinner buffets. The Lamplighter offers a lounge, a wine list, and banquet facilities for up to 400 people. Reservations are suggested. The Lamplighter serves breakfast, lunch, and dinner daily.

Lesley's $$$
327 Mountain View Road, Donegal
(724) 593-6349, (800) 392-7773
www.shol.com/mtviewbb

Lesley's offers intimate dining in a restored chestnut barn nestled in the foothills of the Laurel Highlands at Mountain View Country Inn. Dining is leisurely and memorable here, as you'll enjoy such entrees as scallop pasta with roasted peppers and beef Wellington. The menu changes weekly, but you can get a preview—as well as some of Lesley's most popular recipes and wine list—by visiting the restaurant's Web site. The site also will introduce you to the companion Lesley's Mountain View Country Inn. For more on that, see the Bed-and-Breakfast Inns chapter.

Lesley's offers a full-service bar and an extensive wine list. Smoking is permitted at the bar only. The restaurant serves dinner Monday, Tuesday, and Thursday through Saturday, and reservations are suggested. You'll find the restaurant about 1 mile east of the Donegal exit of the Pennsylvania Turnpike.

Ligonier Country Inn $–$$
U.S. Route 30 East, Laughlintown
(724) 238-3651
www.ligoniercountryinn.com

Located in eastern Westmoreland County, Ligonier Country Inn serves dinner Thursday through Sunday, as well as a Sunday breakfast and a Sunday brunch buffet. It's closed Monday through Wednesday. The menu features beef, chicken, pasta, and seafood selections, as well as specials and a vegetarian feature of the day. You'll find a full-service bar, a wine list, and banquet facilities for up to 300 people. Reservations are recommended.

You can transform your trip here into a relaxing vacation by staying at the adjacent bed-and-breakfast inn, which shares the name Ligonier Country Inn. For more on that, see the Bed-and-Breakfast Inns chapter. Both the restaurant and the bed-and-breakfast are owned and operated by P. J. and Maggie Nied, so you can be assured of uniform service whether you're lodging or dining. There's an outdoor pool here, and the Nieds plan a busy summer schedule of pool parties featuring live music. Call them for details.

Ligonier Tavern $–$$
137 West Main Street, Ligonier
(724) 238-4831
www.ligoniertavern.com

This is a fun spot, where everyone seems to have a good time, whether they're dining indoors or alfresco on the front porch or balcony. Your enjoyment will increase when you discover that the tavern makes all its sauces and desserts from scratch. Popular menu items are the crab cakes and fresh mozzarella and tomato chicken. Make sure you save room for the signature Loyalhanna cheesecake—two layers of New York and chocolate cheesecake over an Oreo cookie crust and topped by fudge icing. Try it and you'll know why everybody's smiling.

The tavern offers a full-service bar and a wine list, as well as catering services and banquet facilities for up to 275 people. Ligonier Tavern is open daily for lunch and dinner. It recommends reservations on Friday, Saturday, and Sunday.

Original Hot Dog Shop $
3901 Forbes Avenue
(412) 621-7388

When you consider the University of Pittsburgh, you may think of such wonders as the towering Cathedral of Learning or the Nationality Classrooms that celebrate the region's ethnic heritage. Ask alumni what they recall about their undergraduate days, however, and the landmark they're most likely to name is "the O," the affectionate nickletter for Original Hot Dog Shop. Since 1960 the O has been serving up hot dogs, burgers, wings, subs, and pizza. French fries are particularly popular here—the O goes through 40,000 pounds of them every 10 days. (Note: A small order of fries could fill a dinner plate, so don't dare order two unless you're dining with four or

> Through its "Dining With Heart" program, University of Pittsburgh Medical Center designates selections at local restaurants that meet program standards in cholesterol, fat, and sodium content. Participating restaurants usually mark those entrees with a small red heart. You can get your free list of participating restaurants from UPMC at (412) 647-UPMC (8762) or (800) 533-UPMC (8762).

five people! Also note that you won't be eating heart-healthy here.) You'll find a full-service bar and a broad selection of beers. The O serves lunch and dinner daily, staying open until 3:30 a.m. during the week and 5:00 a.m. on weekends. It does not accept credit cards or reservations. If you're looking for a leisurely candlelight repast with muted string music in the background, this is not the place for you. But if you want to experience the sights and cacophony of an urban college hangout in motion, the O is a go.

Pamela's   *2-1ˢᵗ Ave, Strip District* $
5527 Walnut Street   *– walked & ate brk.*
(412) 683-1003
3703 Forbes Avenue   *on Sat 10/3/09*
(412) 683-4066

5813 Forbes Avenue
(412) 422-9457

If you like your hotcakes stacked high and stuffed full, Pamela's is the place for you. Each of Pamela's three locations—Shadyside, Oakland, Squirrel Hill—specializes in breakfasts that are available in the afternoon as well. Pamela's offers banana walnut, strawberry, chocolate chip, and apple-walnut hotcakes, a variety so tasty and appealing that Pamela's won the silver medal for Best Breakfast in *Pittsburgh Magazine* Reader's Choice Awards for several years running. Breakfast fare also includes waffles, omelets, and French toast. For lunch Pamela's offers sandwiches and salads.

Pamela's does not serve alcohol and does not accept reservations or credit cards. The restaurants are open daily for breakfast and lunch.

Peppermill Inn $$$
4733 William Penn Highway, Monroeville
(412) 372-9878

You won't find many restaurants with a separate lobster menu, but that's an attraction of Peppermill Inn. You can enjoy lobster tails, lobster Newberg, or lobster in a surf and turf combination. The eclectic menu also offers homemade pasta selections as well as beef, veal, chicken, and additional seafood entrees. It would be hard not to find something you like at the Peppermill. The restaurant offers a full-service bar, a wine list, catering services, and banquet facilities for up to 70 people. Reservations are recommended for weekends and accepted at all times. Peppermill Inn does not designate smoking and nonsmoking sections. It serves lunch and dinner daily.

Pittsburgh Deli Co. $
728 Copeland Street
(412) 682-DELI (3354)
www.pghdeli.com

This bright, airy Shadyside deli serves lunch and dinner daily; you also can enjoy a late-night bite, as the deli is open until 2:00 a.m. daily. You'll find gourmet sandwiches, Jewish-style foods, and homemade baked goods, and you can enjoy it all in the downstairs dining area or the bar area upstairs. Speaking of the bar, Pittsburgh Deli Co. offers a full array of drinks and roughly 100 varieties of beer. It provides catering services and can accommodate banquets of up to 100 people on-site. Smoking is permitted in the second-floor bar area only. The deli features live jazz, rock, and acoustical bands on some Friday evenings. The entertainment schedule is irregular, so it's best to call for details.

Red Room Café and Lounge $$$-$$$$
134 South Highland Avenue
(412) 362-5800
www.redroomcafe.net

Red Room is just one of several new restaurants that have opened in this up and coming neighborhood in East Liberty. Once a vacant corner property, Red Room is now a popular destination for diners who appreciate fusion cuisine and great wine. Some representative entrees include seared day boat sea scallops, served with squid ink linguini; roasted corn, lump crab, and saffron jus; spicy basil noodles, served with honey cashew tofu, and carrot chips; and pan roasted, bacon barded, pork tenderloin served with cheesy grits, wilted greens, and a blackberry demi. Enjoy your meal with a selection from their extensive wine list.

Red Room is open for dinner Monday through Saturday.

The Road Toad $-$$
US 30 East, Ligonier
(724) 539-7623

The Road Toad is one of those places that fairly hops with energy—diners indoors, diners outdoors, the Loyalhanna Creek rushing by just below the restaurant. The menu features beef, chicken, seafood, and pasta selections as well as a lengthy list of sandwiches and pitas. Outdoors at the Back Bay Grill, they'll grill just about anything you order. The Road Toad offers a full-service bar and accepts reservations for parties of eight or more. It can accommodate 50 people for indoor banquets, 150 for outdoor affairs. The restaurant offers occasional live music; it's best to call for details. The Road Toad offers lunch and dinner Tuesday through Sunday.

Ruthie's Diner $
US 30 East, Ligonier
(724) 238-6030

If you're a diner fan, make sure you drop by Ruthie's for the homemade soups, pies, and apple dumplings. The fare is filling and economically priced. Ruthie's serves breakfast, lunch, and dinner daily, and it's open until midnight on Friday and Saturday. Ruthie's does not serve alcohol, and it does not accept credit cards. It accepts reservations Monday through Friday only.

Square Café $
1137 South Braddock Avenue
(412) 244-8002
www.square-cafe.com

There is nothing "square" about this popular spot in Regent Square. Guests sit at 1950s tables surrounded by modern décor. Opened in 2003, Square Café offers breakfast and lunch, occasionally serves as a local performance venue, and provides on- and off-site catering. In the morning, choose from a great list of yummy breakfasts, including the veggie overload omelet, nutella crepes, and pumpkin walnut pancakes. Square Café offers savory crepes, wraps, sandwiches, soups, and salads for lunch. Some of our favorites: the vegetarian white bean chili, chicken and butternut squash crepe, and Italian beef sandwich.

Square Café is a member of Diner Ladies, a group of five women-owned diners in the Pittsburgh area. They share ideas and promote the importance of supporting small, locally-owned businesses. (For details, visit www.dinerladies.com.)

Breakfast and lunch are served Monday through Saturday 7:00 a.m. until 3:00 p.m. and Sunday 8:00 a.m. to 3:00 p.m.

Tessaro's $$
4601 Liberty Avenue
(412) 682-6809

Hardwood-grilled steaks, the best hamburgers in town, and fish top the menu at this bustling spot in the Bloomfield neighborhood. The atmosphere is casual, but don't be surprised if you wait a long time for a table and then get seated near a local celebrity—everyone goes to Tessaro's, unless they're vegetarian, that is. Open Monday through Saturday for lunch and dinner until late.

Union Grill $–$$$
413 South Craig Street
(412) 681-8620

South Craig Street is a happening venue in Oakland, situated between the campuses of the University of Pittsburgh and Carnegie Mel-

lon University and drawing considerable traffic from each. Union Grill is one of the chief contributors to the bustle of activity, offering indoor and outdoor dining and a menu that's sure to please almost everyone. It offers such specialties as Bourbon Street Pasta, fresh vegetables and fettuccine tossed in a spicy Cajun sauce and flavored with a shot of Jim Beam bourbon, and Calypso Chicken, a chicken breast rubbed with calypso spices and topped with peppers, mushrooms, onions, tomatoes, and mangoes.

The selections don't stop there. Union Grill offers seafood and salsa specials each evening, a "Build a Burger" feature, dinner salads, sandwiches, and vegetarian selections. For libations, you'll find a full-service bar and a wine list offering what the house calls "rock bottom prices." Union Grill serves lunch and dinner daily, and it also offers a late night menu each day. Reservations are accepted for parties of seven or more.

Caribbean

Donsvilles' Jamaica Jamaica $
6008 Broad Street
(412) 361-1631

Donsvilles' specializes in such Jamaican dishes as curry shrimp, curry goat, jerk chicken, and escovitch—a red- or yellow-tailed snapper fried and sautéed with spicy peppers, vinegar, tomatoes, and onions. The menu is rich in Jamaican foods—make sure that's what you want, since you won't find any alternative selections. Donsvilles' accepts reservations. It does not serve alcohol or designate smoking and nonsmoking sections. The restaurant serves lunch and dinner daily. You'll find Donsvilles' in Pittsburgh's East Liberty neighborhood near North Highland Avenue, one of the neighborhood's principal thoroughfares.

Belgian

Point Brugge Café $$$
401 Hastings Street, Point Breeze
(412) 441-3334
www.pointbrugge.com

Tucked away in Point Breeze, Point Brugge Cafe may be somewhat difficult to find, but do try. Your efforts will be rewarded with an enjoyable lunch or dinner at this neighborhood gathering spot which was modeled on cafes found in European cities.

Formerly the location of The Point Restaurant, Point Brugge Café opened in 2005. They serve a variety of bistro dishes as small plates and dinners. We prefer the steamed mussels served with brugge fries, or the carbonnade flamande, Belgian pot roast. Delicious food choices are accompanied by a tremendous beer selection.

The café is open for lunch and dinner Tuesday through Saturday, with brunch served on Sunday from 11:00 a.m. until 3:00 p.m. Sorry, reservations are not accepted.

Chinese

China Palace $$
5440 Walnut Street
(412) 687-7423

4059 William Penn Highway, Monroeville
(412) 373-7423

409 Broad Street, Sewickley
(412) 741-7423
www.chinapalacepittsburgh.com
China Palace offers some of the best Chinese food in the area, with the nicest ambience. China Palace offers a compelling variety of entrees, including salmon sizzler; orange-flavored beef; and Three's Company, which combines lemon chicken, General Tso's chicken, and chicken with vegetables. You'll find a broad variety of seafood, beef, chicken, and pork selections, with hot and spicy items noted on the menu. China Palace offers a bar and a wine list, but it does not accept reservations. It serves dinner daily, lunch Monday through Saturday. Note that the phone number of each restaurant sports the same last four digits, which spell the word RICE.

Chopsticks $$
2018 Murray Avenue
(412) 421-1920

Since 1960, Chopsticks has been pleasing Squirrel Hill diners with its broad menu representative of all Chinese regions. You'll find such entrees as Szechuan spicy eggplant; ginger chicken with spicy sauce; and Happy Family, a medley of shrimp, beef, chicken, and roast pork with Chinese vegetables and topped by a brown sauce. Hot and spicy items are so noted on the menu. Chopsticks serves lunch and dinner daily and offers a limited wine list. It accepts reservations, but it does not permit smoking.

Evergreen Chinese Restaurant $
3500 William Penn Highway,
Monroeville
(412) 825-8088
Evergreen offers a varied menu that features beef, chicken, pork, and seafood selections, but the most popular item here is the daily lunch and dinner buffet. The buffet features nearly 40 items, including about one dozen entrees. Evergreen offers a special buffet price for children, and senior citizens receive a discount on any order. The restaurant accepts reservations, and it offers banquet facilities for up to 70 people. It does not serve alcohol. Evergreen is located about 2 miles from exit 57 of the Pennsylvania Turnpike on US Business 22, a commercial corridor that spans Wilkins Township and Monroeville.

The House of Chiang $–$$
120 McKee Place
(412) 681-5169
The House of Chiang, located near the western edge of the University of Pittsburgh campus, serves lunch and dinner daily. It specializes in Cantonese and Szechuan fare, including such favorites as moo goo gai pan over rice and cashew chicken. The diverse menu offers an uncommon number of lunch specials, highlighted by 20 combination plates. Although you won't find a bar here, the waitstaff will serve alcohol you've brought yourself. Reservations are not accepted.

If you spot unsanitary conditions at an Allegheny County restaurant, call the county health department, (412) 687-ACHD (2243). They pledge to investigate.

Jade Garden $–$$
4450 William Penn Highway, Murrysville
(724) 733-2281
www.jadegardenrestaurant.com

If you like to share plates with your dining companions, try Jade Garden's "Happy Family Dinners." They're specially priced, and you can select from 13 entrees. The menu also offers beef, lamb, pork, chicken, vegetarian, and seafood selections. General Tso's chicken is a popular pick, as is Seafood in Bird's Nest, which features sautéed shrimp, scallops, and lobster with Chinese vegetables over a crispy base. The restaurant offers a full-service bar and a wine list, and it can accommodate banquets of up to 40 people. Reservations for parties of five or more are accepted. You'll find Jade Garden on US 22 in Westmoreland County, just east of the Allegheny County line.

Jimmy Tsang's Chinese
Restaurant and Korean Grill $$–$$$
5700 Centre Avenue
(412) 661-4226

Jimmy Tsang's offers selections representing the four major Chinese styles—Mandarin, Hunan and Szechuan, Shanghai, and Cantonese. Popular features of the lunch and dinner menu include shrimp with lobster sauce; Manchurian noodles; and a whole fish, which might be red snapper or sea bass. If you order that whole fish, the folks in the kitchen will need about 40 minutes to prepare it. The restaurant in Pittsburgh's Shadyside neighborhood also offers an extensive roster of vegetarian entrees, combination dinners for up to six people, daily lunch specials, and a limited early-bird menu with specially priced entrees.

Jimmy Tsang's features a full-service bar and an extensive wine list, as well as banquet facilities for up to 300 people. Reservations are accepted for parties of four or more. Jimmy Tsang's is open daily but serves only dinner on Sunday. Prices for the most expensive entrees are at the lower end of $$$.

P. F. Chang's China Bistro $$
The Waterfront
148 West Bridge Street, West Homestead
(412) 464-0640

Once impossible to get into without a long wait, Chang's is no longer the new kid at the waterfront. Yet depending on when the last movie ended at nearby Lowe's Cineplex, there can still be a line; whiling away the time at the small bar is a pleasant enough pastime. The atmosphere is geared toward adults with mood lighting and upbeat background music. The cuisine is from Canton, Shanghai, Hunan, and Mongolia, and there's wine by the glass, as well as a decent by-the-bottle list. Start with Chang's spicy chicken or vegetarian wraps, where you'll scoop ground chicken or wok-seared tofu into lettuce leaves that you fold and then drizzle with a selection of sauces—a tasty appetizer. Even the wonton soup tastes fresh and different here. Mild to spicy entrees—typical Chinese fare but again with a flair—are served with steamed rice. The prices are reasonable. Chang's is open every day, 11:00 a.m. to 10:30 p.m., later on weekends, and reservations are not accepted.

Sichuan House $$
1335 Freeport Road
(412) 967-0789

1717 Cochran Road, Mt. Lebanon
(412) 563-5252

If you like broad menu variety, you'll love Sichuan House, which features 175 distinct entrees at both of its locations—in the city's Squirrel Hill neighborhood, in the South Hills, only a few miles from Downtown. Beef, seafood, chicken, pork—all are well represented at Sichuan House, which serves both lunch and dinner. Among diners' favorites here are shrimp with snow peas; stuffed bean curd; pan-fried Cantonese noodles with seafood; and leeks with smoked ham, Taiwanese style.

The menu clearly highlights "hot and spicy" items in red, so you'll always know what's in store for you. Sichuan House offers a small selection of "lean" entrees and free delivery, within a limited service area for take-out selections. The restaurants accept reservations for parties of five or more.

When you want to enjoy the food at Sichuan House at a slightly reduced rate, try their "family dinner." It features a flat rate for each member of your party, no matter what entree each selects. It's a great way to work your way through that menu.

Soba Lounge $$$
5847 Ellsworth Avenue
(412) 362-5656
www.bigburrito.com

Rising like a phoenix from the ashes of an electrical fire that closed the building for more than a year, Soba has been reborn with revamped, award-winning Pan-Asian cuisine and a cozier ambience, complete with two-story waterfall and wood-burning fireplaces. Try the seared rare tuna with Korean barbecue sauce or one of the many vegetarian dishes. The wine list is now more extensive. Reservations are suggested on weekends.

The rooftop patio offers a breeze in summer and a warm meeting spot when the heaters are on. The side bar downstairs with banquet seating makes a much-needed addition to this very hip restaurant.

Continental

Cafe Zinho $$–$$$
238 Spahr Street
(412) 363-1500

This garage-turned-bistro features tasty nouveau continental cuisine—French, American, and Portuguese influenced—that changes seasonally. Just off Ellsworth Avenue, this sister restaurant to Baum Vivant (sharing the

same owners) has its own young, top-gun chefs turning out terrific food at a surprisingly reasonable price. Many appetizers prove meals in themselves. Daily specials are definitely special.

The funky decor plus outdoor dining when weather permits made this an instant hit with fashionable East-Enders as soon as it opened. Disappointingly, on the other hand, there's little for vegetarians here. Open Tuesday through Saturday for lunch and dinner. Cash only. You're welcome to bring your own wine.

Casbah $$$
229 South Highland Avenue
(412) 661-5656

Feast on French, Italian, and Spanish offerings with influences from the Middle East and North Africa. Dine downstairs in a more formal setting, upstairs in the noisy bar and adjacent area packed with Gen-Xers, or relax outside on the front patio. Dress ranges from casual to dressy.

The award-winning food is a main draw, and as a wine bar Casbah has no equal. Several cheese plates make a good accompaniment to the two-ounce selections in the wine flights—more than 40 wines by the glass or the large selection of wines by the bottle and half bottle. Check for new wine listings on the blackboards behind the bar.

Open every day for lunch and dinner, Casbah serves a popular brunch on Sunday. It accepts reservations.

Lucca $$–$$$
317 South Craig Street
(412) 682-3310

Lucca styles its food as European, inspired by Italian flair. Read the menu and you'll get an idea of the international flavor. You'll find Crisfield County crab cakes, calamari gaetta, lump crabmeat spring roll, and shrimp taquito. The menu changes daily for lunch and dinner and offers seasonal complements; for instance, it features lamb in spring, pasta in summer. Staples of the menu are the mixed grille—samplings of filet mignon, lamp chop, leg of duck, and Italian sausage—and the seafood mixed grille.

You'll find a full-service bar, and a sommelier will guide you through the ample wine list. Reservations are recommended. Lucca offers banquet facilities for up to 30 people. The restaurant serves lunch and dinner Monday through Saturday. Eat out on the patio when the weather is nice—if you can grab a table.

Filipino/Thai

Sweet Basil and La Filipiniana $–$$
5321 Butler Street
(412) 781-8724

2022 Murray Avenue (Squirrel Hill)
(412) 422-8950
www.mysweetbasil.com
Here you'll find the only combination Thai and Filipino restaurant in the region. A feature on the menu is the Taste of La Filipiniana, a seven-course dinner for two that features entrees representing three geographic regions of the Philippines. Thai dishes are one of a kind and prepared with only the very best of fresh ingredients. Groups of 10 or more can make arrangements to dine any day of the week. The Lawrenceville location is open Tuesday to Sunday from 5:00 to 10:00 p.m. The Squirrel Hill location is open Tuesday to Friday 11:30 a.m. to 3:00 p.m. for lunch and 5:00 to 10:00 p.m. for dinner; noon to 10:00 p.m. Saturday and Sunday. Bring your own wine or beer; no corkage fee.

Indian

India Garden $–$$
328 Atwood Street
(412) 682-3000

3815 William Penn Highway, Monroeville
(412) 372-0400
www.indiagarden.net
India Garden's dining room is large and inviting, and the daily lunch buffet features more than 25 items. India Garden prepares its food

in a clay oven, giving it a distinctive taste. The extensive menu offers popular tandoori entrees as well as a generous selection of vegetarian entrees.

Reservations are required. The restaurants, which serve lunch and dinner daily, offer banquet facilities for up to 230 people. You'll find the Pittsburgh restaurant on the University of Pittsburgh's Oakland campus, the Monroeville location on US Business 22 near the Pennsylvania Turnpike. The Oakland location has a full bar.

Prince of India Restaurant
and Tavern $–$$
3614 Fifth Avenue
(412) 687-0888
Located near the University of Pittsburgh campus and the Oakland medical complex, Prince of India serves lunch and dinner daily. Its daily lunch buffet is popular, as is its mix grill tandoori—a medley of seekh kabob, boti kabob, chicken tikka, and tandoori chicken and shrimp, served with chutney. The menu includes beef, lamb, seafood, vegetarian, and biryani entrees, and you'll enjoy the selection of 10 breads baked in Prince of India's clay oven. The restaurant offers a bar and a wine list. Smoking is permitted at the bar only. Prince of India does not accept reservations.

Sree's Foods $
2103 Murray Avenue
(412) 288-2992

606 Main Street, Sharpsburg
(412) 781-4765
www.srees.com
Where else but Sree's can you find an entire Indian meal to go for under $5? Mr. and Mrs. Sree started their business with a take-out cart at Carnegie Mellon. Now they offer take-out from more prestigious digs as well—restaurants in Squirrel Hill and Sharpsburg. Prices are a couple of dollars higher at the restaurant in Sharpsburg, but you can eat in there on Friday and Saturday evenings when

the restaurant is open for dinner. You can't eat in at the Squirrel Hill location, but when you get home you'll enjoy this delicious, medium to very spicy food. Vegetarian entrees are always offered.

Star of India $–$$
412 South Craig Street
(412) 681-5700

Dinner fare includes a variety of chicken, lamb, beef, and shrimp selections as well as biryani—a rice and raisin base topped by shrimp, chicken, lamb, or beef. You'll find a number of vegetarian entrees, and the Monday-through-Thursday lunch buffet includes vegetarian choices. Star of India does not serve alcohol, but you can bring in your own. It accepts reservations. The restaurant does not offer designated smoking or nonsmoking sections. If you become a regular patron here, the personable Star of India waiters will greet you as a friend.

Italian

Carbone's $–$$
U.S. Route 119, Crabtree
(724) 834-3430

Carbone's accepts reservations for parties of six or more, but you probably don't have to worry about getting seated here. With a seating capacity of 650, Carbone's can pretty much guarantee a table whenever you arrive. It's operated by Natale "Buzzy" Carbone and his sister Natalie Carbone—Carbone's has been in their family since its opening in 1938. An interesting bit of family lore: Natale and Natalie were named to honor their grandfather, who was born on Christmas—"Natal" in Italian.

It will seem like Natal when you dine here. A house specialty is braciole, steak stuffed and rolled in tomato sauce. Save room for Carbone's homemade desserts such as angel pie, made with strawberries, coconut, and whipped cream cavorting on a vanilla wafer crust. Carbone's offers a bar, a wine list, and banquet facilities for up to 300 people. It

serves dinner only Monday through Saturday, closing on Sunday. Carbone's is about 6 miles north of Greensburg in Westmoreland County on US 119.

Del's Bar & Ristorante DelPizzo $–$$
4428 Liberty Avenue
(412) 683-1448
www.delsrest.com

Del's, as this establishment is popularly known, has been a Bloomfield fixture since the DelPizzo family opened it in 1949. It offers lunch and dinner daily, providing a broad selection of steaks and chops, pasta, chicken, veal, and seafood dishes. You can easily make a meal of Del's Gourmet pizza. The restaurant offers daily luncheon specials, with specially priced drinks if you eat at the bar. Del's offers a Wednesday lunch buffet, Monday dinner buffet, and Sunday brunch (discount coupons available online). Del's offers irregularly scheduled entertainment in the form of karaoke—it's best to call for details. The restaurant offers a wine list, and it accepts reservations. Banquet facilities for up to 100 people are available.

DeNunzio's Italian Restaurant $$
700 Lowry Avenue, Jeannette
(724) 527-5552
www.denunziosrestaurant.com

You'll enjoy the creative menu at DeNunzio's. It features veal, chicken, beef, and seafood entries, as well as two pages of pasta entrees. But the show stoppers may be the tenderloins of beef garnished with shrimp and prepared in a Cajun style, and the veal Florentine, which is layered with shrimp and lump crabmeat and prepared in a white wine sauce. DeNunzio's offers a bar, an extensive wine list, and banquet facilities for up to 100 people. The restaurant can accommodate two banquets simultaneously. Reservations are recommended. DeNunzio's serves lunch and dinner daily. You'll find it in Westmoreland County about 1 mile north of US 30. DeNunzio's has three additional locations: Monroeville (see listing below), Latrobe (Arnold Palmer Regional Airport), and Youngwood (Cherry Creek Golf Club).

DeNunzio's Italian Restaurant $$–$$$
2644 Mosside Boulevard, Monroeville
(412) 374-7120
www.denunziosrestaurant.com

This is a sister restaurant of the Jeannette DeNunzio's but offers a somewhat less-extensive menu. It also aims more for families, offering more booths than its Jeannette counterpart and covering the tables with paper on which kids are invited to color. In fact, the restaurant holds occasional coloring contests for its young patrons. Another difference: the Monroeville restaurant cooks in a wood-fired oven, providing a distinctive taste for its food. The restaurant offers a full-service bar and an extensive wine list. It serves lunch and dinner daily. Reservations are accepted for parties of four or more; others may call ahead for priority seating. The Monroeville DeNunzio's is about 1 mile west of the Pennsylvania Turnpike.

D'Imperio's Restaurant $$–$$$
3412 William Penn Highway, Wilkins
(412) 823-4800

D'Imperio's is a classy restaurant with an appetite for fun as well. Shrimp Sorrento, enhanced with a taste of lemon and vodka, is a popular selection, and you'll find a wide variety of veal, lamb, chicken, seafood, and pasta entrees. Executive chef Joseph Schilling offers at least three soups—including his signature seafood bisque—for every meal, and he also offers what D'Imperio's calls its "Culinary Geek" showcase of daily entree specials. The restaurant accepts reservations, and it offers a full-service bar and banquet facilities for up to 250 people. It serves dinner Monday through Saturday, lunch Tuesday through Friday. D'Imperio's is closed on Sunday.

A restaurant that calls its specials a "Culinary Geek" showcase clearly knows how to

entertain, and you'll find a number of entertaining touches here. As you walk in you'll enjoy viewing the ample wine collection in cabinets decorating the lobby areas. You can participate in the restaurant's wine-tasting events, held on most Friday evenings, and you can trip the light fantastic at a summer series of "Al Fresco Friday Feasts," which feature dinner and drinks as well as dancing. Al and the geeks move indoors if it rains on their feast. Call D'Imperio's for a schedule of special events.

DiSalvo's Station Restaurant $$–$$$
325 McKinley Avenue, Latrobe
(724) 539-0500
http://disalvosrestaurant.com

Some enterprising entrepreneurs locate their businesses in renovated train stations. The DiSalvo family has done them one better, creating a dining complex in an active train station. You'll find this Westmoreland County restaurant, as well as a sister restaurant called Prima Classe, in the Latrobe Train Station, where two Amtrak trains stop daily. In addition to deploying a railway motif in their decor, the DiSalvos have created a special Steelers training-camp package built around Amtrak's service. The package, offered only when the Steelers are training at nearby St. Vincent College in July and August, includes round-trip train fare from Pittsburgh, lunch at DiSalvo's, and an afternoon at training camp.

The menu offers beef, chicken, seafood, and pasta selections. Favorites include Filet DiSalvo, filet mignon stuffed with prosciutto and provolone cheese and laced with bordelaise sauce and mushrooms; and DiSalvo's Station Seafood Platter, a medley of lobster, clams, shrimp, scallops, deviled crab, oysters, and sole. You'll also enjoy the early-bird menu featuring a limited selection of specially priced dinner entrees from Tuesday through Sunday. Reservations are suggested for all meals. DiSalvo's offers an extensive wine list and can accommodate up to 350 people for banquets. The restaurant is non-smoking, but if you want to light up, you can repair to the adjoining Joey D's Sala Da Fumo, a cigar smokers' lair that's part of the complex.

DiSalvo's serves dinner Tuesday through Sunday, lunch Tuesday through Friday, and brunch on Sunday. It's closed on Monday. The most expensive entrees are priced at the lower end of $$$. (For more on Prima Classe, see following page.)

Girasole $$
733 Copeland Street
(412) 682-2130

This basement restaurant with tables lining the walls may be tiny but its portions are large, and as soon as Girasole opened, it became a popular (nonsmoking) addition to the Shadyside scene. Start with bruschetta or an antipasto platter; then have a fresh house salad with olives, garbanzo beans, and Gorgonzola; and pick a fresh selection of the season. Most of the yummy desserts are made in-house. There is some seating on the patio, and it too is close together—you'll get to know your neighbors. Closed Monday. No reservations.

Lombardozzi Restaurant $–$$
4786 Liberty Avenue
(412) 682-5785

Lombardozzi is one of a number of fine Italian restaurants in Pittsburgh's Bloomfield neighborhood, where you can still hear Italian spoken all along Liberty Avenue. The restaurant features pasta, seafood, veal, chicken, and beef entrees. It's particularly proud of its fettuccine Lombardozzi, which includes lump crabmeat, shrimp, scallops, and clams in a red or white sauce, and its veal Lombardozzi, which is crowned with lump crabmeat and shrimp. Lombardozzi offers a popular lunch buffet—the lineup changes daily—as well as a full-service bar and an extensive wine list. It accepts reservations for lunch and dinner.

The restaurant provides banquet facilities, with a special menu for up to 150 people. Several entrees are priced slightly higher than $$.

Minutello's Restaurant & Lounge $–$$
226 Shady Avenue
(412) 361-9311

The Minutello family has operated this East Liberty restaurant for more than 40 years, attracting a loyal clientele. The restaurant features a diverse menu, with veal, beef, chicken, seafood, and pasta entrees. You'll also find specialty pizzas and salad and sandwich selections. Minutello's offers a full-service bar, a wine list, and an extensive selection of domestic and imported beers and micro-brews. Reservations are accepted. The restaurant is open daily for dinner and serves lunch Monday through Friday; it's open from 1:00 to 9:00 p.m. on Sunday. Takeout, catering, and delivery are available.

Persichetti's Restaurant & Lounge $–$$
101 South Third Street, Jeannette
(724) 527-5553

This Westmoreland County restaurant offers a diverse menu that's especially strong on seafood, with such selections as Persichetti's Lobster Crock and the land and sea trio—a medley of chicken breast, jumbo Gulf shrimp, and sea scallops. You'll also find beef, veal, chicken, and pasta selections as well as dinner salads, sandwiches, and pizza. Persichetti's offers daily specials; on Wednesday, the special is barbecued ribs. The restaurant offers a lounge, a wine list, and banquet facilities for up to 30 people. It serves lunch and dinner Tuesday through Sunday; closed on Monday. Reservations are accepted on weekends for parties of five or more, on weekdays for parties of any size.

Pleasure Bar and Restaurant $–$$
4729 Liberty Avenue
(412) 682-9603

The Pleasure Bar and Restaurant has been a fixture in Bloomfield since the 1940s; the

Mariana family has operated it since 1963. The atmosphere is cozy here, the menu strong on pasta dishes. The Pleasure Bar, as it's popularly known, also offers beef, chicken, veal, and seafood selections, as well as a children's menu. Patrons are especially fond of the Italian tripe, served with mushrooms and sweet or hot peppers in tomato sauce; the eggplant parmigiana; and the homemade manicotti. The list of daily specials is extensive. The Pleasure Bar offers a full-service bar, a limited wine list, and banquet facilities for up to 50 people. It accepts reservations for parties of four or more on weekends, for parties of any number at other times. It's open daily Monday through Thursday until 10:30 p.m., Friday and Saturday until 11:30 p.m., and on Sunday from 4:00 to 9:00 p.m.

Prima Classe $$$$
325 McKinley Avenue, Latrobe
(724) 539-0500
http://disalvosrestaurant.com
This small, elegant restaurant is set in a turn-of-the-20th-century railway dining car. That's fitting, since it's located at the still-active Latrobe Train Station, where Joseph DiSalvo and his father, Gaetano, have created a dining complex. The DiSalvos will make your dining experience here memorable. Joe himself will wait on you, while Gaetano—the executive chef for the complex—will prepare your food. The menu is aural, so you won't need your glasses here. It features such gourmet Italian entrees as veal stuffed with proscuitto and provolone and sautéed in a wine and mushroom sauce, and shellfish in a red bouillabaisse.

Prima Classe offers an extensive wine list. Reservations and proper attire are required. The restaurant is nonsmoking, but you can puff to your heart's content at the adjoining Joey D's Sala Da Fumo, a cigar salon that hosts several cigar-based special events each year and offers private lockers for members. Prima Classe serves only dinner, and only on

Friday and Saturday evenings. For a visit to its sister restaurant, DiSalvo's Station Restaurant and Banquet Facilities, see above.

J G's Tarentum Station Grille Restaurant $$–$$$
101 Station Drive, Tarentum
(724) 226-3301
The Tarentum station was constructed in 1892 as a stop for the Pennsylvania Railroad. Such notables as William Howard Taft, William Jennings Bryan, Kit Carson, Carrie Nation, and Chief Ironstone rode the Pennsylvania to Tarentum, an Allegheny River town. When train traffic declined, the station was converted to a restaurant in 1983. When you dine here, you'll get a little flavor of the train station—and a lot of flavor in your meal.

The menu features beef, seafood, veal, chicken, and pasta selections, as well as dinner salads, such as an enticing grilled eggplant salad. Among the most popular selections is the Pittsburgh steak, a New York strip steak marinated in seasoned butter, then placed in a white-hot cast-iron skillet, resulting in a charred exterior and a rare interior. You'll find a bar and a wine list that includes domestic, Italian, and Australian selections but eschews French brands. J G's Tarentum Station Grille offers banquet facilities for up to 40 people. It serves dinner daily, lunch Monday through Friday. Reservations are recommended. You can get here by taking the Tarentum exit off Route 28.

Vallozzi's $–$$
US 30 East, Greensburg
(724) 836-7663
Vallozzi's is a veritable oasis amid the arid shopping malls and heavy traffic that mark this section of US 30. It's a warm and inviting restaurant—an Italian villa, the proprietors call it—that's been honored by Distinguished Restaurants of North America, The National Restaurant Association, and *Wine Spectator* magazine. The menu has a distinct Italian

flavor, with such entrees as cappelletti lobster, with spinach and portabella mushrooms in a buttery tomato sauce, and Salmon Vallozzi, grilled salmon with artichokes, tomatoes, scallions, and portabella mushrooms, served in an Asiago cream sauce over angelhair pasta.

The wine list offers 325 different selections, and you'll also find a lounge. Parties up to 16 people will enjoy seating in the secluded Wine Cellar or the semiprivate Arbor Room. Reservations are recommended. Vallozzi's serves lunch and dinner Monday through Friday, dinner only on Saturday. It's closed on Sunday.

Japanese

Sushi Too $–$$
5432 Walnut Street
(412) 687-8744
As its sister restaurant on the South Side, this Shadyside establishment features sushi—its phone number spells out 68-SUSHI—and such other Japanese fare as tempura and teriyaki. You'll find an attractive list of chef's specials, including garlic shrimp and lemon chicken. You'll enjoy a visual treat if you order the beef or seafood shabu shabu; both of these meals for two are prepared at your table. Sushi Too offers a bar, a wine list, and a Tatami Room that can accommodate banquets of up to 30 people. Reservations are accepted for parties of six or more. When you enter Sushi Too, take a minute to admire the replica Japanese garden in the lobby; it will help set an appropriate mood for your meal. (By the way, no smart comments about the editors. The Shadyside restaurant is Sushi Too; the South Side restaurant is Sushi Two.)

Korean

Young Bin Kwan $–$$
4305 Main Street
(412) 687-2222
In ancient times, Young Bin Kwan was the name of a house in Korea that hosted the Chinese ambassador and his retinue on official visits. That blending of cultures is the defining feature of this Bloomfield restaurant, which features Korean, Chinese, and Japanese fare—and a separate chef for the dishes of each nationality. Be advised that because the menu is so eclectic, prices vary widely. Young Bin Kwan serves lunch and dinner. It offers a full-service bar, a limited wine list, and banquet facilities for up to 100 guests. Reservations are accepted.

Mexican

Cozumel $–$$
US 30 East, Greensburg
(724) 836-2653
Cozumel offers a diverse menu at both its Greensburg location, but you're most likely to remember the ostrich fajitas and taco salad. The restaurant features a number of tempting combination platters as well as limited children's and vegetarian menus. Cozumel offers a full-service bar, a wine list, and a broad selection of Mexican beers. It features live music each Saturday night—there is a cover charge even if you're dining there. Cozumel serves lunch and dinner daily.

The Fajita Grill $$
5865 Ellsworth Avenue
(412) 362-3030
www.thefajitagrill.com
This Shadyside restaurant offers dishes from four Mexican regions—Central, Puebla, Gulf Coast, and Caribbean. In addition to a broad selection of fajitas, you'll find such intriguing entrees as marinated jumbo shrimp in chipotle sauce and chicken in a pumpkin-seed sauce. The restaurant does accept reservations and does not serve alcohol—you're invited to bring your own. There's no smoking here, even if you're dining on the patio. The Fajita Grill serves lunch and dinner daily.

Middle Eastern

Ali Baba $–$$
404 South Craig Street
(412) 682-2829
Ali Baba has been pleasing Oakland patrons since 1972. Particularly popular are its shish

kebab and its hummus, which are part of a broad selection of entrees and a la carte items. The restaurant serves beer but no other alcohol, and it accepts reservations for parties of five or more. It provides take-out service. Ali Baba serves dinner daily, lunch Monday through Friday. It's located between the campuses of the University of Pittsburgh and Carnegie Mellon University and easily accessible from each. Don't miss it.

Khalil's II　　　　　　　　　　$–$$
4757 Baum Boulevard
(412) 683-4757
www.khalils.com
Before he opened Khalil's II, Mikhail Khalil worked for years as the chef at a predecessor restaurant at the same Shadyside site, so you know this restaurant is a labor of love. Shish kebab is a popular entree, as is samket el pasha—catch of the day baked in lemon and garlic and topped with pine nuts and sesame sauce. You won't find much in the way of fried foods here, as Khalil grills, broils, or oven-bakes most of the fare. The restaurant features a full-service bar, a wine list, and banquet facilities for up to 130 people. It's open for dinner only from Tuesday through Sunday, and it's closed on Monday. If you're wondering about the name, Khalil also operated Khalil's I and Khalil's III some years ago, but these no longer are extant.

Pan Asian

Spice Island Tea House　　　　$
253 Atwood Street
(412) 687-8821
When you visit Spice Island you'll be embarking on a culinary journey of Southeast Asia. The restaurant features the cuisine of Burma, Indonesia, Malaysia, Singapore, Thailand, and lesser-known regions of Southeast Asia. Among the intriguing selections are five-spiced chicken of Malaysia; Burmese barbecued chicken; pad Thai; Singapore rice noodle; Java fried rice; Sumatran corn and shrimp fritters; and gado gado, an Indonesian salad. There are plenty of vegetarian choices.

Dining here is a fulfilling—and filling—journey; it's a trip you'll want to take. The restaurant is near the University of Pittsburgh campus in Oakland, and is owned by a Carnegie Mellon graduate. It serves lunch and dinner Monday through Saturday, closing on Sunday. It does not serve alcohol, and it does not accept reservations. The Spice Island dining room is nonsmoking.

Peruvian

La Feria　　　　　　　　　　$
5527 Walnut Street
(412) 682-4501
Unique is an overused word, but we're pretty sure La Feria is unique in this regard: You won't find another combination Peruvian restaurant and imported crafts store in Southwestern Pennsylvania. Owners Luisa Porras and Pamela Cohen founded this Shadyside complex in 1992, not really sure how the market would respond. They needn't have worried. Residents and visitors alike have been charmed by the products of Peruvian artisans as well as the Peruvian cuisine.

The restaurant features rotating specials—there's always a vegetarian dish—that include such entrees as locro de zapallo, a pumpkin and potato stew; tacutacu, a black bean and rice casserole baked with hot peppers and served with fried bananas and sweet potato chips; and ajide gallina, shredded chicken cooked in a creamy sauce with crushed peanuts, aji peppers, garlic, and onions. La Feria serves lunch and dinner Monday through Saturday, closing on Sunday. It does not serve alcohol but invites patrons to bring their own. The restaurant seats only 36 people, so the smoking section is rather small. Reservations are accepted for parties of six or more.

Pizza

Mineo's Pizza House　　　　$
2128 Murray Avenue
(412) 521-9864

713A Washington Road, Mt. Lebanon
(412) 344-9467

Most pizza lovers have their favorites; for many Pittsburgh residents, their favorite pizza comes from Mineo's. In fact, Mineo's was named the town's best pizzeria for six years in a row by City Paper. The restaurant offers outlets in Pittsburgh's Squirrel Hill neighborhood and in Mt. Lebanon in the South Hills. In addition to its standard pizza, Mineo's offers Sicilian and white varieties as well as options for thick crust and extra sauce. The menu also features subs, calzones, and largely pasta-based entrees. You can order pasta party trays as well. Mineo's does not serve alcohol, and it doesn't accept reservations or credit cards. It does not designate smoking and nonsmoking sections, as most orders here are for takeout rather than to be enjoyed in the small dining area. It's open daily for lunch and dinner.

Vento's Pizza & Dairy $
420 North Highland Avenue
(412) 361-9197
How important is this 50-plus-year-old establishment to its East Liberty neighborhood? In 1998 when the city moved to acquire the buildings in this block to make way for an important new Home Depot store, it worked with Al Vento to find a convenient new location for his restaurant. The result: Vento's and Home Depot are neighbors.

In addition to its signature pizza, Vento's offers such lunch and dinner specials as pepper steak, fish, and chicken Parmesan, as well as a variety of hoagies and other sandwiches. Vento's does not serve liquor, and it does not accept reservations or credit cards. The seating area is small, so there are no smoking and nonsmoking sections. Vento's is closed on Sunday.

Seafood

The Nest $$$
407 Clay Avenue, Jeannette
(724) 527-9880
Lobster and shrimp dominate the interesting menu at this Westmoreland County restaurant. No fewer than 11 entrees feature lobster or shrimp, and the lobster and shrimp scampi includes both. The headliner of the lobster group is the 22-ounce lobster tail; this must have been one of those tails that wagged the lobster. You'll also find crab cakes, orange roughy, and scallops on the menu as well as a few beef, veal, and lamb selections. The Nest offers a full-service bar, a wine list, and banquet facilities for up to 150 people. Reservations are suggested for weekends and accepted at all times. The Nest serves dinner only from Tuesday through Saturday, closing on Sunday and Monday.

Simmie's Restaurant and Lounge $–$$
8500 Frankstown Road, Penn Hills
(412) 731-4689
Located just over the city line in Penn Hills, Simmie's offers such seafood dishes as Caribbean shrimp scampi and twin Maine lobster tails and a variety of fresh fish specials that change with the catch. Barbecued ribs also are popular here. If you'd like to enjoy both seafood and beef, try the surf and turf combination. Happy hour each Monday through Friday from 5:00 to 7:00 p.m. brings specially priced cocktails and hors d'oeuvres, and senior citizens enjoy a discount on their meals each Wednesday.

Simmie's serves lunch and dinner Monday through Saturday, opening at 1:00 p.m. on Saturday. It opens on Sunday only for some holidays. It offers a full-service bar and a wine list, and it accepts reservations for parties of seven or more. If you leave Simmie's with an enduring taste for fresh fish to take home, you can satisfy your urge at the adjacent Frankstown Fish Company.

Thai

Thai Place $$–$$$
5528 Walnut Street
(412) 687-8586
www.thaiplacepgh.com
When you're in Pittsburgh's Shadyside neighborhood and ready for a taste of pad Thai—that signature Thai dish that here is prepared with shrimp and ground peanuts in a flavor-

ful sauce—Thai Place is the place to go. The diverse menu also includes such favorites as tiger prawns, which are spiced with red curry sauce and coconut milk and served with mixed vegetables, as well as a broad selection of beef, chicken, pork, seafood, curry, vegetarian entrees. Thai Place offers a wine list and a retail section, where you can purchase crafts, silk products, and neck-ties—all fashioned in Thailand. The restaurant offers a wine list, and it recommends reservations. Thai Place serves lunch and dinner daily.

Vegetarian

East End Food Co-op Cafe $
7516 Meade Street
(412) 242-3598

Many Pittsburgh shoppers appreciate the East End Food Co-op as a great source of organic and natural foods. In the rear of the co-op is a nice find for vegetarians and veg-ans, and anyone else wishing to have a healthy, tasty meal—the Co-op Cafe. The cafe offers seating for about 20 people, and foods are served cafeteria-style from a hot bar and a salad bar. The cafe features break-fast, lunch, and dinner daily from 9:00 a.m. to 9:00 p.m. The breakfast menu includes hotcakes, omelets, and a variety of tofu dishes. The lunch and dinner menu offers a limited number of soups, salads, and entrees that change daily, including linguine primav-era and spinach quesadilla. The cafe's soups are vegan, and other vegan options are avail-able. Smoothies and fresh juices are also served, and you may want to pick up one of the cafe's cookies made without white flour and sugar, if you've got a sweet tooth. They're really satisfying.

The Co-op Cafe does not serve alcohol, and it does not accept reservations or permit smoking. The cafe can be a little noisy, what with shoppers checking out the adjacent deli case and the kids that are a constant feature of this environment, so don't plan that crucial business lunch or romantic rendezvous here. Come here if you want to meet other like-minded souls or enjoy a quick bite, though—and pick up your groceries at the same time. If you're interested in joining the Food Co-op, management would be happy to explore that with you. The Co-op Cafe is in the North Point Breeze neighborhood, about 2 miles from the Edgewood-Swissvale exit of I-376 (the Park-way East).

SOUTH

American

Armstrong's Restaurant $
Baptist and Grove Roads
Castle Village Shopping Center
Whitehall, Castle Shannon
(412) 885-1033

When you're out shopping at Castle Village Shopping Center, you'll enjoy a respite at Armstrong's, which is located in the mall. You'll find the same menu for lunch and din-ner here—an Italian-accented menu with selections such as pasta and manicotti. Daily specials include such items as stuffed chicken breast, beer-battered fish with macaroni and cheese, and meat loaf. It's hearty fare. In fact, Armstrong's has received a "Best Buy for the Buck" award from *Pittsburgh Magazine*. The restaurant features a full-service bar. It offers catering services, and its entire menu is avail-able for takeout. Armstrong's doesn't take reservations.

The Back Porch $$
114 Speers Street, Lower Speers
(724) 483-4500
www.backporchrestaurant.com/bpr.htm

The Back Porch is set in a restored, antique-packed 1806 home along the Monongahela River in Washington County. You'll enjoy din-ing on the veranda or on the sunporch and choosing from a diverse menu. Appealing selections include charcoal-broiled ribs mari-nated in brown sugar and soy sauce, tuna topped with feta cheese and a lemon-herb vinaigrette, and a mixed grill that highlights three different items each day. The Back Porch offers a full-service bar, an extensive wine list, and banquet facilities for up to 50 people. (The banquet space is not available on Saturday.) Smoking is permitted only in the Side Door, a casual dining room located downstairs. The Back Porch serves dinner Tuesday through Sunday, lunch Tuesday through Saturday, and reservations are recommended for all meals. It's closed on Monday.

Cafe Allegro $$–$$$
51 South 12th Street
(412) 481-7788
www.cafeallegropittsburgh.com
The Pittsburgh Steelers may have won five Super Bowls, but Cafe Allegro has an even more impressive championship record. For six consecutive years, 1993 through 1999, *Pittsburgh Magazine* and its readers named Cafe Allegro Pittsburgh's "Best Overall Restaurant." Considering that the region sports about 7,200 restaurants and taverns, that's a remarkable distinction, indeed. When you visit Cafe Allegro, you'll see the blue quartz trophy emblematic of the title.

Chef Nolan changes the menu with the seasons. Depending on the season, you may find such entrees as horseradish-crusted red snapper with garden salsa; veal saltimbocca; or Chef Nolan's bouillabaisse, prepared with market-selection seafood. One specialty impervious to seasonal changes is the grilled calamari—it's enjoyed a run on the menu year after year. Cafe Allegro offers a full-service bar and an extensive wine list, as well as banquet facilities for up to 40 people. It's open daily for dinner only.

Cafe du Jour $$
1107 East Carson Street
(412) 488-9695
Discovered and rediscovered several times over the years by food critics, this little restaurant on the less-rowdy end of Carson Street has built the following it deserves. On weekends seating can be a problem, either inside the narrow cafe or out back in the charming, brick-wall-enclosed patio. The atmosphere is casual, with the two owner/chefs and usually

one waitperson chatting with diners before or after the dinner. A large fresh salad divides into two satisfying starters with crunchy nuts, greens, and homemade dressings. The portions of comfort food are large, satisfying, and reasonably priced. For example, we found the roasted chicken accompanied by a heaping portion of garlic mashed potatoes quite filling. Bring your own bottle of wine. Cash only. Closed Sunday.

City Grill $–$$
2019 East Carson Street
(412) 431-1770
When you're cruising the South Side and get that hankering for something from the grill, try City Grill. Burgers are the most popular items here, but City Grill also grills steaks, shrimp, and a variety of appetizers. Salads and a delicious grilled chicken sandwich are also available. The desserts are popular here, too. City Grill offers a full-service bar and a wine list, but it does not accept reservations or designate smoking and nonsmoking sections.

Fat Head's South Side Saloon $
1805 East Carson Street
(412) 431-7433
When you have an appetite that won't quit, bring it to Fat Head's for one of their oversized sandwiches called "Headwiches." They headline a menu that includes primarily informal selections—burgers, subs, wings, salads, and munchies—as well as a limited selection of full entrees. Fat Head's offers a full-service bar that draws heavy evening crowds. It does not accept reservations, and it does not designate smoking and nonsmoking sections. Fat Head's serves lunch and dinner daily.

Houlihan's $
15 Freight House Shops, Station Square
(412) 232-0302
You'll usually find something inviting happening at Houlihan's. The Station Square restaurant serves lunch and dinner daily; it also

offers a late-night menu, serving until 12:30 a.m. For dinner you'll find beef selections that are prepared on a wood-fired grill, as well as chicken and fajita entrees and salads and sandwiches. A specialty of the house is an appetizer called 'Shrooms—jumbo mushroom caps filled with herbs and garlic cheese, then lightly battered and fried and served with a horseradish and Dijon sauce. The restaurant offers a lounge, a wine list, and banquet facilities for up to 75 people. For entertainment Houlihan's provides either a DJ or a band—sometimes both—each evening as well as nightly happy hours with complimentary hors d'oeuvres and specially priced drinks. The restaurant accepts reservations Sunday through Thursday but not on Friday and Saturday. The dining room offers a section for smokers after 5:00 p.m.; before then, you can smoke in the lounge.

LeMont Restaurant $$–$$$
1114 Grandview Avenue
(412) 431-3100
www.lemontpittsburgh.com/LeMont

LeMont has been an important Pittsburgh institution since 1960, offering both a splendid Mt. Washington view of Pittsburgh from 20-foot windows and an elegant dining experience. LeMont has been honored by the Distinguished Restaurants of North America and *Wine Spectator*, and has been designated a AAA Four Diamond restaurant. That recognition suggests the comprehensive excellence you'll enjoy here. Popular entrees include roasted raspberry duck and steak Diane, which is prepared tableside, as well as such game specials as antelope and zebra. Vegetarians will enjoy the vegetable strudel, an herb-laced medley of garden vegetables and rice nestled in strudel dough.

The wine list is extensive, as is the selection of coffees and the array of desserts. Crepes Suzette and strawberries and bananas flambé are two of the more tantalizing desserts. Banquets are an important component of LeMont's services, so important that they've captured their banquet menus in a helpful four-color pamphlet that you can request. The restaurant can accommodate up to 250 people for a special event. LeMont serves dinner daily, and reservations are suggested.

Tambellini's on 51 $$
860 Saw Mill Run Boulevard
(412) 481-1118

Just for the heck of it, we counted the entrees Tambellini's was offering on the night we visited. When we reached 44 regular entrees and 19 dinner specials, we were too hungry to bother with the salads and sandwiches, though those are plentiful as well. We were more than ready to eat. The extensive menu here will tempt you, and the restaurant will satisfy your temptation. You'll find beef, veal, seafood, and pasta selections. Specials include such entrees as filet of Norwegian salmon, filet of Florida grouper, and steak filet with sweetbreads and bacon strips. The restaurant offers a full-service bar, a wine list, and banquet facilities for up to 120 people. Banquets are not booked for Saturday night. Tambellini's on 51 serves lunch and dinner Monday through Saturday, closing on Sunday. Reservations for parties of eight or more are accepted. You'll find the restaurant just south of the Liberty Tunnels on Route 51.

The Tin Angel $$$$
1200 Grandview Avenue
(412) 381-1919
www.tinangelpittsburgh.com

When you dine at the Tin Angel, you'll enjoy that splendid Mt. Washington view of the city below, as well as the delights of an innovative menu. You'll get that sense of creativity right away, with the restaurant's signature fresh vegetable boat and homemade clam dip. The boat brings such unusual starters as stuffed grape leaves and baby pickled eggplant. When you're ready for your entree, try the Black Forest Filet—charbroiled filet mignon stuffed with pitted black cherries and topped with a béarnaise sauce. You'll also find other beef, chicken, veal, and seafood selections.

The Tin Angel offers a full-service bar, a wine list, and banquet facilities for up to 50 people on weeknights, up to 30 people on Saturday night. The restaurant serves dinner Monday through Saturday, closing on Sunday. Reservations are suggested.

Belgian

Point Brugge Café $$$
401 Hastings Street, Point Breeze
(412) 441-3334
www.pointbrugge.com
Tucked away in Point Breeze, Point Brugge Cafe may be somewhat difficult to find, but do try. Your efforts will be rewarded with an enjoyable lunch or dinner at this neighborhood gathering spot which was modeled on cafes found in European cities.

Formerly the location of The Point Restaurant, Point Brugge Café opened in 2005. They serve variety of bistro dishes as small plates and dinners. We prefer the steamed mussels served with brugge fries, or the carbonnade flamande, Belgian pot roast. Delicious food choices are accompanied by a tremendous beer selection.

The café is open for lunch and dinner Tuesday through Saturday, with brunch served on Sunday from 11:00 a.m. until 3:00 p.m. Sorry, reservations are not accepted.

Chinese

Golden Palace $
206 Shiloh Street
(412) 481-8500
Golden Palace can't boast of the spectacular city view that other Mt. Washington restaurants offer, but it does provide a diverse menu and tasty food. If offers entrees representing all regions of China. Among the more interesting selections are Golden Palace Seafood Combination—shrimp, scallops, lobster, and crabmeat with black mushrooms, broccoli, baby corn, and snow peas; and The Four Happiness—chicken, shrimp, beef, and roast pork sautéed with vegetables in a brown sauce. Golden Palace serves lunch

and dinner daily. It offers a full-service bar, a wine list, and banquet facilities for up to 75 people. Reservations are accepted for parties of 10 or more.

Sesame Inn $
1 Station Square
(412) 281-8282

715 Washington Road, Mt. Lebanon
(412) 341-2555

2975 Washington Road, McMurray
(724) 942-2888

711 Browns Lane, Ross
(412) 366-1838
www.sesameinn.net
Sesame Inn operates four restaurants in our primary service area—one at Station Square, two in the South Hills, the fourth in the North Hills. The menu is the same at each, so no matter which one you choose, you can be sure of the quality that persuaded both the *Pittsburgh Post-Gazette* and the *Tribune-Review* to name Sesame Inn the region's Best Chinese Restaurant.

The lunch and dinner menus are quite extensive, featuring poultry, beef, lamb, pork, seafood, and vegetarian selections. Among the most popular dinner choice are General Tso's chicken, salmon with black bean sauce, and the four duck entrees on the menu. Hot and spicy dishes are marked with a star, so you shouldn't be taken by surprise. Sesame Inn offers a full-service bar and a wine list, and it accepts reservations. Each restaurant offers banquet facilities for up to 60 people.

French

Le Pommier $$$
2104 East Carson Street
(412) 431-1901
www.lepommier.com
The number of French restaurants in the region is seriously limited; once you've dined here you'll likely agree that one is more than enough when it's as satisfying as Le Pommier. Among the specialties are Muscovy duck, served on currant–red wine sauce, and

Elysian Fields farm lamb, served with spicy brown mustard sauce. Also featured are a nightly seafood selection and chef's specials, which include such unusual fare as Thai-style curried seasonal vegetables. French wines dominate the extensive wine list, but you'll also find American wines. Le Pommier offers a full-service bar and banquet facilities for up to 90 people. It serves dinner only Monday through Saturday, closing on Sunday. Reservations are accepted.

Italian

Angelo's Restaurant $–$$
955 West Chestnut Street, Washington
(724) 222-7120
www.angelosrestaurant.com/index.cfm
You won't have to worry about the track record here. The Passalacqua family has operated Angelo's at the same location for more than 60 years, a tribute to the quality of the food and service. It's fitting that one of the signature entrees bears the family name. It's called Pasta Lacqua, and it features sautéed green beans tossed with a light tomato sauce and served with fettuccini and Romano cheese. You'll find a full-service bar and an extensive wine and liquor list. Angelo's is a nonsmoking restaurant. Reservations are preferred at Angelo's, which is located in downtown Washington.

Bella Vista Ristorante Italiano $$–$$$
1204 Grandview Avenue
(412) 431-1660
www.bellavistapgh.com/index.html
Pittsburgh's newest restaurant on Grandview Avenue, the family owned and operated Bella Vista affords diners a great Mt. Washington view of the city. The restaurant offers American/Italian cuisine served amid a Northern Italian decor, with veal, chicken, meat, fish, and pasta dishes such as baked stuffed Ecuadorian shrimp, New York strip steak, and homemade manicotti. Bella Vista is open for dinner daily. The restaurant has an extensive wine list and can accommodate parties up to 70 people for special occasions.

Bruschetta's $$–$$$
183 East Carson Street
(412) 431-3535
www.bruschettas.com
Bruschetta's is a cozy South Side spot that features both indoor and outdoor dining. The menu offers beef, chicken, seafood, and pasta entrees as well as such interesting veal selections as veal Zurich, which is sautéed with fried onions and Swiss cheese in a Marsala wine sauce. If you're in the mood for pasta, try the rotolo—pasta rolled with sausage, mushrooms, and onions and topped with marinara and fontinella cheese. Bruschetta's serves lunch and dinner Monday through Saturday, closing on Sunday. The restaurant offers a full-service bar, and it accepts reservations for parties of six or more. It does not designate smoking and nonsmoking sections.

Calabria's $–$$
3107 Library Road, Castle Shannon
(412) 885-1030
Hearty portions are the theme at this South Hills restaurant. Each dinner entree comes with two side dishes, a popular feature with patrons. The diverse menu includes pastas and seafood selections as well as such specials as meat loaf and stuffed chicken breast. Each Monday, Calabria's offers a lunch buffet—it's never the same as it was the previous Monday. The restaurant offers a wine list, a limited-service bar, and banquet facilities for up to 65 people. Calabria's accepts reservations for parties of six or more.

The Union Grill $$
13½ East Wheeling Street, Washington
(724) 222-2860
www.theuniongrill.com
The diverse menu at the Union Grill is likely to satisfy most tastes. Italian selections include an appealing assortment of pastas and specialty pizzas as well as fried zucchini. If you're in the mood for American fare, try the popular Reuben sandwich. The Union Grill—not to be confused with a different but similarly

named restaurant in Pittsburgh's Oakland neighborhood—offers a full-service bar, a wine list, and banquet facilities for up to 40 people. Reservations are suggested for weekends and accepted at all times. Union Grill serves lunch and dinner Monday through Saturday; closed on Sunday.

Japanese

Kiku Japanese Restaurant $–$$$
225 West Station Square Drive
(412) 765-3200
www.kikupittsburgh.net
Sushi and tempura for lunch and dinner are Kiku's specialties and its most popular menu items. You'll find plenty of other entrees at this Station Square restaurant, however, including chicken and swordfish teriyaki and shabu shabu, featuring thinly sliced beef and fresh vegetables. You dip the ingredients into a boiling broth, cook them to your liking, and enhance to taste with ponzu and sesame sauce.

Kiku offers an interesting selection of specialty cocktails and Japanese wines and beers, as well as a list of domestic and European wines. Reservations are suggested for dinner. Kiku can accommodate up to 30 people for banquets.

Mexican

Hungry Jose's $
227 South Main Street, Washington
(724) 228-1311
If business takes you to Washington, take your dining business to Hungry Jose's—it's only 2 blocks from the county courthouse. In addition to a wide variety of Mexican fare, Hungry Jose's also offers Italian and American entrees. The restaurant's Cantina bar offers a number of specialty margaritas as well as a generous selection of beers on tap. Hungry Jose's offers banquet facilities for up to 50 people. It does not designate smoking and nonsmoking sections. The restaurant serves dinner each day and lunch each day but Sunday.

Jose and Tony's Mexican Restaurant $
1573 McFarland Road, Mt. Lebanon
(412) 561-2025
Here's an unpretentious restaurant in the South Hills. You'll order at the counter and transport your food to your table without the intervention of waitstaff, but you'll be pleased with the broad selection of tacos, burritos, tostadas, and other Mexican treats. The restaurant offers combination entrees, Mexican-style pizzas, and a limited children's menu. From Monday through Thursday you'll enjoy "Taco Hour" from 5:00 to 7:00 p.m. when tacos and pitchers of beer and soda pop are half price. Jose and Tony's offers a full bar—with specially priced margaritas each Monday—and a limited wine list.

Middle Eastern

Amel's $
435 McNeilly Road, Baldwin Township
(412) 563-3466
www.amelsrestaurant.com
Amel's is an institution—it's been serving customers in the South Hills since 1952 and has been operated continuously by the Reiland family since 1968. You'll appreciate that experience and commitment when you dine on fresh seafood on a bed of homemade pasta, or the lamb kabobs that may be the most popular menu item. Amel's offers daily lunch and dinner specials as well as a full-service bar. It accepts reservations and provides banquet facilities for up to 30 people.

Scottish $–$$

Piper's Pub
1828 East Carson Street
(412) 381-3977
www.piperspub.com
For a hearty, great-tasting meal in a bustling pub, stop by Piper's in the South Side. Here, you'll find "a taste of the British Isles"—*bangers and mash* (English sausages and half-mashed potatoes), fish and chips, Guinness stew, corned beef and cabbage, and much more. Soups, salads and sandwiches are also served.

Piper's Pub is open seven days a week from 11:00 a.m. until 1:00 a.m. The restaurant serves lunch and dinner Monday through Saturday, and brunch on Sunday.

Seafood

Grand Concourse $$–$$$
100 West Station Square Drive
(412) 261-1717
www.stationsquare.com/grandconcourse
The former P&LE Railroad Station is now a National Historic Landmark and restaurant, where you can dine surrounded by near-regal architecture. The restaurant concentrates on seafood and has an all-you-can-eat Sunday brunch that won acclaim in *Pittsburgh Magazine*'s readers' poll. The River Room's view of the city on the water is worth the wait. Open daily for lunch and dinner, the concourse is a popular tourist attraction, so reservations are suggested.

Monterey Bay Fish Grotto $$
1411 Grandview Avenue
(412) 481-4414
If you have any doubts that this is a bright, classy Mt. Washington establishment, take a close look at the waiters. They're all sporting bright aqua vests with schools of fish cavorting across them. The menu and its rich selection of seafood will provide another clue. Among the favorite entrees here are Maryland crab cakes, ahi tuna—served sesame style with a lemon-butter soy sauce—and an Atlantic salmon dish called Rido Grille House, salmon marinated in a house teriyaki sauce, chargrilled, and topped with a honey-lime glaze. The restaurant also offers beef, chicken, and pasta selections.

You'll find a bar and an extensive wine list; Monterey Bay pledges to sell its wines at only $10 more than cost. It also offers banquet facilities for 50 to 90 people. It serves dinner daily, lunch Monday through Friday. Reservations are recommended. We probably don't have to remind you, but don't forget to admire the particularly fine view of the city,

enhanced by Monterey Bay's 10th-story location and its glass elevator.

Solomon Seafood $$
222 Hall Avenue, Washington
(724) 222-0898
Solomon is a popular Washington County spot for salmon, orange roughy, and tuna, and it supplements its seafood offerings with steak and pasta entrees. It's located near I-70 and a few minutes from the campus of Washington and Jefferson College. The Solomon waitstaff will serve your liquor orders. The restaurant serves lunch and dinner Monday through Thursday from 11:00 a.m. to 9:00 p.m. and Friday and Saturday from 11:00 a.m. to 10:00 p.m.; closed on Sunday. You can't reserve tables on Friday and Saturday, but your reservations will be accepted at other times.

Sicilian

Dish Osteria $$-$$$
128 South 17th Street
(412) 390-2012
www.dishosteria.com
Many folks walk around the block for several minutes before finding Dish, a small, stylish restaurant tucked away in a residential neighborhood just two blocks off East Carson Street in the heart of the city's South Side. Most do not give up the search as they have heard of the consistently rave reviews that this restaurant has received since its opening in 2000. Owners Cindy and Michele Savoia renovated the building, which used to be a corner bar, into a simple, but stylish space featuring wood floors, a copper-topped bar, and candlelight. (Michele, who is Sicilian, moved here with his wife after working in the restaurant business in New York.) Serving Sicilian and Mediterranean specialties, Dish's menu is not extensive, but the food is delicious. Favorite appetizers include the bresaola (air-dried beef), carpaccio di manzo, and the calamari alla griglia. As for entrees, the filet mignon is a wonderful treat, and the sea scallops are pan roasted to perfection. Dish also offers pork, fish, and pasta

dishes. Leave enough room for dessert—you don't want to miss the homemade tiramisu and chocolate bread pudding.

Dish is open Monday through Saturday from 5:00 p.m. until 2:00 a.m. The kitchen opens at 5:00 p.m. and closes at midnight. Reservations are recommended.

Spanish

Mallorca $$
2228 East Carson Street
(412) 488-1818
www.mallorcapittsburgh.com

As the sun streams through the skylight, accenting the colors in the hanging plants, and the tuxedoed waitstaff attends your every need, you'd swear you were actually in Spain, enjoying the creative recipes of proprietor Antonio Pereira. It's a touch of Spain on the South Side. Mallorca offers a full-service bar, a robust wine list more than 200 brands deep, and outdoor garden seating seasonally. It accepts weekday reservations for parties of any number and weekend reservations for parties of five or more. Mallorca serves lunch and dinner daily. In fact, it closes only one day—Christmas Eve. "My staff cooks for me 364 days a year," Periera says. "On Christmas Eve I cook for them."

Vegetarian

The Zenith $
26th and Sarah Streets
(412) 481-4833
www.zenithpgh.com

The Zenith offers such vegetarian fare as soups, salads, sandwiches, and daily specials for lunch and dinner. Representative specials include linguini with onions, walnuts, and Gorgonzola, and wild rice pilaf with celery, onions, cashews, and mushrooms. The menu changes weekly. If you leave your e-mail address with owners Mary Kay Morrow and David Goldstein, they'll send out weekly updates, which are also available on the Web site listed above. If you follow the stricter vegan diet, the Zenith will strive to accommodate your needs with various menu items as well on request.

The Zenith does not serve alcohol, but you're invited to bring your own. It does not accept reservations or allow smoking. The cafe can accommodate up to 40 people for banquets. It's located in the same South Side building as the delightful and quirky Zenith Gallery and antiques shop—in fact, you'll be seated among antiques and art in the dining area.

The cafe serves lunch and dinner Thursday through Saturday, brunch only on Sunday. The Zenith is closed Monday through Wednesday. It's located in a residential area and is not particularly well marked. You'll find it just by following the numbered streets. Don't give up; this is one of our favorite restaurants. Vegetarian is gourmet here, and the portions are large, too.

WEST

American

Alexion's Bar & Grill $
141 Hawthorne Avenue, Carnegie
(412) 276-2018

Here's a nice neighborhood restaurant where you can enjoy lighter fare and sports—both spectator and participant. For your culinary enjoyment, Alexion's offers a large sandwich menu as well as salads, pizza, and wings. You'll enjoy lunch and dinner specials as well as discounted drinks during happy hour each Monday through Friday. If you're a sports buff, you'll enjoy the restaurant's seven televisions and its darts and other games, as well as the sports posters that grace the walls. Alexion's offers a full-service bar. It does not accept reservations, and it does not designate smoking and nonsmoking sections for dinner. For lunch, nonsmokers are invited to eat in the upstairs dining room away from the bar. Alexion's is near the Crafton–Green Tree exit of Interstate 279 (the Parkway West), a few miles from Downtown. It serves lunch and dinner Monday through Saturday and offers special entertainment on Christmas, Halloween, and St. Patrick's Day. Call for details.

Casey's Grill $–$$
7195 Eastwood Road, Beaver Falls
(724) 846-3700
You'll enjoy breakfast, lunch, and dinner at Casey's Grill, which is located in the Holiday Inn on Route 18. (For more on this Holiday Inn, see the Accommodations chapter.) The dinner menu includes steak and seafood selections as well as such specialty salads as tuna almond salad, steak salad, and Cajun chicken salad. Each Saturday night there's a surf and turf buffet and a champagne brunch each Sunday.

Casey's Grill provides entertainment— either a disc jockey or a band—on Friday and Saturday night. The restaurant offers a full-service bar and a wine list. Reservations are suggested for Friday and Saturday and holidays. Casey's is open daily but closes from 2:00 to 4:30 p.m. each day. It's located just off exit 13 of the Pennsylvania Turnpike.

Grand Valley Inn $$$
452 Constitution Boulevard, Fallston
(724) 843-9000
This Beaver County restaurant offers a menu that's interesting and diverse. Entrees range from crab cakes to a filet mignon dinner for two, to dinner salads, including a popular pork loin salad. You'll also find chicken and pasta selections as well as lunch and dinner specials. Grand Valley offers a full-service bar, a wine list, and banquet facilities for up to 100 people. It accepts reservations. Grand Valley is open Tuesday through Sunday.

If you enjoy the restaurant's player piano music, you might seek out Grand Valley co-owner Scott Watson and tip your cap. He created the instrument from an unused piano he had around the house.

The Hop House $
2749 Noblestown Road, Green Tree
(412) 922-9560
www.thehophouse.com
The food at the Hop House (formerly the Idlewood Inn) includes pizza, burgers, wings (16 flavors!), salads and wraps, pasta, and "com-

fort food" like meat loaf. This casual eatery offers a full-service bar, and you can watch your favorite sports event on one of four large-screen plasma TVs. The Hop House does not accept reservations, and it does not designate smoking and nonsmoking sections. Lunch and dinner are served daily, and the kitchen is open till midnight on Friday and Saturday. If you're in a hurry at lunchtime, you can call in your order and have it ready when you arrive.

It's happy hour from 5:00 to 7:00 p.m. Monday through Friday, with discounted prices on wine and martini selections, and on Saturday evening you'll enjoy live bands starting at 10:00 p.m., with no cover charge. In fact, there's some type of special every day of the week, including a free halftime buffet every Sunday there's a Steelers game.

The Hop House is located off the Green Tree–Crafton exit of I-279 (the Parkway West).

J. W. Hall's Steak and Seafood Inn $–$$
2284 Brodhead Road, Aliquippa
(724) 375-6860
As the name suggests, J. W. Hall specializes in steak and seafood for both lunch and dinner. It also features such homemade desserts as Dutch apple pie; peanut butter fudge pie; and turtle cheesecake, which is covered with caramel, hot fudge, and pecans. Maybe they need to add desserts to their name. The restaurant, located in the Hopewell Shopping Center, offers a full-service bar and a wine list, as well as banquet facilities for up to 40 people. Lunch and dinner are served daily, and the restaurant does not accept reservations.

Kathy's Country Kitchen $
3403 Old Darlington Road, Darlington
(724) 827-2558
Kathy's is one of those old-fashioned restaurants that offers solid American food at reasonable prices. Breakfast, lunch, dinner—you can get them all here seven days a week, and Kathy's stays open round the clock on Friday and Saturday. Staples of the menu include

sausage over homemade biscuits, breaded vegetables and zucchini, and Kathy's Large Steak and Cheese Sandwich. For dessert try the bread pudding or rice pudding. Kathy's does not accept reservations or credit cards, and it does not serve alcohol. Kathy's will close off part of the dining room to accommodate banquets.

Manny's Rook Station Cafe $
201 Hawthorne Street, Green Tree
(412) 429-9353

Manny's is a neighborhood restaurant, set near an abandoned railroad station, and it offers primarily informal fare. Wings, sandwiches, turkey burgers, and Maryland crab cake sandwiches are popular selections. Manny's offers lunch and dinner specials as well as a full-service bar, where you'll enjoy happy hour discounted beers. Reservations are not accepted. Manny's serves lunch and dinner every day.

Tramp's Grill & Bar $
412 Greentree Road
(412) 921-7194

The owners of this West End establishment operated a downtown restaurant for years but found they preferred a neighborhood atmosphere. You'll like it, too. Tramp's offers lunch and dinner specials, a lot of sandwiches, and a limited dinner entree list. Its "jumbo cut" wings are a popular selection. You'll find a full-service bar and draft beer specials each Monday and Thursday. Tramp's offers banquet facilities for up to 50 people. Reservations are not accepted, and there is no designated smoking section. It's open Monday through Saturday and on Sunday when the Steelers play at home.

Willows Inn Family Smorgasbord $
1830 Midland Beaver Road, Industry
(724) 643-4500
www.willowsinnpa.com

No need to describe the menu here—there isn't any. This Beaver County restaurant offers exclusively buffet dining, serving dinner Tues-

day through Sunday, lunch Tuesday through Saturday, and brunch Sunday. That's not to say that the fare is the same every day. The DiMaggio family, which owns both the restaurant and the adjoining Willows Inn hotel, vary the buffet lineup to provide some fun. Wednesday is Italian Night, while the Friday buffets feature seafood. On Thursday and Saturday, barbecued pork ribs are the featured item. Willows Inn offers a lounge and banquet facilities for up to 215. Reservations are recommended for parties of eight or more.

You can watch a ball game or a movie on the adjacent pub's widescreen TV. The pub is open from 3:00 p.m. till late Monday through Saturday and 11:30 a.m. to 6:30 p.m. on Sunday, with extended hours for *Monday Night Football* and special events. Willows Inn is near Beaver, the county seat of Beaver County. Note that seniors get a discount on the cost of the buffet.

Wooden Angel Restaurant $$–$$$
308 Leopard Lane, Beaver
(724) 774-7880
www.wooden-angel.com

For more than 30 years, Alex Sebastian has operated this Beaver County restaurant on his personal philosophy of customer satisfaction. For example, Wooden Angel offers an extensive wine list that features only American brands, which Sebastian believes should be promoted. It's a personal vision to be sure, but Wooden Angel executes it so well that many regard it as one of the region's finest restaurants.

The menu is attractive and diverse, featuring such entrees as rack of lamp; lobster cannelloni; Tuscany sautéed chicken; and angel hair Cantonese, with Gulf shrimp and sea scallops atop the pasta bed. Wooden Angel offers a full-service bar. It can accommodate up to 100 for banquets. Reservations are recommended. If you want to smoke, you can sit in the more informal Casual Cafe, a bistro located within Wooden Angel, which shares the same service and menu as the larger dining room. The Wooden Angel and the cafe are open for lunch and dinner Tuesday through Friday, dinner only on Saturday; closed Sunday and Monday.

Italian

Aracri's Greentree Inn $
1006 Greentree Road, Green Tree
(412) 921-4601
www.aracrisgreentreeinn.com
Aracri's serves lunch and dinner Monday through Saturday, offering a healthy selection of special entrees that changes regularly. You'll find seafood, pasta, beef, chicken, and veal selections, including such entrees as Norwegian salmon prepared "lightly Cajun" with linguini and red clam sauce, and linguini al Scoglio—a linguini base topped with clams, shrimp, scallops, and lump crabmeat in a white or a red sauce. Aracri offers a full-service bar and a limited wine list as well as banquet facilities for up to 75 people. It accepts reservations.

Giuseppe's Italian Restaurant $–$$
Route 18, Beaver Falls
(724) 843-5656
In addition to its broad selection of Italian food for lunch and dinner, Giuseppe's offers dining themes Thursday through Sunday evenings. Thursday's specialty is prime rib. Fresh Seafood is featured on Friday, while family-style dining is Sunday's concept. The restaurant offers a full-service bar and a wine list, and it offers banquet facilities for up to 20 people in one room and 30 in another.

Mario's Family Italian Restaurant $
926 Brodhead Road, Moon
(412) 262-3020
The breadth of its menu and wine list is a strong appeal of Mario's, which is located near Pittsburgh International Airport. The menu offers beef, veal, seafood, and pasta selections, as well as homemade soups. A favorite of diners is Mario's Own Hot Sausage Casserole, featuring ziti and hot Italian sausage baked with provolone cheese and a

plum tomato sauce. The wine list runs to 190 selections, and you can enjoy the full-service bar as well.

Mario's can accommodate banquets of up to 20 people. It offers dinner only Monday through Saturday. Reservations are accepted. The restaurant is closed on Sunday.

The Primadonna Restaurant $–$$
801 Broadway Avenue, McKees Rocks
(412) 331-1001
Primadonna has won a clutch of awards for its food and service. The *Post Gazette*, *Pittsburgh Magazine*, and *City Paper* have all called it the Best Local Italian Restaurant. But the most important tribute to Proprietor Joseph Costanzo Jr. that hangs on a Primadonna wall is from one Tommy Lasorda, Los Angeles Dodger executive and sometime gourmand, when he's not hawking weight-control products. "You, the Dodgers, and the Italians are all great," Lasorda wrote. We agree with all that, except maybe the part about the Dodgers. You will find great things on the menu here, highlighted by 33 different made-to-order pastas. Seafood, beef, chicken, and veal entrees complement the pasta selections. Popular selections include *portafoglio-delizia*—a pocket of veal filled with ham, cheese, artichokes, and mushrooms and simmered in sauce—and *chicken zummo*, chicken breast filled with a hot stuffed pepper, pepperoni, melted provolone cheese, and prosciutto ham, all breaded, baked, and topped with a tangy tomato sauce.

Primadonna serves dinner from Monday through Saturday. Reservations are accepted for parties of six or more. It offers a full-service bar and a wine list. You'll find it in the western suburb of McKees Rocks, about 5 miles from downtown Pittsburgh.

MULTIPLE-LOCATION RESTAURANTS

Our region boasts a number of locally owned restaurant chains. Each offers family dining, and each is quite popular. Rather than numb you with lengthy lists of addresses and phone numbers, the food and experiences that pretty much apply to all restaurants in the chain are described. The phone number and address listed are those of corporate headquarters; they'll be happy to help you locate a specific restaurant within the chain.

Eat 'n Park $
285 East Waterfront Drive
(412) 461-2000
www.eatnpark.com

It was in 1949 that Eat 'n Park rolled out its first restaurant, a 13-seater in the South Hills section that featured a revolutionary concept: patrons, attended by carhops, could eat in their automobiles. The concept was wildly popular, so popular that Eat 'n Park had to close early on opening day due to the crush of curious patrons. Carhop service has vanished along with the Ramblers, Packards, and Studebakers that queued up that first day, but Eat 'n Park's popularity remains. It's the region's largest restaurant chain, boasting more than 70 locations in Pennsylvania, Ohio, and West Virginia. With more than 7,000 employees and annual sales exceeding $150 million, Eat 'n Park is a major corporate player in the region ...and a responsible one. It donates at least 5 percent of its annual pretax profits to community initiatives.

The restaurants are family-oriented, featuring menus with more than 150 choices. Most offer such features as a breakfast buffet; a soup and salad bar; a Sunday brunch; and a bakery, where you can order homemade pies for takeout and pick up some of Eat 'n Park's signature Smiley cookies. Many of the restaurants are open 'round the clock and offer a midnight buffet. If you contact Eat 'n Park, they'll send you a directory of their restaurants, complete with maps and a checklist of features. The restaurants don't serve liquor, and they don't accept reservations. They serve breakfast, lunch, and dinner daily. All Eat 'n Park locations are smoke free.

Kings Family Restaurants $
1180 Long Run Road, McKeesport
(412) 751-0700

Hartley C. King opened his first restaurant in the eastern community of North Versailles in 1967. His concept of economical family restaurants with signature desserts grew so popular so quickly that today, Kings Family Restaurants includes 36 locations in Allegheny, Butler, Westmoreland, Crawford, Mercer, Vanango, Blair, and Lawrence Counties. All Kings restaurants serve breakfast, lunch, and dinner daily, and all offer 20 daily dinner specials priced under $5.

When you're ready for dessert, you'll enjoy Hartley's Choice ice cream, which also is available for takeout. The Hartley's Choice private label also features tea and coffee selections. Kings does not serve alcohol. Some, but not all, restaurants offer banquet facilities.

Primanti Bros. $
79 South 23rd Street
(412) 325-2455
www.primantibrothers.com

In the 1930s when Pittsburgh was primarily a factory town, Primanti Bros. had a brainstorm: Why not pile everything—meats and side dishes—on a sandwich and create a meal that could be eaten during a rushed lunch hour? Some 70 years later that idea is still popular, even though the region no longer depends as heavily on manufacturing. Sandwiches here begin with thick slices of Italian bread; wedged between them are your choice of meats as well as any coleslaw or french fries you order. The result; just about the most robust sandwich you'll find anywhere, imitated by many but equaled by few. If you must break down and cut your sandwich with a knife and fork, it's okay—you won't be the first.

Primanti Bros. offers lunch and dinner at seven restaurants within the city limits and eight locations in surrounding suburbs. Hours at Heinz Field and PNC Park depend on the day's activities at the stadiums—and the Strip District restaurant is open round the clock. Most serve alcohol, but none designates smoking and nonsmoking sections. Reservations and credit cards are not accepted.

Valley Dairy $
1562 Mission Road, Latrobe
(724) 537-7111
www.valleydairy.net
Valley Dairy offers old-fashioned, unpretentious dining where meals are filling and economical. It serves breakfast, lunch, and dinner daily and is especially popular for its breakfasts. Valley Dairy, which has been in business for more than 60 years, boasts award-winning ice creams and desserts. And the desserts are plentiful here; you have more than 20 to choose from, including such traditional favorites as All American Banana Split and rainbow parfait. Valley Dairy does not accept reservations, and it does not serve alcohol. Valley Dairy restaurants has 11 locations. Check the Web site listed for the one nearest you.

NIGHTLIFE

This chapter offers a sampling of entertainment possibilities throughout the coverage area. Admittedly, some Allegheny County neighborhoods, like the Strip District and Station Square, really party the night away—in sharp contrast to the more sedate evenings in rural counties. Yet you'll probably find something appealing from the list of live music venues, bars and brewpubs, coffeehouses, lounges and nightclubs, sports bars, comedy clubs and movie theaters. Each of these categories has been segmented by the traditional geographic breakdown used throughout this guide.

Rest assured, Pittsburgh nightlife isn't always synonymous with roaring crowds and pulsating music. You'll find those elements, for sure. But you'll also discover neighborhood cafes where patrons play board games, sip cappuccino, and make their own entertainment through lively conversation. If artistic venues of the performing arts appeal to you, turn to the Arts chapter for myriad ideas.

For those who do enjoy a spirited evening in the literal sense, let's discuss a few caveats. First, the drinking age in Pennsylvania is 21. Restaurants with a liquor license are permitted to serve alcohol until 2:00 a.m. Sunday sales are based on a formula involving the establishment's ratio of food to alcohol sales. You won't find sales in the state liquor stores (except at a few sites where Sunday sales are now allowed from 9:00 a.m. until 5:00 p.m.) or at beer distributors on Sunday, however.

Second, you may be asked for identification if you look like your under 30 years old, so be prepared if you have that youthful look about you. Also, be ready to pay a cover charge at some clubs. The amounts vary even from night to night at the same club or nightspot, depending upon that night's entertainment.

Third, always designate a driver who won't partake of alcoholic beverages. Be sure to consult this chapter's taxi listing to arrange cab transportation, for your own safety and everyone else's. Unlike some cities, you usually must call for a cab in Pittsburgh unless you're at the airport or a major hotel—you won't necessarily find the cabbies cruising the streets for fares.

Fourth, dress appropriately, or call the phone numbers provided if you're unsure of the dress code. Remember, as a former industrial town, Pittsburgh is a bit more conservative than New York, Los Angeles, or cities in Florida (like Key West, for example).

Finally, there are two factions that deserve mention, and we didn't want you to think we're excluding them. One is the teen scene, and the other is gay nightlife. In our region neither has a wealth of clubs devoted to them, although they're out there if you look. When clubs, concert venues, or other entertainment may be of particular interest to these crowds, it's noted in the text in order to give you some guidance.

Above all, enjoy your night out on our town.

LIVE MUSIC
North

Andy Warhol Museum
117 Sandusky Street
(412) 237-8300
www.warhol.org
Every Friday from 5:00 to 10:00 p.m., The Andy Warhol Museum hosts Good Fridays. Enjoy a cocktail from the cash bar in the gallery's entrance before touring the exhibits or attending a special program. Cover charge is half-price regular museum admission. The

Warhol also offers live music performances by punk and alternative bands, wine tastings, and parties. Visit the calendar on the museum's Web site for a list of upcoming events.

The Brick House
118 North Main Street, Butler
(724) 284-1159
www.brickhousebutler.com

Set in two early 1900s buildings that had originally served as vaudeville theaters, The Brick House offers live music—mostly songs people know from the 1960s through 1990s—on Thursday, Friday, and Saturday nights after 10:00 p.m. Open Mic is Thursday Night. The "House" also features two dance floors and a gameroom with pool tables, dartboards, shuffle board tables, and much more.

Moondogs
378 Freeport Road, Blawnox
(412) 828–2040

Just 2 miles north of the Highland Park Bridge, Moondogs features some of Pittsburgh's finest local rock 'n' roll talent. On different nights you'll hear from local musicians including native rocker Norm Nardini. Most bands and comedy acts are booked in advance and advertised in the alternative weekly papers (see the Media chapter). Past events have included Pajama Party night, open stage comedy, and contests to win a $1,000 guitar. The tunes range from country and rock to reggae and blues. Moondogs' menu is limited to pizzas, tacos, nachos, and a variety of other light snacks.

Mr. Small's Fun House
400 Lincoln Avenue, Millvale
(412) 821-4447
www.mrsmalls.com

With a state-of-the-art theatre, two full-service recording studios, a skate park, and a backstage Rock Hostel for artist housing, Mr. Smalls Funhouse is a one-stop shop for musical artists. The 650-capacity theater was once a church, and now features a full bar, hardwood floors, a VIP balcony, and 40-foot ceilings. The War Room, located in the theatre's

 Check out live theater productions by consulting the Arts chapter.

basement has a smaller bar and performance stage. Both national and local acts (some are all ages shows) play in often sold-out concerts.

The Speakeasy at Sassy Marie's Bar and Restaurant
422 Foreland Street
(412) 246-0355
www.sassymaries.com

The former home of the legendary James Street Tavern, Sassy Marie's continues the tradition of showcasing live music on Friday and Saturday nights. The owners schedule mostly local jazz and blues bands at The Speakeasy, which is located downstairs from the restaurant. Hungry for food and music? The restaurant offers a late-night menu, with special pricing, after 11:00 p.m.

East

31st Street Pub
3101 Penn Avenue
(412) 391-8334
www.31stpub.com

In the 80s, this bar used to be a local watering hole for bikers. Today, you'll find the "31st" is one of Pittsburgh's best bars for the local underground music scene. Located in the Strip District by the 31st Street Bridge, the 31st offers live music from punk and hard core to garage, rockabilly, psych, post-punk and indie. Don't expect glitz and glamour here. This bar keeps it simple—listen to music and drink beer.

Bridge's
100 Lytton Avenue
(412) 682-6200

Set in the Holiday Inn in Oakland, this local night spot features live jazz each Sunday evening from 7:00 until 10:00 p.m. Pittsburgh Jazz Society bands perform, and anyone joining the society at the door receives a discount off drinks and food. Sunday brunch includes a jazz performance.

Brillobox
4101 Penn Avenue
(412) 621-4900
www.brillobox.net

Named in honor of Andy Warhol, Brillobox was opened in 2005 by two Pittsburghers who moved back to their hometown after living in New York City. Here, you can eat dinner on the first floor, then go see underground music acts on the second. Other nights you may find films, DJs, or even karaoke.

The Mr. Roboto Project
722 Wood Street, Wilkinsburg
(412) 247-9639
www.therobotoproject.org

Looking for an all-ages show? The Mr. Roboto Project is an independently, collectively run venue that features live punk, hard core, indie-pop, and math-rock. No alcohol or smoking is allowed.

South

Club Café
56-58 South 12th Street
(412) 431-4950
www.clubcafelive.com

One of the few remaining small venues (150 capacity) where you can see original musical performances by local, regional, and national acts in Pittsburgh. With its simple, but classy décor, small menu selection, and full bar, Club Café remains a favorite of Pittsburghers and visitors alike. All shows at this non-smoking club are 21 and over and either require a ticket or cover charge. Tickets can be purchased through Ticketmaster, ticketmaster.com, or by calling (412) 323-1919.

Diesel Club Lounge
1601 East Carson Street
(412) 431-8800
www.dieselpgh.com

Enjoy live music and DJs five nights a week at this multi-level club in the heart of Pittsburgh's South Side. Music is featured Wednesday through Sunday, 9:00 p.m. until 2:00 a.m. The club features a lounge area, VIP seating, and dance floor. Check out their Web site for concert listings as this club also offers all-ages shows and comedy acts. Doors open at different times depending on the concert schedule. Tickets can usually be purchased in advance through Ticketmaster, ticketmaster.com, or by calling (412) 323-1919.

Excuses Bar & Grill
2526 East Carson Street
(412) 431–4090

If the music menu of live blues, R&B, plus rock 'n' roll doesn't tempt you, then the 24 imported beers surely will. Feast on wings and munchie delights. Thursday night enjoy a jam session. Depending upon the entertainment on Saturdays, there may be a cover charge of $2 or $3.

Hard Rock Café
230 W. Station Square Drive
(412) 481-ROCK
www.hardrock.com

In 2002, Pittsburgh became home to one of the nationally-renowned Hard Rock Cafés. Located in Station Square, the Hard Rock Café Pittsburgh offers live music performed by local, regional, and national rock bands. There are cover charges for some performances so it's best to call or check the Web site for details.

Rex Theatre
1602 East Carson Street
(412) 381-6811
www.rextheatre.com

The historic Rex Theatre, a popular movie theater for more than 90 years, is now a thriving live-music venue on Pittsburgh's South Side where you can find a variety of local, regional, and national music performances. With a capacity of 550 people, The Rex also hosts occasional comedy acts and the longest running open stage in town with singers, poets, and spoken word. Don't forget the full bar and fresh homemade pizza. Tickets are available at Ticketmaster, www.ticketmaster.com, or by calling (4120) 323-1919. You can also purchase tickets at the Culture Shop, next door to the Rex.

Rhythm House Café
3029 Washington Pike (Bridgeville)
(412) 221-5010
www.rhythmhousecafe.com
About a 15-minute drive from Pittsburgh, you'll find live music 6 nights a week at The Rhythm House Café. Every Wednesday night is country night, Thursday night is acoustic night, and every Sunday, you can hear Pittsburgh Jazz Society. On Friday and Saturday nights, there is usually dancing to a DJ spinning Top 40 music in the backroom while local and regional bands play in the front. Last, but not least, if you want to play cards, show up on Tuesdays and Thursdays for Texas Hold 'Em Poker. Beware there is a dress code policy here–no athletic gear, hooded shirts, tossle caps, scullies, backward hats, or baggy clothing of any type are acceptable.

BARS AND BREWPUBS
Downtown

Olive or Twist
140 Sixth Street
(412) 255-0525
www.oliver-twist.com
Known for their martinis, Olive or Twist is located in the heart of Downtown's Cultural District. A sophisticated spot for a drink before a show at one of the nearby theaters, Olive or Twist also offers a full menu from appetizers and salads to sandwiches and entrees. Sports fans, don't forget to try the Black and Gold Martini!

Palomino
Four Gateway Center, 1st Floor
(412) 642-7711
www.palomino.com
On the first floor of Four Gateway Center, one of the towering office buildings in Pittsburgh's Point, Palomino is a contemporary, city restaurant with a bar popular with Pittsburgh's business crowd. The bar, which allows smoking, offers Happy Hour every day from 5:00 until 7:00 p.m. Patio seating is also available, weather permitting.

The Sonoma Grille
947 Penn Avenue
(412) 697-1336
www.thesonomagrille.com
Sonoma Grille, located near the David L. Lawrence Convention Center, is a sophisticated, casual restaurant. However, claiming to have the most extensive wine collection in Pittsburgh with more than 100 wines by the glass, Sonomoa Grille's lounge deserves a mention here for those looking for a nice place to drink wine. Their wine cellar is primarily represented by the west coast region. (A complete wine list is located on their Web site.)

North

Penn Brewery
800 Vinial Street
(412) 237-9402
http://pennbrew.com
Enjoy the ambience of restored 19th-century brewing buildings as you sample at least a dozen varieties of German beers brewed on the premises. This North Side hangout offers an award-winning selection of microbrews, plus its own famous Penn Pilsner beer. There is live Alpine music every Wednesday, with music performances on some weekend nights. German and American cuisine is served in the dining hall with traditional family-style tables (see the Restaurants chapter). The outdoor biergarten is fun in warm weather and the Oktoberfest is a true celebration of microbrews in late September. Plus, there's free parking in the covered lot next door.

i To find the latest GLBT nightlife events, get a copy of *Out*, the newspaper serving the local gay and lesbian community. Free copies can be found at local bookstores, bars, restaurants, and coffeehouses or call (412) 381-3350. *Out* is also on the web at www.outpub.com.

East

Baggy Knee Bistro
9 East Pittsburgh Street, Greensburg
(724) 836-7261
This upscale bar attracts what locals call the courthouse crowd comprised of after-hours professionals. Occasionally a live band will perform, but this is a rarity. It's mostly an eatery for dine-in or take-out service, as well as a place to imbibe favorite beers or mixed drinks. It is reported that Harrison Ford enjoyed himself here while in town.

Bloomfield Bridge Tavern
4412 Liberty Avenue
(412) 682-8611
www.myspace.com/polishpartyhouse
Local bands, including alternative rock, rhythm and blues, and new-wave artists, perform here in Bloomfield, where ethnic food such as pierogies (a Polish specialty) always hits the spot as a late-night treat. And be sure to wash them down with imported beers.

Church Brew Works
3525 Liberty Avenue
(412) 688-8200
www.churchbrew.com
Does the name intrigue you? We admit, it might seem strange, but in Lawrenceville you'll find handcrafted ales and lagers served in a turn-of-the-20th-century Catholic church-turned-pub. In fact, you'll find a gleaming steel and copper kettle sitting behind glass on the famous altar. Strange, we know, but it's true.

Brews featured include Pipe Organ Ale, Bell Tower Brown Ale, and Pious Monk Dunkel. You won't go hungry either, with wood-fired pizzas, buffalo strip steak, and other American cuisine. The outdoor Hop Garden is open every day. If you come because you're curious, you won't be the only ones. The Food Network also visited and featured Church Brew Works on one of its shows.

Mullaney's Harp and Fiddle Irish Pub
2329 Penn Avenue
(412) 642-6622
www.harpandfiddle.com
Not just on St. Patrick's Day but every day, it's Irish Old World atmosphere here in the Strip District. Enjoy at least 10 different draft beers, grilled specialties, outdoor seating, and traditional live music. Tuesdays feature Celtic dancing. Be prepared to pay a $5 cover charge after 8:30 p.m. on weekends, when you'll find Irish bands playing.

Red Star Brewery and Grille
Greensburg Train Station
101 Ehalt Street
(724) 850-7245
www.redstarbrewery.com
Housed in a former train station built in the early 1900s, Red Star Brewery & Grille started brewing beer in 1998. Today, they usually feature six fresh brews on tap, including an English Brown and Irish Dry Stout. A full menu, including pizza, sushi, noodle bowls, fish, steaks, and barbeque (in the summer), is available.

South

Dee's Café
1316 East Carson Street
(412) 431-1314
www.deescafe.com
Located in the heart of Pittsburgh's South Side, Dee's is known by most locals as a great place to buy a modestly-priced drink and play a great game of pool. Of the seven pool tables, four are new championship Brunswick Gold Crown III pool tables. There are also dart boards, a Ping Pong table, and three juke boxes.

Fat Head's Saloon
1805 East Carson Street
(412) 431-7433
www.fatheads.com
Fat Head's Saloon is a neighborhood bar and grill located on Pittsburgh's historic South Side. Besides the great food, this bar features a nice selection of beers, including Rogue Fat

Head's Ale, a beer brewed especially for Fat Head's by Rogue Ales in Oregon. For regular visitors, check out Fat Head's Beer Tours–interesting opportunities for "traveling" your way through a journey of handcrafted beers without leaving your barstool.

Gandy Dancer Saloon
100 West Station Square Drive
(412) 261-1717
www.stationsquare.com/grandconcourse
In what was once the main passenger waiting area of the Pittsburgh & Lake Erie Railroad, the Gandy Dancer at the Grand Concourse makes natives and those from out of town feel right at home. The Gandy Dancer is located in the station's former baggage area. Today, crowds come here for the cozy feel this bar affords, complete with nightly music from the baby grand piano. Listen to every tune imaginable, from Gershwin to ragtime and even the Pittsburgh Steelers fight song. You can also enjoy special pricing for appetizers during Happy Hour, 4:30 to 6:30 p.m., Monday through Friday.

Tiki Lounge
2003 East Carson Street
(412) 381-TIKI
www.tikilounge.biz
Escape to a Polynesian Paradise on Pittsburgh's South Side by visiting Tiki Lounge, a retro recreation of those high-style Tiki bars popular in the 1950s and 1960s. You have to see it to believe it–three waterfalls, numerous statuaries, and, of course, the bars where you can order your favorite cocktail such as a Volcano, Blue Shark, or Coconut Kiss, in one of their special mugs. Thanks to the DJs, this is also a popular weekend dance spot.

West

Kelly's Down By The Riverside Saloon
1458 Riverside Drive, Bridgewater
(724) 728-0222
www.myhometownlinks.com/kellys/
Kelly's is one of a kind in this Beaver County community. Set on the banks of the Beaver

River, Kelly's advertises itself as "An Irish Pub – A Caribbean Island." Inside, you'll find an old Irish style pub where you can listen to Irish balladeers. Step outside to enjoy the tropical island they've set up with palm trees, equatorial plants, and lots of sand. During the summer months there is live music. During winter it's usually blues bands for your listening pleasure. A bar menu features sandwiches and burgers.

Sharp Edge Beer Emporium
288 West Steuben Street
(412) 922-8118
www.sharpedgebeer.com
Just off the Crafton exit of I-79, Sharp Edge's Creekhouse location features two floors and an outside deck where many of the locals gather to drink beer and eat thin crust pizza. On tap, you'll find a great selection of world-class, award-winning beers from around the world. And, if you want more than beer, try the buffalo meat loaf, the ostrich burger, or the kobe beef burger. Sharp Edge has two other locations: The Sharp Edge Bistro in Sewickley and the Sharp Edge Beer Emporium in Friendship.

COFFEEHOUSES
Downtown

La Prima Espresso
205 Twenty-first Street
(412) 681-1922
www.laprima.com
Originally, Sam Patti founded La Prima in 1988 to sell and service commercial espresso machines from the first store located at the corner of Penn Avenue and 21st Street in the Strip District. That showroom evolved into an Italian-style espresso bar where many of the locals today stop to enjoy their morning espresso. La Prima is open from 6:00 a.m. until 4:00 p.m. You'll also find La Prima coffee being served at many local restaurants and independently owned coffee shops.

Getting a Cab

Remember: Most of the time, you can't hail a cab in Pittsburgh. It's just one of those things. But be sure to call one if you're unable to drive home safely.

Yellow Cab Company of Pittsburgh
(412) 321-8100

Peoples Cab Company
(412) 466-8300

A Limousine Service
(412) 782-5466

Starbucks Coffee
www.starbucks.com

This national retailer operates more than 60 locations within 50 miles of Pittsburgh. You can find Starbucks in hotels, suburban malls, downtown office buildings, and even in some Giant Eagles (a local supermarket). There are also several drive-thru Starbucks such as the one at Robinson Town Centre. Serving coffees, Tazo teas, and pastries. Starbucks also provides high-speed wireless Internet through T-Mobile Hot-Spot. To find the Starbuck nearest you, visit their Web site.

North

Borders Books & Music
1170 Northway Mall
(412) 635-7661
www.borders.com

There are more than a dozen Borders and Borders Express retailers in the Pittsburgh region. Most of the locations—East Side, Bethel Park, North Hills, Monroeville, and The Mills—provides a monthly newsletter with its literary as well as music offerings. If you're looking for a more sedate evening sipping a cappuccino and listening to the sounds of jazz, guitar, acoustic music, and many other varieties, then hang out here. Other locations include Monroeville Mall Boulevard in the east

suburbs and at Norwin Center in the South Hills (see the Shopping chapter).

Coffee Tree Roasters
48 Fox Chapel Road
(412) 782-5622

Founded in 1993 by father and son Bill and Bill Swoope, The Coffee Tree Roasters started with one small in-store roaster and now boasts four retail locations in the Pittsburgh area. Offering specialty coffees, pastries, coffee accessories, gift baskets and gift cards, customers can sip their favorite drink in a relaxing atmosphere. Locations are also found in Shadyside, Squirrel Hill, and the South Hills.

East

61C Café
1839 Murray Avenue
(412) 521-6161
www.61ccafe.com

Started at a time when coffeehouses were not yet high style in Pittsburgh, 61C Café is a neighborhood treasure in Squirrel Hill. Serving great coffee in a friendly environment, 61C is a great place to stop after seeing a nearby movie or taking a break from a long day of shopping. Open most nights until 11:00 p.m. or midnight, they offer free, wireless internet and an outdoor patio, weather permitting. (By the way, 61C is the name of the local bus route.)

Crazy Mocha
5830 Ellsworth Avenue
(412) 441-9344
www.crazymocha.com

With its first store opening in 2000, Crazy Mocha is now a regional chain with more than 10 stores located in the city, and plans to open more in surrounding areas. Each coffeehouse tries to reflect its neighborhood. So, for instance, you find those in the South Side Works and Shadyside neighborhoods looking more like and a hip New York café and staying open until 1:00 a.m. All stores offer La Prima coffee, free wireless internet, and are non-smoking. Other Crazy Mocha stores can be found in Oakland, Bloomfield, Lawrenceville, Sewickley, and downtown Pittsburgh.

Enrico's Tazza D'oro Cafe & Espresso Bar
1125 North Highland Avenue
(412) 362-3676
http://tazzadoro.net
Owner Amy Enrico grew up in an Italian family and created this cafe with European flair. Recently expanded, Tazza D'Oro is a popular neighborhood gathering place offering great coffee and conversation. Open seven days a week, entertainment occurs Friday evening, with brunch on Sunday. Dine on the great sandwiches made on the European panini grill. Also, stop by the coffee shop Web site to learn about events, such as the weekly Tuesday Night Walks, which leave from the coffee shop.

Hemingway's Cafe
3911 Forbes Avenue
(412) 621-4100
Located near the University of Pittsburgh, Hemingway's Café has featured poetry readings every Tuesday at 8:30 p.m. for decades. While there's no live musical entertainment here, you may want to try the appetizers, wings, seafood dishes, and a full range of pastas in addition to the full bar.

South

Beehive Coffee Shop
1327 East Carson Street
(412) 488-4483
www.beehivebuzz.com
Here, you'll find businessfolk and bikers, ministers and punks, artists and chess players. All are drinking great coffee and relaxing in an eclectic space featuring art hanging on the walls and from the ceilings. There is no planned entertainment here at this South Side coffee shop. Board games and chess sets are available to use if you want to join in with this hip, laid-back crowd. Don't forget to check out the courtyard in the back—it's a hidden treasure.

The Bean Cafe
31 East Wheeling Street, Washington
(724) 222-6555
Close to Washington & Jefferson College, this spot is a favorite of college students. On Friday nights, there is music provided by the local radio station, but the ambience here is created more by the conversation and diversity among the patrons. Some of those customers comment that this place is a throwback to the '60s with its rhythmic sounds as background music.

West

Café Kolache
402 Third Street, Beaver
(724) 775-8102
www.cafekolache.com
Featuring Prestogeorge Master Roasted Coffees, this coffee bar offers made-to-order drinks and *kolache,* a slightly sweetened yeast dough filled with apricot, cottage cheese, poppy seed, and/or *levkar* (prune butter) that was a traditional Czech dessert. Owner Kristi DeMaiolo adds a twist to the *kolache* by also filling them with a variety of fruits, meats, cheeses, and/or vegetables. On most Saturday evenings, Café Kolache plays host to a variety of local musical and literary talent.

LOUNGES, DANCING, MUSIC, & MORE

Downtown

Bossa Nova
123 Seventh Street
(412) 232-3030
www.bossanovapgh.com
Located in downtown Pittsburgh's Cultural District, Bossa Nova serves global tapas, exotic cocktails, and great martinis. No cover charge, but you must be 21 with proper dress.

Pegasus
818 Liberty Avenue
(412) 281-2131
www.pittpegasus.com
It's got a glittery look and a techno sound for dancing. Watch for drink specials as well. This is perhaps Pittsburgh's most visible gay bar. Open Wednesday through Sunday from 10:00 p.m. until 2:00 a.m.

ℹ️ Please remember, don't drink and drive. Always have a designated driver in your group.

North

Ghost Riders
1805 North Main Street Extension, Butler
(724) 283-4401

Ghost Riders is a big place with a big dance floor. No, we're not kidding. This 24,000-square-foot complex has a 7,200 square foot dance floor. Playing country music, Ghost Riders is open on Saturday nights from 7:00 p.m. until 2:00 a.m. to all ages. If you want to learn line dancing, Ghost Riders offer free lessons from 8:00 until 9:00 p.m. There's no liquor license here, so it's bring your own bottle. Cover charge is $8.00.

Jetz
2801 Freeport Road, Harmarville
(412) 828-9500
www.jetznightclub.com

Jetz attracts the younger, under-21 crowd on Friday, Saturday, and Sunday. Since there aren't that many clubs for this age group, you can see it's a popular place on weekends. The club was closed for remodeling in late 2007, so call for details.

Pittsburgh Eagle
1740 Eckert Street
(412) 766-7222
www.pitteagle.com

This club for gay men also offers special events, celebrations, and features. From the West End Bridge, take Chateau Street on the North Side and head toward the penitentiary, several miles from Downtown. At night the building is most impressive: Four brick stories stretch toward a bridge high above. Inside is even better; a pressed-tin ceiling, 14-feet high, covers a spacious bar where a diverse gay crowd, some women and all ages, mingles. The pace picks up on the second floor, where the beat and the heat hit you immediately.

Unwind in the third-floor lounge where couches surround a huge TV showing dance videos. On weekends the dance floor is packed to the beat of Hi-NRG music from years past. Expect a weekend cover, typically $3 to $5 depending on the theme or entertainer.

East

The Altar
1620 Penn Avenue
(412) 263–2877
www.altarbar.com

Convert a 19th-century Slovak Catholic church into a nightclub and what do you get? A three-level, upscale hot spot for dancing and drinking. Open Thursday through Sunday from 9:00 p.m. until 2:00 a.m. Expect to pay a cover.

dejAVu Lounge
2106 Penn Avenue
(412) 434-1144
www.dejavulive.net

Open from Tuesday through Saturday, dejAVu Lounge offers a casual atmosphere where you can find drinks, food, and music. dejAVu offers weekly specials, karaoke on Tuesday, and Sunday nights hosted by WAMO, a local radio station.

PURO Pittsburgh
108-114 19th Street
(412) 434-1310
www.purepgh.com

Located in the heart of Pittsburgh's Strip District, PURO is an upscale venue with three, fully stocked bars, exclusive indoor and outdoor VIP areas, and a unique glass dance floor. The all-white décor adds to the elegance of this nightclub, which does enforce a strict dress code. Isoldi's on The Strip, a fine-dining restaurant featuring Italian cuisine is located on the lower floor.

Shadow Lounge
5972 Baum Boulevard
(412) 363-8277
www.shadowlounge.net

Shadow Lounge features live events five to seven days each week, including music performances and poetry readings. Music acts including local and regional acts performing jazz, indie-rock, salsa, hip hop, and much more. Cover charge is usually $5.00, but sometimes varies. All shows are 18 and older.

Tequila Willies
1501 Smallman Street
(412) 281–3680
www.tequilawillies.com
Tequila Willies, on the shores of the Allegheny River in what's known as the Strip District, attracts boaters who dock and climb aboard these floating barges anchored to the shore. Different music is featured on different nights, including disco, oldies, and steel band rhythms.

South

Lava Lounge
2204 East Carson Street
(412) 431–5282
www.lavaloungepgh.com
Most every night disc jockeys keep the pace hopping at the Lava Lounge. The mood here is set by the different decor—the feeling of a subterranean organic environment with a deep-cushioned pit booth. DJs spin music on Wednesday, Friday, and Saturday. Sunday is Karaoke Night and Thursday features live bands. Covers vary.

Matrix
7 East Station Square
(412) 261-2220
www.matrixpgh.com
Matrix features four nightclubs in one facility. You can hop from Miami-style trance music in Liquid's futuristic décor to '80s party music and movie clips at Exit. Or go to Club Goddess to grind to Top 40 and the underground before taking a break to rest at Velvet, a comfortable and luxurious lounge area. Over 21 and proper dress required. Cover charge varies.

Nitelite
Holiday Inn Meadowlands
340 Racetrack Road, Washington, D.C.
(724) 222–6200
Join the upscale crowd assembled here for dancing, drinks, and wonderful evening entertainment. Nitelite isn't far from the race track, so once your wagering is finished for the evening, head on over.

Pepsi-Cola Roadhouse
Route 18, Burgettsown
(724) 947–1900
www.pepsiroadhouse.com
Pepsi-Cola Roadhouse is a unique dining and entertainment experience, with a seating capacity in excess of 800. With tables of four, every seat yields an up close and personal view of the performers, who range from country and western entertainers to pro boxing and night-at-the-races events. Take Route 22 west (off the Parkway West) and continue until you reach the Burgettstown-Florence exit.

The Sandbar at Sandcastle Waterpark
1000 Sandcastle Drive
(412) 462–6666
www.sandcastlewaterpark.com
If you didn't spot a glimpse of the Gateway Clipper Fleet, you'd think you were on Venice Beach. So says their ad for this beach bar along the banks of the Monongahela River. Having experienced Sandcastle's family fun during the day (see the Kidstuff chapter), adults claim this spot at night to enjoy a little alcoholic refreshment. Open Friday and Saturday during the summer months.

SPORTS BARS
North

Clark Bar & Grill
503 Martindale Street
(412) 231-5720
Housed in the old Clark Candy Building on the North Side, there's a definite sports atmosphere to this popular hangout across from Gate B at Three Rivers Stadium. Come in for

the great grilled entrees, delicious salads, sandwiches, and supreme pastas. Drinks are moderately priced. Even better than the food and libation, however, is the Art Deco atmosphere, including autographed jerseys, baseballs, hockey sticks, and much more celebrating Pittsburgh sports.

East

Dino's Sports Lounge
3883 US 30, Latrobe
(724) 539-2566

Dino's is a popular spot for sports fans. If you don't want to watch the 10-foot big-screen television, park yourself near one of the 16 to 18 smaller sets. In addition to the great sandwiches and wings for which the lounge is known, there are also video and pinball games.

Oakmont Tavern
814 Allegheny River Boulevard, Oakmont
(412) 828-4155
www.oakmonttavern.com

With five televisions that let you see your favorite sports action, we'll term this a sports bar, even though you can have lunch or dinner also. After all, the walls are adorned with old photos of Forbes Field, Pirates baseball, and more. The menu features sandwiches, hoagies, and appetizers. Mexican dishes are apparently the hit of the house. They offer free half-time buffets during Sunday Steeler football games and promise to broadcast every Penn State football game.

Sports Rock Café
1400 Smallman Street (Strip District)
(412) 552-1199
www.sportsrockcafepgh.com

With 60 televisions, including personal televisions in each of the booths, 10 big-screen televisions around the cafe, and televisions behind all three bars, this is a great place to watch sports. Or, if you want to play yourself, check out the café's pool tables, video games, football toss machine, or basketball hoops. Menu and drink specials are available. Call for hours of operation, as they vary by season.

William Penn Tavern
739 Bellefonte Street, South of Elmer
(412) 621-1000

Nestled in Shadyside's shopping district, just off Walnut Street, William Penn Tavern is a haven for sports fans. Watch a game, or play one yourself as this small bar has dartboards, a foosball table, and video poker machines. The Tavern also features great wings, hamburgers, and sandwiches.

South

Jay's Sports Bar and Restaurant
114 Southpoint Boulevard, Canonsburg
(724) 746-2250
www.jaysatsouthpointe.com

Located at Southpointe's Iceoplex, Jays Sports Bar and Restaurant is open everyday from 11:30 a.m. until 2:00 a.m., with a full menu available until 1:00 a.m. There are games and entertainment for all ages, including karaoke and trivia nights and live music on the weekends.

Piper's Pub
1828 East Carson Street
(412) 381-3977
www.piperspub.com

If you want to watch "football" (a.k.a. European soccer), Piper's Pub is the place. They show live English Premier League, Champions League, Scottish Premier League, the FA Cup, and much, much more on Piper's four televisions. Fans gather to drink beer, eat great food, and root for their favorite teams. The menu includes traditional Scottish, Irish, and English fare, including boxty, a version of a potato pancake, and *bangers and mash* (sausage and potatoes). Pipers Pub is open seven days a week from 11:00 a.m. until 1:00 a.m., with the exception of Sunday, when brunch starts at 9:00 a.m.

West

Butya's Tavern
5580 Steubenville Pike, Route 60
McKees Rocks
(412) 787-1919

The autographed memorabilia hanging on the walls gives just the right team spirit to watch popular games on television while enjoying good food and drink. Available for the summer season is a sand volleyball court with an adjacent pavilion for outdoor serving. Based in Robinson Township, Butya's is known for its tasty fish sandwiches.

Zooky's Sports Tavern
Route 51, Fallston
(724) 843-9464
www.zookys.com
Between Beaver and Chippewa, Zooky's offers more than just great wings and beer. There's the trivia game patrons play on television, competing against participants in other bars around the country. Of course that's when fans aren't watching a major sporting event. So whether it's food, beverages, or just plain fun, Zooky's has all three.

COMEDY AND MORE
South

Charlie Murdoch's Dueling Pianos
1005 East Carson Street
(412) 431-SING
www.charliemurdochspittsburgh.com
Located in a renovated church in Pittsburgh's South Side, Charlie Murdoch's is a great place to see world-class piano players perform songs from today's hits to yesterday's classics. An interactive show, the audience is singing, clapping, and laughing in no time. Full bar and menu available. Open Wednesday through Saturday from 6:00 p.m. until 2:00 a.m., with the show beginning at 8:00 p.m. No cover charge on Wednesday and Thursday nights.

Dave and Buster's
180 Waterfront Drive East, Homestead
(412) 462-1500
www.daveandbusters.com
Part of the Dave and Buster's national chain, this location offers food and drinks, plus more than 200 games to choose from, including billiards, shuffleboard, and video games. Open Monday through Thursday and

Sunday from 11:30 a.m. until 12:00 a.m. On Friday and Saturday nights they remain open until 2:00 a.m. Guests under 18 years old must be accompanied by a parent or guardian over 25 years old. Rooms for private parties are available.

Funny Bone
242 West Station Square Drive
(412) 281-3130
www.funnybonepgh.com
If you couldn't guess from the name, this club will keep you laughing with its evenings of comedy, music, and magic. Showtime is 7:30 p.m. most nights. Tuesday, Funny Bone showcases the best of local and regional touring comedians. Cover charge is $8, plus two-beverage minimum, Tuesday through Thursday, with the cover increasing to $15 on Friday and Saturday. Friday and Saturday be prepared for shows at 8:00 and 10:15 p.m. Reservations are recommended.

Gateway Clipper Fleet
350 West Station Square Drive
(412) 355-7980
www.gatewayclipperfleet.com
For almost fifty years, the Gateway Clipper Fleet has sailed the rivers of Pittsburgh. The fleet, comprised of five boats with a total capacity of 2,500 passengers, offers its own unique nightlife on the rivers. Cruises include the Captains Dinner Dance Cruise, Jazz on the Three Rivers, Oldies Dinner Dance Cruise, and much more. Call or visit their Web site for a list of cruises and costs.

Pittsburgh Improv Comedy Club
166 East Bridge Street, Homestead
(412) 462-5233
www.improv.com
The Improv originated in 1963 in New York City. This world famous club brings nationally-known acts to Pittsburgh. Dinner and drinks are available. Shows on Friday and Saturday are 21 and over. Showtimes and cover charges vary. You can make reservations online at their Web site or by calling (412) 462-5233.

Sing Sing Dueling Piano Bar
171 East Bridge Street, Homestead
(412) 461-7426
www.singsing.com
Featuring musical comedy, Sing Sing's entertainers perform a non-stop dueling piano act
that features rock 'n' roll and great times. Sing
Sing is open Wednesday through Saturday
with doors opening at 6:00 p.m. and shows
beginning at 8:00 p.m. A full dinner menu and
party packages are available.

MOVIE THEATERS

This obviously is not a comprehensive list, but
here we've given the largest and the most
popular theaters and spots for movie lovers.

AMC Loews Waterfront 22
300 West Waterfront Drive, Homestead
(412) 462-6923
www.amctheatres.com
With 22 theaters, one word defines this movie
theater—BIG. Inside, "big" also applies: from its
vast lobby with a high ceiling, a huge concession stand, and a cafe for a leisurely coffee to a
full-service restaurant and bar upstairs. The
screens and sound are big, too. Some of the
theaters offer VIP areas with the opportunity to
purchase tickets in advance.

Andy Warhol Museum
117 Sandusky Street
(412) 237-8300
www.warhol.org
While the art is most of the attraction here,
there is a theater that screens Andy Warhol
films. It's on the first floor of the museum
and sometimes easily missed by those who
only browse the exhibits or eat in the cafe.
The Warhol is open Tuesday, Wednesday,
Thursday, Saturday, and Sunday from 10:00
a.m. to 5:00 p.m. and Friday from 10:00 a.m.
to 10:00 p.m. It's closed Monday. Admission
to the theater is included in the cost of a
museum ticket. Adults will pay $15, seniors
(age 55+) $9, and students and children $8
for admission. Carnegie members pay nothing to enter.

Carmike Cinemas—Cranberry
U.S. Route 19 North, Cranberry
(724) 772-3180
www.carmike.com
Carmike Cinemas is a chain with several suburban locations throughout the Pittsburgh
region. This cinema in Cranberry has eight
screens showing popular first-run movies. Try
the others closer to you at South Hills Village,
(412) 835-7700; the Galleria in Mt. Lebanon,
(412) 531-5720; Pleasant Hills, (412) 655-
0511; Greensburg, (724) 834-1190; Beaver
Falls, (724) 846-2945; and Delmont, (724)
468-3555.

Carnegie Science Center Rangos Omnimax
One Allegheny Avenue
(412) 237-3400
www.carnegiesciencecenter.org
Read more about this attraction in both the
Attractions and Kidstuff chapters. However,
here we wanted to highlight the Rangos Omnimax Theater, which shows one or two different films on any given day. Double-feature
presentations are the norm on weekends.
Expect to pay approximately $6 to $8 for tickets ($5 to $7 for members), unless you attend
a double feature.

Comcast Cinema in the Park
(412) 937-3039
www.city.pittsburgh.pa.us
For a unique Pittsburgh experience, bring a
blanket and enjoy cinema under the stars
through this special program, run by the City
of Pittsburgh and sponsored by Comcast.
Every night of the week, you can find a movie
playing in one of the city's parks: Flagstaff Hill
in Schenley Park, Riverview Park, Grandview
Park, Arsenal Park, Brookline Memorial Park,
East Liberty an Elliot Overlook in the city's
West End. The Cinema in the Park runs June
through August. Movies start at dusk and are
free and open to the public.

Dependable Drive-In
Moon Clinton Road, Coraopolis
(412) 264-7011
www.dependabledrivein.com

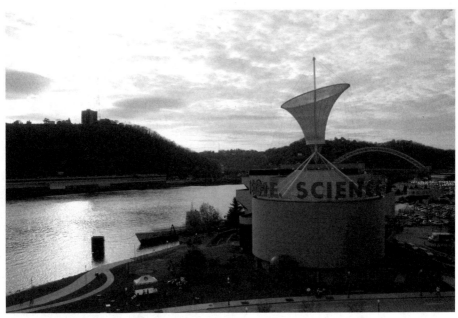

The Carnegie Science Center. ALAN AND BARBARA VENTO

Drive-in theaters are so rare, we've chosen to list this one. Why not enjoy a throwback to the 1950s and take the family out to this theater? Open year round with double-features starting at dusk. Cost is $6 for an adult and $2 for a child.

Destinta Theatres
1701 Lincoln Highway, North Versailles
(412) 824-9200 (movie recording line)
www.destinta.com
This 20-screen complex bills itself as "luxury for less" because it boasts VIP luxury boxes, high-back recliner seats, large party rooms, a video arcade, a full concession stand, and a gourmet coffee bar. Visit another location in the west suburbs at 1025 Washington Pike (Route 50 West) in Bridgeville, (412) 914-0999.

Harris Theater
809 Liberty Avenue
(412) 471-9700
www.pghfilmmakers.org
Operated by Pittsburgh Filmmakers and located in Pittsburgh's Cultural District, Harris

Theater is great place to see independent and foreign films. You can read more about both the theater and the organization in the Arts chapter.

Regent Square Theater
1035 South Braddock Avenue
(412) 682-4111
www.pghfilmmakers.org
Like the Harris Theater, this facility is operated by the Pittsburgh Filmmakers. Find out about the showings by calling the phone number, checking the Web site, or reviewing the listings in local newspapers.

Showcase Cinemas
9700 McKnight Road
(412) 931-1870
www.showcasecinemas.com
Built in the 1970s, many of these cinemas have been added on to. The North Hills location on McKnight Road boasts 11 screens; Showcase Cinemas West in Robinson Township, (412) 787-5788, has 12 screens.

South Side Works Cinema
425 Cinema Drive
(412) 381-7335
www.southsideworks.com
SouthSide Works Cinema is Pittsburgh's newest theater with 10 screens. A great place to see a movie before or after eating or shopping at the South Side Works, the cinema offers discounts to South Side residents on Tuesday and to students on Thursday. (Valid identification or school identification is required.)

Check the weekend entertainment sections in the local newspapers for listings of movies currently playing and a whole host of other nightlife possibilities. Most of these sections appear on Friday, although some may be published on Thursday.

SHOPPING

If you've read other chapters so far, you probably know that Pittsburghers are proud of our sports teams. But there's one sport we love that you won't read about in that chapter: shopping.

Indeed, browsing for bargains, finding fresh produce, or uncovering valuable antiques is a true treasure hunt in these parts. Then there's gearing up for your garden, outfitting the kids, or finding a fun flea market. If all these venues don't complete your search, your local mall surely will. Throughout the region, major malls and strip plazas dot the landscape.

Whether it's window-shopping or stockpiling for the next snowstorm, you're set. Peruse the following list, which we hope will help you on your way. Using this guide's normal geographic breakdown for the most part, this chapter is also broken into other sections, beginning with places where you can boost the Downtown economy, then focusing on shopping within the city limits before heading out to the suburbs. In addition, particular types of stores were felt to deserve their own sections within this chapter, so look for added focus on books and music, specialty merchants, consignment shops, antiques dealers and flea markets, and farmers' markets. Hardly comprehensive, we've tried to include highlights such as major malls and outlets, while also steering you toward out-of-the-way shops and independent merchants you won't want to miss. Several of these entrepreneurs have stellar reputations in the region for providing only the finest.

DOWNTOWN SHOPPING

Pittsburgh is fortunate to have a rather compact central business district, defined by the banks of its rivers on each side. From Point State Park to the Mellon Arena, we call this area the Golden Triangle. Here you will find two major department stores, smaller fine-clothing stores, and chic boutiques. You will also find several downtown office buildings with arcades of shops that sell everything from gourmet chocolate to Rolex watches. For those looking for a bargain, the Golden Triangle offers a Burlington Coat Factory, several designer discount stores, and dollar stores.

Clark Building
717 Liberty Avenue
Pittsburgh's diamond district is actually contained on the floors of the Clark Building, Here you will find diamond wholesalers, retailers, and cutters. You will also discover antique and estate jewelry as well as designers who will create your very own piece.

Fifth Avenue Place
Fifth and Liberty Avenues
(412) 544-4675
www.fifthavenueplacepa.com
Featuring a mix of clothing stores, specialty shops, and eateries, the lower levels of Fifth Avenue Place are where many Pittsburghers stop for a quick shopping spree. On the finer side, stop by Betsy Ann Chocolates for handmade sweets, Lydell's for fine men's clothing, or King's Jewelry for that special gift. Fifth Avenue Place is also home to Faber Coe & Gregg, a one-stop shop for sundries.

Larrimor's
501 Grant Street
(412) 471-5727
Larrimor's, locally owned and operated since 1939, features fine clothing for men and women. Today the store carries designer lines

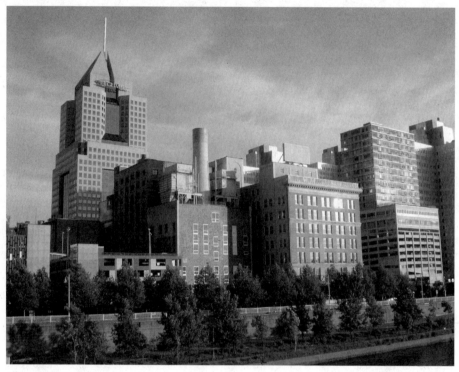

Fifth Avenue Place. MICHEL D. REED

like Ero for women and Ermenegildo Zegna for men. Parking is validated. Also visit Larrimor's store in the Galleria on Washington Road.

Macy's
400 Fifth Avenue
(412) 232-2000
www.macys.com

For decades the department store on Fifth and Smithfield was known as Kaufmann's, home of the famous Kaufmann's clock, which hangs outside the store and acts as a special marker for people to meet downtown. (To learn more about the building itself, the Kaufmann family, and their legendary summer retreat, Fallingwater, go to the Architecture chapter.)

In 2006 the Federated Department Stores purchased the chain of Kaufmann stores, and the department store is now known as Macy's. (Beware; Pittsburghers still call the building Kaufmann's, which can be quite confusing if you try to find it as a landmark!)

Now the area's premier department store, Macy's carries moderately priced to expensive merchandise including jewelry and cosmetics; men's, women's, and children's fashions; home furnishings; and housewares.

This downtown store offers a parking garage across the street with a convenient skyway. Macy's suburban locations include Beaver Valley, Ross Park, Monroeville, and Westmoreland Malls, Robinson Town Centre; Century III Mall; South Hills Village; and Shenango Valley Mall in Mercer County.

Saks Fifth Avenue
513 Smithfield Street
(412) 297-5388
www.saksfifthavenue.com

While much smaller than the world-famous Saks Fifth Avenue in Manhattan, this location holds an appeal to certain upscale clientele. It's got all the same top names in fashion and fragrance as its New York counterpart. Within easy walking distance of the other major department stores, it rounds out Pittsburgh's list of major downtown retailers.

The Shops at One Oxford Centre
Fourth Avenue and Grant Street
(412) 391-5300
www.shopoxford.com

On the lower floors of this office tower, you can find high-fashion boutiques for women like Emphatics and Adornments, as well as fine clothing stores for men like Kountz & Rider and N. J. Richetti's Fine Men's Clothing. One Oxford Centre also includes Hardy & Hayes; representing fine jewelers like Patek Phillipe, and Rolex, and Four Winds Gallery, featuring Southwestern art.

SHOPPING DISTRICTS ON THE OUTSKIRTS

While not within the Golden Triangle, many other areas boast wonderful shopping. Several are within city limits.

East

Lawrenceville

From 16th Street to 62nd Street in Lawrenceville, you will find more than 90 businesses in the 16:62 Design Zone. From hip and trendy to high end, there are galleries, boutiques, and "mom and pop" shops here. Some of our favorites are Divertido, (412) 687-3701, for cool gifts; Who New? Retro Mod Décor, (412) 781-0588, for vintage furniture; and Julep, (412) 478-6160, for handcrafted jewelry.

Shadyside Shopping—Part 1
Walnut Street
www.shadysideshops.com

Not far off Fifth Avenue, heading east, is the fashionable Walnut Street of Shadyside. This 6-block-long shopping area is known for cafes, restaurants, national retailers, and local specialty shops and galleries. In addition to Ann

Taylor, Gap, J. Crew, Pottery Barn, and Williams Sonoma, you will also find independently owned boutiques like Cheeks, (412) 681-5414; e.b. Pepper, (412) 683-3815; and Moda, (412) 681-8640. Find treasures at Toadflax, (412) 621-2500, and gifts for the kids at S. W. Randall Toyes, (412) 562-9252; the Picket Fence, (412) 246-0350; and Shadyside Variety Store, (412) 681-1716.

Shadyside Shopping—Part 2
Ellsworth Avenue

When you've shopped the stores on Walnut Street, head to nearby Ellsworth Avenue for an eclectic mix of locally owned stores, galleries, and restaurants. For unique gifts stop by Articulation, (412) 661-1963, and Hiptique, (412) 361-5817. Or visit one of several galleries in the area featuring fine art, glassworks, and antiques. Ellsworth Avenue also features many locally owned clothing boutiques. You will find Eons and Hey Betty here, two antique and resale clothing stores detailed later in this chapter.

South Craig Street Shopping
Oakland section of Pittsburgh
www.onlyinoakland.org

In the heart of Pittsburgh's education and health-care community, you'll find one-of-a-kind gifts and other worldly surprises. Check out Caliban Book Shop, (412) 681-9111, for books of the scholarly variety or Phantom of the Attic, (412) 621-1210, for comic books and games. The Irish Design Center, (412) 682-6125, is filled with such Irish imports as sweaters, fashionable woolens, and decorative household items, or stop by Watermelon Blues, (412) 681-8451, for unique and wonderful gifts.

Squirrel Hill Shopping District
Forbes and Murray Avenues

The heart of Pittsburgh's Jewish community, the Squirrel Hill shopping district features kosher grocery stores and Pinskers Judaica Center, (800) JUDAISM, a Judaica book and gift store. The district, which runs along Murray and Forbes Avenues, also features wares from many other cultures, with a 10,000 Villages gift store and several Moroccan import stores. There are also fashionable clothing and accessory stores such as Charles Spiegel, (412) 421-9311, for men and Cheryl W., (412) 422-9099, for women. Another favorite is Little's Shoe Store, (412) 421-3530, which is actually big! That's right, no matter whose feet you intend to fit into the shoes, you should be able to find a pair here. And after a day of heavy-duty shopping, why not walk to the recently renovated branch of the Carnegie Library or Barnes & Noble (see Books & Music below) for some coffee and a relaxing book.

Strip District
Several blocks from Downtown at 11th Street to 33rd Street

Named for the strip of flat land that runs from the edge of downtown to the beginning of Lawrenceville, one thing is for sure: People come to the Strip for the hectic atmosphere, novel merchandise, and, above all else, great food! As stated in other chapters, the Strip is very decent!

Gourmet delights abound, including the wonderful seafood selection at Robert Wholey & Co., (412) 391-3737, and Benkovitz Seafoods, (412) 263-3000.

Looking for Italian bread, buckets of fresh olives, imported cheeses, and a variety of pastas? Head to the Pennsylvania Macaroni Co., (412) 471-8330; Jimmy & Nino Sunseri Co., (412) 255-1100; or Prestogeorge Fine Foods, Inc., (412) 471-0133.

While it's true that you'll breathe in a new aroma on virtually every corner of the Strip, there are a few other nonedible finds in this trendy shopping district. Known for its noise-activated toys and wacky gadgets, the Mike Feinberg Co., (412) 471-2922, supplies everything from partyware and gifts to Pittsburgh sports team merchandise. Come Halloween, look your spookiest with the help of Costume World, (412) 281-3277.

Sidewalk vendors in the Strip peddle everything from T-shirts to compact discs and DVDs. And you will not go hungry while you shop. Sidewalk grills offer barbecue ribs, chicken, and pork; Chinese specialties; plus hot dogs and hamburgers. Stop in at a coffee shop or bakery for a cup of fresh brew and a freshly baked pastry or biscotti. It's all here—dozens of stores to tempt your palate and pocketbook—in Pittsburgh's Strip District.

South
The Shops at Station Square
Across the Smithfield Street Bridge
at Carson Street
(412) 261-2811
www.stationsquare.com

Imagine an old railroad station with its freight house and passenger operations. That hurried exchange of merchandise between boxcars and wagons is somewhat replicated today as savvy shoppers dart in and out of the chic stores that make up the Shops at Station Square.

Since the 1970s, when the Pittsburgh History & Landmarks Foundation launched a site study and plan for a retail complex, the Shops at Station Square have brought distinction to this section of the South Side.

Today this indoor mall boasts 20 unique retailers. St. Brendan's Crossing, (412) 471-0700, features Celtic charm with fisherman's knit sweaters, woolens, and wraps. And Hometowne Sports, (412) 471-7280, is the place to go for the latest Pittsburgh sports team merchandise.

Parking and restaurants are nearby, as is the Monongahela Incline, taking visitors or commuters to the heights of Mt. Washington. The "T" light-rail station is also a permanent fixture. Indeed, many downtown shoppers park at Station Square and ride the "T" across the river.

SouthSide Works
East Carson and 27th Streets
(412) 481-8800
www.southsideworks.com

Located on the former site of LTV Steel Mill, SouthSide Works is one of the most exciting new additions to Pittsburgh's shopping scene.

Sunrise over Pittsburgh from West End. ALAN AND BARBARA VENTO

Here you will find locally owned boutiques and Madison Avenue retailers, many of which aren't found anywhere else in the region. Joseph Beth Booksellers, an independent bookseller, and REI, the world's premier outdoor gear store, are here. So are Sur La Table, Steve Madden, Urban Outfitters, Cole Haan, and Z. Gallerie. Tired of shopping? Take in a movie at SouthSide Works Cinema, tempt your palate at the Cheesecake Factory, or just sit in the "Town Square" and enjoy watching the children play in the fountain.

The Waterfront
285 East Waterfront Drive, West Homestead
(412) 476-8889
www.waterfronttowncenter.com
The Waterfront is Pittsburgh's newest shopping and entertainment development—and also its biggest, occupying more than 260 acres. It's been attracting crowds since it opened. On the site of the former Homestead steel mills, this complex features a mix of stores, from Filene's Basement to Barnes &

Noble to Abercrombie and Fitch, a Loews Cineplex, and restaurants in every price range. There's even a village square surrounded by smaller shops. Take the Homestead Hi-Level Bridge over the Monongahela River. The huge brick chimneys to the right mark the spot, and there's plenty of free parking.

West

West End Village
More than 30 businesses have opened in this up-and-coming neighborhood. Many are drawn to the possibilities and potential of its small business district. Some Pittsburghers know this area as the West End, but its new moniker is the West End Village. It's worth an afternoon's visit to see James Gallery, (412) 922-9800; the delicacies at the Vanilla Pastry Studio, (412) 922-2173; the handmade collector pieces at Buon Sapore, (412) 922-6530; and, if you're in the holiday spirit, the ornaments at European Treasures Christmas Shop, (412) 920-2720.

SHOPPING

It's a taxing subject, but you will want to know that in Pennsylvania, most clothing is not subject to the state's 6 percent sales tax. Within Allegheny County, the sales tax levied is 7 percent.

SUBURBAN MALLS
East

Westmoreland Mall
Route 30 East, Greensburg
(724) 836-5025
www.westmorelandmall.com
Anchor tenants here include Macy's, JCPenney, Sears, and the Bon-Ton. In terms of size, Westmoreland ranks second in the region. You'll find the usual stores here— the Disney Store, Victoria's Secret, Limited and Limited II, Champs, and Old Navy—and a few unique ones. Built in the late '70s, Westmoreland Mall was refurbished in the mid-'90s, taking on a thoroughly modern look.

Monroeville Mall
Monroeville Mall Boulevard off Route 22, Monroeville
(412) 243-8511
www.monroevillemall.com
Built in 1969, this was one of the region's first major malls. In addition to large department stores such as Macy's, Boscov's, and JCPenney, Monroeville Mall boasts more than 180 stores, including the usual regimen of franchises and national chains such as Victoria's Secret, the Disney Store, Payless Shoe Source, Mimi Maternity, White House Black Market, Abercrombie & Fitch, Kay Jewelers, and more. Behind the mall itself sits the Monroeville Mall Annex, with Burlington Coat Factory, Best Buy, Dick's Sporting Goods, and other merchants. The food court and full-service restaurants keep you well fed. There's Playtime Creative, (412) 380-4330, for the kids, and stroller rentals and wheelchairs are available.

South

Century III Mall
3075 Clairton Boulevard, West Mifflin
(412) 653-1220
www.simon.com
Century III offers 160 stores, including anchor department stores Macy's, JCPenney, and Sears in addition to specialty retailers Old Navy and Macy's Furniture. National chains such as American Eagle Outfitters, the Disney Store, NY & Co., Steve & Barney's, Motherhood Maternity, and d.e.m.o. are located here. A food court and full-service restaurants are available.

The Galleria
1500 Washington Road, Mt. Lebanon
(412) 561-4000
www.galleriapgh.com
This upscale mall property boasts some national chains and other retailers that operate solely at this location in Pittsburgh. Enclosed parking for inclement weather is one perk at the Galleria. Shops include Chico's, Anthropologie, Godiva Chocolatier, Restoration Hardware, Williams-Sonoma, Talbots, and Ann Taylor. There are several restaurants in the complex, including Mitchell's Fish Market.

Washington Crown Center
1500 West Chestnut Street, Washington
(724) 228-4270
www.shopwashingtoncrown.com
Anchor tenants at this Washington County mall include Macy's, Sears, and the Bon-Ton (a smaller regional department store). Banks, jewelers, and shoe stores are found here in addition to names you'll recognize such as Gap, Old Navy, American Eagle Outfitters, Victoria's Secret, and Bath & Bodyworks. There is a small food court on the premises. Customer services include stroller rental and wheelchair loans, shopping bags, and senior citizen discount cards.

South Hills Village
301 South Hills Village, Bethel Park
(412) 831-2900
www.simon.com
South Hills Village is an amenity for the South

Hills communities of Bethel Park, Mt. Lebanon, and Upper St. Clair. Macy's, Boscov's, and Sears department stores anchor this mall, with the usual national chains and franchises such as Banana Republic, Brookstone, Build-a-Bear Workshop, J.Jill, Coach, and the Disney Store. In recent years, strip malls and other merchants have taken up camp nearby this 130-store mall.

Washington Mall
301 Oak Spring Road, Washington
(724) 222-7390
There are no major department stores here. However, the mall has several "big box" retailers such as Staples and Toys 'R Us outside the main building. Inside you will find JoAnn Fabrics and Barbara's Hallmark, as well as several banks, barbers, and hair salons.

West

Airmall
Pittsburgh International Airport
(800) 487-3247
www.airmall.com
If you arrive at the airport early for your flight, you might want to consider carrying more than your suitcase on your next trip. Try a shopping agenda and credit cards! That's right, with 90 shops, the Airmall makes it possible to shop for much more than last-minute souvenirs. In fact, Pittsburgh International consistently scores as one of the nation's leading airports based upon the stellar shopping alone.

BAA Pittsburgh oversees the airport shopping mall, and one rule for retailers here is that prices are guaranteed to be the same as they are at local malls. And while you will find some familiar names here (Eckerd Drugs, The Body Shop, and Victoria's Secret), you'll also find such niche stores as Brookstone, Crocs, GNC, Perfumania, Tie Rack, and the PGA Tour Shop. Food court vendors as well as sit-down restaurants are available, and there is Kidsport if the youngsters need to play a spell. (Unfortunately, for security reasons the Airmall's AirSide shops are only available for those traveling. See the Getting Here, Getting

Around chapter for more details on the airport.)

Beaver Valley Mall
380 Beaver Valley Mall, Monaca
(724) 774-5573
www.shopbeavervalley.com
Beaver County's major shopping locale, this mall has all the major department stores in the region—Boscov's, Macy's, Sears, and JCPenney. In addition, you'll find the typical mall stores such as American Eagle Outfitters, Borders Express, Dick's Sporting Goods, and a convenient food court.

The Mall at Robinson
100 Robinson Centre Drive, Robinson Township
(412) 788-0816
www.shoprobinsonmall.com
Located off Parkway West between the airport and downtown Pittsburgh, opposite the Pointe at North Fayette and behind Robinson Town Centre, The Mall at Robinson is the most recent addition to this rapidly growing shopping district. The two-story enclosed mall is anchored by Macy's, Sears, JCPenney, and Dick's Sporting Goods and contains more than 100 shops and a food court with large TV screens that just can't be ignored.

The Pointe at North Fayette
Summit Park Drive at Quinn Drive, North Fayette Township
(412) 787-0722
Directly across from Robinson Town Centre on the other side of the Parkway West sits the Pointe, which looks a little like a strip mall but is almost more of a shopping district because its buildings are not connected in many locations. Don't miss Barnes & Noble, Home Place, Sam's Club, Wal-Mart, Home Depot, and many other major retailers. You won't go hungry either. (Turn to the Restaurants chapter for more detail on dining options here.) To get to the Pointe, take the bridge from Robinson Town Centre. Or if you're coming from the airport on Interstate 279, exit at Montour Run. You'll find Summit Park Drive about 0.5 mile up the road on your left.

Robinson Town Centre
Route 60, Robinson Township
(412) 391-7887
www.robinsontowncentre.com
Featuring more than 50 shops, this outdoor strip mall includes both freestanding stores and buildings. Ikea (see Specialty Stores in this chapter) is an anchor retailer along with Dick's Sporting Goods, Marshalls, and T.J. Maxx. Family Christian Stores have a location here, along with Toys 'R Us and many other chains.

North

Clearview Mall
101 Clearview Circle, Center Township
(724) 285-5722
www.shopclearviewmall.com
Anchor tenants include JCPenney, Sears, The Bon-Ton, and Boscov's. Typical mall outlets and chain stores such as Zale's and King's jewelry stores, Bath & Body Works, and American Eagle Outfitters also make their home in the Clearview Mall. There is a food court, as well as plenty of restaurants and eateries within the complex and along the mall periphery.

Pittsburgh Mills
590 Pittsburgh Mills Circle, Tarentum
(724) 904-9000
www.pittsburghmills.com
Pittsburgh Mills, one of the newer shopping malls in the region, is located in Frazer Township, 16 miles northeast of downtown Pittsburgh. The Galleria at The Mills features hundreds of the best names in retail—H&M, Macy's, Victoria Secret, and American Eagle Outfitters. The location also features a Cinemark 18 Theater; a variety of restaurants, including Abate and Chef Steff's Ristorante; and even a walking club, Mills Milers.

Ross Park Mall
1000 Ross Park Mall Drive, Ross Township
(412) 369-4400
www.simon.com
Nestled in the North Hills, Ross Park Mall offers 150 stores, including a collection of major department stores such as Macy's, Boscov's, JCPenney, and Sears. Nordstrom's will open at the mall in 2008. Here you'll also find all the other stores you've grown accustomed to in mall locations, such as Ann Taylor, Baby Gap and GapKids, Talbot Kids, Bailey Banks & Biddle, J. Crew, Frederick's of Hollywood, Nine West, and Le Gourmet Chef.

The Waterworks Mall
Freeport Road, O'Hara Township
(412) 366-2252
This outdoor strip mall, located in the Fox Chapel Area, has the usual merchants you would find at most indoor locations, such as Avenue, Dress Barn, Toy Kingdom, The Children's Place, Old Navy, and Famous Footwear. No major department stores have branches here except for discounters Marshall's, T.J. Maxx, and Dunham Sports. However, you will find gourmet groceries within the Giant Eagle supermarket, as well as musical selections in the Barnes & Noble.

BOOKS, COMIC BOOKS, & MUSIC

Downtown

Eide's Entertainment
1121 Penn Avenue
(412) 261-0900
Billing itself as "the only store that matters," Eide's—to some—isn't exaggerating. Founded in 1972, Eide's quickly became Pittsburgh's first and foremost comic shop, winning *City Paper*'s award for best comic-book store nine years in a row. Eide's also began hawking videos, magazines, and music, winning awards as "best record store" and "best place to buy used CDs" as well. Today this "entertainment superstore" offers alternative press and cutting-edge books and magazines.

Kirner's Catholic Bookstore
219 Fourth Avenue
(412) 261-2326
Since Kirner's carries much more than books within this family-run store, we classify this as

more of a gift shop. It's been in business for more than 115 years. Merchandise includes a most extensive selection of Catholic Bibles, books, clerical apparel, first communion merchandise, and gifts for all occasions, including Christmas, Easter, weddings, baby congratulations, and confirmation.

East

Barnes & Noble Booksellers
1723 Murray Avenue
(412) 521-3600
www.barnsandnoble.com

As with all Barnes & Noble stores in the area, there is a Starbucks coffee bar serving up cappuccinos, fancy desserts, and other goodies. Author events and children's story times are held regularly. Check the in-store bulletins for dates and times. There are several Barnes & Nobles in Greater Pittsburgh. Additional locations are at the Waterfront, South Hills Village, the Pointe, Cranberry Township, Greensburg, Monroeville, and the Waterworks.

Basilica Gift Shop
St. Vincent College, Latrobe
(724) 532-5060

Gifts for the soul abound here. This shop is a project of the St. Vincent Archabbey, whose 190 Benedictine monks, many of whom teach at the college, operate priories worldwide. The spiritual stock includes religious medals, prayer books and Bibles, small statuary, and artwork, as well as cookbooks and gift items.

The Book Center
University of Pittsburgh
(412) 648-1455

The main supplier of textbooks to University students, this store (colloquially called the Pitt Book Store) offers a full range of consumer and trade books as well as periodicals and children's books. Merchandise such as Pitt sweatshirts, T-shirts, mugs, and other mementos are also available.

ℹ️ General Nutrition Center (GNC), with more than 4,800 locations in the United States, was founded in Pittsburgh in 1935 as a health-food store. Back then, the main product was yogurt. Today GNC stocks a variety of vitamins, health foods, and natural products. Visit www.gnc.com for information.

Borders Books & Music
5986 Penn Circle South
(412) 441-1080
www.borderstores.com

The most recent location in the Borders chain to open in Pittsburgh, the East Liberty store offers book lovers and music fans a "wall-less" concept in shopping. Unique spaces are designed for the children's area and the cafe, which serves coffee, soft drinks, pastries, salads, and desserts. The store's music department is located on the first floor. Author signings and discussions are regularly held, along with a full array of children's story times and events. Check the current newsletter for details. Additional Borders and Borders Express locations in the area are in South Hills Village, Monroeville, Beaver Valley Mall, Bethel Park, North Hills, Robinson Center, The Pittsburgh Mills, Greensburg, Butler, and Washington.

Caliban Books
410 South Craig Street
(412) 681-9111
www.calibanbooks.com

A great little store with a surprisingly large number of books on hand, Caliban offers more than 35,000 used and rare first editions. In addition to poetry, fine arts, and travel, Caliban also stocks contemporary fiction and local history. The bookstore is well situated in a lovely little shopping area near the Carnegie Museums, where you'll also find some excellent restaurants, such as Ali Baba, serving Middle Eastern fare, and LuLu's Noodles.

Journeys of Life
810 Bellefonte Street, Shadyside
(412) 681-8755

On the second floor of this New Age gift store,

you will discover a selection of wonderful books for kids and adults, many with creative and alternative spiritual themes. Lots of 12-step recovery books and materials are found here as well. While you're there, don't forget to check out the gifts—feng shui cures, hand-crafted meditation fountains, candles, and aromatherapy products—on the store's first floor.

Mystery Lovers Bookshop
514 Allegheny River Boulevard, Oakmont
(412) 828-4877
www.mysterylovers.com
The only bookstore in Pittsburgh devoted exclusively to the passion of mystery novels, Mystery Lovers Bookshop offers a warm atmosphere, knowledgeable staff, author signings, writers' group meetings, children's events, and an in-store coffee bar. Orders by phone can be placed using their toll-free number, (888) 800-6078.

Phantom of the Attic
3766 William Penn Highway
Route 22, Monroeville
(412) 856-4403
www.pota-oakland.com
There aren't many stores specializing in comic books, magic cards, and collectible cards. But you'll find those items here.

North

Aspinwall Bookshop
20 Brilliant Avenue, Aspinwall
(412) 782-7072
www.aspinwallbookshop.com
The owner of this local bookshop offers knowledgeable service. An avid reader himself, John Towle provides visitors with excellent recommendations of books to read, as well as hosts book signings and other events in this intimate bookshop in Aspinwall.

Cokesbury Books & Church Supplies
19015 Perry Highway, Mars
(724) 776-6150
www.cokesbury.com
Stocking church supplies and curriculum

materials, this store also carries books and gift items merchandised to the general public. Compact discs, cassettes, videos, pictures, and greeting cards are also available.

Duncan Comic Books and Accessories
1047 Perry Highway
(412) 635-0886
Find more than just comic books here; there are toys, gifts, and cards to choose from as well as a large selection of action figures. You'll also find a plentiful array of used books to browse through.

Family Christian Stores
Morning Star Bible Bookstore
1717 Route 228, Cranberry Township
(724) 779-7082
www.familychristian.com
Carrying a full range of Christian Bibles, storybooks, music, gifts, and church supplies, this chain used to be known as Family Bookstores. You'll find additional locations at Natrona Heights, West Mifflin, Monroeville, Robinson Town Centre, and Bridgeville.

New Dimension Comics
20550 US 19, Mars
(724) 776-0433
Located in Cranberry Township, New Dimension stocks more than 60,000 back issues of comic books, and a 40-foot wall of new releases. This is the place to browse for collectible card games, too. Your children will also delight in the action figures.

South

Dave's Music Mine
1210 East Carson Street
(412) 488-8800
www.davesmusicmine.com
Dave's is an independent store in Pittsburgh's South Side that sells new and used music and movies. You can purchase concert tickets for Club Café, Mr. Small's, and The Rex and Diesel at this location. At their Squirrel Hill store on Murray Avenue, Dave's Music Mine claims to have over 10,000 used CDs, all for under $1.

Buy Fresh, Buy Local

Most communities offer farmers' markets beginning in May and running through the fall harvest season. Markets don't just offer vegetables; some feature freshly baked bread, biscotti, and pies; canned fruits and jellies; organic produce (even chocolate), farm-raised meats; and even homemade pierogies, a Slavic dumpling. Check with your municipality or borough for more details. For a list of all farmers' markets in the city, call (412) 422-6523. Additional markets can be found through www.farmersmarketalliance.com. Here's a list of a few of the more popular farmers' markets.

Downtown
City-County Building Farmers' Market
400 Grant Street
Friday from 10:00 a.m. to 2:00 p.m.

East
Farmers @ Firehouse
2216 Penn Avenue
Saturday from 9:30 a.m. to 1:30 p.m.

East Liberty Farmers' Cooperative
Market
344 North Sheridan Avenue
Saturday from 5:00 a.m. to noon;
open year-round

Greensburg Market
Behind the City Hall, Greensburg
Tuesday from 3:00 to 6:00 p.m.

Ligonier Country Market
Springer Road and West Main Street
Saturday from 7:00 a.m. to noon

Monroeville Lions Club
Farmers' Market
Gateway High School, Monroeville
Saturday from 9:00 a.m. to 12:30 p.m.

South
Mt. Lebanon Farmers' Market
975 Washington Road
Wednesday from 4:00 to 7:00 p.m.

South Side Farmers' Market
South 18th Street and Carson Street
Tuesday from 3:30 to 7:30 p.m.

Washington Farmers' Market
139 Main Street, Washington
Thursday from 3:00 to 6:00 p.m.

West
Ambridge Farmers' Market
Park Road and Route 65
Thursday from 4:00 to 7:00 p.m.

Beaver Farmers' Market
Beaver County Courthouse
parking lot
Saturday from 10:00 a.m. to 1:00 p.m.

North
Farmers' Market
Chestnut and Diamond Streets, Butler
Wednesdays from 2:00 to 6:00 p.m.

North Side Farmers' Market
East Park (across from main
entrance to Allegheny General
Hospital at Cedar Avenue)
Friday from 3:30 to 7:30 p.m.

Eljay's Used Books
1309 East Carson Street
(412) 381-7444
www.eljaysbooks.com
Carrying used paperback and hardcover books, Eljay's is a funky little bookshop where you can lose yourself for hours, searching among the stacks on the shelves and on the floor. Here you will find an eclectic collection of a little bit of everything—sci-fi, philosophy, and even some signed modern first editions. And if you can't find it, just ask Frank or Louise to see if they can find it for you.

f.y.e.
477 South Hills Village, Bethel Park
(412) 835-6930
www.fye.com
This chain of music stores can be found all around Pittsburgh, with locations at South Hills Village, Century III, Monroeville Mall, and The Mall at Robinson.

Joseph-Beth Booksellers
2705 East Carson Street
(412) 381-3600
www.josephbeth.com
With five locations in the Eastern United States, Joseph-Beth Booksellers is one of the nation's strongest and most prosperous independent bookselling companies. The Pittsburgh store, located in the South Side Works, opened in late 2004. This large, two-story bookstore offers a huge selection of books, CDs, and DVDs along with personal, friendly service. The store organizes a number of book clubs, such as the Cookbook Pot-Luck Club and the Gay and Lesbian Book Club. Each month, Joseph-Beth publishes a calendar of events featuring book signings, author lectures, and social gatherings. For the kids, Joseph-Beth offers story times for preschoolers and young children, a Harry Potter Withdrawal Club, American Girl Tea Parties, and performances by local performing arts groups, such as UMOJA. Even further showing its commitment to the local community, this bookseller supports a number of local charities. So

grab a coffee at Caribou Coffee, the adjacent cafe, and stop by to browse at Joseph-Beth.

West
The Open Mind Bookstore
439 Beaver Street, Sewickley
(412) 741-1888
www.theopenmind.com
New Age, spirituality, self-help, and recovery books stock the shelves along with a limited children's selection. Gift items include jewelry, incense, candles, bath salts, greeting cards, music, and videos. Call to find out when you might catch appearances by a massage therapist, palm reader, or psychic.

Penguin Book Shop
420 Beaver Street, Sewickley
(412) 741-3838
Here's another independent bookstore of a general nature. Kids can browse upstairs while adults look over the selection of fiction, nonfiction, current best-sellers, and greeting cards.

SPECIALTY SHOPS & BOUTIQUES
Downtown
Bailey Banks & Biddle Jewelers
500 Grant Street
(412) 391-4440
You'll find this store in the lower lobby of One Mellon Bank Center along Grant Street, Downtown. This leading jeweler offers the finest in jewelry, watches, corporate gifts, and giftware, including crystal and porcelain pieces. Clients come here for custom design work and repairs. With 29 windows, it's a great place to window-shop as well! Look for additional locations at South Hills Village and Ross Park Mall.

Chick
717 Liberty Avenue
(412) 434-0100
www.chickdowntown.com
New Yorker Amy Reed and her husband opened this clothing boutique in 2007 with the

goal of bringing New York and Lost Angeles fashion designers' clothing lines to Pittsburgh. Besides carrying women's formal and casual wear, Chick offers belts, purses, and jewelry.

Curtain Call
545 Penn Avenue
(412) 392-3313

Stop by this unique store run by the Pittsburgh Symphony—a perfect complement to the Cultural District according to many arts patrons. Here you'll find great gifts for music lovers such as CDs, books, jewelry, and symphony-related merchandise.

Honus Wagner Co.
320 Forbes Avenue
(412) 471-3045

Sports fanatics will flock to this store named for one of the greatest Pirate players ever, since many sporting goods and apparel items are stocked here. This includes athletic shoes; team merchandise; brand-name athletic workout suits, coats, shorts, and shirts; footballs; baseballs and gloves; tennis, racquetball, and squash racquets; and golf accessories. Really, anything that's sports related and small is available here. Because of its downtown location, Honus Wagner Co. doesn't stock golf clubs and other large items. But with almost 75 years in business, it's a store to check out.

S.W. Randall Toyes & Giftes
630 Smithfield Street
(412) 562-9252

Step back in time to the days of small, independently owned toy stores when you walk into S.W. Randall's shop. Featuring an extensive selection of educational toys, games, puzzles, and plush animals, the store carries the complete line of Madame Alexander dolls and Wee Forest Folk. The downtown location also features a year-round Christmas shop, train, and hobby department. Additional stores are located in Shadyside, Station Square, and Squirrel Hill.

East

Ambiance
1039 South Braddock Avenue
(412) 243-5523
www.ambianceboutique.org

Ambiance is a wholly owned subsidiary of Bethlehem Haven, a nonprofit organization that supports homeless women. This boutique carries new and consigned designer clothing, shoes, and accessories. You can shop with a purpose here, as proceeds go directly toward Bethlehem Haven's mission. Ambiance recently opened a second location in Oakmont.

D's SixPax & Dogz Shoppe
1118 South Braddock Avenue
(412) 241-4666
www.regentsquare.net

Thirsty? Why not take home a six pack? D's carries over 900 domestic, import, and microbrew beers that are available for "mix and match" takeout. Whether you are looking for an old favorite or want to try something made in Western Pennsylvania, D's should have it. Don't forget to ask them about their Beer Gift Baskets.

Delallo Italian Market Place
Route 30, Jeannette
(724) 523-5000

Since 1950 this family name has supplied its own brand of pastas, peppers, tomato sauce, oils, and vinegar to Pittsburgh-area supermarkets. In Jeannette you can visit the large Italian market where the complete selection of Delallo products is stocked on the shelves. In addition, you'll find an extensive counter of ready-made foods (both hot and cold entrees and salads), fresh breads, candies, and Italian supplies.

Palate Partners
2013 Penn Avenue
(800) 565-2816
www.palatepartners.com

With kitchen gadgets, wine accessories and distinctive gifts, this store is a must-stop for

Shop the Museum Shops

Pittsburgh is home to many museums, and some of the greatest gifts can be found in the museum shops. So after you're through with the exhibits, take some time to tour the stores. You may just find a treasure that you can take home with you!

- Andy Warhol Store, 118 Sandusky Street, (412) 237-8303. Find posters, videos, calendars, stationary, clothing, books, reproductions, and more at this small but very popular shop in the Warhol Museum.
- There are two stores at the Carnegie Museum at 4400 Forbes Avenue in Oakland. The Carnegie Museum of Art Store features books, jewelry, and gifts for children and adults. Kids may also want to stop by the Carnegie Museum of Natural History Store, (412) 622-3309, where they can find dinosaur books, models, and toys, plus much more!
- Another favorite of young and old alike is the XPLOR Store at Carnegie Science Center, (412) 237-3418. From Astronaut Ice Cream to DNA Laboratory kits, science books to IMAX DVDs, you'll find the year's hottest science and technology gifts here.
- If you prefer history, might we suggest a purchase from the Senator John Heinz Pittsburgh Regional History Center Museum Shop, (412) 454-6300; the Frick Art & Historical Center Shop, (412) 371-0600; or the Pennsylvania Trolley Museum Store (724) 228-9256?
- Looking for a gift for someone with a green thumb? Shop no further than Phipps Conservatory & Botanical Gardens Store, (412) 622-6914. This newly expanded store features botanical and horticultural books, educational gardening toys, eco-friendly gifts, and a variety of plants including orchids and bonsai.
- And finally, even though they are not technically museums, we have to mention the shops at the National Aviary, (412) 323-7235, and the Pittsburgh Zoo & PPG Aquarium, (412) 474-4966. Here you'll find great gifts for the little ones, including plush animals, bird feeders, nature music, and much more.

wine connoisseurs. Here you can also order a gift basket (with wine), find out about a local wine tasting led by Dreadnought Wines, or learn about their wine club.

Pittsburgh Center for the Arts Shops
6300 Fifth Avenue
(412) 361-0873
www.pittsburgharts.org
The Pittsburgh Center for the Arts Shops feature original and handcrafted jewelry, ceramics, paintings, prints, glassware, and more. You'll find this location at Fifth and Shady Avenues in Shadyside. Galleries and shops are open Monday through Saturday, from 10:00

a.m. to 5:30 p.m. and on Sunday from noon to 5:00 p.m. The store is accessible for those with physical challenges. In prior years there were other suburban locations, but all operations and sales have been consolidated into this location.

The Pussycat
5824 Forbes Avenue
(412) 521-5977
www.anotherpussycat.com
With more than 35 years of intimate apparel retailing, the Pussycat offers top-quality merchandise, knowledgeable service, and a great selection.

Sugar
3703 Butler Street
(412) 681-5100
www.sugarboutique.com
In the shopping district known as 16:62, you
will find this hip boutique featuring independent designers, one-of-a-kind T-shirts, and
accessories that are, well . . . sweet.

Trader Joe's
6343 Penn Avenue
(412) 363-5748
www.traderjoes.com
Just down the road from Whole Foods, you'll
find Trader Joe's, another national chain that
recently opened a location in Pittsburgh.
Although not as large, nor as serious as
Whole Foods (Trader Joe's crew members
wear Hawaiian shirts), this store has a great
selection of organic foods, prepared entrees,
and yummy snacks.

The Toy Box
108 South Market Street, Ligonier
(724) 238-6233
www.toyboxligonier.com
You'll find quality toys, games, and puzzles for
children of all ages here. Phone orders are
welcome as well. Popular brand names
include Avanti, Brio, Bburago, Erector, Folkma-
nis, Playmobile, Steiff, and Tucker Jones.

Whole Foods Markets
5880 Centre Avenue
(412) 441-7960
www.wholefoodmarket.com
Founded in 1980 in Texas, Whole Foods is
now the world's leading retailer of natural
and organic foods. The Pittsburgh location
opened in East Liberty in 2002 and has
become a popular stop for Pittsburghers,
no matter where they live in the city.

Willi's Ski Shop
3838 William Penn Highway
Route 22, Monroeville
(412) 856-1230
www.skiandboard.net

Shop here for complete ski furnishings,
including clothing and equipment in addition
to snowboarding and tennis accessories.
Additional locations are at Seven Springs Ski
Resort, in the North Hills and South Hills.

West

The Country Mercantile
220 Route 30, Imperial
(412) 695-7251
Country crafts fill the shelves of this quaint little store in rural Imperial, not far from Pittsburgh International Airport and just minutes
from Robinson Town Centre. Fresh-ground coffees, unique teas, candles, crafts, bears, baby
items, and other gift suggestions stock the
store. Visitors who sign the guest register are
invited to special open houses held throughout the year for refreshments and an advance
peek at new holiday-themed merchandise.

Ikea
2001 Park Manor Boulevard
Robinson Town Centre
(412) 747-0747
The only store of its kind in the Pittsburgh
region, this Swedish furniture and home furnishings retailer offers a thoroughly modern
and well-stocked showroom, cafeteria-style
restaurant and cafe areas, and a supervised
ballroom for young children, as well as convenient self-service and efficient checkout. Known
for its inventiveness and thriftiness, the Ikea
concept will be kind on your budget. Most components are easy to assemble, but it's best to
take your measurements carefully before coming to the store. Design specialists are on hand
to assist you. Ikea is open every day except
Thanksgiving, Christmas, and Easter Sunday.

Volkwein's Music
138 Industry Drive, RIDC Park West
(412) 788-5900
www.volkweins.com
Anyone who is serious about music in Pittsburgh knows Volkwein's for its fine reputation
selling musical instruments, band and orchestra accessories, and sheet music. Private

instruction, voice lessons, and instrument rentals are also available. Phone orders are welcome. There is also a Volkwein's located in Ligonier.

North

Alpaca de Moda
120 Three Degree Road, Butler
(724) 586-2412
www.sunsethillsalpaca.com
Featuring handcrafted Peruvian fashions made from alpaca fleece, "From farm to fashion," Alpaca de Moda carries a variety of sweaters, shawls, coats, hats, and more. They also feature toys and home products such as blankets and afghans.

Carlisle's of Pittsburgh
2549 Penn Avenue
(412) 562-5800
www.bridalwear.com
Carlisle's is truly a Pittsburgh wedding tradition. For the past five generations, since 1888, Carlisle's has offered wedding fashions. Here you'll find names such as Vera Wang and Janell Berté on the racks. In 2001 Carlisle's moved from its former North Side location into the new Big Day Wedding and Events Center. Touted as a "wedding mini-mall, this center offers a one-stop shop for the bride and groom.

Wendell August Forge
620 Madison Avenue, Grove City
(724) 748-4132
Allow some time for a tour of the Wendell August Forge in Mercer County, established in 1923 in Brockway and moved to Grove City in 1932. Signs are well placed along major routes into town. It's one of the few remaining forges in the country that continue to produce forged aluminum, pewter, bronze, sterling, and silver articles entirely by hand, using no production machinery.

The showroom houses a historical collection of artifacts and a complete line of giftware that has been commissioned by corporate executives, leading companies, and even the U.S. Congress. Visitors witness the artisans hammering and chiseling artforms as part of the free, self-guided tours available Monday through Saturday. Do call before making the trip to make sure that the forge and/or showroom is open, since it's a bit of a drive from some communities in our coverage area.

South

The Cuckoo's Nest
1513 East Carson Street
(412) 481-4411
www.thecuckoosnest.com
Carrying magic tricks, illusions, books, and DVDs, the Cuckoo's Nest is an aspiring magician's one-stop shop. They will demonstrate tricks and also offer classes and magicians for hire.

Decade Pittsburgh
1407 East Carson Street
(412) 720-1677
www.decadepittsburgh.com
A block away from Slacker, you'll find Decade Pittsburgh, a hip little shop that carries jeans, handbags, hats, and even Punkster, a line of baby onesies and tanks designed by the owner's sister. Steven Ford used to work for Worn Free; now he owns this shop that features the T-shirt line, which features licensed reprints of shirts worn by famous musicians in the '60s and '70s.

The E House Company
1511 East Carson Street
(412) 488-7455
www.ehousecompany.com
Calling itself the "home for green living," E House features organic cotton adult and baby clothing, unique recycled accessories and gifts, and natural household products. From Burt's Bees to Little Earth, Inc., products, E House offers a wonderful and clever variety of goods.

Fireborn Studios
2338 Sarah Street
(412) 488-6835
www.fireborn.com
Established in 1985, Fireborn Studios features a full line of functional and decorative pottery—

Close-up

Pittsburgh Products

Pittsburgh Pride extends to gift giving. No matter if you're a sports fan, beer connoisseur, Christmas collector, or card player, there's a Pittsburgh product for you or your loved one. Here's a sampling of hometown products we've found:

- Couch potatoes will want to curl up with more than 20 different videos produced by WQED/Pittsburgh. From Frank Lloyd Wright's House on the Waterfall or Kennywood Memories to The Strip Show or Pittsburgh's Greatest Sport Heroes, each video costs $19.95 plus tax. These are available online at www.wqed.org, or call (412) 622-1370.
- Also from WQED, find products based on Mister Roger's Neighborhood, including Play Time, a 128-page book packed with ideas for entertaining activities. You can also give Daniel Striped Tiger or Henrietta Pussycat to your favorite little someone.
- For music loving adults, we'd suggest one of the Grammy-nominated CDs from the MCG Jazz collection ($15 each). These recordings, produced locally through Manchester Craftsmen's Guild on Pittsburgh's North Side, feature jazz greats such as Nancy Wilson, Paquito D'Rivera, Stanley Turentine, and Dizzie Gillespie. Purchase online at www.mcgjazz.org, or call (412) 322-1733.
- Looking for something stylish and made in Pittsburgh? Try Little Earth Productions, Inc. (www.littleearth.com, 800-545-3784). Founded in 1993, they create eco-fashion, making purses and CD cases out of recycled licenses plates and belts from recycled bottle caps and rubber tires. Their new line, Pro-FANity, includes purses made from recycled materials and featuring one of 32 NFL team logos.
- "You went to Pittsburgh, and brought me back a towel?" That's not just any towel, it's a Terrible Towel, the gold terrycloth sensation created by the late local broadcasting legend Myron Cope. Steeler fans wave the towels, fast and furious, at football games, cheering their team to victory. Available for $6.95 plus tax/shipping from www.steelers.com or (800) 832-6883.
- Last, but certainly not least, how about some notecards. Remember Pittsburgh is a line of notecards, T-shirts, and other items featuring black-and-white photographs of "the old days" in the "Burgh. There are more than 57,000 photos in the catalog, all available as reprints. Visit www.rememberpittsburgh.org or call (412) 622-3154 for more details.

sushi ware, dinnerware, serving pieces, vases and more—made by the proprietors and other craftspeople on-site. Fireborn also offers pottery classes for children and adults.

Gals On and Off the Green
7440 McKnight Road
(412) 630-8808
www.galsonandoffthegreen.com
Focusing on moderate to high-priced highly fashionable golf apparel and country club leisure wear, Gals also stocks gifts, home accents, and even some whimsical offerings.

Gram & Gramps
1720 Washington Road, Upper St. Clair
(412) 831-4726
Not only will you find a great selection of top-quality toys (including Neuro Smith, Thomas, and Playmobile), but you'll also be able to out-fit the kids in this all-in-one store. Named for doting grandparents, it's probably appropriate. While prices on the toy merchandise are competitive, the clothing lines are a little upscale. But then, grandparents want only the best!

McGinnis Sisters Specialty Foods
3825 Saw Mill Run Boulevard
Route 51, Brentwood
(412) 882-6400
If you're in the market for supreme cuts of meat, plentiful produce, fresh fish, gourmet cheeses, and ready-made pasta salads, McGinnis Sisters is the place to go. With one other location at 4311 Northern Pike, Monroeville, the McGinnis Sisters stores host occasional Saturday events with samples of seasonal items. Special orders are accepted. Why not join in a cooking class also? Find out more by calling the store near you.

Original Cin
1922 East Carson Street
(412) 431-6246
www.originalcin.org
With price points ranging from $14 to $600, Original Cin has something for everyone—fun

women's designer wear, Ts for men, gifts for all, and accessories galore. Owned by a mother and daughter who love to shop, the store's design concept is based on the Garden of Eden.

The Riverside Shoppes
127 Speers Street, Lower Speers
(724) 483-2290
Situated midway between Washington and New Stanton and just two minutes off Route 70, this complex sits along a wooden walkway and cozy courtyard. In this colonial setting you'll find 16 shops awaiting you with everything for the home, for the luxurious bathroom, for a gourmet kitchen, and much more.

Slacker
1321 East Carson Street
(412) 381-3911
The inventory at this alternative clothing store, founded in the 1990s, includes clothing by AnarchTee and Rebel 8, body jewelry, Special Effects hair dye, vintage Ts, and even Mexican wrestler masks.

Trunk Show Boutique
30 Donati Road
(412) 833-6467
www.trunkshowboutique.com
With clothing and accessories for ladies, this boutique also offers hostess gift ideas, custom tailoring, and a unique collection of designers.

CONSIGNMENT STORES
East
Music Go Round
431 Old William Penn Highway, Monroeville
(412) 856-8742
If you need musical instruments that don't cost bundles, then head here. This store is great for the parents of aspiring musicians just taking up an instrument in school. You'll find guitars, drums, clarinets, flutes, and all the other popular instruments as well as speakers, amplifiers, and accessories.

South

Yesterday's Best
141 Main Street, New Eagle
(724) 258-8112
Located in Washington County, this old house is full of everything on consignment that's related to the home. Dishes, pots and pans, linens, furniture, and antiques are here, but no clothing.

West

Second Hand Rose
411 Walnut Street, Sewickley
(412) 741-5909
Men's, women's, and children's gently worn apparel is found here, along with accessories, ties, shoes, and hats. Some designer labels are available, as well as selected formal wear, suits, and dresses.

North

Once Upon A Child
3747 William Penn Highway, Monroeville
(412) 374-9932
www.ouac.com
Outfit the kids for less here at Once Upon A Child. Not only will you find play and dressy clothing for the kids, but a selection of quality used toys and children's furnishings. Strollers, portable cribs, and potties prevail, too. The store's location is in Holiday Center Shopping Plaza.

OUTLET SHOPPING

North

Prime Outlets at Grove City
Interstate 79 at the Grove City/
New Wilmington exit
(888) 545-7221
www.primeoutlets.com
In 1994 the Grove City Factory Shops, smack between the towns of New Wilmington and Grove City, put this region in the news as savvy shoppers combed racks and roamed aisles of outlets in search of the ultimate bargain. Now the complex is called the Prime

i Thrift stores such as Goodwill, Salvation Army, and St. Vincent De Paul stores are plentiful throughout the region.

Outlets. With the fourth phase completed, the shops now include 533,000 square feet—a virtual shopper's mecca. The more than 130 stores here include Ann Taylor Factory Store, Liz Claiborne Outlet, Calvin Klein, Eddie Bauer, and many other popular retailers.

From downtown Pittsburgh, count on at least an hour's drive (perhaps less from northern suburbs). Shuttle buses run daily to take shoppers around the outlets—it's that big. Customer services (located in the food court) include gift certificates, stroller rentals, wheelchair loans, area tourist information, coupon books, and lost-and-found services.

East

Georgian Place
707 Georgian Place, Somerset
(814) 443-3818
Just off the Pennsylvania Turnpike at Somerset lies another outlet complex that has been serving up finds for outlet shoppers for many years. Opened in April 1990 as the Horizon Outlet Center, Georgian Place is approximately one hour from Pittsburgh (less perhaps from the eastern suburbs). Retailers here include Cooke's Furniture, Bauer's, Van Heusen, and Express Yourself Gifts. There is also an antiques mall located here.

Lenox Factory Outlet
Route 31 East, Mt. Pleasant
(724) 547-9555
www.lenox.com
Located in Mt. Pleasant, the Lenox Factory Outlet saves you 15 to 20 percent off suggested retail prices on quality china and crystal gifts, dinnerware, stemware, and barware. At the Lenox Factory Clearance Center, save up to 60 percent off suggested retail prices of seconds, overstocks, and discontinued and

ℹ️ For antiquing, try the main drag in the little town of Blawnox, past Fox Chapel on Route 28 North or the "16:62 Design Zone" along Butler Street, between the 16th Street Bridge in the Strip and the 62nd Street Bridge in Lawrenceville. You'll also find numerous other sorts of shops—about 70 in the Design Zone, most of them arts-related in some way.

special products. The outlet is open from 10:00 a.m. to 5:00 p.m. Monday through Saturday and 12:00 to 5:00 p.m. on Sunday.

L.E. Smith Glass Company
1900 Liberty Street, Mt. Pleasant
(724) 547-3544
www.lesmithglass.com
At L.E. Smith Glass Company, they've been crafting handmade glass for nearly a century. Using many techniques of original artisans, today's craftsmen mold, shape, heat, and cool beautiful glassware. Factory tours are available Monday through Friday from 9:00 a.m. to 2:00 p.m. The Factory Outlet & Giftware Store is open daily until 5:00 p.m., but it's closed on weekends from January through March and on all national holidays. Don't miss the annual "Christmas in July" sale held during the first two weeks of the month.

ANTIQUES & FLEA MARKETS
East

Ages Ago Antiques
722 Allegheny River Boulevard, Verona
(412) 828-9800
Moderately priced antiques here include furniture, lamps, lace, glassware, pottery, rugs, collectibles, toys, and paintings. The store is open Monday through Saturday from 10:00 a.m. to 4:30 p.m., but it's closed Sunday. Evening hours are by appointment only.

East End Galleries
600 Clyde Street
(412) 682-6331

Popular with Pittsburgh antiques lovers, East End Galleries displays paintings, objéts d'art, and furniture—genuine antiques only, not reproductions.

Hanna's Town Antiques & Collectibles Show
Between Routes 119 and 819 in Historic Hanna's Town
(724) 836-1800
Three miles north of Greensburg, in a large open field, you'll find this show and sale held several times each year. This one-day market ends up being more like a two-day event, according to those who frequent it. Technically held on the second Sunday of each month (May through September), some bargains can be found throughout Saturday. Hours are usually 7:30 a.m. until early afternoon.

South
Antiques Downtown
88 South Main Street, Washington
(724) 222-6800
This store carries a general line of antiques, including Duncan & Miller and other American handmade glass. They specialize in glass and china. Bring your Civil War (or any war) collector here—the shop offers swords, badges, pins, books, and other military memorabilia.

The Antiques Fair at the Meadows
Race Track Road, North Strabane Township
(724) 228-3045
Voted the best flea market by *Pittsburgh Magazine* readers, this Washington County flea market offers some 600 different dealers who put out their wares the last Sunday of each month from February through November. Better quality antiques and collectibles are featured. There are indoor as well as outdoor dealers from 8:00 a.m. to 3:00 p.m.

Where The Toys Are
45 West Pike Street, Canonsburg
(724) 745-4599
Indeed an antiques store, this place specializes in turn-of-the-20th-century through baby boomer–era toys, old Barbies and other dolls,

trains, vehicles, action figures, TV-show and movie tie-in toys, comic characters, GI Joe and Star Wars figures, and memorabilia. The owner of this unusual store travels to different antiques shows, so it's best to call for updated store hours.

Whiskey Run Antiques Southpointe
US 19 South, Canonsburg
(724) 745-5808
Named because of its location in the 1794 Whiskey Rebellion area, this shop sits between Pittsburgh and Washington off I-79. More than 40 professional dealers offer upscale antiques, including 18th- and 19th-century country and formal furniture along with appropriate accessories such as glassware, pottery, and silver. Appraisals, clock repairs, and lamp repairs are offered as well. It's open daily from 10:00 a.m. to 5:00 p.m.

West

The Antique Emporium
818 Seventh Avenue, Beaver Falls
(724) 847-1919
Here you'll find three floors devoted to antiques and collectibles from more than 75 quality antiques dealers. There are no crafts and only a few reproductions. But you'll find the usual array of furniture, military wares, glass, and collectibles. The store is open Monday through Saturday from 10:00 a.m. until 5:00 p.m. and Sunday from noon until 5:00 p.m.

North

Wildwood Peddlers Fair
2330 Wildwood Road, Hampton Township
(412) 487-2200
This indoor and outdoor flea market is held weekly, featuring an eclectic mixture of brand-new items, coins, collectibles, and antiques to typical yard-sale-quality merchandise. It's open on Sunday from 6:00 a.m. until 3:00 p.m.

ATTRACTIONS

Sightseeing around this diverse city is more than an afternoon's entertainment or a day away from it all. Pittsburgh is particularly rich with memories of eras past, parks as pleasurable as you'll find, and culture that flourishes here.

Whether you choose to spend your leisure time learning, poking through Pittsburgh's past, exploring nature, or simply seeing the sights, opportunities abound for you throughout the entire region.

Note that the usual geographic headers are being deviated from in this chapter—most of these attractions are worth driving to, even if they're not in your immediate area. You can look forward to learning about educational venues, touring famous homes, venturing out to parks and other fun places, and browsing through some of our notable museums.

While many of the most popular attractions are situated in or near the city of Pittsburgh, and within Allegheny County, a fair number await your discovery in surrounding counties. So enjoy the listing presented here. Your fun-filled opportunities will soon transform into fond memories. And you'll keep coming back for more!

EDUCATIONAL ATTRACTIONS

The Carnegie Museums
4400 Forbes Avenue
(412) 622-3131
www.cmoa.org
www.carnegiemuseums.org
www.clpgh.org
Culture, history, and art appreciation abound in our area because of renowned turn-of-the-20th-century Pittsburgher Andrew Carnegie, who resolved at an early age to use his phe-

nomenal wealth for benevolent purposes. This led to the creation of Carnegie Institute and Carnegie Library, as well as the Carnegie Music Hall and Lecture Hall, the Museum of Art, and the Museum of Natural History. Along with the Carnegie Science Center and The Andy Warhol Museum, these entities all fall under the organizational banner of The Carnegie Museums.

Inside, pick up a visitor orientation map of the Museums of Art and Natural History. This will guide you through three floors of exhibits including the newly renovated Dinosaur Hall (see Kidstuff), the natural history gallery, the Benedum Hall of Geology, Hillman Hall of Minerals & Gems, Walton Hall of Ancient Egypt, and the Heinz Architectural Center (see Architecture). Additional displays feature African and North American wildlife, botany, fossils, insects, amphibians, and reptiles, as well as the Wyckoff Hall of Arctic Life.

Upstairs is the permanent collection of the Scaife Galleries as well as exhibitions of limited runs.

Before leaving the Carnegie, walk through the Hall of Sculpture, made famous as a backdrop in the movie *Flashdance*. Each holiday season, the Hall of Architecture hosts a display of beautifully decorated Christmas trees (see Festivals and Annual Events).

A coffee cart is available inside the complex, and the Museum Cafe serves meals during certain hours (see Restaurants). A brown-bag lunch area is located in the basement with vending machines for sandwiches, snacks, and beverages.

Andrew Carnegie's legacy is predominantly felt through his contribution to literacy with the entire system of Carnegie Libraries, with branches throughout the city. The main

Carnegie Music Hall. LINDSEY KEOGH

library is part of the Oakland complex, next to the Music Hall and post office. Highlights here include the Pennsylvania Room, the Foundation Center, and the Ready Reference telephone unit, as well as the general holdings of the book, video, and periodical collections.

Hours at the museum are Monday through Saturday from 10:00 a.m. to 5:00 p.m. and Sunday from noon to 5:00 p.m.

Carnegie Library is open Monday through Thursday from 10:00 a.m. to 8:00 p.m., Friday and Saturday from 10:00 a.m. to 5:30 p.m., and Sunday from 1:00 to 5:00 p.m. Admission to the library is free of charge. Admission to the Carnegie Museum of Natural History and Museum of Art is $10 for adults, $7 for senior citizens, and $6 for children (ages 3 to 18). Children younger than age 3 and members are admitted free of charge.

Carnegie Science Center
One Allegheny Avenue
(412) 237-3400
www.carnegiesciencecenter.org
Along the north shore of the Ohio River is the Carnegie Science Center, recognizable because the USS *Requin* submarine moors along the banks of the river. This facility grew out of the older institution known as Buhl Planetarium. Now it boasts not only a new planetarium and observatory but also indoor displays of science, technology, and health care as well as the miniature railroad display that's open almost year-round (see Annual Events).

Rangos Omnimax Theater film presentations, hands-on learning, and a guided tour of the submarine, commissioned during World War II, are available (see Kidstuff). The center extends its hours in the summer at times.

Close-up

The August Wilson Center for African American Culture

Pittsburgh is known for its multi-cultural heritage resulting from the immigrants who were attracted to the region's booming economy during the Industrial Age. Among these cultures is that of African Americans, who have made significant impact and contributions in the region and around the world.

The August Wilson Center for African American Culture (AWC) is a not-for-profit organization that presents performing, visual and education programs that celebrates the contributions of African Americans within the region and the impact of cultural expressions from Africa to the African Diaspora.

For three years, the AWC has presented a season of performances and exhibits that includes a diverse mix of dance, theater, spoken word, and visual arts. Productions are presented and co-presented in theaters in Pittsburgh's Cultural District and in other neighborhoods. Events have included "A Tribute to African American Heroes," "First Voice: A Pittsburgh International Black Arts Festival," the Drakensber Boys' Choir, and "An Evening with Spike Lee."

In mid-2006, the AWC started construction of a 67,000 square foot facility that will house a vibrant mix of cultural activities through engaging and inter-disciplinary presentations. Named in honor of August Wilson, a Pittsburgh native and Pulitzer-winning playwright, the Center will be more than a museum, including galleries, classrooms, a 500-seat theater, gift shop, café and multi-purpose spaces. The new facility will house exhibits that help tell the story of how African American culture has developed, including both historical and current experiences.

The center is scheduled to open in 2008. For more information, contact the center at (412) 258-2700 or visit www.africanaculture.org.

—With thanks to August Wilson Center for African American Culture

Regular hours, Sunday through Friday 10:00 a.m. until 5:00 p.m. and Saturday 10:00 a.m. to 7:00 p.m. An Explorer Pass for adults costs $14, $10 for children.

Tickets are also sold separately for Omnimax, submarine, laser shows, and exhibits, if you prefer to see only one part of the center. For instance, to see the exhibits only, admission costs $14 for adults and $10 for seniors (ages 65 and above) and children (ages 3 through 18). For the Omnimax theater alone, expect to pay $8 or $6. Combination ticket packages are available, and prices are listed at the desk and given by telephone on the automated information line (call number given above). Senior discounts are extended on Tuesday. Purchasing a membership to the science center allows complimentary admission. Parking is free.

Nationality Rooms
157 Cathedral of Learning
University of Pittsburgh
(412) 624-6000
www.pih.edu/~natrooms
Twenty-six classrooms (and the number con-

tinues to grow) in this towering cathedral depict the city's diverse ethnic heritage through their individual architecture and decor. In the 1920s over a quarter of Pittsburgh's population had been born abroad, and another fifth were the offspring of foreign-born parents. At Pitt, one of every three students was foreign-born or the child of immigrants.

Thus, chancellor John Baggert Bowman and others conceived of these special rooms so as not to disappoint visitors who saw the impressive structure outside. Each was funded by ethnic committees, designed by native architects, and built with materials from the countries they represent. Access to the classrooms is by tour only. Recorded tours are offered if you like. Tours are also available between 11:00 a.m. and 2:30 p.m. on most days. The Nationality Rooms are open Monday through Friday 9:00 a.m. to 2:30 p.m., Saturday 9:30 a.m. to 2:30 p.m., and Sunday 11:00 a.m. to 2:30 p.m. Admission rates are $3 for adults, $2 for seniors (ages 60 and older), and 50 cents for children (ages 8 to 18). Children age 7 and younger are admitted free.

HISTORICAL ATTRACTIONS

Air Heritage Museum
Beaver County Airport
15 Piper Street, Beaver Falls
(724) 843-2820
www.airheritage.org
This museum boasts a rich heritage of aviation with vintage aircraft, warplanes, and aeronautical artifacts. Volunteers at this museum work hard to make some of these old "war birds" or aircraft fly again. Some of the aircraft date from the 1920s. Visitors can shop for flying paraphernalia in the gift shop. Proceeds from the planes' appearances in air shows, movies, and commercials help to support the restoration process, as do donations from the public and gift shop sales. Here you'll find that behind every plane is, of course, a war story to go along with it! The Air Heritage Museum is open to the public

from 10:00 a.m. to 5:00 p.m. Monday through Saturday, 11:00 a.m. to 6:00 p.m. Sunday. A small donation per person is requested.

Beaver Area Historical Museum
East End Avenue, Beaver
(724) 775-7174
www.bchistory.org/beavercounty/Beaver
CountyCommunties/Beaverfolder/History
Museum/HistoryMuseum.html
Housed in the renovated Pittsburgh and Lake Erie Railroad freight station, this museum tells the story of Beaver County. Residents and visitors alike will enjoy the collection of artifacts and information about life in years past. Some of the exhibits include a Revolutionary War uniform and equipment, Civil War weaponry, archaeological specimens from area digs, and examples of local pottery. Publications and gifts are features in the museum shop. The historical attraction is open on Wednesday and Saturday from 10:00 a.m. until 4:00 p.m. and on Sunday from 1:00 to 4:00 p.m. Admission is free of charge. Donations are welcome.

Butler County Heritage Center
119 West New Castle Street, Butler
(724) 283-8116
www.butlercountyhistoricalsociety-pa.org
/heritagecenter.html
After searching for more than 20 years for a place to archive its artifacts and memorabilia, residents of Butler County found just such a site. In 1994 the Butler County Heritage Society purchased a three-story building that opened the following year, with a 4,500-square-foot exhibit entitled "Made in Butler County," which includes an original Bantam jeep, the Bantam Hollywood prototype convertible sports car, and displays representative of Butler industries both past and

i A total of 218 covered bridges remain standing throughout Pennsylvania. The common nickname for many of these structures was "the kissin' bridges." Well, you can probably figure out why!

present. Metered on-street parking is available. The Heritage Center is open weekends May through October.

Fort Ligonier
U.S. Route 30 and Route 711, Ligonier
(724) 238-9701
www.fortligonier.org
A battle site of the French and Indian War, Fort Ligonier is located on US 30 and Route 711 in Westmoreland County. On October 12, 1758, the British overcame a few French and only a few hundred Indian forces. The fort is open daily May 1 through October 31 from 10:00 a.m. to 4:30 p.m. Monday through Saturday and noon to 4:30 p.m. Sunday. Fort Ligonier Days are held each October (see the Annual Events chapter). Admission fees are $8.00 for adults, $4.75 for children ages 6 to 14, and $7.50 for seniors. Children younger than age 6 are admitted free of charge.

Fort Necessity National Battlefield and Braddock's Grave
One Washington Parkway, Farmington
(724) 329-5512
www.nps.gov/fone/home.htm
Along what's called the National Road (otherwise known as U.S. Route 40), there's a little bit of history from the French and Indian War. Here, on July 3, 1754, a French and Indian force surrounded George Washington's "fort of necessity" and forced his only military surrender. Fort Necessity park grounds and visitor center are run by the National Park Service and open to the public daily from 9:00 a.m. to 5:00 p.m. throughout the year (except for Veterans Day, Thanksgiving, Christmas Day, New Year's Day, Martin Luther King Jr. Day, and President's Day. Besides the battlefield, don't miss other related sites, including the grave of British general Edward Braddock, a commanding officer who was mortally wounded in the war and buried just up the road. Jumonville Glen was the site of Washington's first skirmish with the French. And the park also operates the Mount Washington Tavern, built in 1828 to serve travelers along the National Road.

Picnic facilities are available during summer months. Start at the visitor center with the audiovisual program and exhibits before moving through the grounds, where on a warm day you'll see Indians demonstrating crafts and telling the story of survival at Fort Necessity. Admission to Fort Necessity, which includes the fort, the museum exhibits, and the Mount Washington Tavern, costs $5 per person. Children age 15 and younger are admitted free of charge.

Harmony Museum
218 Mercer Street, Harmony
(724) 452-7341, (888) 821-4822
www.harmonymuseum.org
Surrounding the diamond in the village of Harmony are many of the original buildings erected by the Harmonists, immigrant German separatists, in the early 1800s. Johann George Rapp was a German vinetender-turned-prophet. Several of his followers traveled with him to the New World, fleeing religious persecution and finding the freedom here they could not have in their European homeland. Rapp purchased acreage in Western Pennsylvania. Their religious fervor prospered until 1807, when they adopted celibacy, a step toward the ultimate extinction of the group. Subsequently, the Mennonites settled here from 1815 through much of the 19th century.

The Harmony Museum, including the Wagner House and Ziegler log house, as well as the Harmonist cemetery, Father Rapp's hillside seat, and the Mennonite meetinghouse and cemetery, are under the direction of Historic Harmony. Appointments are recommended for the weekends. Tours are given Tuesday through Sunday, 1:00 to 4:00 p.m. year-round. General admission is $3.50; seniors (ages 60 and older) pay $3.00; children (ages 6 through 12) get in for $1.50; children age 6 and younger are admitted free of charge.

Meadowcroft Museum of Rural Life
401 Meadowcroft Road, Avella
(724) 587-3412
http://meadowcroft.pghhistory.org

Experience life in the 19th century, as it was in Western Pennsylvania. This 200-acre living-history museum in Washington County offers lessons on rural life for the entire family (see Kidstuff). Meadowcroft introduces you to the Native Americans, frontier settlers, farmers, lumbermen, coal miners, and conservationists who have shaped rural Western Pennsylvania You'll get to try your hands at spinning wool or attend a class in a one-room school. Included on the grounds are wooded paths, gardens, a picnic area, a gift shop, a cafe, and a modern visitor center. Meadowcroft is open Memorial Day through Labor Day Wednesday through Saturday from noon to 5:00 p.m. and on Sunday from 1:00 to 5:00 p.m. Groups of 20 or more can call for appointments. To enter, adults pay $10; seniors pay $9; and children (ages 6 through 16), $5. Children younger than age 6 are admitted free of charge.

Old Economy Village
270 Sixteenth Street, Ambridge
(724) 266-4500, (724) 266-1803
www.oldeconomyvillage.org

Visit the third and final home of the Harmony Society here at Old Economy Village in Beaver County. This National Historic Landmark is administered by the Pennsylvania Historical and Museum Commission. The Harmonists were one of America's most successful Christian communal groups. Wearing Harmonist dress, interpreters take you through the museum building, cabinet shop, community kitchen, baker house, wine cellar, store, and George and Frederick Rapp Houses, all of which were built between 1825 and 1830. Browse through four buildings and the gardens independently. Original objects owned by the Harmonists are displayed.

Tours are conducted Tuesday through Saturday 9:00 a.m. to 5:00 p.m. and Sunday noon to 5:00 p.m. If you're visiting in fall or winter, the tours end at 2:30 p.m. Old Economy Village is closed Monday and winter holidays and during January and February. Special holiday decorations and activities are seen at particular times throughout the year (see Annual Events). Admission costs $7 for adults (18

years and older), $6 for seniors (60 years and older), $5 for youths (6 years to 17 years), and no charge for those younger than 6 years old.

Pennsylvania Trolley Museum
1 Museum Road (Off Race Track Road), Washington
(724) 228-9256
www.pa-trolley.org

South of Pittsburgh in Washington County, vintage streetcars depict transportation from another era. Home of "A Streetcar Named Desire," this museum rebuilds and restores these relics for your enjoyment. Kids especially enjoy the special events such as Santa's visit each year (see our Kidstuff and Annual Events chapters).

Allow at least two hours to completely experience the museum. Please note the museum is closed during the months of January and February. From March 1 through December 31, the museum is open from 10:00 a.m. to 5:00 p.m. Monday through Thursday and 11:00 a.m. to 5:00 p.m. Saturday and Sunday. It's open weekdays also, Memorial Day through Labor Day, from 10:00 a.m. to 4:00 p.m. Admission costs $8 for adults, $7 for seniors (age 62 and older), and $5 for children (ages 3 to 15). Children age 2 and younger receive free admission.

Senator John Heinz Pittsburgh Regional History Center
1212 Smallman Street
(412) 454-6000
www.pghhistory.org

Named in memory of the late U.S. Senator John Heinz, this center in the Strip District is home to the Historical Society of Western Pennsylvania and serves as a museum and depository of regional history. Four floors of exhibits tell of building a life in Western Pennsylvania from 1750 to the present. Many of the displays are interactive, informative, and entertaining. A library and archives are housed on the sixth floor.

The center's first floor offers a video inside an actual trolley car, reminiscent of Pittsburgh's past. There are also famous neon

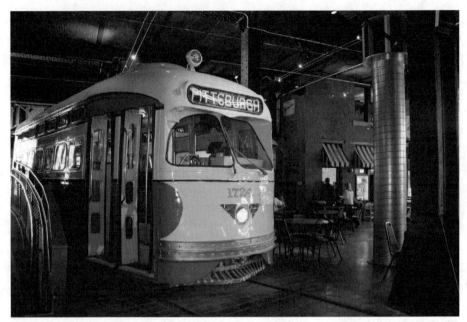

The Senator John Heinz Pittsburgh Regional History Center. ALAN AND BARBARA VENTO

signs depicting well-known merchants and companies through the years. Large staircases and elevators take you to the exhibit areas, starting with the second floor and its dramatic contrast of Pittsburgh in the pioneer days with its status today (as seen through a large screen image). A 10-minute orientation video introduces the exhibits you'll see on this floor of the permanent collection.

On the museum's third floor, children enjoy the Discovery Place (see Kidstuff). Changing exhibit galleries grace the fourth floor, where past displays have included "Toy Bop," "Glass: Shattering Notions," and the "History of Heinz 57" (a history of the Heinz Company).

The center is also home to the Western Pennsylvania Sports Museum, which spans 20,000 square feet of exhibit space over two floors. This "museum within a museum" highlights Pittsburgh's impact as a sports leader over more than a century, from amateur to pro and across the spectrum of sports. The Sports Museum features hundreds of artifacts, more than 70 hands-on interactive exhibits and 20

audio-visual programs. Here, you can see Franco Harris' "Immaculate Reception" shoes; Mario Lemieux's hockey skates, and Chip Ganassi's 2000 Indy 500–winning race car. There are also hundreds of Pirates baseball cards, and much, much more.

The Heinz History Center is open daily from 10:00 a.m. to 5:00 p.m. The library is open Thursday through Saturday 10:00 a.m. until 5:00 p.m. The center is closed Easter, Thanksgiving, Christmas, and New Year's Day. Cost for adults is $9.00, $7.00 for seniors (ages 65 and above) and students (with ID), and $5.00 for children (ages 6 to 18). Children younger than age 6 are admitted at no cost. All rates include admission to both the History Center and the Western Pennsylvania Sports Museum.

HERALDED HOMES

Armstrong County Historical Museum
300 North McKean Street and Vine Street, Kittanning
(724) 548-5707

This Federal-style house was built in 1842 and added on to with a spacious wing in 1990. It was known as the McCain House before the change to its present name. Today it's a museum offering the public seasonal exhibits, a historical and genealogical library, and an educational classroom center. It's open Wednesday noon to 4:00 p.m. During the winter months, this attraction is closed. Special tours can be arranged by appointment.

Clayton
Penn and Homewood Avenues
(412) 371-0600
www.frickart.org/home
Henry Clay Frick and his wife, Adelaide, purchased this as their home in Pointe Breeze in 1882. Clayton, as the house was called, was an example of the Italianate homes built following the Civil War. But the Fricks, wanting a new look, had the house remodeled, giving it steep roofs and gables. (See the Architecture chapter.)

The Fricks' daughter, Helen Clay Frick, inherited the home, and after she died in 1984, it was willed to the family's foundation. In 1990 Clayton opened to the public and is now part of the Frick Art & Historical Center (see the Arts chapter). There is free parking. The center is open Tuesday through Saturday from 10:00 a.m. until 5:00 p.m. and on Sunday from noon until 6:00 p.m. Clayton is closed on Monday. Tours of Clayton cost $10 for adults, and $8 for seniors and students. Members are admitted free of charge.

Fallingwater
Mill Run (off US 40), Fayette County
(724) 329-8501
www.wpconline.org/fallingwaterhome.htm
Frank Lloyd Wright's spectacular house set atop a waterfall is an architectural masterpiece of the 20th century. Back in the 1930s, Pittsburgh department store owner Edgar J. Kaufmann and his wife, Liliane, commissioned Wright to design their weekend retreat at Bear Run, 90 minutes south of Pittsburgh. Tucked among the rhododen-

drons, the house uses cantilevers, enabling the terraces of the living and bedroom levels to extend over the rushing falls without visible support.

Now under the care of the Western Pennsylvania Conservancy, the house can be toured by visitors, but reservations are suggested. Fallingwater is open daily except Wednesday, mid-March through Thanksgiving weekend, from 10:00 a.m. to 4:00 p.m. Winter hours (weather permitting) are 11:00 a.m. to 3:00 p.m. December weekends, the week between Christmas and New Year's, and the first two weekends in March. Regular tours are $16 for adults and $10 for youths (ages 6 to 12). In-depth tours cost $55, and sunset tours are $100. You may explore the grounds only for $6 per person.

Children younger than age 6 are not permitted, but group babysitting is available at $2 per hour per child at the Visitors Pavilion. With the many stairs, considerable walking is required, so make arrangements in advance for special assistance if you feel you'll need it.

Hartwood
200 Hartwood Acres
(412) 767-9200
In the northeastern suburbs of Pittsburgh lies the Hartwood estate, 629 equestrian acres with stables, gardens, and summer music and theater performances. The Tudor-style mansion is fully furnished with English and American antiques, and there is a gate lodge designed by Alfred Hopkins. This is the site of the special holiday lights tour (see Annual Events). Mansion tours are conducted by reservation only. Hartwood is open April 1 through December 31; closed January through March and major holidays. Hartwood opens its doors Wednesday through Saturday, 10:00 a.m. to 3:00 p.m. and Sunday noon to 4:00 p.m. It's closed Monday and Tuesday. Admission costs $5 per adult, $3 for seniors (age 60 and older), $3 for children ages 13 to 17, $2 for children ages 6 to 12, and $1 for children age 5 and younger.

Kentuck Knob
Chalk Hill, Ohiopyle
(724) 329-1901
www.kentuckknob.com

High above a mountain overlooking the Youghiogheny River Gorge near Fallingwater is another of Frank Lloyd Wright's creations. Built of native stone and tidewater cypress, this house was commissioned by the I. N. Hagan family of Uniontown. Contemporary sculpture and historic artifacts enhance the secluded setting. Kentuck Knob is open daily 9:00 a.m. to 4:00 p.m. Regular tours are $16 for adults and $10 for children ages 6 to 12. In-depth tours ($55 per person) are available Tuesday through Sunday, 1:15 to 2:30 p.m. Sunset tours (3:00 to 5:00 p.m.) cost $100 per person and include complimentary wine and hors d'oeuvres in the living room. Children younger than age 6 are not permitted.

LeMoyne House
49 East Maiden Street, Washington
(724) 225-6740
www.wchspa.org/html/house.htm

Discover why LeMoyne House is a trail to the Civil War. This historic 1812 structure once was an abolitionist home and shelter to escaping slaves. The house is named for Dr. Francis Julius LeMoyne, who converted words into action, at great personal risk, as he sheltered escaping slaves on the Underground Railroad, established a college for African Americans, and rescued Washington College from bankruptcy. LeMoyne House is administered by the Washington County Historical Society, which makes tours available. The property is open from February through mid-December, Tuesday through Friday, 11:00 a.m. to 4:00 p.m. and Saturday by appointment. Admission is $4 for adults and $2 for students.

Linden Hall
432 Linden Hall Road, Dawson
(724) 529-7543, (800) 944-3238
www.lindenhallpa.com

Listed on the National Register of Historical Places, Linden Hall Mansion and Recreation Center was built in Fayette County in 1913, with its grand view of the Laurel Highlands. Enjoy 35 rooms of the exquisite English Tudor mansion featuring signed Tiffany windows, an Aeolian pipe organ, wonderfully restored Victorian furnishings, and original paintings. In addition, there are gardens and trails for warm-weather walks. The estate offers lodging, dining, and recreation. Tours are conducted daily April through October, 11:00 a.m. to 3:00 p.m. (weekends, by reservation). Tours are available only for groups of 25 or more.

If you want to visit in November and December, you may, but by appointment only. To enter, each person can expect to pay $7.

Passavant House & Buhl House
243 and 221 South Main Street, Zelienople
(724) 4529457
boro.zelienople.pa.us/historical_society.htm

Local history abounds in this Butler County community, where these two homes have been converted to museums. Baron Dettmar Freiderich Basse, an aristocrat, invited daughter Zelie and her husband, Philipp Louis Passavant, to join him at the land he'd purchased in the early 1800s. The couple's five children were born in Passavant House, which dates from 1808. Their progeny continued their hardworking tradition, establishing churches, hospitals, orphanages, and schools in the area.

Son Charles married the granddaughter of Christian and Fredericka Buhl, another famous name to Western Pennsylvania, associated with the Buhl Planetarium and the former Boggs and Buhl Department Store on the city's North Side. Buhl House, built in 1805, houses a museum of the Buhl family in its 10 rooms. Contact the Zelienople Historical Society (telephone listed above) for tours. Admission includes a guided tour of both homes, with the general admission price set at $3.50 per person. Children ages 6 through 17 and students cost $2.50. Children younger than age 6 are admitted free of charge.

Rachel Carson Homestead
613 Marion Avenue, Springdale
(724) 274-5459
www.rachelcarsonhomestead.org
At the birthplace and childhood home of ecol-
ogist Rachel Carson (1907–1964), there are
guided tours available to homestead visitors.
Carson's 1962 best-seller *Silent Spring* helped
launch the environmental movement. This
legendary home has seasonal hours, so call
before heading here. Admission costs $4.00
for adults, $3.00 for seniors, and $2.50 for
kids ages 5 to 12.

ON THE WILD SIDE

Idlewild Park and SoakZone
U.S. Route 30, Ligonier
(724) 238-3666
www.idlewild.com
Set in the Laurel Highlands of Westmoreland
County, Idlewild is an amusement park where
you'll want to pack for a picnic. Theme areas
include Story Book Forest, Mister Rogers'
Neighborhood of Make-Believe, SoakZone,
Jumpin' Jungle, Hootin' Holler, and Raccoon
Lagoon. Enjoy major amusement rides in the
Olde Idlewild area and live entertainment
occurring on stage. (See the Kidstuff chapter
for more.) This family fun land is open from
May 26 to Labor Day but is closed every Monday in June. Adults and children pay $26.95
every day, and seniors (age 55 and older) are
charged $17.95. Children age 2 and younger
are admitted free of charge. For those who
discover there is simply too much fun to
explore in one day, ask about the "Next Day
Pass" ($14.50) at guest services. There's no
cost to park at Idlewild.

Kennywood Park
4800 Kennywood Boulevard, West Mifflin
(412) 461-0500
www.kennywood.com
A historic park and roller-coaster capital,
Kennywood has long had a commitment to
upgrading its rides and keeping its Allegheny
County grounds family-friendly. (See the Kidstuff chapter.) Kennywood has brought generations of Pittsburghers lots of thrills and old-
fashioned fun. Enjoy live performances, community and school picnics, ethnic pride days,
and fall fantasy parades. Ride-all-day passes
cost $32 for adults, $19 for juniors (under 46
inches tall), and $15 for seniors (ages 55 and
up). During the last week of August, there is a
Fun Finale each evening. A ride-all-evening
pass costs $17.

Sandcastle
1000 Sandcastle Drive, West Homestead
(412) 462-6666
www.sandcastlewaterpark.com
Set along the Monongahela riverbanks in
Allegheny County, this is where Pittsburgh
beats the heat during the summer. That's
because there are 15 twisting and turning
waterslides, a gentle Lazy River to float down,
several pools, and the self-proclaimed World's
Largest Hot Tub for adults. The park has
undergone renovations that added the
20,000-square-foot Mon-Tsunami wave pool.

Landlubbers play volleyball, snack on
food, or visit the gift shops along the old-fashioned boardwalk. Oasis Miniature Golf and the
exciting Formula One Speedway provide additional activities. The adjacent Riverplex entertainment complex boasts an amphitheater,
big-top circus tent, grassy areas, and tree-
lined walkways.

Sandcastle is open daily from early June
through early September. Hours are 11:00
a.m. to 6:00 p.m. in June and September and
11:00 a.m. to 7:00 p.m. in July and August. A
Whitewater Pass entitles you to all water
attractions and costs $25.95 for adults,
$18.95 for seniors (age 55+), and $13.95 for
juniors (under 46 inches tall). The Season Pass
costs $59.95. Children age 2 and younger are
admitted free of charge. Parking is $5.00;
boat docking is free of charge.

Whitewater Rafting
Ohiopyle
(800) 272-4141
Ohiopyle Falls in Fayette County derives its
name from the native words *Ohio pehelle*,
which means white frothy water. Indeed,

thousands enjoy whitewater rafting in this famous site in the Appalachians. Ohiopyle State Park has hiking and bicycle trails, picnic areas, and camping, as well as cold- and warmwater fishing. During the winter months, many enjoy sledding, cross-country skiing, and snowmobile trails. Whitewater rafting trips are available through Wilderness Voyageurs, at the telephone listed above, April 1 through November 1. The reservation office is open year-round. Anyone can use the bike trail free of charge, but it's best to call when reserving pavilions or organizing a rafting trip.

NATURE'S BEST

The National Aviary
Allegheny Commons West, Ridge Avenue
(412) 323-7235
www.aviary.org
This bird zoo is indeed called the National Aviary. Although it receives no federal funding, Congress granted the North Side aviary the national designation in 1993. More than 600 of the world's most colorful and exotic birds live here in this, the nation's largest indoor bird display independent of a larger zoo. The aviary is open daily, except Christmas Day, 10:00 a.m. to 5:00 p.m. (open 9:00 a.m. in summer). Adults will pay $9 and seniors (over age 60) $8. Admission for children (ages 2 to 12) costs $7.50; those younger than age 2 and aviary members are admitted free of charge.

Phipps Conservatory and Botanical Gardens
One Schenley Drive
(412) 622-6914
www.phipps.conservatory.org
Donated by Henry Phipps, one of the city's turn-of-the-20th-century millionaire industrialists and philanthropists, this conservatory is a 13-room Victorian glasshouse full of beautiful gardens. Visit one of the country's finest bonsai collections, or take the kids to the Discovery Garden (see Kidstuff). You don't need to fly to Arizona to view desert plants or head to

ⓘ Powdermill Nature Reserve, in the Laurel Highlands, offers woodlands, streams, fields, and ponds for its educational programs, run through the Carnegie Museum of Natural History. It's open during the warm-weather months.

the Caribbean to see tropical palms, ferns, and other flora—they are right here for you to enjoy. A $30 million expansion project that will quadruple the size of this facility broke ground in mid-2003. To date, the new Welcome Center, Production Greenhouses and Tropical Forest Conservatory have been completed, Expanded parking areas and a new administration and education building are also planned.

Phipps is open Tuesday through Sunday, 9:00 a.m. to 5:00 p.m. On Friday it is open until 9:00 p.m. Phipps admission is $10.00 for adults, $9.00 for seniors ages 62 and older, $9.00 for students with ID, and $7.00 for children (ages 2 through 12). Children younger than age 2 and Phipps members enter without charge. Metered parking is right in front of the conservatory.

Pittsburgh Zoo & PPG Aquarium
One Wild Place
(412) 665-3640, (800) 474-4966
www.zoo.pgh.pa.us
If you feel like monkeying around, head to Highland Park, where the primates show off just for you. The elephants, zebras, and giraffes roam the African Savanna, and the Siberian tigers and snow leopards explore the Asian forest. Youngsters can enjoy Kids Kingdom (see Kidstuff). The PPG Aquarium, which opened in 2000, features state-of-the-art exhibits such as a two-story shark tank and a wide array of aquatic species, including penguins, octopus, jellyfish, seahorses, and electric eels. Water's Edge, the zoo's newest exhibit features polar bears, seat otters, and—in the future—walruses. Did you know that the zoo is open year-round? Well, it is, closing only on Thanksgiving, Christmas Day,

and New Year's Day. Don't miss the special evening hours during the holiday season (see the Annual Events chapter). Hours at other times are 9:00 a.m. to 5:00 a.m. April 1 through Friday before Memorial Day and Tuesday after Labor Day through December 31; 9:00 a.m. to 4:00 p.m. January 2 through March 31; and 9:00 a.m. to 6:00 a.m. Saturday before Memorial Day through Labor Day. Entrance gates close an hour before the park closes. Admission is as follows. April 1 through November 30: adults $10, seniors $9, and children (ages 2 to 13) $8. December 1 through March 31: adults $8, seniors and children $7. Children younger than age 2 are admitted free. Members of the zoo are also admitted free of charge. Strollers are available for rent at a nominal charge.

PIVOTAL POINTS OF INTEREST

Andy Warhol Museum
117 Sandusky Street
(412) 237-8300
www.warhol.org
Pop artist Andy Warhol, born into a Pittsburgh family that emigrated from Eastern Europe, began his career right in this city. After attending Saturday art classes and college at Carnegie Institute and what now is Carnegie Mellon University, Warhol moved to New York, working as a commercial artist and becoming famous for his experimentation with silk screens (from which he made photographically derived paintings). Upon his sudden death in 1987, the Andy Warhol Museum was constructed on the city's North Side. Seven floors house celebrity portraits, pop paintings (including Heinz boxes, Marilyns, and Campbell's soup cans), Warhol's sketchbooks, and a film gallery.

The Warhol is open Tuesday, Wednesday, Thursday, Saturday, and Sunday, 10:00 a.m. to 5:00 p.m. and Friday from 10:00 a.m. to 10:00 p.m. The museum is closed on Monday; also closed New Year's Day, Martin Luther King Jr.

Day, Easter Sunday, Memorial Day, Independence Day, Labor Day, Thanksgiving, and Christmas Day. Adults will pay $15, seniors (age 55+) are charged $9, and students and children older than age 3 pay $8 for admission. Members of the Carnegie Museums of Pittsburgh pay nothing to enter.

Jimmy Stewart Museum
845 Philadelphia Street, Third Floor
Indiana
(724) 349-6112, (800) 835-4669
www.jimmy.org
Though an attraction of Indiana County, this museum is a definite Western Pennsylvania highlight for those who follow Hollywood and its legends. Located in Jimmy's hometown of Indiana, where his father once owned a hardware store, the museum gives you a chance to see many of Stewart's accomplishments in film, radio, and television. Tributes to Jimmy Stewart's military service, family life, and public service are also housed here. The museum is closed Christmas Day, New Year's Day, Easter Sunday, Independence Day, Labor Day, and Thanksgiving. At all other times it's open 10:00 a.m. to 5:00 p.m. six days a week; on Sunday noon to 5:00 p.m.; and closing at 1:00 on Christmas and New Year's Eves. Adults pay $5; seniors (ages 62 and older), students, and military, $4; and children (ages 7 to 17), $3. Children younger than 7 get in for free.

Pittsburgh's Inclines
Carson Street
(412) 442-2000 (Monongahela Incline)
(412) 381-1665 (Duquesne Incline)
members.tripod.com/~riid/inclines.html
Pittsburgh had over a dozen working inclines at the turn of the 20th century. Now only the Monongahela and Duquesne Inclines remain, transporting commuters and tourists to and from Grandview Avenue atop Mt. Washington to the city of Pittsburgh below. The Monongahela Incline was the city's first in 1870. Declared

163

Downtown and the Duquesne Incline. ALAN AND BARBARA VENTO

a historic structure by the Pittsburgh History and Landmarks Foundation, it's been registered a National Historic Landmark as well. Today it's operated by the Port Authority Transit (PAT). For a panoramic view, a ride on one of these is a must, night or day. (See the Getting Here, Getting Around chapter.) The inclines operate daily starting at 5:30 a.m. until 12:45 a.m. On Sunday, service begins at 8:45 a.m.

Washington County Covered Bridges
Various Locations, Washington County
(800) 531-4114
Travel back in time to some century-old covered bridges (of which there are 25 in this county alone). All are listed on the National Register of Historic Places. Romantics call these "kissing bridges" for their seclusion, and animal lovers herald their barnlike appearance for helping animals cross streams. A helpful map is offered through the Washington County Tourism office (telephone number listed above). A covered bridge festival is held each fall (see Annual Events).

KIDSTUFF

To see the world through a child's eyes lends a new perspective, particularly on Pittsburgh. Kids, this chapter is for you mostly, but it's also for Mom and Dad, family and friends, and anyone else who simply wants to have fun.

Since play is the child's work, it's impossible to list every spot across so many counties where kids can enjoy themselves as they learn and grow. In these pages you'll find the highlights and the things you most definitely won't want to miss.

Savvy parents might also peruse the Attractions and even the Arts chapters, particularly for older children or those who have interests in more sophisticated subjects such as history, art appreciation, and landmarks. As another entire chapter, Recreation offers a range of equally fun activities that can burn off some of that boundless energy.

Separate chapters cover Shopping and Restaurants as well, so if you're looking for family-friendly places to eat or shops in which to outfit the kids, or if you need to stock your home with a few new toys, it's best to turn to these listings. However, you'll find that most of the museums and attractions listed in these pages do offer gift shops with appropriate memorabilia and merchandise. That can be a double-edged sword—bringing on the chorus of "Mom, can I have that?"—but these stores are often very educational in nature.

Because children teach us to throw structure to the wind sometimes, the usual geographic breakdown has been abandoned for this chapter. Instead, get ready to stretch your mind, discover and explore, go a little crazy in between, and savor the delights of Pittsburgh's seasons.

We've tried to present current prices, but there are instances where class or exhibit fees do fluctuate. It's best to call before heading out (and perhaps disappointing a child).

So lace up your sneakers and get ready to enjoy a day (or several) of being inquisitive, overjoyed, and, yes, probably tired at the end of it all. Oh, but the fun you'll have!

ACTING UP

The Gemini Theater Company
7501 Penn Avenue
(412) 243-6464,
(412) 243-5201 (Showtimes/Tickets)
www.geminitheater.org
The Gemini Theater offers fun, interactive musical children's theater for children ages one through ten. Each production is an original retelling of a children's classic and uniquely designed to bring the children into the magic of the story. Past performances have included *Pocahontas, Beauty and the Beast, Alice in Wonderland* and many more.

All performances are held on Saturdays and Sundays at 1:00 and 3:00 p.m. Ticket price is $9. Gemini also offers summer drama camps, birthday party room rentals, and education and outreach programs.

Pittsburgh International Children's Festival
182 Allegheny Center Mall
(412) 321-5520
www.pghkids.org
Now in it's 22nd year, the Pittsburgh International Children's Festival offers children and their families five days of world-class international theater. Held for five days each May, the festival includes acrobatics, puppets, music and movement, and theatrical performances, just to name a few. In 2008, the festival will

debut at a new site in Oakland with the festival grounds to be located on the lawns of the University of Pittsburgh campus and Schenley Plaza. The festival, which is cosponsored by Citiparks, is one of only four international festivals for children in the United States. Single performance tickets are $8, with special rates available for school groups and groups of 15 or more. Advanced tickets can be purchased by calling the Pittsburgh International Children's Theater at (412) 321-5520 or visiting the Web site. A limited number of ticket donations for groups that work with underserved children are available by calling Tickets for Kids Charities at (412) 781-KIDS.

Pittsburgh International Children's Theater
182 Allegheny Center Mall
(412) 321-5520
www.pghkids.org

Each year, Pittsburgh International Children's Theater presents and promotes professional theater experiences for children, typically age 3 to 8, at affordable prices in convenient neighborhood locations. Past productions have featured *Winnie the Pooh* (Two Beans Productions), *Pinkalicious–The Musical* (Vital Theatre Company), and *Don't Let the Pigeon Drive the Bus!* (Big Wooden Horse Theatre Company.

The theater series for families is held October through March at locations such as the Byham Theater (Downtown Pittsburgh), Pine-Richland Middle School (Gibsonia), Laughlin Auditorium at St. Paul Seminary (Crafton), Upper St. Clair High School (Upper St. Clair), and Gateway High School (Monroeville). Single ticket prices are $9.50, with Flex-Pack Tickets and Lap Passes available.

ARTS AND CRAFTS

The Bead Mine
1703 East Carson Street
(412) 381-8822
www.beadmine.net

Since 1992, The Bead Mine has offered jewelry makers of every age a wide selection of beads and jewelry making supplies. Located in the city's historic South Side, Bead Mine is a great place for children to try their hand at making a bracelet or necklace. Bead Mine also offers bead parties for birthday celebrations and jewelry making classes.

Color Me Mine
5887 Forbes Avenue
(412) 421-2909
www.pittsburgh.colormemine.com

A great place to spend an afternoon making a gift with your little ones, Color Me Mine offers over 400 different bisque items from their garden, kids, bathroom and interior décor section. Whether it be a vase, cookie jar, platter or coffee mug, there is truly something for everyone, no matter the age or artistic ability. Prices for pieces ranging from $3.50 to $35.00. The studio fee, which includes glazing and firing, is a flat rate all day Monday through Friday, $9 for adults and $7 for kids 10 and under. Saturday and Sunday is an hourly rate, $6 for adults, $4 for kids 10 and under. Pieces are usually available for pick up a week after your visit.

Manchester Craftsmens Guild
Summer Arts Studios
(412) 322-1773
www.manchesterguild.org

MCG Youth was founded in the knowledge that deep creative engagement leads to a gateway for personal development. Today, MCG Youth offers programs for middle and high school students and their teachers during the school day, after school, and in summer studios. The summer studios, free to eligible Pittsburgh teens from 13 to 18 years of age, are usually held in June and July. Courses in ceramics, photography, and digital

Contact the Special Kids Network at (800) 986-4550 for information on services for children with special health needs. Directories of summer day camps, residential camps, and leisure and recreational activities are available.

or design arts usually meet Monday through Thursday from 1:00 until 4:00 p.m. Enrollment in all studios is limited.

STRETCHING THE MIND

Carnegie Science Center
One Allegheny Avenue
(412) 237-3400
www.carnegiesciencecenter.org
With its focus on science and technology, it's no wonder the Carnegie Science Center on the North Side makes kids feel like inventors, young astronauts, and even magicians. The center isn't limited to children's activities, but certainly kids can learn so much from the interactive exhibits and Omnimax large-format films. They can momentarily pretend they are meteorologists on the evening news, and they can watch a demonstration of science in the kitchen.

Ports of Discovery is a three-part water-related area featuring a living Pacific coral reef aquarium. Kids can explore the planets and stars at the Henry Buhn, Jr. Planetarium & Observatory. Young history buffs shouldn't miss a tour of the USS *Requin*, a World War II diesel-electric submarine moored on the banks of the river (this one's not recommended for very young children). And do note that the miniature train display, while closed a few weeks in June for refurbishing, is open most other months of the year. The train exhibit is a must see—an 83-foot long by 30-foot wide display featuring towns, an amusement park, farmlands, a baseball field, several lakes, and a mountain region—all built in miniature! You'll avoid the crowds if you time your visit outside the holiday season (see the Annual Events chapter).

The center features an educational division with programs for school groups, students, families, and educators. Scouts can earn badges at the science center's Scout workshops. Using NASA resources, there's even a young astronauts program exploring space travel. Periodically, school students

compete in science fairs sponsored by the museum. The Carnegie also offers workshops, summer camps, and parent/child sleepovers.

Parents of young children (ages three to six years old) will appreciate the Exploration Station Jr., located on the fourth floor. This 8,000 square foot exhibit offers fun-filled activities that encourage open-ended exploration and problem-solving. Children can splash at the water table, "work" in the ball factory, build a structure in the construction zone, or take a break in the Quiet Spot.

The whole family will enjoy Laser Nights at the planetarium and observatory. Watch laser shows while listening to great music. ($8 per person for the first show; $5 per person for each additional show. Free for members.)

The center extends its hours in the summer at times. Regular hours are Sunday through Friday 10:00 a.m. to 5:00 p.m., and Saturday 10:00 a.m. to 7:00 p.m. General admission is $14 for adults, $10 for children (age 3 to 6) and seniors (62 and older); members are admitted free of charge.

General admission tickets include entry to the exhibits, Buhl Planetarium, and the submarine. Admission to the Omnimax theater alone is $8 for adults, $6 for children and seniors. Combination ticket packages are available; prices are listed at the desk and available by telephone on the automated information line (call the number given previously) and on the Web site. Additional senior discounts are extended on Tuesday. Purchasing a membership to the science center allows complimentary admission to the museum and discounted rates at the theater. Parking costs $3.

Children's Museum of Pittsburgh
10 Children's Way
(412) 322-5058
www.pittsburghkids.org
Located in the historic landmark Old Post Office Building on the city's North Side, this museum offers outstanding exhibits for children throughout its three floors.

A Major Makeover for Dinosaur Hall

Carnegie Museum of Natural History has created a dinosaur experience like no other and is now the best place in the world to see and learn about dinosaurs!

In mid-2005, Dinosaur Hall was closed for two years. Phase One opened on November 21, 2007, and features the Triassic, Jurassic, and early Cretaceous periods, as well as the Cretaceous Seaway. Phase Two opened in Spring 2008 and features the remainder of the Cretaceous Period. The 18,600-square-foot exhibit, which cost $36 million to construct, features more than three times the exhibition space of the original Dinosaur Hall and displays 19 mounted dinosaur skeletons, 11 of which consist almost entirely of real fossils. *Dinosaurs in Their Time* is unique in that the dinosaurs are arranged by their respective ecosystems, which are reconstructed in extraordinary detail.

Visitors will journey forward in time through the periods of the Mesozoic Era or Age of Dinosaurs, 251 to 66 million years ago. They'll see dinosaurs arranged in scenes, with many of them engaged in life-or-death struggles, and surrounded by extraordinarily detailed, scientifically accurate environments that include fossils and reconstructions of plants, invertebrates, fishes, amphibians, mammals, birds, and other reptiles that lived alongside the dinosaurs. Phase One composes about three-quarters of the exhibit. The highlight of Phase Two will be the two fighting T. rex specimens.

—with thanks to Carnegie Museum of Natural History

Kids, take a turn on Luckey's Climber, an amazing two-story indoor jungle gym. In The Attic, fly down the slide made from an old bowling lane alley or create your own virtual puppet. Build things and take them apart in The Garage. Or, climb the rope ladder to the second floor and throw mini-parachutes to those below. Visit the Neighborhood Trolley and Daniel Tiger's Clock in Mister Roger's Neighborhood.

Are you ready to get wet? Head to the third floor where you can build your own fountains and boats! (On the way, parents with young children can visit The Nursery, a special area designed specifically for infants and toddlers.) Stop by The Theater and visit with Stuffee, the museum's health-teaching exhibit. (Don't worry, he doesn't mind at all if he's poked and prodded.) There is so much to do, both you and the grown ups will be ready for a rest at day's end!

The Children's Museum is closed on major holidays, but open Monday through Saturday from 10:00 a.m. to 5:00 p.m.; on Sunday the museum is open from noon to 5:00 p.m. Adults pay $9 per person for admission, with $8 charged for seniors (over 65) and children (ages 2 to 18) and $7 for museum guests. Children younger than age 2 are admitted free of charge. Each Thursday, everyone's admission is discounted to $7.

Classes at The Carnegie Museums
4400 Forbes Avenue
(412) 622-3288
www.carnegiemuseums.org
Culture, history, science, and art appreciation abound here at the home of the Carnegie Museum of Natural History, the Carnegie Museum of Art, Carnegie Science Center and The Andy Warhol Museum. Each museum offers classes, camps, and scout programs. Some even offer overnight stays!

The schedule changes each semester, so it's best to call for a catalog, or visit the Website. Previous offerings have included painting, puppet-making, sculpting, and architectural classes on the art side. Explore everything from bugs and bears to dinosaurs, Disney animals, reptiles, and archeological findings. Also, there are classes specifically designed for homeschoolers. The prices for these always fluctuate, so it's best to call for further details.

Kids' Classes
Community College of Allegheny County
Main Campus
800 Allegheny Avenue
(412) 369-3703
www.ccac.edu

Think of The Kids Summer of Discovery as a kids' college of sorts, as youngsters attend a variety of classes at one of the community college campuses near you. Kids can acquire new skills or sharpen existing ones as they take art, acting, basketball, babysitting, cheerleading, dance, computer, language, writing, fencing, swimming, or other classes. There are also specialty interest programs like The Robotics Challenge, Junior Golf Camp, and Extreme Builders. Sessions are offered in June and July, Monday through Friday, either in the morning (9:00 a.m. until 12:00 p.m.) or the afternoon (1:00 p.m. until 4:00 p.m.).

CCAC also offers learning enrichment classes for middle and high school students and remedial courses for grades 6 through 12.

In outlying counties, many community colleges offer similar fare for the younger set. It's best to contact the schools in your area for their continuing-education brochures. Use these numbers to help you:

Butler County Community College (724) 287-8711

Community College of Beaver County (724) 775-8561

Westmoreland County Community College (724) 925-4000

Dinosaur Hall
Carnegie Museum of Natural History
4400 Forbes Avenue
(412) 622-3131
www.carnegiemnh.org

This world-famous collection of dinosaur bones and fossils is perhaps the most popular attraction at the museum with children of all ages. Eleven different species are on display in addition to the other fossils of animals that lived around the same Mesozoic era. For children, these nonthreatening monsters are simply amazing, especially in size. The *Tyrannosaurus rex* stands 20 feet tall and dominates the far end of Dinosaur Hall. While at the Museum of Natural History, don't miss Bonehunters Quarry, an interactive exhibit that re-creates an area of Dinosaur National Monument in Colorado and Utah.

Hours at the Carnegie museums are Tuesday through Saturday, 10:00 a.m. to 5:00 p.m. and Sunday noon to 5:00 p.m. The museums stay open until 9:00 p.m. on Thursday and is open on Monday between July 4 and Labor Day from 10:00 a.m. to 5:00 p.m. Admission to the Carnegie Museum of Natural History and Museum of Art is $15 for adults, $12 for seniors, and $11 for students with ID and children (ages 3 to 18). Children younger than age 3 and members are admitted free of charge.

The Discovery Room
440 Forbes Avenue
(412) 622-1950
www.carnegiemnh.org

Tucked away downstairs in this museum is a room where kids can touch, explore, ask questions, and discover many intriguing facts. Individual boxes of artifacts can be checked out to explore while in the room (grown-up supervision with these sets is requested). The room's handful of aquariums contain fish, hermit crabs, and turtles.

Kids can sniff spices and learn where they come from and, in general, explore to their heart's (and hands'!) content. All children younger than age 12 must be accompanied by an adult.

Water, Water, Everywhere!

Hot? Tired of the pool? Pittsburgh offers three unique water features that are open to the public, free of charge.

The Water Feature at PPG Place pulses water from the surface up to a height of over 15 feet, with no barrier between the fountain and the rest of the plaza. The water disappears into the plaza surface and is recycled. The 140 columns of water are dramatically accented by 280 underground lights. Children must be supervised by an adult at all times. Running, beachwear, and sunbathing is not permitted.

At the heart of Station Square, next to the river, sits the Fountain at Bessemer Court. This state-of-the-art Waltzing Waters Liquid Fireworks Show features hundreds of multi-colored jets soaring 40 feet in the air, choreographed to music. (Get close enough and you will get wet!) The Fountain performs over a dozen different shows, favorites include the Frank Sinatra Show, Disney Spectacular Show, and Diva Disco. Open from late-April through the Friday before Thanksgiving, the shows begin at 9:00 a.m. and end at midnight daily.

Last, but not least, check out The Water Steps, a popular destination feature in the North Shore Riverfront Park. The steps offer a playful element to the park and a beautiful display of water landscaping. Located just west of PNC Park, between the Equitable Building and the Allegheny River, the Water Steps are constructed of nearly 500 blocks of sandstone and more than 1,000 smaller pieces of sandstone. Young and old alike gather at the Water Steps to wade in the shallow pools or simply sit alongside and watch the children play.

Discovery Room hours are Tuesday through Friday 1:00 to 3:00 p.m., Saturday 10:00 a.m. to 4:00 p.m., and Sunday 1:00 to 4:00 p.m. during the school year. July and August the room is open weekdays and Saturday 10:00 a.m. to 4:00 p.m. and on Sunday from 1:00 to 4:00 p.m. Admission to The Carnegie Museum of Natural History and Museum of Art is $15 for adults, $12 for seniors and $11 for students with ID and children (ages 3 to 18). Children younger than age 3 and members are admitted free of charge.

Kindermusik
Various locations
(800) 628-5687
This flexible curriculum that brings out the magic in music appeals to children between the ages of 18 months and 5 years. The goal isn't necessarily to make a musician out of your child, but to make your little one eager to learn and become more alive through musical activities. These include 30-minute classes of singing, moving, listening, and playing simple instruments for those younger than 3, and 45-minute classes for kids ages 3 to 5. Those who enroll can take advantage of the parent orientation, family newsletters, and bring-a-friend days. Early registrants receive a 10 percent discount. The eastern suburbs location at Beulah Church may provide information for this site. Contact them at (412) 798-SONG (7664). To find a Kindermusik location closer to you, call the toll-free number above or do a class locator search on the kindermusik.com Web site.

DISCOVERING HISTORY

Fort Ligonier
U.S. Route 30 and Route 711, Ligonier
(724) 238-9701
www.fortligonier.org

If your children studied the French & Indian War, visit Fort Ligonier in Westmoreland County, which served as a staging area for the 1758 Forbes campaign that resulted in the capture of Fort Duquesne (Pittsburgh). The enemy arrived here October 12, 1758, with about 1,200 French and only a few hundred Indians, who were retreating to begin preparations for the long winter ahead. With their strength in numbers and mortar fire, the British were victorious. The new battery, constructed in a $2.3 million restoration project, is built on the site of the original defense fortification of 1758. This historic site is open daily, May 1 through October 31. Fort Ligonier Days are held each October (see the Annual Events chapter). It's open from 10:00 a.m. to 4:30 p.m. Monday through Saturday and noon to 4:30 p.m. on Sundays. Admission rates are $8 for adults, $4.75 for children ages 6 to 14, and $7 for seniors. Children younger than age 6 are admitted free of charge.

Fort Necessity National Battlefield and Braddock's Grave
One Washington Parkway, Farmington
(724) 329-5512
www.nps.gov/fone/home.htm
Most kids have had to study about the French and Indian War in school, so why not show them a little history to supplement the studies! Right off U.S. Route 40 in Fayette County, or what is commonly called the National Road, visit George Washington's "fort of necessity," so named because a large force of French and Indians attacked Washington's army of 400 here. While this battle wasn't a success for Washington, the war's outcome had great impact on global affairs. The French lost much influence in North America, while the English colonies began to pay taxes levied upon them to help pay for this expensive war. Independence became a dream of some settlers.

Quietly up the road from Fort Necessity, a single marker memorializes the final resting place of British Major General Edward Braddock. Braddock was the leader of an ill-fated expedition along the Ohio River trying to cap-

Bookstores throughout the region often feature story times, Saturday craft and story sessions, and other events for children during school breaks and throughout the summer months. Check with your local bookseller, particularly the large superstores, for their individual offerings.

ture the French-held Fort Duquesne. Don't drive too fast along this road, for you just might miss it.

Fort Necessity park grounds and visitor center open daily from 9:00 a.m. to 5:00 p.m. Picnic facilities are available during summer months. It's best to start your visit at the visitor center with its audiovisual program and exhibits before moving through the grounds. On a warm day you'll find costumed Indians demonstrating crafts and telling the story of survival at the fort.

In addition to the battlefield and the aforementioned grave of General Braddock, Fort Necessity features other historical sites of interest to kids. Jumonville Glen was the site of Washington's first skirmish with the French. The park also operates the Mount Washington Tavern, built in 1828 to serve travelers along the National Road. Admission to Fort Necessity, which includes the fort, the museum exhibits, and the Mount Washington Tavern, costs $5 per person. Children age 15 and younger are admitted free of charge.

Meadowcroft Rockshelter and Museum of Rural Life
401 Meadowcroft Road, Avella
(724) 587-3412
www.meadowcroft.pghhistory.org
This 200-acre living-history museum in Washington County offers lessons on rural life for the youngsters as well. Each summer there's a hands-on history day camp where children experience life in 19th-century Western Pennsylvania. Kids shop at the general store, visit the blacksmith, and join Ma in preparing a meal on a woodstove. Then, after lunch, there's class in a one-room school, learning a

Close-up

Everyone's Favorite Neighbor

Fred Rogers' life was honored formally in a public memorial service at Heinz Hall in Pittsburgh on May 3, 2003 that was attended by more than 3,000 people. Fred's life was also honored informally in myriad other ways, at a special gathering at Carnegie Mellon University for students, for example.

Fortunately for Mister Rogers' "television neighbors," the series continues to be broadcast on public television stations across the country. Fred Rogers' intention over the years was to produce the *Neighborhood* series as a "video library" of programs that could be available to children in future years. Thus, for children the relationship with their "television neighbor" didn't change with his death. As one child said, "But I can still see him on TV, can't I?" Through these television visits, Mister Rogers can still help children feel good about who they are and appreciate others and the world around them.

Fred McFeely Rogers (1928–2003) was born in Latrobe, Westmoreland County. After graduating from Rollins College, Fred surprised everyone with his decision to work in television. He rejected the pies-in-the-face humor aimed at young audiences in the 1950s and was determined to find a better approach to this powerful medium.

In New York he worked briefly as an NBC floor manager, but later he wanted to return to Pittsburgh and a start-up station—the first community-supported public television station in the country. "My friends thought I was crazy. I was in line to be a network director," he told us in a 2000 interview. And though it took eight years to complete additional studies at Pittsburgh Theological Seminary, Rogers was ordained with the special mission of working through the media.

While gaining that seminary degree, Rogers was influenced by what he calls the "giants" in the field of child development—people like the late Margaret McFarland, Benjamin Spock, and Eric Erikson. Much of the *Mister Rogers' Neighborhood* material, all written by Fred himself, emerged from the insights he gained from his mentors.

---

craft skill, and playing historical games. This five-day camp is for ages 8 through 13 and runs from 10:00 a.m. to 3:00 p.m. Registration costs $160 per child. (See the Attractions chapter for more information on Meadowcroft.)

Pennsylvania Trolley Museum
1 Museum Road (off Race Track Road), Washington
(724) 228-9256
www.pa-trolley.org

Just 30 minutes south of Pittsburgh, kids can climb aboard a streetcar, hear the clang of the bell, and feel the powerful electric motors and the heavy clatter of steel wheels over the rails. These vintage streetcars are fun to ride and learn about. Volunteer craftsmen rebuild and restore these relics. Allow at least two hours to completely experience the museum. Please note the museum is closed during the months of January, February, and March, but reopens on

Family Communications, Inc. (www.misterrogers.org), the nonprofit company that Fred Rogers founded in 1971, carries on his legacy. Building on its beginnings in broadcast television production, Family Communications has expanded into a wide range of media—books for children and adults, audio- and videotapes, training workshops, the Internet, DVDs, a planetarium show, and traveling exhibits. The company's ongoing work continues to be guided by Fred Rogers' mission of communicating in open, honest, and nurturing ways—ways that support the relationships between children and their families as well as those with the professionals who often care for them.

While over the years some parents have poked fun at Mister Rogers and his slow, quiet approach, most have grown to admire the way he reaches out to their youngsters, becoming an important teacher in their lives, even now, as his broadcasts continue. "Any adult who is honest with children and cares to spend time with them and cares to appreciate them can make a difference," he asserted. "Parents need to know how important they are in the life of their children. They really are their preschool child's world. They are their axis."

The world showed its thanks with numerous awards and recognition. During the course of his lifetime, Fred Rogers received two Peabody Awards; four Emmys; a "Lifetime Achievement" award from the National Academy of Television Arts and Sciences; and the nation's highest civilian honor, the Presidential Medal of Freedom.

A favorite quote that guided Fred Rogers perhaps gives us the most personal insight into this man. Translated from Saint-Exupery's *The Little Prince*: "What is essential is invisible to the eye." Indeed, this great television neighbor appreciated every day, every person, "just the way they are." We Pittsburghers cherished him—and still cherish the legacy his television program and the staff at Family Communications continue to provide.

weekends in early April through December 31 from 11:00 a.m. to 5:00 p.m. It's open weekdays also, Memorial Day through Labor Day from 10:00 a.m. to 4:00 p.m. Admission costs $8 for adults, $7 for seniors (age 62 and older), and $5 for children (ages 3 to 15). Children age 2 and younger receive free admission.

Senator John Heinz History Center
1212 Smallman Street
(412) 454-6000
www.pghhistory.org
Home of the Historical Society of Western Pennsylvania, this museum and depository of regional history isn't limited to children alone (see the Attractions chapter). However, there are several displays and features that will interest your youngsters. Start on the first floor of the Strip District museum, where kids

can board an old streetcar, the way it used to be in Pittsburgh before the days of light-rail transit and PAT buses. Kids will also delight at the robots giving them directions.

Children are certainly welcome to browse the exhibits throughout the building, but they will especially enjoy the Discovery Place (no relation to the Discovery room mentioned earlier) on the third floor, which is just for them. This room offers hands-on exploration with interactive exhibits and games. Kids can travel through time, interview a shoe, and climb in a steel mill. Sports lovers will enjoy visiting the Western Pennsylvania Sports Museum, a 20,000-piece exhibit of sports artifacts, interactive exhibits, and audio-visual programs.

The Heinz History Center is open from 10:00 a.m. to 5:00 p.m. The library is open Thursday through Saturday, 10:00 a.m. until 5:00 p.m. The center is closed Easter, Thanksgiving, Christmas, and New Year's Day. Cost for adults is $9, $7 for seniors (age 65 and older), and $5 for students (with ID) and children (ages 6 to 18). Children age 5 and under are admitted at no cost.

GOING CRAZY

Chuck E. Cheese's
1025 Washington Pike, Bridgeville
(412) 257-2570

101 Clearview Circle, Butler
(724) 282-4659

5256 Route 30, Greensburg
(724) 837-2455

3800 William Penn Highway, Monroeville
(412) 856-5044

Chuck E. Cheese and his band are on stage for you at several locations in the area. So take the kids to this popular restaurant for pizza, music, and lots of fast-paced indoor fun. Watch them climb their way to the sky-crawls or shimmy down a slide. Tiny tots are bound for the ball pit and pint-size rides, and there are plenty of arcade games for your preteens, too.

Chuck E. Cheeses has a hand-check child-identification system to keep children from leaving without their parents. Party packages are available, but do make weekend party reservations at least one month in advance. Enjoy the nonstop fun (and noise!) Sunday through Thursday from 9:00 a.m. to 10:00 p.m. On Friday and Saturday, hours are 9:00 a.m. to 11:00 p.m. Prices vary on the menu, so call if you're curious.

Fun Fest Entertainment Center
2525 Freeport Road, Hamarville
(412) 828-1100
www.funfest.myfastsite.com

Tagged as "Not Your Grandfather's Bowling Alley," Fun Fest offers a range of activities at this indoor entertainment complex. Pick from cosmic bowling with laser lights and fog rising above the lanes, laser-tag games with computerized scorekeeping, and much more. Bowling costs $5.25 per game Monday through Thursday. On weekends it costs a little more—$5.95 per game, per person. Laser Tag costs $6.99 per game per person during the week. Reservations are strongly suggested. Fun Fest is open daily, starting at 9:00 a.m.

Gymboree Play Programs
1500 Washington Road #120
Galleria Mall
(724) 933-0033

Wexford Plaza
10628 Perry Highway, Wexford
(724) 933-0033

Gymboree specializes in developmental play programs for newborns through 5-year-olds, with more than 40 pieces of colorful play equipment, upbeat music, movement, creative games, and activities to improve self-esteem. It's a great opportunity for youngsters to socialize with children their own age. Call for class schedules and rates.

Idlewild Park and SoakZone
US 30, Ligonier
(724) 238-3666
www.idlewild.com

This family theme park in Westmoreland County includes Storybook Forest, Mister Rogers' Neighborhood of Make-Believe (the only one in the country), SoakZone (water slides and pool), Jumpin' Jungle, Hootin' Holler, and Raccoon Lagoon (kiddie rides). Kids will enjoy such major amusement rides as a Ferris wheel and other traditional amusement park attractions in the Olde Idlewild area, and live entertainment on stage. Idlewild offers shaded picnic tables and grills, so be sure to pack a basket in this beautiful area of the Laurel Highlands. Pavilions can be reserved for large groups. Refreshment stands are numerous, and there's a large restaurant.

Previous highlights at Idlewild have included the Royal Hanneford Circus, and annual appearances of everyone's favorite characters from *Mister Rogers' Neighborhood*. Height requirements apply on the park's faster rides. There are changing facilities for the water attractions and lockers for rent to store your belongings. But they aren't large, so pack light.

This family fun land is open from May 26 to Labor Day but is closed on Monday in June. Adults and children pay $26.95 everyday and seniors (age 55 and older) are charged $17.95. Children age 2 and younger get in free. For those who discover there is simply too much fun to explore in one day, ask about the "Next Day Pass" at guest services, which gives you a discount ($14.50) on your second day's visit. There's no cost to park at Idlewild.

Just Ducky Tours
Station Square
(412) 402-DUCK (3825)
www.justduckytours.com
It's a boat, it's a truck . . . no, it's a duck! That's right, Just Ducky tours offers an amphibious tour vehicle to shuttle passengers throughout the city as they learn a little about Pittsburgh and its waterways. This fully narrated tour begins at Station Square, a building formerly housing the Pennsylvania and Lake Erie Railroad and now a shopping/restaurant mecca on

If Just Ducky's amphibious tour vehicle is a bit much for your youngster (or you!), why not take a ride on the Good Ship Lollipop. Operated by the Gateway Clipper Fleet, this popular riverboat ride sails for an hour along with Lolli the Clown, who entertains the kids. The fleet also offers Sunday Ice Cream Social Cruises and Kids Showtime Cruises. For details, call (412) 355-7980 or visit www.gatewayclipper.com.

the city's South Side. Quacking your way along, you'll see Pittsburgh's past and present along Grant Street and the historic Penn Station before moving into the Strip District (yes, it's G-rated—the Strip is the infamous produce/food shopping area) and then the Cultural District.

Kids squeal with delight at the tour's highlight, when the Duck boat makes its way effortlessly off the dry land, splashing down into the Allegheny River to continue the tour! Adults ride for $19, children ages 3 to 12 pay $15, and children age 2 and under are $5. The duck tour is wheelchair accessible, and the boats are equipped with heat and canopies for inclement weather. Tours operate daily from April through October at various times throughout the day beginning at 10:30 a.m. and ending at 6:00 p.m. (weekends only in November). Call to book your reservation and get ready to quack away!

Kennywood Park
4800 Kennywood Boulevard, West Mifflin
(412) 461-0500
www.kennywood.com
Named as a Pennsylvania Historic Landmark and having celebrated its 100th year anniversary in 1998, Kennywood in Allegheny County is a roller-coaster capital. The park has been named the favorite traditional amusement park of the National Amusement Park Historical Association for more than a decade running.

One of the most popular rides is the Pitt Fall, which hoists riders to the top of a black-and-gold tower, then plummets them at a free fall of nearly 65 miles per hour. Technology and innovation have set Kennywood apart for years. Noah's Ark, a walk-through "haunted" ark built in the 1930s, was totally refurbished in 1996–1997 so that it might sail into the 21st century. Guests are now thrilled by such high-tech scenes as the Elevator of Doom, which provides the illusion that you're in a falling, crumbling elevator.

Coasters at Kennywood are the main attraction. Don't miss the Thunderbolt and the Jack Rabbit roller coasters, if your children are old enough (and brave enough!). There's also the Racer and the Exterminator to thrill you. Be prepared to get drenched on the Log Jammer flume ride. And, here at Kennywood, you don't need a learner's permit to drive the Turnpike.

Throughout the year, but especially in summer, Kennywood features live performances, community and school picnics, ethnic pride days, and fall fantasy parades. A cafeteria-style restaurant is available as well as numerous refreshment stands. Height requirements do apply on some rides.

Ride-all-day passes cost $32 for adults, $19 for juniors (under 46 inches tall), and $15 for seniors (ages 55 and up). General admission tickets (rides not included) are available to adults for $8.00 and to seniors (age 65 and older) for $7.00. During the last week of August, there's a Fun Finale each night. Ride-all-evening passes cost $17 per person.

Sandcastle
1000 Sandcastle Drive, West Homestead
(412) 462-6666
www.sandcastlewaterpark.com
This is Pittsburgh's wettest playground, just minutes outside the Golden Triangle along the Monongahela River in Allegheny County. With 15 twisting and turning waterslides, a gentle Lazy River to float down, several pools, and the self-proclaimed World's Largest Hot Tub

i In 2002 the trade magazine *Amusement Today* voted Kennywood the fourth-best amusement park in the nation.

(for adults), you understand why people flock to Sandcastle when the mercury soars. Little tykes love Wet Willie's Waterworks.

There's plenty of fun on land as well, with volleyball, food and gift shops, and an arcade on the boardwalk. Oasis Miniature Golf and the Formula 1 add landlubber fun to your trip to Sandcastle.

Sandcastle is open daily from early June through early September. Hours of operation are 11:00 a.m. to 6:00 p.m. June and September, and 11:00 a.m. to 7:00 p.m. in July and August. A Whitewater Pass entitles you to all water attractions and costs $25.95 for adults, $18.95 for seniors (age 55+), and $13.95 for juniors (under 46 inches tall). The Season Pass costs $59.95. Children age three and younger are admitted to pools free of charge, and parking is $5.00. Boat docking, if you get here via the river, is free.

Wildwood Highlands
2330 Wildwood Road
(412) 487-5517
www.wildwoodpa.com
Wildwood Highlands is North Park's family fun center, with miniature golf, go-karts, bumper boats, a driving range, an arcade, and a complete menu for meals and snacks. Woody's Den is an area of the park especially suited for kids age 10 and younger. This site can accommodate small groups of children as well as large corporate gatherings. Arrangements for teen parties are also available. Wildwood Peddlers Flea Market is adjacent to this family fun center (see the Shopping chapter).

The center sells tickets for go-karts, bumper boats, and Woody's Den. Tokens are required for the driving range, miniature golf, and game room. Call the automated information line (number above) for complete price information. However, miniature golf costs $5.25 for adults and $3.75 for children ages 4 to 10, and it's free for kids age 3 and younger with a paying customer. Indoor play costs $4.00 for children age 4 and older, $3.00 for 2- and 3-year-olds; it's free for babies age one and younger. Tickets are available in different price amounts, but for $20 you can receive 25 tickets.

Wildwood Highlands is open year-round, but the hours vary seasonally. Generally, it's open Sunday through Thursday from 11:00 a.m. to 10:00 p.m. and on Friday and Saturday from 11:00 a.m. to 11:00 p.m.

TALKIN' TOYS

Pittsburgh Toy Lending Library
5401 Centre Avenue
(412) 682-4430
www.pghtoys.com
Created as a safe, clean, inexpensive place for children, parents, and caregivers, the Toy Lending Library operates from the First United Methodist Church at the corner of South Aiken Avenue and Baum Boulevard. Children from birth through kindergarten are welcome to come and explore. Developmentally appropriate toys enhance motor, social, sensory, cognitive, imaginative, and language skills.

A resource reference library helps parents and caregivers, and informal meetings provide friendly information exchange of such topics as nursing and potty training to selecting a school. Family memberships costs range from $25 to $130 per year. Lower membership amounts require volunteer commitments. Visitors are also welcome to stop by on a pay-per-visit basis. Cost is $5 per child older than one year of age, with a maximum of $10 per family. Adults are admitted free. Members enjoy toy borrowing and party privileges as well as newsletter subscription. This toy library is open Monday through Saturday, generally 9:30 a.m. until 2:30 p.m., but it varies depending upon the day. Please call before heading out with your little ones!

EXPLORING NATURE

The National Aviary
Allegheny Commons West
(412) 323-7235
www.aviary.org
While it receives no federal funding, the

Giant Eagle supermarkets make shopping just a bit easier with the Eagle's Nest play center in many of the larger stores. It's free for children ages 3 to 9. Check with your store for requirements.

National Aviary on Pittsburgh's North Side was granted the national designation by Congress in 1993. This sanctuary proves that the Pittsburgh Penguins hockey players aren't the only birds in town! More than 500 of the world's most colorful and exotic birds live here in this, the nation's largest indoor bird display independent of a larger zoo. Kids will love the cacophony and the mysterious-looking birds flying overhead. The Aviary is open daily, except Christmas Day, 10:00 a.m. to 5:00 p.m. (open 9:00 a.m. in summer). Adults will pay $9 and seniors (over age 60) $8. Admission for children (ages 2 to 12) costs $7.50; those younger than age 2 and aviary members are admitted free of charge.

Pittsburgh Zoo & PPG Aquarium
One Wild Place
(412) 665-3640, (800) 474-4966
www.pittsburghzoo.org
If your idea of fun is seeing others act out, head to the Pittsburgh Zoo & PPG Aquarium. At this 77-acre natural habitat facility, primates show off their antics in the fog-shrouded indoor rain forest; elephants, zebras, and giraffes roam the African Savanna; and Siberian tigers and snow leopards explore the Asian forest. Your own children can act as animalistic as they like (under your supervision, of course!) at Kids Kingdom, where they'll have a roaring good time on play equipment that replicates animal motions and behaviors. They'll pass through a petting area to touch a friendly goat or see the Australian gray kangaroos up close.

Children also enjoy the PPG Aquarium where they can crawl through the stingray tunnel, watch the sharks swim in the two-story tank and, of course, find the clown fish (also known as "Nemo!")

Down on the Farm

Another great way to experience the seasons is to visit local farms. Pumpkin patches in the Fall and strawberry picking in the summer are two great, "hands-on" experiences for kids. Here are a few of the better-known farms in the area:

Janoski's Farm, U.S. Route 30, Clinton (3 miles from the airport), (724) 899-3438

Kaelin Farm Market, 2547 Brandt School Road, Franklin Park, (724) 935-6780

Reilly's Summer Seat Farm, Ohio Township, (412) 364-86662

Schramm's Farm Market & Greenhouse, 291 Criswell Road, Butler, (724) 282-3714

Schramm's Farms & Orchard, Harrison City Road, Westmoreland County, (724) 744-7320

Soergel's Farm, Brandt School Road, Wexford, (724) 935-1743

Trax Farms, Route 88, Finleyville, (412) 835-3246

Simmons Farms, 170 Simmons Road, McMurray, (724) 941-1490

Water's Edge, the Zoo's newest exhibit, features polar bears, sea otters, and—in the future—walruses. With seven strategically placed viewing windows and two huge underwater tunnels, Water's Edge provides an opportunity to get up close and personal with these wonderful animals.

The Pittsburgh Zoo is open year-round. Special evening hours are held during the holiday season (see Annual Events). Hours at other times are 9:00 a.m. to 5:00 p.m. April 1 through Friday before Memorial Day and Tuesday after Labor Day through December 31; 9:00 a.m. to 4:00 p.m. January 2 through March 31; and 9:00 a.m. to 6:00 p.m. Saturday before Memorial Day through Labor Day.

Entrance gates close an hour before the park closes. Admission is as follows. April 1 through November 30: adults $10, seniors $9, and children (ages 2 to 13) $8. December 1 through March 31: adults $8, seniors and children $7. Children younger than age 2 are admitted free. Members of the zoo are also admitted free of charge. Strollers and wagons are also available for rent at a nominal charge.

Round Hill Farm
651 Round Hill Road, Elizabeth
(412) 384-8555

Take the kids to see a real working farm. Open year-round with tours conducted from April through November, Round Hill in southern Allegheny County has picnic areas in the summer, so be sure to pack a lunch. Kids will enjoy the self-guided tour, especially if there's a cow that needs some milking. Though retired, the county police department's riding horses remain on the farm along with their friends, the sheep and chickens. In fact, exotic chickens that they are, some even lay beautifully colored eggs. Ask about the "Day on the Farm" program for fifth and sixth graders whereby the students go on hayrides, have snacks, and fix their own lunches on the farm. Normal hours are from 9:00 a.m. to 2:30 p.m.

SAVORING THE SEASONS

Discovery Garden
Phipps Conservatory and Botanical Gardens, Schenley Park
(412) 622-6914

Located in Schenley Park in Pittsburgh's Oakland section, among the blossoms and bonsai, the indoor and outdoor Discovery Garden is designed especially for children. Kids can pot their own plants, learn about botany with the garden ambassadors, and partake of other special activities. The Discovery Garden is open May 2 through October 31, and the hours vary depending upon the weather. A $30 million expansion project that will quadruple the size of this entire facility began construction in mid-2003.

Phipps is open Tuesday through Sunday, 9:00 a.m. to 5:00 p.m. weather permitting. Admission is $10 for adults, $9 for seniors age 62 and older, $9 for students with ID, and $7 for children (ages 2 to 18). Children younger than age 2 and Phipps members enter without charge. Metered parking is in front of the conservatory.

FESTIVALS AND ANNUAL EVENTS

No matter what your favorite interest, hobby, sport, or recreation, chances are good you'll find events throughout the Greater Pittsburgh area that will make you smile, and keep you plenty busy. Perusing this list will give you an overall picture of the broad range of activities and events our area has to offer at special times of the year—everything from county fairs and farm shows, marathons and parades, to ethnic celebrations and holiday festivities.

Unless indicated otherwise, events can be enjoyed free of charge, although specific portions of a festival or event—like food or a special performance—might require some cash outlay. For those festivals or special events that require an admission or entry fee, the most current price level is given. Please remember that these are subject to change each year, so it's best to check before heading out.

Also given are approximate dates and times for anything particularly special occurring within the activities and celebrations listed, but again, it's always best to call the sponsoring organization or group before making plans to attend. Where expositions are listed spanning many days, even entire weekends, the times are left out because they vary. Again, call in advance. Many of the shows at the David L. Lawrence Convention Center run well into the evening. And of course, bring along enough money to any festival to cover the food, beverages, and crafts you might want to purchase. This is often the case even if there is no formal admission charged.

Rather than format this chapter geographically, we've followed the calendar, starting in January and ending up at the holidays. So grab your camera, put on your walking shoes, and get ready to have some fun.

JANUARY

Beaver County Annual Snow Shovel Contest
Economy Park
Legionville Hollow Road, Ambridge
(724) 846-5600
Contestants in this event ride on their favorite snow shovels, trying for the fastest time as they slide down a 160-foot hill. You must be at least 5 years old to participate. Four different divisions are offered—for boys age 13 and younger, girls age 13 and younger, adults, and a modified race for all ages. This modified class simply means those with "improved shovels." Registration starts at 11:00 a.m., and the contest begins at 1:00 p.m. The winner is the person with the fastest time to the bottom, where a trophy awaits. There is no charge to participate, so bundle up, grab your shovel, and enjoy!

Recreational Vehicle Show
David L. Lawrence Convention Center
1001 Penn Avenue
(412) 565-6000
www.pghrvshow.com
The latest in recreational vehicles, including travel trailers, motor homes, fifth wheels, custom and conversion vans, campers, park models, pop-up camping trailers, truck caps, and utility trailers, are on display on the convention center floor. Representatives are handy to answer questions you might have or help put you behind the wheel of your own Winnebago. If nothing else, just seeing the limitless camping possibilities primes you for summer and all its allure in the months ahead. Admission costs $7 for adults, $6 for seniors, and $5 for children ages 6 to 16. Those younger than age 6 are admitted free of charge.

Pittsburgh Boat Show
David L. Lawrence Convention Center
1001 Penn Avenue
(412) 798-8858
www.pittsburghboatshow.net
This annual display of boats, big and small, along with the latest in other assorted watercraft, makes people in this boat-crazy region pray for an early spring on the three rivers. Included on the showroom floor are personal watercraft (such as Jet Skis), fishing boats, ski boats, plus houseboats. You can even take boating exams and classes for various safety certifications, though advance registration may be necessary. As of January 2000, anyone operating a personal watercraft in Pennsylvania must possess a valid boating-safety certificate. Be sure to enter the contests (sometimes there's a cash giveaway contest) and peruse the accompanying flea market to find a bargain treasure to add to your watercraft. Admission costs $9 for adults, $4 for children age 6 to 12. Younger children are admitted free of charge if accompanied by an adult.

FEBRUARY

Winterlude Festival
Various locations throughout Greensburg
(724) 838-4362
This monthlong major arts extravaganza celebrates the performing and visual arts all across Westmoreland County. The Grand Finale concludes the event at the restored Palace Theatre, Greensburg. Hours vary, with locations throughout the county. As the event is diverse, with many different activities, please check your local paper for particular listings and the prices charged at any particular show, display, concert, or screening.

Pittsburgh Automobile Show
David L. Lawrence Convention Center
1001 Penn Avenue
(412) 565-6000
A Pittsburgh tradition, this show brings out the best in local automobile dealerships. Local dealers' newest models, plus manufacturers'

prototype cars of the future, are on display. So picture yourself driving the car of your dreams. Here you can hop right in behind the wheel (at least for a brief moment of glory!). The admission charge for adults is $8, with children ages 6 to 16 paying $6 and those younger than age 6 admitted free of charge.

South Side Mid-Winter Soup Contest
South Side Local Development Company
(412) 481-0651
www.southsidepgh.com
Stop by the historic South Side to sip soup during the South Side Mid-Winter Soup Contest. Participating South Side shops feature kettles of soup prepared by neighborhood restaurants. Attendees who donate at least $5 and one can of soup to the Brashear Association Food Pantry will be given a wristband and a map allowing them to "soup hop" all afternoon.

MARCH

Pittsburgh Home & Garden Show
David L. Lawrence Convention Center
1001 Penn Avenue
(412) 565-6000
www.pghhome.com
A very large and popular event among Pittsburghers, the Home & Garden Show usually features more than 1,400 exhibits highlighting the latest in products for your house, yard, and garden. Information on interior design, landscaping, lawn care, furnishings, cooking, and other related topics is plentiful, and you won't want to miss your chance at winning any number of prizes in various contests and giveaways. Adult admission costs $10, and children ages 6 to 12 pay $4. Those younger than age 6 enter free of charge.

St. Patrick's Day Parade
Downtown
(412) 621-0600
www.pittsburghirish.org/parade
Usually held the Saturday morning before St. Patrick's Day, this annual parade brings out

the best Irish eyes in the city. The parade runs from Mellon Arena down Grant Street to the Boulevard of Allies, and there's a reviewing stand at Stanwix Street. Sponsored by the Irish Society for Education and Charities, the parade includes everything you'd expect on St. Patty's Day: floats, celebrities, and lots of green on display. Usually you can count on seeing approximately 200 different parade entries, and it seems to be a tradition to watch the parade from parking garages (for a better view, and to stay dry in the unpredictable March weather). There's no charge to view the parade, so come out, wear your green shirts and hats, and be a little Irish for the day! Plenty of parties follow throughout the day in the Downtown area.

Spring Flower Show
Phipps Conservatory and Botanical Gardens, Schenley Park
(412) 622-6914

The arrival of spring brings new blossoms and a bouquet of color at this Schenley Park conservatory in the Oakland neighborhood. Call for notice of special activities, including the annual Mother's Day Flower Sale, held each spring. The Flower Show lasts for about a month, while the Mother's Day sale runs the weekend of that special holiday. Phipps is open Tuesday through Sunday 9:00 a.m. to 5:00 p.m. Admission is $10 for adults, $9 for seniors (age 62 and older), and for students with ID, and $7 for children (ages 2 to 18). Children younger than 2 years old and Phipps members enter without charge. Metered parking is right in front of the conservatory.

APRIL

Shrine Circus
Mellon Arena, 66 Mario Lemieux Place
(412) 642-1800

The Shriners have all that it takes for a festive circus adventure, with traditional clowns, wild animals and their trainers, magic tricks, illusions, and other zany surprises. Kids' eyes may light up at the fire rings lit for animals to

jump through in the darkened arena. Ticket prices average approximately $10. There are usually eight shows (including three on Saturday) over the course of a long weekend.

Easter Egg Hunts
Trax Farms, 528 Trax Road, Finleyville
(412) 835-3246
www.traxfarms.com/events.htm

Held on numerous weekends leading up to Easter in this South Hills town, kids hunt for Easter eggs, enjoy pony rides, learn button-making, have their faces painted, and walk away with a bag of goodies, treats, and other surprises. Of course no egg hunt would be complete without a visit from the celebrated rabbit himself—the Easter Bunny. There's no admission charge for kids to hunt, although some of the other activities require money.

Antiques Show at the Carnegie
Carnegie Museum of Art
4400 Forbes Avenue, Oakland
(412) 622-3131

This show runs concurrently with other regular museum attractions and exhibits and features fine quality glass, furniture, jewelry, porcelain, silver, and various other works of art. The antiques are brought in and displayed by more than 50 different dealers, representing many states across the country. This isn't garage-sale stuff—items can be quite pricey, but certainly worth the look and price of the extra charge. Tickets for the Antiques Show cost $10 for members of the Carnegie and $15 for nonmembers. To browse the exhibits and/or make a purchase, you'll spend your time in the Music Hall Foyer and Hall of Architecture for the most part, which are consumed by this annual show.

Maple Syrup Festival
Brady's Run Park, off Route 51
Beaver County
(724) 774-7090

Held at the Brady's Run Park Lodge in April or the end of March, this festival celebrates the annual spring bounty of the area's millions of maple trees. Come for the all-you-can-eat pancake breakfast and stay for demonstrations and old-time crafts, including lace-making. The lines for breakfast can be long, but locals report that the wait is worth it. The concept is to tap the trees and explain the boiling-down process through which maple syrup is made. Admission (including breakfast) is $4 for adults. Children age 10 and younger are admitted free of charge. The event runs from 8:00 a.m. until 4:30 p.m.

Spring Festival
Trax Farms, 528 Trax Road, Finleyville
(412) 835-3246
www.traxfarms.com/events.htm
Step into spring with three days of celebrating flowers and sunshine and getting back into the fresh air at this South Hills farm. Garden lectures, display gardens, kids' activities, farm animals, demonstrations, giveaways, and other prizes are all part of this long weekend of celebrating the outdoors. There's no admission charge for the spring festival, so come, learn, and just have fun.

MAY

Fort Pitt Museum Colonial Fair
Point State Park
(412) 281-9285
www.fortpittmuseum.com
The Fort Pitt Colonial Fair weekend is usually held one or two weekends before Memorial Day at the Fort Pitt Museum downtown in Point State Park. The museum itself is located in part of a re-created 18th-century British fort at the confluence of the mighty Allegheny and Monongahela Rivers, which converge to form the Ohio River at this location. Military reenactments and performances are the attraction.

Greek Food Festival
419 South Dithridge Street
(412) 682-3866
In years past, more than 20,000 people have stopped in for an appetizing dose of Greek food and culture at this weeklong festival in the Oakland neighborhood. Greek lunches and dinners, plus dancing and live entertainment each evening, are found at St. Nicholas Greek Orthodox Cathedral's community center. Imagine smelling the aroma of dishes you typically do not cook at home, such as moussaka, pastita, and baklava. Normal hours run Sunday noon to 8:00 p.m., Monday through Friday 10:00 a.m. until 2:00 p.m. (lunch), and Monday through Thursday 5:00 to 9:00 p.m. (dinner). On Friday dinner is served from 4:00 until 10:00 p.m. Prices for various parts of the festival vary each year, so call closer to the actual event for updated information.

Ambridge Nationality Days
Merchants Street from Fourth to Eighth Streets, Ambridge
(412) 266-3040
www.nationalitydays.org
Held as an open-air street fair, this three- or four-day celebration of ethnic pride offers tasty foods from all over the world along with live entertainment, crafts, and special children's activities and attractions. Traditional dancing has always been a part of the event, and you can count on 3 blocks of fabulous food stands with the aromas of Greek, American, Italian, and other cuisines wafting through the air. Italian, German, Croatian, Greek, Russian, Vietnamese, Scottish, Caribbean, Argentinean, Peruvian, Polish, Bosnian, and African-American dishes are represented. The festival begins at 10:00 a.m. and lasts until 9:30 p.m. As this is a street fair, there is no admission charge, just the cost of your food and beverages purchased.

National Pike Festival
U.S. Route 40
Washington, Fayette, and Somerset Counties
(724) 437-9877, (800) 840-0274
Numerous towns in three counties participate in this festival along the historic National Road, which we know today as US 40. Washington (Washington County) and Uniontown (Fayette County) are two of the larger cities

the road passes through as it cuts diagonally across the southwest corner of the state. Arts and crafts, antique cars, displays, food, and entertainment are all a part of the event. In years past, two wagon trains started at opposite ends of the route, traveling along and making encampments along the way. The best advice we can give you is to check the local newspapers closer to the actual festival (or call the number above) for particular offerings you're interested in, as this event covers three large counties. So get ready for a full range of fun as you travel back in history.

Pittsburgh International Folk Festival
David L. Lawrence Convention Center
1001 Penn Avenue
(412) 565-6000
www.pghfolkfest.org

Usually held around Memorial Day weekend, this is a festive three-day ethnic event. More than 20 nationalities prevalent in the Pittsburgh area celebrate their heritages with colorful costumes, authentic folk dancing, native dishes, delicious desserts, and an international marketplace. In years past, tickets cost $5. Children age 12 and younger enjoy free admission.

JUNE

Three Rivers Arts Festival
Gateway Plaza and Point State Park
(412) 281-8723
www.artsfestival.net

A Downtown tradition for decades, new exhibitions and performers are introduced daily as a part of this 17-day festival. All types of art, crafts, dance, music, and food make this a memorable start to anyone's summer. Lunchtime for downtown office workers will never be the same after meandering the line of food booths at the entrance of Point State Park.

Just imagine the aroma of sizzling steak sandwiches and fried vegetables, let alone hot sausage, Chinese foods, and dozens of other tasty treats.

Most artists offer their work for sale, including handcrafted jewelry, pottery, photography, paintings, fiber art, and finished calligraphy. As years go by, the expanse of the arts festival has covered more of the downtown urban setting, including the Art Institute of Pittsburgh and Wood Street Gallery (on the second floor of the Wood Street "T" station at Liberty Avenue).

The Three Rivers Arts Festival runs from the beginning of June through midmonth and is free to the public. (See the Getting Around chapter for tips on parking downtown or taking public transportation.)

Historic Harmony House Tour
Harmony Museum, 218 Mercer Street
Harmony, Butler County
(724) 452-7341

Normally held the first Saturday in June, this event gives visitors the chance to tour the historically and architecturally significant Harmony House that lies in the historic district (exit 27 off Interstate 79, east of Zelienople). The site actually consists of five houses in addition to the museum buildings. Since the tour is self-guided, you can use the map to go at your own pace, and it costs $20 per person. Tours are given Tuesday through Sunday, 1:00 to 4:00 p.m., year-round. General admission is $3.50 for adults, $3.00 for seniors (age 60 and older), and $1.50 for children ages 6 through 12. Children younger than 6 years of age are admitted free of charge.

Mountain Top Bluegrass and Craft Festival
Mountain Top Park, Tarentum
Armstrong County
(724) 224-1511

Some of the top national bluegrass pickers and strummers come to Pittsburgh for the region's premier bluegrass festival. It brings a touch of Appalachia to Pittsburgh no doubt! This event, typically the first weekend in June, features the family fun of live music, crafts, workshops, horse-drawn wagon rides, camping, a petting zoo, and much more. There's also been a pig roast in previous years. A day pass costs $25 per person Thursday and Friday and $30 per person on Saturday. Children ages 10 to 16 get in for half price, and children younger than 10 years old are admitted free.

JULY

Ellwood City Arts, Crafts & Food Festival
Ewing Park, Ellwood City
(724) 758-5630
www.ellwood-city-festival.net
More than 200 craft booths, art shows, entertainers, and food booths are offered at this annual Beaver County event held in Ewing Park, Ellwood City. The fun begins at 11:00 a.m. and keeps going strong until 10:00 p.m. Enjoy the free admission. On-site parking is available for $3, though you might park at no charge in outlying areas if you're willing to walk a few blocks.

Fourth of July Fireworks at the Point
Point State Park
(412) 471-0235
Fireworks displays are ignited in numerous Western Pennsylvania communities, but this one is perhaps the most spectacular. The Pittsburgh Symphony Orchestra performs a rousing patriotic concert under the stars and fireworks at the Point. Fireworks are courtesy of Zambelli International of New Castle, Lawrence County (also known as the fireworks capital of the world). The music and fireworks extravaganza comes at no cost, but bring a blanket to spread out in Point State Park, and be prepared for the massive crowds and traffic jam exiting the city. The festivities get under way at dusk.

Greenberg's Train & Dollhouse Show
ExpoMart, 105 Mall Boulevard, Monroeville
(412) 856-8100
This is America's premier toy train and miniature railroad event, complete with a dramatic train layout, displays, and a huge dollhouse marketplace. In addition, there are ongoing

i Many boroughs or municipalities host community days over the summer. Keep tabs with the local newspapers for dates and times.

how-to clinics, door prizes, and the latest in hobby books. This show will definitely give you plenty of project ideas to fill those upcoming winter days! Adults will pay approximately $7 and children younger than 11 are free. The show also comes to ExpoMart in November.

Pittsburgh Vintage Grand Prix
Schenley Park
(412) 471-7847
Since 1983 the Pittsburgh Vintage Grand Prix has grown from a one-day vintage car race to a full week of activities. In addition to a rally at Point State Park and the main attraction, the race itself, which weaves along twisty turns in a gem of a city park, you can watch drivers compete in qualifying races, check out several classic car shows, buy automotive memorabilia, and perhaps participate in a mystery run as well.

Three Rivers Regatta
Point State Park
(412) 875-4841
www.pghregatta.com
This free, family-oriented weekend is full of thrilling air shows, on-land events, Formula 1 powerboat races, hot-air balloon races, fireworks, and waterskiing demonstrations. In prior years, the live music made coming out to the Regatta special, even if you never saw the water attractions. Local musician Donnie Iris has performed as well as the group Blood, Sweat and Tears. The "Anything That Floats Race" has also been a regular event, with teams creating some type of seaworthy (in theory, anyway) transportation out of materials not usually used for boatmaking. And one year, beer lovers not only sipped their favorite brew but also learned how it was made in a trailer-classroom created for the event.

Westmoreland Arts & Heritage Festival
Twin Lakes Park, off US 30
Westmoreland County
(724) 834-7474
www.artsandheritage.com

Art comes alive at the kaleidoscope of creative expression usually held around the July 4th holiday in Unity Township. What makes the booths appealing is their juxtaposition around the lake. Get ready for arts, crafts, and music—everything from woodworking, painting, and photography. Past festivalgoers have enjoyed poetry readings and performances by the Westmoreland Symphony, polka bands, fiddlers, and oldies music, country, and rock 'n' roll groups. International food booths offer a culinary complement. This festival begins at 11:00 a.m. and runs until 8:00 p.m. Shuttles and wheelchair-accessible vans run from the University of Pittsburgh at Greensburg. Round-trip shuttle tickets cost $2 per person.

AUGUST

Beaver County Riverfest
Ohio River at Riverfront Park, Rochester
(724) 775-1200

This celebration of the region's rivers brings out residents of Beaver County for outdoor activities, fireworks, food, and great music. Bands typically perform on a stage constructed on the riverfront, and boaters enter a contest to determine the best decorated among them. Look up and you'll see skydivers, too.

As this is open air, there's no admission charge, but you'll pay for food and other purchases.

Two Shadyside Arts Festivals
Walnut Street and Ellsworth Avenue
(412) 621-8481

There is a little rivalry of sorts between these two Shadyside festivals, but we couldn't alert you to one without the other. One festival encompasses the area of Walnut Street between South Negley and South Aiken Avenues. The Ellsworth Avenue celebration takes place between Maryland Avenue and Spahr Street.

Nightly outdoor jazz performances, workshops, and more than 200 designers of American collectibles exhibiting their wares are a part of these large community events. Recycled art and neon art plus multidimensional pieces have been on display for serious art aficionados in years past. Both festivals showcase local talent, and there is shuttle service from various points in Shadyside to avoid parking nightmares. A few of these shuttle points include Shadyside Hospital, the Pittsburgh Center for the Arts, and Sacred Heart Academy.

Greater Pittsburgh Renaissance Festival
Route 31E, west of New Stanton
(724) 872-1670
www.pgh-renfest.com

From August 14 through September 19, this re-creation of a 16th-century village brings together crafters, acting troupes, combat jousters, musicians, and food purveyors in a village setting to celebrate the arrival of the king and queen. The Westmoreland County festival is an appealing history experience for all ages. Children will particularly enjoy the Children's Dell and petting zoo. Held over five weekends, the event was moved to a new site in recent years on Route 31 East, 7 miles west of New Stanton in southwestern Westmoreland County. Take exit 51A of Interstate 70 (for those of you traveling that route). Admission is $11.95 in advance or $13.95 at the gate for adults; children ages 5 to 12 pay $3.95 in advance or $5.95 at the gate.

SEPTEMBER

Ligonier Highland Games
Idlewild Park, US 30, Ligonier
(724) 851-9900

The first weekend after Labor Day brings a Scottish fair to Ligonier, featuring bagpipe bands, highland dancing, Scottish fiddling, children's games, exhibits, and more. Friday ℹ️ There are many county fairs held throughout the region during the summer. For a comprehensive list contact the Pennsylvania State Association of County Fairs at www.pafairs.org.

and Saturday evening activities include dinner and entertainment at Mountain View Inn, by reservation only. Event hours for Saturday and Sunday are 9:00 a.m. until 6:00 p.m. Admission charges are $15 for adults and $5 for children ages 6 to 12. Those younger than age 6 enter at no cost. Parking is free as well. Group discounts are available.

Annual Pennsylvania Arts & Crafts Colonial Festival
Westmoreland Fairgrounds
RD 2, Greensburg
(724) 863-4577

Experience the pride and skill of colonial men and women in more than 170 booths as they create hand-thrown pottery, handcrafted furniture, dried floral arrangement, stained glass, tole and decorative painting, and much more. In years past there have been military encampments, a fife and drum group, a Civil War string band, carriage rides, children's activities, and refreshments at this multiday event. Rates for adults are $5.00, $4.50 for seniors, and $1.00 for children ages 6 to 12. There are indoor as well as outdoor exhibits, so come rain or shine!

Pittsburgh Irish Festival
Chevrolet Amphitheatre, Station Square
(412) 422-1113

Irish and Celtic folk music is the focus of this festival, usually held around the second weekend in September, running from Friday night through most of Sunday. Get ready for a long list of performers and bands. Previous years, the talent has included the Great Big Sea band, Tommy Makem and the Makem Brothers, David Kincaid, and Mike Gallagher. There's plenty of traditional Irish dancing, too. Admission in past years has been $9 for adults, $3 for children ages 3 to 12, and complimentary

tickets for children age 2 and younger. A three-day pass costs around $16.

Penn's Colony Festival
Allison Park, Allegheny County
(724) 352-9922

This is the closest thing you'll find to Colonial Williamsburg outside Virginia, and we've got it here in Western Pennsylvania! This is an 18th-century colonial marketplace featuring 230 American folk artists and cottage craftsmen with authentic entertainment and food. Demonstrations here have included sheep clipping and wool preparation, soapmaking as done in colonial times, and hand-stenciling for the kids. Come on Friday from 1:00 to 5:00 p.m., Saturday from 10:00 a.m. until 6:00 p.m., and Sunday 10:00 a.m. until 5:00 p.m. Admission in prior years has been $6.50 for adults, $4.50 for seniors (ages 65 and older), and $3.50 for children (ages 8 to 15). Children age 7 and younger receive complimentary admission. Parking is free of charge.

Covered Bridge Festival
Various locations throughout Washington County
(724) 228-5520

Traditionally held the third weekend in September, there's old-fashioned hospitality in store at this festival among the rolling hills of Southwestern Pennsylvania. Old-time fiddlers perform in addition to the arts and crafts, antique cars and engines, guns, and other artifacts that are displayed. Country-style food is also available at different covered bridges throughout Washington County. In prior years, just under a dozen of the covered bridges in the county were featured, and each one has its own natural flavor. Approximately 218 covered bridges remain standing in the Commonwealth of Pennsylvania. The exploring begins at 10:00 a.m. and continues until 5:00 p.m. Admission and parking for the festival are free of charge.

i During the month of December, many churches offer dramatic presentations of the journey to Bethlehem, free of charge, as a gift to their communities. Keep an eye out for mentions of these in community newspapers, church bulletins, and through word of mouth.

Richard S. Caliguiri/City of Pittsburgh Great Race & Walk
Frick Park to Point State Park
(412) 255-2493

This race is always held the last Sunday in September. Nearly 11,000 runners from around the world, many donning hilarious costumes, compete in this annual 10K great race, 5K run, and 5K walk, held in honor of the late Richard S. Caliguiri, former mayor of Pittsburgh. Caliguiri died in 1988 after a lingering illness in the prime of his political career. The race begins at Frick Park and moves to Point State Park downtown, where it concludes. Early-bird registrations save you money. If you submit them before July 16, the fee is $16. Those registering before September 3, pay $18.95. Thereafter, it costs $25 to register.

Oktoberfest
Penn Brewery, Troy Hill Road and Vinial Street
(412) 237-9402

This traditional event is held on the last two weekends in September to coincide with the actual Oktoberfest in Germany. The North Side's German heritage is in full swing as the Pennsylvania Brewing Company marks this event. Dine in the brewery restaurant on such traditional German fare as schnitzel, sauerbraten, and potato pancakes. In the outdoor tent there's often grilled wurst and chicken, pork, and strudel. Ongoing entertainment provided by German bands and a strolling accordionist complete the ambience. And of course there are plenty of beers to sample. Celebrate your German heritage (or pretend you're German!) on Friday and Saturday from 5:00 p.m. to midnight, or on Sunday from 4:00 to 10:00 p.m. The hearty aromas will tempt you, so bring along money for your food and beverage purchases.

OCTOBER

Fort Ligonier Days
US 30 and Route 711, Ligonier
(724) 238-9701

This three-day Westmoreland County festival commemorates the battle at Fort Ligonier in 1758 during the French and Indian War. It's the largest celebration in town with 150 juried craftspeople, merchant sidewalk sales, entertainment, antique window displays, and a huge parade on Saturday at 11:00 a.m. There are more than 30 food booths around the diamond, or bandstand area. Look for an official program to guide you through the festival. It's a supplement to the *Ligonier Echo* newspaper. Admission rates are $6.75 for adults and $3.75 for children (ages 6 to 14). Children younger than age 6 are admitted free of charge.

Fall Foliage Cruises
Along the Allegheny River
Armstrong County
(724) 548-3226

All month long, you're invited to board boats of the Gateway Clipper Fleet to experience the beautiful autumn foliage along the Allegheny River in Armstrong County northeast of Pittsburgh. The atmosphere is relaxing as you see the region from a totally different (waterfront) perspective. Cruises, which have in the past cost around $20 per person, are offered throughout the month of October and sail from 1:30 until 4:30 p.m.

Fall Flower Show
Phipps Conservatory and Botanical Gardens, Schenley Park
(412) 622-6914

Fall foliage is on display indoors with the splendor of autumn accented in the various rooms of the Schenley Park Conservatory in Oakland.

Phipps is open Tuesday through Sunday, 9:00 a.m. to 5:00 p.m. Phipps admission is

$10 for adults, $9 for seniors (age 62 and older), and $9 for students with ID, and $7 for children (ages 2 to 18). Children younger than 2 years old and Phipps members enter without charge. Metered parking is right in front of the conservatory.

The Pennsylvania Arts
& Crafts Christmas Festival
Washington Fairgrounds
2151 North Main Street, Washington
(724) 863-4577
This festival, held in late October and early November, boasts more than 165 exhibit booths with artists and craftspeople displaying hand-thrown pottery, handcrafted furniture, dried floral arrangements, stained glass, clothing, quilts, children's toys, wrought iron, and lots more. Santa Claus and Emmett the Elf are here for children. Trolley rides are also available. Exhibits are displayed in five heated buildings Friday, Saturday, and Sunday 10:00 a.m. until 6:00 p.m. Admission is $5.00 for adults $4.50 for seniors (ages 65 and older), $1.00 for kids (ages 6 to 12), and complimentary for children younger than age 6.

NOVEMBER AND DECEMBER

Sparkle Season & Light Up Night
Various locations throughout Downtown
(412) 566-4190
Light Up Night traditionally kicks off the holiday shopping season within the Golden Triangle, known as Sparkle Season. Light Up Night begins at 5:00 p.m. on a Friday evening and lasts until midnight. Downtown office buildings remain lit, and retailers have their holiday displays illuminated.

PPG Place is aglow in luminaria and its own towering tree. Several trees, including the Unity Tree (formerly the Joseph Horne Co. tree) at Penn Avenue Place, are unveiled, and there is the creche at the USX Plaza. (Read more about it in the Worship chapter.)

Looking down at the city from Mt. Washington is a great vantage point, especially for the fireworks.

Throughout the rest of Sparkle Season, activities, events, and displays appear throughout the city to celebrate Christmas, Chanukah, Kwanzaa, and New Year's. One such display is the Santa Exhibit at the PPG Wintergarden. The "Celebrate the Season" parade is the Saturday after Thanksgiving. And if you feel worn out, take the Holly Trolley shuttling downtown shoppers throughout the Golden Triangle. It's free of charge and stops at the major plazas and department stores, in the Cultural District, and at the Heinz History Center in the Strip District.

Sparkle Season brochures are available at the major downtown buildings with a complete list of events and special shopping hours during the holiday season.

Beaver County Festival of Trees
Brady's Run Park, off of Route 51
Beaver County
(724) 846-2411
www.beavercountyfestivaloftrees.org
This winter wonderland—indoors, mind you—lasts a long weekend and has approximately 58 decorated trees, continuous entertainment, a Santa snack bar, visits by Santa, and a talking Frosty the Snowman. Community groups and businesses decorate these trees, which are sold at the end of the festival. There's a Santa's gift shop and a model railroad on display in the park's large recreation center. Thursday hours are from 5:00 to 9:00 p.m. All other days, come around noon and stay until 9:00 p.m. Admission costs $3 for everyone ages 13 to 60, $2 for seniors, 50 cents for children ages 6 to 12, and free for those age 5 and under.

Clayton Holiday Tours
The Frick Art & Historical Center
7227 Reynolds Street
(412) 371-0600
www.frickart.org
From mid-November through the New Year's Holiday, visitors to the Frick Art & Historical Center can enjoy extended hours and special holiday tours of Henry Clay Frick's Clayton. This

ℹ️ Don't miss the display of life-size Santas from around the world at the PPG Place Wintergarden in downtown Pittsburgh each holiday season.

23-room, turn-of-the-20th-century residence is the only surviving estate in Pittsburgh's East End (Pointe Breeze), the once-fabled million-aires' row. Watchful holiday guests at Clayton might even catch a glimpse of Father Christmas, dressed in Victorian costume. They certainly gather a sense of the closeness associated with Frick holidays at Clayton. The mansion is decorated with pine, poinsettias, and other winter blooms, and the scent of evergreens prevails. For families with children ages 6 to 12, the Frick presents Family Holidays at Clayton, special tours for kids, on several Saturdays in December from 9:30 until 11:30 a.m. Cost is $10 for one adult/one child for nonmembers and $7 for members. Additional children cost $5 ($3 for members).

Hours during the holiday season are Tuesday through Saturday from 10:00 a.m. until 5:00 p.m. and Sunday from noon until 6:00 p.m. Evening tours (which run until 8:00 p.m.) are offered on selected days, so it's best to call for the exact dates each year. Tours of Clayton cost $10 for adults, $8 for seniors, and $6 for students. Members are admitted free of charge.

For more information about Clayton and the Frick museums, turn to the Architecture and Arts chapters.

ZooLights
Pittsburgh Zoo & PPG Aquarium
One Hill Road
(412) 665-3640
Brought to the zoo by AT&T, ZooLights transforms the zoo into a display of more than 500,000 lights from 5:30 until 8:30 p.m. closing time each night for approximately six weeks. Visitors can stop at various indoor locations for hot cocoa, to see the indoor zoo exhibits, or merely to warm up from the brisk night air. The Pittsburgh Zoo is closed on Christmas Eve and Christmas Day. Admission

to ZooLights costs approximately $4 for nonmembers and $3 for zoo members. Parking for ZooLights is free.

Santa's Trolley
Pennsylvania Trolley Museum
1 Museum Road (off Race Track Road)
Washington
(724) 228-9256
www.pa-trolley.org
The trolley begins operation the day after Thanksgiving and runs for three weekends. All aboard the Santa Express! Kris Kringle arrives in true trolley fashion to kick off the holiday season's popular Santa's Trolley. Children and their families can ride with Santa aboard one of the vintage trolleys while listening to the sounds of Christmas carols. Kids can make special crafts, and visitors can operate the Lionel trains on the museum's large "you run it" display. Santa's Trolley pulls out regularly from 11:00 a.m. until 5:00 p.m. Admission rates are $8 for adults, $7 for seniors (age 62 and older), and $5 for children (ages 3 to 15). Those age 2 and younger are admitted free.

Miniature Railroad & Village
Carnegie Science Center
One Allegheny Avenue (next to Three Rivers Stadium)
(412) 237-3400
Whereas many other train displays close up shop after the holiday season, this North Side one stays open Thanksgiving through the end of January, and throughout many months of the year.

This is a true Pittsburgh tradition. The railroad display began in the 1950s but, because of the limited space, had to be dismantled each spring. Now the 2,300-square-foot

ℹ️ If you plan to attend the Miniature Railroad Village at the Carnegie Science Center, know in advance that holidays are the peak period. More than 6,000 visitors each day pass through in the week between Christmas and New Year's. So plan to stand in line.

exhibit, featuring new models each year, is left in place, closed only periodically for refurbishment (for a week in June and again from September 27 through mid-November). The miles of train displays feature an O-gauge railroad and beautiful animated scenery showing the region's history.

Regular hours run Sunday through Friday from 10:00 a.m. until 5:00 p.m. and on Saturday from 10:00 a.m. to 9:00 p.m.

Admission costs vary. Adults can see the exhibits for $14, children (ages 3 to 12) and seniors (age 62 and older) pay $10, and science center members are free. For more detailed prices for the rest of the science center facility and attractions, turn to the Attractions chapter.

LeMoyne House Candlelight Tours
East Maiden Street, Washington
(724) 225-6740
Typically this event is held the first weekend in December. Sponsored by the Washington County Historical Society, these evening candlelight tours show the LeMoyne House decorated for Christmas with costumed actors portraying members of the LeMoyne family. Admission rates are $5 for adults and $3 for students. Candlelight hours run from 5:00 to 9:00 p.m. on Saturday and 2:00 to 6:00 p.m. on Sunday.

Candlelight Christmas at Old Economy Village
14th and Church Streets, Ambridge
(724) 266-1803, (724) 266-4500
Traditional German Christmas decorations and legends are displayed in the historic village of the 19th-century Harmony Society, here in Beaver County. Food, crafts, and entertainment are always a part of the annual festivities. More than 25 rooms are decorated for the season, nightly from 5:00 until 9:00 p.m. This event is held for only two days, usually at the start of December, so call in advance or you might miss out. The village, lit only by the glow of candlelight and with the scent of pine prevailing, is sure to put you in

the holiday spirit! The tour takes you out of the hustle and bustle of the season, allowing you to focus on simplicity. Cost is $6 per person. For those interested in the special Christmas Dinner Tour, the cost is $45 per person, and reservations are necessary. The dinner typically takes place after the two-day tours, but again, call for the exact day and times.

Holidays at The Carnegie
4400 Forbes Avenue
(412) 622-3131
Stop in to see this annual Christmas tree exhibit that illuminates the Hall of Architecture. Each year, there's a different theme. Past trees have celebrated the Russian czars, French impressionists, and Victorian England. Traditional carols echo throughout the great halls of the museum and art galleries. Previous exhibits have included rare nativity scenes and spiritual paintings. Concerts are performed most days.

Admission to the Carnegie Museum of Natural History and Museum of Art is $15 for adults, $12 for seniors, and $11 for students with ID and children (ages 3 to 18). Children younger than age 3 and members are admitted free of charge. Call for the Carnegie's *Holiday Program Guide*.

Candlelight Evenings at Phipps Conservatory and Botanical Gardens
Schenley Park
(412) 622-6914
www.phipps.conservatory.org
Throughout December each year, the conservatory remains open later than usual during the holiday season. The rooms are dressed for the holidays with lights and festive decorations. Special tours can be arranged.

Phipps admission is $10 for adults, $9 for seniors age 62 and older, $9 for students with ID, and $7 for children (ages 2 to 18). Children younger than age 2 and Phipps members enter without charge. Metered parking is right in front of the conservatory.

First Night
Various locations throughout Downtown
(888) PGH-FEST (744-3378)
www.firstnightpgh.com

Go out with a big bang, as the expression says! Pittsburgh's First Night celebration occurs each year for families. It's the city's way of planning a safe alternative for New Year's Eve. Events and locations vary, but package deals are available so that families can book a room at a Downtown hotel. Public transportation into the Downtown area is also offered. Performances in years past have included Joe Negri from *Mister Rogers' Neighborhood* and Margo Loveland puppets, among others. Fireworks are courtesy of Zambelli International of New Castle, Lawrence County (also known as the fireworks capital of the world).

i Many small train displays are presented locally each December, such as the one the Penn Hills Police display at their municipal building. Call your own borough or municipality for local exhibits.

In past years, those who wanted to attend all events had to purchase a First Night button costing $15 for adults and $5 for children (ages 6 to 12). Children younger than age 6 did not have to pay. But if you just want to see what's happening in the open-air spaces, there is no cost for First Night. Check the daily newspaper for particulars each year, including special parking and public transportation hours.

ARCHITECTURE

As the sun sets on Pittsburgh's Golden Triangle, it lights the pinnacles of PPG Place and reflects off several other shimmering skyscrapers that are the city's architectural gems. These dominant corporate headquarters, including the mighty U.S. Steel Tower, add aesthetically as well as economically to the city. Often the modern buildings reflect the transitions our companies have undergone—companies such as PPG industries (Pittsburgh Plate Glass decades ago) and U.S. Steel.

Today nothing is half-veiled in smoke the way many buildings erected in 19th-century Pittsburgh were back when heavy industry polluted the skies. And plenty of these structures merit close attention, especially for aficionados of great architecture. In this chapter discover the highlights, including the works of famous architects and a brief tour of architectural masterpieces you won't want to miss.

Of course with any remarkable achievement and improvement comes controversy, and Pittsburgh has had its share. For instance, downtown Pittsburgh was a picture of urban vitality back in the late 1940s. Well before shopping malls, many downtown merchants thrived in Italianate, Victorian Gothic, or Art Deco buildings.

In an effort to restore such commercial vitality to the downtown area and encourage new housing developments, City of Pittsburgh officials have struggled with plans that would forge into the future while saving at least some semblance of the past. As you might guess, it's hard to merge the wishes of preservationists with the need of modern merchants, corporations, and developers. At this writing, it's hoped that many important facades and the city's skyline can be maintained while making way for renovations and

new construction of entertainment, corporate and housing complexes.

You will notice in this chapter that we depart from the geographic breakdown used in other chapters throughout this book. Instead we start with information on history and preservation efforts and close the chapter with a short list of important buildings and bridges, some of which are broken down by region. The highlight of the chapter is our downtown walking tour, which features many of Pittsburgh's most important buildings. If you've never taken a walking tour, now's your chance.

In keeping with the architectural theme, this chapter focuses more on the structural aspects of design than the historical appeal. So you won't find descriptions of buildings simply because they are old. Of course architecture and history overlap, and where appropriate, you might want to refer to the History chapter.

Now get ready to read about the fascinating creations and works of building art brought about by names such as Hornbostel, Janssen, Klauder, Osterling, Richardson, and Wright. Their contributions quite literally made our city what it is today.

ARCHITECTURAL PERIODS

From the formation of Fort Pitt after the British took hold of Pittsburgh Point in 1758, this city has enjoyed a rich structural heritage. The settlement phase was followed by the Georgian simplicity of 1785 to 1830. The latter-day form of Georgian style is what we now call the Federal style.

The Greek Revival period came next, followed by the mid-Victorian era. The Manchester and Mexican War Streets neighborhoods on the city's North Side remain primarily Victorian examples of architecture. Unfortunately, this mid-Victorian style was thought by some to have a harsh appearance.

New ideas characterized the years following the Civil War. Helping to propel these insights was the American Institute of Architects, which became a national organization in 1857. Architectural schools, exhibitions, and journals became recognized forces. All of this focus culminated in a time of experimentation, most notably in East Coast cities such as Boston and Philadelphia. Henry Hobson Richardson was one of these experimental architects.

Richardson, his firm based in Brookline, Massachusetts, submitted his plans to rebuild the Allegheny County Courthouse and Jail in 1883. (In May 1882, fire had gutted the rotunda of the second county courthouse, reducing the building to a sandstone shell.) The first and original jail structure had been built in the Downtown Market Square area (known as the Diamond in years prior).

The simplicity of Richardson's Romanesque design was alluring with its rounded arches, rugged stone walls, and Byzantine leaf carving. He was formally chosen for the job from among competitors in 1884.

The original jail and courthouse site was 10 feet higher due to a hump, commonly referred to as Grant's Hill, that was eventually lowered in 1912. Subsequent widening of Grant Street required that the entrances be lengthened in the 1920s. But to look upon the finished structure is to see the beauty of the intricate carvings, the rise of the tower, the way in which the sun grazes the exterior stone, and most certainly the handsome grand staircase Richardson created.

The Allegheny County Courthouse and jail are regarded as the finest works of architecture in the city. Richardson is quoted as saying, "If they honor me for the pygmy things I have already done, what will they say when they see Pittsburgh finished?" Sadly, the architect passed away before his vision was realized. Work did not conclude on these structures until 1888, two years after his death. (See walking tour below.)

ADDITIONAL ARCHITECTURAL STRIDES

As the application of architecture became more professional around the country, Pittsburgh felt the effects as well. The Carnegie Technical Schools, founded in 1900 and the predecessor of today's Carnegie Mellon University, incorporated architecture into its curriculum in 1905. Architects sought more modern ways of designing. American architects practicing their trade between 1890 and 1930 are loosely categorized as Eclectics.

Henry Hornbostel, a partner in the New York firm of Palmer & Hornbostel, won the 1904 competition for the master plan of the Carnegie Technical Schools. During the next two decades, Hornbostel carved out his architectural domain, quite literally, in the Oakland-Shadyside area. Among the buildings he designed were the Rodef Shalom Temple, Soldiers' and Sailors' Memorial, the U.S. Bureau of Mines building (now a part of CMU), the Schenley Apartments, and the University Club in Oakland. Two downtown buildings, the City-County Building and the Grant Building, are also among Hornbostel's creations.

Major Eclectic buildings erected during the Great Depression include the Gulf Building and Mellon Institute (both Downtown), East Liberty Presbyterian Church (in East Liberty), Buhl Planetarium (on the North Side), and the Cathedral of Learning and Heinz Chapel (both in Oakland at the University of Pittsburgh). Engineers, contractors, and suppliers were accustomed to the whims, even fantasies, of architects during this time. However, as material became more expensive and money in short supply during the war years, Eclecticism steadily declined. (Read more detail of these noteworthy buildings later in this chapter.)

PITTSBURGH'S RENAISSANCE

It wasn't until the 1950s that the architectural effects of Pittsburgh's first Renaissance could actually be seen, although plans for revitalization had begun years before. Soon after World War II ended, smoke abatement became one of the city's priorities. Business and government leaders—Republican Richard King Mellon and Democrat David L. Lawrence, chief among them—joined forces for the future. Mellon and Lawrence were indeed a powerful pair, convincing the city's populace to listen to their ideas for Pittsburgh's Renaissance.

The Fort Pitt Blockhouse was saved, but freight terminals at what is now Point State Park gave way to create the Gateway Center office complex. It's interesting to note that many ideas had surfaced to create the Point as we know it today. Among the visions tabled were those Edgar J. Kaufmann, the department store owner, commissioned from his own architect, Frank Lloyd Wright. Grandiose schemes were quietly put aside, for they lacked any concern over cost and were considered to be extravagant for the times.

The building boom continued all over the region. In the 1950s the lower Hill District was cleared to make room for the Civic Arena, now known as the Mellon Arena. Structures on the North Side in the former city of Allegheny made way for Allegheny Center. Other buildings, particularly those of historical significance, were saved in part by the Pittsburgh History & Landmarks Foundation, founded in 1964.

Also during this time, buildings began to display their corporate products. The firm of Harrison & Abramovitz showed off the functional and decorative uses of aluminum in the Alcoa Building, erected in the early 1950s. The firm did the same years later in 1970, designing the U.S. Steel Building (also known as the U.S. Steel).

In the mid-1970s Landmarks, as the foundation is known, turned its attention to another large-scale property, the Pittsburgh & Lake Erie Railroad complex. With an eye toward commercial revitalization, Landmarks saw potential in this site along the south shore of the Monongahela River. Why not try the notion of historic preservation coupled with urban development? The result is what we know today as Station Square on the South Side. Five historic railroad buildings were saved and adapted to stand beside several new buildings.

Renaissance II

Pittsburgh's second Renaissance altered the skyline yet again. Although the 680-foot main tower of PPG Place still doesn't match the height of the USX Tower (at 841 feet), the complex architecturally changed the city forever. Perhaps no other structure since Klauder's Cathedral of Learning or Richardson's County Courthouse has had the impact of PPG Place.

Here we see Gothic translated into plate glass by architect John Burgee with Philip Johnson. The six buildings that make up PPG Place were completed in 1984 and are leased to various retailers and businesses.

Also in the 1980s, the old Jenkins Arcade was razed to make way for Fifth Avenue Place. This and the Dominion Tower (formerly known as CNG Tower) are smaller, yet substantial additions to the city as well, since the former houses an upscale shopping complex (see the Shopping chapter) and the latter the corporate headquarters of Dominion.

Add to the delicate balance between developers and preservationists, the local architectural design community. The city, home to two internationally known programs in architectural education, at Carnegie Mellon University and the University of Pittsburgh, boasts an amazing group of architects and planners who practice their crafts professionally in the region. More importantly, these men and women volunteer to serve community development organizations, historic review commissions, and zoning and planning boards. As the city moves forward, whether it is the redevelopment of the downtown's Market Square, the addition of a the first casino on the North Shore, or the redevelopment of

Thinking Green

Western Pennsylvania is one of the "greenest" regions in the country. According to the Green Building Alliance, the region is a national leader in LEED-certified buildings, whether you measure by the number of LEED-certified buildings, or the overall square footage of LEED-certified space. FYI, green buildings incorporate design and construction practices that reduce or eliminate the negative impact of buildings on the environment and occupants in five broad areas: sustainable site planning, safeguarding water and water efficiency, energy efficiency and renewable energy, conservation of materials and resources, and indoor environmental quality. Energy savings of between 25 and 50 percent are common for green buildings, and a few cases have documented 90 percent savings!

Mellon Arena area in the Hill District, citizens can expect spirited public debate, more government transparency, and continued opportunities for development. Rest assured, architecturally, the future of Pittsburgh will be beautiful to behold.

ARCHITECTURAL EXHIBITS

Hall of Architecture
Carnegie Museum of Art, 4400 Forbes Avenue
(412) 622-3131
www.cmoa.org
In this grand space, architecture has been an important part of the Carnegie since it opened in 1895. Carnegie Institute, designed by Longfellow, Alden & Harlow, was an outstanding example of academic Classicism. The Hall of Architecture, which opened in 1907, became a major feature of the Carnegie, with 144 full-scale plaster casts of building fragments—pulpits, columns, portals, and pediments, even an entire facade capturing the history of Western architecture.

Here you can see the east and west fronts of the Parthenon as well as a portal of the north transept of the Cathedral of Sainte-Andre at Bordeaux. Browsing through this skylit space, designed especially for the display of these casts, you will see samples of columns, pillars, and doorways from Romanesque, Italian Byzantine, French Gothic, and many other periods of historic architecture.

The Hall of Architecture is one of three surviving cast courts today, and it is the only one in North America. It's not uncommon to see groups of students gathered within the room studying the displays. Indeed, the purpose of the hall's creation was so that everyone, not just those who could afford to travel abroad, could study the form and detail of architecture in full scale.

The Hall of Architecture is open during regular museum hours, Tuesday, Wednesday, Friday, and Saturday 10:00 a.m. to 5:00 p.m.; Thursday 10:00 a.m. to 8:00 p.m.; and Sunday noon to 5:00 p.m. Admission is $15 for adults, $12 for seniors, and $11 for students and children (ages 3 to 18). Children younger than age 3 and members are admitted free of charge.

The Heinz Architectural Center
Carnegie Museum of Art, 4400 Forbes Avenue
(412) 622-3131
www.cmoa.org
Founded in 1990, the Heinz Architectural Center honors the memory of Henry J. Heinz II, who during his lifetime combined a deep interest in architecture with a commitment to Pittsburgh. Here you'll find architectural drawings, photographs, models, artifacts, and related items. While the center's scope is international, it still places significance on the architecture of Western Pennsylvania.

Cicognani Kalla Architects designed the Heinz Architectural Center with galleries specifically suited for the exhibition of drawings, a study room, and support spaces. Every few months these exhibits change.

Throughout the rest of the center, much of the collection of drawings, models, prints, and photographs represents the 19th and 20th centuries. Designs for residential, institutional, commercial, and industrial buildings are included, as well as examples of engineering, landscape, furniture, and interior design.

A special affiliation between the Heinz Architectural Center at the Carnegie Museum of Art and the Royal Academy of Arts in London allows these two institutions to collaborate on exhibitions, publications, and programs of mutual interest. Exhibits at the center change every few months, usually with one of the exhibits featuring art from Andrew Carnegie's own collection.

The Architectural Center is open during regular museum hours: Tuesday, Wednesday, Friday, and Saturday 10:00 a.m. to 5:00 p.m.; Thursday 10:00 a.m. to 8:00; and Sunday noon to 5:00 p.m. Admission is $15 for adults, $12 for seniors, and $11 for students and children (ages 3 to 18). Children younger than age 3 and members are admitted free of charge.

ARCHITECTURAL PRESERVATION

Pittsburgh History & Landmarks Foundation
100 West Station Square Drive, Suite 450
(412) 471-5808
www.phlf.org
This nonprofit historic preservation organization was founded in 1964 to explore and assess regional architecture and preserve Pittsburgh's history.

Landmarks, as the foundation is known, compiled the first countywide architectural site survey in the nation and has published many studies of regional architects, buildings, and landscape design, including the hefty book *Pittsburgh's Landmark Architecture,* written by Walter C. Kidney, published in 1997, and revised in 2001. Many books and publications produced by Landmarks can be found at the Carnegie Library, in local bookstores, or through their Web site.

Since 1965 the Pittsburgh History & Landmarks Foundation has offered a variety of walking tours throughout the Golden Triangle where visitors and even lifetime Pittsburghers can learn from trained docents. These range from one-hour walking tours of the downtown area to customized, in-depth excursions filling one or two days. Walking tour field trips for school groups can also be arranged. Hours are Monday through Friday, 9:00 a.m. to 5:00 p.m. excluding holidays.

By becoming a member of the Pittsburgh History & Landmarks Foundation, you'll save on tours, publications, and educational programs; get special invitations and a *PHLF News;* 10 per cent discount at many local historic bed and breakfast and inns; and have access to the foundation's James D. Van Trump Library of architecture and historical materials.

10/1/09

DOWNTOWN WALKING TOUR

Though there are guided tours available, there's nothing to keep you from discovering Pittsburgh's streets, structural facades, and architectural highlights on your own. Lace up your comfortable walking shoes, and come along on our own Insiders' tour of Downtown. The tour will be as brief or as long as you prefer. There may be some buildings in which you'll want to browse for a while and other facades you may want to skip. The choice is yours. But if you took a few minutes to stop, read, and look at each mention, we're guessing you'll complete the tour in about two hours. As we said, it all depends upon your gait and your curiosity.

Our starting point will be Station Square, where you can easily park your car in the parking garage or outdoor lot. Our best advice is to bring along this book, and plan your walking adventure in good weather. That way you can stop along the sidewalk, follow the directions of where to turn next, and read about the structure you're passing.

started from our hotel,
Omni Wm. Penn

Station Square
South Side

On a 40-acre site on the south bank of the Monongahela River that was once the center of a bustling railroad and a complex of operational buildings sits a major tourist attraction, office complex, and shopping mall called Station Square.

In the late 1870s the Pittsburgh & Lake Erie Railroad consisted of coal freight, boxcar leasing, and passenger service at the northwest corner of Carson and Smithfield Streets.

Architect William George Burns was chosen to create a new train station, which was extolled in an 1896 issue of the *American Architect*. Building began in 1899. Upon completion, the structure and its interior were extensively praised. The Chicago firm of Crossman and Sturdy was responsible for the interior, and the watercolor for the waiting room was written about in the *Pittsburgh Architectural Club Exhibition Catalog of 1900*.

The vestibule and waiting room were filled with decorative details—marble, mosaic, and stained-glass elements. Pittsburgh historian James Van Trump called it "the finest Edwardian interior in the city," second only to the Carnegie Music Hall foyer.

By 1970, when other forms of transportation had made the railroad somewhat obsolete, the ornate spaces were empty, and the terminal complex, with a great barrel-vaulted ceiling in the waiting room, was a prime focus of restoration. The Allegheny Foundation, a Scaife family trust, provided the necessary funding to the Pittsburgh History & Landmarks Foundation to sponsor this restored site, which would be dubbed Station Square.

Today the old waiting room is now the Grand Concourse restaurant (see the Restaurant chapter), and natural light shines through the clean stained glass. The Gandy Dancer Bar was fashioned out of part of the former baggage area.

The dingy, tarnished, and faded facades have been polished in other buildings as well. The former shovel warehouse was transformed into an office complex. The freight house underwent a metamorphosis into a modern-day arcade of shops, restaurants, and entertainment possibilities. Smaller structures such as the gatehouse and express house were also remodeled. Several years ago, an additional entertainment complex, including a "dancing fountain with music shows and a marina, were added. For a complete listing of attractions, visit www.stationsquare.com.

Plenty of commuters find the parking at Station Square convenient for workdays or stadium games as they board the Gateway Clipper Fleet of sightseeing and dinner cruise vessels. Special events are sometimes held on the grounds as well (see Annual Events).

Standing just outside the Landmarks Building at Station Square, we'll step onto the bridge deck to continue our tour. One of the oldest and most remarkable bridges in Allegheny County, the Smithfield Street Bridge used to be called the Monongahela Bridge.

Smithfield Street Bridge
Downtown and South Side

Visitors to Station Square can't miss this bridge spanning the Monongahela River—it's one of Pittsburgh's oldest and most remarkable. When engineer Gustav Lindenthal designed it between 1981 and 1983 (with Stanley L. Roush, the architect for the bridge's portals), it replaced the Monongahela Bridge, a covered wood truss. The forces of the two 360-foot main lenticular-truss-type spans seem to cancel each other out. An arch thrusts outward on the upper cord. The lower cord pulls inward. Several restorations have taken place since the original design. In 1995 the Roush portals and main spans were repainted in their original colors—deep blue for the trusses, brown for the flooring, and a creamy yellow for the portals. The bridge has been designated a National Historic Civil Engineering Landmark. Notice as you walk across the bridge that the upper cord visually cancels out the lower cord.

Victorian Fronts
Various locations along Fort Pitt Boulevard

Standing at the traffic light across the bridge, you'll see to your left the Victorian fronts of a row of commercial buildings along the 200 block of Fort Pitt Boulevard.

Cross Fort Pitt Boulevard at the light, and walk 1 block north on Smithfield Street to First Avenue.

Keep walking 3 more blocks, crossing the Boulevard of the Allies and Third Avenue and stopping at Fourth Avenue. Here at the corner of Smithfield Street and Fourth Avenue, you could take a rest if you like on one of the outdoor benches right outside Dollar Bank.

Dollar Bank
340 Fourth Avenue
(412) 261-7538

Philadelphia architects Isaac Hobbs & Sons designed this bank in a era when the word Victorian was usually the equivalent of "monstrosity." This structure was begun in 1868 and completed in 1871. The strong columns at the Fourth Avenue entrance suggest solidity. The lions on each side are masculine in detail. Fourth Avenue used to be the investment district, and many buildings here have a rather masculine look to them.

When you get up from your brief bench reprieve, turn left down Fourth Avenue, quickly passing the Times Building (336 Fourth Avenue). This is one of architect Frederick J. Osterling's most successful designs, in Richardson Romanesque fashion, with its rounded arches.

Shortly, across the street you'll see the awnings and brass sign that designate the Bank Tower (307 Fourth Avenue), built in the 1890s. Architects Alden and Harlow are responsible for the semicircular grand staircase. Cross the street and stroll into the Bank Tower's lobby (if the building is open). Glancing up the stairwell, you'll see the marble intarsia of the balustrade.

Once you have finished admiring the building, exit on Fourth Avenue and turn right, continuing toward the shimmering glass tower we know as PPG Place. You'll cross Wood Street, passing both the Investment Building (239 Fourth Avenue) and the Benedum-Trees Building (221, 223, 225 Fourth Avenue) on your right.

Burke's Building
209 Fourth Avenue
www.city.pittsburgh.pa.us/wt/html/burke_s_building.html

Immediately before PPG Place on the right is a tiny building of great architectural significance. This is the Burke's Building, Pittsburgh's oldest commercial structure.

As the oldest commercial building in the Golden Triangle, the Burke's Building is what remains of the city's Greek Revival period. When the great Downtown Fire of 1845 destroyed many buildings, this one was fortunately spared. This small building was designed by architect John Chislett in 1836. It's small, but with the plaque outside, you shouldn't have any trouble finding it. It's literally right next door to PPG Place.

PPG Place
One PPG Place

Witness the spectacle of PPG Place, the shimmering tower we've been saying you'd find. You can't miss this plate-glass complex with the tower rising 680 feet into the downtown sky. In fact, young movie fans affectionately refer to the structure as "the Inspector Gadget building," since that Disney film used Pittsburgh and PPG Place as its backdrops. But this is only its more recent claim to fame.

In 1979 PPG Industries, wanting to make a one-time gift of significant proportions to the city, commissioned architects to show off the company's product of plate glass. The site chosen was a stretch of land from the Boulevard of the Allies, through Third and Fourth Avenues, to Market Square. But you don't just decide to construct a towering complex without a lot of scrutiny.

PPG heard the many fears that their design might block the midday light and forever harm the appeal of nearby Market

Square. The company involved city planners in selecting architects Philip Johnson and John Burgee. While the original intent might have been to build a single tower, the final plan included six buildings, with the tower (One PPG Place) serving as corporate headquarters for PPG Industries. The complex was completed in 1984.

To meet the city's 20 percent open space requirement, the architects and planners created a formal plaza on the east side of the tower between Third and Fourth Avenues. In 2003, the Plaza at PPG Place was redesigned to include a water feature that shoots 140 columns of water into the air. Both children and adults can access the water feature, providing much entertainment for those enjoying their lunch at nearby tables. Now a year-round attraction, that feature is replaced in winter months with a 104-foot-by-104-foot ice-skating rink, complete with a decorated Christmas tree.

Philip Johnson saw Pittsburgh as Gothic. The tower, with its silver-gray glass that you can't see through, has eight wonderful pinnacles reaching up to the sky. The building is glazed with nearly 20,000 pieces of reflective glass—the company's flagship product—that catch the sunset over the Point nightly. Inside the lobby of this headquarters building sits the PPG Wintergarden, where the annual Christmas Santa display is a popular attraction (see the Annual Events chapter).

From the Burke's Building, keep walking along Fourth Avenue, literally a few steps, and open the glass doors to Two PPG Place, one of the complex's six buildings, on your right. Go through the second set of doors entering the retail arcade (the food-court escalators greet you, should you need a beverage by now). Out the glass doors directly ahead of you is Market Square, once known as the Diamond. From the mid-1790s until 1852, it accommodated not only market stalls but also the First Allegheny County Courthouse.

Market Square is currently used as a small, open-air space for rallies, political announcements, and even concerts in warm weather. Workers often eat lunch on the benches, appreciating the ambience and sunshine. Continue straight from your glass door departure point with one warning. Duck the pigeons! They flock in Market Square, much to the chagrin of most every resident and visitor. As you walk you will pass several small shops and the 1902 Landmark Tavern. This building, along with the Oyster House restaurant, are Market Square's oldest structures.

The street you are walking on is not marked with a street sign. When you get to the intersection at Fifth Avenue, however, you will find an inscription on the curb stating this is Graeme Street.

From Fifth Avenue On

Turn right onto Fifth Avenue and begin walking east toward Macy's, formerly known as Kaufmann's. A 2-block walk will put you at the intersection of Fifth Avenue and Smithfield Street, with Macy's on the far right corner. Notice the popular Kaufmann's Clock, under which many a rendezvous for Pittsburghers have taken place. But wait! Don't cross the street (unless you're meeting someone, of course).

We want you to turn left at this juncture, crossing Fifth Avenue as you proceed north on Smithfield Street. Walk 2 blocks (passing Saks Fifth Avenue on your left) until you come to Sixth Avenue, where you will take another left to explore two of Pittsburgh's architecturally significant churches and a club for the powers that be.

Trinity Cathedral
328 Sixth Avenue
(412) 232-6404
www.trinitycathedralpgh.org
You'll know you're in the right place when you see Trinity Cathedral. Detroit architect Gordon Lloyd designed this house of worship in 1871 using the decorated Gothic of early 14th-century England as his style for this Episcopal cathedral. While a fire in 1969 damaged portions of the structure, the interior still reflects its original mid-Victorian appeal. Outside

there's a historic courtyard, and the cemetery holds some of Pittsburgh's oldest graves.

First Presbyterian Church of Pittsburgh
320 Sixth Avenue
(412) 471-3436
www.fpcp.org

First Presbyterian Church is next door to Trinity, just a step away. On property donated by the Penn family (William Penn was the founder of Pennsylvania), Philadelphia architect Theophilus Parsons Chandler began constructing the church in 1903, completing it two years later. The cathedral-like front is reminiscent of 13th- and 14th-century English Gothic. Inside, the nave windows (all but one) are by the Tiffany Studios, and the sanctuary boasts rectangular preaching space. Notice also the raised side galleries.

Duquesne Club
325 Sixth Avenue
(412) 391-1500
www.duquesne.org

Directly across the street from First Presbyterian on Sixth Avenue sits the bastion of what some would say was the "old boy network" in Pittsburgh. Women were once excluded from the Duquesne Club as leading industrialists conducted countless business transactions. The architectural firm of Longfellow, Alden & Harlow designed the club between 1887 and 1889. Alden & Harlow added to the main front in 1902, and further remodeling was completed by Janssen & Cocken, which added a tower in 1930 to 1931.

Return up Sixth Avenue to Smithfield Street and proceed past Mellon Square, an outdoor park atop an underground parking garage, on your right. This puts you at a street called William Penn Place (the same street is named Cherry Way a few blocks south of here). Walk 1 more block to Grant Street, and cross it. You can't miss the skyscrapers such as the USX Tower, the tallest building in downtown Pittsburgh.

Turn left and walk past the USX Tower, which we'll describe in detail soon. En route,

i Books on Western Pennsylvania and Pittsburgh architecture are on display in the Heinz Architectural Center. Many of these are also available on the shelves of Carnegie Library next door.

notice how Grant Street offers a handsome view of old architecture juxtaposed next to modern-day skyscrapers.

There's the First English Evangelical Lutheran Church (615 Grant Street), the Gulf Tower, and the Koppers Building (both at Seventh Avenue and Grant Street). Continue your walk to the end of Grant Street.

At the traffic light you will see where Port Authority buses turn onto the East Busway. Cross this stretch of pavement at the light to the Pennsylvanian.

The Pennsylvanian
Grant Street and Liberty Avenue
www.thepennsylvanian.com

You'll know you are in the right place as you peer up at the former train station's Beaux Arts rotunda—a 1900 architectural student's dream and the first sight rail passengers used to see of the city upon arrival.

Inside the rotunda, on pendentives beneath the skylit dome, four women's heads once smiled down upon tablets naming four destinations of the Pennsylvania Railroad. Passenger service diminished in the 1940s, and soon buses used the rotunda, so large was its scale. Eventually the bus traffic ceased as well. In 1988 a restored Union Station became the Pennsylvanian apartment complex. Many of the architectural highlights from the heyday of the trains remain in place today.

We'll soon end the walking tour, taking you past the gem of Pittsburgh architecture—Richardson's Allegheny County Courthouse. But there are a few more substantial structures for you to recognize. For instance, there's the USX Tower as you make your way south back along Grant Street (in the opposite direction you came from).

U.S. Steel Tower
600 Grant Street

At 841 feet high, the USX Tower is the tallest building in downtown Pittsburgh, and one of the tallest buildings between New York City and Chicago. Once known as the U.S. Steel Building (before the company merged with Marathon Oil), it towers 64 stories into the sky. Harrison & Abramovitz started construction in 1968 and completed the project in 1971. The skyscraper is made of an exposed frame of Cor-Ten weathering steel, a rust-resistant steel originally developed for the insides of grain hopper railcars that could not be painted. However, the Cor-Ten finish did need to be painted, as the rust that formed washed off onto other nearby sidewalks. Interestingly, the columns and girders are filled with water to resist fire (and antifreeze to prevent the expansion of frozen water).

If you keep walking on the left sidewalk next to the USX Tower, you will pass One Mellon Center, corporate headquarters of Mellon Financial Corporation. If you're on the other side of Grant Street (across the street from the U.S. Steel Tower), you'll pass both the Omni William Penn Hotel and Union Trust Building on your right.

Omni William Penn Hotel
530 William Penn Place
(412) 281-7100
www.omnihotels.com

The Omni William Penn Hotel is an American Renaissance masterpiece erected by industrialist Henry Clay Frick between 1914 and 1916. Designed by Janssen & Abbott, the hotel was enlarged in the late 1920s by their successor firm, Janssen & Cocken. *(now has a Starbucks)*

Inside, the Palm Court Lobby has been restored to its original splendor. This is where guests today enjoy afternoon tea and piano music. For a lovely dining experience, the setting is the Terrace Room, framed in carved walnut with original rococo detailing and murals depicting Fort Duquesne during the Revolutionary War.

The centerpiece of this hotel, however, is the Art Deco classic of black marble and Carrara glass, gold detailing, and exotic murals in the Urban Room, named for designer Joseph Urban. This famed room resides on the 17th floor. For years this hotel was known simply as the William Penn Hotel—named for Pennsylvania's founder—until its purchase by the Westin hotel chain in 1984, and its most recent change from Westin to Omni.

Union Trust Building
501 Grant Street

— wonderful interior + roof, must be viewed from a distance

First called the Union Arcade, this was one of Henry Clay Frick's buildings all in a row. He chose architect Frederick J. Osterling to build the Union Arcade, with its prominent rotunda roof. The project was begun in 1915 and finished two years later. Osterling designed this 237-foot Gothic building using carved gray sandstone, terra-cotta, and green granite exterior trim, with plenty of bronze, marble, and terra-cotta inside. You'll also notice the specially designed light fixtures and leaded glass.

In 1922 the Union Trust Company purchased the building from the Frick estate and remodeled the building the next year, naming it the Union Trust Building. The main vault held more than a billion dollars in silver, cash, and securities. The most significant architectural change was Grecian, but it blended well with the original Gothic design.

The Union Trust Company merged with Mellon National Bank in 1946, and the character of the building changed a bit as the new owner closed in and floored over the excess corridor space from the second through fourth floors. When Mellon completed its new corporate headquarters in the 1980s, this site became Two Mellon Bank Center. After additional corporate mergers, Mellon vacated the building in 2007, and it reverted to its former name, the Union Trust Building. Although offices occupy the upper floors, the first floor still contains several shops. If nothing more, cut through the building on a rainy day to escape the elements and admire the rotunda.

From where you stand on either side of the street, you can't miss the beautiful detailing of Richardson's Romanesque design in the Allegheny County Courthouse and Jail.

Allegheny Courthouse and Jail
Between Grant and Ross Streets
(412) 350-5300 (for courthouse tours)

New technical approaches to design may have originated elsewhere, but they soon found their way into downtown Pittsburgh. When Henry Hobson Richardson's Romanesque design was selected, its simplicity was the alluring element, with its rounded arches, rugged stone walls, and Byzantine leaf carving. Richardson was formally chosen from competitors in 1883 to move ahead with this project to replace the second County Courthouse, which had been gutted by fire.

Since Richardson hailed from Boston (where his famous Trinity Church stands), the stone brought in for the courthouse was quarried in Massachusetts, and many Boston stone carvers and contractors came to Pittsburgh to work for the architect.

Richardson designed each court facility to be self-contained and lighted both from the courtyard and the street. Judges' chambers and jury and consultation rooms were planned for the building's turrets. The tower, at 325 feet high, dominated the skyline until the Frick Building forever altered the view in 1901.

One courtroom—Judge Raymond Novak's courtroom—has been restored to its original splendor. The lighting and paint were replicated, and a beam in Richardson's work exposed (rather than have drop or artificial ceilings). Much of the furniture used in the restored courtroom today is vintage. Shepley, Rutan & Coolidge, an architectural firm led by Richardson's son-in-law, George Shepley, designed and purchased much of the courthouse furniture.

County offices frequented by the public were situated below the courtrooms. Prisoners were transported securely across a built-in bridge, known as the "bridge of sighs," over

Ross Street. One theory regarding this peculiar name was that prisoners walking the raised bridge would sigh upon finishing their route to the courthouse. Others say the name comes from the 16th-century bridge between the Doge's palace and the city prison in Venice, Italy.

A plaque affixed to the courthouse details what used to be called Grant's Hill. This section of street you are standing on used to be significantly higher, so much so that the original entrance was on what's now the second floor. In 1912 the hump was leveled to ease traffic.

The Allegheny County Courthouse and Jail are regarded as the finest works of architecture in the city. Richardson passed away in 1886, and the buildings were completed after his death. The inscription near the grand staircase at the entrance of the old law library reads: "IN MEMORY OF HENRY HOBSON RICHARDSON, ARCHITECT (1838–1886). GENIUS AND TRAINING MADE HIM MASTER IN HIS PROFESSION. ALTHOUGH HE DIED IN THE PRIME OF LIFE, HE LEFT TO HIS COUNTRY MANY MONUMENTS OF ART, FOREMOST AMONG THEM THIS TEMPLE OF JUSTICE."

Classical and Gothic architecture were used when Richardson employed the rounded arch, his best-known element, adapted from Romanesque architecture of the early 11th century. Indeed, his style has been called Richardson Romanesque, a distinction that means that the architect built the structure. A building said to be Richardsonian Romanesque was inspired by the famous architect but not built by Richardson himself. Two R's, one written backward and sharing

Whirlwind Downtown Walking Tour, a 37-page booklet listing a selection of architectural landmarks and public spaces in downtown Pittsburgh can be downloaded free of charge from Pittsburgh History and Landmarks' Web site, www.phlf.org. Or, go to www.visitpittsburgh.com to download audio and video podcast walking tours of areas in and around Pittsburgh.

the straight line with the next R, is the signature logo carved into one of the architect's great works.

Richardson used granite in such a way that the stone carver's skill revealed rather than concealed the natural stone. Frank Ellis Alden, a senior member of Richardson's design staff, supervised the construction of both the courthouse and jail. Eight months after the jail's completion in June 1886, and by now after his boss's passing, Alden formed his own architectural firm in Pittsburgh—Longfellow, Alden & Harlow, later Alden & Harlow. The courthouse was completed in April 1888 by Shepley, Rutan & Coolidge, a firm that completed several Richardson designs and went on to construct others in the Pittsburgh area.

In 1904 Frederick J. Osterling was commissioned to expand the county jail. A new round tower at Fifth Avenue and Ross Street was added in keeping with Richardson's original ideas. In 1976 trees and shrubbery were planted and benches added, transforming the courthouse courtyard into a public park that's now a popular summer lunchtime spot for downtown workers.

Having outgrown the space, the jail was vacated in 1995; prisoners are now housed in a new facility along Second Avenue, with its exceptional view of the river. The accommodations have been jokingly dubbed "the Hilton on the Mon." The old jail that Richardson built has been renovated for additional courtroom space.

You can take a self-guided tour of the Allegheny County Courthouse, using a pamphlet available at the Visitor's Center. For a fee, larger group tours can be arranged through the Pittsburgh History and Landmarks Foundation,

By the way, don't forget to stop to admire the design of the three-story staircase, made of Indiana limestone with original lighting fixtures. It's a celebration of the Richardson Romanesque arch—the architectural style this famous architect created with his artistry and talent!

City-County Building
414 Grant Street

line –up for photos next to trophies

Next door to the courthouse, the City-County Building, along Grant Street between Forbes and Fourth Avenues, is one of Henry Hornbostel's contributions to the skyline. Civil proceedings within Allegheny County take place here. It represents work toward the end of this architect's career in the Art Deco mode.

Beginning his work in 1915 and finishing two years later, the architect had one distinct advantage—by the time he began working, the hump on Grant Street had been lowered. The open corridor inside the structure allows light to shine through. At the bottom of the outside steps, a statue of Pittsburgh's beloved mayor, the late Richard S. Caliguiri, stands as a tribute to his legacy.

This ends the walking tour of downtown Pittsburgh. From reading other entries in this chapter, there might be additional buildings or bridges you'd like to explore. However, this tour has given you the highlights (and a little healthy exercise!).

From the City-County Building, return to your starting point at Station Square by following Fourth Avenue 1 block west to Smithfield Street. Turn left and walk back to the Smithfield Street Bridge, crossing it to Station Square. Or, if you're tired out, take the "T" (light-rail transit) from Gateway Center, Wood Street, Steel Plaza, of First Avenue Stations and get off at Station Square. The fare is minimal.

OTHER ARCHITECTURE IN DETAIL

Downtown

Frick Building
437 Grant Street
(412) 281-1260

Directly across the street from the courthouse, Henry Clay Frick made a number of real-estate investments in a closely aligned group of buildings. His Frick Building robbed the county buildings of their dominance. Finished in 1902, the building included the new and unusual for that time, things such as hydraulic elevator machinery, a basement generating plant, and washrooms for the whole building (on the 10th floor). Bronze telephone booths remain in the lobby. Chicago architects D.H. Burnbaum & Co. built this building between 1901 and 1902.

Heinz Hall
600 Penn Avenue
(412) 392-4900
In the late 1960s the Howard Heinz Endowment bought the old Penn Theatre, one of many silent-movie theaters that also had a stage. Originally built between 1925 and 1926 by the Chicago firm of Rapp & Rapp, Heinz Hall was remodeled in the early 1970s by the local firm of Stotz, Hess, MacLachlan & Fosner. The firm turned the old entrance into a large foyer window, and it used the architectural terracotta to match the off-white exterior. Viennese baroque is the style for this center of performing arts, which is home to the Pittsburgh Symphony (see the Arts chapter).

Bouquet's Redoubt
Point State Park
This 1764 structure is better known as the Fort Pitt Blockhouse. Of the original Fort Pitt, only one structure remains, known as Bouquet's Redoubt (better known as the blockhouse). Built too late to see any action in the French and Indian War, it has suffered its drama during peacetime through floods and a variety of uses. In 1894 the wealthy Mary Croghan Schenley gave the blockhouse to the Daughters of the American Revolution. The Fort Pitt Society restored the structure and has maintained it as a museum that is open to the public to this day. Please note that Point State Park is undergoing a major renovation, scheduled to be completed at the end of 2008. During the park renovation, the building should be accessible and the museum is scheduled to remain open. However, we recommend calling (412) 281-9284 to confirm before visiting.

Special Distinctions

As you tour the region, take special note of buildings bearing the National Historic Landmark designation, the highest possible recognition conferred upon a building or site by the Secretary of the United States Department of the Interior.

Additionally, the National Register of Historic Places is the official listing of the country's historic sites worthy of preservation. The Pittsburgh History & Landmarks Foundation awards the Historic Landmark plaque to architecturally significant buildings in Allegheny County. Although such a plaque identifies the property for its heritage, it does not guarantee protection. In Pittsburgh, however, there are City Historic Districts and City Historic Structures, which cannot be legally altered or demolished without approval of a review commission.

Koppers Building
436 Seventh Avenue
(412) 227-2001
www.aviewoncities.com/building/koppersbuilding.htm
The Koppers building, completed in 1929, was the headquarters of Heinrich Koppers's company. Koppers was the 1908 inventor of a byproduct coke oven, one that captured wastes, recycling and utilizing a product that would have otherwise been dispersed into the air and rendered useless. He had moved his business to Pittsburgh in 1915. This building's chateau roof was made of copper, and the lobby spaces are among the best Art Deco works in the city.

Gulf Building
707 Grant Street
(412) 263-6000
In the 1920s Grant Street was extended northward, and more real estate became available in the city. Directly opposite the new Koppers Building, the Gulf Oil Company built a 44-story, 582-foot tower that would be the city's tallest building until the USX Tower was constructed in 1970. Trowbridge & Livingston, an architectural firm from New York, was commissioned. E. P. Mellon served as an associate architect for the project. At the top of the building, neon tubes forecast the weather. When Gulf and Chevron merged in 1984, New York developers acquired the property, and today it has become office space rented out to companies. Note, some Pittsburghers refer to this building as the Gulf Tower.

Regional Enterprise Tower
425 Sixth Avenue
www.spcregion.org/ret/
Built by Alcoa in 1953, this building served as the company's headquarters until 1999, when everyone moved to a new facility on Pittsburgh's North Side. The firm of Harrison & Abramovitz designed the building that sits between Smithfield and Grant Streets, and of course the idea was to showcase aluminum in every possible way—from the electrical work to cladding. It's a wonder of industrial design, with a system in place that allows all windows to be washed from the inside. The windows swing completely around and are sealed with inflatable gaskets that have rounded corners. And the rounded corners, necessitated by the

i Learn more about Armstrong County architecture by taking a walking tour where you can walk past private properties and see inside some public ones. To obtain a brochure guide on Apollo, Dayton, Ford City, Freeport, Kittanning, Leechburg, or Parker City, call (724) 548-3226.

window-cleaning system, change this structure's entire appeal. When completed, the building was hailed as a daring experiment in modern office buildings. Today the 31-story Regional Enterprise Tower has become a regional resource center, housing economic development groups, among others.

North
Allegheny Post Office (now the Pittsburgh Children's Museum)
10 Children's Way
(412) 322-5058
www.pittsburghkids.org
Though now converted into a museum for children (see the Kidstuff chapter), the former Allegheny Post Office on the North Side is architecturally significant for its Early Italian Renaissance style. The central domed space inside is tall and much like a mosque. In a sense, Pittsburghers get to see more of the building as a children's museum, since they were restricted to the counter and outer corridors when it was a post office.

Armstrong County Courthouse
450 East Market Street, Kittanning
(724) 543-2500
This courthouse is a late Greek Revival structure that boasts a Corinthian porticoed central pavilion. It was erected in 1858, and a left wing was added in 1871. The courthouse was constructed first, and the jail was built in 1873. Clarion County sandstone was used in both.

Butler County Courthouse
124 West Diamond Street, Butler
(724) 285-4731
Built in 1886, the Butler County Courthouse is Richardsonian in its style of mixed Gothic and French architecture. James P. Bailey of Pittsburgh was its architect. Later enlarged and modernized between 1907 and 1908, this building contains a clock at least 100 years old, which dutifully ran without motorized assistance until 1940.

Carnegie Library of Pittsburgh
5 Allegheny Square
(412) 237-1890
www.carnegielibrary.org/locations/allegheny/
Completed in 1890, this was the first Carnegie
Library commissioned. Designed by architects
Smithmeyer & Pelz of Washington, D.C., the
library interior has been updated over the
years. In 2006, lightning struck the building's
clock tower, causing $2 million in damage
when large chunks of rock fell into the second-floor lecture hall and destroyed the building's heating and cooling system. Though the
damage has been repaired, the building is yet
to reopen as library officials and local residents debate the possibility of relocation the
branch to Federal Street.

Hartwood Acres
200 Hartwood Acres
(412) 767-9200
New York architect Alfred W. Hopkins constructed this large country estate in 1929 in
Indiana Township. It was the property of Mary
Flinn Lawrence, daughter of well-known con-
tractor William Flinn. Its main house, which
can be toured by the public, is typical of 1920s
rural Tudor styling. Allegheny County maintains the property today for recreational and
cultural use. (See the Attractions chapter.)

Mother House of the Sisters
of Divine Providence
La Roche College
9000 Babcock Boulevard
(412) 367-9300
Religious and academic buildings are clustered around the towering Mother House with
its chapel, here on the North Hills campus of
La Roche College. John E. Kauzor was its
architect in 1927. While many of the other
buildings are nondescript, the Mother House
maintains a splendid North Italian
Romanesque style.

East

Allegheny Cemetery
(Butler Street Entrance)
4734 Butler Street
www.alleghenycemetery.com
John Chislett was the architect for this gateway to the Allegheny Cemetery in 1847. You
can see his work on the Butler Street
entrance, a Tudor Gothic gateway in warm
gray sandstone. The cemetery was enlarged
20 years later with a chapel and office. The
Penn Avenue gates were added in 1887.

Board of Education Building
341 South Bellefield Avenue
(412) 622-3500
Built between 1926 and 1927, this structure
resembles an Italian Renaissance town palace
with a few Baroque touches. Architects Ing-
ham and Boyd deserve the honors. Inside,
you'll find a landscaped courtyard.

The Carnegie Museums and the Carnegie
Library of Pittsburgh (Main)
4400 Forbes Avenue
(412) 622-3114
www.carnegiemuseums.org
www.clpgh.org
On land donated by Mary Croghan Schenley,
another renowned philanthropist, Andrew
Carnegie, offered Pittsburgh a cultural entity
that reigns today. Architects Longfellow, Alden
& Harlow created Carnegie Institute and the
Carnegie Library of Pittsburgh in 1892.

The Italian Renaissance library building
was first on the scene, followed by the Music
Hall and museums. Outside the institute, you
can't miss the four statues—Gallileo,
Michelangelo, Bach, and Shakespeare—representing the four branches of science, art,
music, and literature.

The wealthy Sarah Mellon Scaife donated
a massive collection of art. To house it,
Edward Larabee Barnes built the Scaife
Gallery at the Carnegie Museum of Art in
1974 (see the Arts chapter).

Year-round hours at the museums are Tuesday, Wednesday, Friday, and Saturday 10:00 a.m. to 5:00 p.m.; Thursday 10:00 a.m. to 8:00; and Sunday noon to 5:00 p.m. Admission is $15 for adults, $12 for seniors, and $11 for students and children (ages 3 to 18). Children younger than 3 and members are admitted free of charge.

Cathedral of Learning
The University of Pittsburgh
Bigelow Boulevard and Fifth Avenue
(412) 624-4141 (Main Number)
(412) 624-6000 (Nationality Rooms)
www.pitt.edu/~natrooms
John Gabbert Bowman, who was named chancellor of the University of Pittsburgh in 1921, inherited a less than spectacular campus. Although a university skyscraper was virtually unheard of, Bowman had a vision for one here; he hired Charles Zeller Klauder to ignite and carry it through.

Klauder, an Eclectic architect from Philadelphia and a specialist in college design, tried to create the perfect plan. Bowman insisted that the building must inspire his students. The chancellor's concept was best articulated when, upon hearing the "Magic Fire Music" from *Die Walküre,* Bowman suggested that he wanted a climax building, towering higher and higher.

Indeed, Bowman had quite a selling job on his hands. However, with the help of benevolent donors, ordinary laborers, and even young children who took up collections to create the cathedral, the campaign was successful.

Most considered the results beautiful, though some thought it absurd. It's said that Frank Lloyd Wright called the creation "the world's largest keep-off-the-grass sign." Today the Gothic Cathedral of Learning, at 535 feet with 42 stories, towers over much more modest Oakland rooftops.

The Commons Room inside is cavernous and inspiring. On any given day you'll find students at quiet study or occasionally taking a nap between classes.

Chancellor Bowman wanted to use the Cathedral of Learning to showcase world cultures. Thus dozens of classrooms within the cathedral depict the city's ethnic diversity through their individual architecture. Since so many immigrants settled here in the 1920s, these Nationality Rooms seemed a fitting tribute to that heritage (see the Attractions chapter).

But an important stipulation in creating these nationality displays was that each room had to be used as a classroom. In addition, no person who was alive could be portrayed in the room. Each is different. The English is patterned after the House of Commons in 16th-century Tudor. The Yugoslav room features pocketknife wood carvings. And the French were the only group that selected the room's location, in this case to be closer to Heinz Chapel. Each room was funded by ethnic committees, designed by native architects, and built with materials from the countries they represent.

You can tour the Nationality Rooms from 9:00 a.m. until 2:30 p.m. Monday through Saturday or 9:00 a.m. until 2:30 p.m. on Sunday. Note that the rooms are closed on the following days – December 24th through 26th and January 1st. Also, during the academic year, classes are scheduled in the rooms, guests are invited to tour those rooms that are unoccupied.

While touring, you can listen to a 90-minute tape of remarks about each room. Simply stop by the Information Center on the Cathedral's first floor. Cost for these taped tours are $3 for adults and $1 for ages 8 to 18 years old. Last but not least, check out the virtual tours of the rooms, which can be found on the Web site.

Clayton
Penn and Homewood Avenues
(412) 371-0600
http://frickart.org/features/clayton/
In 1882 Henry Clay Frick and his wife, the former Adelaide Howard Childs, purchased this modest example of an Italianate house built

The Cathedral of Learning. ALAN AND BARBARA VENTO

Altering Your Home?

If you are a resident of the city of Pittsburgh and live in a building or neighborhood that has been designated by the City of Pittsburgh as historically significant, you may need permission to make any exterior changes to the front of your home. The Historic Review Commission must review and approve visible exterior alterations, including demolition, new construction, and additions. For more information, call (412) 255-2243.

after the Civil War in Pittsburgh's Point Breeze neighborhood. Several years later, in 1890, the Fricks decided to expand and remodel the home, hiring Pittsburgh architect Frederick J. Osterling to carry out the task. Although Osterling proposed a much more elaborate vision than what he finally built, today's Clayton boasts a chateauesque appearance, with steep roofs and gables that bespeak Osterling's style. This architect patterned his remodeling efforts after houses in France's Loire River Valley.

Other buildings, including the conservatory, sprouted up along the property. Upon Mr. Frick's death in 1919, his daughter, Helen Clay Frick, inherited the property. It's reported she was very fond of the home. Although she lived in New York, she visited often and maintained the property. Helen Clay Frick died in 1984, willing the home to the family's foundation. Following her wishes, Clayton was opened as a museum in 1990.

Today Clayton is part of the Frick Art & Historical Center (see the Arts chapter). You can reserve a spot for a tour of Clayton, where you'll notice the renowned art collection the Fricks amassed during their many trips abroad. The stained-glass window illuminating the main stairs is by Cottier and Company in New York and depicts heroines from

literature. Many of Mr. Frick's acquisitions remain as they were in the oak-paneled sitting room. The family used to gather for meals in the formal dining room, where they received Theodore Roosevelt in 1902 as the U.S. Marine Corps Band entertained luncheon guests with marches from the lawn.

When you visit Clayton, free parking is available, and there is access for visitors with disabilities. The center is open Tuesday through Sunday from 10:00 a.m. to 5:00 p.m. Clayton is closed on Monday. Tours of Clayton (reservations recommended) cost $12 for adults, $10 for seniors, students, and military. Members are admitted free of charge.

Pittsburgh Athletic Association
4215 Fifth Avenue
(412) 621-2400
Architect Benno Janssen was responsible for the Pittsburgh Athletic Association, a clubhouse in the manner of a Venetian Renaissance palace. It was constructed between 1909 and 1911 of limestone and matching terra-cotta. Don't miss the carved ceilings and murals inside.

Soldiers' and Sailors' Memorial
4141 Fifth Avenue
(412) 621-4253
www.soldiersandsailorshall.org
Built between 1907 and 1911 as a memorial to Civil War veterans, this building was also designed to add to Oakland's cultural scene. Architect Henry Hornbostel modeled the memorial after the Mausoleum at Helicarnassus, one of the seven wonders of the ancient world. Today it contains a museum remembering all American wars, as well as a ballroom and large public auditorium available for rent. The building is open Monday through Saturday from 10:00 a.m. until 4:00 p.m. It is open on Memorial Day and Veteran's Day. Admission is $5 for adults, $3 for seniors, veterans (over 60), and children (age 6 to 13). Children age five and under are admitted free of charge.

Stephen Foster Memorial
The University of Pittsburgh
Forbes Avenue
(412) 624-4100
www.pitt.edu/~amerimus/museum.htm
Built tight against the Cathedral in 1937 is the
Stephen Foster Memorial, a museum to the
Pittsburgh-born composer. It's a combination
theater, research library, social center, and
shrine to honor another of the city's native
sons. The auditorium seats nearly 700. The
west wing houses the Foster Hall collection of
more than 20,000 items pertaining to the
composer. Regular hours for the Stephen Foster Memorial are Monday through Friday from
9:00 a.m. until 4:00 p.m. (except during University holidays). Weekend and library hours
are made by appointment only. Guided tours
(call number above) cost $1.50 for adults and
$1.00 for seniors and children. Unguided
tours are free.

Westmoreland County Courthouse
North Main Street, Greensburg
(724) 830-3000, (724) 830-3110
www.co.westmoreland.pa.us
Built between 1906 and 1908, this public
building's style is French Renaissance. The
bell from a 1798 brick courthouse has been
placed in the old jail tower and preserved by
the county's historical society.

South

LeMoyne House
49 East Maiden Street, Washington
(724) 225-6740
www.wchspa.org
LeMoyne House is a fine example of early
Greek Revival architecture. Built in 1812 by a
French family that had come to America during
the French Revolution, the home was passed
down through the generations. Tours are available (see the Attractions and Festival chapters).

Thomas Jefferson Garden Mausoleum
Jefferson Memorial Cemetery
401 Curry Hollow Road
(412) 655-4500

At this South Hills cemetery you'll find portions of the former Bank of Pittsburgh building, which came down in 1944. An admirer of
this building asked the property's owner to
save the temple front. Thus its permanent
home is this memorial park, which is the final
resting place for many generations of Pittsburghers.

Washington County Courthouse
South Main and West Beau Streets
Washington
(724) 228-6700
www.courthousecentennial.org
This is the county's fourth courthouse erected
between 1898 and the fall of 1900. It's modeled in the Beaux Arts classical style from the
Italian Renaissance. Rising 25 feet above the
courthouse roof are four highly ornamental
cupolas, whose terra-cotta domes rest on
sandstone Ionic columns.

Within these cupolas rises a large dome.
From this summit rises a cupola on top of
which rests an 18-foot bronze statue of
George Washington. An original statue of
Washington stood atop the building from
1900 until 1917, when lightning strikes damaged it beyond repair. The present-day statue
was erected in 1927 and is protected by lightning rods.

West

Beaver County Courthouse
810 Third Street, Beaver
(724) 728-5700
Built between 1876 and 1877, the Beaver
County Courthouse is made of stone. Additions to the building were completed in 1907,
remodeling took place in 1933 following a fire
the year before, and another addition was
added between 1973 and 1974. Philadelphia
architect David S. Geredel was responsible for
the present courthouse.

BEST OF THE BRIDGES

When you learn about Pittsburgh's path to progress, you learn of some struggle to bring about improvements. Well, for those who thought Plan B—the plan by which voters registered their thoughts on new stadium construction—was controversial, you should have been around for the debate about bridges back in the 1920s.

In 1924 the county's Ultimate Highway System was designed to carry the road system into the 21st century. New boulevards and radial roads connected the city to outlying areas. But what would span the deep ravines, so prevalent in this region?

The Ultimate Highway System was never quite completed, though portions of the plan were built as late as the 1950s. But the plan's legacy remains in the form of magnificent bridges—at Sixth, Seventh, and Ninth Streets, plus the West End and McKees Rocks Bridges, the Liberty, South 10th Street, and Westinghouse Memorial Bridges—all erected between 1924 and 1940. This achievement cemented Pittsburgh's reputation as the "City of Bridges." Here's a peek at the best of these engineering marvels.

Sixth, Seventh, and Ninth Street Bridges
Allegheny River
Affectionately called the "Three Sisters," these three suspension bridges span the Allegheny River between Downtown and the North Side. Their lyrical design was created in the 1920s as they replaced three adjoining Victorian bridges considered to be too ugly for the times. In 1928 the American Institute of Steel Construction bestowed an award on the Sixth Street Bridge. While several engineers from the Allegheny County Department of Public Works participated in the construction of these impressive spans, Stanley L. Roush served as the architect. In particular, at the site of the Sixth Street Bridge, engineer and designer John Roebling built one of his earlier structures. Roebling, who would go on to construct the Brooklyn Bridge, came from Germany to Pittsburgh in 1832, for he thought

Pittsburgh would become the world's industrial center. Roebling invented wire rope and used that technology to build a number of Pittsburgh's early suspension bridges.

It's worth noting that in recent years these three bridges have been renamed to honor famous Pittsburghers. The Sixth Street Bridge is now the Roberto Clemente Bridge, the Seventh Street Bridge is now the Andy Warhol Bridge, and the Ninth Street Bridge is now the Rachel Carson Bridge. Beware when asking for directions, most Pittsburghers still refer to the bridges' former names!

16th Street Bridge
Allegheny River
www.pghbridges.com
Spanning the water between 16th Street in the Strip District and Chestnut Street on the North Side, the 16th Street Bridge was designed in 1923 by Warren and Wetmore, the same architects responsible for New York's Grand Central Station. Three truss-arch spans and four masonry piers highlight this bridge. New York's Leo Lentelli created the sea horses that make crossing this bridge even more appealing.

10th Street Bridge
Monongahela River
www.pghbridges.com
This bridge runs between South 10th Street on the South Side and the Armstrong Tunnel on the Bluff (near Duquesne University). Sydney A. Shubin was the engineer in 1931 for this modernistic bridge. Apart from the "Three Sisters" (see description for Sixth, Seventh, and Ninth Street Bridges), this is Pittsburgh's only extant suspension bridge.

George Westinghouse Memorial Bridge
U.S. Route 30
www.pghbridges.com
Connecting East Pittsburgh and North Versailles Township, the George Westinghouse Memorial Bridge served as an entrance for railroad passengers for more than 50 years. Built in 1930, it has five concrete arches and a

i If you're a high school senior interested in Pittsburgh's history or architecture, apply for the scholarship awarded by the Pittsburgh History & Landmarks Foundation. Call (412) 471-5808.

total length of 1,596 feet. Each side's entrance has tall concrete pylons honoring George Westinghouse's development of the Turtle Creek Valley below. The George Westinghouse Memorial Bridge was once compared with other engineering marvels of its era, including the Hoover Dam, the George Washington Bridge, and the Holland Tunnel.

HOUSES OF WORSHIP

Downtown

First English Evangelical Lutheran Church
615 Grant Street
(412) 471-8125
www.flcpittsburgh.org/Index2.htm
Steep-roofed with a 170-foot spired tower and Gothic elements, this church was built by Andrew Peebles in 1887 and 1888. Inside, worshippers enjoy the Tiffany glass window of the Good Shepherd in the church's sanctuary. Established in 1938, this congregation was the first English-speaking Lutheran congregation west of the Allegheny Mountains.

First Presbyterian Church
320 Sixth Avenue
(412) 471-3436
www.fpcp.org
This Downtown church, with its 13th- and 14th-century English Gothic cathedral front, is covered in the Downtown walking tour. Turn to that listing for more detail.

Trinity Cathedral
328 Sixth Avenue
(412) 232-6404
www.trinitycathedralpgh.org
Trinity is right next door to First Presbyterian Church. The cathedral also is covered exten-

sively in the Downtown walking tour, described earlier.

St. Mary of Mercy Roman Catholic Church
202 Stanwix Street
(412) 261-0110
www.stmaryofmercy.org
Somewhat dwarfed by towering PPG Place, this church holds its own simplicity and strength. Built in 1936 by architect William P. Hutchins, there are two redbrick walls gracing the sidewalks on the church's Stanwix Street and Third Avenue sides.

East

East Liberty Presbyterian Church
116 South Highland Avenue
(412) 441-3800
www.cathedralofhope.org
East Liberty Presbyterian Church in its namesake neighborhood of East Liberty was built according to cathedral dimensions as a gift from Richard Beatty and Jennie King Mellon. Boston architects Cram and Ferguson created this Gothic house of worship, which consumes an entire city block.

Heinz Memorial Chapel
East Lawn of the Cathedral of Learning
The University of Pittsburgh
(412) 624-4157
www.heinzchapel.pitt.edu
Next door to the Cathedral of Learning at the University of Pittsburgh is an interdenominational chapel. Chancellor Bowman had insisted upon such a chapel to inspire his students. Thus, in 1938 Charles Zeller Klauder created the flamboyant 15th-century French-style Heinz Chapel, built with donations from Henry John Heinz and his children. Klauder used several models as inspiration, including Mont-St-Michel, King Louis IV's Sainte-Chapelle, and St.-Maclou at Rouen.

Charles J. Connick, a noted glassmaker from Boston, had responsibility for the spectacular stained-glass windows in this structure that is set off by its tall spire atop the center.

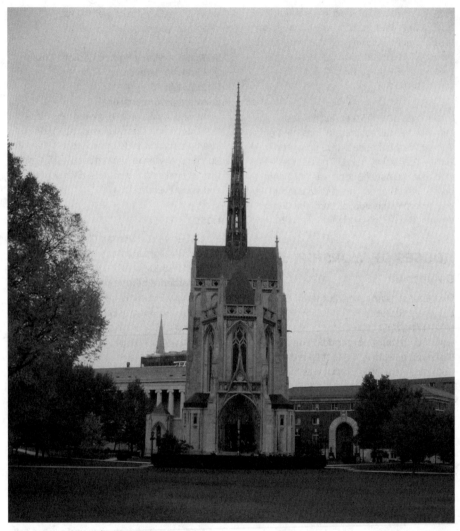

Heinz Memorial Chapel. LINDSEY KEOGH

Four transept windows represent courage, tolerance, temperance, and truth; each is 73 feet high.

The present pipe organ in the chapel was made possible through a generous gift of the Howard Heinz Endowment. The third organ to serve this chapel, it has 4,272 pipes (73 ranks) and three electronic pedal stops. The organ, re-created in 1994 through 1995, represents a trend in American organ building to reuse existing materials in an environmentally friendly and musically sound manner. When you hear the organ in this setting, you can literally feel the vibrations around you.

Heinz Chapel is the site of approximately 1,500 events each year, including lectures, memorial services, weddings, and guided tours. The first funeral to be held in this chapel was that of the late Senator H. J. (John) Heinz III, who died tragically in an airplane accident in April 1991.

ℹ️ Only University of Pittsburgh students, alumni, faculty, staff and members of their immediate families may reserve the Heinz Memorial Chapel at the University of Pittsburgh for wedding ceremonies. Visit the Web site for details.

Rodef Shalom
4905 Fifth Avenue
(412) 621-6566
http://rodefshalom.org/
Rodef Shalom Congregation, in Shadyside, is one of the two synagogues designed by Henry Hornbostel. Here the architect used his favorite materials—cream-colored brick and terra-cotta. Inside, Hornbostel made use of the light from the skylight, which beams down upon his rich mahogany-and-gilt interior. The temple also contains stained-glass windows and beautiful blue-and-gold chandeliers.

Sri Venkateswara Temple
1230 South McCully Drive
(412) 373-3380
www.svtemple.org
This Penn Hills temple, constructed in 1979, was the second Hindu temple to be built in the United States. The Indian scientific and professional community contributed greatly to its establishment.

The Tirupathi Shrine from seventh-century southern India served as the model here. Two temple domes are constructed of inch-thick stucco over brick and concrete. The *sikhara* (spire towers) are similarly made.

St. Paul's Cathedral
Fifth Avenue and Craig Street
(412) 621-4951
www.catholic-church.org/st.paulcathedralpgh/
Chicago architects Egan & Prindeville designed the twin spires at St. Paul's Cathedral, its Victorian design prominent on the Oakland skyline. The main structure was built between 1903 and 1906. Two Roman Catholic cathedrals had been downtown on the site of the Union Arcade (see listing for Two Mellon Center), but

Mr. Frick's desire to construct the arcade prompted the cathedral's move to Oakland.

This new cathedral turned away from Victorian colors, yet the actual design was reminiscent of Victorian style. There are no flying buttresses, as are found on many large cathedrals. Two prominent Catholic architects from our city contributed to the complex. Edward J. Weber created the Synod Hall and Chancery of 1914, with its 15th-century English look, and Carlton Strong built the Rectory in 1926 in a Tudor style.

West

St. Nicholas Chapel
5400 Tuscarawas Road, Beaver
(724) 495-3400, (800) 722-4428
www.gcuusa.com/snc.htm
Constructed in 1992 by architect Tom Terpack, St. Nicholas Chapel, with its three onion domes, is quite a sight in suburban Beaver County. Because it is crafted of cedar logs and shingles, it resembles traditional chapels in eastern Slovakia and western Ukraine. Windows are located in the upper areas of the church so as not to weaken the main log structure. The wooden entrance doors are carved and framed with logs.

THE WRIGHT STUFF

Since Western Pennsylvania is so fortunate to have two great works of legendary architect Frank Lloyd Wright, we've chosen to give you the highlights in their own special category. Please note that both of these homes are outside the coverage area, but they're included because they're significant in the architectural scheme of things. Turn to the Day Trips chapter for more on these architectural gems.

Fallingwater
Mill Run (off U.S. Route 40), Fayette County
(724) 329-8501
www.paconserve.org/index-fw1.asp
Back in the 1930s, Pittsburgh department store owner Edgar J. Kaufmann and his wife, Liliane, commissioned architect Frank Lloyd

> **i** To learn more about efforts that recently restored Frank Lloyd Wright's Western Pennsylvania masterpiece called Fallingwater, watch Saving Fallingwater, a film by Kenneth Love. The DVD can be purchased for $36 from the Western Pennsylvania Conservancy's shop located at Fallingwater or online at www.wpcshop.com.

Wright to design their weekend retreat at Bear Run in the Laurel Highlands, 90 minutes south of Pittsburgh. Tucked among the rhododendrons and sitting atop a waterfall, this masterpiece is more reminiscent of the 1960s than the Great Depression.

A devotee of organic architecture, Wright decided to locate the house on top of the waterfall rather than to the side. Who would have thought? Construction began in spring 1936, with local contractors quickly trained to implement Wright's techniques.

The structure was built of sandstone quarried on the property, and Wright used natural stone to reinforce the concrete and create the image of man-made land meeting nature and vice versa. The elements cause the eye to focus outside. Glass and steel were among the other materials used in this massive project, which back in the 1930s cost approximately $155,000 to construct—modest by today's standards, but consider the times.

The architect believed the Kaufmann family should live with the water, not merely look upon it. Cantilevers enable the terraces of the living and bedroom levels to extend over the rushing falls without visible support. A guest and service wing was added in 1939, and Albert Einstein was among the celebrated guests reported to have stayed with the Kaufmanns.

Inside the house, Wright designed the furniture to echo his themes. Southwestern colors were used throughout the property. While touring the home, you'll notice the stairway opens to the sound of the rushing falls. Nature indeed takes over when the windows on the

cantilevers are opened—there is no physical window structure as we normally experience.

When the Kaufmanns' son, Edgar Jr., turned the home over to the Western Pennsylvania Conservancy in 1963, the family requested that the home remain as original as possible. Thus you'll see Tiffany lamps, Japanese prints, and artwork along with Wright's furniture. Much detail was put into the home—from the novel way the windows open to caning in the closet shelves, allowing air to flow in such a damp climate. Even ship-quality wood was used to prevent warping. In 1976 the National Park Service designated the property a National Historic Landmark.

Ironically, when Edgar Kaufmann had Wright build this home, he was concerned about the structural soundness of his project. He sought the reassurance of a Pittsburgh firm of registered engineers and steel suppliers for concrete, who advised that Kaufmann use twice the amount of steel his architect had recommended. Kaufmann took the firm's advice, which reportedly infuriated Wright to the point of a near break in the two men's working relationship. Wright felt the steel would weigh too much and cause the terrace to deflect more than it would naturally.

This disagreement was prescient. In 1997 temporary shoring was installed under the main floor cantilever because of the gradual but continuing deflection of the first and second levels. In fact, at this writing if you stand at just the right part of the surrounding woods, you can see the famous home's slope whereby the master terrace is 7 inches lower than the living room. Computerized analysis along with historical research revealed that the main house had not stopped deflecting since its construction in 1936 through 1938. This was due to the inadequate steel reinforcement in the concrete beams of the first and second levels.

Robert Silman Associates, a structural engineering firm in New York, designed the final repair plan. Strengthening the main floor concrete beams eliminated the need for further vertical support from beneath. At that juncture, the temporary shoring was removed. To fund this massive restoration, the Western Pennsylvania Conservancy has conducted a fund-raising campaign. This 20th-century architectural masterpiece is open daily except Wednesday, mid-March through Thanksgiving weekend, from 10:00 a.m. to 4:00 p.m. Winter hours (weather permitting) are 11:00 a.m. to 3:00 p.m. December weekends, the week between Christmas and New Year's, and the first two weekends in March. Regular tours are $16 for adults and $10 for youths (ages 6 to 12). In-depth tours cost $55, and sunset tours are $100. Reservations are suggested. You may explore the grounds only for $6 per person. Tickets may be purchased online or by calling (724) 329-8501.

Children younger than age 6 are not permitted, but group babysitting is available at $2 per hour per child at the Visitors Pavilion. With many stairs, considerable walking is required, so call ahead to make arrangements if you need special assistance (see also the Attractions and Day Trips chapters). Note that staircases are narrow, and the stone can be a bit slippery if you aren't agile. No picture-taking or large bags are allowed.

The best route to Fallingwater is to take the Pennsylvania Turnpike to exit 91 (Donegal). Turn left onto Route 31 East, and travel 2 miles. Turn right onto Route 381 South, and follow this route for approximately 19 miles to Fallingwater.

Kentuck Knob
Chalk Hill, Ohiopyle
(724) 329-1901
www.kentuckknob.com

Not far from Fallingwater is another of Frank Lloyd Wright's famous homes, Kentuck Knob, overlooking the Youghiogheny River Gorge. Kentuck (yes, without the "y") Knob was commissioned by the I. N. Hagan family of Uniontown, who owned the Hagan Ice Cream Company. They had come to know the Kaufmanns and fell in love with the idea of a Wright creation of their own (only of a little more modest dimension).

This lesser known Wright home was built of fieldstone boulders found on the site and tidewater red cypress from South Carolina. Wright based the design on a hexagonal modular grid on one main level because it allows for openness. That hexagonal motif is repeated inside and out, even allowing light to shine through in that geometric pattern. It reflects Usonian design, a precursor to the ranch home that most could afford.

Famous for incorporating nature into each site, Wright made sure light permeated every room at Kentuck Knob. The outdoors is always present, from the morning sun until dusk. A steep, narrow causeway winds its way up from the road and opens to a gravel courtyard, as you ride in the small tour van leading you to the homesite. The double glass entry doors welcome guests just as the copper roof offers shelter to curious tourists. The architect also designed the house's furniture, much of which is built-in, such as the cypress table that conforms to the angles of the dining room. Today, however, Wright's furniture sits beside some contemporary pieces reflecting the tastes of its current owners.

The home is now the property of Great Britain's Lord and Lady Palumbo, dedicated patrons of the arts both in the United States and across the Atlantic. Contemporary sculpture and historic artifacts also enhance the secluded setting. The Palumbo family's photographs give the house a warm, lived-in feel. Notice the rather striking photo of the late Princess Diana, shaking hands in her chic black dress. And do enjoy the many outdoor sculptures that the Palumbos have added throughout the 79-acre property.

But don't expect to meet the owners on your tour. While the Palumbos occasionally entertain in the house when visiting the United States, they live in the nearby valley.

Kentuck Knob is open daily, 9:00 a.m. to 4:00 p.m. Regular tours are $16 for adults and $10 for children ages 6 to 12. In-depth tours ($55 per person) are available Tuesday through Sunday, 1:15 to 2:30 p.m. Sunset tours (3:00 to 5:00 p.m.) cost $100 per person and include complimentary wine and hors d'oeuvres in the living room. Children younger than age 6 are not permitted, and no organized child care is provided for touring parents.

ARCHITECTURAL TOURISM

It used to be that misbehavior unintentionally rewarded you with a tourist's treat. Yes, career criminals were given a sneak peek at one of the greatest works of 19th-century architecture—the Allegheny County Courthouse and Jail.

Well, now you don't have to misbehave at all to see the same site. "Living Architecture . . . Alive in Pittsburgh" debuted in 1998 to highlight the region's architectural charm. Aficionados of design, engineering, and architecture can book a package tour and then partake of the work of two of America's most revered architects—H. H. Richardson and Frank Lloyd Wright.

VisitPittsburgh (formerly the Greater Pittsburgh Convention & Visitor Bureau, C&VB) gauged the interest in architectural tourism, found it was there, and has marketed a packaged tour ever since. Pittsburgh History & Landmarks Foundation created pamphlets for tours of the courthouse, and cassette tapes also help visitors take self-guided tours of the North Side and Downtown.

If you'd like more information, contact VisitPittsburgh at (800) 359-0758, or visit their Web site at www.visitpittsburgh.com/.

Another tourism option, the "American Landmarks Getaway" package is marketed by the Laurel Highlands Visitors Bureau. It focuses on Frank Lloyd Wrights' Fallingwater and Kentuck Knob but includes a tour of Fort Necessity National Battlefield. Available April to mid-November, prices start at $370 (based on double occupancy). If you're interested, contact the visitor bureau at (800) 333-5661 or visit its Web site at www.laurelhighlands.org.

THE ARTS

You don't have to be a connoisseur of fine art or a season subscriber to the symphony to appreciate cultural life in Western Pennsylvania. There are dozens of opportunities for aficionados of all forms of the arts. In fact, it surprises some visitors and newcomers to learn that Pittsburghers are followers of the opera, in addition to being fans of their football team. But such is the scene here.

For a city its size, Pittsburgh has hidden wealth in its passion for excellent performances, dramatic theater, roving exhibitions, unique films, and the latest in literature and poetry. Combine that passion with plenty of raw talent, and the dedication of organizations that support artistic growth, and you have that rare combination that any arts lover needs to feel challenged, yet overwhelmingly satisfied with the offerings.

In this chapter the usual geographic breakdown is abandoned, as the cultural opportunities available here cross regional boundaries. We'll first explore some of the key places where Pittsburgh takes to the stage for theater, dance, and film. There's a sampling of local galleries and museums and a listing of outlets for you creative types, including writers, actors, and musicians. We've also noted some of the area's best artistic support groups.

The Pittsburgh Cultural Trust oversees the development and operation of several theaters and galleries, including the Benedum Center for the Performing Arts, the Byham Theater, the OReilly Theater, and the Harris Theatre—all located in the 14-block downtown area known as the Cultural District.

The Pittsburgh Cultural Trust was formed in 1984 as the result of the effort of Henry John "Jack" Heinz II. His vision for a downtown cultural district was turned into reality with

strikingly restored building facades, murals, and other public art. Handsome brick sidewalks and granite curbs line the district. There's new energy brought about by the economic revitalization of business and the arts community. In December 1999 the O'Reilly Theater opened for public theater patrons to enjoy. Again, Pittsburgh's Cultural Trust was instrumental in this achievement.

We'll close the chapter with a few of the organizations you might turn to for enhancement of your own artistic flair. One thing is certain. In Pittsburgh you will be pleased with the sounds of symphonies and orchestras, with the sights at major galleries, and with the appeal of theater companies performing a range of works, from Broadway musicals and opera to comedies and dramatic plays.

IN THE LIMELIGHT

Benedum Center for the Performing Arts
719 Liberty Avenue
(412) 456-6666
This center for the performing arts used to be known as the Stanley Theater, a movie palace dating from 1927. Today this building is the cornerstone of Pittsburgh's Cultural District. Reopened in 1987 after a $42 million renovation, the Benedum seats 3,100 and is home to the Pittsburgh CLO, Pittsburgh Ballet Theatre, Pittsburgh Dance Council, and the Pittsburgh Opera. Registered with the National Trust for Historic Places, the Benedum (as it's known for short) is one of the few theaters in the country large enough to stage full-cast, first-run Broadway shows.

You'd never guess from the outside the ornate details and ambience you'll find within. Feast your eyes on the sweeping staircases, then let your eyes travel up to the domed ceiling, where the crystal chandelier glitters.

Byham Theater
101 Sixth Street
(412) 456-1350

Opened in 1903 as a vaudeville house, and later serving as a 1930s talking motion picture house, the Byham today is Pittsburgh's oldest performing-arts facility. With 1,342 seats, the Byham functions as stage for small to mid-size performing arts productions as well as touring companies in music, dance, and the performing arts for children.

Heinz Hall for the Performing Arts
600 Penn Avenue
(412) 392-4900

No other landmark in this city enjoys the cultural reputation of Heinz Hall, for this great concert hall boasts an international reputation. Back in the 1920s it was called the Penn Theater. But the Howard Heinz Endowment saved this theater, with its Breche opal and Lavanto marble interior, from the wrecking ball after it closed in 1968. Reopened in 1970 after a 16-month, $10-million renovation, it's now known as Heinz Hall. With 2,847 seats, it's home to the Pittsburgh Symphony Orchestra, the Pittsburgh Pops, and the Pittsburgh Youth Symphony Orchestra.

O'Reilly Theater
621 Penn Avenue
(412) 316-8200

The most recent addition to Pittsburgh's Cultural District is the O'Reilly Theater. Designed by architect Michael Graves and opened in 1999, the theater's balcony overlooks the lobby's floor laid with a checkerboard of green and black slate. This theater moved from the Hazlet Theater of Pittsburgh's North Side and is now home to the Pittsburgh Public Theater. There are many elegant elements to Graves's design, including the two-story, semi-circular wall of seven windows facing the street entrance. Looking at the 650-seat theater as you enter, you can't miss the grand overhanging effect created by the windows and the copper-covered roof above you. In honor of his leadership of the H. J. Heinz Co. and undisclosed contributions toward the theater's construction, the building is named for former chairman Anthony J. F. O'Reilly.

The Palace Theatre
21 West Otterman Street, Greensburg
(724) 836-8000
www.palacetheatre.org

The Palace Theatre, opened in 1926 as the Manos Theatre. Since 1990 the Westmoreland Cultural Trust has owned and operated the theater, restoring the building through a series of renovations. Today visitors will find Old World charm mixed with modern amenities at this 1,320-seat facility. Used by both local and traveling art and musical groups, the Palace Theatre is home to the Westmoreland Symphony Orchestra.

DANCE

Dance Alloy Theater
5530 Penn Avenue
(412) 363-4321
www.dancealloy.org

Committed to exploring dance as a creative performance medium as well as an educational process, the Dance Alloy Theater, under the direction of Beth Corning, is Pittsburgh's premier modern dance company. Founded in 1976, Dance Alloy presents works by national and international choreographers. Tickets for single performances range from $15 to $20.

Dance Alloy's dance center, which opened in 1995 as part of the Friendship neighborhood's revitalization efforts, offers noncompetitive classes and outreach activi-

To find out what's happening in the local arts scene during your visit, go to www.proartstickets.org or www.pgh arts.org. Or check out Thursday's issue of the *Pittsburgh Post-Gazette*, Friday's issue of the *Pittsburgh Tribune Review*, or the weekly *City Paper*.

ties to more than 5,000 students of all ages. Class offerings range from traditional dance to culturally diverse dance and movement classes.

Duquesne University Tamburitzans
1801 Boulevard of the Allies
(412) 396-5185
www.tamburitzans.duq.edu
Pittsburgh's Eastern European heritage is showcased through America's longest running multicultural song and dance company, the Duquesne University Tamburitzans. Started in 1937 as a musical group of 12 young men who played the *tamburitza*—a traditional East European stringed instrument—today's Tamburitzans feature 40 men and women from here and around the world who perform music, songs, and dances of Eastern Europe in a rousing production of color and sound. Under the direction of Paul G. Stafura, the Tamburitzans perform an average of 80 shows in Pittsburgh and across the country—all on weekends and semester breaks, as these performers also attend Duquesne University as college students!

Laurel Ballet
813 Highland Avenue, Greensburg
(724) 837-7230, (724) 832-7391
www.laurelballet.com
Founded in the mid-1980s by artistic director Eleanor Tornblom, the Laurel Youth Ballet is a semiprofessional performing company in Westmoreland County introducing hundreds to the world of dance. Former students have gone on to perform with larger companies, including the Pittsburgh Ballet Theatre and the San Francisco Ballet. Each year's schedule includes *The Nutcracker*.

Pittsburgh Ballet Theatre
2900 Liberty Avenue
(412) 281-0360
www.pbt.org
Founded in 1969, the Pittsburgh Ballet Theatre features both contemporary and classical productions with Terrence S. Orr as its artistic

director. Past performances have included *Giselle, The Nutcracker, Swan Lake, Coppella, Peter Pan, Don Quixote,* and the works of George Balanchine. This dance company takes the stage at the prestigious Benedum Center (see earlier write-up) for its season each October through April. Tickets range from approximately $20 to $88, depending upon seating in the various tiers. Subscribers receive a convenient ticket exchange policy, discount savings of 20 percent on additional single tickets, and pre-performance lectures. To purchase ballet tickets, call the Benedum Box Office at (412) 456-6666.

In addition to fostering its own program, the ballet offers more than 12 levels of dance instruction, with graduates performing with the Pittsburgh Ballet or other national ballet companies. To contact the Pittsburgh Ballet Theatre School, call (412) 281-6727. Classes are offered for children age 2 and older.

Pittsburgh Dance Council
Benedum Center, 719 Liberty Avenue
(412) 456-1390
www.pgharts.org/dance
The Pittsburgh Dance Council offers contemporary dance productions by international and emerging artists. In addition to its nationally recognized presenting series, the Dance Council regularly commissions new works for its October through April season. Previous shows featured works by Les Ballet de Monte Carlo, Cricus Oz, and Lucy Guerin, Inc. Each performance is priced differently, but tickets range from $19 to $40.

UMOJA African Arts Co.
601 Wood Street
(412) 471-1121
www.umojacompany.com
UMOJA, meaning "unity" in Swahili, works to bring together diverse cultures through African art and performances. Created in 1989, the company provides African dance, drumming, storytelling, drum making, and other creative arts. UMOJA and UMOJA Jr.'s lively and engaging performances occur

throughout the city at different venues and events. They also offer a series of programs and workshops and the newly created African Arts in the Parks Festival.

FILM

Pittsburgh Filmmakers
477 Melwood Avenue
(412) 681-5449
www.pghfilmmakers.org
You can see independent and foreign films at any of the three theaters operated by Pittsburgh Filmmakers: Harris Theater (809 Liberty Avenue) in downtown Pittsburgh, Regent Square Theater (1035 South Braddock Avenue) in Edgewood, or occasionally at the Melwood Screening Room (477 Melwood Avenue) in North Oakland). Filmmakers also host the region's largest and oldest film festival, the Three Rivers Film Festival, a two-week-long annual celebration that features over 40 films. The festival features parties throughout the city, visiting filmmakers, and informal post-screening discussions.

GALLERIES & MUSEUMS

Andy Warhol Museum
117 Sandusky Street
(412) 237-8300
www.warhol.org
Andy Warhola was the son of Eastern European immigrants (he would shorten his name later in life). Beginning in the fourth grade, Warhol attended free Saturday art classes and later graduated from Carnegie Tech's College of Fine Arts.

Warhol moved to New York to work as a commercial artist, taking with him from Pittsburgh an appreciation of working-class life. Thus he created art that played on everyone's fantasies of inaccessible glamour and celebrity, embodied in his famous works of Marilyn Monroe, Elvis, Jackie Onassis, and Mick Jagger.

Regardless of whether he was correct that everyone would have 15 minutes of fame, Warhol has received that many times over. Who else could create art out of a soup can or ketchup box? Today the Warhol Museum is one of the Carnegie Museums of Pittsburgh and is a collaborative project of the Carnegie Institute, the Dia Center for the Arts, and the Andy Warhol Foundation for the Visual Arts.

The collection includes over 4,000 works in all media and provides an in-depth view of every period of Warhol's life from the 1940s to the 1980s. From this collection, approximately 500 works are on view at one time alongside special exhibits of work by related artists (Basquiat, Billy Name, Mariko Mori) and opportunities to view work from the Warhol's film and video collection. If visiting on the weekend, create your own Warhol-style art through the Weekend Factory, one of the museum's most popular education programs.

The Warhol is open Tuesday, Wednesday, Thursday, Saturday, and Sunday from 10:00 a.m. to 5:00 p.m. and Friday from 10:00 a.m. to 10:00 p.m. The museum is closed on Monday; also closed New Year's Day, Martin Luther King Jr. Day, Easter Sunday, Memorial Day, Independence Day, Labor Day, Thanksgiving, and Christmas Day. Adults pay $15, seniors (55+) are charged $9, and students and children pay $8 for admission. Members of the Carnegie Museums of Pittsburgh receive free admission. Parking is available 1 block north of the Museum on Sandusky Street ($6).

Carnegie Museum of Art
4400 Forbes Avenue
(412) 622-3131
www.cmoa.org
One of Andrew Carnegie's benevolent gifts to this city was the Museum of Art, which is operated under the umbrella of the Carnegie Museums. The Carnegie Institute's original Renaissance-style building was designed by the firm of Longfellow, Alden & Harlow between 1891 and 1895. Alden & Harlow completed new galleries in 1907. And in 1974 the Sarah Scaife Gallery, designed by Edward Larrabee Barnes, tripled the exhibition space in the Museum of Art.

While many turn-of-the-20th-century art museums focused on amassing work of old masters, Mr. Carnegie envisioned a museum collection consisting of "the old masters of tomorrow." In 1896 he initiated a series of exhibitions of contemporary art, proposing that the museum's collection be formed through purchases from this series.

Early acquisitions included work by Winslow Homer, James Abbott, McNeill Whistler, and Camille Pissarro. Today's collection includes a continuum of strength in American art from the late-19th century to the present, along with French impressionists, post-impressionist paintings, and other highly significant works of the 20th century.

The permanent collection is housed in the newly renovated Scaife Galleries, and special exhibitions are reserved for the Heinz Galleries (or the Alisa Mellon Bruce Galleries for decorative arts). While there, you can also visit the Heinz Architectural Center, the Hall of Sculpture, and the Hall of Architecture, which will celebrate its 100th anniversary in 2008. The 55th Carnegie International, curated by Douglas Fogle, will be on exhibit May 3, 2008, through January 11, 2009. The oldest invitational survey of contemporary art in North America, this exhibit features an exciting and diverse array of established and emerging contemporary artists.

The Carnegie offers an extensive selection of programs, classes, and lectures throughout the year and for all ages. Enjoy the Carengie's ARTventures drop-in programs for families, or check out one of the Lunch & Learns, a lecture followed by lunch in the Carnegie Café. (See the Kidstuff chapter for more information on childrens classes.)

Hours at the museums are Tuesday, Wednesday, Friday, and Saturday 10:00 a.m. to 5:00 p.m.; Thursday 10:00 a.m. to 8:00 p.m.; and noon to 5:00 p.m. on Sunday. The museums are closed most Mondays, with the following exceptions: Martin Luther King Jr. Day, Presidents' Day, and Mondays from July 9 through August 27. Admission is $15 for adults, $12 for seniors, and $11 for students and children (ages 3 to 18). Children younger than age 3 and members are admitted free of charge.

Concept Art Gallery
1031 South Braddock Avenue
(412) 242-9200
www.conceptgallery.com
One of the oldest galleries in Pittsburgh, the Concept Gallery represents established and emerging local and national artists. Gallery hours are Tuesday through Saturday from 10:00 a.m. to 5:30 p.m. and Thursday from 10:00 a.m. to 8:00 p.m. The gallery is also open on Sunday noon to 5:00 p.m. from September through May.

The Frick Art & Historical Center
7227 Reynolds Street
(412) 371-0600
www.frickart.org
This six-acre complex in Point Breeze is elegantly landscaped with museums and turn-of-the-20th-century buildings, the legacy left by Helen Clay Frick to the people of Western Pennsylvania. Step into the Victorian past to appreciate the architecture and artifacts in addition to the collection of pre-20th-century European art. Helen, the daughter of industrialist Henry Clay Frick and his wife, the former Adelaide Childs, grew up on the estate in Pittsburgh's fashionable East End. After her parents took her to New York, Miss Frick maintained her heartfelt feelings toward the home and property.

Today the Frick Art & Historical Center comprises the Frick Art Museum, Clayton (the restored home of Henry Clay Frick), the Car and Carriage Museum, the Greenhouse, the Museum Shop, the Playhouse, The Café, and six acres of sprawling lawns and gardens. Free parking is available in the museum lot. The center is open Tuesday through Sunday from 10:00 a.m. until 5:00 p.m. Clayton is closed on Monday. Tours of Clayton cost $12 for adults and $10 for seniors and students; members are admitted free of charge. Reservations for tours are recommended. Architecture aficionados can turn to that chapter for more information about touring Clayton.

Hoyt Institute of Fine Arts
124 East Leasure Avenue, New Castle
(724) 652-2882
www.hoytartcenter.org

Tucked away from the commercial district of New Castle (Lawrence County) sits the former home of Miss May Emma Hoyt. Today the mansion is part of Hoyt Institute of Fine Arts, which serves as a local art gallery offering monthly exhibitions upstairs and downstairs. Classes range from watercolors, stained glass, and ceramics to photography, dance, and even writing. The institute is open Wednesday, Friday, and Saturday 10:00 a.m. to 5:00 p.m., Tuesday and Thursday 10:00 a.m. until 8:00 p.m.; closed Sunday and Monday. Free admission.

James Gallery
413 South Main Street
(412) 922-9800
www.jamesgallery.net

Located in Pittsburgh's West End, James Gallery exhibits art by regional, national, and international artists working in all media. The gallery is open Monday through Saturday from 9:00 p.m. to 5:00 p.m. and by also appointment.

The Mattress Factory
500 Sampsonia Way
(412) 231-3169
www.mattress.org

No, it's not a place to outfit your boudoir! We're talking about a former mattress factory warehouse turned art museum. Here you'll now find room-size contemporary artworks called installations created on-site by artists. Located in the historic Mexican War Streets of Pittsburgh's North Side, the Mattress Factory houses a growing—and distinctive—permanent collection, featuring artists James Turrell, Yayoi Kusama, and Winifred Lutz. Since 1977 the museum has also supported over 300 artists through its world-renowned residency program. Hours are 10:00 a.m. to 5:00 p.m.

Tuesday through Saturday and 1:00 to 5:00 p.m. on Sunday. Closed Monday, New Year's Day, Easter, Memorial Day, Independence Day, Thanksgiving, and Christmas. Admission is $9 for adults, $6 for students, and $7 for seniors. Members and children under 6 are admitted free.

Merrick Free Art Gallery
1100 Fifth Avenue, New Brighton
(724) 846-1130
www.merrickartgallery.org

Edward Dempster Merrick wanted to be an artist when he was coming of age in New Brighton, Beaver County, back in the mid-1860s. But like others with similar goals, he was told to find a real job rather than live the life of a starving artist. So he did that, working as a telegraph operator, a soldier, and a cowboy before retiring at age 53 to pursue collecting things, including artwork. Merrick's international travels and studies abroad helped him garner an impressive collection of 18th-and 19th-century art, including a prominent group of Hudson River School paintings. Perhaps not as wealthy as Frick and Carnegie, who also donated their names and money to museums, Merrick's gallery is the only fine arts museum in Beaver County. Also look for the 19th-century library, the rock and mineral collection, and the zoological collection. Ask about Saturday art classes and summer art camp for kids. Gallery hours vary depending upon the season (Labor Day through Memorial Day and the summer months), so do call ahead. Admission is free, and group tours can be arranged.

Silver Eye Center for Photography
1015 East Carson Street
(412) 431-1810
www.silvereye.org

This nonprofit organization premieres contemporary photography exhibits of work by local, national, and internationally recognized photographers. Silver Eye offers educational programming, gallery tours, and workshops. Admission is free. The center's hours are

Wednesday, Friday, and Saturday from noon to 5:00 p.m. and Thursday from noon until 9:00 p.m. The center is closed on Monday and Tuesday for educational programs.

SPACE
812 Liberty Avenue
(412) 325-7723
www.spacepittsburgh.org
The Pittsburgh Cultural Trust turned this building, formerly home to an adult bookstore, into one of Downtown's newest galleries, offering works in multiple disciplines by local and regional artists who use both established and contemporary technologies. Don't forget to look for SPACE as part of the Pittsburgh Cultural Trust's Gallery Crawl, held quarterly and featuring a free night of great art and music in downtown Pittsburgh.

Westmoreland Museum of American Art
221 North Main Street, Greensburg
(724) 837-1500
www.wmuseumaa.org
Built at the crest of a hill in downtown Greensburg, the Westmoreland Museum of American Art was established in 1949 with the support of the Woods Marchand Foundation. Ten years later, the museum opened to the public with its mission of acquiring and exhibiting American art. Today the museum features nationally recognized and regionally significant work by artists like Mary Cassatt, Winslow Homer, and Louis Comfort Tiffany. Educational programs offered include art classes, school outreach, docent-guided tours, lectures, demonstrations, and other special events.

One holiday tradition that families look forward to is the Holiday Toy and Train Exhibition. First begun out of whimsy, it's become a serious collection within the museum. Museum hours are Wednesday through Sunday 11:00 a.m. to 5:00 p.m. and Thursday from 11:00 a.m. to 9:00 p.m. It's closed Monday and Tuesday, as well as most holidays. Admission is free of charge, but there is a $5 suggested donation per visitor.

i A limited number of scholarships for the Carnegie Museum of Art adult programs are available through the Scaife Family Foundation. Apply early by calling (412) 622-3288.

Wood Street Galleries
601 Wood Street
(412) 471-5605
www.woodstreetgalleries.org
The Wood Street Galleries, operated by the Pittsburgh Cultural Trust, showcase various artists' work from around the world. Illustrations, paintings, and other forms of art are presented. Gallery hours are Tuesday through Thursday 11:00 a.m. to 6:00 p.m. and Friday and Saturday 11:00 a.m. to 8:00 p.m. The gallery is closed Sunday, Monday, and holidays.

LITERARY ARTS

Gist Street Reading Series
305 Gist Street, Third Floor
www.giststreet.org
Declaring that "it's not about suffering," this reading series is an unpretentious and fun way to listen to works by emerging local and national poets and writers. Held at the James Simon's Sculpture Studio in Uptown, the Gist Street Reading Series isn't just about the work. There is also social time and sometimes even music and homemade ice cream. Events are typically held the first Friday of each month at 8:00 p.m. Admission is $5.00 per person.

International Poetry Forum
Grace Library, 3333 Fifth Avenue
(412) 621-9893
www.thepoetryforum.org
Founded in 1966 by Samuel Hazo, Pennsylvania's Poet Laureate (1993–2003), this poetry forum continues as a cultural outreach in Pittsburgh and proves that there is a resurgence of poetry here and around the nation. Poets and performers have included Nobel Prize awardees and many Pulitzer Prize winners. Poets-in-Public is a series at the core of the forum's mission. Poets-in-Person offers

educational outreach and poetry workshops as Pennsylvania poets visit juniors and seniors in high schools. Single ticket prices for readings at the forum are $12 general admission and $8 for students and seniors. Subscription and group rates are also available.

Pittsburgh Arts and Lectures
Carnegie Music Hall, 4400 Forbes Avenue
(412) 622-8866
www.pittsburghlectures.org

Hear from influential, entertaining, and informative speakers through one of three Pittsburgh Arts and Lectures series. The Drue Heinz Lectures offers talks by 12 influential speakers during its fall and spring seasons. Past speakers have included Orhan Pamuk, Azar Nafisi, and Elizabeth Kolbert. Families love Black White & Read All Over, a series featuring six award-winning children's authors and illustrators. And for those who enjoy fiction, the American Shorts Reading delivers classic and contemporary short works of fiction at the New Hazlett Theater on Pittsburgh's North Side. Prices vary; subscription packages are available for the Drue Heinz Lectures.

Pittsburgh Speakers Series
(412) 392-4900
www.pittsburghspeakersseries.org

Presented by Robert Morris University and held at Heinz Hall, the Pittsburgh Speakers Series brings "the world to Pittsburgh" through provocative and insightful speakers. Past guests have included Madeleine Albright, Salmon Rushdie, and George Will. Tickets are sold by subscription only for the entire series and start at $275.

MUSIC

Butler County Symphony Orchestra
259 South Main Street, Butler
(724) 283-1402
www.butlersymphony.org

The Butler County Symphony Orchestra is a regional treasure offering six concerts between October and May. Under the tutelage of Elizabeth "Betsy" Heath Charles, musical director and conductor, the symphony features talented musicians and invited guests. Concerts take place at the Butler Intermediate High School. Single season tickets cost approximately $65 for adults and $35 for students. Other pricing plans are available for contributors.

Calliope: Pittsburgh Folk Music Society
6300 Fifth Avenue, Third Floor
412-361-1915
www.calliopehouse.org

Founded in 1976, Calliope is a nonprofit educational and presenting organization that preserves and promotes traditional and contemporary folk music and its allied arts. All Calliope programs are unique to Western Pennsylvania. The Calliope Concerts, featuring the legends of folk music, holds eight concerts between September and April in the acoustically acclaimed Carnegie Lecture Hall in the city's Oakland area. Classes taught at Calliope Folk Music School include guitar, banjo, fiddle, harmonica, bagpipes, songwriting, and even belly dancing!

Manchester Craftsmen's Guild—MCG Jazz
1815 Metropolitan Street
(412) 322-0800
www.mcgjazz.org

For the past 20 years MCG Jazz has celebrated the rich tradition of jazz through concerts, live recordings, and educational programs. Here jazz greats like Joe Williams, Billy Taylor, Dizzy Gillespie, Stanley Turrentine, and Ray Brown have arrived to perform for audiences and left talking about the spirit and joy of the place. Concerts are held at the 350-seat concert hall in Manchester Craftsmen's Guild, a minority-directed arts education and presenting organization that was founded by Bill Strickland in 1968 with the goal to help inner-city youth. Under the direction of Marty Ashby, MCG Jazz's recording label has produced 22 releases and continues to garner national attention through GRAMMY nominations and awards. The jazz concert season runs September through May, with ticket prices ranging from $37 to $42 and subscriptions for the eight-concert series starting at $140.

Pittsburgh Chamber Music Society
315 South Bellefield Avenue
(412) 624-4129
www.pittsburghchambermusic.org

This society brings some of the finest chamber music groups to Pittsburgh through two concert series. Chamber Music at Carnegie Music Hall is a series of seven concerts featuring traditional chamber music. The Bridges series, four concerts held at the New Hazlett Theater on Pittsburgh's North Side, explore string quartets. The season runs from late October through late May. Ticket prices vary.

Pittsburgh CLO
Benedum Center, 719 Liberty Avenue
(412) 281-2822
www.pittsburghclo.org

Subscribers to Pittsburgh CLO enjoy a delightful series of summer Broadway musicals each year performed in the Benedum Center. Past summer series have included the national tour of *Doctor Dolittle*, Barry Manilow's *Copacabana, Lunch,* and *Casper the Musical.* In 2004 the CLO introduced year-round entertainment with the opening of the CLO Cabaret at Theater Square.

Prices for Pittsburgh CLO's three-show Broadway package range from $49.50 to $139.50; a six-show Broadway package costs between $99 and $279. Thursday matinees are available, and subscribers can secure guaranteed seats, a newsletter, free ticket exchange privileges, and discounts to selected restaurants.

The CLO also offers many outreach and education programs, including the Academy of Musical Theater. Here students ages 5 through 18 can attend evening or Saturday classes with the finest training in dance, music, and drama.

Pittsburgh Opera
801 Penn Avenue
(412) 281-0912
www.pghopera.org

Under the direction of Mark J. Weinstein, the Pittsburgh Opera is world renowned. One of the first to offer English translations, it breathes new life into the classics and takes to the stage at the beautiful Benedum Center in the heart of Pittsburgh's Cultural District. Past performances have included *Tosca, Madama Butterfly,* and *Aida.* Tickets range in price from around $20 to $190. Subscribers get a free opera highlights recording, an option to purchase parking passes, and ticket exchange privileges.

Pittsburgh Symphony Orchestra
Heinz Hall, 600 Penn Avenue
(412) 392-4900
www.pittsburghsymphony.com

Under the leadership of Music Director Designate Manfred Honeck, the Pittsburgh Symphony Orchestra continues its heritage of presenting the most talented conductors and musicians. The symphony has completed more than 30 international tours, making the PSO truly a world-class orchestra. Previous conductors have included Maestro Lorin Maazel, André Previn, and Mariss Jansens. At home the orchestra offers 22 weeks of subscription concerts annually between September and June, and a Pops series under the direction of Marvin Hamlisch. Concerts are staged in the elegant Heinz Hall for the Performing Arts. Free summer concerts are also offered at various parks. For children, Fiddlesticks, the tuxedoed mascot, teaches lessons in classical music at selected performances.

Pittsburgh Youth Symphony Orchestra
Heinz Hall, 600 Penn Avenue
(412) 392-4872
www.pittsburghyouthsymphony.org

Comprising 85 young musicians, ages 14 to 21, the Pittsburgh Youth Symphony Orchestra was selected as one of five youth orchestras

i The Heinz Chapel Choir presents several concerts throughout the year. If you miss it, recordings are available from the Book Center at (412) 648-1455 or bookcenter@bc.pitt.edu.

to participate in the 2002 National Youth Orchestra Festival. The musicians take direction from conductor Daniel Meyer. Since 1962 the youth symphony has enjoyed affiliation with the Pittsburgh Symphony Orchestra. Admission is free; however, tickets are required for admission and can be obtained by calling the number listed or e-mailing info@pyso.us.

River City Brass Band
Various locations
(412) 434-7222
www.rcbb.com

While the word "band" might conjure up images of John Philip Sousa marches, this one is very different. Each year more than 120,000 people enjoy the sounds of the River City Brass Band under the direction of Maestro Denis Colwell. The band plays at least 49 concert series in seven different Western Pennsylvania locales and tours to more than 60 venues and festivals in the nation. Season subscribers enjoy concerts at various locations throughout Allegheny County and in Greensburg, Westmoreland County. "Take 5" flex plans and single concert ticket sales are available. Senior citizens, students, and groups of 10 or more receive discounted rates. Depending upon the location of the concert, tickets cost between $17 and $42.

Squonk Opera
468 Broadway Boulevard
(412) 372-4264
www.squonkopera.org

Focused on theater created from sound and image and inspired by a rust-belt love of spectacle and humor, Squonk Opera created its first show more than a decade ago. Since then, Squonk Opera has created eight original shows, including bigsmorgasbordwunderwerk,

an Off-Broadway and On-Broadway hit. Under the artistic direction of Jackie Dempsey and Steve O'Hearn, the company tours around the world but still returns home to perform at Pittsburgh venues, including the Kelly Strayhorn Theater in Pittsburgh's East Liberty neighborhood.

Westmoreland Symphony Orchestra
Palace Theatre, Greensburg
(724) 837-1850
www.westmorelandsymphony.org

Performing in the beautiful Palace Theatre in Greensburg, the Westmoreland Symphony Orchestra has provided musical experiences for decades. Under the direction of Kypros Markou, the season includes five classical concerts and one holiday concert. Two Young People's Concerts are held during the school day to introduce youth to classical music. The orchestra also sponsors a youth symphony. Single tickets range from approximately $10 to $36. Subscription prices vary according to seating.

THEATER

City Theatre
1300 Bingham Street
(412) 431-CITY (2489)
www.citytheatrecompany.org

On the city's South Side, the City Theatre makes its home in a restored building that was once the Bingham Street United Methodist Church. Specializing in new plays, City Theatre has brought to Pittsburgh playwrights such as Adam Rapp, Christopher Durang, and Jeffrey Hatcher and introduced Momentum, a new play festival that is now held each year. Shows appear on City Theatre's 270-seat main stage and in the 100-seat Lester Hamburg Studio. Call for ticket and subscription prices.

Greensburg Civic Theatre
951 Old Salem Road, Greensburg
(724) 836-7529
www.gctheatre.org

More than 100 people volunteer their time

and talent on and off stage to bring Greens-burg Civic Theatre to life. Entering its 55th season, the company offers both adult plays and children's theatrical productions. Past productions have included *The King and I, Fiddler on the Roof,* and *The Fantastiks.* Ticket prices vary; drama classes are also available.

Kuntu Repertory Theatre
(412) 624-7298
www.kuntu.org

From joyous musicals celebrating gospel singers to moving dramas about avoiding the pitfalls of inner-city living, Kuntu performances explore Africana life from a sociopolitical-historical perspective. Since its start in 1974, Kuntu has produced more than 80 plays by such playwrights as Kathleen Collins, Langston Hughes, and August Wilson. The season includes four to six productions, with ticket prices ranging from $11 to $20.

Mountain Playhouse
Route 985, Jennerstown
(814) 629-9201
www.mountainplayhouse.com

Pennsylvania's oldest professional stock theater, the Mountain Playhouse offers musicals, dramas, and farce during its June through October season. The 393-seat theater is housed in a restored 1805 gristmill that was moved log by log in 1939 to its current location in the Laurel Highlands. Ticket prices range from $15 to $30, with student and senior discounts available.

Pittsburgh Irish & Classical Theatre
222 Craft Avenue
(412) 561-6000
www.picttheatre.org

Pittsburgh Irish & Classical Theatre (PICT) has, in just 10 years, emerged as one of Pittsburgh's most celebrated new theater companies, with an annual attendance of over 23,000. Here you'll find undertakings like *BeckettFest,* the production of all 19 of Samuel Beckett's stage plays, and the premier of *Faith Healer.* Under the direction of Andrew

S. Paul, PICT presents both classic and new works that appear on stage at Charity Randall Theatre and Henry Heymann Theatre at the Stephen Foster Memorial in Oakland.

Pittsburgh Playhouse of Point Park University
222 Craft Avenue
(412) 621-4445
www.pittsburghplayhouse.com

The Playhouse is the performing arts center for Point Park University and offers a rigorous calendar with 18 major productions and 235 performances annually. The playhouse is home to The REP, a professional theater company, and three student companies—the Conservatory Theatre Company, Playhouse Dance Company, and Playhouse "Jr." The curtain goes up at the Main Stage of Rockwell & Hamlet Theater and at the Rauh Studio. Depending on the performance company, single tickets cost between $7 and $27; subscription packages range from $15 to $72.

Pittsburgh Public Theater
O'Reilly Theater, 621 Penn Avenue
(412) 316-1600
www.ppt.org

When this theater burst onto the Pittsburgh scene in September 1975, theater had nearly vanished from the city except for community and college theater companies. But patrons of the arts and benefactors from many Pittsburgh foundations helped to found the public theater in the early 1970s. Formerly housed on the city's North Side in a building more than 100 years old (the original Carnegie Music Hall, in fact), the theater moved into the state-of-the-art O'Reilly Theater in 1999. Recent premieres have included *The Secret Letters of Jackie and Marilyn* and *The Glorious Ones.*

More than 100,000 theatergoers attend presentations at the Public every year, and many more are served through educational outreach programs, including student matinees, post-performance discussions, internships, and classes.

Subscriptions range from approximately $120 to $300, with single performance tickets ranging from $34 to $60. Subscribers receive guaranteed and discounted parking and discounts at selected restaurants.

Quantum Theatre
67 Bedford Square
(412) 697-2929
www.quantumtheatre.com
Going to the theater? Not for Quantum productions. Instead you may find yourself in an abandoned warehouse, a defunct brewery, or even the zoo, watching contemporary plays or adaptations of classic works. The company's unique approach attracts artists from around the world to collaborate on productions, which are under the direction of founder Karla Boos. Tickets are available through ProArts (412-394-3353), or call the theater to purchase season subscriptions, which start at $95.

Theatre Factory
Third and Cavitt Avenues, Trafford
(412) 374-9200
www.thetheatrefactory.com
This small theater company delights audiences with a variety of performances for adults and families. The season runs from September through July and features musicals, drama, comedy, plus several children's productions. Tickets are $18 for adults and $16 for seniors, with $6 tickets for Kidsworks performances.

ARTISTIC & LITERARY SUPPORT GROUPS

Associated Artists of Butler County
The Art Center
344 South Main Street, Butler
(724) 283-6922
www.butlerartcenter.net
Dedicated to promoting the arts, this group encourages participation in the creative process and assists the community in finding ways to incorporate the arts into daily life. As the oldest cultural organization in Butler County, the AABC relies upon volunteers and now resides in its own facility on South Main

Street. The more than 300 members host exhibits throughout the year. Lectures, poetry readings, musical performances, and art classes are also a part of this group's mission.

Ligonier Valley Writers
Ligonier, Westmoreland County
www.ligoniervalleywriters.org
A nonprofit organization dedicated to encouraging and promoting the craft and business of writing, this group meets informally six times a year to hear from speakers and instructors.

The *Loyalhanna Review* provides talented writers with an outlet for their work. Social events, library resource materials, periodic newsletters, and other seminars are the perks of membership. Annual dues are approximately $30 for members ($45 for two members at the same address) and $15 for students. For information write in care of P.O. Box B, Ligonier, PA 15658.

Pennwriters
Statewide gatherings at various locations
www.pennwriters.org
Pennwriters is a rapidly growing, independent network of writers covering many genres. Established in 1988, the group includes members from all over the Commonwealth who share their knowledge and support fellow writers penning mystery, science fiction, fantasy, romance, women's fiction, children's books, poetry, nonfiction books and articles, greeting cards, and other work. The group now boasts more than 300 members.

Held in either Pittsburgh or in the Harrisburg area, a major writer's conference draws attention (and new members) each May. Throughout the year, area groups meet to learn from guest speakers or fellow members, or simply to network over lunch. Pittsburgh is considered to be in Area 3 of the group's six areas. Officers are elected by members. Author advocacy and other services, including a subscription to the *Penn Writer* newsletter, are the perks of becoming a Pennwriter. Dues cost approximately $55 for first-time members and $45 for renewals.

Various literary prizes are offered to area writers. One of these, the Drue Heinz Literature Prize, is administered by the University of Pittsburgh Press and carries a $15,000 cash award and a promise to publish. Manuscripts are accepted in May and June for short stories or novellas. For a copy of the rules, write to the University of Pittsburgh Press, 3400 Forbes Avenue, PA 15260.

Pittsburgh Center for the Arts School
6300 Fifth Avenue
(412) 361-0455
www.pittsburgharts.org
With classes in everything from ceramics, drawing, and music, to yoga, stretch, and meditation, the Pittsburgh Center for the Arts offers instruction at its Shadyside location. Annually there are hundreds of different classes, workshops, and camps provided for adults and children in 20 artistic disciplines. Some say this is the largest community-based art school in the country.

The Center for the Arts Galleries showcase exhibitions of emerging and recognized artists. And the Center for the Arts Shop features original and handcrafted jewelry, ceramics, functional and decorative works, paintings, prints, glassware, and more. Galleries and shops are open Tuesday through Saturday 10:00 a.m. to 5:00 p.m. and Sunday noon to 5:00 p.m. Closed Monday.

Pittsburgh Filmmakers
477 Melwood Avenue
(412) 681-5449
www.pghfilmmakers.org
Founded in 1971, Pittsburgh Filmmakers is a media-arts center devoted to artistic expression through film, video, and photography.

The organization provides exhibitions of alternative work ranging from off-beat foreign films to radical showings. Classes are available for credit or noncredit learning. Artists have access to necessary filming equipment.

Society for Contemporary Craft
2100 Smallman Street
(412) 261-7003, ext. 25
www.contemporarycraft.org
Founded by Betty Raphael in 1971 as the Store for Arts and Crafts and People-Made Things, this organization—now called the Society for Contemporary Craft—is a nationally recognized nonprofit contemporary arts organization. Exhibits, family workshops, and a drop-in studio are open for hands-on activities during all public hours. Previous workshops have included bookmaking, metalsmithing, woodworking, and fiber arts. Purchases from the store benefit the society as well as the individual artist. Guided tours and activities are available for schools and groups. The society is free to the public and open Tuesday through Saturday, 10:00 a.m. to 5:00 p.m. and on Monday by appointment. Closed Sunday.

Sweetwater Center for the Arts
200 Broad Street, Sewickley
(412) 741-4405
www.sweetwaterart.org
Founded in 1975, this regional center seeks to stimulate broad-based support for interest in the arts. Artist-instructors have outstanding qualifications for lectures and demonstrations, as well as classes for beginners and experienced artists. The schedule of classes and workshops includes ceramics and sculpture, drawing, and Raku.

PARKS

The hills, mountains, streams, and woodlands of Western Pennsylvania provide spacious and splendid settings for parks. In the region you'll find a happy balance between development and greenways. To its credit, local government has long recognized the value of parks for its citizens. In an era when both the public and private sectors actively seek new revenue sources from growth, they've tended to view the region's parklands as natural resources already producing riches aplenty.

Many of the region's parks were founded through private sector and government cooperation. If you trace the history of parks development here, you'll find that quite a few sit on land once privately owned, then bequeathed to the public by industrialists and philanthropists. Knowing the gems that they inherited, governments tended to buy up adjacent tracts to expand their new parks.

The result is a rich variety of parks ranging from the playground apparatus and tennis courts on the corner to the sweep and majesty of the Allegheny National Forest, Western Pennsylvania's largest scenic and recreation area.

In our descriptions we've sketched the attractions of 24 municipal parks, 16 state parks, and 6 federal recreation areas. You'll find many more municipal parks that you'll want to get to know. We've tried to capture both the most popular and heavily used parks as well as those with particularly compelling features. For more information on activities

i For the scoop on state parks, forests, rail trails, and other opportunities for outdoor adventure, check out the Department of Conservation and Natural Resource's Web site: www.dcnr.state.pa.us.

offered in the parks, see the Recreation chapter, where you'll find descriptions and opportunities for many sports and activities.

MUNICIPAL PARKS

Municipalities in Western Pennsylvania know the value of parks. Virtually every municipality in the region maintains green areas for the relaxation and enjoyment of its citizens. The City of Pittsburgh, for example, operates 29 parks offering picnic shelters, to say nothing of smaller parks and parklets. Included descriptions are only the "crown jewels" of the Pittsburgh parks system—Frick, Highland, Riverview, and Schenley. The City of Pittsburgh, along with The Pittsburgh Parks Conservancy, is working to renew, revitalize, and preserve these four parks. Visit the conservancy's Web site (www.pittsburghparks.org) to learn about current projects at these parks. Clearly you'll find a great deal more to explore than we could capture here. An excellent place to begin exploring, on a rainy, early-spring day perhaps, is the county parks' Web site: www.county.allegheny.pa.us/parks.

If you want to reserve a shelter or ball field in the City of Pittsburgh or Allegheny County, you'll need to be familiar with the permitting process in each case. For shelters, the City of Pittsburgh launches its permitting period with a "Shelter Day," held each spring in the lobby of the City-County Building. That opening day is reserved for City of Pittsburgh residents, who participate in a lottery for permits. Thereafter, you can reserve your shelter by calling (412) 255-2370. Fees, which include a mandatory alcohol permit, range from $42 to $262. The city will hold your reservation for seven days, and your payment must be by money order or business check only.

For City of Pittsburgh ball fields, organizations currently using fields are entitled to automatic renewals. For the fields that remain, the city permits time slots of 1 hour and 45 minutes. Fees range from $150 to $300 for the spring season. Call (412) 255-2370 for your ball field permits. Updated fees are available on the Web site www.city .pittsburgh.pa.us/pw/html/ballfield_permits.html.

Allegheny County's procedures are significantly different from the City of Pittsburgh's. You can reserve shelters, groves, and buildings up to one year in advance—a good idea if you're eyeing one of the large facilities at North Park or South Park. You can make your reservations at the parks (except for Hartwood Acres) or by calling the county at (412) 350-2474. Fees range from $20 to $275. Checks, cash, and money orders are accepted at all the parks; North and South Parks accept credit cards. For ball fields at North, South, and Boyce Parks, again, call the county at (412) 350-2474; you can reserve fields at other parks at the parks themselves. You must pay your fee in person—$30 for a three-hour slot—within 48 hours of your reservation.

North

Belmont Complex
415 Butler Road, Kittanning
(724) 548-1067
www.co.armstrong.pa.us
It would be hard to find a municipal park that offers more comprehensive ice-skating facilities than you'll find at Belmont Complex. Operated by the Armstrong County Recreation Authority, the complex features ice-skating and hockey programs August through April. The budding hockey stars in your family will enjoy skating instruction and youth leagues, while adult teams can compete in the league operated by the complex. If you don't belong to a league, complex officials will find one for you.

The complex also hosts skating shows and high-school hockey matches. Perhaps best of all, you can rent the ice complex for your personal or group use. With ice time as precious as it is in the region, that's a rare attraction indeed.

Skating and hockey are far from the only activities at Belmont Complex. The Olympic-size swimming pool is available on a daily admission basis and to members who pay an annual fee; members are welcome to host their guests. There is also a 150-foot water slide. This is a fun place.

Deer Lakes Park
1090 Bailies Run Road, Tarentum
(724) 265-3520
www.alleghenycounty.us/parks/dlfac.aspx
Fishing is the primary theme at Deer Lakes Park, a facility administered by Allegheny County. Over the years, the county augmented the park's existing lake with two additional lakes; all are interconnected and use the same watershed. The state stocks the lake with bluegill, crappie, perch, sunfish, and trout; bass and catfish also bite. The park's picnic areas all bear the names of fish. Nine picnic shelters and nine groves may be reserved through Allegheny County. The park also features a children's play area, disc golf course, the Wagman Observatory, and hiking and jogging trails.

Harrison Hills Park
5200 Freeport Road, Natrona Heights
(724) 295-3570
www.alleghenycounty.us/parks/hhfac.aspx
This 500-acre park in the extreme northeastern corner of Allegheny County offers some of the most enticing vistas of any municipal park in the region. From the Watts Memorial Overlook, you'll view a vast expanse of the Allegheny River, and your view will take in parts of three neighboring counties—Armstrong, Butler, and Westmoreland. You'll find groves and shelters for relaxation as you enjoy the view, and walking trails, soccer fields, and a children's play area, if you're in the mood for something less sedentary.

Hartwood Acres
200 Hartwood Acres
(412) 767-9200
www.allegheny county.us/parks/hwfac.aspx
The centerpieces of Hartwood Acres are the mansion and riding stables that once were the property of the estate's former owner, Mary Flinn Lawrence, who sold the estate to Allegheny County in 1969. The county has maintained the stables and riding trails and offers tours of the mansion. Hartwood also offers cross country skiing, hiking and walking trails, and off-leash dog areas.

Among municipal parks in the region, Hartwood Acres may be unequaled for its beauty, whether lush and green in summer or a snow-covered picture postcard in winter. For all that, the principal current attractions are cultural. Hartwood Acres hosts theater, dance, symphony, and other musical programs in warm-weather months. Local restaurants sometimes provide box dinners to patrons of Hartwood performances. A picnic dinner on the lush lawn followed by an evening of music or theater in the park: Now that's entertainment!

North Park
Pearce Mill Road, Allison Park
(724) 935-1766
www.alleghenycounty.us/parks/npfac.aspx
North Park and South Park are the reigning monarchs of the Allegheny County park system. Visit this sprawling 3,075-acre park located in Hampton, McCandless, and Pine Townships, and you'll agree that it deserves its crown. Its 75-acre lake, considered the largest man-made body of water in the county, is bordered by 4½ miles of natural woodlands. If you're a jogger, you won't earn your spurs until you jog around the lake, a popular pastime for many. Anglers utilize the well-stocked lake; even if you don't fish, you can enjoy the lake by renting a boat from the park's concessionaire.

Bicyclists also circumnavigate the lake—the park provides bicycles for rent. The swimming pool may be the largest you'll ever see. Don't count on lap swimming here, though.

There are too many swimmers enjoying the pool and waterslide to allow for that. North Park's 18-hole golf course is exceptionally popular. (You'll find a more detailed description in the Golf chapter.)

For hobbyists, North Park also features a remote control airplane field, the Marshall Island Wildfowl Reserve, and a horse show area. Play a game of horseshoes, tour the nature center—the list of activities offered is quite extensive!

Other amenities include tennis courts, one football field, nine ball fields, eight soccer fields, a skating rink, and numerous groves and shelters of varying sizes and amenities. The ball fields and groves attract heavy use. If you're planning an outing, it's mandatory that you reserve your grove or picnic area, and we suggest that you do so well in advance. For costs associated with renting fields or groves call the park's office or visit the Web site.

Riverview Park
Riverview Avenue
(412) 323-7209
www.pittsburghparks.org
When the North Side of Pittsburgh was a separate municipality known as Allegheny, local residents raised money to purchase land for a park, which they donated to the community. That land became Riverview Park, a 251-acre facility now operated by the City of Pittsburgh. The park offers many attractive features, including hiking trails that will carry you so deeply into thick woods that you'll swear you've left the city for virgin forest.

You'll enjoy bridle trails—rare enough within the city—as well as a swimming pool, three tennis courts, horseshoe pits, a ball field, and five playgrounds. Picnickers can utilize six shelters—you'll need permits and reservations for three of them.

The Allegheny Observatory stands near the park's main entrance. Used primarily as a research facility by the University of Pittsburgh, the observatory also hosts credit and informal courses and meetings of the region's amateur astronomers.

East

Boyce Park
675 Frankstown Road, Plum
(724) 327-0338
www.alleghenycounty.us/parks/bpfac.aspx
If you're looking for downhill skiing in Allegheny County, Boyce Park is the place. In fact, it's the only place. This park at the extreme eastern edge of Allegheny County offers both lifts and a large ski lodge called Four Seasons. (For more on Boyce Park's skiing, see the Recreation chapter.) This area of the park reopened in early 2008 after a $1 million renovation project that included upgraded and new chair lifts, new elevated snow-making equipment, and a new tubing park. The ski area now offers six runs for skiing. The Boyce Park Ski Area is open Monday through Thursday from 3:30 until 10:00 p.m., Friday 3:30 until 10:30 p.m., and on Saturday, Sunday and holidays from 9:00 until 4:30 p.m. Call (724) 733-4665 for details.

Skiing is just one of many attractions here—the county-run park also features a popular wave pool and a large recreational complex. The 1,096-acre park offers tennis courts and picnic groves and shelters all named with a Boy Scouts motif. That's to honor William D. Boyce, the founder of the Boy Scouts, who was born nearby.

Cedar Creek Park
Route 51, Belle Vernon
(724) 929-4352
www.co.westmoreland.pa.us/parks
The scenic Youghiogheny River provides the northern border for Cedar Creek . . . as well as a host of recreational activities. The Yough offers fishing and canoeing, with river access through a boat launch. You'll also enjoy hiking and bicycling along the Yough River Trail. The Trail is now complete from Cedar Creek north to McKeesport in Allegheny County, approximately 21 miles, and south to Meyersdale, approximately 79 miles. The 10-foot-wide trail is finished with crushed limestone, making it wheelchair accessible.

The park also features 19 pavilions available for rental, bicycle and cross-country ski rentals, ball fields, basketball and volleyball courts, horseshoe pits, and sledding and tobogganing areas. You may hunt in certain areas of the park.

You'll take particular pleasure in several special features of the park. Cedar Creek has cut a deep gorge in the northern section of the park—water cascades down the shale steps amid steep, forested slopes. The park's amphitheater accommodates up to 2,500 visitors for its free summer concert series. The Mon Valley RC Club operates from Cedar Creek Park, so you can expect to see some low-flying craft.

Frick Park
2005 Beechwood Boulevard
(412) 422-6538
www.pittsburghparks.org
If there were no Frick Park, someone would have to invent one. Operated by the City of Pittsburgh, this huge urban park touches five city neighborhoods—Squirrel Hill, Point Breeze, Park Place, Regent Square, and Swisshelm Park—and reaches into the adjacent municipality of Swissvale. At 600 acres, it's large enough to host many simultaneous activities without seeming overly crowded, even when dog lovers and their pooches congregate each weekend morning for socializing and play. Frick's walking and jogging trails wind along the park's hills, giving you a workout that few other municipal parks can.

For recreation, Frick Park offers six clay tennis courts, a basketball court, two playgrounds, three ball fields, and a lawn bowling green. (For more on lawn bowling in Frick Park, see the Recreation chapter.)

The park was bequeathed to the city by industrialist and philanthropist Henry Clay Frick. In accordance with the bequest, 150 acres of the park have been designated Frick Woods Nature Reserve. Unfortunately, the Frick Environmental Center building burned down in 2002, but year-round programs for the public are still available. Contact (412) 422-6538 for details.

Within the reserve you'll find a meadow, woodlands, and gardens that host a treasure trove of native plant life and are one of the region's most popular birding areas—home and migratory "stopover" to more than 150 different species.

Highland Park
Highland Avenue and Bunkerhill Street
(412) 665-3632
www.pittsburghparks.org

For a true Pittsburgh scene, drop by the reservoir at Highland Park any morning at dawn or shortly thereafter. You'll see a parade of walkers and joggers getting in their laps around Reservoir No. 1, part of the daily regime for many residents of Pittsburgh's East End. Don't be surprised if you're inspired to join them.

Operated by the City of Pittsburgh, the 380-acre park offers eight shelters—all of which you must get a permit to use—woodland trails, a large swimming pool, and a companion wading pool. You'll find nine tennis courts, a softball field, and multiple areas with play apparatus. Lake Carnegie is popular with anglers; it's a good place for an afternoon of laid-back fishing, but don't expect to walk away with that trout you've been wanting to mount on your wall. The reservoir notwithstanding, the most popular attraction of the park is the Pittsburgh Zoo & PPG Aquarium, which is detailed for you in the Kidstuff chapter.

Mammoth Park
Off Blacksmith Road, Mt. Pleasant
(724) 830-3950
www.co.westmoreland.pa.us/parks

As you drive through eastern Westmoreland County, you'll come across a lake that's mammoth, ergo the name, Mammoth Park. Mammoth Lake spans 24 acres, and it's stocked with trout by the Pennsylvania Fish and Boat Commission. When frozen, the lake provides both ice fishing and ice-skating. The park offers wheelchair-accessible fishing decks.

Another popular water-based activity is the giant waterslide, which descends 96 feet from a hillside into the lake. Sounds like a "must-do" for the kids.

When you're dried off and ready for land-based activities, you'll find numerous pavilions available for rental as well as ball fields, play apparatus, sledding and tobogganing areas, and courts for volleyball, boccie ball, shuffleboard, basketball, street hockey, and tennis. You can take it all in from the Mammoth Park observation deck, which provides a panoramic view ranging for almost 10 miles.

Both the Laurel Highlands Radio-Controlled Airplane Club and a BMX club base their operations at the park.

Mt. Odin Park
Tollgate Hill Road, Greensburg
(724) 834-2640
www.city.greensburg.pa.us

Operated by the city of Greensburg, Mt. Odin Park features several picnic pavilions, tennis courts, and a golf course. (For more about that amenity, see the Golf chapter.) The most compelling attraction of the park, however, is its play area, where you'll find replicas of downtown Greensburg buildings, including city hall, the Westmoreland County Courthouse, and Westmoreland Hospital. The replicas have an open design, so kids can walk through and play inside them. Sounds like an intriguing way to familiarize your youngsters with life in the city.

Northmoreland Park
Route 356, Allegheny Township
(724) 727-7616
www.co.westmoreland.pa.us/parks

Once you get used to the idea of traveling east to Northmoreland in Westmoreland County (we're dizzy just writing it), you'll find a lovely facility developed around the 17-acre Northmoreland Lake. The lake features a winter and spring trout fishery, as well as quality bass and pan fishing. Since the lake is designated a conservation lake, special Fish and Boat Commission rules apply. Northmoreland provides a wheelchair-accessible fishing deck.

The Boathouse Building offers boat rental and picnic facilities. You'll find 11 pavilions available for rental, as well as ball fields, play apparatus, cross-country ski trails, and courts for shuffleboard and volleyball. Also available for rental is the Activities Building, which features a small kitchen and an air-conditioned reception/meeting room. You may hunt in some areas of the park. The park sports a model radio-controlled airfield and a BMX track, as well as opportunities for horseback riding and equestrian lessons, using either your own horse or one of the park's.

Renziehausen Park
Eden Park Boulevard, McKeesport
(412) 675-5068
This urban park operated by the city of McKeesport offers both recreational and cultural delights. For recreation you can enjoy the park's ball field, splash pool for kids, seven shelters and a pavilion available for rental, and fishing in Lake Emily, which hosts an annual fishing derby.

For culture and entertainment, visit the International Village, which since 1960 has been hosting a three-day celebration of the region's ethnic heritage, complete with music, dancing, and food. You'll also enjoy The Little Red Schoolhouse—a replication of the city's first schoolhouse, erected in 1832—and entertainment at the park's band shell. Make sure you save time to tour the Rose Garden maintained by the Garden Club of McKeesport. It features 1,500 rose bushes as well as perennials and beds of grasses and herbs. In addition, the club uses the garden as a test bed to introduce new roses to the region. You'll find it difficult to tear yourself away from this beautiful spot.

Schenley Park
Schenley Drive
(412) 622-6904
www.pittsburghparks.org
Schenley Park, in the Oakland neighborhood bordering the campuses of both the University of Pittsburgh and Carnegie Mellon University, is one of the crown jewels of the City of Pittsburgh park system. You'll enjoy activities that are marvelously diverse. You'll find a swimming pool, six playground areas, walking and jogging trails, 13 tennis courts, and 3 ball fields. With permits and reservations, picnickers can utilize all five shelters—rent Schenley Park Visitor Center, a popular site for small receptions.

The park's ice rink is one of the region's most popular venues for ice-skating. (For more information on this activity, see the Recreation chapter.) Schenley hosts a number of popular annual events, including the Vintage Grand Prix and the Smoky City Folk Festival. You can lounge on the lawn at Flagstaff Hill—a popular pastime of CMU students—where the city stages its Comcast Cinema in the Parks program each summer or take in the flower shows at Phipps Conservatory and Botanical Gardens.

Schenley Park is rich in history as well as amenities. Much of the park was donated by philanthropist Mary Schenley, and the park's "Oval" for decades was home to harness racing and horse stables. A horrific fire in the early 1970s destroyed the stables and ended the park's equine involvement.

The park also offers a popular nine-hole golf course—the only golf course within City of Pittsburgh limits—and a flying disc golf course that hosts organized competition. For more on these activities, see the Golf and Recreation chapters.

Twin Lakes Park
Twin Lakes Road, Luxor
(724) 837-8611
The park takes its name from its twin lakes that provide boating, fishing, ice fishing, and ice-skating opportunities. At the Lower Lake's Boating & Concession building, you can load up on fishing and picnic supplies and rent pedal boats, rowboats, and canoes. The park features three wheelchair-accessible fishing decks.

The reservoir at Schenley Park. MICHAEL D. REED

A broad network of recreational trails is a major attraction at this Westmoreland County–operated facility. You'll find trails for walking, cross-country skiing, and jogging—joggers also can test the exercise stations staged along the trails. If you enjoy the Wilderness Trail, you'll also enjoy the park's environmental and nature center, which provides interpretive programs for school, groups, and any interested visitors.

For outings you can rent any of the seven pavilions or the Activities Building, which features a kitchen and a reception hall/meeting room. Twin Lakes also offers play apparatus as well as hunting in designated areas.

South

Cross Creek Park
Route 50, Rea
(724) 228-6867

Operated by Washington County, Cross Creek Park offers hunting and fishing and boating on the 258-acre lake. Bring your own boat and boating permit. (Annual permits are available from the county.) Picnic sites are available free of charge, but shelters must be rented. All shelters feature grills and electrical outlets. You'll enjoy the park's hiking trails.

Mingo Creek Park
Route 136, Nottingham
(724) 228-6867

Mingo Creek Park features a number of activities with an equine theme. You'll find 15 miles of bridle trails for horseback riding—you're responsible for bringing the horse and purchasing an annual permit—and hourly hayrides from 5:00 a.m. through 8:00 p.m. on Fridays and usually 6:00 p.m. through 8:00 p.m. on Saturdays in October. (Hours do vary depending on the date, please call to confirm.) Cost for a hayride is $50 per hour for a maximum of 25 people.

The park offers 10 shelters of varying sizes, which must be reserved in season, as well as picnic sites available free of charge. Organized groups may camp in the park, and nature walks are available for all. Mingo Creek Park is operated by Washington County.

Round Hill Park and Farm
651 Round Hill Road, Elizabeth
(412) 384-4701

This is a park with an agrarian theme. In fact, the 1,100-acre park is built around a modern working farm that's a popular destination for student groups. The park offers interpretive sessions to thousands of students and other visitors each year. Other attractions of Round Hill, which is located in the southeastern corner of Allegheny County and administered by the county, include walking trails and picnic groves and shelters.

South Park
Buffalo Drive, South Park
(412) 835-5710
www.allegheny.us/parks/spfac.aspx

At more than 2,000 acres, South Park is one of the most capacious and diverse of the region's municipal parks, and it offers just about every recreational activity you would hope to find in a municipal facility. Its wave pool attracts about 100,000 people per season, and its two golf courses totaling 27 holes are exceptionally popular. For more on golf at South Park, see the Golf chapter.

After the wave pool, check out the bumper boats, go carts, and miniature golf course at the South Park VIP. For kids, the park also offers a pony rink. You'll also find picnic tables and shelters as well as walking, jogging, and hiking trails. The trails wind through areas that feature both woodlands and open glades. For all that, many joggers eschew the trails for a run along Corrigan Drive, the park's main thoroughfare that was named for the famous "Wrong Way Corrigan." Other amenities include 33 lighted tennis courts, 6 ball fields, 1 soccer field, horseshoe pits, a deck hockey facility, and a skating rink.

You'll get an eyeful of history at the park as well. Allegheny County, which operates the park, has preserved the homestead of Oliver Miller; it was near that estate that the first shots of the 1794 Whiskey Rebellion were fired. The bathhouse near the wave pool was patterned after the Miller house. You'll also find on Corrigan Drive a memorial to poet Joyce Kilmer, who penned the famous poem "Trees"... an appropriate tribute to this lush park.

Ten Mile Creek County Park
Clarksville Road, Fredericktown
(724) 228-6867
www.co.washington.pa.us/

As you might guess, the main attraction in 25-acre Ten Mile Creek County Park is the creek, where boating is a popular activity. Bring your own boat and annual permit issued by Washington County, which operates this park. (Permit applications can be downloaded from the Web site.) You may also fish from the shore of the creek. Shelters with grills and electrical outlets are available for rental. Picnic sites are offered on a first-come, first-served basis.

White Oak Park
3 Muse Lane, McKeesport
(412) 678-3774
www.alleghenycounty.us/

Operated by Allegheny County, White Oak Park is a botanist's delight, featuring a broad variety of plants and trees, some of them found nowhere else in Pennsylvania. You'll get plenty of exercise if you explore the flora, as some of White Oak's terrain is quite steep. You can unwind in the park's rental picnic groves and shelters when you've finished exploring the 810 acres. The park is open daily from 8:00 a.m. to sunset.

West

Brady's Run Park
526 Brady's Run Road, Beaver Falls
(724) 846-5600
www.co.beaver.pa.us

Brady's Run Park is named for Captain Samuel Brady, an early pioneer and merciless killer of Native Americans, whose ferocity was fueled by the death of his father and brother in the Indian wars of the 1770s. In one of the most interesting examples of early American jurisprudence, Brady was charged with killing Native Americans—and acquitted largely on the strength of testimony of Chief Guyasuta, whose tribe had been relentlessly hunted by Brady.

While this 2,000-acre park pays homage to Brady, it is a gentle and peaceful facility operated by Beaver County. It features the Beaver County Ice Arena and the Calland Arboretum, a natural area with walking trails. You'll also enjoy Brady's Run Lodge, a popular site for weddings and other special events; an indoor facility for tennis and walking, with an observation deck; an arena for horse shows; and horseshoe courts that have hosted state championship events.

Settler's Cabin Park
1225 Green Road, Oakdale
(412) 787-2750
www.alleghenycounty.us/parks/scfac.aspx
Settler's Cabin spans 1,610 acres, unusually large for a municipal park, and it has more of a rugged feel than most municipal parks. Named for an 18th-century log cabin that was found on the site, the park's attractive meadows in many cases have been left largely untouched. Allegheny County, which operates the park, has preserved the log cabin for visitors. If you're looking for a getaway only a few minutes from downtown Pittsburgh and Pittsburgh International Airport, you can feel like a settler at Settler's Cabin. It will be easy to feel as if you're exploring a brave new frontier: The park extends to Collier and Robinson Townships and even into northern Fayette County.

You'll find plenty of amenities, including reasonably priced rental shelters and groves named for Native American tribes. The wave pool and diving platform are extremely popular, as are the park's tennis courts.

STATE PARKS

When the Commonwealth of Pennsylvania established its Department of Environmental Resources in 1971 under Secretary Maurice K. Goddard, it was with the avowed purpose of situating at least one public park within a 25-mile drive of each resident of the state. It might take a surveyor to determine if the state achieved exactly the goal, but one thing the Commonwealth did accomplish was development of a public park system rich in recreational opportunities and environmental wonders.

The state operates 116 parks with a varied and compelling recreational menu. At most, natural or man-made waterways offer fishing, boating, and swimming. Hunting is permitted in most areas of the parks, and you'll find miles of scenic hiking trails, campsites, and picnic areas. Winter brings ice-skating, ice fishing, ice boating, sled riding, cross-country skiing, and snowmobiling. Not all activities are offered everywhere, but most parks are diverse enough to satisfy your outdoor needs.

State parks are open year-round, typically from 8:00 a.m. until sunset, although some activities are seasonal. Some activities require fees, reservations, or rentals. You may bring your pets to day-use areas, provided you keep them on leashes. The state imposes a number of restrictions on certain activities and uses, including limitation on the horsepower of motorized boats and the length of your stay at certain cabins and campsites. For instance, to boat, in most cases, you'll also need at least one of the following: 1) a state park launching permit, available at most state park offices; 2) a state park mooring permit; 3) a current certificate and number of watercraft registration; 4) current registration for your motorized (electric) boats; or, for your boat registered in another state, 5) a Pennsylvania State Park launch permit and the boat's current registration.

If you call the Bureau of State Parks at (888) PA–PARKS (727-2757), they'll be happy to provide you with a useful brochure and map of all 116 parks, indicating the activities that each park offers as well as introducing you to park rules and regulations. They'll also send you more detailed brochures on individual parks—they will charge a nominal fee if you ask for more than a few brochures.

We've profiled 16 state parks. To do so, we've had to step out of the six-county coverage area on occasion. We think you'll find the trip worth taking.

Point State Park
101 Commonwealth Place
(412) 471-0235
www.dcnr.state.pa.us/stateparks/parks
/point.aspx

A state park in downtown Pittsburgh? It's not a misprint—the Commonwealth maintains this 36-acre downtown oasis right at the Point, where the Allegheny and Monongahela Rivers meet to form the Ohio River. The park is steeped in historical significance. It was the site of the original Fort Pitt, where the British routed the French and founded the city. You can see a portion of the old fort at the park's Fort Pitt Blockhouse museum. The park was created just after World War II as part of the city's renaissance, yet another historical note.

The park hosts the Three Rivers Arts Festival and a variety of concerts and serves as the finishing point for the Pittsburgh Marathon. The emphasis here, however, is not on doing but on relaxing and, dare we say it, contemplating. With benches that provide views of river traffic and the giant fountain, you can slip away from the day's challenges for a few moments of peace and quiet. This is a rare and welcome city amenity.

To celebrate Pittsburgh's 250th anniversary in 2008, Point State Park is undergoing a major renovation. The project includes restoring and enhancing utilities in the park, providing a Great Lawn for performances, installing a new stage on the Festival Grounds, and adding new trees, native flora, signage, lighting, furniture, and concessions. During the multi-phase project, the fountain will be restored and enhanced, and water steps at the confluence of the three rivers will be installed.

The project, which is being executed through public/private partnerships between several organizations, began in 2001 with a master-planning process. The entire project will not be completed until at least 2009. Until that time, the majority of the park will be closed. For more information about the renovation, visit www.pointstatepark.com.

North

Clear Creek State Park
Clear Creek State Park Road, Sigel
(814) 752-2368
www.dcnr.state.pa.us/stateparks/parks/clear
creek.aspx

Set in Jefferson County just north of the six-county coverage area, 1,676-acre Clear Creek State Park is popular for its own attractions as well as its proximity to Clear Creek State Forest, Cook Forest State Park, and the Allegheny National Forest. If you want to stay long enough to hit all those highlights, you can use this park's family campground, with 53 tent and trailer sites, or opt for cozier accommodations in one of the park's two yurts or 22 rustic family cabins.

Anglers will find stocked and native brook trout in Clear Creek and northern pike, smallmouth bass, walleye, trout, and panfish in the nearby Clarion River. Hunters can stalk white-tailed deer, bear, squirrel, and wild turkey on 677 acres. The park offers 15 miles of hiking trails, a 180-foot guarded swimming beach, more than 300 picnic tables, and 5 pavilions available for rental.

For a special treat while you're here, try canoeing on the Clarion River, one of the region's most scenic and pristine waterways. Canoe rental is available from private concessionaires just outside the park.

ℹ️ Many park Web sites now offer maps that can be downloaded for no fee. Or, to obtain a printed park map, try one of these park offices: Westmoreland County Bureau of Parks and Recreation, (724) 830-3950 or (724) 830-3951; Washington County Department of Parks and Recreation, (724) 228-6867; and Armstrong County Recreation Authority, (724) 548-1067.

Cook Forest State Park
Route 36, Cooksburg
(814) 744-8407
www.dcnr.state.pa.us/stateparks/parks/cook
forest.aspx

Cook Forest State Park spans 8,500 acres in three counties—Clarion, Forest, and Jefferson. It's north of the coverage area but such a recreational and historical gem that you'll want to visit this park. It's named for John Cook, an early settler whose descendants are buried in a private cemetery adjoining the park. In the 1930s the park was the site of a Civilian Conservation Corps (CCC) camp; CCC workers helped construct the park's cabins, roads, and trails.

The trails remain an attraction. These include 27 miles of hiking trails, featuring a portion of the 140-mile Baker Trail, which stretches from Freeport in Armstrong County to the Allegheny National Forest. The trails wind through magnificent stands of virgin white pine and hemlock timber stands, which have earned the park the nickname "the Black Forest of Pennsylvania." The trail network includes 4.5 miles of bridle trails and 20 miles of snowmobile trails.

Anglers enjoy the scenic Clarion River, which flows along the park's border and yields trout, warmwater game fish, and panfish; hunters utilize more than 4,000 acres in search of deer, squirrel, and turkey. You're welcome to canoe on the Clarion, but you'll have to go outside the park for canoe rentals. Cook Forest offers a swimming pool and such winter activities as ice-skating, sledding, and cross-country skiing, with ski rentals available.

Picnickers will find tables and two pavilions available for rental. The park offers two organized group tenting areas as well as 24 rustic cabins for rental. Don't miss the Sawmill Craft Center and Theater for plays, musical performances, and displays of crafts by local artisans.

Jennings Environmental Education Center
2951 Prospect Road, Slippery Rock
(724) 794-6011
www.dcnr.state.pa.us/stateparks/parks/
jennings.aspx

You can't swim, snowmobile, hunt, or fish here—Jennings isn't that kind of park. You can, however, learn about ecological and environmental issues . . . then traverse the 300-acre facility and get a hands-on feel for those issues. Jennings just happens to encompass one of the only prairies left in the Pennsylvania area.

The center strives to protect natural ecosystems and provide public education in ecological responsibility. It does so through displays, exhibits, and the natural wonders of the park. These include the blazing star, a prairie plant that sports a cluster of rose-purple flowers at their most colorful in August, and 220 acres of woodland trails that display nearly 400 species of plants and 134 species of birds. Stay on those trails, please, or you may encounter the Massasauga rattlesnake. This guy is endangered and not keen on being disturbed.

Kids, this is one place you'll want to take your parents.

Maurice K. Goddard State Park
684 Lake Wilhelm Road, Sandy Lake
(724) 253-4833
www.dcnr.state.pa.us/stateparks/parks
/mauricekgoddard.aspx

The park is named for Dr. Maurice K. Goddard, father of Pennsylvania's environmental movement, who served as the founding secretary of the state's Department of Environmental Resources in 1971. Lake Wilhelm dominates the park, spanning more than 60 percent of the facility's 2,856 acres. As you might expect, water-based activities are popular here.

The park features a 200-slip marina and a 48-space dry land seasonal mooring area; the marina provides parking space for 371 cars and trailers. Other amenities include boat rentals and seven launching areas. Nonpowered boats and those up to 10 horsepower are permitted. Anglers enjoy the lake as well, pursuing largemouth and smallmouth bass, walleyes, northern pike, muskellunge, bluegill, crappie, catfish, perch, and sunfish.

More than 1,155 acres are available for hunting—deer and waterfowl are abundant. You'll find 14 miles of hiking trails, 6 miles of mountain bike trails, and 150 picnic tables in the park. Winter activities include ice-skating, ice fishing, ice boating, cross-country skiing, and snowmobiling. The park is just north of the principal coverage area.

McConnells Mill State Park
1761 McConnells Mill Road, Portersville
(724) 368-8091
www.dcnr.state.pa.us/stateparks/parks
/mcconnellsmill.aspx

The centerpieces of McConnells Mill are the deep gorges of Slippery Rock Creek, formed by glacial activity more than 100,000 years ago, and a man-made attraction, the restored rolling gristmill from which the park derives its name. The gorge creates some of the region's best—and most challenging—opportunities for modern-day hikers, climbers, and whitewater boaters.

Hikers will enjoy 11 miles of rugged trails that provide unparalleled views of the creek. Whitewater boaters can take to the creek in rubber rafts, whitewater canoes, and kayaks, none of which can be rented at the park. Climbing and rappelling are available at the Rim Road Climbing Area and Breakneck Bridge. Warning: They don't call it Breakneck for nothing. You may hunt in designated areas—you'll likely encounter grouse, deer, turkey, rabbit, and squirrel.

Anglers will find trout and bass in the creek as well as a "Delayed Harvest—Fly Fish-ing Only" area. You won't have camping or swimming opportunities at McConnells Mill, but you can enjoy more than 150 picnic tables and a ball field.

Moraine State Park
225 Pleasant Valley Road, Portersville
(724) 368-8811
www.dcnr.state.pa.us/stateparks/parks
/moraine.aspx

When you take in the majesty of Moraine's 16,725 acres, you may not believe that this treasured public resource was pocked by the scars of coal mining and oil-well drilling as late as the 1950s. The Commonwealth of Pennsylvania undertook the reclamation of strip-mined land, plugged 422 gas and oil wells, and created the 3,225-acre Lake Arthur—a restoration of the glacial lake that covered most of Northwestern Pennsylvania more than 10,000 years ago. The result: one of the state's most beautiful and useful parks.

Much of the activity at Moraine centers on Lake Arthur. The lake features 10 boat-launching areas—motorized boats up to 10 horsepower are permitted—and you can rent canoes, rowboats, paddleboats, motorized fishing boats, and pontoon boats. Sailing is especially popular on the lake, with sailboats available for rental. The colorful sails form an appealing vista that you can view from picnic areas high above the lake. The Barber Point area of the lake is even suitable for windsurfing. Anglers pursue muskellunge, northern pike, tiger muskellunge, striper, largemouth bass, walleye, channel catfish, black crappie, and bluegill. For swimmers the park offers two large, guarded beaches.

You'll find plenty to do away from the lake. A 14-mile portion of the North Country National Scenic Trail courses through the park. A 7-mile paved bicycle trail parallels the north shore of the lake, and you'll also find a 6-mile mountain bike trail that is targeted to experienced off-road bikers. Numerous other trails also offer opportunities for adventure. Approximately 13,600 of Moraine's acres are open seasonally for hunters. Picnickers will

Close-up

Urban, Suburban, and Wilderness Trails

Frick Park Trail System
(412) 422-6538
www.pittsburghparks.org
This is an extensive woodland trail network, including designated areas where dogs may run off-leash. Like the park, it runs from Point Breeze into Squirrel Hill, borders Edgewood, and dips under the Parkway East. A highlight is the Frick Environmental Center, near the Beechwood Avenue entrance in Squirrel Hill, which provides information about the park's history, habitat, and ecology.

Three Rivers Heritage Trail System
(412) 488-0212
www.friendsoftheriverfront.org
This 37-mile trail and greenway system connects the heart of downtown Pittsburgh with surrounding neighborhoods, including Oakland, the North Shore, South Side, and the Strip District. The trail runs along both sides of the Allegheny, Monongahela, and Ohio Rivers and was built by the city of Pittsburgh in partnership with Friends of the Riverfront. These trails are suitable for walking, running, and biking.

Montour Trail
(412) 831-2030
www.montourtrail.org
The Montour Trail stretches for 42 miles between Coraopolis and Clairton and will ultimately extend 46 miles. The trail is suitable for hiking, biking, cross-country skiing, and horseback riding in some areas.

Steel Valley Trail
www.steelvalleytrail.org
When completed, this 19-mile urban trail will connect with the Three Rivers Heritage Trail System and the Montour, Nine Mile Run, and Youghiogheny Trails, as well as numerous historic Pittsburgh areas. It's a highlight of the Rivers of Steel National Heritage Area.

discover more than 1,200 picnic tables as well as seven pavilions available for rent.

In winter Lake Arthur offers ice-skating, ice boating, and ice fishing; you also may enjoy sledding, tobogganing, cross-country skiing, and snowmobiling. For overnight stays, the park provides 11 modern cabins and 2 organized youth group camping areas. You won't find family campsites, but the area surrounding the park offers plenty of privately operated campsites.

Oh, and just in case you're wondering, "moraine" refers to the soil, rocks, and debris that accumulate at the edges of and underneath a glacier. Now aren't you glad half of Pennsylvania was once covered in ice?

Youghiogheny River Trail
(724) 872-5586
www.youghrivertrail.com
Including 71 miles of limestone-surfaced trail and accessible to individuals of all ages and physical abilities, this trail winds through Allegheny, Westmoreland, and Fayette Counties. Called "one of the world's best walks" by *Travel + Leisure* magazine, the trail draws more than 200,000 visitors each year. The trail is suitable for walking, running, biking, and studying nature.

Great Allegheny Passage
www.atatrail.org
Completed in 2006, this 150-mile system of biking and hiking trails connects Pittsburgh to Cumberland, Maryland. The system actually includes seven trails that are organized under the Allegheny Trail Alliance and include the Montour Trail. Once you reach Maryland, you can continue on the passage to Washington, D.C. Go to ATA's Web site to learn more, including details about lodging, camping, and food.

Laurel Highlands Hiking Trail
(724) 455-3744
This 70-mile path follows the Laurel Ridge from the Youghiogheny River at Ohiopyle to the Conemaugh Gorge near Johnstown. Known among hikers and backpackers, the trail features eight overnight shelter areas, located every 8 to 10 miles along the trail. Overnight reservations are mandatory; call the number above.

Laurel Caverns
(800) 515-4150
www.laurelcaverns.com
Hike inside Pennsylvania's largest cave. Tours for individuals, families, and groups, as well as a more advanced caving excursion or rappelling seminar are available. Open daily from May to October and on the weekends in March, April, and November.

—With thanks to VisitPittsburgh

Oil Creek State Park
305 State Park Road, Oil City
(814) 676-5915
www.dcnr.state.pa.us/stateparks/parks/oilcreek.aspx
It was along Oil Creek that Col. Edwin Drake struck oil in 1859, helping to launch the petroleum industry. Part of the mission of Oil Creek State Park is to preserve and perpetuate the heritage of the oil boomtowns that grew up around Drake Well. The park features displays and historical programs at the Petroleum Centre, once a focal point of the petroleum boom and now the park's visitor center.

Hiking is an important activity in the 7,075-acre park. It provides more than 52

More on Outdoor Activities

Through the guiding principles of awareness and training, Venture Outdoors (formerly known as the Western Pennsylvania Field Institute) strives to increase participation in outdoor activities in Western Pennsylvania. Their ultimate goal is to create a sense of community among participants and a better understanding of and a deeper appreciation for the environment and wilderness among residents and visitors. Venture Outdoors provides a comprehensive list of all scheduled outings on their website (www.wpfi.org) organized by clubs and other organizations in the region. They also publish The Adventures Times, Contours e-newsletter and a blog featuring additional information about outdoor activities in the area. Whether you want to kayak the rivers, climb the mountains or hike the trails, check out Venture Outdoors to learn more!

miles of hiking trails that double as biking and cross-country ski trails, and there's one trail exclusively for bikes.There are shelters as well, which should be reserved in advance. Warning: If you see railroad tracks along the trails, stay off the tracks. The railroad is active.

Anglers flock to Oil Creek, which is known for its bass and trout. If you prefer to be on the water, bring your canoe. Oil Creek is classified as a beginner's stream. You'll find a paved portage path around the creek's ice-control dam. Approximately 6,250 acres of the park are open to hunting, with rabbit, deer, squirrel, turkey, and ruffed grouse the most common prey. You'll find picnic areas and shelters, although not nearly as many as other state parks offer. Oil Creek State Park is north of our six-county coverage area.

Pymatuning State Park
2660 Williamsfield Road, Jamestown
(724) 932-3141
www.dcnr.state.pa.us/stateparks/parks/pymatuning.aspx

Pymatuning is somewhat north of the principal coverage area, but if you're an outdoors type, you won't mind the extra drive. An act of the Pennsylvania Legislature decrees that the principal purposes of Pymatuning Lake and dam are for controlling floods and the flow of water in the Beaver and Shenango Rivers. The recreational opportunities that follow in the wake of those objectives are awesome.

The lake, spanning Pennsylvania and Ohio, is one of the region's most productive for anglers, yielding walleye, muskellunge, carp, crappie, and largemouth and smallmouth bass, among many species. In one of those jurisdictional quirks that will drive you crazy, if you're a licensed angler in Pennsylvania, you can't fish from the Ohio shore. Similarly, Pennsylvania bans Ohio licensees on its side of the water. On the water itself, however, licensees from both states are welcome. The lake is a popular site for ice fishing in winter.

Hunting is available in much of the park, including the Goose Management Area, where controlled shooting is permitted during the annual waterfowl season. The park features a large protected area for migratory waterfowl. Swimmers will find four guarded beaches. Nonpowered boats and those up to 10 horsepower are permitted on the lake, and you can rent floatboats, rowboats, canoes, and motors, or try ice boating in winter.

Pymatuning offers a variety of overnight facilities, including 657 family camping sites, an organized group camping area that can accommodate up to 400 people, 194 modern tent and trailer campsites, and modern family cabins. You'll enjoy many picnic tables and 11 pavilions available for rental. Make sure you check out the Linesville spillway, where you may feed the fish and ducks.

Unofficially, this park boasts the most mispronounced name in the region. Try it this way: *pie-muh-TOO-ning*.

East

Keystone State Park
1150 Keystone Park Road, Derry
(724) 668-2939
www.dcnr.state.pa.us/stateparks/parks
/keystone.aspx

If your family has a diversity of outdoor interests, you'll find that Keystone State Park has facilities to match those interests—all within easy driving distance of Pittsburgh. The recreational theme of this 1,200-acre park is variety. Keystone Lake offers up trout and a variety of other fish for anglers and a venue for nonpowered and electric-powered boats. You can rent rowboats, sailboats, and canoes. In winter the lake provides ice fishing and ice-skating, while you can sled and snowmobile elsewhere in the park. Swimmers will enjoy a 1,000-foot turf-and-sand beach.

Hunters can pursue white-tailed deer, pheasant, and grouse. Campers will find 100 tent and trailer sites for family camping as well as 11 modern cabins available for rental. Keystone State Park offers 443 picnic tables, several shelters, a ball field, and hiking and biking trails.

Laurel Hill State Park
1454 Laurel Hill Park Road, Somerset
(814) 445-7725
www.dcnr.state.pa.us/stateparks/parks
/laurelhill.aspx

In 1794 during the Whiskey Rebellion, George Washington's troops camped on the site of what is now Laurel Hill State Park. You won't feel the need to rebel here, except perhaps against drudgery. There is much to do and enjoy at Laurel Hill.

The 3,935-acre park offers 12 splendid miles for hiking, including the Hemlock Trail, which features a stand of virgin timber. You'll find four picnic areas with a total of 564 tables, playground equipment, and horseshoe pits. Hunting is permitted in 2,100 acres, and you'll enjoy 70 miles of snowmobile trails in Laurel Hill and the adjacent Forbes State Forest.

Laurel Hill Lake provides many water-based activities, including swimming along a 1,200-foot sandy beach and renting paddle-boats, canoes, and rowboats. Both nonpowered boats and electric-powered boats are permitted on the lake. Anglers can test the lake 24 hours a day for bass, trout, catfish, suckers, bluegill, perch, crappie, and sunfish. You'll enjoy ice fishing and ice boating when the lake is frozen. If you want to spend some time to enjoy all the amenities, try the family camping areas. Organized groups may camp in tents or in large cabins.

Though technically a bit outside the six-county coverage area, Laurel Hill is part of a trio of adjacent state facilities—along with Linn Run State Park and Forbes State Forest—well worthy of coverage.

Linn Run State Park
Linn Run Road (off Route 381), Rector
(724) 238-6623
www.dcnr.state.pa.us/stateparks/parks
/linnrun.aspx

Set on 612 acres within the Forbes State Forest, in the heart of the Laurel Mountains, Linn Run is a scenic park used primarily for picnicking, hiking, hunting, and fishing, although it offers other opportunities as well. The Adams Falls and Grove Run areas provide a total of 137 picnic tables; Adams Falls also offers a pavilion and play apparatus. If you find you really like the place, you can rent one of the park's 10 rustic cabins for up to a week in season—slightly longer out of season.

More than 400 acres are open for hunting, typically providing squirrel, turkey, deer, and black bear. Anglers will like the availability of trout in Linn Run Stream, while hikers will enjoy a variety of delights. The park itself

ℹ️ Each May the city of Pittsburgh Parks & Recreation (Citiparks) publishes a "summer magazine," a comprehensive guide to its recreational facilities, including 18 outdoor pools, 25 picnic shelters, 24 community and senior community centers, and a variety of special programs. To get your free copy, contact Citiparks at (412) 255-2539.

offers 5 miles of trails, and it's near three other trails in Forbes State Forest as well as the Laurel Highlands Hiking Trail, which spans 70 miles from Ohiopyle to the Conemaugh River.

Linn Run offers limited horseback riding and snowmobiling, and it is near such other outdoor attractions as Laurel Mountain ski area.

Ohiopyle State Park
Route 381, Ohiopyle
(724) 329-8591
www.dcnr.sate.pa.us/stateparks/parks/ohiopyle.aspx

Ohiopyle State Park is primarily in Fayette County, just outside our coverage area, but its more than 19,000 acres are so spectacular and rich with recreational opportunities that it would be a significant omission.

The focal point of the park is the more than 14 miles of the Youghiogheny River Gorge that passes through the heart of the park, providing some of the best whitewater boating in the mid-Atlantic region. Just watching the churning water is excitement enough for some; if you're in that category, you'll enjoy a number of scenic overlooks.

Bicycling, too, is a popular Ohiopyle activity. The park features a 27-mile biking trail, converted from abandoned railroad rights-of-way, that parallels the Yough; bikers will share 9.4 miles of the trail with equestrians. The trail also is suitable for hiking, jogging, and cross-country skiing. Both the Yough and the tamer Meadow Run offer trout to anglers; a wheelchair-access area is available. Nearly the entire park is open for hunting and trapping, with typical quarry including deer, turkey, grouse, rabbit, and squirrel. Winter activities include cross-country skiing, sledding, tobogganing, and snowmobiling, with numerous snowmobiling trails carved from Sugarloaf Knob at an elevation of 2,640 feet.

Picnic areas feature play apparatus, a pavilion available for rental, a softball field, and a volleyball court. If it's all too much to enjoy in one day, extend your stay by reserving a campsite. Ohiopyle offers 226 campsites

that you can reserve from March through December.

Yellow Creek State Park
170 Route 259 Highway, Penn Run
(724) 357-7913
www.dcnr.state.pa.us/stateparks/parks/yellowcreek.aspx

When winter brings a thick snow cover, Yellow Creek is a wonderland of outdoor activities. These begin with ice-skating, ice fishing, and ice boating on Yellow Creek Lake—which makes up about one-quarter of the park's 2,981 acres—and include cross-country skiing, snowshoeing, sledding, tobogganing, and snowmobiling in 350 designated acres.

When the weather warms, you can enjoy your nonpowered boats and boats up to 10 horsepower; swim along an 800-foot guarded beach; and cast your fishing lines for smallmouth and largemouth bass, walleye, muskellunge, tiger muskellunge, northern pike, yellow perch, bluegill, and catfish. (Ice fishing is also available in the winter.) The park's picnic and parking areas can accommodate more than 4,000 people.

Most areas of the park are open for hunting. While the facility is not known for hiking, you will find a number of pleasant, short trails, one of which is dotted with wildflowers in season. Yellow Creek is in Indiana County, just outside our six-county coverage area. State parks are so popular, however, that we want to detail all those within a comfortable drive of Pittsburgh.

West

Raccoon Creek State Park
3000 Route 18, Hookstown
(724) 899-2200
www.dcnr.state.pa.us/stateparks/parks/raccooncreek.aspx

Raccoon Creek is one of the larger state parks, spanning 7,572 acres, including the beautiful Raccoon Creek Lake. Camping is a particularly popular attraction here. The park offers 172 tent and trailer sites for family camping from mid-April through mid-

December, as well as group campsites; group tent camping; and 10 modern family cabins with a furnished living area, kitchen space, and two or three bedrooms. For a special treat, try Lakeside Lodge, a three-bedroom cottage that sleeps nine and is open all year.

The lake yields a wide variety of fish: bluegill, sunfish, bullhead, catfish, yellow perch, walleye, muskellunge, crappie, sauger, largemouth and smallmouth bass, and brook and rainbow trout. You'll find a turf beach for swimming, a boat launch area, and 42 mooring spaces. Nonpowered boats and electric-powered boats are permitted, and you can rent several types of nonpowered boats at the park. You can also ice fish and ice-skate on the lake in season and enjoy sledding, snowmobiling, and cross-country skiing in other areas of the park.

More than 5,000 acres are available for hunting the park's deer, wild turkey, grouse, squirrel, and rabbit. Raccoon Creek offers 16 miles of bridle trails and 5 miles of hiking trails, along which you'll find some of the most singular stands of native wildflowers in the Western Pennsylvania region. You may want to call the Wildflower Reserve and Interpretive Center before you head out to check when your favorite flowers will be in bloom; the number is (724) 899-3611. You'll also find 600 picnic tables in the park—some shelters must be reserved. For a historical touch to your outing, visit King's Creek Cemetery on the park's western boundary, where many of the area's pioneers are buried.

Ryerson Station State Park
361 Bristoria Road, Wind Ridge
(724) 428-4254
www.dcnr.state.pa.us/stateparks/parks/ryersonstation.aspx
Technically outside the six-county coverage area, Ryerson Station deserves mention as one of the finest facilities in sparsely populated Green County. Named for the 18th-century Fort Ryerson, which stood nearby, the 1,164-acre park features a variant of winter sports, including ice-skating, ice fishing, snowmobiling on 6 miles of trails, and cross-country skiing. You'll find a guarded swimming pool, 10 miles of hiking trails, more than 275 picnic tables, and five pavilions—three of the pavilions are available by reservation only.

Anglers will find trout, warmwater game fish, and panfish in Duke Lake. You can use nonpowered boats and electric-powered boats on the lake. The park provides a launching ramp and a limited number of mooring spaces. For camping you'll find a 48-site family campground for tents or trailers, as well as organized group tenting areas. Hunting, trapping, and dog training are only allowed the day following Labor Day to March 31 in designated hunting areas.

FEDERAL RECREATION AREAS

The Pittsburgh District of the U.S. Army Corps of Engineers operates 16 flood-control projects in the multi-state area. The principal purpose of course is to prevent, or reduce, the damage from flooding. Because the dams hold a pool of water that forms a lake, they also serve a variety of recreational purposes. So popular are these areas that they draw more than 15 million visitors annually.

Generally you'll find fishing, boating, camping, picnicking, hunting, and cross-country skiing opportunities, as well as hiking, snowmobile, and interpretive trails, although the lineup varies from dam to dam. You may bring your pets to all federal recreation areas. Five of these outdoor playgrounds fall within the six-county coverage area, or close enough to merit description below. For unusually well-written and easy-to-follow brochures about all 16 areas, contact the Corps at (412) 395-7152.

Along with descriptions of these recreation areas, we've included information about the Allegheny National Forest. Pennsylvania's only national forest is outside the principal coverage area, but it's such an unusually rich resource that it attracts many visitors from Southwestern Pennsylvania.

North

Allegheny National Forest
222 Liberty Street, Warren
(814) 723-5150
www.fs.fed.us/r9/forests/allegheny/
For outdoor enthusiasts, the Allegheny National Forest is as much paradise as it is park. It spans 513,325 acres in Elk, McKean, Forest, and Warren Counties, about a three-hour drive from Pittsburgh. The only national forest in the state, Allegheny National Forest sits in the rugged plateau country of Northwestern Pennsylvania, with elevation ranging from 1,046 feet to 2,263 feet above sea level. Many creeks and streams cut deeply into the plateau, creating some of the most majestic vistas in the region.

The 12,000-acre Allegheny Reservoir, created by the impoundment of the Kinzua (*KIN zoo*) Dam, provides a diversity of water-based activities. The reservoir is the centerpiece of 700 miles of waterways that offer anglers muskellunge, smallmouth bass, walleye, northern perch, channel catfish, and some types of trout. To give you an idea of the scale of fish available, the park is annually the site for Cabela's North American Walleye Anglers Team Event. You can boat in the Allegheny and Tionesta Reservoirs—many launching areas are available—or try canoeing on such venues as the scenic Clarion and Allegheny Rivers or the Brokenstraw and Tionesta Creeks. If swimming or waterskiing is your thing, you'll find the Allegheny Reservoir most accommodating.

Hunters can stalk white-tailed deer, black bear, and wild turkey; campers will find 20 campgrounds, including primitive camping areas that you can reach only by boat or hiking trail. Speaking of hiking, you'll find plenty of opportunities here—201 miles of the North Country National Scenic Trail traverse the forest. Cross-country skiers, snowmobilers, and dirt bikers will enjoy the loop trails that wind through the hills, while bikers will discover several special treats: Both the Iowa to Maine trail and a cross-Pennsylvania bike route pass through the forest.

Many Western Pennsylvanians plan fall foliage excursions to the forest. If you go, check out the Tionesta Scenic Area, part of a 4,000-acre tract of old-growth forest that features venerable beech, hemlock, and sugar maples trees—some of them up to 400 years old. Fall's colors will blaze brightly for you in the Allegheny National Forest. If you're looking for a pretty drive, try the 29-mile Longhouse National Scenic Byway.

You're welcome to bring your pets to the forest, provided you keep them leashed. Saddle and pack animals are permitted in all areas, except on the forest's hiking and cross-country ski trails.

Crooked Creek Lake
114 Park Main Road, Ford City
(724) 763-2764
www.lrp.usace.army.mil/rec/lakes/crookedc.htm
Crooked Creek is a delight for water enthusiasts, no matter the season. In warm weather, swimmers and sunbathers utilize the sandy peninsula beach, water-skiers dot the lake, while anglers reel in bass and sunfish. In cold weather, the park offers two ice-skating ponds, a sled-riding area, and cross-country skiing. You'll also find a boat-launching ramp and no horsepower limit.

Crooked Creek offers hunting; hiking and horse trails; and tent, trailer, and group camping. A special feature is the Environmental Learning Center, an interpretive center for groups. Crooked Creek Horse Park, detailed in the Recreation chapter, adjoins the recreation area.

Mahoning Creek Lake
145 Dam Site Road, New Bethlehem
(814) 257-8017
www.lrp.usace.army.mil/rec/lakes/mahoning.htm
Anglers especially will enjoy Mahoning Creek Lake—its waters yield northern pike, walleye, muskie, and bass. (The lake is stocked by the Pennsylvania Fish and Boat Commission.) You can score when you hunt here as well—the

Pennsylvania Game Commission leases nearly 1,300 acres for wildlife management and public hunting.

The lake features two boat-launching ramps, with boats up to 10 horsepower permitted. Swimming is not permitted, but you will enjoy 28 acres of campgrounds, with all sites featuring restrooms, showers, and electricity.

East

Conemaugh River Lake
1665 Auen Road, Suite A, Saltsburg
(724) 639-3785
www.lrp.usace.army.mil/rec/lakes/conemaug.htm

The Pennsylvania Game Commission leases 8,954 acres around the lake for public hunting and wildlife management. The park provides a canoe launch but no other public boating due to limited accessibility to the lake. You'll enjoy a picnic area with two pavilions, play apparatus, and nature and hiking trails.

The park contains several sites of historical interest, including traces of the Pennsylvania Mainland Canal and sections of early Pennsylvania railroads.

Loyalhanna Lake
440 Loyalhanna Dam Road, Saltsburg
(724) 639-3785
www.lrp.usace.army.mil/rec/lakes/loyalhan.htm

The Loyalhanna Watershed is one of the most scenic areas in Western Pennsylvania, and Loyalhanna Lake captures that majesty. One of the most popular activities here is picnicking at the Damsite Picnic Area—the view of the dam and surrounding woodlands will soothe your jangled nerves.

The Commonwealth of Pennsylvania invites you to hunt in many areas of its public parks ... except for woodchucks, also known as groundhogs, which are protected on most parklands. Sounds like Punxsutawney Phil (of Groundhog Day fame) has been an effective lobbyist.

If you're looking for more active entertainment, try the Black Willow Water Trail, the lake's self-guided boating trail with stations marking natural and man-made features. Anglers will find inlets and coves that yield bass, walleye, crappie, bullhead, and bluegill. The lake offers two boat-launching areas and no horsepower limit. You can camp and hunt at Loyalhanna; the Pennsylvania Game Commission leases 2,894 acres for hunting and wildlife management.

South

Youghiogheny River Lake
497 Flanigan Road, Confluence
(814) 395-3166
www.lrp.usace.army.mil/rec/lakes/youghiog.htm

Principal activities at Youghiogheny are boating, waterskiing, and fishing. Just below the dam, the Youghiogheny River offers some of the most popular rafting and canoeing waters in the Mid-Atlantic region. One boulder-strewn stretch is so popular and challenging it frequently hosts national kayak championships. The lake features five boat-launching ramps.

Anglers find the backwaters and coves rich with walleye and smallmouth bass. You can choose from three campgrounds, with facilities ranging from primitive to modern.

RECREATION

The recreation scene in Western Pennsylvania is diverse, creative, and inviting. You'll find an arena and an association for just about every sport and activity that might interest you. If you're not sure just what interests you, don't be afraid to jump feet first into something new. Most of the groups profiled below welcome newcomers and offer an instructional component.

Several factors have contributed to the breadth of recreational opportunities. One is the success of the city's professional teams. As the Steelers, Pirates, and Penguins have captured championships that brought them increasing support and media exposure, thousands have been inspired to take to the fields, courts, and rinks to achieve their own levels of athletic enjoyment and rewards. The region's college campuses have played a key role in the growth of certain sports such as rugby; former college players, lacking vehicles to extend their playing days, founded clubs of their own.

Natural geographic resources contribute to the popularity of outdoor activities. The region is blessed with an excellent inland waterway system that provides varied opportunities for fishing, boating, and swimming. The woods of Western Pennsylvania are a hunter's delight, while the region's slopes provide a natural—sometimes stunning—setting for hiking, climbing, and skiing. Add the welcome cycle of the four seasons, and you have a region where virtually every sport has its moment in the sun—or snow, as the case may be.

In the profiles of Western Pennsylvania's recreational activities, we've tried to avoid describing commercial establishments in the belief that you have plenty of other resources to find these. Instead, we offer information on coordinating associations and interest groups that could be hard to track down otherwise. You won't find descriptions of the region's bowling alleys, for example, but you will learn about the organizations that sanction bowling leagues and tournaments. The exception to this is in the "yoga" section, where several yoga centers are listed. They're hard to find if you don't know where to look.

One caution about phone numbers and addresses. In the case of clubs, these may be accurate only as long as the president or captain keeps the job. As a hedge against shifting organizational responsibilities, we've tried to list the venues where clubs practice and perform so that you always can make contact by dropping by.

ARCHERY

Allegheny County Sportsmen's League
www.acslpa.org/
Archery is a popular activity in Western Pennsylvania, but it's sometimes difficult to identify appropriate sites and organizations. That's because much of the activity occurs inside private shooting clubs; you'd be hard pressed to know that archery takes place at the club. Allegheny County Sportsmen League's Web site can provide you with a directory of shooting clubs. You can use that to find archery facilities.

Chieftain Archery Club in New Kensington, (724) 335-7135, is one of the few in the area dedicated exclusively to archery. You'll need to join the club and provide your own equipment to participate.

AUTO RACING

Don Martin's Lernerville Speedway
278 North Pike Road, Sarver
(724) 353-1511
www.lernerville.com

Sprints, late models, modifieds, pure stocks ... Don Martin's Lernerville Speedway has all the variety you could desire in dirt-track racing. The track often features its division in competition on the same evening, creating an unusually diverse program that's sometimes spiced with such special events as demolition derbies. You'll find the track in action from late March/April through September, as weather permits. If you plan to enjoy the action from the stands, general admission prices range from $6 to $39, with discounts for kids and senior citizens. Children under 10 years old are admitted free of charge. If you'd prefer to get down and dirty on the track, the speedway will welcome your entry as long as your car meets safety specs.

BASEBALL

Most communities feature an organized youth baseball program. The city of Pittsburgh goes that one better through its BIG ("Baseball Is Great") League Sports program, (412) 488-8585, which hosts a variety of programs that include baseball, softball, hockey, soccer, flag football, track and field, and special programs for teams. BIG coordinates rookie, pony, and colt leagues that involve about 1,500 youths in organized baseball. The Pittsburgh Pirates invite all BIG participants to a Pirate game each year at PNC Park.

BIG conducts clinics in association with the Pittsburgh Pirates and also enables community programs to acquire their equipment through BIG and realize the discounts the city of Pittsburgh often enjoys on bulk purchases. BIG administrators will refer you to an organized program in your neighborhood. Perhaps best of all, if youngsters don't have opportunities to play in their neighborhood, BIG will find spots for them in its program.

Kids in the region's inner-city neighborhoods—encompassing both Pittsburgh and its suburbs—will find additional opportunities through Reviving Baseball in the Inner-City (RBI), (412) 782-5710 (administrative office). Major League Baseball sponsors RBI in 70 cities in 6 countries. In Western Pennsylvania, it's run by the Boys and Girls Clubs of Western Pennsylvania in cooperation with Pittsburgh's BIG League Program. Funding for the program is provided in partnership with the Pittsburgh Pirates Charities.

Locally, about 300 boys and girls ages 13 to 18 participate—boys in baseball, girls in fast-pitch softball. An All-Star team selected from local participants is eligible for national post-season competition that culminates in a World Series typically held in a Major League Baseball stadium, a thrill for the young players. The program goes beyond baseball to offer career development counseling and advice on conflict resolution. A nice added touch: All teams in the local program sport names and uniforms that honor Negro League teams, such as the Pittsburgh Crawfords and the Homestead Grays.

BASKETBALL

The city game is healthy in Western Pennsylvania—men and women of all ages compete regularly in gyms provided by schools, churches, and other institutions. Many such competitions aren't really leagues, as the players "pick up" teams each evening. The best way to find out about these games is through word of mouth or by checking with those schools and churches to determine when games are played.

For youths, many city of Pittsburgh recreation centers sponsor regular competition—3-on-3 for the youngest kids, 5-on-5 for teenagers. Check with your local recreation center for its schedule.

The Pittsburgh Sports League, a program of PUMP, hosts a basketball league each winter that includes men's and co-ed teams. Call

(412) 338-2133 or visit PUMP's Web site at www.pump.org.

BIKING

On-road or off-road, you will find plenty of opportunities to bike in the region. If you are biking in the city of Pittsburgh, we suggest checking out Bike Pittsburgh's Web site (www.bike-pgh.org). Here you'll find the Pittsburgh Cycling Events Calendar, which includes organized rides and other events of interest to bikers. Bike Pittsburgh also offers commuter bike maps, advocates bike safety, and installs new and unique public art bike racks around the city.

A great way to see the city and get some exercise is with Bikers in Pittsburgh, who have their own signature event, PNC Pedal Pittsburgh. Sponsored by the Community Design Center of Pittsburgh, this fun, educational bicycle ride draws 2,000 riders annually. The course for this ride (it's not a race!) ranges from 6 to 60 miles and highlights Pittsburgh neighborhoods and landmarks. For details, call (412) 391-4144 or visit www.pedalpitts burgh.org.

Western Pennsylvania Wheelmen Bicycle Club
www.wpwbikeclub.org
The premier touring organization in the region, the WPW Bicycle Club boasts more than 1,000 members who typically ride from March through November, weather permitting. The club meets monthly and publishes a monthly newspaper and maps depicting nearly 7,000 miles of bicycle routes. Join them and you'll be able to participate in a highlight ride each month as well as the annual Fall Rally in September.

You can keep up with club activities by visiting its Web site.

BILLIARDS

Oh so quietly, billiards has become one of the faster growing sports in the region. You'll find more than three dozen establishments that sport multiple tables, to say nothing of the countless taverns that have installed a table to satisfy the clientele. If you are interested in playing in a league, call Chuck Farinella at (412) 215-3130. He runs The Players' League, Pittsburgh's premier nine-ball league. The league's Web site lists weekly nine-ball tournaments and charity fundraisers.

BIRDING

Audubon Society of Western Pennsylvania at Beechwood Farms Nature Reserve
614 Dorseyville Road, Fox Chapel
(412) 963-6100
www.aswp.org
Experience the sights and sounds of a night hike along a moonlit trail. Search for turtles and other creatures in a pond teeming with aquatic life. Follow the colorful tracings of butterflies in a meadow awash with wildflowers. Explore the fascinating lives of birds on a walk through a singing woodland. These and many other experiences await you at Beechwood Farms Nature Reserve, home of the Audubon Society of Western Pennsylvania.

Known as "Pittsburgh's Outdoor Classroom," Audubon at Beechwood offers extensive, year-round environmental programs for the entire family, from young children to adults. Offerings range from Outdoor Discovery Programs, which provide thousands of school-age children each year with hands-on guided experiences of nature, to programs designed for family participation. Programs range in duration from weeklong summer nature camps for children in grades K–5 to 2 innovative programs for preschool children as young as 2 months old. Audubon at Beechwood also offers a monthly series of bird outings to regional sites; guided bird walks on Wednesday morning; the annual Christmas Bird Count; and other popular events such as the Secret Gardens Tour of spectacular Fox Chapel gardens and Applejamm, one of the oldest fall festivals in the area.

Thousands of people visit Beechwood Farms year-round to enjoy informal outdoor

For additional resources regarding birding in the region, visit the Carnegie Library of Pittsburgh's Web site www.carnegielibrary.org/research/sports/birding/html.

activities on its 5 miles of nature trails and 134 acres of woodlands, meadows, ponds, and wetlands. Others visit Beechwood to shop at the Audubon Nature Store, with its wide selection of bird feeders, birdseed, and other nature-related items. Beechwood also features a modern education center with facilities for children's birthday parties, the Audubon Center for the Native Plants, and a natural history reference and reading library. Beechwood's trails are open 365 days a year, dawn to dusk.

BOATING

Western Pennsylvania's waterways beckon to boaters. Whether you're sailing, canoeing, kayaking, paddling, rafting, or motoring under electrical power, you'll find waters in the region that will accommodate you. Perhaps the best place to start is with a comprehensive state map available free from the Pennsylvania Fish and Boat Commission, (717) 705–7835; www.fish.state.pa.us/. The map depicts nearly 1,000 boating and fishing opportunities in the state and provides a guide to parking, launch ramps, and horsepower limits. Other free publications are also available.

You'll also want a copy of the commission's *Pennsylvania Boating Handbook* for boating rules and advice. Several of those regulations are particularly noteworthy. You will need to register your boat; the fee, good for two years, ranges from $10 for unpowered boats to $40 for craft more than 20 feet long. You'll need to display your boat registration number on your boat; kayaks, sculls, and sailboards are exempt from this requirement. The state also provides boat titling, at a cost of $15, to help deter theft. The handbook will familiarize you with state requirements for

personal flotation devices and regulations regarding alcohol consumption while you're boating. The commission can provide you with brochures on each topic. The handbook is available online at www.fish.state.pa.us/bookboat.htm.

If you're a boater and an angler, you'll get a particular kick from *Pennsylvania Angler & Boater,* the commission's official magazine. It's published six times each year and offers lush color photography, how-to pieces, and commission updates. Cost is $12 annually.

The Parks chapter will introduce you to boating opportunities at state parks and federal recreation areas. For more specific information about any state or federal facility, contact the Pennsylvania Parks Information and Reservation line, (888) PA-PARKS (888-727-2757), Monday through Saturday 7:00 a.m. to 5:00 p.m. or the U.S. Army Corps of Engineers, (412) 395-7500.

Three Rivers Rowing Association
300 Waterfront Drive
(412) 231-8772
www.threeriversrowing.org

One of the city's most compelling sights is that of crews plying the Allegheny River, intermittently visible through the early-morning mist. That vista is brought to you by Three Rivers Rowing Association (TRRA), a group founded in 1984 with the mission of providing broad-based rowing opportunities in the Pittsburgh area. The group is headquartered on Washington's Landing, an Allegheny River island about 2 miles north of downtown Pittsburgh. The island houses the group's 15,000-

i To see the city of Pittsburgh from a unique perspective, try kayaking. Kayak Pittsburgh Downtown rents solo and tandem kayaks by the hour. These flat-water kayaks can be used by beginners after a few minutes of instruction. The shop is located just below the Roberto Clemente Bridge. Call (412) 969-9090 or visit www.kayakpittsburgh.org for details.

Close-up

Fun on the Water

Pittsburgh's three rivers easily accommodate fishing, kayaking, canoeing, and boating. In partnership with various related groups, such as Venture Outdoors and the Three Rivers Rowing Association, Three Rivers Water Trail provides a good source of information for boaters, fishers, and other water thrills seekers about river safety, how to use the area's locks and dams, and historical and natural points of interest along the rivers. Call (866) 3KEEPER (866-353-3737) or visit www.friendsof theriverfront.org.

Ohiopyle State Park and the Youghiogheny River are hailed as the birthplace of whitewater rafting. To arrange a whitewater ride, call or visit the Web sites of these reputable tour companies:

Laurel Highlands River Tours
(800) 472-3846
www.laurelhighlands.com

Ohiopyle Trading Post
(888) 644-6795
www.ohiopyletradingpost.com

White Water Adventures
(800) 992-7238
www.wwaraft.com

Wilderness Voyageurs
(800) 272-4141
www.wilderness-voyageurs.com
Also offering historic float tours, showcasing the rich history of the times during the French and Indian War and the Whiskey Rebellion.

square-foot boathouse, which features large boat storage bays, exercise equipment, lockers and showers, and meeting space.

The association offers orientations, clinics, and other instructional activities to get you started. Of particular interest are the club's programs for special populations. These include programs for youths, seniors, and rowers with certain disabilities. There is also a special summer corporate rowing program. TRRA also offers a variety of sprint rac-

ing and tours for kayaks. A basic adult membership allows you to participate in one or more of the association's programs. Call or check the Web site for details and cost.

Among the highlights of the rowing year is the Head of the Ohio Regatta, typically held in early fall along the Allegheny just before it merges with the Monongahela to form the Ohio. It's a prestigious event, generally drawing several thousand entries. You may not be ready to enter, but you'll love the spectacle.

BOWLING

Greater Pittsburgh Ten Pin Bowling Association
Pittsburgh Women's Bowling
105 Penn Plaza, 600 Penn Avenue, Turtle Creek
(412) 823-2118
www.gptpba.com

Bowling is such a popular pastime in Pittsburgh that you really don't need the help of an organization to get started; just visit your local lanes and ask about leagues. In fact, if you're not in a league, you may find open alleys hard to come by during peak times. That said, the Greater Pittsburgh Ten-Pin Bowling Association and Pittsburgh Women's Bowling perform important functions for local keglers.

The companion organizations, which are run from the same office, sanction leagues and tournaments with the American Bowling Congress. Since more than 15,000 men and women compete locally in sanctioned events, this is a key service. The organizations also sponsor tournaments, present awards for high scores, sponsor a junior bowling program, and publish yearbooks that feature most area lanes and leagues.

BOXING

As it is at the national level, administration of boxing activities in Western Pennsylvania is somewhat fragmented. However, this is all sorted out on the amateur level with the Golden Gloves tournament held each March. Visit www.pagoldengloves.com to find a comprehensive listing of the registered clubs where boxing is held in your neighborhood.

BRIDGE

A true story about bridge in Pittsburgh: A newcomer to town some years ago was invited to a veteran bridge player's house for a private game featuring some of the area's elite players. As the evening progressed, the newcomer smelled something burning. Sure enough, when she looked up she saw orange flames shooting ever higher from a wastebasket. "There's a fire in the garbage can," she said. No one moved. No one looked up. Finally, overcoming her shyness as the newest player, she arose and stamped out the fire. No one thanked her or even noticed that she had been gone.

That incident tells you something about bridge in our area. It's not that players are unfriendly, but they are intense. A little thing like a wastebasket fire won't bother them. If you aspire to that level, you can learn bridge at the Jewish Community Center of Greater Pittsburgh, (412) 521-8011, ext. 225, in Pittsburgh's Squirrel Hill neighborhood, which sponsors instruction at various levels. Older Adult Service and Information System (OASIS), (412) 232-9584, offers bridge classes for senior citizens; the classes usually are fully subscribed. OASIS is located on the 10th floor of Macy's department store in downtown Pittsburgh.

Pittsburgh Bridge Association
(412) 683-GAME (412-683-4263)
www.pittsburghbridge.org/

If duplicate bridge is your game, you'll want to be in touch with the Pittsburgh Bridge Association, an affiliate of the American Contract Bridge League. Association members will make you aware of as many as 40 games throughout the region each week. The association also stages its own games and publishes a directory including games and the names and phone numbers of 1,400 players. The directory is available online at www.pittsburgh bridge.org/ClubDirectory.htm.

CAMPING

If you're an avid camper, you're likely to become mighty familiar with Pennsylvania's state park system. The Commonwealth maintains more than 7,000 campsites in 57 state parks, many of them within an easy ride of Pittsburgh. Check out the Parks chapter for an introduction to camping at Western Pennsylvania state parks, or call the Pennsylvania Parks Information and reservations line, (888) PA-PARKS (888-727-2757), for more comprehensive information and a fee schedule.

State parks offer a variety of overnight options. These include family campsites; group cabins and tent areas; and cabins, both modern and rustic. Whichever option you select, you'll find more campsites and cabins open from early April until late October. Some sites welcome campers through December, and a handful are open year-round. From Memorial Day through Labor Day, your stay will be limited to 14 consecutive days. At other times your maximum stay is 21 consecutive days. Most sites are available on a first-come, first-served basis, although you can reserve other sites. The state prohibits alcohol and pets at its sites.

The U.S. Army Corps of Engineers maintains campsites at its recreation areas, although the number can't compare with the total offered by the state. If you lack appropriate camping gear, ask about the "Rent-A-Tent" program, which will provide you with enough equipment to host up to five friends. For information call the Corps at (412) 395-7500.

You'll find many private campground operators who have opened businesses near state and federal facilities to capitalize on any overflow. You can get a useful list of 200 privately operated campgrounds from the Pennsylvania Campground Owners Association, (888) 660-7262 or online at www.pacamping.com. The list is not comprehensive, since some operators don't belong to the association, but it's a great place to start.

CAVING

Several local outdoors groups, while not devoted exclusively to the activity, feature caving on their roster of events. The Explorers Club of Pittsburgh, www.pittecp.org, occa-sionally explores caves in West Virginia. Sierra Club Allegheny Group, Pennsylvania Chapter, (412) 802-6161; www.alleghenysc.org, ventures to caves on Chestnut Ridge. If you contact Allegheny Group, they'll advise you on the degree of difficulty of each outing.

CHESS

Pittsburgh Chess Club
5604 Solway Street
(412) 421-1881
www.pittsburghcc.org
The Pittsburgh Chess Club has been staging tournaments for more than 50 years, making it one of the older chess organizations in the country. Located in a former elementary school in the city's Squirrel Hill neighborhood, the organization stages both club tournaments and those rated by the United States Chess Federation. In addition, the club sponsors instruction and competition at local schools and has reached about 6,000 students through these efforts.

The club's nearly 200 members engage in open play on Wednesday and Saturday and in tournament play on Tuesday. Visitors always are welcome. When you drop by, make sure to check out the extensive chess library, an asset utilized by many researchers.

Every year the Pittsburgh Chess Club and the Carnegie Library jointly sponsor an annual series of free chess tournaments for young people known as the Carnegie Library Chess Tournaments. In recent years, about 40 to 45 branch libraries throughout Allegheny County participate each year. Beginning in year 2000, the Pittsburgh Chess Club also started to host free beginner's chess classes at various libraries in conjunction with the tournaments.

CLIMBING

Explorers Club of Pittsburgh
www.pittecp.org
Founded in 1948, the Explorers Club of Pittsburgh is dedicated to two purposes: exploration at home and abroad, and the

i According to Explorers Club of Pittsburgh, climbing and mountaineering are distinct activities. Climbing involves scaling the face of a peak, while mountaineering means a more lateral traversing of mountains and coping with snow, ice, and crevasses.

For a climb within the city limits, stop by REI Pittsburgh at 412 South 27th Street in the South Side and climb the Pinnacle, the freestanding indoor climbing wall. Or, head to The Climbing Wall, 7501 Penn Avenue (412) 247-7334 where they offer 14,000 square feet of climbing surface. Equipment rentals and all-day passes are available for purchase.

promotion and instruction of exploratory sciences. The club's members meet monthly and offer instruction in mountaineering and basic and advanced rock climbing. If you enjoy travel, you'll find this group cheerfully peripatetic. Their outings have included rock climbing at West Virginia's Seneca Rocks and ice climbing in Colorado, Canada, and the Adirondack Mountains. They've climbed the Andes and the Himalayas and enjoyed scuba diving in the Bahamas. Other club expeditions include caving and mountain biking. For your annual membership fee, you'll receive the club's monthly newsletter.

DOG SHOWS

Western Pennsylvania Kennel Association
208 Old McBride Road, Canonsburg
(412) 920-1332
The largest kennel club in Western Pennsylvania, the Western Pennsylvania Kennel Association stages two all-breed shows each spring, most commonly at the David L. Lawrence Convention Center in downtown Pittsburgh. A portion of the proceeds benefit the American Kennel Club's Canine Health Foundation and the local humane societies, so there's a great reason for patronizing the shows.

Annual association dues range from $15 to $20; membership entitles you to free admission to the association's shows as well as its newsletter. There are other kennel clubs in the region. A comprehensive listing is available from the *AKC Gazette*. Subscriptions (12 issues, $24.95) are available by calling (800) 533-7323.

FENCING

Fencers in Western Pennsylvania are relatively small in number, but they are dedicated. With a little help from us, you'll be sure to find a sale—a studio where fencing takes place.

Fencing Institute of America
(412) 931-0235
www.fencinginstituteusa.com
Fencing is a movable feast at the institute. This nonprofit organization provides fencing opportunities in a number of Greater Pittsburgh neighborhoods, including Squirrel Hill, Monroeville, Mt. Lebanon, the North Hills, Ligonier, and Washington. In some cases, the municipalities engage the institute to provide fencing opportunities for the public. You will be charged for group and private lessons, and open fencing is available for a fee. The institute does solicit donations to help defray costs.

The institute boasts several strengths. First, its coaches and apprentices are accredited by the U.S. Fencing Association. In addition, it offers instructions in all three of the sport's weapons: foil, épée, and saber. They'll provide you with all the equipment you need to get started.

Three Rivers Fencing Center
7501 Penn Avenue, Point Breeze
(412) 731-4454
http://trfc.typepad.com
Three Rivers Fencing Center offers both group and private instruction in foil and saber as well as open fencing on Tuesday and Thursday. The center offers full-time professional coaches, and its members compete in tournaments locally and throughout the country.

Dress in regular workout clothes when you visit, and don't worry about equipment if you're new to the sport. The center will provide your weapons, jackets, masks, and gloves. You will be responsible for fees for any lessons, and a per-night charge for open fencing. If you join the center and pay annual dues, open fencing is included. Check the Web site for classes and fees.

FISHING

Fishing in Pennsylvania is a joy that can be utterly different each time you take to the waters. How extensive are the state's fishing opportunities? Consider that a map of state fishing and boating opportunities provided by the Pennsylvania Fish and Boat Commission depicts nearly 1,000 locations for those activities. You'll find state and federal lakes, streams, and impoundments (waters behind a dam) marked on the map, as well as a guide to parking and other facilities. Once you've studied your map, you'll be ready for more specific brochures that detail where you can find trout and warmwater species. All these publications are available from the commission, 1601 Elmerton Avenue, Harrisburg, PA 17101, (717) 705-7800, or online at www .fish.state.pa.us/pubonl.htm.

When you contact the commission, you'll also want to acquire the state's Summary of Fishing Regulations and Laws, a must for all anglers. Some of the regulations won't surprise you. You'll learn that all anglers age 16 and older must have a license, with fees ranging from $11 for resident senior citizens to $52 for nonresidents. If you're fishing in Lake Erie or for trout or salmon, you'll need a special permit at an additional cost. You'll also learn about "special regulation" waters, including catch-and-release areas and those reserved for children and anglers with certain disabilities. Did you know that each year the state sponsors two "Fish-for-Free" days, when licenses are not required? You'll find this information—and much more—in the summary.

Among the commission's many publications, you'll find two others especially useful. One is the commission's official magazine, *Pennsylvania Angler & Boater.* This is a slick, four-color journal with great photography; first-person articles; tips on where they're biting; and commission updates on seasons, sizes, and regulation modifications. Cost is $12 annually.

The second piece is the commission's pocket guide to seasons, sizes, and creel limits. With this guide tucked into your pocket,

you'll never be out of season or over the limit. For an introduction to fishing opportunities at state parks and federal recreation areas, see the Parks chapter.

FLYING DISC

Pittsburgh Flying Disc Society
153 LaBelle Street
(412) 734-0321
www.pfds.org

The Pittsburgh Flying Disc Society administers two types of activities. The first is a golf league, which plays at Schenley Park and Phillips Park in the city of Pittsburgh and Knob Hill Community Park in the North Hills. In golf, players throw discs into a basket posted on a pole about 2 feet off the ground. The courses wind through wooded areas, so it's a scenic activity as well. The society, which was formed in 1978, awards prizes at each competition. Don't worry if you're new to the sport—you'll receive a handicap that will make you the equal of veteran players.

The second activity is more demanding. It's called ultimate—a blend of football, basketball, and soccer with continuous action. The sport is coed, and you can keep up with it by phoning the ultimate hotline, (412) 521-2441. Ultimate is not a sedentary activity.

The society coordinates clinics, the Professional Disc Golf Association Tour's annual stop at Knob Hill, and Pittsburgh's participation in the World's Biggest Disc Golf Weekend, an international event that attracts 17,000 players. "Why not?" says society president Gary Dropcho. "You don't have to be Arnold Schwarzenegger, run really fast, or jump really high." Sounds like our kind of sport.

FOOTBALL

In the hometown of "The Stillers," you would expect football to be a popular activity. You would be correct, but at the participant level, the game you're most likely to see differs in key areas from the one they play at Three Rivers Stadium. This variation is called "flag

Close-up

Pittsburgh Sports League

In September 2000 the Pittsburgh Sports League (PSL) offered its first sport, a flag football league for 150 people. PSL is a program of PUMP, an organization that advances issues affecting young and "young-thinking" people in Pittsburgh. PUMP started PSL to engage young people in activities that showcase the region's recreations and offers opportunities for socializing.

That strategy has worked. Since 2000 over 6,000 Pittsburghers, from ages 18 to 40, have participated and played on over 920 teams in 125 different leagues. Today, PSL offers basketball, bowling, broomball, cornhole, darts, dek hockey, dodgeball, flag football, kickball, softball, soccer, tennis, and volleyball. A running club and indoor tennis clinic are also offered.

To learn more contact PSL at (412) 338-2133 or visit www.pump.org.

football," and it's played on sandlots throughout Western Pennsylvania. In this variation, players wear belts to which two "flags"—strips of cloth or plastic—are attached. A ball carrier is "tackled" when a flag is pulled off his belt.

It can be a hard-hitting game complete with certain oddities. If you've never seen the game before, this will be your first opportunity to witness unsportsmanlike conduct penalties for "shielding the flag." The trouble here is that leagues and personnel are ever shifting. Some leagues are organized by team captains, others by officials' groups. It's hard to find a central organization that stays put. One idea: Check with municipal and county field permitting offices. They'll always be able to tell you which groups have fields reserved.

If your youngster wants to play, the path to participation is much easier. Just contact the Boys & Girls Clubs of Western Pennsylvania, 5432 Butler Street, Pittsburgh, (412) 276-3151, or visit the Web site at www.bgcwpa.org. The organization runs the Dapper Dan Charities/Pittsburgh Steelers Flag Football League, which each year involves about 600 youths as players . . . and another 75 as officials, scorekeepers, timers, and statisticians. The league plays at eight city fields and includes both boys and girls—some playing together on coed teams.

GYMNASTICS

The sight of young girls and boys twirling gracefully and perilously over imposing apparatus has contributed to an explosive growth of gymnastics facilities in Western Pennsylvania. The region boasts about three dozen gymnastics schools and facilities—more if you include dance schools that also offer gymnastics instruction. Your best bet for information may be USA Gymnastics, (800) 345-4719, which can tell you about its affiliates in our region.

HIKING

With its far-reaching inland waterway network, vast expanses of forest, and many miles of abandoned railroad rights-of-way, Western Pennsylvania is a hiker's paradise. In fact, there are so many outstanding hiking opportunities here that you may want to familiarize yourself with local trails before you set out. You'll find a number of useful resources.

For trails in City of Pittsburgh parks, the Pittsburgh City Planning Department has produced a colorful brochure called *Pittsburgh Outdoors*. You can get your free copy by contacting the department at (412) 255-2200. For information on a group of longer and more challenging trails called Heritage Trails of

Southwestern Pennsylvania, contact the Southwestern Pennsylvania Heritage Preservation Commission, 105 Zee Plaza, P.O. Box 565, Hollidaysburg, PA 16648-0565, (814) 696-9380. The commission also can provide you with a useful guide to the rails-to-trails program in the state. Pennsylvania's *Rail-Trails* details more than 700 miles of such trails. Cost is $15, including postage and handling.

Another useful guide, *Hiking Pennsylvania,* by John L. Young (FalconGuides, 2008), features hikes of varying difficulty across the Keystone State.

Sierra Club Allegheny Group
3109 Forbes Avenue, Suite 100, Oakland
(412) 802-6161
www.alleghenysc.org
You'll enjoy the varied outings of the Allegheny Group. The group's hikes average 8 to 9 miles along the region's most scenic trails on Laurel Ridge, Chestnut Ridge, and in such state parks as Moraine, McConnells Mill, and Raccoon Creek. Allegheny Group rates its hikes as "easy," "intermediate," "strenuous," and "strenuous and exploratory," so you'll always know what awaits you. For the most leisurely outings, try the club's Wednesday rambles. These seldom exceed 4 miles.

The group also organizes backpacking events throughout the region and offers a Basic Backpacking Course each April. Some of the group's activities are held at the national club's Oakland office (see above). The best way to keep up with events is through the club's newsletter. For subscription information, write to the group at P.O. Box 8241, Pittsburgh PA 15217 or send an e-mail to info@alleghenysc.org .

i Sierra Club Allegheny Group welcomes volunteers to help maintain hiking trails throughout the region. So does Friends of the Riverfront, www .friendsoftheriverfront.org, which developed the 11.5-mile trail around Pittsburgh's three rivers.

HORSE SHOWS

Fort Armstrong Horsemen's Association
P.O. Box 266, Ford City, PA 16226
(724) 845-4502
www.crookedcreekhorsepark-faha.com
Crooked Creek Horse Park, operated by the Fort Armstrong Horsemen's Association, is one of the Mid-Atlantic's most comprehensive equine facilities. Encompassing 113 acres, the park features stable facilities for nearly 150 horses during events only, barns, outdoor arenas, electrical hook-ups for trailers and recreational vehicles, an equine museum, and 300 miles of riding trails. You'll also find pavilions sprinkled through the park. The association sponsors quarter horse, walking horse, and Arabian shows as well as an annual 100-mile sanctioned race. You can lease the park and also utilize the adjoining Crooked Creek Lake and the federal recreation area encompassing it. For more on Crooked Creek Lake, see the Parks chapter.

The Paper Horse
HCR 67, Box OH95, Mifflin, PA 17058
(717) 436-8893
www.thepaperhorse.com
Fort Armstrong is one of the region's most prominent horse organizations, but dozens of others are active. To keep up with all their events, try the *Paper Horse,* a monthly magazine that will keep you current with many shows in Western Pennsylvania and throughout the Commonwealth. You can subscribe for $14 (third-class mail) or $30 (first-class mail).

Pennsylvania Equine Council
P.O. Box 1461, Harrisburg, PA 17105-1469
(888) 304-0281
www.pennsylvaniaequinecouncil.com
The council is a good place to find a horsemen's group to suit your needs and tastes. It publishes a directory of 30 to 40 such groups as well as a newsletter that will update you on events as well as legislative and other activities. Annual membership costs $25 with dis-

> **i** Each year the city of Washington in Washington County hosts the Pony League World Series at—where else?—Pony League Field.

counts for families and those younger than age 18.

If you belong to an equine group, you might want to take advantage of the council's fire prevention and rescue program—they'll travel to your barn to offer instruction.

HUNTING

Hunting in the Commonwealth is the preserve of the Pennsylvania Game Commission. The commission provides many opportunities for hunters in Southwestern Pennsylvania—check out the Parks chapter for an introduction to which state parks permit hunting—but it's best to know some of the rules before you begin.

It's easy to remember that you must be licensed and wear fluorescent-orange safety clothing. But do you know the seasons for each species? The limit on kills for each species? The regulations on goose blinds, dog training, and hunting from tree stands? If you're new to hunting in the state, chances are you'll need some help in becoming familiar with Pennsylvania regulations. If you contact the commission, 2001 Elmerton Avenue, Harrisburg, PA 17110-9797; (717) 787-4250, they'll send you *A Digest of Pennsylvania Hunting & Trapping Regulations*. You'll want to spend some time with it—it runs 55 pages.

Once you know the rules, you're ready to enjoy the approximately 1.4 million acres in Southwestern Pennsylvania that are open to public hunting. Common quarry include grouse, squirrel, deer, raccoon, rabbit, turkey, and pheasant. Trappers will find both beaver and red fox within sight of Pittsburgh's suburbs. If you venture east to the Chestnut, Laurel, and Allegheny ridges, you may encounter black bear. One of the better guides to area game is the commission's *Hunting in Southwestern Pennsylvania.* You'll find detailed acreage and game lists for each hunting tract.

A good way to keep up with hunting news in the state is through the official monthly magazine of the Pennsylvania Game Commission. It's called *Game News,* and you can subscribe for $18 per year.

ICE HOCKEY

B. M. L. (Before Mario Lemieux), ice hockey was an informal kids' game played whenever the pond froze over. Today, thanks to the influence of Mario Lemieux and the success of the National Hockey League's Pittsburgh Penguins, youth ice hockey in Western Pennsylvania is a sophisticated, complex business that has given rise to hundreds of organizations as well as occasional jurisdictional squabbling. We'll try to sort out the organizational structure for you.

The Mid-American District of USA Hockey is the coordinating body for amateur youth hockey in Western Pennsylvania, Ohio, West Virginia, Indiana, and Kentucky. Within its region, the district keeps track of 280 organizations, 2,400 teams, and more than 30,000 players and coaches. If you're looking for a hockey organization based in your community, the district will point you in the right direction. You can call their hotline at (412) 884-2922.

The South Hills Amateur Hockey Association (SHAHA), (412) 833-8500, unlike TAHA or the Mid-American District, is not an administrative body. Rather, it stages playoffs for local organizations that include 7,000 kids. The league's Web site, pahockey.com, is a great source for information on local organizations and tournaments.

That's a quick guide to the structure of youth ice hockey. Here's a look at some of the most prominent organizations.

**Pittsburgh Amateur Penguins
Hockey Association
66 Alpha Drive
(412) 628-6997
www.amateurpenguins.com**
This program is affiliated with the Pittsburgh Penguins, a relationship that dates from 1983.

The Amateur Penguins compete at the highest level of amateur hockey, in the Buffalo-based Empire West League. The program is for youths ages 8 to 20 with a serious commitment to hockey. They practice two or three times a week at BladeRunners Ice Complex in Warrendale and Harmarville, pay about $1,500 to the association, and adhere to the group's dress code.

ICE SKATING

Ice-skating in the region is inextricably linked with ice hockey. Not every ice skater is a hockey player, of course, but hockey teams snap up so much ice time at commercial facilities that it's sometimes difficult for others to find ice time at convenient hours. Public facilities may be your best bet, and two of these merit special attention.

The Schenley Park Skating Rink, operated by the city of Pittsburgh in the Oakland neighborhood, is open year-round for ice-skating and in-line skating. In addition to public sessions, the city operates leagues and pickup hockey programs for ice hockey and roller hockey and rents rink and meeting-room time. Call the rink at (412) 422-6523 for schedules and fees.

You also will find ice time for rent at the Belmont Complex, (724) 548-1067, operated by the Armstrong County Recreation Authority, where skating and hockey are two of the principal activities. For more on Schenley Park and Belmont Complex, see the Parks chapter.

Ice-skating is a special treat at state parks and federal recreation areas—no hockey teams to contend with here—though you will need cooperation from the

i For a special treat, go ice-skating just outside PPG Place, one of downtown Pittsburgh's skyscrapers. The Rink at PPG is open daily and provides skate rentals and skating lessons. Call (412) 394-3641 or visit www.ppgplace .com for details.

weather. The Parks chapter will introduce you to ice-skating opportunities at these facilities. For more comprehensive brochures, contact the Pennsylvania Parks information and reservations line, (888) PA-PARKS (800-727-2757).

LAWN BOWLING

**Frick Park Lawn Bowling Association
427 Dorseyville Road, O'Hara
(412) 782-0848**
Lawn bowling in the region is the domain of the Pittsburgh Lawn Bowling Association ... literally. As far as we know, you won't find lawn bowling anywhere else in the state. The city of Pittsburgh provides lawn-bowling greens at Frick Park, but the association, founded in 1938, raises funds to maintain the facility through private donations and several plant-selling fund-raisers each year.

The genteel game is played on greens that are 120 feet long and 15 feet wide and is distinct from boccie ball, where the course is a gravel pit with sidewalls. The season generally begins in May and lasts until Labor Day, or as long as weather permits. The association engages in league play on Tuesday and Wednesday, while pickup action occurs Thursday and Friday evenings. The action is pretty much continuous on weekends. Newcomers are always welcome—in fact, veteran bowlers will provide complimentary lessons. So give it a try!

Annual membership in the club includes equipment; call for membership rates and available packages,. There's also a youth league offering free supplies and lessons for four weeks. If you're an adult new to the sport, you can play for free in May to determine if you like it. When you join, beyond helping with plant sales, you will be required to wear traditional white dress in tournaments; "No white, no play," is a venerable club rule. Don't knock it. The sight of the bowlers in their tourney whites on the perfectly smooth green is one of the city's most appealing and relaxing tableaux.

POLO

Darlington Polo Club
6517 Mars Road, Darlington
(724) 827-2160
www.us-polo.org/clubs/darlington.htm
In 1937 Glenn Watterson founded the Darlington Polo Club. Today Glenn Watterson III operates the club, maintaining this unusual asset for the region. The club competes—at the Beaver County field it owns—in the Mid-States Circuit, which also includes clubs from Grand Rapids, Toronto, Lexington, Cincinnati, Virginia, Cleveland, and Columbus. You can catch the club each Friday at 8:00 p.m. from May through August. It's best to call ahead if skies are threatening, because rain will force cancellation of the match.

The club welcomes new members, but you must provide your own equine partner.

RUGBY

Western Pennsylvania is a hotbed of rugby, although the participants themselves aren't sure why. Some attribute it to the popularity of collegiate rugby in the region. As college players graduate, this theory goes, they've created clubs to extend their opportunities to play. All the clubs profiled below feature spring and fall seasons; most practice during the week and play their matches on Saturday afternoon.

Before you begin play, talk to club members to gauge their intensity. Each of the clubs has developed a "culture," so to speak. You'll want to select the club that best fits you; you're sure to fit in somewhere. Also, if rugby is a little rugged for your tastes, but you'd like to get involved anyway, think about officiating. There's a chronic shortage of officials. You can reach the Allegheny Rugby Union Referee Society at (412) 351-3455.

Pittsburgh Rugby Football Club
www.pghrugby.com
The Pittsburgh Rugby Football Club was established in 1964. Since that time, the club has identified itself as an organization of diverse and colorful people with one common passion: to play the best rugby possible.

The Pittsburgh Women's Rugby Club was founded in the spring of 1976. They're nicknamed the "Angels," but there's nothing angelic about the game these women play. The Angels became the sister club of the Pittsburgh Men's Rugby Football Club in the fall of 2002 after the team split from the University of Pittsburgh Women's Team.

Both the men's and women's teams welcome new players of all experience levels. If you'd rather watch than play, "social" memberships are also available.

For more information on joining the club, e-mail Dan Talbert at djtal10@att.net (men) or Jaimie Sullivan at jsulli223@yahoo.com (women).

South Pittsburgh Rugby Football Club
1604 McFarland Road
(412) 734-8998
www.southpittrugby.com
Formed in 1978, the Hooligans, as these players are known, perform in both the Allegheny Rugby Union and the Midwest Rugby Union. Edgebrook Field in South Park serves as home field. By their own admission the Hooligans are perhaps the most social of the area's rugby clubs. It's not that they don't take their rugby seriously. It's just that they take the postgame party just as seriously.

Greensburg Area Rugby Football Club
104 North Sixth Street, Youngwood
(724) 331-2749
Their nickname is "Gorillas" and they play at Mammoth Park. Does that tell you what you need to know about this club? The club plays in the Allegheny Rugby Union and practices at Lynch Field in Greensburg. The organization welcomes new Gorillas.

Westmoreland Highlanders REC
126 Cedar Avenue
(412) 260-3644
The Highlanders' home games in the Allegheny Rugby Union, part of which is a

national organization, take place in Pittsburgh. The Highlanders are a Division 3 team and a good venue for developing your game. The 160-member club is always looking for new members.

RUNNING

You can run to your heart's content in Western Pennsylvania. Many parks offer walking and jogging trails—see the Parks chapter for which parks have the most appropriate facilities. More commonly, runners in the region practice their sport informally, tackling the region's hilly terrain with gusto. A warning is in order: If you're not used to hill running, introduce yourself to Pittsburgh's terrain gradually. You might not realize how taxing hill running can be.

One premier running event in the region is the Richard S. Caliguiri Great Race, a 10-kilometer event staged each September. The course begins at Frick Park in Squirrel Hill and ends at Point State Park downtown. The Great Race is extremely popular, typically drawing more than 10,000 runners, so it's a great place to socialize as well.

In addition to the Great Race, there are hundreds of other races in the area. *The Pittsburgh Post-Gazette* publishes a schedule of running events each Sunday and produces an annual calendar of races each March. In addition, two organizations can keep you posted on coming events.

Runner's High, 83 Cranberry Road, Grove City, (724) 458-4435, www.runhigh.com, provides timing services for many of the region's races and publishes an online road race directory providing details for approximately 500 races per year in Western Pennsylvania, as well as all such race results. (S. Mark Courtney, founder and principal of Runner's High, meticulously records the names of all finishers in important races.) For information on the directory visit the organization's Web site: runhigh.com.

A second race timing service, operated by Dave Mapes, provides a free race calendar that catalogues about 80 races per year. You can write this service at 1502 Grandview Avenue, Somerset, PA 15501, or call (814) 445-6213. If you send a self-addressed, stamped envelope with your request, Dave will send you his calendar free of charge.

SHOOTING

Allegheny County Sportsmen's League
1028 Hulton Road, Verona
(412) 882-9115
www.acslpa.org
Shooting is a popular Western Pennsylvania activity, as witnessed by the more than 40 organized sportsmen's clubs. The Allegheny County Sportsmen's League serves as their umbrella organization, publishing an annual directory of clubs and their facilities. You can contact the organization for a current directory. You'll find facilities for a broad variety of shooting, including skeet- and trap-, high-powered rifle-, and handgun-shooting, as well as a civilian marksmanship program that utilizes older military rifles. Many of the clubs host competitions and leagues, and some feature archery ranges and private lakes for fishing.

Greater Pittsburgh Gun Club
920 King Road, Bulger
(724) 796-9111
www.greaterpghgunclb.com
Most area sportsmen's clubs are private. Greater Pittsburgh Gun Club is one of the few exceptions, offering public facilities as well as hosting a private club. Skeet, trap, and sporting clays are the organization's most popular offerings. You'll also enjoy rifle-, pistol-, and combat-shooting, as well as an archery range, with all facilities available daily. NSCA shoots are held once a month.

For relaxation, the clubhouse is open all weekend, plus Wednesday and Thursday evenings. Pay by the day or hour, and if you need equipment, ammunition, or ear protection, just knock on the door of proprietor Tex Freund, who lives on the premises. He'll be happy to rent you whatever you need. The guess here is that Tex goes through a lot of ear protection equipment himself.

SKIING

The hills elsewhere may be alive with the sound of music, but in Western Pennsylvania, they're alive with the sights of skiers. With its climate and topography, the region provides excellent skiing venues. You'll find plenty of opportunities for cross-country and downhill skiing, as well as a skiing community that loves its après ski (the after-ski party). We've highlighted Western Pennsylvania slopes and cross-country trails, but keep in mind that you'll find additional opportunities nearby in West Virginia, Maryland, and New York. Our region boasts a run for just about every skier, whatever your level of experience. Here's the dope on slopes.

Cross-Country Skiing

Cross-country skiing is a staple of many state parks and federal recreation areas. The Parks chapter will introduce you to local facilities that offer this activity. Keep in mind that some parks offer well-delineated trails, while at others the skiers just go with the flow. For more detailed information on particular parks or recreation areas, contact the Pennsylvania Bureau of State Parks, (888) PA-PARKS (800-727-2757), or the U.S. Army Corps of Engineers, (412) 395-7500.

Several local organizations organize cross-country ski outings. Sierra Club Allegheny Group (724) 327-8737, hosts ski-touring treks at such locations as the Laurel Mountains and West Virginia's Canaan Valley. Often the group doesn't determine its destination until several days before the outing, in the hope of encountering the best weather conditions. It's always best to call ahead. They'll rent you all the gear you need. Participants carpool for most outings, so you'll be expected to pony up your fair share.

Also, don't forget to check out Venture Outdoors online listing of resources at

www.wpfi.org. Here, you'll find scheduled outings and also ski clubs.

Downhill Skiing

Boyce Park
675 Old Frankstown Road, Plum
(724) 733-4665
www.county.allegheny.pa.us/parks/bpfac.aspx
You can't beat the convenience of Boyce Park, which is operated by Allegheny County. You'll find it in the easternmost portion of the county, no more than a 30-minute drive from anywhere in the county. This area of the park reopened in early 2008 after a $1 million renovation project that included upgraded and new chair lifts, new elevated snow making equipment, and a new tubing park. The ski area now offers six runs for skiing. The Boyce Park Ski Area is open Monday through Thursday from 3:30 until 10:00 p.m., Friday 3:30 until 10:30 p.m., and on Saturday, Sunday and holidays from 9:00 until 4:30 p.m. You can pay by the day or purchase a season pass. The park provides equipment rentals as well as special group rates on lift tickets. Call (724) 733-4665 for details.

Kids will have a grand time here with several special events, including an annual Mini-Junior Olympics for boys and girls from 5 to 12 years of age. You can learn the sport at the ski school and try cross-country skiing along the park's trails and hills using your own equipment. Snowboarders will fancy the Alpine Terrain Park and its 200-foot halfpipe. Whichever activity you choose, you'll enjoy après ski at the Four Seasons Ski Lodge. For more on Boyce Park, see the Parks chapter.

Hidden Valley Four Seasons Resort
One Craighead Drive, Hidden Valley
(814) 443-8000
www.myhiddenvalleyresort.com
Under new ownership, Hidden Valley reopened on December 15, 2007. This 1,500-acre resort offers 28 slopes and trails for skiing and snowboarding, a tubing course, and downhill and cross country trails, and many other ameni-

ties. The vertical drop ranges from 340 feet to 430 feet, so you know you're in for a fun ride.

The new owners have started a three-year improvement plan that will include new snow-making systems, groomers, chairs for chair-lifts, and ski rental equipment. Significant improvements are also planned for the lodge and recreational amenities at Hidden Valley. New residential and commercial developments are also in the works.

Cross country and downhill skis, snow-boards, and snowshoes are available for rent daily.

Hidden Valley offers day, twilight, night and full-day sessions. Lift tickets range from $20 to $52 depending on the day and skier's age. Children 5 and under pay $10 per session any day of the week. Seniors 70 and over pay $15 per session any day of the week. Mul-tiday and season passes are available.

You can take advantage of a variety of instructional packages at the Ski & Snow-board School. Private or group lessons for ski or snowboard are available. A Youth Ski Racing Clinic is also available for ages 7 and up. Reservations are required.

When you're ready to relax, you'll have the entire resort at your fingertips. You'll find more about the amenities of Hidden Valley in the Accommodations and Golf chapters.

Mystic Mountain, Nemacolin Woodlands Resort
1001 La Fayette Drive, Farmington
(724) 329-8555, (800) 422-2736
www.nemacolin.com
Mystic Mountain ski area is part of Nemacolin Woodlands Resort, which tells you right out of the chute that you're in for top-quality activi-ties and amenities. When you leave that chute, the vertical drop is 300 feet. Mystic Mountain is equipped with one regular quad chairlift and one handlebar. You'll find a full line of rental equipment, including cross-country skis and snowboards. Groups of 20 or more receive special discounts on ski tickets and rentals. Hours are 9:00 a.m. to 8:00 p.m. on Friday and Saturday and 9:00 a.m. to 4:00

p.m. on Sunday. If you need some help before you tackle the mountain, the resort offers pri-vate lessons.

Lift ticket day passes are $38 for adults and $30 for juniors (ages 6 to 11). Night passes (3:00 until 8:00 p.m.) are $20 for adults and $15 for juniors.

For other Nemacolin features, see the Accommodations and Golf chapters.

Seven Springs Mountain Resort
777 Waterwheel Drive, Seven Springs
(814) 352-7777, (800) 452-2223
www.7springs.com
You've reached a certain pinnacle when you ski at Seven Springs—the vertical drop ranges from 360 feet to 750 feet, while the skiable terrain measures 500 acres. Just as breathtak-ing are the facilities, which include 31 slopes and trails, 3 quad chairlifts, 7 triples, and 8 tows. The lift capacity is 24,600 per hour, and the longest run stretches for 1.25 miles. If you're ready to tackle all this, you can rent all the equipment you need and enjoy such related activities as snow tubing. There are also snowmobile tours and Sno-Cat rides available. If ever you need help on the slopes, the resort maintains a 150-member ski patrol to assist you.

The resort's Kids' Corner offers child-care services as well as a Tiny Tots instructional program. Seven Springs provides a variety of lodging packages, instructional programs, and skiing packages. Of course you're always welcome to pay by the day. The resort is an accommodating place for après ski—make sure you try the outdoor hot tubs! Check the hotline, (800) 523-7777, for a report on current ski conditions. See the Accommodations and Golf chapters for more about Seven Springs.

SNOWMOBILING

You'll find some of the best snowmobiling trails in the region at state parks, forests and game lands, and federal recreation areas. The season generally runs until about April 1, or until the weather no longer is conducive.

ℹ️ To check the condition of snowmobile trails at state parks, call the
state's Snowmobile Hotline, (877)
SNOMBLE (766-6253).

Remember that on state terrain you'll need a
valid snowmobile registration as well as proof
of liability insurance coverage. The Parks
chapter will tell you which local facilities offer
snowmobiling. For more comprehensive
brochures, contact the Pennsylvania Parks
Information and Reservations line, (888) PA-
PARKS (800-727-2757); the Pennsylvania
Game Commission, (717) 787-4250; or the
U.S. Army Corps of Engineers, (412) 395-
7500. For a nominal fee, the Game Commission also will provide you with detailed maps
of its lands.

McKean Snowriders Club
P.O. Box 27, McKean, PA 16426
(814) 476-7221
If you're willing to travel a bit for your snowmobiling thrills, you'll find some like-minded
riders in Northwestern Pennsylvania. The
McKean Snowriders Club belongs to the Erie
County Snowmobile Affiliation, an alliance of
five groups that plans exciting and challenging outings while undertaking useful projects,
such as mapping snowmobile trails. One of
the club's favorite rides is along a 175-mile
loop in the Allegheny National Forest. The
snowriders welcome participants from Southwestern Pennsylvania.

SOCCER

Though it may seem like sacrilege in what
was traditionally football country, soccer has
become the sport of choice for many area
youths. In fact, it's estimated that there are
more than 55,000 registered players in the
region. It would be difficult, if not impossible,
to detail all the region's soccer organizations.
Instead, we offer you information on the coordinating agency as well as several of the most
important clubs that operate in different geographic regions.

PA West State Soccer Association
855 MacBeth Drive, Monroeville
(412) 856-8011
www.pawest-soccer.org
Through the United States Soccer Federation,
PA West Soccer serves as the overall coordinator for all nonscholastic soccer in this half
of the state. Its numbers are impressive—it
encompasses 131 youth clubs with 154,000
members as well as 11 adult leagues and
4,000 members. For its members, the association handles registrations; scheduling; and
referees, who number 2,500 strong.

Of special interest are the association's
programs targeted to disadvantaged youths
and those with physical and mental challenges. If you're looking for the best soccer
opportunity for your particular situation, this
is the best place to start.

Beadling Soccer Club
P.O. Box 435, Bridgeville, PA 15017
(412) 221-3880
www.beadling.com
If you visit Beadling in Pittsburgh's South Hills,
they'll be pleased to show you a photograph
of the 1898 Beadling club. Needless to say,
Beadling is one of the oldest soccer organizations anywhere. Today the club administers
20 boys' and girls' teams that play in the Classic League. Beadling also boasts membership
in the Continental Alliance, a group of 22 elite
clubs. Players range in age from 12 to 20 and
must try out for the teams. Some of the
teams enter tournaments that take them as
far away as France. Youths accepted for the
program must provide $500 to cover the
club's costs. Club members also participate in
less formal adult men's leagues.

Penns Forest Football Club
435½ Cabbot Avenue, Trafford
(412) 646-2625
www.pennsforest.com
The club sports 15 teams of youths ages 11
to 21. They play in a number of leagues,
including the Classic League, the Premier

League, USL Super-Y League, and the National League, with home fields located in Trafford. Players must try out for teams and are responsible for all expenses.

Pittsburgh Strikers
(724) 898-8090
www.pittsburghstrikers.com
Boys and girls between the ages of 12 and 18 are eligible to try out for the Strikers, who play at a number of fields in the North Hills. The club participates in the Classic League. Be sure to ask about costs, as the Strikers don't publish a fee schedule.

SOFTBALL

Softball—the slow-pitch variety—is a popular warm-weather activity in Western Pennsylvania, so much so that it's hard to find an open field at the height of the season. While leagues abound, the sport lacks an overall coordinating body, so a league appropriate for your skill level may be hard to locate at once. Many teams are company based, meaning you can play only if you work there. Word of mouth may be the best way to find a league, but here are a few suggestions, whether you're searching for a team or your team is looking for a league or tournament play.

One of the neatest opportunities is with the 55 and Older Softball League. There are 110 players ages 55 to 83 who play twice-weekly games at a ball diamonds around the South Hill area, including their home field, Texas Field, in South Park. Your $35 fee includes a jersey and cap. The league uses standard American Softball Association (ASA) rules, with some modifications for safety. For example, players may not slide into home plate. For details, call co-commissioners David Sheridan (412) 882-7702 or Bob Wagler (412) 884-2029.

If your team is looking for a highly competitive league, try the Amateur Softball Association of Pennsylvania. Each year the league brings together about 85 men's and women's teams that play at fields throughout Allegheny County. The best teams travel to national tournaments, and the league also sponsors touring youth teams. You can reach them at (717) 285-2050 (executive offices).

The Penn Hills Sports Shop Softball League, (412) 795-3636, typically fields a league of about 30 men's teams, most based in the city of Pittsburgh's eastern suburbs. The teams are grouped by ability to assure the most enjoyable competition. One variation here: since the league is not run by a municipality, teams are expected to provide their own permitted fields.

SWIMMING

The city of Pittsburgh operates an extensive network of pools, with the outdoor season generally from early June through Labor Day. The network includes 18 outdoor pools as well as the Oliver Bath House on the South Side, which is open year-round. The pools are open to city residents and nonresidents alike, although city dwellers receive discounts on admissions fees. The city also offers a discount for recipients of public assistance. For schedules and fee information, contact Citiparks' pool hotline at (412) 594-4645.

You'll also find swimming opportunities at other municipal pools and at state parks and federal recreation areas. The Parks chapter will suggest some swimming venues for you. Keep in mind that some state and federal facilities offer sand beaches, others turf beaches. Some without lakes have large swimming pools. Food concessions and changing and showering facilities also vary. For comprehensive brochures, contact the Pennsylvania Parks Information and Reservations line, (888) PA-PARKS, (800)-727-2757, and the U.S. Army Corps of Engineers, (412) 395-7500.

TENNIS

The tennis boom may be long over, but the sport continues to flourish here. Most of the courts constructed during the boom of the 1970s remain, and they're more available than ever before. You'll find indoor and out-door courts aplenty at municipal parks, as well as courts at commercial facilities and private clubs.

The City of Pittsburgh's Citiparks, (412) 255-2539, offers a broad variety of tennis opportunities. If you're a beginner, you'll benefit from free group lessons provided through USA Tennis, a tennis industry program that also barnstorms Pittsburgh's neighborhoods with youth clinics. Citiparks also offers group clinics with varying fees.

You'll soon be ready for the Citiparks Adult Grand Prix Tennis League, which matches singles and doubles players of comparable skills. Some fees are involved. Finally, the Citiparks program includes clinics specially tailored to senior citizens and "munchkins" from 5 to 7 years of age. Munchkins is their word, not ours. When we're charging the net, we have great respect for anyone with a racquet—munchkin or not—on the other side.

YOGA AND MEDITATION

You'll find yoga and meditation being practiced in all kinds of venues in the Pittsburgh area: hospitals, health clubs, yoga centers, churches and synagogues, community centers, local colleges and universities, holistic health centers, and meditation rooms in private homes. There are almost as many forms of yoga and meditation being practiced as there are venues: various schools of Hatha yoga, such as Iyengar, Kirpalu, and Ashtanga yoga; Zen meditation; and Kundalini yoga. Because Zen meditation is associated with Zen Buddhism, some information is included in the Worship chapter. Note also that all forms of yoga represented here teach some type of meditation as well.

Several of the forms, including Kundalini yoga and gentle forms of Hatha yoga, offer special benefits and/or exercises for pregnant women. Kundalini is especially good for people trying to build strength and balance the internal systems of the body, particularly the immune and glandular systems. That includes people recovering from or coping with severe illness.

Below are contacts for some of the main groups or centers that offer yoga and meditation. Health clubs, due to their commercial nature, have not been included. We encourage you, however, to check out clubs through the Yellow Pages. When you're looking for a yoga teacher, you'll want to find out what form she or he teaches; how the form will help you achieve the results you want; where the teacher was trained and how extensive the training was; and how many years the teacher has been practicing yoga.

Breathe Yoga Studio
1113 East Carson Street, Third Floor
(412) 481-YOGA (412-481-9642)
www.breathe-yogastudio.com
Located on Pittsburgh's South Side, this studio is on the third floor of an old office building. The space is beautiful with hardwood floors, high ceilings, and windows that offer a view of the sky as well as the gargoyles on the building next door. It's great to stretch up during Cobra pose and catch a glimpse of those gargoyles! Courses in a variety of forms of yoga, dance, and related disciplines are offered at the center daily. When we called, classes scheduled were beginning, intermediate, and advanced Hatha yoga, Vinyasa (or "flow") yoga, Kundalini yoga, Middle Eastern dance, and Ashtanga yoga. The studio is continually adding new classes, and workshops on various topics are held there regularly. Integrative Yoga therapy and massage are also available. Drop in for a class for $13. Check out the variety of discount class cards available when you pay a lump sum from $40 to $96 and make a regular commitment to your health and well-being.

The studio shares its home with Labco Dance, a modern dance company with up-and-coming choreographers. An art gallery is on the second floor of the building the studio shares. Come, relax, get cultured! Breathe Yoga Studio is a fun and peaceful place.

Yoga Training Association of Pittsburgh (YTAP)
(412) 421-1506
www.ytap.org
Founded by a small group of yoga teachers more than 25 years ago, YTAP's purpose "is to foster education about the teaching and practice of the ancient science and art of yoga." Currently YTAP membership is a mixture of yoga teachers and yoga students of varying levels. Except during summer months, YTAP holds monthly meetings during which a teacher of yoga or a related discipline presents a class. The group also brings in several nationally or regionally known yoga teachers each year and hosts an annual "Yoga Day Out" devoted to showcasing a variety of the forms of yoga and related disciplines available in the Pittsburgh area. YTAP also offers the opportunity for those practicing yoga to stay in touch with other like-minded individuals, to make new friends, and to network.

The group publishes five newsletters per year advertising the dates of some of the major yoga events in the area and offering various philosophical meanderings related to yoga and meditation. Periodically the newsletter includes a simple directory of members; the names of teachers are marked with a "T." If you're a yoga teacher looking for a substitute for one of your classes, this list is one of the best places to start. Yearly membership in the organization is $25. We've not listed an address for YTAP, because the organization meets at a different location each month in an effort to make meetings convenient for members living in the various Pittsburgh neighborhoods.

GOLF

Golf in Western Pennsylvania is more than a sport or hobby—it's something approaching a regional passion. The relatively short season may be a handicap, but there are several compelling reasons why golf is so popular here.

Pittsburgh was for many years a leading corporate headquarters town—at one time outranked only by New York and Chicago—as well as a center for manufacturing. Golf always has been a popular getaway for corporate executives, a fondness that tended to trickle down throughout such organizations. Today, even though the region boasts a more diversified economy, that heritage of golf as the ideal vehicle for relaxation and competition remains.

A second pillar of golf's foundation in Western Pennsylvania can be summarized in two words—Arnold Palmer. One of golf's legends, Palmer was reared in Westmoreland County, created several golf courses here, and remains highly visible, staging tournaments for charity, maintaining his offices near his hometown of Latrobe, and popping up on countless television commercials. The rage for golf in Western Pennsylvania is part of Arnold Palmer's gift to the community.

The statistics are impressive. Of Pennsylvania's 705 public and private golf courses, the National Golf Foundation reports that Allegheny County and Westmoreland County rank second and third in the state, respectively, in the number of courses, with a combined total of 81 18-hole equivalents. Butler County is not far behind, ranking sixth.

Of 309 metropolitan areas in the country for which the foundation keeps records, the average golf hole per population rate is 76 holes per 100,000 people. In Pittsburgh the rate is 101 holes per 100,000 people.

The region boasts courses to suit all tastes and talents, ranging from quick-play executive courses to storied Oakmont Country Club, site of a number of major Professional Golf Association tournaments over the years. You'll find courses carved from mountainsides, a course built atop a slag heap, even a municipal course operated by a university.

In the descriptions below, we've tried to feature most public courses in our service area, although the rate of construction and course openings makes development of a comprehensive list nearly impossible. Unless otherwise noted, costs cited include the price of electric cart rental. Keep in mind that prices change from season to season—you might find slight variations from those we've provided. We've noted where starting times are available, suggested, or required, and we've tried to describe unusual or compelling features of the courses.

Your tour through Pittsburgh's golf courses will be enjoyable, but take care. When you put "the sticks" in your car trunk permanently, because you never know when you'll get a chance to "hit a few," you'll know that the Pittsburgh golf bug has bitten you.

PUBLIC GOLF COURSES
North
Aubrey's Dubbs Dred Golf Course
140 Aubrey Drive, Butler
(724) 287-4832
www.aubreysdubbsdred.com
At Dubbs Dred you'll be playing target golf, hitting over ravines and gullies to tight landing areas. It's a challenging course from stem to stern. Distance for the par-71 course ranges from 6,500 yards to 6,850 yards. Starting

times are required on weekends and holidays, but are optional during the week. Cost to play 18 holes during the week is $18 and on weekends is $34. Dubbs Dred offers a limited-service pro shop and a small lounge.

Bostonia Country Club
Route 66 / 28, Distant
(814) 275-2553

The semiprivate Bostonia Country Club is located at the northernmost reaches of Armstrong County. Its relatively remote location means you can get on and off the course quickly, and without a starting time. The nine-hole, par-35 course covers 2,800 yards. The cost for nine holes during the week is $12, on weekends $14; for 18 holes during the week it's $18, on weekends $20. Annual memberships priced from $200 for students (ages 18 and younger) to $720 for families allow unlimited golf. You'll find a pro shop and a snack bar.

Buffalo Golf Course
201 Monroe Road, Sarver
(724) 353-2440
www.buffalogolfpa.com/

Perhaps the most challenging hole on Buffalo Golf Course is No. 15, a 446-yard par 4. The course has a pond along the right side of a rising fairway, and trees reach out and hang over the green. Distance of this flat, par-71 course ranges from 6,138 yards to 6,324 yards. Weekend and holiday starting times are available. Cost is $18.50 weekdays and $23.50 on weekends, with senior citizen discounts offered during the week. You'll find a pro shop and a snack bar.

Cabin Greens Golf Course
361 Ford City Road, Freeport
(724) 295-3744
www.cabingreens.com

Cabin Greens is a pleasant, unpretentious nine-hole course that's a great place to get in a quick round after work. The par-36 course ranges from 2,462 yards to 2,907 yards. Cost is $18 for 18 holes, $11 for 9 holes, with senior citizen discounts available. Starting times are available on weekends and holidays only. Cabin Greens offers a pro shop, a snack bar, and a full-service bar.

Cherry Wood Golf Course
212 Truxall Road, Apollo
(724) 727-2546

When Carol and John Chernega designed Cherry Wood, they had golf in mind, of course, and much more. The Chernegas participate in the national Audubon Cooperative Sanctuary Program to promote native habitats and more natural environments. The course design so complements wildlife habitats that the Chernagas have recorded sightings of 50 species—including foxes, mink, wild turkeys, and vultures—on Cherry Wood. Perhaps the most important residents are such birds as woodpeckers, which feed on insects and reduce the need for pesticide application.

If you interrupt your commune with nature to golf, you'll find a nine-hole, par-35 course. Distance ranges from 1,895 yards to 3,115 yards. Starting times are not offered. Cost for a round of nine holes is $20 during the week and $4 more on weekends. Senior citizens enjoy a special discount during the week. Amenities include a pro shop, a snack bar, and a driving range with grass tees.

Clover Hill Golf Course
2200 Reis Run Road, Franklin Park
(412) 364-2447

While this 2,300-yard, par-32 course won't test your long-driving ability over its nine holes, it does place a premium on shot making. That's especially true at No. 7, a 173-yard par 3, where you'll hit over a lake to a two-tiered green.

Cost for a round of nine holes is $10, and you can play a second nine for $4. Seniors receive a daily $2.50 discount. Clover Hill offers neither starting times nor dining facilities, but you will find vending machines in the small clubhouse.

Conley Resort Inn
740 Pittsburgh Road, Route 8, Butler
(724) 586-7711, (800) 344-7303
Could it be that Coleridge was describing Conley's course when he wrote "Water, water everywhere?" Probably not, but you may feel like the Ancient Mariner when you play Conley. Both irrigation and scenic water hazards come into play on five holes. These include No. 7, a 520-yard par 5, where you must hit over water to reach the green.

Distance ranges from 6,200 to 6,515 yards, with par varying from 70 to 72. Tee times are required. The fee to play 18 holes Monday through Thursday is $30; Friday through Sunday it is $40. They also offer specials and golf packages. You'll find a pro shop as well as a full-service restaurant called the Tavern. For more on Conley Resort Inn, see the Accommodations chapter.

Deer Run Golf Club
287 Monier Road, Gibsonia
(724) 265-4800
This semiprivate club is open to nonmembers, although members get first crack at tee times. You will enjoy the facilities, which include a pro shop, locker rooms, full-service grill room, bar, and banquet areas.

Distances on the par-72 course range from 6,345 yards to 7,066 yards. Pay special attention to No. 11, a scenic 382-yard par 4. Your second shot must carry over water to a green sheltered behind by a steep hill dotted with flowers. Tee times may be made up to four days in advance by calling the pro shop. Cost to play 18 holes is $28 Monday through Thursday and $36 Friday through Sunday.

Hartmann's Deep Valley Golf Course
169 Hartmann Road, Harmony
(724) 452-8021
www.hartmannsresort.com/
This is an easy walking 18-hole course, popular with senior citizens, with a back nine dotted by picturesque water hazards. The par-72

Going Public

Golf in Western Pennsylvania can be a rich and rewarding experience . . . if you can find the dozens of public courses the region offers. You'll find several useful guides. Both the *Pittsburgh Post-Gazette* (www.post-gazette.com) and the *Pittsburgh Tribune Review* (www.pittsburghlive.com) print annual golf directories. Also, check out *Golfer's Lifestyle Magazine,* a free publication that can usually be found at the entrances of local Dick's Sporting Goods stores and local golf courses. Or go online to www.golferslifestyle.com.

The Pennsylvania Golf Course Owners (PGO) publishes the Pennsylvania Golf Trail Pass, which offers great golf deals at more than 110 PGO courses across Pennsylvania. Not all Pennsylvania courses are listed, since some are not PGO members,but those courses that are listed will get you off to a swinging start. You can purchase the Golf Trail Pass for $29.99 at any participating PGO golf course. Call (800) 872-1483 for more information, or go to PGO's Web site at www.golfinpa.com.

course covers 6,310 yards, with no starting times necessary. For 18 holes the cost is $14 during the week and $19 on weekends and holidays; for nine holes it's $7.50 on weekdays and $10.50 on weekends. (These prices don't include electric carts, since the course isn't difficult to walk, but carts are available for an extra charge.) Senior citizens receive discounts during the week. Take advantage of the picnic and banquet facilities, as well as the pro shop, snack bar, and the Waterhole Restaurant & Lounge.

Lake Arthur Country Club
255 Isle Road, Butler
(724) 865-2765
www.lakearthur.com

Lake Arthur offers a great fishing hole, and the entire course was upgraded recently. The fairway on No. 18 is flanked by lakes with a small landing area between them. Even if you find the fairway, getting your par 4 on this 451-yard challenge is hardly a sure bet.

Distance for the par-69 course is 6,629 yards. Cost (without cart) is $17 on weekdays and $23 on weekends, with senior citizen discount cards available in the pro shop. Lake Arthur offers starting times every day. In addition to the pro shop, you'll find a chipping green, a bar and lounge, and banquet facilities. If you play the Lake Arthur and have time for even more fun, stop at nearby Moraine State Park.

LakeVue North Golf Course
591 Pittsburgh Road, Butler
(724) 586-7097
www.lakevuenorthgolf.com

LakeVue North offers many picturesque holes that feature water hazards and elevated or hidden greens. Distance for the par-72 course is 6,055 yards. Weekend starting times are available. An 18-hole round will cost $15 during the week and $18 during the weekend; a nine-hole round will cost $9 during the week and $12 during the weekend. Carts and weekday senior discounts are available. LakeVue North's newly renovated clubhouse includes a restaurant and dining area, bar and lounge, locker rooms, and well-equipped pro shop. An outdoor outing shelter is also available. The course is open March 1 to November 1, weather permitting.

Lenape Heights Golf Course
950 Golf Course Road (Route 66), Ford City
(724) 763-2201
http://lenapeheights.com

Lenape Heights is a 6,245-yard, par-71 course that features a pro shop and a sandwich shop. The cost to play this 18-hole course is $30 on weekdays and $37 on weekends, with weekend starting times available.

The signature hole is No. 13, an unusual 531-yard par 5. What makes it so striking is an island, which measures about 20 yards across. If your ball somehow stays on the island, it's in play. In addition to its restaurant and full-service bar, Lenape now has meeting rooms that can accommodate up to 400 guests.

North Park Golf Course
Pearce Mill Road, Allison Park
(724) 935-1967

One of two golf courses administered by Allegheny County—South Park is the other—North Park is exceptionally popular and does not offer starting times. To avoid the crowds, try to play the course during the late morning, the early afternoon, and on Friday, when things are a bit slower. The 6,805-yard, par-72 course is an open, gently rolling affair with large greens and no water, a fun outing no matter what your level of play.

Cost for an 18-hole round is $15 on weekdays and $18 on weekends. North Park offers a pro shop, a putting green, a driving range, and a full-service restaurant. The course is open year-round. For more on the amenities of North Park, see the Parks chapter.

Pittsburgh North Golf Club
3800 Bakerstown Road, Gibsonia
(724) 443-3800
www.pittsburghnorthgolf.com

Pittsburgh North offers both an 18-hole course and a 9-hole course known to habitués as "the Fox." The 18-hole course, with a 134 slope rating from the back tees, can be challenging. Distance ranges from 5,075 yards to 7,000 yards, with par at 72 or 73 depending on which tees you play. The course features several tough par-3 holes, including No. 14, a 232-yard challenge where you must hit over water and avoid a sand trap guarding the right of the green. If you miss to the left, you're likely in the water or the accompanying dam.

The Fox, a par-35 course, ranges from 2,051 yards to 2,800 yards. Weekend and holiday starting times are available. Cost for 18 holes is $18 on weekdays and $36 on weekends, while you can play the Fox for $15. The club features a pro shop, a bar, and a seasonal driving range. Pittsburgh North regularly hosts group functions, including outdoor barbecues. Two PGA pros are on staff; they offer a golf school.

Rose Ridge Golf Course
4769 Route 910, Allison Park
(724) 443-5020
At Rose Ridge starting times begin at dawn during the weekends, and the course maintains a fleet of 90 carts. The par-72 course measures 6,520 yards. You'll enjoy No. 11, a 165-yard par 3 with an elevated tee and a lake guarding the green. You'll also like the sight of Deer Creek, which winds its way for nearly a mile through the course.

Cost is $27, with weekend and holiday starting times available. Rose Ridge features a driving range, a lounge, and a sandwich shop.

Saxon Golf Course
839 Ekastown Road, Sarver
(724) 353-2130
Saxon Golf Course is a duffer's dream. It offers 27 holes, with nary a water hazard or sand bunker to be found, and both the 18-hole course and the 9-hole layout are flat. Distance for the par-72, 18-hole course ranges from 5,131 to 6,177 yards; the tight little 9-hole course, a par 34, covers 2,255 yards.

Starting times are available on weekends and holidays. Cost for the 18-hole course on weekdays is $19, on weekends $23; for the 9-hole course it's $9.50 on weekdays, $11.50 on weekends. You'll find a snack bar, a driving range, chipping areas, and a picnic shelter you can reserve for a group outing. When you get to know course operators Frank Ekas Sr. and Frank Ekas Jr., you'll be encountering a bit of local history—Ekastown Road was named for their family, early blacksmiths who helped settle the Saxonburg area.

The Western Pennsylvania Golf Association, (412) 826-2180, performs several useful services for local golfers. It publishes an annual schedule of amateur tournaments, provides a list of course ratings and slope ratings, and can help you establish your handicap. On the Web visit www.wpga.org.

Shamrock Public Golf Course
481 Grove City Road, Slippery Rock
(724) 794-3030
This par-35, nine-hole course is deceptive. While its layout of 2,686 yards seems inviting, there are three par 4s longer than 400 yards. You'll also encounter a challenge at No. 2, a 155-yard par 3 with a green surrounded by steep hills. Miss in any direction and you're in double-bogey territory.

Cost for a round of nine holes is $7.50, and you can play 18 for $13.00. Carts are available at an additional cost. Starting times are not offered. You'll enjoy the chipping area, snack bar, and banquet facilities.

Stoughton Acres Golf Course
904 Sunset Drive, Butler
(724) 285-3633
No. 13 at Stoughton Acres will challenge you. It's a 524-yard par 5 that forces you to cross both water and a highway to reach the green. The par-71 course covers 6,054 yards. Reserved tee times are required on weekends. You'll find a pro shop and a snack bar. Stoughton Acres does not publish its very reasonable green fees and cart charges. We recommend that you check Stoughton Acres out, especially if you want to play a nice round without emptying your wallet.

Suncrest Golf Course
137 Brownsdale Road, Butler
(724) 586-5508
www.suncrestgolf.com
The front nine at Suncrest is flat—that will get you in shape for the hillier back nine. Distance

for the par-72 layout ranges from 5,415 yards to 6,243 yards. Cost for an 18-hole round is $32.50, with weekend starting times available. Suncrest offers senior citizen discounts during the week. Facilities include a pro shop, a snack bar, and a full-service bar.

Woodlawn Golf Course
917 Bull Creek Road, Tarentum
(724) 224-4730

Woodlawn is an enticing par-32, nine-hole course that's not as easy as it looks, despite measuring only 2,376 yards. That's because Bull Creek, a natural phenomenon that still supports fish and other aquatic life, runs through the course, coming into play on five holes.

The cost for a round is $10 on weekdays, $11 on weekends for nine holes; $15.50 on weekdays, $16.50 on weekends for 18 holes. Senior citizens discounts are available. Woodlawn offers a pavilion for group outings.

East

Carradam Golf Course
2151 Hahntown Wendell Road, North Huntington
(724) 863-6860

This Jim Harrison–designed course features great finishing holes—No. 9 and No. 18 sport tree-lined fairways and mounding around the greens. At press time, this course was a par-71 that measured 5,904 yards, but the owners will be lengthening holes, so the play may change. When you're planning your golf outing, note that reserved starting times are available on weekends and holidays only, and that Carradam entertains leagues most evenings. The cost for 18 holes is $18 on weekends; the cost for 9 is $9 on weekdays and $11 on weekends. You'll enjoy country club–quality greens, a fully stocked pro shop, a snack bar, full-service bar, and a picnic pavilion.

Champion Lakes Golf Course
Route 71 North, Boliver
P.O. Box 4743 Rte 711 Boliver
(724) 238-5440
www.pagolf.com

Champion Lakes is located in the Laurel Mountains, and the 13th hole offers a particularly beautiful view of the mountains. The fairway on the 380-yard par-4 hole is part of a valley that splits two soaring peaks, while a picturesque lake guards the green.

The fee for the 6,608-yard, par-71 course is $40 on weekdays and $49 on weekends. Reserving a tee time is imperative because of the regular schedule of tournaments. Facilities include a restaurant, a bar, a pro shop, banquet capabilities, and a bed-and-breakfast inn.

Champion Lakes is the creation of former Pittsburgh Pirates Jerry Lynch and Dick Groat. Groat still resides there during the summer, and so can you—for a little while, anyway. That's because Champion Lakes Bed & Breakfast adjoins the course, with all sleeping rooms named for former Pirates. For more on this bed-and-breakfast, see the Bed-and-Breakfast Inns chapter.

Cherry Creek Golf Course
1000 Spyglass Hill, Greensburg
(724) 925-8665

This par-70, 18-hole course is styled as an "executive course" because of its appealing 4,500-yard length. During the week the cost is $10 for 9 holes and $16 for 18; on weekends the cost is $16 for 9 holes and $24 for 18. (We haven't included the cost of carts, since you'll probably enjoy walking this course.) Senior citizen discounts are available. You'll enjoy the pro shop and snack bar, known as Duffers Deli. Cherry Creek takes pride in its smooth, well-manicured greens.

Cloverleaf Golf Club
P.O. Box 55, Delmont, PA 15626
(724) 468-4173

Cloverleaf offers three nine-hole courses; for your round of 18 you can select any two of the courses. Depending on the combination, the yardage for 18 holes ranges from 6,016 to 6,215 yards, while par ranges from 70 to 72. Your round of 18 will cost you $25, and starting times are not available. You'll find a limited-service pro shop, a snack bar, and a tree-shaded pavilion that is popular with Cloverleaf's 30 leagues.

Donegal Highlands Golf Course
P.O. Box 130, Donegal, PA 15628
(724) 423-7888
www.donegalhighlandsgolf.com
The Laurel Highlands provide a scenic locale for Donegal Highlands, which is located at an elevation of 1,850 feet in southeastern Westmoreland County. Pro Ken Ivory Jr. doesn't believe the elevation will help your length, but he does commend the view on No. 15—a 487-yard par 5 that, in addition to featuring a hard dogleg right and water on both sides of the green, is flanked by Chestnut Ridge and Laurel Ridge.

The 6,018-yard, par-72 course is demanding; its slope rating is 12. Starting times are required daily. Cost for a round is $32 for cart and greens, $40 on weekends; senior citizens can play Monday to Friday for $25 each day. You'll enjoy the pro shop, a two-tier driving range with grass tees, and a tavern called the Rusty Putter Pavilion.

Grand View Golf Club
1000 Club House Drive, North Braddock
(412) 351-5390
www.pittsburghgolf.com
If there's a golf course that says "Pittsburgh," it's Grand View. The course sits atop a converted heap of slag, a useless by-product of industrial operations. The club's owners have done a commendable job reclaiming the land, although if you're interested, you can still make out evidence of the slag at several points along the course.

A round over the 6,111-yard, par-71 course will cost you $36 on weekdays and $46 on weekends; senior citizen discounts are offered during the week. Starting times are available, and you'll enjoy a pro shop, a driving range, and a full-service restaurant. Club pro Thomas Beeler points out that from the lofty perch of Grand View, you can see as far

away as downtown Pittsburgh to the west and the Laurel Mountains to the east.

Irwin Country Club
594 Simpson Road, Irwin
(724) 863-6016
www.irwincountryclub.com
You'll especially like the back nine at Irwin Country Club—that portion of the course was carved from surrounding woods and offers many scenic vistas. The par-70 course covers 5,577 yards. Cost for a round is $22.50 on weekdays and $31.50 on weekends, with starting times available on weekends and holidays. The club features a pro shop, a lunch counter, and a bar.

Linden Hall
432 Linden Hall Road, Dawson
(724) 529-2366
www.lindenhallpa.com/golfing.html
Golf is one of many attractive features at this resort about 37 miles from Pittsburgh. The course is scenic, offering compelling views of the Youghiogheny River, but as the Linden Hall pro points out, it's also a stern test. Most holes have sand traps, and seven holes present water hazards. Yardage on the par-72 course ranges from 5,900 to 6,675.

Cost for a round is $47 on weekdays and $56 on weekends, with senior citizen discounts available. You also can purchase golf packages from the resort. Starting times begin at 6:00 a.m. In addition to the amenities of the resort, the course features a pro shop; a bar; a restaurant; and a "halfway house," a snack shack after the ninth hole. Linden Hall hosts group outings each year as well as leagues virtually every weeknight. The Accommodations chapter provides a fuller description of Linden Hall's recreation and hotel facilities.

The Madison Club
519 Yukon Road, Madison
(724) 446-4000
www.themadisonclub.com
Bill Sarsfield, pro and general manager at the

upscale Madison Club, challenges you to test your shot-making skills on No. 8, a 181-yard par 3. You'll hit downhill along a fairway guarded by a massive stone wall. The green is protected by a lake in the rear, a steep hill on the right, and a venerable red oak tree on the left.

Distance for the par-72 course ranges from 4,905 to 6,847 yards. Starting times are required daily. Cost is $39 on weekdays and $49 on weekends. Amenities include a driving range, a snack bar, a full-service bar and restaurant, and a picnic pavilion that your group can reserve.

Mannito Golf Club
P.O. Box 258, New Alexandria, PA 15670
(724) 668-8150

To master Mannito, you'll need a sharp game throughout, as the course features two tough closing holes. No. 9 is a 245-yard par 3, while No. 18 is an even longer par 3 at 254 yards. If you get home on regulation on those two tough nuts, you can consider your round a success.

Par for the 6,709-yard course is 71. Cost to play 18 holes is $24 on weekdays and $33 on weekends, with senior citizen discounts available. You can reserve a starting time on weekends. Facilities include a pro shop, a restaurant and full-service bar, a driving range, a chipping area, and a picnic shelter that your group of up to 150 may book.

Manor Valley Golf Course
2095 Denmark Manor Road, Export
(724) 744-4242

If you've ever had that sinking feeling as darkness closed in and shortened your round, you'll appreciate Manor Valley. The course is one of the few in the region with lights for evening play, Monday through Friday. A number of Manor Valley leagues don't get under way until 7:00 or 8:00 p.m.

The par-72 course measures 5,853 yards. Weekend and holiday starting times are available. Cost to play 18 holes (without carts) is $21 during the week and $22 during weekends and on holidays. Carts and senior citizen discounts are available. Manor Valley offers a pro shop, a snack bar, a bar, several chipping greens, and banquet facilities.

Maplecrest-Monroeville Golf Course
3892 Logans Ferry Road, Monroeville
(412) 372-7770

Tucked away in a wooded area far from the frenzy of Monroeville's shopping district, Maplecrest is a scenic nine-hole course where relaxation and quick play are the norm. The par-33 course covers only 2,100 yards and presents no bunkers or water hazards.

Cost is $12.75 on weekdays and $14.49 on weekends. Senior citizens enjoy daily discounts, and starting times are available. Maplecrest sports a pro shop, a snack bar, and many junior leagues—this is one course that courts kids.

Meadowink Golf Course
4076 Bulltown Road, Murrysville
(724) 327-8243
www.meadowinkgolf.com

To play this 6,139-yard, par-72 course, the cost is $21 on weekdays and $28 on weekends, with senior citizen discounts available during the week. (Carts aren't included in these prices, since many people prefer to walk this course.) You can reserve a starting time every day. Meadowink offers a pro shop and a snack bar, as well as one of the toughest par 3s around. From the elevated tee at No. 11, you'll see the green 149 yards away guarded by sand and water in front and left, a steep hillside to the right, and woods in the rear.

"You really need to hit the green," says the Meadowink operations manager. "If you can do it, it's a routine hole. If you don't, it's trouble. This is not a place to miss."

Mt. Odin Golf Course
Mt. Odin Park Road, Greensburg
(724) 834-2640

Operated by the city of Greensburg as part of a municipal park, Mt. Odin is an 18-hole course that features a pro shop, a snack bar, a driving range, and considerable league play. Distance ranges from 4,743 to 5,445 yards, with a par of 70. Cost for nine holes during the week is $14, on weekends $16 for 18 holes; during the week you'll pay $25, on weekends $26. Senior citizens can purchase a restricted pass ($400) or an unrestricted pass ($350) that covers greens fees for the entire season. For more on Mt. Odin, see the Parks chapter.

Murrysville Golf Club
3804 Sardis Road, Murrysville
(724) 327-0726
www.murrysvillegolfclub.com
Murrysville Golf Club opened in 1930 with a classic Scottish design—plenty of grass bunkers but no sand. It maintains that philosophy today. The par-72 course spans 6,036 yards but features tricky winds to compensate for the moderate distance. Starting times are available during the week. Cost is $36, with senior citizen discounts daily. You'll find a pro shop, a snack bar, and a putting green.

Norvelt Golf Club
Off Route 981, Mt. Pleasant
(724) 423-5400
www.norveltgolfclub.com
This par-72 course covers 6,417 yards. You can reserve starting times on weekends and holidays and enjoy the club's pro shop, restaurant and bar, and snack bar. Cost for a round is $25 on weekdays and $36 on weekends, with senior citizen discounts offered on Wednesday.

Oak Lake Golf Course
1208 Oak Lake Road, New Kensington
(724) 727-2400
The Conley family owns and operates this 5,485-yard, par-71 course, and they've created several signature holes. You'll be tempted by No. 17, a 496-yard par 5 that invites you to go for the green in two shots. First you must contend with a double dogleg as well as a large sand trap guarding the green. The more conservative approach is to lay up, but if your round needs a pick-me-up, go for it!

Fabled Oakmont Country Club, about 10 miles east of downtown Pittsburgh, has played host to more than a dozen major tournaments, including the 2007 U.S. Open. The course is not written about in this chapter because it's not open for public play. However, Oakmont East Course, the next best thing to the actual club's course, is usually open to the public. Unfortunately that course was used by the U.S. Open for support services (tents, vendors, etc.) and has since been closed for at least a year for repairs and renovations. With no scheduled opening, it's best to call (412) 828-5335 to see if the course is available for play.

Starting times are offered on weekends. Cost for a round of 18 holes is $30, with weekday senior citizen discounts available. Oak Lake features a pro shop, a bar and lounge, and pavilions for group outings.

RidgeView Golf Course
Gravel Hill Road, Ligonier
(724) 238-7655
This nine-hole course provides a sweeping view of Chestnut Ridge in the Laurel Highlands; you'll enjoy that view for much of the 2,650 yards of this par-36 course. Cost is $8.00 for a round of nine on weekdays and $9.50 on weekends, $13.00 on weekdays and $14.50 on weekends for 18 holes. RidgeView offers starting times, a snack bar, a lounge, an outdoor deck, and a limited-service pro shop.

Rolling Fields Golf Course
Hankey Church Road, Murrysville
(724) 335-7522
www.rollingfieldsgolfcourse.com
You'll be rolling along at Rolling Fields when you reach the challenging No. 13, a 375-yard par 4 with a dogleg left and a severely undulating green. Did we mention that you must hit over water to reach the green? Get home in four here and you'll have earned your par.

Cost to play 18 holes on this 6,210-yard,

i In the Pittsburgh Metro area, there were 2,682 golf holes in 2006 (according to the National Golf Foundation).

par-70 course is $23 during the week and $25 during the weekend. After your round, you can relax in the snack bar. Rolling Fields also offers a limited-service pro shop.

The Bob O'Connor Golf Course at Schenley Park
5370 Schenley Drive
(412) 622-6959
www.thefirstteepittsburgh.org/scripts/golf/view

Club pro Bruce Stephen likes to say that Schenley offers the best golfing in the city of Pittsburgh. That's indisputable, since this is the only course within city limits. Part of Schenley Park, the course is owned by the city of Pittsburgh and operated through a lease agreement by a nonprofit corporation affiliated with Carnegie Mellon University.

The par-67 course measures 4,620 yards, which is considered executive length. You won't find bunkers or water hazards, but you will have a unique opportunity to hit across roads protected from stray balls by fences, and you'll enjoy a beautiful view of the city skyline as you play. You'll encounter highway hazards no fewer than six times. For your troubles you'll be rewarded at No. 5, a 122-yard par 3 that probably produces more aces than any other hole in the area. A number of nonprofit organizations stage hole-in-one contests on No. 5.

Cost for a round with a pull cart—electric carts aren't available—is $21. Schenley offers a pro shop, putting greens, and lessons. The course is open year-round. For more on Schenley Park, see the Parks chapter.

Seven Springs Mountain Resort
777 Water Wheel Drive, Seven Springs
(814) 352-7777, (800) 452-2223
www.7springs.com

The golf course at Seven Springs is very much in keeping with the resort. It's beautiful and

well appointed. You'll enjoy the facilities, which include a pro shop, locker rooms, and the Tee Top Lounge. The 11th hole is particularly appealing. It's a 195-yard par 3 where the undulating green is guarded by a lake, a bunker, and a large mound. Distance for the par-71 course ranges from 4,913 to 6,360 yards.

Cost to play 18 holes during the week is $58 for guests of the resort, $70 for nonguests; on weekends it's $67 for guests, $75 for nonguests. Resort guests may reserve starting times two weeks in advance, while others can get their tee times two days in advance. You can get a good feel for the course by taking a virtual tour of all 18 holes on the course's Web site.

For more information on Seven Springs, see the Accommodations and Recreation chapters.

Timber Ridge Golf Course
Mulberry Hill Road, Mt. Pleasant
(724) 547-1909

You'll enjoy your round at Timber Ridge, if you hit straight. Otherwise you may get up close and personal with the bunkers featured on just about every hole, as well as the water hazards on three holes. Distance for the par-72 course ranges from 5,277 to 6,340 yards. Reserved starting times are available on weekends. Cost is $28 during the week and $30 on weekends, with weekday discounts for seniors. You'll find a pro shop, a bar/restaurant, and banquet facilities for up to 200 people.

Timberlink Golf Course
Route 30 West, Ligonier
(814) 629-9064

This executive length course—a par 55 that covers 2,375 yards—is attractive in itself, and it's also one of the many features that draw visitors to Ligonier. During the week the cost to play nine holes is $6; $7 on weekends. An 18-hole round during the week is $11; on weekends it's $12. Timberlink does not offer starting times, but you will enjoy the small pro shop and snack bar.

Valley Green Golf & Country Club
2249 Valley Green Road, Greensburg
(724) 837-6366
www.valleygreengolfclub.com
Club pro Larry Liprando calls Valley Green one
of the region's best walking courses—it's
uncharacteristically flat for a Western Pennsylvania layout. The par-72 course measures
6,580 yards. Cost for a round is $28.50 on
weekdays and $33.50 on weekends, with
weekend and holiday starting times available.
You'll find a pro shop, a bar, and a snack bar.

Vandergrift Golf Club
1223 Tee Lane, Vandergrift
(724) 567-7413
Vandergrift Golf Club is semiprivate—nonmembers are welcome to play, but call ahead
for weekend starting times. During the week
it's first-come, first served.

Cost to play this par-36, nine-hole course
is $11. You can play 18 holes, using the sec-
ond set of tees, for $19. (Prices do not include
carts, although they are available.) The pro
shop is limited, but you'll enjoy a snack
bar/grill, a driving range, and a chipping area.

South

Butler's Golf Course
800 Rock Run Road, Elizabeth
(412) 751-9121
www.butlersgolf.com
The unusual design of Butler's Golf Course
includes four nine-hole courses that you can
combine according to your preference, unless
heavy crowds prevent that. Whichever two
nines you play, the distance is 6,606 yards
and the par 72. Cost is $38 on weekdays and
$49 on weekends, with starting times
required every day.

The course also entertains many leagues—
59 during one recent season. If you're interested in joining a league, the club pros will
match you with a group looking for players.
One of the great attractions for leagues is the
Rock Run Inn, the course's spacious, full-
service restaurant that offers a huge and varied menu. In fact, it's a destination dining spot

in the Elizabeth area, whether you golf or not,
and it offers full banquet and outing facilities.

Enjoy the driving range, putting green,
par-3 practice course, and the popular shot-
gun outings offered at this course. Call for
more information about the latter.

Carmichaels Golf Club
471 Harts Road, Carmichaels
(724) 966-7500
www.carmichaelsgolf.com
Located in Greene County, Carmichaels Golf
Club technically is beyond the coverage area,
but we thought it worth noting because of the
scarcity of courses in the sparsely populated
county in the state's southwestern corner.
Distance for the par-70 course ranges from
4,584 to 5,393 yards. On the back nine, be
prepared to contend with several ponds and
many hills. Cost for an 18-hole round is $29
during the week and $32 on the weekend,
with starting times available on weekends and
holidays. The club offers a pro shop, a snack
bar, and bar.

Cedarbrook Golf Course
215 Route 981, Belle Vernon
(724) 929-8300
www.cedarbrookgolfcourse.com
You can select from two 18-hole courses at
Cedarbrook. The par-72 Gold Course ranges
in distance from 5,138 to 6,710 yards; the
par-71 Red Course ranges from 4,577 to
6,154 yards. Cost to play 18 holes on either
course is $50 on weekdays and $60 on weekends. Senior citizen discounts are available on
weekdays, and starting times are required.
You can visit the pro shop and relax in the full-
service Clubhouse Grille.

Golf course architect Dr. Michael Hurdzan
designed Cedarbrook's courses, which feature large flat greens. Don't be deceived—the
courses offer some stiff challenges. No. 6 on
the Gold Course is a monstrous 578-yard par
5 with ever-narrowing fairways. "I don't know
if it's ever been reached in two from the back
tees," says club pro Bryon Palonder.

On the Red Course, the 531-yard, par-5
No. 10 offers a split fairway divided by an

uninviting thicket. The right fairway is longer, the left more dangerous. Which one does Palonder choose? "Whichever one the ball lands in," he says diplomatically.

Chippewa Golf Club
128 Chippewa Road, Bentleyville
(724) 239-4841
www.golfchippewa.com

Architect Jim Harrison designed plenty of water hazards into Chippewa, but he spared you the heartbreak of sand. There's not a single sand bunker on the course. Distance for the par-70 layout ranges from 5,104 to 6,051 yards. Starting times are available each day. Cost to play 18 holes is $30 on weekdays and $35 on weekends, with weekday discounts for senior citizens. Chippewa offers a limited-service pro shop, a snack bar, a bar serving beer only, and a picnic pavilion. Soft spikes are required.

Eighty Four Golf Course
1344 Route 519, Eighty Four
(724) 746-1510

This course features one of the longest holes around. No. 4, a par 5, measures 600 yards with a dogleg right. Get out your driving clothes for this one. The par-70 course measures 5,450 yards. Starting times are not available. Cost is $29.50, with weekday discounts for senior citizens. You'll find a pro shop, a lounge, and a full-service restaurant.

Fort Cherry Golf Club
80 Fort Cherry Road, McDonald
(724) 926-4182
http://fortcherrygolfclub.com

Fort Cherry has a number of scenic and challenging holes, perhaps none tougher than No. 4. The par-3, 201-yard hole features water left and right as well as bunkers guarding the green's right side. Distance for the par-70 course ranges from 5,888 to 6,205 yards. Starting times are available in season. Cost is $31 on weekdays and $39 on weekends, with weekday discounts for senior citizens.

Frosty Valley Golf Course
2652 Hidden Valley Drive, Upper St. Clair
(724) 941-5003

Frosty Valley once was the course of Hidden Valley Country Club, which relocated some years ago, and this nine-hole course still resembles a country club layout in some ways. The flat course is easy to walk, but water hazards affect six of the nine holes. The par-36 course plays from 2,371 to 3,250 yards. The cost is $13 during the week and $15 on weekends; cart rentals start at $7. Reserved starting times are available on weekends and holidays.

Amenities include a driving range, putting area, pro shop, Mickey's on the Green restaurant, and banquet facilities.

Mt. Lebanon Golf Course
1000 Pine Avenue, Mt. Lebanon
(412) 561-9761
http://mtlebanon.org/index.asp?NID=194

This nine-hole course is operated by the municipality of Mt. Lebanon. While only residents and their guests can play on weekends and holidays, nonresidents are welcome at other times. Cost is $13 per weekday and on weekends for nonresidents. Discounts are available for juniors and seniors citizens. You'll find a pro shop and vending machines.

Distance for the par-34 course is 3,034 yards. You'll like No. 2, a 400-yard, tree-lined par 4 with its two-tier green protected by a bunker. The hole typically plays longer due to a stiff wind. If you'd like a tip or two, look up pro Matthew Kluck.

Nemacolin Woodlands Resort & Spa
1001 Lafayette Drive, Farmington
(724) 329-6111, (800) 422-2736
www.nemacolin.com

When noted golf course architect Pete Dye designed Mystic Rock at Nemacolin Woodlands, he had a lavish $19 million budget to work with. The course shows it. The 6,832-yard, par-72 course utilizes Nemacolin's natural assets to create a course as beautiful as it is challenging, with a 146 slope rating. You'll

GOLF

find undulating greens and plenty of water and rock that connect fairways with foliage. Nemacolin hosts the Mystic Rock Charity Pro-Am, which in 1997 attracted no less a player than Tiger Woods. If you think you'd like a tip or two in order to play your best game, look up pro Delo Mees.

Nemacolin also features a second handsome course called the Woodlands Links, a 6,643-yard, par-71 adventure with thick woods, high rough, and lakes aplenty surrounding the fairways. The Links is no slouch—the slope rating is 131—but it may seem like a vacation after Mystic Rock.

Resort guests can reserve starting times two weeks in advance; others can reserve their starting times a week ahead of time. Guests can play Mystic Rock for $130, while others pay $150. For The Links, the cost is $84 for all. Whichever course you play, you'll enjoy the extensive facilities, which include a pro shop, a driving range, practice greens and sand traps, and locker rooms. If hunger strikes as you approach the ninth tee at Mystic Rock, pick up the courtesy phone and order from the restaurant just off the ninth green. After you sink that birdie putt, your lunch will be ready for you. For more on Nemacolin, see the Accommodations chapter.

Riverview Golf Course
Bunola Road, Elizabeth
(412) 384-7596

Riverview is an 18-hole layout with dual personalities. The front nine is tight, demanding precision shot making, while the back nine is more open. You'll need most of the clubs in your bag for Riverview.

Distance for the par-71 course ranges from 4,817 to 6,382 yards. You can arrange a starting time in season and take advantage of the pro shop and snack bar. Cost is $34 on weekdays and $44 on weekends, with senior citizen discounts available on weekday mornings.

Rolling Green Golf Course
2426 Route 136, Eighty Four
(724) 222-9671

Distance for this par-71 course ranges from 6,011 to 6,621 yards. Weekend and holiday tee times are available. Cost is $29 on weekdays and $33 on weekends, with senior discounts available on weekdays until 3:00 p.m. Facilities at Rolling Green include a limited-service pro shop, a snack bar, and a picnic pavilion your group can reserve for $40.

Seven Springs of Elizabeth Golf Course
357 Pineview Drive, Elizabeth
(412) 384-7730
www.golf7springs.com

If your ball has an unerring nose for the water, you'll enjoy Seven Springs of Elizabeth (not to be confused with the similarly named resort). There are no significant water hazards on the 18-hole, par-71 course, or the 9 hole, par-35 course, although both courses feature liberally bunkered greens. The length of the 18-hole course ranges from 5,582 to 6,503 yards. You can reserve a starting time every day, and management suggests that you do. They also ask that you call for rates. The course features a driving range, a pro shop, a lunch counter, and bar and banquet facilities.

South Park Golf Course
East Park Drive, Library
(412) 835-3545

South Park offers both an 18-hole course and a 9-hole course. As with North Park, the other course operated by Allegheny County, crowds can be huge. Starting times are not offered, so you may have to wait to play.

The par-72, 18-hole course covers 6,584 yards. It offers a number of tree-lined fairways with tight landing areas. Bring all your clubs, the pro advises. The nine-hole course is a par 34 that spans 2,652 yards. South Park offers a putting green, a chipping area, a pro shop, and a full-service restaurant.

Costs for 18 holes are $15 during the week and $18 on weekends; for 9 holes you'll pay $10 during the week and $12 on the weekends. Carts are available for an additional fee. If you're age 60 or older, you can purchase a $60 season pass. The Parks chapter provides a more detailed look at the features of South Park.

Village Green Golf Course
4050 Henderson Avenue, Hickory
(724) 356-4653
www.golfvillagegreen.com

Enjoy the first half of your outing at Village Green—the back nine is a lot hillier than the front. Distance for the par-71 course measures 6,489 yards. A round will cost you $32 during the week and $40 on weekends. If those hills leave you huffing and puffing, you can relax in the pro shop, the bar, or the full-service restaurant.

Willowbrook Golf Course
Route 201 North, Belle Vernon
(724) 872-7272
www.willowbrook.9f.com

At 3,019 yards, this nine-hole, par-36 course can be deceptive. Just when you think you can take it by storm, you'll find the creek that runs through five holes. Cost for nine holes is $18.75, and you'll enjoy a reduced rate for a second round of nine. Seniors (over age 55) can play nine holes for $16.50. Willowbrook does not offer starting times, but it does have a snack bar.

West

Black Hawk Golf Course
644 Blackhawk Road, Beaver Falls
(724) 843-5512
www.blackhawkgolfcourse.com

Black Hawk features 36 holes, ranging in distance from 6,114 yards (No. 1 and No. 2 courses) to 6,300 yards (No. 3 and No. 4 courses). Watch out for the fifth hole on No. 3 course. This 420-yard par 4 was voted by local golfers the "Toughest Hole in Beaver County."

"The fairway slopes left to right, so you never have a level lie," says Garen Steele, club pro. "You're hitting into a blind green. You can't miss on any side because of the big hills. Most people take a shorter club and look for bogies and double bogies."

Cost is $30 during the week and $38 on weekends, with senior citizen discounts offered on weekdays before 3:00 p.m. You can relax in the full-service restaurant or book the course and its pavilion for a group outing.

Fox Run Public Golf Course
River Road, Beaver Falls
(724) 847-3568
www.foxrungolfcourse.net

If you like water, you'll love Fox Run. All of the course's par-3 holes feature water hazards. The par-72 course covers 6,508 yards. Tee times beginning as early as 6:00 a.m. are offered on weekends and holidays. Cost for a round is $27 on weekdays and $32 on weekends, with senior citizen discounts available on weekdays. In addition to the pro shop, you'll enjoy the driving range and snack bar.

Grassy Lane Golf Club
470 McCaughtry Run Road, Darlington
(724) 336-5006

Watch out for the hole they call "The Chute." It's No. 4, a 363-yard par 4 with a narrow, tree-lined fairway that broadens as it approaches the green. This nine-hole, par-36 course covers 3,035 yards. Cost is $12 with a $2 discount for your second round of nine. Senior citizen discounts are offered during the week.

Only large groups may reserve starting times. Amenities include a limited-service pro shop, a snack bar, a chipping area, and a picnic shelter your group can book.

Hawthorne Valley Golf Club
122 Daniels Drive, Midland
(724) 643-9091

This 18-hole course is popular with evening leagues. If that's when you're planning to play, you might want to call ahead to check whether it's a league night. Starting times are available on weekends.

The par-72 course measures 6,237 yards. A round of 18 will cost you $15 during the week and $17 on weekends, with carts available for an additional $11. Senior citizens receive discounts during the week. Hawthorne Valley offers a pro shop and a snack bar.

Marada Golf Course
1434 U.S. Route 30, Clinton
(724) 899-2600

Only 2 miles from Pittsburgh International Airport, Marada draws quite a few players laying over at the airport. Distance for the nine-hole, par-35 course ranges from 2,485 to 3,090 yards. Arrival and departure times are important here, but you won't need a reserved tee time. For nine holes the cost is $11.00 on weekdays and $12.50 on weekends. For 18 holes you'll pay $17.50 during the week and $20.00 on weekends. These prices do not include carts. Senior citizens receive discounts during the week. Marada offers a small clubhouse and a snack bar.

Moon Golf Course
505 McCormick Road, Moon Township
(412) 262-2992
www.moongolfclub.com

Moon is a popular course with visitors staying at hotels near Pittsburgh International Airport, which is only minutes away. Under new management, this 5,800-yard, par-71 course generally plays quickly, so there's plenty of time to enjoy a round and still make your meeting or flight. Cost to play 18 holes is $33 during the week and $36 on the weekend. Weekend and holiday starting times are available. You'll find a snack bar, a bar and grille, and a limited-service pro shop.

Oglebay Resort and Conference Center
Route 88 North, Wheeling, WV
(304) 243-4000, (800) 624-6988
www.oglebay-resort.com

If you long to play a course that tempts and challenges the pros, try the Speidel Championship Golf Course at Oglebay, longtime host of the West Virginia LPGA Classic. Designed by the legendary Robert Trent Jones Sr., Speidel is a gorgeous course with compelling views of the hillsides that surround the resort. It's those same hills, however, that create the course's challenge.

One of the toughest holes is No. 17, a 456-yard par 4 with narrow landing areas protected by a line of trees and a steep hill. The green is enormous—about 32 yards deep. The par-71 course plays from 5,515 to 7,000 yards, with a fee of $60—modest, considering the course's heritage. Arnold Palmer recently designed a new par-71 course at Oglebay. You'll pay $70 to play that one.

You'll enjoy the pro shop, locker room facilities, and the Hamm clubhouse for dining.

If you're not quite comfortable with the challenge of Speidel or the Arnold Palmer course, you can enjoy the same great Oglebay vistas at the resort's Crispin Golf Course, a 5,670-yard, par-71 course. Cost for a round at Crispin is $30.

Oglebay offers a variety of golf packages that include such features as overnight accommodations, breakfast buffets, and a second round at a 50 percent discount. Call Oglebay for details, and see the Accommodations and Day Trips chapters for more information about the resort.

Ponderosa Golf Lands
2728 Route 168, Hookstown
(724) 947-4745

Just as Ben Cartwright was concerned about irrigating his Ponderosa, the owners of Ponderosa Golf Lands have lavished attention on their watering system. It's all computerized, keeping the course green throughout the season.

Distance for the par-71 course ranges from 5,525 to 6,283 yards. Starting times are available in season. Cost for a round is $30.25 on weekdays and $36.00 on weekends. Facilities include a pro shop, showers and locker rooms, and a full-service restaurant.

Quicksilver Golf Club
2000 Quicksilver Road, Midway
(724) 796-1594

Quicksilver has hosted five events on the Senior PGA tour and three events on the Buy.com tour (formerly the Nike Tour), as well as many tristate PGA and USGA events. That will give you some idea of the quality of the course. The amenities will reinforce that idea. You'll find a pro shop, a driving range with grass tees, Murphy's Restaurant, and Murphy's Pub. The club's owner, if you hadn't guessed, is Bob Murphy.

Distance for the par-72 course ranges from 5,067 yards to 7,083 yards. One of the favorite holes of general manager Sean Parees is No. 8, a 199-yard par 3 with a green guarded on three sides by water and sand. The course is a "fair challenge for all golfers with ability," according to Parees. Cost is $65 during peak season, with reduced rates for out-of-season and twilight play. For a $2,000 annual membership, you'll receive a locker, handicap service, a charge account, and the opportunity to reserve starting times 14 days in advance. Nonmembers can reserve tee times six days ahead of time.

Rolling Acres Golf Course
350 Achor Town Road, Beaver Falls
(724) 843-6736

You'll love the unusual timber-frame club-house at Rolling Acres. It's a popular spot for banquets, accommodating up to 300 people. In addition, you'll find a snack bar and lounge.

Rolling Acres offers three nine-hole courses, with staff determining your configuration based on the day's volume. The distance for 18 holes ranges from 5,878 yards to 6,518 yards, with par varying from 71 to 73. While the courses are mostly free of sand and water, you will find many mounds and grass bunkers. Starting times are offered each day. Cost for 18 holes is $28 during the week and $34 on weekends, with senior citizen discounts available during the week.

SPECTATOR SPORTS

In Western Pennsylvania, the term "spectator sports" is almost an oxymoron. The identification of residents with local sports teams is active, emotional, and deep. Spectators in Pittsburgh may be outside the white lines, but we participate nonetheless with our sports teams.

Some have suggested that the local love for sports is rooted in the economic and social history of Pittsburgh. Because many Pittsburgh residents labored long and hard in coal mines and steel mills to feed their families, this theory goes, they turned to sports for recreation, relaxation, and the rewards that were few and far between on the job. They found physical and psychic satisfaction both in their own play and in the success of the teams that represented them.

If that's true, it must be added that the region's emphasis on family helps broaden the affection for sports. In Pittsburgh, sports tends to be a family pursuit. If you check out youth basketball or football games in the area, in addition to the young athletes on the field, you'll most often find Mom and Dad out there, too, volunteering as yard-line markers, concession booth operators, and team chauffeurs.

For whatever reasons, we love our sports teams. The metropolitan area supports professional teams in baseball, football, and ice hockey; top-level collegiate football and basketball programs; a harness-racing track; and a radio station that features sports programming almost exclusively. In few other communities will you find baseball's home opener regarded as a civic holiday. Here otherwise dutiful parents cheerfully falsify school excuses to allow their children to attend the game, perpetuating a generations-old tradition.

When our teams win, we dress up in the colors of the local heroes, hang signs of support from office buildings, and party hearty. When the local teams lose, we phone the talk shows to offer heartfelt advice on how the teams can improve—"Get ridda de bums!" would be one example.

The new century is an especially exciting time to be a sports fan in Pittsburgh, as both our baseball and football teams have moved into new stadiums. For 30 years both the Pirates and Steelers played at Three Rivers Stadium, but in 2001 the franchises went their separate ways. (See the sidebar in this chapter for details on the new stadiums.)

Broadcast coverage of local teams deserves special mention. Some who may not appreciate Pittsburgh look at our sometimes half-empty arenas and label us a "bad sports town." What they may not fully understand it that, for reasons that sociologists someday will probe, many local residents—particularly those of a certain age—are notorious stay-at-homers who follow their teams religiously on radio and television but who seldom make it out to the game. For them and for you, details of the broadcast schedules and personnel for each team are provided.

We've also gathered information on transportation options, points of interest about the various sporting venues, and specifics about ticket prices. A word of caution about prices: These can—and do—vary from season to season, and many of the teams offer more packages than could be detailed here. This is especially true for the teams preparing to move to greener pastures. We've noted the most popular package and provided the most current pricing information available, but you may encounter some variations.

BASEBALL

Pittsburgh Pirates

http://pittsburgh.pirates.mlb.com

In 1889 the Pittsburgh professional baseball franchise was accused of stealing a second baseman from the Philadelphia organization. Pirates, these rascals from Pittsburgh were called. The name stuck, and today the Pittsburgh Pirates continue as one of the bedrock franchises of Major League Baseball.

The Bucs (short for Buccaneers), as local fans affectionately call them, have a storied past, with World Series victories in 1909, 1925, 1960, 1971, and 1979. The club has produced 41 Hall of Famers over the years, including Honus Wagner, Pie Traynor, brothers Paul and Lloyd Waner (known as "Big Poison" and "Little Poison"), Ralph Kiner, and such contemporary greats as Roberto Clemente, Willie Stargell, and Rich "Goose" Gossage. The Pirates were involved in what may be the most dramatic moment in baseball history— Bill Mazeroski's home run to defeat the heavily favored Yankees in the 1960 World Series.

The Bucs compete in the National League's Central Division, where their rivals are the Chicago Cubs, Milwaukee Brewers, St. Louis Cardinals, Cincinnati Reds, and Houston Astros. In 2007, Robert Nutting replaced Kevin McClatchy as majority owner. Mr. Nutting quickly began to assemble a new leadership team by appointing Frank Coonelly as President & CEO, Neal Huntington as General Manager, and John Russell as Manager. Only time will tell if these changes will result in more wins.

The 2000 season was the Pirates' last in Three Rivers Stadium. In April 2001 the team christened PNC Park, a new "old-style" park a few blocks up the Allegheny River. PNC Park is the latest in a nationwide trend toward retro ballparks. It features natural grass (as opposed to the artificial turf at Three Rivers), an asymmetrical outfield, and a spectacular view of the Downtown skyline. The park is designed by HOK Inc. of Kansas City, the firm that designed a number of retro parks around the country, including Oriole Park at Camden Yards in Baltimore.

The new park seats 38,127 people, and includes 69 suites and two restaurants. A 21-foot wall in right field honors Pirate great Roberto Clemente. The park is bordered by General Robinson Street, Federal Street, Stadium Drive East, and the Allegheny River, and there is a pedestrian walk along the water.

For those games when you can't make it to the stadium, the Pirates maintain a heavy broadcast schedule to bring the action to you. After 52 seasons with KDKA AM, the Pirates changed their flagstation affiliate to WPGB FM Newstalk 104.7. For television, cable's Fox Sports Net Pittsburgh typically carries a healthy schedule of games each season and is available on most local cable television systems. In addition, Pirates games sometimes are featured on national broadcasts.

Make sure you pay particular attention to game starting times, as the Pirates vary them to accommodate school schedules and fans concerned about the possibility of chilly weather.

The Pirates offer a variety of ticket plans. Prices for individual game tickets range from $10 to $35. The club also features season tickets, multiple-game plans, and discounted packages for groups. If you really want to treat your group to a memorable night at the ball yard, reserve the Grand Slam Box, which doubles as the football press box. Your group of 50 or more will dine in style and enjoy discounted tickets.

You can purchase your tickets at the Advance Ticket Window beneath the stadium's Gate A. You also can make credit-card purchases over the phone by calling (412) 321-BUCS or (800) BUY-BUCS or online at http://pittsburgh.pirates.mlb.com.

i The Pirates, who have won five World Series to date, were originally called the Alleghenies. They earned their new name when they "pirated" star player Louie Bierauer from the Philadelphia Athletics in the 1890s.

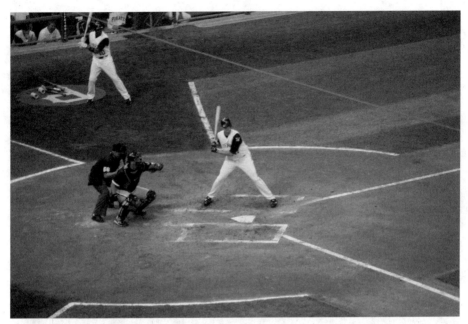

A Pittsburgh Pirate at bat. ALAN AND BARBARA VENTO

For most games you'll find $5 parking in the lots that circle the stadium. Other options include public transportation or parking downtown and walking across the Fort Duquesne Bridge to the stadium.

One of the neatest aspects of the Pirates' operation is the club's extensive involvement in the community. The Bucs have a special unit called Pirates Partners to coordinate a far-reaching program of school appearances, youth clinics, neighborhood athletic field restorations, donations of memorabilia, ticket giveaways to disadvantaged youths, and autograph appearances—including an annual event at the Pittsburgh Zoo & PPG Aquarium.

BASKETBALL

Who says you need a professional basketball team to generate fan excitement and loyalty? While Pittsburgh lacks an NBA team, it doesn't lack for basketball thrills. The city sports three institutions that compete in NCAA Division I, the best college basketball in the land. Rare is

the evening during the season when you can't enjoy a major college game, either in person or in the comfort of your living room.

Actually, Pittsburgh has featured several professional franchises, none of them in the NBA. The Pittsburgh Rens—short for Renaissance—performed in the old American Basketball Association. Later, in the American Basketball League of the late 1960s—the league of the red-white-and-blue balls—the Pittsburgh Condors won the league's inaugural championship behind the swooping grace of Connie Hawkins, who used that experience as a springboard to NBA fame. In the 1990s Pittsburgh was the brief home of the Piranhas entry in the Continental Basketball Association.

All three franchises were short-lived. That entrepreneurs launched them here, however, gives you some sense of basketball's popularity in Western Pennsylvania. If you're new to town and wondering if quality basketball is available, have no fear. The city game is alive and well in Pittsburgh.

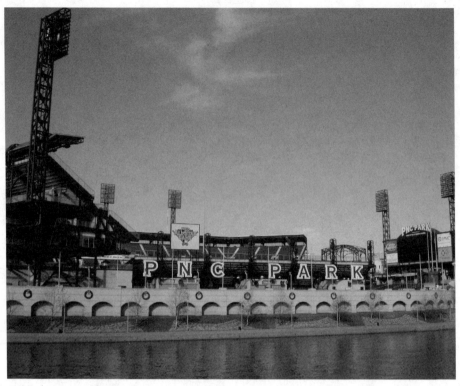

PNC Park. MICHAEL D. REED

Duquesne University

www.goduquesne.cstv.com

The men's basketball program at Duquesne University has long been both an artistic and a popular success. The Dukes have been to the NCAA tournament five times and to the National Invitation Tournament 16 times, capturing the NIT in 1955. Its legendary alumni include Chuck Cooper, Sihugo Green, Willie Somerset, and Norm Nixon—perhaps the most recognizable name for current fans, as Nixon was one of the key players in the Magic Johnson–led Los Angeles Lakers dynasty.

The Dukes, coached by Ron Everhart, compete in the Western Division of the Atlantic 10, a conference that features such traditional basketball powerhouses as Temple, Massachusetts, George Washington, Xavier, and Dayton.

Duquesne's home court is the A.J. Palumbo Center, an attractive building that opened in 1988, seats 6,200, and retains the feeling of newness. The center is located on Duquesne's campus along Forbes Avenue, making it quite accessible, as it is only a few blocks from downtown. Parking lots are available near campus as well as around the Civic Arena a few blocks away. You can also shoot for limited on-street parking. Forbes Avenue and the parallel Fifth Avenue are part of many Port Authority of Allegheny County bus routes, so using public transportation to see the Dukes is easy.

Individual tickets can be purchased by visiting www.ticketmaster.com or by calling (412) 232-DUKE (3853). Individual tickets range from $9 to $13. You also may purchase season tickets or 6 Pack tickets.

Duquesne's TV appearances are limited and difficult to predict from season to season. Typically, regional cable network Fox Sports Pittsburgh offers several games; check local TV listings for those. While we don't recommend staying home to catch the Dukes, if you do find yourself listening to them on KQV-AM (1410 on the dial), you're in for a treat. Ray Goss is worth not paying the price of admission. Goss, who has been broadcasting Dukes' games since 1968, can squeeze more words into a broadcast—intelligibly—than can any other announcer we've heard.

One other Duquesne note: When you're at the Palumbo Center, several times each game you'll see the crowd rise and chant as one, "Shoo Shoo, Rah Rah." It may sound like a weird new mantra, but it's really a cheer developed by Duquesne's No. 1 all-time fan, the late Maurice "Mossie" Murphy.

Robert Morris University

www.rmucolonials.com

For much of its basketball history, Robert Morris University played at the junior college level. In 1976, however, the Colonials jumped all the way to NCAA Division I—and they did it with flair. The Colonials have reached the NCAA tournament five times since then and have been a mainstay of Division I basketball ever since.

Coached by Mike Rice, the Colonials play in the Northeast Conference, which also features such schools as Long Island, Monmouth, St. Francis (New York) and St. Francis (Pennsylvania). Home arena for Robert Morris is the Charles L. Sewall Center for Leadership, a facility that also serves as a business training and meeting hub. Located on the college's Moon Township campus, Sewall Center is only a few miles from Greater Pittsburgh Airport.

While seating capacity at Sewall Center is 3,056, you'll find that tickets on most occasions are readily available. General admission is $5 for adults, and $3 for children (12 and under) and seniors (65 and older). Center court reserved seats cost $6. Season tickets also are available, with costs ranging from

$60 to $75. To purchase single-game, season or group tickets, call (412) 262-8449.

When you watch Robert Morris play, you'll find that most fans are students . . . some in outlandish garb. During one recent season, some students were so involved with the game that the officials assessed the Colonials a technical foul for student misbehavior. That's the kind of excitement that will capture you when you watch the Colonials.

Catching the Colonials on the air is a bit more difficult. Their games are broadcast on WPIT-AM (730 on the dial) with likable Chirs Shovlin handling play-by-play. On rare occasions, Fox Sports Net will televise games. Check your local cable television listings to see if your system carries WBGN. If you live in Beaver County, you may be able to pick up the station directly over the air.

University of Pittsburgh

www.pittsburghpanthers.cstv.com

The University of Pittsburgh has fielded a men's basketball team in every season since 1910, a remarkable achievement that has carried through several wars and a variety of other dislocations.

From 2001–2007, the Panthers (under first Ben Howland and then Jamie Dixon) have been one of the most successful programs in major college basketball, winning three straight Big East regular season titles, and the Big East Tournament in 2003. They also have had success in the NCAA Tournament, advancing to three straight "Sweet 16" appearances from 2002–2004. Pitt basketball compiled one of the nation's three best winning percentages (0.846 with an 88-16 record) from 2001 through 2004. Among the highlights: the magical season of 1973–1974, when the upstart Panthers, largely a home-grown squad led by future NBA star Billy Knight, compiled a 25–4 record, losing in the NCAA tournament's Eastern Regional final to eventual champion North Carolina State.

Coach Jamie Dixon and his Panthers compete in the Big East, one of the premier basketball conferences in the nation.

If you follow the Panthers, you'll enjoy such top teams as Georgetown, Villanova, Connecticut, Syracuse, St. John's, and West Virginia—all conference members—as well as an attractive nonconference schedule. Big East teams typically contend for top national honors, and Pitt is more than competitive in the conference, with a 1987–1988 Big East title to its credit. The brand of basketball you'll see is both fast-paced and physical.

If you're a fan of college basketball, you'll want to catch the Panthers in person in their new arena, the Petersen Events Center, located on the school's upper campus. The "Pete" provides a state-of-the-art 12,500-seat venue "that promises to be one of the finest college basketball arenas in the country."

When you can't make it to the "Pete," you can follow the Panthers on Fox Sports 970-AM, which carries the complete Panthers schedule. There is no set television schedule, but local stations and cable and broadcast networks find Pittsburgh and the Big East so attractive that they combine to show about a dozen games each season. The ticket policy requires a bit of explanation. When Pittsburgh joined the Big East in 1982, interest in the team skyrocketed, and a seat at a conference game became one of the tougher tickets in town. Day-of-game tickets typically are available for nonconference opponents but may be scarce for Big East foes. Tickets for field-house games are typically less expensive than games at the Mellon Arena, and games against West Virginia and Syracuse usually carry a premium. Single game tickets can usually be had for $20 or less. You can make credit-card purchases over the phone at (800) 643-PITT (7488), and you can access the ticket hotline at (412) 648-PITT (7488).

Season tickets are another matter. These are available at prices ranging from $210 to $310, but you must make a contribution of at least $1,000 to the school to be eligible for season tickets.

The university maintains several parking lots on its upper campus to accommodate fans, but if the truth be told, parking on the upper campus can be a crunch. A good way to beat that crunch: Park on the lower campus, which offers more on-street parking, and ride the campus shuttle bus to the Field House.

FOOTBALL
Pittsburgh Steelers

www.steelers.com

The romance between the Pittsburgh Steelers and their adoring fans is one of the enduring love affairs of sports. The team was founded in 1933 by the late Arthur J. Rooney, one of the grand old men of the National Football League and one of the game's great sportsmen. He launched the Steelers with money won at the race track, and he remained a sharp and successful handicapper until his death. Success couldn't spoil Rooney. He never moved from his house near Three Rivers Stadium, walked to work each day, gave generously to anyone in need, and "loafed," to use the expression he favored, with the friends he had grown up with.

Rooney was beloved, but the Steelers had a hard time winning until the 1970s, when the team under Coach Chuck Noll won four Super Bowls and became a dynasty. Nine Steelers from that era—including Rooney, Noll, Joe Greene, Jack Ham, Mel Blount, Terry Bradshaw, Franco Harris, Jack Ham, and Mike Webster—have been enshrined in the Pro Football Hall of Fame.

Rooney and Noll are gone, but the Steelers success continues under club President Daniel M. Rooney, Arthur Rooney's son, and former Coach Bill Cowher, who led the Steelers to postseason appearances in each of his first six years at the helm, an unprecedented coaching performance. Cowher left the team, after 15 years at the helm of the franchise. The Steelers then hired former Minnesota Vikings defensive coordinator Mike Tomlin as Cowher's replacement.

Steelers fans show their support in a big way. Every Steelers home game since mid-1972 has sold out the 58,729-seat Three Rivers Stadium. The waiting list for season

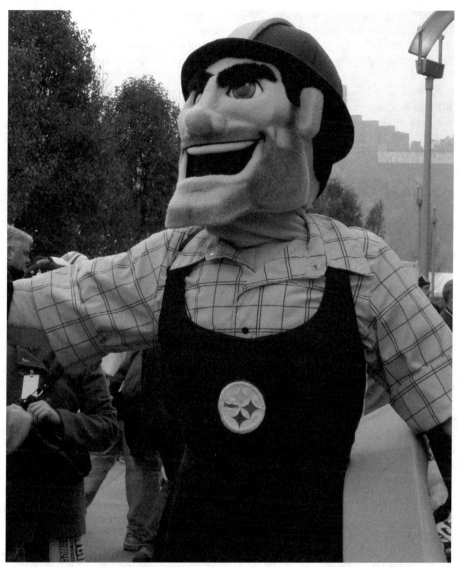

Steely McBeam, the Steelers' mascot. ALAN AND BARBARA VENTO

tickets is 6,000 names long. Like the Pirates, the Steelers have left Three Rivers Stadium. See this chapter's sidebar for details on the Steelers' new stadium.

Because the games are sold out well in advance, the Steelers are able to televise every contest, home or away, preseason, reg-ular season, or postseason. During the regular season, one of the local network affiliates will play the games depending on the day and opponent. Since area cable television systems assign these networks different channel numbers, make sure you check local listings to determine where to catch the Steelers.

ℹ️ A good place to see the Steelers in person is at their summer-training site—St. Vincent College in Latrobe, about 40 miles east of downtown Pittsburgh.

Steelers radio broadcasts on WDVE-FM (102.5 on the dial) and WBGG-AM (920 on the dial). For the 14th straight season, Bill Hillgrove capably handles the play-by-play. Until his death in early 2008, Myron Cope excited the crowds with his colorful analysis and catch phrases like "Yoi!" and "Okel dokel."

Since home games are always sold out, traffic and parking can be troublesome. Most Steelers fans are veterans and know the parking rope. If you do manage to come by tickets for a game, make sure you leave home early enough for the obligatory tailgate party. Before Steelers games, the parking lots around the stadium resemble sprawling picnic grounds, with parties ranging from elaborate catered affairs to simple munchfests with center-cut jumbo. What's center-cut jumbo? It's a 'Burgh thing. You'll catch on.

University of Pittsburgh

What do Mike Ditka, Tony Dorsett, and Dan Marino have in common? They all are National Football League greats, and they all played collegiate football at the University of Pittsburgh. The Panthers long have been a major college football power, producing such standouts as Joe Schmidt, Hugh Green, Matt Cavanaugh, Bill Fralic, Bill Maas, and Craig "Ironhead" Hayward, in addition to Ditka, Dorsett, and Marino. In all, 46 Panthers have won All-America honors, ranking Pittsburgh No. 6 among all NCAA Division I-A schools.

Pittsburgh plays in the Big East conference, which means that when Coach Dave Wannstedt and company take the field, they line up against such name opponents as Syracuse and West Virginia, as well as tough non-conference opponents. Pittsburgh won a national championship behind Dorsett in 1976—its third unanimous national title—and has appeared in 19 bowl games.

The Panthers play at the new football stadium. For three-quarters of a century, the team played at venerable Pitt Stadium on campus, an antiquated facility that was razed to make room for a new convocation center.

Saturday at the stadium on a glorious fall day is a memorable event, and typically an accessible one. While games with such traditional rivals as Penn State, Notre Dame, and West Virginia can sell out, tickets tend to be available for most games. Ticket prices are $25, with youth discounts offered. For "backyard brawls" against West Virginia and Penn State, ticket prices are higher. You also can purchase season tickets and multigame packages. You can get your tickets by calling (800) 643-PITT (7488) and using your credit card. For the status of seats for any game, call the ticket hotline at (412) 648–PITT (7488).

HORSE RACING
Ladbroke at the Meadows

If you've ever thrilled to the beauty of equine athletes as they thunder toward the finish line, then Ladbroke at the Meadows is the place where you'll find that thrill. Located in the Washington County town of Meadow Lands, about 25 miles from downtown Pittsburgh, Ladbroke features live harness racing—the type where the horses pull a sulky with a driver in it—five nights a week during warm-weather months, four nights a week during the winter. The races begin at 6:40 p.m. every Tuesday, Thursday, and Saturday; 4:00 p.m. Friday.

When you come to enjoy the races, you'll find much to do. Ladbroke features a full-service restaurant, a sports bar, and a cafe for lighter fare. The kids will enjoy Ladbroke's pinball arcade.

But for the dedicated horseplayer, the real attraction of Ladbroke is the amazing menu of simulcast races that the track offers. The concept is simple. To enhance its own card, Ladbroke imports races from up to 25 harness and thoroughbred tracks across North America—there's even thoroughbred racing from Australia—and shows them to patrons at monitors placed throughout the facility. You can wager on any or all races at any of the tracks featured. The action typically begins just after noon and usually lasts until about midnight, seven days a week.

That's not all. Ladbroke offers that full racing menu at six wagering and dining facilities in the area. Thus, if you can't make it to the Washington County track, you can visit a Ladbroke facility in Greensburg, New Castle, Harmar, Moon, West Mifflin, or Johnstown and take advantage of the same viewing, wagering, and dining options that patrons at the track are enjoying.

Ladbroke heightens convenience even more by broadcasting its live races—as well as about 100 simulcast races from other tracks—into viewers' homes over satellite and via affiliation with local cable television companies. If your cable company features the Ladbroke Racing Network, or if you acquire the appropriate satellite signal decoder, you'll receive 12 hours of racing each day in the comfort of your home. Plus you can wager by phone by opening a Call-A-Bet account with a cash, check, or credit-card deposit. To do so, call (800) 242-RACE (7223). Ladbroke won't let you bet more than you have in your account, although you can replenish your account at will. If you plan to participate from your home, you can pick up race programs at dozens of neighborhood newsstands and convenience stores.

Finally, the track offers aficionados a high-tech enhancement. If you visit the Web site brisnet.com, you can view real-time betting odds at racetracks across the country.

Your experience at Ladbroke can be as simple or as complicated as you like. Some will find a wagering interest—however modest—heightens the enjoyment of the races. For others, the beauty of equine and human athletes in action will be enjoyment enough. Ladbroke also offers group outings that include such features as a race named for your group and a photo of you and your guests in the winner's circle, posed with the winning horse and driver.

When 65,000 people descend on Heinz Field for a Steelers game, you may be looking for a way to avoid traffic and parking hassles. Port Authority of Allegheny County may have that alternative for you. For information about special shuttle buses, call PAT at (412) 442-2000 or go to www.portauthority.org.

ICE HOCKEY

Pittsburgh Penguins

For many years the Pittsburgh Penguins were synonymous with their superstar, Mario Lemieux, arguably the greatest National Hockey League performer of all time. When chronic back problems forced Lemieux's retirement at the end of the 1996–1997 season, he went out with a flourish, leading the league in scoring for the sixth time and winning First All-Star Team honors for the fifth time. Most important to Penguins fans, he led the club to two Stanley Cups in 1991 and 1992. After retirement, Mario bought the team, ensuring the future of hockey in Pittsburgh.

Yet even during the apex of Lemieux's career, the Penguins were much more than a one-man team. In their Stanley Cup seasons, they played championship-caliber hockey during Lemieux's prolonged injury-related absences. In the P.M. (Post-Mario) era, led by such stars as Jaromir Jagr, they continue to excel as one of the NHL's top clubs.

The Penguins under Coach Michel Therrien perform in the Northeast Division of the Eastern Conference. That means they skate against Buffalo, Montreal, Ottawa, and Boston on a regular basis. If the regular season isn't enough hockey for you, you also can catch the Penguins in training; their preseason drills are public and take place at the Iceoplex at Southpointe in Washington County.

Home ice for the Pens is the Mellon Arena, but you won't want to call it that. To local fans, it's "the Igloo." The arena in downtown Pittsburgh seats 16,958 for hockey and features the world's largest retractable stainless-steel roof. Chances are you won't get to see the roof in action during hockey season.

Stadium Stats!

Quick—name the third professional franchise to call Pittsburgh's former Three Rivers Stadium home. Steelers, Pirates, and—no shame in forgetting—the hapless Maulers of the defunct United States Football League. Hardly a highlight, they went 3–15 in their only season (1984). Blame it on the team's purple-and-orange color scheme.

Games in the town are played in black and gold and, until its implosion on February 11, 2001, on the Tartan then Astro turf at Three Rivers Stadium. For 30 years, this gargantuan yet aesthetically mundane concrete structure hosted some of Pittsburgh's most memorable sports moments, including perhaps the premier call in NFL history—Franco Harris's 1972 "Immaculate Reception."

Three Rivers also saw Roberto Clemente's 3,000th hit; the first World Series night game; four Super Bowl Championship teams; two World Series champions; and for diehard facility fans, the largest crowd ever to see a concert in Pittsburgh—nearly 66,000 for Bruce Springsteen in 1985. But that was then. It took just 19 seconds that February morning for 4,800 pounds of dynamite to put the stadium on the disabled list forever...and usher in Pittsburgh's next generation of hallowed sports ground: PNC Park and Heinz Field.

PNC Park
115 Federal Street on Pittsburgh's North Shore
Tickets: (800) 289-2827; $9 to $185
The Pirates have had five residences in their 116-year history, including the newest domain, PNC Park, which opened April 9, 2001. Ironically, it seats just over 38,000, roughly 3,300 more than Forbes Field, where the "Bucs" played before Three Rivers. Named for the financial institution founded and headquartered here, the park sports an old-time feel whose design intimacy—at the highest point, fans are only 88 feet above the field—contrasts artfully with the scenic view of the city's skyline to create one majestic background for America's pastime.

Add in a riverside location, classic archways, the silkiness of a natural grass surface, an architecture that seems to naturally place it within the cityscape, and the nostalgia permeates like warm apple pie with each crack of the bat. Other features include an outfield picnic area and party pavilion, an outdoor amphitheater, an arcade with a restaurant, an interactive theater and Pirates Hall of Fame, and a 500-person party deck in left field.

In *USA Today* (March 3, 2003), Jay Ahuja, author of *Fields of Dreams: A Guide to Visiting and Enjoying All 30 Major League Ballparks* (Kensington Books), cites PNC Park as one of the top 10 places to watch a game. The charm resonates from the structure right out to the retail and restaurant rows along Federal and General Robinson Streets on the North Side, just across the bridge from the stadium. Parking is fairly plentiful around the facility, but

Clemente Bridge from the stands in PNC Park. ALAN AND BARBARA VENTO

there's added convenience in leaving the car downtown and taking the five-minute walk across the Roberto Clemente Bridge, which closes to vehicle traffic during events. Or access the $216 million park by river walk or boat. For $10 round-trip, the Gateway Clipper Fleet at Station Square will shuttle you back and forth every 15 to 30 minutes starting two hours before the game until a half hour after it ends.

Heinz Field
400 Art Rooney Avenue on Pittsburgh's North Shore
Tickets: (412) 323-1200 for the Steelers;
(800) 643-PITT (7488) for the Panthers
The Ketchup Bowl? For the first NFL stadium named for a global food company, such a game may not be far behind. Welcome to Heinz Field, home of the NFL Pittsburgh Steelers and the University of Pittsburgh Panthers, located about a kickoff return from PNC Park. The world's condiments king, Pittsburgh's H.J. Heinz Company, is pouring out a cool $2.85 million per year for 20-year naming rights to the facility, which features two 35-foot-tall, 8,000-pound neon, animated ketchup bottles attached to the scoreboard. They dump their virtual contents when the home team reaches the "Red Zone" (20 yards from the end zone).

Like its baseball counterpart, Heinz Field combines two-tiered construction, real grass surface, terrific sight lines, and a horseshoe shape with the

continued

Heinz Field. ALAN AND BARBARA VENTO

open end offering a dramatic downtown view of city highlights such as Point State Park, PPG Place, Fort Pitt Bridge, and Duquesne Incline. The stadium seats close to 65,000 people, about 6,000 more than Three Rivers, but getting a season ticket may be tougher than tackling a 300-pound lineman—the waiting list is 10 years. At Gate B, step inside the Coca-Cola Great Hall, a 4,000-square-foot area of fun, food, and football entertainment—and a celebration of Panthers and Steelers history. Savory concessions include hometown favorites such as Benkovitz Fish and the legendary Primanti Brothers, offering their sandwiches with the fries inside. Six interactive displays offer trivia and games and also showcase team memorabilia. Marvel at the Lombardi Trophy columns commemorating the Steelers' five Super Bowl victories. A Steelers Hall of Fame showcases memorabilia from star players.

—Michael J. Dongilli

One of the best features about the Igloo is its accessibility. Many Port Authority of Allegheny County bus routes end in, or depart from, downtown, making it easy to reach or leave the arena by public transportation. If you drive you'll find parking in both the arena lots and in several nearby indoor garages, but parking can get sticky when crowds are large.

Another good idea—get your tickets in advance. Tickets are accessible for many games, but fans turn out in big numbers for the best teams and for contests they consider important. The Pens offer season and partial-season plans as well as discounted group packages. For ticket information, call (412) 642-PENS (7367).

If you can't make it to the Igloo, it's still easy to follow the Pens. WXDX-FM (105.9 on the dial) serves as the flagship radio station for the Penguins. On the television side, Penguins games are broadcast on Fox Sports Net Pittsburgh, Versus, NBC, and TSN.

(Note: A new arena is being planned to replace the Igloo. Expected to be open for the 2010-11 NHL Season, the arena is expected to have a capacity of about 18,500 people.)

The Penguins maintain a close relationship with their fans through an active community involvement program. Their initiatives include school visits, scholarships, development of youth hockey, and financial support for nonprofit organizations. Perhaps the most innovative aspect of the program is the Penguins Information Booth at the arena, which nonprofit organizations can use on game days to distribute information to fans. For information about the booth, call (412) 642-1800.

DAY TRIPS AND WEEKEND GETAWAYS

We frankly believe that there's so much to see and do in and around Pittsburgh that you'd never need to leave! But for those of you stricken with a case of wanderlust, or just itching to get out in the country, we present a number of destinations for your consideration within a half-day's drive (at most) of the city.

Whether you venture just 30 minutes from your home base, take to the highway for a leisurely drive, or even opt for the express airline service offered locally, there are plenty of fascinating escapes just hours from Pittsburgh.

Some of these lend themselves to the affordable family getaway. Others might have the word "golf" written all over them (for more focus on that subject, turn to the Golf chapter in this book). Educational exploration is certainly prevalent in the area. So is boosting the economy of several sites in Western Pennsylvania. Finally, a few of the destinations you might consider remind us of romance—dare we say, even reminiscent of the second honeymoon you've put off. Well, now is the time to take it!

The day excursions and weekend trips presented in this chapter fall within approximately three hours of Pittsburgh. From the western communities, count on some extra time when traveling east, and vice versa. The only other caveat is to let go, relax, and enjoy yourself exploring new sights, loading your car with new wares, and sampling fine food, entertainment, and hospitality.

Bon voyage!

ERIE COUNTY

Find out why areas north are Erie-sistible. Roughly three hours from Pittsburgh, Erie County offers something for every member of the family, from amusement parks and water recreation to arts, museums, and fun shopping.

Getting There

Reach the Erie area by taking Interstate 79 north from Pittsburgh. It's a straight shot up one single highway! Once in the area, the 36-passenger *Presque Isle Express* will taxi you across the water from Dobbins Landing to Presque Isle (which isn't really an island but a nice park with a beach). Weather permitting, the water taxi operates seven days a week from 10:00 a.m. until 6:00 p.m. It's wheelchair and bicycle accessible and maintains a 60-minute schedule.

Erie County Attractions

As you might have guessed from the name, Erie County borders Lake Erie, one of the five Great Lakes, and the lake is an integral piece of life here. You'll want to explore the waters of Lake Erie, and what better way to do it than at the Erie Maritime Museum, 150 East Front Street, (814) 452-2744, on the bayfront.

At the Erie Zoo & Botanical Gardens, 423 West 38th Street, (814) 864-4091, kids can visit 300 animals exhibited indoors and out. Especially enticing are the dual-level otter exhibit, the white Bengal tiger, and the African wild-bird exhibit. Sightseeing train rides are also popular.

Summer is always fun at Waldameer Park and Water World, located at the entrance to Presque Isle State Park, where you'll experience more than 75 rides, slides, and attractions. There are fun games, great gift houses, snacks, and food to help pass the time. Call (814) 838-7435 or visit www.waldameer.com

for details. In the winter months, Splash Lagoon's indoor water park is a favorite with nine twisting water slides and a 1,000-gallon Tipping Bucket. Call (866) 3- SPLASH or visit www.splashlagoon.com. Conneaut Lake Park, 12832 Center Street, Conneaut Lake (25 miles southwest of Erie), (814) 382-5115, also boasts rides, festivals, and family fun.

Presque Isle State Park, (814) 883-7424, www.presqueisle.org, has been rated by *Birder's World* magazine as one of the top birding spots in the country. In addition, you'll find approximately 13 miles of hiking trails in the park (bicycles are not permitted on the hiking trails). A good place to begin your visit is at the Stull Interpretive Center, located near Barracks Beach. Here you'll learn about the park's many resources, including its access for people with disabilities. There's no charge to enter the park. Water sports abound in Erie. Motor boats, paddle boats, jet skis, water skis, canoes, and kayaks can be rented through Port Erie Sports, 402 West Bayfront Parkway, (814) 452-BOAT (2628). They also offer bikes and fishing gear for rent.

The Presque Isle Lighthouse, in the park, was built in 1872 and first lit on July 12, 1873. The U.S. Coast Guard still maintains it with its flashing white light. Visitors aren't allowed inside the lighthouse. At Misery Bay and the Perry Monument, you'll find the temporary home of the fleet of ships commanded by Commodore Oliver Hazard Perry in the Battle of Lake Erie. Six of his nine vessels, including two brigs—the *Niagara* and the *Lawrence*—were constructed from local trees along Erie Bay. It was his victory and the War of 1812 that assured we didn't become Canadians!

The Lake Shore Railway Museum, 31 Wall Street at Robinson Street, (814) 825-2724, welcomes visitors Wednesday through Sunday from Memorial Day weekend through Labor Day weekend, in addition to Saturday and Sunday in May, September, and October. Admission is free of charge to relive the days of the steam locomotive-powered trains that ran along Pennsylvania's picturesque North East countryside. Walk through a 1926 "Night-

For a complete listing of attractions, accommodations and events, call VisitErie, (800) 524-ERIE (3743), the area's local travel bureau.

star" sleeping car built by Pullman and see the Centralized Traffic Control board, built in 1943, showing how a single dispatcher controlled large stretches of track at one time.

Presque Isle Downs Casino & Racetrack provides an evening of entertainment. Opened in 2007, The Downs offers 2000 slot machines and 170 flat-screen plasma TVs for simulcasting racing, Live thoroughbred racing is also planned. Open daily. Call (866) ERIE-FUN (374-3386 or visit www.presqueisle downs.com for details.

A day trip for the grown-ups wouldn't be complete without a sampling of Pennsylvania wine. Stop at the Penn Shore Winery, 10225 East Lake Road, Route 5, North East, (814) 725-8688—one of the largest and longest established wineries in the state. Mazza Vineyards, 11815 East Lake Road, North East, (814) 725-8695 or (800) 796-9463, offers wine-tasting tours daily, seven days a week, year-round.

Erie County Shopping

Are you in the mood for souvenirs? The Nature Shop, at Presque Isle State Park (see write-up above), has books, field guides, and other nature-related items for you to purchase and enjoy from your day trip. Proceeds benefit the state park. Also, Penn Shore Winery (see above) can ship its vintage, table, and sparkling wines in Pennsylvania via United Parcel Service (UPS), if you don't want to carry the bottles home with you.

Each season the Mason Farms Country Market, 839 Peninsula Drive, (814) 833-9933, brings exciting treats and experiences to store customers. Choose from a large selection of perennials, annuals, and shrubs in spring; fresh fruit and vegetables over the summer months; pumpkins around Halloween; and country crafts for Christmas.

The Bayfront Gallery, part of the waterfront revitalization, is Erie's artists' co-op located at 17 East Dobbins Landing, (814) 455-6632. It's open seasonally for its unique blend of antique wares and local artistry.

Customary shopping at chain establishments and some local merchants is found at the Millcreek Mall, Peach Street and Interchange Roads, (814) 868-9000, www.millcreekmall.net. Boasting a Macy's, Elder-Beerman, JC Penney, Sears, and more than 200 specialty shops, it's no wonder you could spend the entire day shopping. In fact, the entire Summit Township area has been peppered with more stores and restaurants (see below).

Erie County Accommodations

Independently owned, the Downtown Erie Hotel, 18 West 18th Street, (814) 456-2961, features 141 rooms, an outdoor pool, laundry facilities, and a continental breakfast.

The Bel-Aire Clarion Hotel & Conference Center, 2800 West Eighth Street, (814) 833-1116, www.clarionhotel-erie.com, has an indoor heated pool, Jacuzzi, and fitness center for its guests, as well as restaurants and room service. The Hampton Inn Erie-South, 8050 Old Oliver Road, (814) 866-6800, www.hamptoninn.com, has a heated indoor pool, complimentary hot breakfast, a free movie channel, and free high-speed Internet access. The hotel is accessible to Interstate 90 and nearby I-79. Avalon Hotel & Conference Center, 16 West 10th Street, (814) 459-2220, www.avalonerle.com, is in the heart of downtown Erie, near the Erie Art Museum and the Erie Playhouse. And, for business travel, the Courtyard by Marriott, 7792 Peach Street, at I-90, exit 6 (Scott Drive), www.scottenterprises.org, boasts a full-service hotel with 110 guest rooms, an indoor pool, and several suites. Or consider staying in one of the area's dozen bed and breakfasts. A listing can be found at www.visiterirepa.com.

Families might prefer renting a cottage near Presque Isle State Park. The Cottages at Presque Isle, 320 Peninsula Drive, (814) 833-4956, offers one-, two-, or three-bedroom individual and deluxe cottages, all with kitchenettes, carpeting, private baths, and porches, and some with living rooms as well as decks. There's even a central playground for the kids. Camping is also available at a number of sites in the area, including Lampe Marina Campground, located at the foot of Port Access Road, (814) 454-5830, www.porterie.org/camping, where you will find 42 waterfront campsites along Lampe Marina.

Erie County Restaurants

Oh, the waters—and what better way to experience the wonder of Lake Erie than on a dinner cruise aboard the *Victorian Princess*. Leisurely dinner sailings are offered in Victorian style from April 1 through November 1. Cost is $29.95 per person for dinner cruises. Group and children's rates are also available. For reservations, call ahead at (814) 459-9696. Dinner (as well as sightseeing only) cruises board at Dobbins Landing.

You can sample various cuisines at area restaurants. Hibachi Japanese Steak & Sea House, 3000 West 12th Street, (814) 838-6718, features food as the name implies. As we mentioned in the shopping description, restaurants have been part of the Upper Peach Street expansion, adding chains such as, Applebee's, Eat'n Park, TGI Friday's, and Quaker Steak & Lube (read a description in Lawrence and Mercer Counties, below). Pufferbelly Restaurant, 414 French Street, (814) 454-1557, operates out of an old Erie firehouse while The Brewerie at Union Station, (814) 454-2200, can be found in an renovated train station.

Dock your boats near Dobbins Landing for a casual dinner at Rum Runners, (814) 455-4292, or sit on the veranda at Smuggler's Wharf, 3 State Street, (814) 459-4273, www.smugglerswharfinc.com. There's also the Waterfront Seafood & Steakhouse, (814) 456-8642, with seating on three decks.

LAWRENCE AND MERCER COUNTIES

What you know of Lawrence and Mercer Counties may be through your children—each fall, another mass exodus begins for families with college students attending Westminster, Grove City, and Thiel Colleges; the Penn State Shenango campus; and nearby Slippery Rock University. Perhaps you've noticed the beauty of the farm fields on your trips here, but never stopped to truly enjoy the countryside. Maybe you've visited a shop or two, but you haven't taken the time to explore the hidden treasures off the beaten path.

For more information on traipsing through Lawrence and Mercer Counties, call the Lawrence County Tourist Promotion Agency at (888) 284-7599, or the Mercer County Tourist Agency at (800) 637-2370.

Getting There

From Pittsburgh you can reach these counties by driving north on I-79, U.S. Route 19, or Route 60, if you're starting out from Pittsburgh's west suburbs. Route 208 runs between the towns of New Wilmington and Grove City, crossing over I-79.

Mercer and Lawrence County Attractions

If you thought Tara was found only in the South, guess again. Tours of Tara—A Country Inn, nestled in the little village of Clark, outside Sharon, are popular for day-trippers. Visitors peruse the antique furniture, books, and an original jacket worn by Vivian Leigh's Scarlet O'Hara in *Gone with the Wind*. There's an antique slave cradle and many other rare finds. The custom-made glass doors in the entry hall, handcrafted and beveled by Bob Lutz & Sons of New Castle, most definitely add to the elegance of the mansion (see more about Tara on following pages).

If you're like most visitors, you'll want to allow time to explore the Wendell August Forge, 620 Madison Avenue, Grove City, established in 1923 in Brockway before moving in

1932 to its current location. You can't miss the signs, well placed along the major routes into town. Free tours are available, but to make sure the forge is open when you want to visit, it's best to call (724) 458-8360 or (800) 923-4438 or visit www.wendallaugust.com.

The forge is one of the few remaining in the country that continue to produce forged aluminum, pewter, bronze, sterling silver articles entirely by hand, using no production machinery. The showroom/museum houses a historical collection of artifacts and a complete line of giftware that has been commissioned by corporate executives, leading companies, even the U.S. Congress. Visitors get to see the artisans hammering and chiseling these art forms when they take the free, self-guided tour.

Mercer and Lawrence County Shopping

Adventurous shoppers seeking the best prices will track down the authentic Amish shops that make a trip north fun in itself. Visitors can ponder a selection of quilt supplies and fabrics, baby and children's shoes, and have also been known to drive to the Amish harness shops for their custom-made saddles and leather goods. If you get lost, ask the locals to head you on your way to your next stop, since many of these are tucked off on back roads in private homes, without noticeable signage to guide you. (See the Amish Close-up in this chapter.)

Market Street in New Wilmington is the center of retail activity with crafts, antiques, and gift merchandise. The Silk Road Fair Trade Market, 115 North Main Street, offers products from around the world.

If you take I-79 and Route 208 to New Wilmington, you'll drive through Volant, a unique village of quaint shops and restaurants, where you can't miss Volant Mills, a major tourist stop featuring Amish goods and furniture. Built in 1812, it operated as a gristmill and flour mill until 1963. Today it sits across the street from the min of refurbished train shops.

Downtown Sharon, sometimes referred to as the world's largest small town, is full of shopping. It's known for the Winner, 32 West State Street, which owners Jim and Donna Winner proclaim to be the world's largest off-price fashion store; Reyers, Sharon City Centre, (800) 245-1550, which locals say is the world's largest shoe store, claiming to stock every size; Daffin's Candies, 496 East State Street, (724) 342-7502, where candy making is an art; and Kraynak's, 2525 East State Street, (724) 347-4511,with special Christmas and Easter displays. For more traditional types of chain stores, head to the Shenango Valley Mall located at 3303 East State Street. Anchor stores include Macy's, JCPenney, and Sears.

Of course, if you want to shop until you are absolutely exhausted or spent (literally!), then head to the Prime Outlets along I-79 and Route 208. Here you'll find every type of store you could possibly imagine, and prices that sometimes can't be beat. (See the Shopping chapter for more details.)

Mercer and Lawrence County Accommodations

With so much to see, you're most likely looking for a place to rest your weary feet. Sprawling development has brought along with it a choice of popular chain motels and hotels, usually clustered off Interstates 79 and 80. But don't overlook the small and elegant, the rural and charming. Several bed-and-breakfast establishments have thrived, offer a delightful alternative for guests.

At the most elegant end of the spectrum is Tara—A Country Inn, at 2844 Lake Road, Clark, (724) 962-3535 or (800) 782-2803, www.tara-inn.com. A home whose refurbishing was inspired by the movie *Gone with the Wind,* Tara is a graceful 1854 antebellum home—the embodiment of the Old South. Purchased in 1984 by innkeepers Jim and Donna Winner, it's a frequent stop for travelers who want to tour the grounds and mansion or dine in one of three restaurants.

Visiting Tara isn't just a culinary experience, or tourist stop to tour. There's a little history lesson as well, as your guide tells you about the property, including the formal gardens overlooking the beautiful 450-acre Shenango Lake. No tour is complete without walking through the mansion—a virtual museum of rare and priceless antiques, works of art, and collectibles, many of which the owners purchased on trips abroad.

Each room is decorated differently—many with canopy beds, crystal lamps, marble fireplaces, and sunken whirlpool baths. Guests enjoy swimming in the indoor spa, sipping afternoon tea on the sunporch, or curling up with a favorite book or videotape checked out of the library.

The Winners own not only Tara but also the Buhl Mansion in Sharon, Mercer County. An art gallery, guesthouse, and spa, this home was built in 1890; it's listed on the National Register of Historical Places. The grand oak staircase ascends to the second and third floors. Each suite has a gas fireplace and luxurious bath. For reservations, call (724) 962-3535 or (800) 782-2803.

In recent years, several chain hotels have established themselves, due in large part to the tourist attractions and the outlet shopping. Spend the night in West Middlesex at the Radisson Hotel Sharon, off I-80, on Route 18, (724) 528-2501, and relax in the heated indoor pool. Right across the street is the Holiday Inn Express and Suites of Sharon/Hermitage, 3060 Spangler Road, (724) 982-4600, with its golf packages and outdoor pool facility. The Comfort Inn Shenango Valley, 2700 Wilson Road, Hermitage, (724) 342-7200, has an indoor heated pool, whirlpool suites, and complimentary breakfasts available.

The Howard Johnson Inn, 835 Perry Highway (US 19) in Mercer, (800) 542-7674, is just 10 minutes from the outlet shops. In Grove City itself, choose from bed-and-breakfasts such as Terra Nova House, (724) 450-0712, at 322 West Poplar Street, or the Snow Goose Inn, (724) 458–4644, at 112 East Main Street. The Snow Goose is across the street from Grove City College.

Within New Wilmington, charming bed-and-breakfasts abound as well. Consider the Beechwood Inn, an old Civil War home with Victorian decor, found on the road by the same name (175 Beechwood Road to be exact). When your day is complete, sit on one of three covered porches at this inn. Call Beechwood at (724) 946-2342. Or, contact The Veazey House Bed and Breakfast, 188 Beechwood Road, (724) 946-2918, another inn located nearby.

Mercer and Lawrence County Restaurants

At Tara, guests can enjoy Ashley's for gourmet dining and Stonewall's Tavern for lighter fare, including great steaks and salads. Ashley's menu features wine selections honored by the coveted *Wine Spectator* Award of Excellence. Call for reservations at (724) 962-3535.

Quaker Steak & Lube, a popular watering hole famous for its atomic wings and unusual display of race cars and auto memorabilia, is located in the heart of downtown Sharon, 101 Chestnut Street, (724) 981-3121, as well as in Hermitage, on East State Street, (724) 983-8646. Locals call it "the Lube."

Likewise, the Iron Bridge Inn, 1438 Perry Highway, (724) 748-3626, is popular for its good food and rustic charm. Despite the name, there's no lodging here, just a restaurant that bills itself as "food merchants and brewmasters." Conveniently located on US 19 between Westminster and Grove City, it attracts tourists by day, college crowds by night. Also along US 19 is Rachel's Roadhouse, 1253 Perry Highway, (724) 748-3193, a sister restaurant literally just down the road, between the Iron Bridge and Route 208.

Longtime area visitors still enjoy pleasant meals at The Tavern on the Square in New Wilmington, (724) 946-2020, or step back in time by visiting the Mercer Mercantile & Soda Shoppe, 108 North Pitt Street, (724) 662-2231, where you will find original tin ceilings, an antique Coke machine, a "juke" box playing "45s" from the 1940s to the 1970s. While there enjoy a malted milkshake, "flavored Cokes," chili dogs, and penny novelty candy.

LAUREL HIGHLANDS

This scenic expanse in Southwestern Pennsylvania encompasses a broad stretch of more than 100 miles throughout several counties to the south and east of Pittsburgh. With the region named in deference to the mountain laurel, you could be in the Laurel Highlands if you're in Greene, Fayette, Somerset, or Westmoreland County. Since this last county is a part of this book's general coverage area, we'll cover only the highlights here. Indeed, exploring the Laurel Highlands for a day, or perhaps several, is a pleasant option.

The Laurel Highlands is a vast area for day-trippers, but if you need assistance, write the Laurel Highlands Visitors Bureau at 120 East Main Street, Ligonier, PA 15658, or call (724) 238-5661.

Getting There

There are several routes to take to the Laurel Highlands, depending upon where you depart and which area you'd like to visit. The Pennsylvania Turnpike is popular, with exits at Donegal, Somerset, and New Stanton. Traveling along U.S. Route 30 or U.S. Route 40 (the former National Road) in Fayette County will also take you to many of the sites described here.

Laurel Highlands Attractions

Fallingwater, in Mill Run, (724) 329-8501, www.paconserve.org, was once the weekend retreat of department store owner Edgar J. Kaufmann and his wife, Liliane. Tucked away in the Laurel Highlands, architect Frank Lloyd Wright designed this outstanding example of organic architecture. Though there is much walking and many stairs to climb, the curious love to tour Fallingwater. Similarly, Kentuck Knob, located at Chalk Hill, Ohiopyle, (724) 329-1901, www.kentuckknob.com, is another of Frank Lloyd Wright's creations, though less popular than Fallingwater. Regular tours of Fallingwater are available (see the Architecture and Attrac-

Close-up

New Wilmington's Old Order Amish

Beyond the bonnets and wide-brimmed hats, the plain white farmhouses, and the strict code of conduct, the Old Order Amish thrive in the New Wilmington area, approximately one hour north of Pittsburgh. Visitors come to browse in the craft shops, ponder a carpenter's handiwork, or merely enjoy the drive through farm pastures and life at its simplest.

While there are many retailers displaying Amish-made goods, adventurous shoppers seek out their own best buys directly from these creators of country quilts; custom-made leather saddles; and solid wood rockers, cradles, toys, or complete dining and bedroom sets. In warmer weather you'll spot Amish women selling homemade baked goods at roadside stands.

For the Amish, their cottage industries are just that. Many make their living from the bounty of the land or the skill of their hands, using diesel power (with car batteries to start their equipment) instead of electricity and horse-drawn buggies and farm equipment rather than cars and tractors. The average family boasts 8 to 10 children, and hard work is a way of life.

Amish education takes place in a one-room schoolhouse where children learn reading, writing, and arithmetic. Religion is taught in the home, not in churches, as small groups gather in homes one Sunday and visit other Amish the next.

Baptism is saved for adulthood, not undertaken at birth. So vital is this passage that teenagers yearn to experience the English world, as they call it, before the commitment is made. Finding young people to hang around with is hardly a problem here, as New Wilmington is also home to Westminster College, a four-year liberal arts college related to the Presbyterian Church.

As you drive along Route 18 (north from New Castle or south from Sharon), you'll spot Amish homes and farms by the tell-tale white sheets tied back as curtains in the windows. New Wilmington's Amish are entrepreneurial in spirit, but far less so than their neighbors across the state. There are signs, but they won't knock you over. Most establishments are open year-round except on Sunday and major holidays. Do stop in and chat, but please don't take pictures at close distances. The Amish prefer to live in the world; they just don't like to be of the world. They're a friendly, honest, and hardworking group of people!

tions chapters for details). Reservations are required to guarantee admission.

Travel back to the French and Indian War at Fort Necessity National Battlefield, along US 40, (724) 329-5512, www.nps.gov/fone, in Fayette County just southeast of Uniontown.

This became George Washington's "fort of necessity" because a large force of French and Indians attacked his army of 400.

Ligonier, in the far reaches of Westmoreland County, is a charming town, known for "the Diamond" town square with its old-fashioned gazebo, ice-cream parlor, and antiques and craft shops. But most historic is Fort Ligonier, named in honor of Sir John Ligonier, a British commander-in-chief. In 1946 the Fort Ligonier Association was charged with re-creating the 1758–1766 garrison, and with building a museum. Although never occupied by the enemy, this fort, and its three-day festival every October, commemorates the battle at Fort Ligonier in 1758 during the French and Indian War. Fort Ligonier Days (see Annual Events) features craftspeople, merchant sidewalk sales, entertainment, and a huge Saturday parade. Of course, there's plenty of great food to sample.

Families will love the beautiful setting of Idlewild Park and SoakZone, (724) 238-3666, www.idlewild.com, with its theme areas, especially suited for kids who want to have fun (see Kidstuff). Other areas of noted interest in the Laurel Highlands are Seven Springs Mountain Resort and Hidden Valley Four Season Resort (see "Skiing" in the Recreation chapter). For thrills of another kind, you won't want to miss white-water rafting on the Youghiogheny River at Ohiopyle (see Attractions). In addition, there are miles of excellent bike and walking trails throughout the highlands.

The Laurel Highlands also boasts the largest natural cave north of the Mason-Dixon line. Laurel Caverns, 5 miles west of US 40 on Caverns Road near Uniontown, offers guided and self-guided tours through this limestone catacomb cave with more than 2 miles of passages. Visitors should dress warmly, as the average temperature hovers around 52 degrees Fahrenheit year-round. For information call (724) 438-2070 or (800) 515-4150.

Laurel Highlands Shopping

Outlet shopping in Somerset and Mt. Pleasant is plentiful, but you'll also find many small shops scattered around the Laurel Highlands. Major malls, specialty merchants, and factory outlets are covered in the Shopping chapter; it's best to include this reading in your research.

i If you plan to shop in a traditional Amish establishment, do arrive well before dusk, since there are no electric lights to help you size up the merchandise.

In Fayette County you'll find the Uniontown Mall at 1368 West Main Street, (724) 437-9411, www.shopuniontownmall.com. In Connellsville shop at Youghiogheny Station: Glass & Gallery at 900 West Crawford Avenue, (724) 628-0332, www.youghioghenyglass .com. It's the beautifully refurbished P&LE passenger station just minutes from Fallingwater, Ohiopyle, Nemacolin Woodlands, and Greensburg. The shop offers everything glass, from paperweights to perfume bottles and lamps. Of course the tourist attractions maintain their own gift shops, which you'll want to browse for souvenirs or unique gifts, including Frank Lloyd Wright references and works at Fallingwater.

Laurel Highlands Restaurants

In Somerset the Oakhurst Tea Room, 2409 Glades Pike Road (Route 31), (814) 443-2897, established in 1933, is famous for its smorgasbord and desserts. There's a Friday seafood buffet and Sunday brunch among other items on the menu. Seven Springs Mountain Resort boasts several restaurants, ranging from snacks at the coffee shop to elegant dining at Helen's Slopeslide Dining Room, (800) 452-2223.

Look for the innkeeper's menu selections at the Mountain View Inn, 121 Village Drive, (724) 834-5300. Favorites include salmon Oscar, lobster Delmonico, and scallops of lamb with apple butter. Family-style meals are served on Sunday. There are also health-conscious menu items and early-bird specials.

Vallozzi's, approximately 4 miles east of the U.S. Route 199 junction, on US 30 East near Greensburg, features northern Italian specialties for lunch or dinner. It's closed on major holidays and Sunday. Call for reservations at (724) 836-7663.

Nemacolin Woodlands offers full-service restaurants, as well as casual corners to catch a bite. At Lautrec, the menu is French and on the expensive side, with such appetizers as escargots and entrees such as chateaubriand or roast rack of lamb. For casual dining, try The Tavern, Nemacolin's version of an English style pub or the Hungry Moose Café, the place to stop for a quick bite. Or, try Elements, located at the workout facility, for a fruit-based smoothie, salad, or wrap-style sandwich. (For a much more detailed listing of Nemacolin, see the Accommodations chapter.)

For more casual dining in a relaxed setting, head to the Sun Porch Restaurant along US 40 in the Hopwood Business District, east of Uniontown, (724) 439-5734. River's Edge Café, 203 Yough Street, in Confluence features both indoor and outside dining for lunch and dinner. Call for seasonal operating hours, (814) 395-5059.

Laurel Highlands Accommodations

Because much of the Laurel Highlands exists in and around the Pennsylvania Turnpike and other major highways, accommodations are plentiful. Among the highlights is Mountain View Inn, conveniently located between Greensburg and Latrobe in central Westmoreland County. Guest rooms are all unique, some with king-size beds, whirlpool tubs, and fireplaces. Some have the elegant formality of the 18th century, while others are early American in charm. It's the perfect venue for a romantic weekend. To book a room call (724) 834-5300.

Seven Springs Mountain Resort (see the Accommodations chapter) is certainly an option, as is the Holiday Inn, 202 Harmon Street, Somerset, (814) 445-9611, or the Hampton Inn, at 324 Laurel Crest Road, (814) 445-9161. In addition to the resort and spa setting of Fayette County's Nemacolin Woodlands, you might also be interested in the Summit Inn Resort at the Summit in Farmington (800) 433-8594.

ALTOONA/STATE COLLEGE/JOHNSTOWN AREA

This area around two hours east of Pittsburgh is popular for day trips, especially for Penn State fans venturing in the fall to Nittany Lion football games. While the area is accessible for a day, why not stay the night and make it a weekend?

To obtain a visitor's map or area information, call the Allegheny Mountains Convention and Visitors Bureau at (814) 943-4183 or (800) 842-5866, or visit www.alleghenymountains .com. In State College, the staff of the Central Pennsylvania Convention and Visitors Bureau is available at (800) 358-5466 or www.central pacvb.org. For specific Johnstown information, contact the Greater Johnstown Convention and Visitors Bureau at (800) 237-8590 or www.visitjohnstownpa.com.

Getting There

There are several routes to take to these destinations. If you're headed to Altoona and State College from Pittsburgh, follow U.S. Route 22 east and U.S. Route 200/Interstate 99 north to Altoona and Blair County. Continue on US 220/I-99 and make a right onto Route 322 for your destination of State College.

En route to Johnstown, follow US 22 east and you'll find the signs for Johnstown long before Altoona and State College. You could also reach Johnstown going north on U.S. Route 219 from the Pennsylvania Turnpike.

Altoona/State College/Johnstown Attractions

The Frost Entomological Museum, Headhouse III, (814) 863-2865, www.ento.psu.edu/home /frost/, in State College has more than 500,000 insects and arthropods, all well preserved and labeled for public display. Each October, highlights at the Great Insect Fair include an insect deli, an insect zoo, and Phydeaux's Flying Flea Circus with George. Also in State College, the Matson Museum of Anthropology, in the Carpenter Building, (814) 865-

3853, www.anthro.psu.edu/matson_museum/index.shtml tracks human evolution with a genetics exhibit, artifacts, needlework, and ceramics of far ranging cultures. Pennsylvania's prehistoric treasures are found here as well.

Just minutes from I-80 in Nittany Lion Country is Penn's Cave, Centre Hall, 222 Penns Cave Road, (814) 364-1664, www.pennscave.com, filled with glittering stalactites and stalagmites reminiscent of national tourist attractions. You tour this all-water cavern by boat, learning the legend of Indian princess Nitanee, for whom the Penn State Nittany Lion was named.

Speaking of the Nittany Lion, Penn State's mascot since 1904, stop at the Nittany Lion Shrine near the recreation building, on campus. This landmark was created by Heinz Warneke in 1940 from a 13-ton block of Indiana limestone. During the second week of July each year, plan to browse the Central Pennsylvania Festival of the Arts, (814) 237-3682, www.arts-festival.com.

Altoona's Horseshoe Curve, 1300 Ninth Avenue, (814) 946-0834, www.railroadcity.com, is a historic landmark that tells the story of how railroads were the key in coast-to-coast commerce. The challenge of carrying the Pennsylvania Railroad Mainline over the mountainous terrain was met with the construction of the Horseshoe Curve. You can board a train, say in Pittsburgh, and ride along Lakemont Park & The Island Waterpark, 700 Park Avenue, Altoona, (800) 434-8006, www.lakemontparkfun.com, offers more than 30 rides and attractions, go-karts, miniature golf, and picnic facilities. Or stop by Del-Grosso's Amusement Park, Old Route 220 in Tipton, (814) 684-3538, www.delgrossos.com. Fred DelGrosso (yes, the maker of spaghetti sauce fame) bought the park in 1946. Today, the park offers 30 rides, an extensive waterpark, go-karts, and miniature golf.

To learn the devastation of natural disaster, set out for the Johnstown Flood Museum, 304 Washington Street, Johnstown, (814) 539-1889, www.jaha.org, where state-of-the-art

For a more extensive listing of bed-and-breakfasts throughout the region, write to the Western Pennsylvania Bed & Breakfast Association at 1174 Greenfield Road, Hermitage, PA 16148, or visit their Web site at www.westernpabandb.com. Or, contact the Pennsylvania Mid-State Bed & Breakfast Association at (814) 466-6481 or www.bedandbreakfastpa.com.

exhibits and an Academy Award–winning documentary re-create the powerful force that swept through town in May 1889. The Johnstown Flood National Memorial overlooks the ruins of the South Fork Dam, which burst that May 31. It was indeed one of the worst, if not the worst, flood in American history. The Grandview Cemetery there is where 777 unidentified victims of the flood are buried in the Plot of the Unknown. The museum is open daily 10:00 a.m. to 5:00 p.m. No admission is charged.

The Johnstown Inclined Plane, at Route 56 and Johns Street, (814) 536-1816, was built in 1891 and is one of the steepest vehicular inclines in the world. It is 996 feet long with a 71 percent grade. Witness the spectacular Johnstown view from the observation deck.

Altoona/State College/Johnstown Shopping

In State College, head to the shops downtown. Looking for gifts for the little ones? Stop by the Animal Kingdom, 103 South Allen Street, (814) 237-2402 which claims to be the "huggable heart of the downtown" or the Growing Tree Toys, 202 South Allen Street, (814) 237-3655. Jewelry stores and art supplies, antiques and boutiques—they can all be found downtown.

When you're done, don't forget to visit the Penn State Creamery, 119 Food Science Building, University Park, (814) 865-7535, www.creamery.psu.edu, to sample and take home some of Penn State's famous ice cream. At Mount Nittany Vineyards & Winery, 300

Houser Road, Centre Hall, (814) 466-6373, you can sip and purchase local wine.

There are specialty shops in Historic Hollidaysburg, (814) 696-0544. Or stop by Benzel's Pretzel Bakery Outlet Store, 5200 Sixth Avenue, Altoona, (814) 942-5062, for a variety of pretzels. Boyer Candy Factory Outlet & Emporium, 821 17th Street, (814) 944-9401, contains gift baskets, tins, baking ingredients, and of course lots of candy for those family members with a sweet tooth!

Johnstown offers shoppers the Johnstown Galleria, 500 Galleria Drive, www.johnstown galleria-pa.com, with more than 100 specialty shops. In addition, there is lots of shopping along Johnstown's Scalp Avenue. Twenty minutes south you'll find outlet shopping in Somerset (see the Shopping chapter).

Altoona/State College/Johnstown Accommodations

In State College, many opt for the Nittany Lion Inn, 200 West Park Avenue, (800) 233-7505, www.pshs.psu.edu/NittanyLionInn/nlhome.asp, located near the Nittany Lion Shrine sculpture. Others head to Toftrees Golf Resort and Conference Center, One Country Club Lane, (814) 234–8000 or (800) 252-3551, featuring designer guest rooms, golf villa suites, four-star golf, tennis, and swimming. The Atherton Hotel, 125 South Atherton Street, (814) 231-2100 or (800) 832-0132, is just a block from campus. Located downtown, and also a block away from PSU is the Days Inn Penn State, 240 South Pugh Street, (814) 238-8454, with its heated indoor pool, sauna, tanning beds, free weights, and Nautilus equipment for guests.

If you're looking for a bed-and-breakfast establishment, try Gladwin House B&B, 257 Ridge Avenue, (814) 234-2381 or Home at Town Center, 119 South Barnard Street, (814) 238-8304, in downtown State College. Ten miles away, Reynolds Mansion, 101 West Linn Street, Bellefonte, (800) 899-3929, is Victorian with fireplaces, whirlpool tubs, private baths, and a billiards room.

The Holiday Inn, 250 Market Street, Johnstown, (814) 535-7777, is conveniently located at the intersection of Route 56 and US 219. It's within walking distance of the flood museum and inclined plane, and boasts an indoor pool, hot tub, and exercise room. Just east of US 219, stay at the Comfort Inn & Suites, 455 Theatre Drive, (814) 266-3678. While the indoor heated pool is small, some rooms have microwaves, radios, and refrigerators. Special amenities include the free breakfast and newspaper.

Bed-and-breakfast establishments are also available for a quiet stay in Johnstown. Try the Homestead Retreat & Guest House, 1077 Crest Avenue, (814) 539-2273, or the Meadowbrook School Bed & Breakfast, 160 Engbert Road, (814) 539-1756. The Meadowbrook is a former one-room schoolhouse that now features two guest rooms with private baths, outdoor hot tubs, and a fireplace in the great room.

Altoona/State College/Johnstown Restaurants

At Toftrees Golf Resort & Conference Center, (814) 234-8000, www.toftrees.com, there are three restaurants—the Down Under Steak House, the Patio on the Green, and Le Papillon—for special functions and occasions.

At the Allen Street Grill, 100 West College Avenue, (814) 231–4745, entrees are served in the ambience of the restaurant's historic porch overlooking downtown. Mario & Luigi's, 1272 North Atherton Street, (814) 234-4273, has wood-burning ovens and rotisserie in view, health-conscious menu items, and carry-out service available. Whisker's Lounge and Courtyard at the Nittany Lion Inn features a pub menu (see previous listing).

The Tavern Restaurant, 220 East College Avenue, (814) 238-6116, is another popular pick for American cuisine. Here you'll find photos of Penn State and Pennsylvania on the walls.

A trip to Penn State wouldn't be complete with out stopping by Ye Olde College Diner, 126 West College Avenue, (814) 237-2379, for one of their famous Diner Stickies, a sweet, sticky sourdough pastry. (They're so popular the Diner also sells them online at www.the dineronline.com to Penn Staters across the country!) Or, join the locals for a hearty breakfast at the Original Waffle Shop, 1610 West College Avenue, (814) 235-1816.

In Johnstown, visit the Johnstown Brewing Company Restaurant & Pub, where you can enjoy fillet, salmon, porkchops, and other dishes while tasting the local brew. Surf 'n' Turf Inn, 100 Valley Pike, Johnstown, (814) 536-9250, specializes in steaks and fresh seafood.

Within these areas of Altoona, State College, and Johnstown, there are plenty of casual, family-oriented, and inexpensive chain restaurants as well.

CLEVELAND

Approximately two hours from Pittsburgh, a drive northwest into Ohio brings you to Cleveland. Yes, the rivalry among football fans is fierce, with the Cleveland Browns pro football team back in the league. But putting those feelings aside, there's plenty to do for families, business travelers, and anyone who wants to see a different set of scenery.

To obtain a visitor's guide to the area, or any additional information, call Positively Cleveland (Convention and Visitors Bureau of Greater Cleveland) at (216) 875-6680 or (800) 321-1001, or visit the Web at www.positively cleveland.com.

Getting There

Cleveland is easily accessible from several major interstate highways. From Pittsburgh take the Pennsylvania Turnpike west to the Ohio Turnpike and continue on Ohio 76 until you join Interstate 77 north. I-80 will also lead you to I-77.

Cleveland Attractions

The Rock and Roll Hall of Fame and Museum, 1 Key Plaza, opened in 1995, with improvements in 1998, to provide information on each of the Hall of Fame inductees. Multimedia productions combine film footage, music,

interviews, animation, and still photography to tell the stories of these famous musicians. During the holidays and peak tourist periods, advance reservations are available by calling Ticketmaster at (800) 493-ROLL (7655).

Amusement parks are popular in Cleveland, especially Cedar Point in nearby Sandusky. Cedar Point is a 364-acre amusement park and resort home to 75 rides and 17 roller coasters. The newest ride, Skyscraper, is a towering new thrill ride that spins guests in a full circle using two giant propeller arms. At its highest point, riders will be upside down 160 feet above the ground! You can also get wet at Soak City, and take the little ones to Planet Snoopy, and the Early Petting Farm. For details and hotel packages, call (419) 627-2350, or visit www.cedarpoint.com.

There are more than 300 golf courses in the area, abundant waterways, and many museums located in Cleveland, including the Cleveland Museum of Art, 11150 East Boulevard, (216) 421-7340, where admission is free. Football fans won't want to miss the Pro Football Hall of Fame, 2121 George Halas Drive NW, Canton, (330) 456-8207, about 45 minutes south of Cleveland. Visit the five-building complex, movie theater, displays, museum, enshrinement halls, and the museum store.

True Pittsburghers would have a hard time admitting they "might" root for the Cleveland Browns, but if you're going there to cheer on the Steelers, check out the $283 million Cleveland Browns Stadium, seating 73,200 people and standing 12 stories tall.

Leisurely excursions can be had aboard the *Goodtime III,* a 1,000-passenger, triple-decker sightseeing ship on the Cuyahoga River and Lake Erie. For reservations, call (216) 861-5110, or visit www.goodtimeiii.com.

Positively Cleveland offers *Walk Cleveland,* a pedestrian's guide to Cleveland architecture and public art. Download the booklet at www.positivelycleveland.com/pdf/walk _cleveland07_reduced.pdf.

Cleveland also has lakefront parks and beaches, fishing expeditions, trolley tours, wineries, and breweries to visit. In the winter months, there's even ski resorts to try. Read on for the visitor's guide later in this section, which will help you find a weekend (or several) of fun possibilities.

Cleveland Shopping

Downtown Cleveland boasts shopping that includes the Avenue at Tower City Center, 230 West Huron Road, (216) 623-4750, www.tower citycenter.com, where you will find 100 specialty shops, six full-service restaurants, an 11-screen theater, and an amphitheater. Browse the Galleria at Erieview, East Ninth and St. Clair, (216) 861-4343, www.galleria aterieview.com, with its glass-enclosed stores such as Williams Sonoma, Eddie Bauer, and the Cleveland Indians Team Shop. In addition, the Colonial Marketplace has combined two unique and historic retail arcades—the Colonial Arcade and the Euclid Arcade. Call (216) 621-0057.

Beachwood Place, 26300 Cedar Road, (216) 464-9460, is Cleveland's premier fashion destination, with such department stores as Dillard's, Saks Fifth Avenue, and Nordstroms. Factory outlets include the Aurora Farms Premium Outlets, 549 South Chillicothe Road, Aurora, (330) 562-2000, and the Prime Outlets at Lodi, 9911 Avon Lake Road, Burbank (888) 746-7563, 40 minutes south of Cleveland. Information about both outlets can be found at www.premiumoutlets.com.

Also within Cleveland is a 10-block shopping district on Larchmere Boulevard, where you'll find more than 15 antiques shops and art galleries. European pastry shops and fine restaurants line this boulevard as well.

Cleveland Accommodations

In the Cleveland area, you'll choose from more than 15,000 hotel rooms. Some of these are of the elegant nature that befits the Ritz-Carlton Cleveland, 1515 West Third Street, (216) 623-1300; Renaissance-Cleveland Hotel, 24 Public Square, (216) 696-5600; and Marriott Downtown Key Center, 127 Public Square, (216) 696-9200.

The 293-room Hyatt Regency Cleveland at the Arcade, 420 Superior Avenue, is an archi-

tectural gem featuring the refurbishment of the Arcade's 62,000 square feet of shops and restaurants. To make reservations, call (216) 575-1234.

There are several Holiday Inn locations in Cleveland, including City Center Lakeshore, (216) 241-5100, and Beachwood, (216) 831-3300, as well as some Hampton Inn locations, such as Hampton Inn Cleveland—Downtown, 1460 East Ninth Street, (216) 241-6600, and Hampton Inn & Suites Cleveland—Beechwood, 3840 Orange Place, Beachwood, (216) 831-3735.

In addition, try the Fairfield Inn Willoughby, 35110 Maplegrove Road, (440) 975-9922. Budget and economy-minded motels dot the landscape, including several Travel Lodge, Days Inn, and Red Roof Inn franchises. You'll find an extensive listing in the *Cleveland Official Visitors Guide;* order a copy on the Web at www.positivelycleveland.com or by calling (800) 321-1001.

Cleveland Restaurants

Dining in Cleveland is just as abundant as places to stay. The *Nautica Queen* is a luxury cruise and dining ship featuring lake and river cruises. Docked in the Flats Nautica Entertainment Complex, the ship serves up to 400 passengers and runs from April until December. For reservations, call (216) 696–8888 or (800) 837-0604, or visit www.nauticaqueen.com.

Seafood reigns supreme on the shores of this city. Hornblower's Barge & Grill, 1151 North Marginal Road, (216) 363-1151, is a seafood house to head to, on the shore of Lake Erie. Barnacle Bill's Crab House, 14810 Detroit Avenue, Lakewood, (216) 521-2722, also serves seafood and steaks with its raw bar and beer varieties in a nautical setting. Try some more ales and lagers brewed on the premises of the award-winning local brewery, the Great Lakes Brewing Company, 2516 Market Street, (216) 771-4404, where you'll also dine on fine food.

Sans Souci Restaurant in the Renaissance-Cleveland Hotel (see previous) specializes in French country fare. It's among Cleveland's better and more expensive restaurants. Morton's of Chicago, Cleveland, 1600 West Second Street, (216) 621-6200, is another upscale restaurant serving great steaks and fresh seafood.

Those preferring Chinese can head to Lu Cuisine, 1228 Euclid Avenue, (216) 241-8488, for cuisine from the Shandong province of Northeast China. And for a family-style buffet in a nonsmoking atmosphere with Norman Rockwell decor, there are at least a half dozen Hometown Buffet locations around Cleveland. Check the long list in the visitors guide mentioned in Accommodations.

OGLEBAY RESORT & CONFERENCE CENTER, WEST VIRGINIA

Less than two hours west of Pittsburgh sits a playground, golf spot, and shopping destination, complete with lodging and food, all for your pleasure in Wheeling, West Virginia. Oglebay started as a farm, then became the elegant summer estate of Cleveland industrialist Col. Earl W. Oglebay. Later the property was given to the city of Wheeling for use as a park and recreational site.

There are seasonal attractions that may become favorite traditions, such as the Winter Festival of Lights, a spectacular outdoor light show that you drive through during the holidays. Regardless of the time of year, the people of Wheeling have long known of the wonderful offerings of Oglebay. Now you can also! For reservations or more information on any of the facilities at Oglebay, West Virginia, call (304) 243-4000.

Getting There

Follow I-79 south out of Pittsburgh until you pick up Interstate 70 west in Washington, Pennsylvania. Then follow the signs to Wheeling and Oglebay. It's that simple!

Oglebay Attractions

The Winter Festival of Lights we mentioned above is sometimes called America's largest light display, complete with model trains and a laser light show (every hour, on the hour); admission is priced by age, per person, not by car as some other winter light shows are structured.

During the warmer months, walk through Bissonnette Gardens, with a different floral display each season. These elegant gardens existed at the turn of the 20th century and have been carefully re-created to cover the hilltop region of Oglebay. From April through October you can stroll along winding brick pathways among hanging baskets, fragrant flowers, ever-flowing water displays, and the finest of trees.

The Speidel Championship Golf Course, designed by noted golf architect Robert Trent Jones, is a perfect challenge for the serious golfer who needs a change in scenery. There's also a par-3 golf course and driving range.

At the Good Zoo, bears, otters, bison, and rare red wolves are at home in this specious natural setting.

In addition, at Oglebay there is a huge outdoor swimming pool as well as tennis at the Crispin Center. Get your exercise paddling a boat upon Schenk Lake, right on the grounds. In winter, if there's enough snow, the par-3 golf course becomes some mild ski slopes. Both cross-country and downhill skiers are accommodated.

Less physical fun can be had touring the beautiful, white Mansion Museum's period rooms. Oglebay's Glass Museum features over 3,000 examples of Wheeling Glass made from 1829 to 1939. The museum's Northwood Gallery displays the work of one of the region's most respected glass artisans, Harry C. Northwood .

Oglebay Shopping

Seven distinctive shops complement Oglebay's full range of activities and recreation. But then, shopping is indeed recreation for some!

Start at Carriage House Glass, boasting the area's largest selection of West Virginia decorative glass, with items produced right before your eyes.

i Be sure to familiarize yourself with safety procedures and the rules of the waterways at Deep Creek Lake, Maryland. Police patrol by boat and will pull you over to run safety checks and inspect for fishing licenses. You will be fined if you're caught boating recklessly or under the influence of alcohol.

Gourmet in the Gardens, located in Bissonnette Gardens, specializes in gourmet and regionally produced food products, food- and kitchen-related giftware, wine, gift baskets, candy, and confections. Also in the gardens, Garden Center Gift Shop features silk floral arrangements and other unique items; the Palm Room offers flowering plants, gifts, and seasonal items.

The Resort Shop features logo merchandise and resort clothing. Golfers will find golf apparel and equipment in the Pro Shop, located in the Hamm Club House on the Speidel Golf Course. During the Winter Festival of Lights, the Pro Shop is transformed into a Christmas wonderland featuring a large selection of one-of-a-kind decorations, ornaments, and more.

Finally, you and the children will enjoy the Nature Express store at the Good Zoo.

Oglebay Accommodations

Wilson Lodge provides excellent overnight accommodations with modern luxuries such as an indoor pool, Jacuzzi, and fitness center. See the Accommodations chapter for further details.

For those who require additional space, Oglebay offers a choice of cottages, deluxe or standard, rented by the day, the weekend, or the week. Each has a large living area, a fully equipped kitchen, and either two, four, or six bedrooms.

Oglebay Restaurants

Ihlenfeld Dining Room in Wilson Lodge serves American cuisine at its finest in a family-friendly setting. The menu features gourmet selections as well as entrees the kids

will surely enjoy. Overlooking Schenk Lake and the surrounding countryside, the view is an added attraction each season. Winter guests will enjoy the Festival of Lights, and summer patrons can look out over the lake's 150-foot fountain with its music and colored lights.

DEEP CREEK LAKE, MARYLAND

Once called "Maryland's Best Kept Secret," Deep Creek Lake in Garrett County, western Maryland, is now well known in many seasons.

Each October the annual Autumn Glory Festival is reason for a drive not only to witness the spectacular foliage but also to partake of banjo and fiddle contests, square dancing, bagpipes, bands, baseball card shows, and wonderful food.

When it snows (and boy, does it snow in Garrett County!), the slopes at the Wisp Ski Resort (800) 462-9477, www.wispresort.com, are bustling with downhill activity. There are 22 trails, a halfpipe for snowboarders, snowmaking capability, a lodge, and restaurants to warm the hearty. For more information on such winter recreation, turn to the Recreation chapter.

However fun a downhill run is in December, summer is Deep Creek's most popular season. As the largest freshwater lake in Maryland, Deep Creek boasts 65 miles of shoreline. Built in 1925 by the Youghiogheny Electric Company, the lake was purchased by the Pennsylvania Electric Company in 1942. Currently it's owned by the state of Maryland, and plenty make this their summer playground and weekend retreat.

If you're thinking of spending any time at Deep Creek Lake, pick up a copy of the Deep Creek Lake Area Visitors Guide, updated annually. Write the Garrett County Chamber of Commerce at 15 Visitors Center Drive, McHenry, MD 21541, or call (301) 387-4386. Pick up a guidebook at the visitor center, located along US 219, or contact the promotion council.

Getting There

If you start from south or west of Pittsburgh, take I-79 through Washington (there's a stretch that becomes I-79 and I-70) and continue on I-79 through West Virginia until you pick up Interstate 68. Follow I-68 to the Maryland border and on to the Friendsville exit (approximately 4 miles after the border). Take Maryland 42 to McHenry, Maryland, the first sighting of Deep Creek Lake.

From points south and east of Pittsburgh, take Route 51 south to Uniontown, until you pick up US 40 East. Continue to US 219 at Keyser's Ridge, and follow US 219 south to McHenry, Maryland.

Deep Creek Lake Attractions

Water sports abound here at Deep Creek. Just be sure to learn the rules of the waterways before taking off in your rental boat, towing a water-skier, or cruising around on your Jet Ski. For motorboat rentals, consult the vacation guide listed at the conclusion of this section.

Since the lake is home to the Flying Scot 19-foot daysailer, sailboat races are a popular activity on weekends. The nautical crowd takes to the water in the yacht club. Kids and adults can learn to sail with weeklong classes conducted by the Deep Creek Sailing School, 365 Back Bay Road, Swanton, (301) 387-4497, www.saildeepcreek.com.

Swallow Falls State Park, where four waterfalls cascade along a beautiful backdrop of tall hemlocks, is a perfect place for camping, picnicking, and hiking the scenic trails.

Funland Family Fun Center, across from McHenry Plaza, US 219, (301) 387-6168, is perhaps the best local amusement besides the annual county fair each August. There's a carousel for all ages, a go-kart track for kids ages four and older, bumper cars, miniature golf, and an indoor arcade with video games.

Courses at the Wisp Resort and in Oakland keep the family golfers happy, while area trails are prime for mountain bikers. If you prefer to ride horses, several stables offer pony and horseback rides. Consult the vacation guide listed above.

Deep Creek Lake Shopping

Schoolhouse Earth, 2 miles north of Deep Creek at 1244 Friendsville Road, (800) 223-4930, www.schoolhouseearth.com, is a country shop with gifts for year-round Christmas shoppers, as well as those searching for cards, handcrafted jewelry, lamps, country accessories, framed calligraphy, music, books, rugs, and more. Antique reproduction furniture and custom framing are also available. For the kids, visit the petting zoo, open daily in the summer season and on spring and fall weekends, weather permitting.

There's nothing like a good book to read in the warm sunlight. Head to the Book Mark'et & Antique Mezzanine, 111 South Second Street, Oakland, (301) 334-8778, for books, CDs, and a complete children's area. The addition of antiques makes this a must-stop.

Within Mountain Village Shops, check out The Tourist Trap, (301) 387-7900, for souvenirs, gifts, swimsuits, music, cards, and miscellaneous gifts. The Christmas Chalet, (877) 387-4646, is exactly what the name implies, with Christmas-themed gifts and collectibles.

Arrowhead Market, along US 219 next to Alpine Village, has expanded over the years to be a one-stop shopping establishment for almost any provision you need. Open 24 hours, the store stocks baked and canned goods, fresh meats and produce, roasted chickens, ready-made sandwiches and beverages, as well as newspapers and beer. Located at 19746 Garrett Highway, Arrowhead even has a business service center, photo developing center, gas station, and it's accessible by boat with its own dock. Call (301) 387-4020, or visit www.arrowhead market.com for more information on the store's provisions and services.

Yoder's Country Market, Maryland 669, Grantsville, (301) 895-5148, (800) 321-5148, www.yoderscountrymarket.com, is not at the lake itself, but if you are traveling US 40, or if you plan to eat at Penn Alps, we'd be remiss if we didn't tell you about it. Do stop for county fare, including jams, jellies, baked goods, and other Amish specialties.

Deep Creek Lake Accommodations

Depending upon your personal preferences, you'll find many types of accommodations at Deep Creek Lake. For those families opting to rent a cottage, contact Railey Mountain Lake Vacations, (800) 846-7368, www.rentals.deep creek.com, or Long & Foster Deep Creek Resort Rentals, (800) 336-7303, www.deep creekresort.com. If having direct access to the waterfront is important to you, be sure to ask for it. Cabins advertised as having "lake access" could still mean the lake is a considerable hike from your accommodations.

Campers will find several state parks nearby, with Deep Creek Lake State Park, (301) 387–5563, providing a beach, boat launch, and camping facilities. Camping trailers up to 29 feet in length are permitted in Maryland state parks, and there are electric hookups. Improved campgrounds provide centrally located washhouses, toilets, lavatories, and hot-water showers. Cabins are available, some with wheelchair access. Make your site reservations (888-432-2267) up to one year in advance, especially for the busy summer months. Some parks do permit pets.

For vacationers who prefer motels, hotels, or a bed-and-breakfast inns, there are plenty of these in the area. For a complete listing, consult the vacation guide. Alpine Village Inn, 19638 Garrett Highway, (301) 387-5534, www.alpinevillageinn.com, sits right off US 219 next to Arrowhead Market. With a private beach and outdoor pool, the village includes some cottages and some motel rooms. The Inn at Point View, (301) 387-5555, www.point viewinn.com, also sits along US 219, offering lakefront access, boat docking, a private beach, and a restaurant on the premises.

The Wisp Resort is a center of summer and winter activity. In addition to taking to the ski slopes, golf course, and hiking trails, you can swim a few laps in the indoor pool. However, the Wisp does not have a beach, and it's a walk to the waterfront. For reservations, call (800) 462-9477. Affiliated with the Wisp are the Will O' the Wisp Prestige Condominiums,

US 219, (301) 387–5503, (888) 590-7283, with an indoor pool, whirlpools, a sauna, fireplaces, exercise and game rooms, a sandy beach, boat docking, and a restaurant.

The bed-and-breakfast crowd will want to check out the Carmel Cove Inn, Glendale Road, (301) 387-0067, www.carmecoveinn .com. This former monastery boasts beautifully appointed rooms with fireplaces, whirlpool baths, and private decks. Guests can swim from the dock, fish from shore, or enjoy other amenities such as the great room with billiards and cable television. Lake Pointe Inn, off Marsh Hill Road, (800) 523-LAKE (5253), www.deepcreekinns.com, is 13 feet from the water's edge and a five-minute walk from Wisp Resort. All rooms have lake and/or ski slope views. There's a private dock, too.

Deep Creek Lake Restaurants

Penn Alps Restaurant and Crafts Shop, half a mile east of Grantsville, (301) 895-5985, www.pennalps.com, isn't exactly at Deep Creek, but it's en route from Pittsburgh. Plan to stop for Amish-style food, along with their soup and salad bar. Visit the artisan village next door.

Pine Lodge Steakhouse, 1520 Deep Creek Drive, (301) 387-6500, www.pinelodgesteak house.com, offers fine food in a majestic rustic log lodge with views of Deep Creek Lake. Beef, elk, trout, lobster, duck and crab cakes are just some of the entrees on the menu. Don't forget to have an after-dinner drink at the Pine Lodge Saloon.

Next to Arrowhead Market, UNO Chicago's Grill and Bar, (301) 387-4866, features a great view of the lake if you choose deck seating in the summer. Just a few steps away is the Honi-Honi Bar, (301) 387-9100, www.honi-honi.com, a Deep Creek watering hole for decades. Live music takes the stage on summer weekends, where families or couples often sit out on the open lawn. Both establishments are accessible by boat dock.

If you prefer a more formal sit-down dinner, drive just a bit farther on US 219, turning onto Glendale Road. Here you'll find the Silver

Tree Inn, (301) 387-8333, serving lunch and dinner, including Italian entrees.

Sip a cappuccino with a croissant or enjoy the country French or American cuisine at the Cornish Manor Restaurant & French Bakery, 830 Memorial Drive, Oakland, (301) 334-6499, www.cornishmanor.net, only 10 miles south of Deep Creek Lake. They also offer live entertainment and, in warmer months, serve meals to guests on the charming covered porch.

HERSHEY

Otherwise known as Chocolate Town, U.S.A., Hershey is the sweetest place on earth. To be floating high up in the air at Hersheypark, the popular amusement park, you only need to breathe in the scent of cocoa to know where you are! The sweet smell drifts from the factory into the park.

A three- to four-hour drive east from Pittsburgh, Hershey is definitely a weekend getaway as opposed to a day trip. But if you can spare a few days, head on out to see the town Milton Hershey pretty much created for his employees. The Hershey Entertainment & Resort Company will assist you by supplying information and/or booking your stay. Call them at (800) HERSHEY (437-7439).

Getting There

Take the Pennsylvania Turnpike east about 200 miles to exit 247 (Harrisburg), then follow Interstate 283 North to exit 3 (Route 322). Follow Route 322 East into the town of Hershey. Amtrak runs trains daily to Harrisburg, the state capital. If you book reservations at the Hotel Hershey or Hershey Lodge (see below), you may be able to take advantage of free shuttle service (which is also available for those flying into Harrisburg International Airport, 15 minutes away).

Hershey Attractions

Turn-of-the-20th-century confectioner Milton Snavely Hershey didn't actually start out in chocolate. Caramels were his focus, and he did very well in business. But he made an

i The holiday season at Hershey begins in mid-November with a winter wonderland of horse-drawn carriage rides, carolers, Santa Claus, and of course chocolate! Call (800) HERSHEY (437-7439) for details.

interesting discovery along the way: It was the chocolate adhering to the caramels that children licked off and seemed to enjoy the most. Hershey sold his Lancaster Caramel Company for $1 million but shrewdly reserved the rights to sell chocolate. And sell he did, building a company town rich in benevolence, and just plain fun to visit. Hershey opened his chocolate factory in 1905.

Hersheypark, (717) 534-3900, began as a place for his employees and their families to relax. Built in 1907, it was largely picnic grounds. Today it's one of the cleanest and most exciting amusement parks in the country. Ride the Great Bear, an inverted steel looping roller coaster; the Sidewinder; the Comet; one of several water rides; or some kiddie rides. Children love to determine their ride status by measuring their height against popular candy bars, posted throughout the park.

Adjacent to Hersheypark is ZooAmerica, (717) 534-3860, opened as the Hershey Zoo in 1910 as a place for Mr. Hershey to showcase his wild animal collection. Now there are more than 200 animals for everyone to see. Hours for Hersheypark vary according to the month, but the park generally opens at 10:00 a.m. ZooAmerica is open daily, year-round, from 9:00 or 10:00 a.m. to between 5:00 and 8:00 p.m., depending on the time of year, with the exception of Thanksgiving, Christmas, and New Year's Day. Call the toll-free info line, (800) HERSHEY (437-7439), for more information. Admission for these two attractions falls under the one-priced admission plan, which changes most seasons. Ride height restrictions apply.

Many years ago, tours of the Hershey factory used to attract a million people each year. When the tours became too popular to manage, they were stopped and the education shifted elsewhere. Visit Hershey's Chocolate World for a Disney-like tour of chocolate production and facts. You'll ride through the displays in automated cars, and as you exit, reach out your hand for that complimentary piece of chocolate! Admission to Chocolate World is free. Hours vary depending upon the season, so be sure to call the toll-free Hershey information line listed above.

What better way to learn about the town Mr. Hershey built (complete with chocolate kiss–shaped streetlamps on Chocolate Avenue) than by riding the Hershey Trolley? Visit Hershey Trolley Works, (717) 533-3000, right inside Chocolate World, to purchase your ticket for this fun-filled and educational ride through town. You'll learn how Milton Hershey gave so much back to the community that during the Depression he kept many townspeople employed by building a community center, a sports arena, a stadium, and the palatial Hotel Hershey (see description). In addition, you'll learn that Milton and his wife, Catharine, unable to have children of their own, founded a school for needy children, today known as the Milton Hershey School.

What began as a rose garden in 1937 became the Hershey Gardens, (719) 534-3492, a 23-acre botanical display garden that includes Butterfly House, representing more than 25 different North American plant species. It's located on Hotel Road across from the Hotel Hershey, and is open from 9:00 a.m. until 5:00 p.m. April through May, September, and October; 11:00 to 4:00 p.m. November through March. June through August the gardens stay open until 8:00 p.m. Butterfly House is open late May (around Memorial Day) to the third week in September. Admission is charged according to age.

A short walk from Hersheypark and Chocolate World is the Hershey Museum, (717) 534-3439. It's a self-guided tour that explains how Milton Hershey overcame business failures to create his chocolate empire, and how he became the philanthropist he's remembered as today. There's a Discovery Room for young children. The museum is

open from 10:00 a.m. until 5:00 p.m. Memorial Day through Labor Day, the museum stays open until 8:00 p.m.; closed Thanksgiving, Christmas, and New Year's Day. Admission is charged according to age.

Hershey Shopping

Most of the Hershey attractions have gift shops on the premises. One you won't want to miss is the giant candy feast-land inside Chocolate World. In fact, the ride lets you off at the entrance of the gift area. Here you'll find some types of candies packaged differently from what you're used to in stores back home, in addition to shirts, hats, mugs, ornaments, and more. The Hershey Museum and Hershey Gardens also offer gift shops, and in Hersheypark and ZooAmerica there are multiple chances to purchase souvenirs.

The Factory Stores at Hershey, (717) 520-1236, give you plenty of shopping opportunities. You'll find the usual array of outlet establishments for men's and women's apparel, children's clothing, footwear, books, stationery and gifts, home furnishings and housewares, intimate apparel, leather goods and luggage, and much more. They're located at 46 Outlet Square in Hershey, just 1 block east of Hersheypark, on Hersheypark Drive. Visit Monday through Saturday, 9:30 a.m. until 9:00 p.m. and on Sunday from 11:00 a.m. until 5:00 p.m. Hours may be shorter during the winter months, so do call in advance.

Hershey Accommodations

Built with European charm, the Hotel Hershey is elegant with its Mediterranean design, luxury amenities, and guest services. You'll enjoy valet parking, concierge service, 24-hour room service, babysitting, laundry services, indoor and outdoor pools, bike rentals and carriage rides, therapeutic massages, saunas, tennis, golf, lawn bowling, and much more. The Fountain Lobby, with hand-carved wooden balustrades, custom-painted tile, and the famous painted cloud ceiling, is a wonderful display of craftsmanship. The Hotel Hershey certainly rivals some of the finest hotels in the world.

At the Hershey Lodge and Convention Center, you'll enjoy fitness facilities, indoor and outdoor pools, miniature golf, concierge service, and valet parking as well, in addition to the many meeting and business facilities. Kids will love the free chocolate bars upon check-in!

For reservations at either the Hershey Hotel or the Hershey Lodge and Convention Center, call the reservations and information line at (800) HERSHEY (437-7439).

The Milton Motel, located at 1733 East Chocolate Avenue, (717) 533-4533, offers comfortable, more budget-conscious accommodations. Amenities include free coffee, free HBO/ESPN, a heated swimming pool, and a game room.

Campers will appreciate the Hershey Highmeadow Campground featuring more than 290 campsites on 55 beautiful acres of countryside. Choose from cabins, with electricity and small kitchen equipment, or sites for camping and recreational vehicle hookups. There are two outdoor swimming pools, plus a kiddie pool, playgrounds and a country store, self-service laundry, a game room, recreational facilities, and more. Contact the information line at (800) HERSHEY (437-7439) for further information on camping in Hershey.

Hershey Restaurants

The most exclusive restaurant at Hershey is the Circular Dining Room, built in the Hotel Hershey so that no guest would have to settle for a corner table. The cuisine is contemporary American with an extensive wine list. The dining room overlooks formal gardens and a tranquil reflecting pool. For more casual fare, try the Fountain Café.

Reservations are recommended at any of the Hershey restaurants, with the exception of the Cocoa Beanery coffee shops and the lounges. Call (717) 534-8800 for dining at the Hotel Hershey and (717) 534-8601 for the Lodge and Convention Center.

At Chocolate World, visit the KIT KAT "Gimme a Break" Cafe for overstuffed sandwiches, salads, home-style meals, and great, chocolate-y (what else!) desserts. For more information call (717) 533-2917.

NEIGHBORHOODS, REAL ESTATE, AND RELOCATION

At various times in its history, Pittsburgh has been defined by its rivers and bridges, by its steel mills and coal mines, by its sports teams. More than anything else, however, Pittsburgh is a city of neighborhoods, of residential communities that are both distinct and distinctive. In its relatively small space of 55.5 square miles, the city proper officially includes 90 neighborhoods. Beyond the city itself, Allegheny County spans 130 municipalities. Add the neighborhoods in the other five counties in our coverage area, and you have a region blessed with hundreds of attractive places to live.

Pittsburgh's emphasis on neighborhoods has firm roots in both topography and history. The region's riverfronts and mountains serve as natural boundaries to neighborhoods. Traveling across town in Pittsburgh can mean traversing hills and major waterways, providing some incentive to remain close to home. This was especially true during Pittsburgh's industrial heyday, when workers did not want to live too far from their mills and factories.

Perhaps even more important, Pittsburgh was settled by immigrants who tended to cluster together, taking comfort in the familiarity of people and customs from their native lands. The principal waves of immigration ended many decades ago, yet even today, the center of activity in many neighborhoods remains the local church constructed by early immigrants.

All of which provide Pittsburgh's neighborhoods with unusual solidity. Most neighborhoods in the region feature business districts—ranging from several stores to several blocks or more—to assure that residents can meet their shopping needs without leaving the neighborhood. The region also has witnessed the growth of neighborhood-based development organizations, known locally as community development corporations, which inspire neighborhood development and involve residents in their own well-being.

Most Pittsburghers live in single-family residences, although this is hardly the exclusive style. Many of the city's elegant older homes have been subdivided into apartments, and larger multiunit buildings dot the region as well. Region-wide statistics on apartment life are not completely reliable, but a good guess is that about 30 percent of city of Pittsburgh residents live in rental properties, condominiums, or cooperative housing. Many residents spend their entire lives within their neighborhoods. Call it parochial if you will, but it's an enduring strength of Pittsburgh that contributes to the richness of residential life here.

Outside the city proper you'll find a broad diversity of styles in residential communities. Pittsburgh has many close-in suburbs of both the affluent and working class variety. A number of nearby cities, such as Greensburg and Beaver, blend both sophistication and charm. If rural life is more your style, you can be in lush farm country by driving about 20 minutes—in just about every direction—from downtown Pittsburgh.

From riverfront to mountaintop living, from homes with spacious grounds to those with shared or "party" walls, you're pretty likely to find the style of living you prefer in Pittsburgh's attractive neighborhoods.

In describing some of Pittsburgh's neighborhoods in this chapter, we could present only a fraction of the communities where you might choose to live. We've tried to pick neighborhoods that are interesting in and of themselves and others—such as Kittanning, an Allegheny River town, or Penn Hills, an affluent suburb—that may be representative of a large number of communities.

One final word about Pittsburgh's neighborhoods. Maps may formally delineate neighborhood boundaries, but cartographers don't necessarily have the last word. Pittsburghers will heatedly defend their perceptions of their neighborhoods in utter defiance of what the maps may say. On certain corners in the city, you can talk to residents and discover that you are simultaneously in Brookfield, Garfield, Lawrenceville, Shadyside, and East Liberty. Don't fight it. Ultimately, neighborhood in Pittsburgh is more than a place. It's a state of mind, a creed, a way of life. Don't be surprised if it becomes your way of life very soon.

NEIGHBORHOODS

Downtown

Downtown life offers proximity to the city's vital center, with its primary business facilities—and many of its cultural amenities—within easy walking distance. Remember that you can traverse the entire length or breadth of Downtown in less than 30 minutes. If you're living Downtown, you're close to everywhere.

Downtown living offers a variety of options, including high-rise living in such buildings as Gateway Towers near Point State Park; the Pennsylvanian, a refurbished former railroad station at Downtown's edge approaching the adjacent Strip District; and Washington Plaza, an apartment complex near the Mellon Arena. A number of recently renovated smaller buildings feature lofts and condominiums. In addition, several new construction and renovation projects are under way. A new high-rise with views of the Monongahela River, 151 First Side will offer 84 condominiums. Developers are currently renovating the former Lazarus department store building into Piatt Place, a mixed-use development with residential units.

Most downtown residences bring you both convenience and views of the rivers. Downtown boasts more than 3,000 residents, many of whom belong to a residents' association. For more information about Downtown, go to www.downtownpittsburgh.com or call (412) 566-4190.

North

Aspinwall

A scenic community just north of Pittsburgh, Aspinwall is an appealing blend of the old and new. About half its homes are sturdy brick affairs predating World War II. The town also features recently constructed dwellings. Rental properties are popular in Aspinwall, as fewer than half its homes are owner-occupied.

The business district is particularly appealing. With the Allegheny River as its backdrop, the commercial section features a variety of small specialty shops with a handsome, old-fashioned decor. If you're of a mind to promenade, parasol upon your shoulder, this is the perfect setting for it.

If shopping plazas are more your métier, you'll find the Waterworks Mall conveniently placed along Route 28, which also connects Aspinwall to Pittsburgh's North Side, about 6 miles away. Other amenities include the Pittsburgh Zoo & PPG Aquarium, which is just across the Allegheny River, and UPMC St. Margaret Hospital, which, through the mysteries of politics, is located in the city of Pittsburgh without being contiguous to any part of the city.

With a population of just under 3,000, Aspinwall has been able to preserve its considerable charm. For more information go to www.aspinwallpa.com.

Butler

Between 1992 and 1996, Butler County saw the creation of more manufacturing jobs than any other county in Pennsylvania. That augurs well for employment in Butler County and the city of Butler, the county seat, which has continued to maintain a strong employment base since 1996. Among the leading employers are steelmaker ARMCO Inc., with a major complex just outside Butler, and the Veterans Affairs Medical Center and its sprawling hospital/residential complex.

i In 2007 Pittsburgh was named to Relocate-America's 100 Top Places to Live. Also, Worldwide ERC and Premier Relocation listed the Pittsburgh region as the sixth best metropolitan area for relocating families. The ranking was based on 50 metropolitan areas with populations of 1.25 million or more.

Residential style in Butler is a mix of affordable single-family homes and rental properties. Though no official figures exist, some longtime Butler residents believe that 4 of every 10 Butler residents live in rental units. Renovating older homes is a popular pursuit here.

The city of just more than 15,000 residents was named for a Revolutionary War general. It's accessible from Pittsburgh, about 25 miles away, by Route 8, which also serves as a gateway to communities farther to the north. For more information, go to the county's Web site at www.co.butler.pa.us.

Cranberry

Cranberry has been perhaps the hottest growth area in Western Pennsylvania. This Butler County township was for many years a largely rural community when folks discovered that its location—at the juncture of the Pennsylvania Turnpike, Interstate 79, and U.S. Route 19—meant easy access from and to just about everywhere. That signaled the start of a growth spurt that hasn't stalled yet.

Cranberry is home to new residential developments, apartment complexes, and planned communities. About 17 percent of Cranberry residents live in rental units. Shopping is a breeze at the many malls along US 19.

Cranberry is full of seeming contradictions. Turn away from the busy shopping plazas and you'll quickly find yourself in unspoiled terrain without sidewalks. The shape of the township's development remains a topic of considerable debate among residents. One owner of a large unimproved site, upset with Cranberry's development rules, threatened to cut down every tree on his

property if the process wasn't liberalized. He reached a compromise with elected officials, and the amazing development of Cranberry continued. For more information, go to www.twp.cranberry.pa.us.

Fox Chapel

One statistic tells you much of what you need to know about Fox Chapel: Housing prices beyond $1 million are not uncommon in Fox Chapel, which neighbors Aspinwall.

As you might guess, homes here are large, frequently set back from streets atop winding drives and lush grounds. The community is so woodsy that town fathers on occasion must develop ways to cope with a deer overpopulation that threatens residents' shrubbery.

There's more to Fox Chapel than gorgeous homes. The borough maintains six parks totaling 280 acres, and it's home to the Beechwood Farms Nature Reserve and Hartwood Acres, an Allegheny County park that is a popular summertime site for theatrical and musical performances. For more on Hartwood Acres, see our Parks and Recreation chapters.

You won't find much of a commercial district here, but residents can purchase just about everything they need at the Waterworks Mall and other Route 28 shopping plazas. If you're driving from Downtown, you'll reach Fox Chapel in about 25 minutes. If Fox Chapel is your home, you won't mind the drive. To learn more visit the borough's Web site: www.fox-chapel.pa.us.

Harmony

In 1804 Johann George Rapp and his religious separatist followers abandoned the German duchy of Wurttenberg and began constructing a communal town in what today is Butler County. They gave the name Harmony to the town they built along the banks of the Connoquennessing, in the hope that it would reflect their communal style. The Harmonists developed other communities in Western Pennsylvania as well.

Ultimately the Harmonists' experiments died out, but the town they constructed retains much of its original charm. Its shopping district features an appealing variety of antiques and artisans' shops. Approximately 1,200 people live here, most in single-family dwellings but some in rental units. You'll find no high-rises here.

Among Harmony's leading employers are Sippel Company, a steel fabricator, and Paragon Trade Brands, which produces diapers. To learn more visit Harmony Borough's Web site at www.harmony-pa.us.

Kittanning

The county seat of Armstrong County, Kittanning shares many qualities with its fellow Allegheny River communities, including attractive riverfront homes and vistas. Single-family homes dominate the town, although recent developments include three high-rise buildings featuring housing for the elderly.

Large employers in this community of about 5,100 include Alltel Pennsylvania, a telecommunications provider, and Standard Products, a rubber company. As a county seat, Kittanning boasts its own daily newspaper and proximity to several hospitals and a branch of Indiana University of Pennsylvania.

Kittanning is about a 40-minute drive from Pittsburgh along Route 28, which becomes a high-speed highway once it leaves Pittsburgh.

McCandless

The town of McCandless is representative of Pittsburgh's burgeoning North Hills in many regards. Most residents live in single-family homes, with more than half the town's dwellings built after 1970. Residents have access to the many malls and shops along US 19 and McKnight Road.

What makes McCandless noteworthy, even among Pittsburgh's splendid northern suburbs, is that it sits squarely in the middle of North Park, one of the jewels of the Allegheny County park system. The park offers such activities as fishing, boating, biking, tennis, jogging trails, swimming, golf, and ice-skating. Read more about it in our Parks chapter. If you live in McCandless, North Park is your backyard.

Mexican War Streets

Near as we can tell, Pittsburgh did not play a prominent role in the Mexican-American War. Nevertheless, this city of Pittsburgh North Side neighborhood features streets like Palo Alto and Monterrey named for battles and heroes of that conflict. The community was developed in the 1860s and 1870s—perhaps the freshness of the war in the minds of the developers helps account for the homage to the soldiers who fought it.

The neighborhood is one of the city's architectural showcases. Carefully restored row houses reflect a broad variety of styles, with Greek revival doorways, Gothic turrets, stained glass, and Richardsonian stonework. Many residents are longtime homeowners, while some homes here are purchased as investments. If you live in the Mexican War Streets, downtown is less than 2 miles away, and you'll be within walking distance of such amenities as Allegheny General Hospital, PNC Park, Heinz Field, Children's Museum of Pittsburgh, the National Aviary, and the shopping district of East Ohio Street. Plus, when someone asks what in the heck Buena Vista Street is doing in Pittsburgh, you'll have an answer of sorts. To learn more about this neighborhood, visit www.mexicanwarstreets.org.

Observatory Hill

Not often can you find stately older homes with such features as window seats, carved wooden doors, front porches, and third-floor rental units. That's what you'll find, though, in

Pittsburgh has the second-best home improvement professionals, according to ServiceMagic.com in 2007. The ranking was based on results of a survey of 66,000 customers, who said they would recommend the professional they hired to a friend or relative.

The Region

Pittsburgh
www.city.pittsburgh.pa.us
The people who live and work here are connected by more than the region's famous rivers. They share a history of innovation, the work ethic to get things done, and an affordable, high quality of life. The top three major employers in Pittsburgh are the UPMC Health System, the University of Pittsburgh, and the West Penn Allegheny Health System.

Allegheny County
www.county.allegheny.pa.us
In addition to Pittsburgh, the largest municipalities in Allegheny County are Bethel Park, McKeesport, and Monroeville. The U.S. Government and the Commonwealth of Pennsylvania are large employers in the county.

Armstrong County
www.armstrongidc.org
Armstrong County is recognized as a hub of technology-based industries, carbide tool and die-making, and electro-optics innovation, including the U.S. Navy's National Center of Excellence in Electro-optics Manufacturing. The top three employers are Armstrong County Memorial Hospital, Armstrong School District, and Rosebud Mining Company.

Beaver County
www.beavercountyced.org
www.beavercountychamber.com
The largest municipalities in Beaver County are Aliquippa, Ambridge, and Beaver Falls. The top three major employers are The Medical Center, First Energy, and Horsehead Corporation.

Butler County
www.butlercountycdc.com
Butler County capitalizes upon a strategic location and highly diverse economic and recreational base that includes Cranberry Township—one of the fastest developing communities in the eastern United States. The largest municipalities in the county are Cranberry Township, Butler City, and Butler Township. The top three major employers are A-K Steel; Butler Memorial Hospital; and TRACO, which manufactures windows.

Washington County
www.washcochamber.com
The largest municipalities in Washington County are Peters Township, California, and Canonsburg. While the Commonwealth of Pennsylvania and the County of Washington are major employers here, among other industries the top three are Washington Hospital, Monongahela Valley Hospital, and Wal-Mart, Inc.

Westmoreland County
www.westmorelandcountyidc.org
The largest municipalities in the county are Hempfield, Murrysville, and Greensburg. The top three major employers are Excela Health, United Parcel Service, and Supervalu, Inc.

Information courtesy of the
Pittsburgh Regional Alliance

Observatory Hill, a neighborhood at Pittsburgh's northern boundary.

The neighborhood draws its name from Allegheny Observatory. Perhaps a more important feature for you is Riverview Park, one of the city's grandest, which features acres of open greenery and such activities as picnic shelters and hiking, biking, and riding trails. See our Parks chapter for more on Riverview Park.

Observatory Hill is home to both a public elementary school and a public high school. It's several miles from downtown Pittsburgh, although the steepness of the neighborhood's hills encourages driving to town rather than walking. No matter. If you live here, you won't want to leave too often. To learn more about this neighborhood, visit www.observatory hill.net.

Troy Hill

Whoever coined the term "neighborhood" probably was inspired by a vision of Troy Hill—or a community very like it. Troy Hill was settled by European immigrants, and today this city of Pittsburgh neighborhood retains the look and feel of an Old World village.

From its base near the Allegheny River, Troy Hill winds up a series of steep hills to a plateau that overlooks the city and the river. Here you'll find brick and frame row homes and solid single-family houses, with not much in the way of rental units. With few entrances and exits from the neighborhood, Troy Hill has been able to retain much of its close-knit character, contributing to a low crime rate and a genuine sense of community. For a glimpse into the neighborhood, read *The Women of Troy Hill, The Back-Fence Virtues of Faith and Friendship,* by Clare Ansberry.

East

Bloomfield

While many city of Pittsburgh neighborhoods boast a strong European heritage, in Bloomfield that heritage is alive and well in daily activities. Just east of downtown, Bloomfield was settled by Italian immigrants, many of whom passed on their homes, language, and traditions to their descendants. As a result, the bustling business district along Liberty Avenue is dotted with ristorantes and grocerias. When you walk along Liberty Avenue, don't be surprised when you hear residents conversing in Italian.

Homes here typically are small but well maintained, providing a quaint quality to the narrow streets.

Amenities include Western Pennsylvania Hospital (part of the West Penn Allegheny Health System) and Dean Field, a football field beneath the Bloomfield Bridge where the legendary Johnny Unitas got his start. Dean Field was one of the first gridirons in the city to boast an artificial surface. Never mind that the laying area is only 70 yards long. Johnny U. graduated to the big time from Dean Field, and that's an inspiration for all the kids in Bloomfield.

To learn more about Bloomfield visit www.bloomfield-garfield.org, or check out the shopping district at www.shoppingbloom field.com.

Edgewood

This community just east of the city of Pittsburgh spans less than 1 square mile, yet it is something approaching a living book of the region's history. A farming community until the mid-19th century, Edgewood took on an industrial character with the growth of Union Switch & Signal Company. Today, as industry has declined, Edgewood is a lovely community of just under 4,000 residents, with large, inviting homes throughout the borough but especially prominent along tree-lined Maple Street.

Edgewood boasts two shopping hubs—a string of small shops along South Braddock Avenue, and Edgewood Towne Center, a popular strip mall that draws shoppers from throughout the eastern suburbs and Pittsburgh's eastern neighborhoods. With its location along Interstate 376 (the Parkway East), Edgewood is about a 15-minute drive from both downtown Pittsburgh and the Pennsylvania Turnpike.

An oddity: If you walk a certain 6-block route here, you can pass through four municipalities: Edgewood, Wilkinsburg, Swissvale, and the city of Pittsburgh. You don't win anything. It's just an interesting quirk. To learn more, visit the borough's Web site at www.edgewood.pgh.pa.us.

Friendship

Friendship offering stately old homes on tree-lined streets is a favorite of families with young children, students, and young professionals. Some of the homes have been converted into apartments, as many are attracted to the areas's proximity to Oakland. It is an easy walk to Bloomfield or a quick drive to the stores like Trader Joe's, Whole Foods, and Home Depot that have opened in recent years in nearby East Liberty.

For more information about Friendship, visit www.friendship-pgh.org.

Greenfield

Greenfield borders Squirrel Hill to the east. Here you can still find bargain prices for some homes,although those closer to the conveniences of Squirrel Hill may cost more. Greenfield, too, offers many conveniences, including a senior citizens center, baseball field, and public pool, as well as shops, doctors' offices, and service businesses. A considerable percentage of Greenfield's residents are former steel mill workers, although more and more young families are moving into the area. To discover more about this city neighborhood, visit www.greenfieldorg.com.

Greensburg

Once you spy the gleaming dome of the Westmoreland County Courthouse, you know you're in a city with character. That's Greensburg, a rather small city with an outsized appetite for culture. While Greensburg's population is just over 16,000 and the city spans only about 5 square miles, it is home to three institutions of higher learning—Seton Hill University, the University of Pittsburgh's Greensburg campus, and Westmoreland County Community College—as well as the popular Westmoreland Museum of American Art; the Westmoreland Symphony Orchestra; and the Palace Theatre, a downtown hall for performing arts.

The city offers many large, gracious homes as well as a growing number of planned developments that feature single-family homes, town houses, condominiums, and rental units. Shopping here is fun. You'll have the option of browsing downtown establishments or heading to the large malls that just about surround the city.

Greensburg is about 30 miles east of Pittsburgh along U.S. Route 30. Perhaps more important, it sits at the foothills of the Laurel Highlands and serves as the gateway to the popular recreation areas located there. You'll be delighted by Greensburg, a city of sophistication and charm. To learn more visit the city's Web site at www.city.greensburg.pa.us.

Highland Park

Highland Park is located east of Pittsburgh's downtown and is most known as the home of Pittsburgh Zoo and PPG Aquarium. However, locals recognize the neighborhood for its tree-lined streets, variety of architectural styles, and strong and active community groups.

And then there is the park at the top of Highland Avenue. The 500-acre Highland Park features several tennis courts, a beautiful public swimming pool, trails, a unique playground, and many picnic areas.

Though you won't find a major shopping district in Highland Park, the neighborhood is just minutes away from East Liberty and Shadyside. To learn more, go to the local community group's Web site: www.highlandparkpa.com.

The Hill District

Although it is actually a collection of neighborhoods, many Pittsburghers simply refer to this area of the city as the Hill. In the 1930s through the 1950s, the Hill was considered to be the cultural center of African-American life in Pittsburgh. The area housed many—Stanley Turrentine, Art Blakey, and Billy Eckstine, just to name a few—who went on to become international jazz legends. Pulitzer Prize–winning playwright August Wilson was born here, as was Teeny Harris, a local photographer who documented African-American life in the 20th century.

Unfortunately, in 1950 the Hill was ravaged by an urban renewal project that tore down homes and businesses to make room for the Civic Arena, now called the Mellon Arena. That redevelopment failure, plus rioting in the late 1960s, were serious blows to a community that was once considered to be the "crossroads of the road" by Harlem Renaissance poet Claude McKay.

However, Hill residents today are determined to regain the neighborhood's lost greatness. Working with them are a number of community groups, including the long-standing Hill House Association, an agency that provides numerous services related to child and youth services, workforce development, and senior services.

The Hill is now beginning to enjoy a comeback. In recent years new housing developments have attracted residents thanks to the area's proximity to downtown. One such development, Crawford Square, is a mixture of 500 rental and for-sale units that, with its grand trees and cul-de-sac drives, looks like a suburb plunked down in the heart of the city.

The Pittsburgh Penguins, who play in Mellon Arena, have announced plans to demolish the current arena and build a new $225 million one. Initial plans call for reconnecting the Hill District back to the downtown area once again through this development, which will include the new hockey arena, a hotel, business and retail buildings, and possibly more than 1,000 housing units for rent or sale.

The history, the major new developments, and the easy walk to downtown make the Hill a neighborhood to consider.

Latrobe

Welcome to Mister Rogers' neighborhood. And Arnold Palmer's. And Rolling Rock Beer's. And the banana split's. All had their start in this community of about 9,300 in Westmoreland County, about 35 miles east of Pittsburgh.

Latrobe is rich in history. It was mentioned, although not by its current name, in a 1750 entry in the diary of Christopher Gist, the surveyor credited with being the first explorer to cross the Allegheny Mountains heading west. Today Latrobe is an appealing blend of urban and rural life. You'll find residential styles of all varieties. About 70 percent of Latrobe residents live in single-family homes. Venture just a few minutes outside downtown Latrobe and you'll be surrounded by fertile farmland.

With its central location along US 30, the town is important to the commerce of Westmoreland County. Among the largest employers are Latrobe Area Hospital, with a staff of more than 1,500 at its main facility, and Kennametal, a Fortune 500 company that produces cutting tools.

One of Latrobe's cultural centers is St. Vincent College, which is operated by the Benedictine monks. In addition to hosting a number of important lecture series and being home to the new Fred Rogers Center for Early Learning and Children's Media, the college each summer serves as the training site for the Pittsburgh Steelers.

Can you say, "Go, Stillers"?

To learn more about businesses in the area, visit the local chamber of commerce's Web site at www.latrobearea.com. For general information go to the city's Web site at www.cityoflatrobe.com.

Lawrenceville

Lawrenceville, located just east of downtown, is quickly becoming one of Pittsburgh's hottest redeveloping neighborhoods. With about 11,000 residents, Lawrenceville also is one of the city's oldest and largest neighborhoods. The area features many historic homes—from brick row houses to large, detached homes. In recent years, new condominiums and unique lofts have been created in former warehouses.

Registering to Vote

You can apply to vote at any Pennsylvania Department of Transportation photo license center when you obtain or update your driver's license. Online you can register at www.votespa.com. Or call or visit your county's registration center online to obtain a voter application form.

Allegheny County
(412) 350-4500
www.county.allegheny.pa.us

Butler County
(724) 284-5310
www.co.butler.pa.us

Armstrong County
(724) 548-3222
www.armstrongcounty.com

Washington County
(724) 228-6750
www.co.washington.pa.us

Beaver County
(724) 728-3934
www.co.beaver.pa.us

Westmoreland County
(724) 830-3594
www.co.westmoreland.pa.us

Besides the housing stock, residents are attracted to Lawrenceville's business district, which features hip boutiques and restaurants, cozy coffee shops, fine art galleries, and "mom-and-pop" shops. To learn more go to www.lawrencevillecorp.com.

Ligonier

When Westmoreland County residents refer to "the Diamond," they're not talking about precious stone deposits or a baseball field. Rather, they're referring to downtown Ligonier, where the shopping area—in the shape of a diamond—is one of the region's most charming. You'll find a variety of quaint shops as well as a bandstand that is the center of the town's civic activities.

Ligonier is one of the most prestigious addresses in the region; some who live elsewhere have second homes in Ligonier. Residences can be breathtaking, with woodlands stretching to the backyards and pristine streams coursing through the properties. Not all homes here are quite that spectacular—the Ligonier Valley offers a broad mix of income levels—but it is those picture-postcard dwellings that provide Ligonier with its reputation.

Located in the Laurel Highlands, Ligonier is close to some of the region's most popular resorts as well as Idlewild and SoakZone, an amusement park with an unusual rustic flavor. See our Kidstuff chapter for a more complete description of Idlewild Park. Also an enduring attraction is Fort Ligonier, an important British redoubt in the 18th-century struggles with the French for supremacy. For more information visit www.ligonier.com.

Oakland

Oakland is the hub of the region's university-medical complex and known for its rich variety of residents, visitors, and amenities. The neighborhood is home to the University of Pittsburgh, Carnegie Mellon University, and Carlow University, attracting students, faculty, and visitors who contribute to the neighborhood's vitality.

The medical complex, including the University of Pittsburgh Medical Center, Children's Hospital of Pittsburgh, and UPMC Magee Women's Hospital, is among the most highly regarded in the world. Dr. Jonas Salk developed the polio vaccine here, and it serves as the base for Dr. Thomas Starzl, one of the world's transplant pioneers. See the Health Care chapter for more detail on Oakland's hospitals.

The style of life in Oakland covers a wide range. Beyond the transient community of students, the neighborhood boasts a solid residential base. South Oakland features streets of closely built homes that stretch all the way to I-376 (the Parkway East), where they overlook the Monongahela River. You will find many rental properties here, although there are still pockets of owner-occupied homes. Schenley Heights features large older homes, while at Oakland's eastern end you'll find many attractive high-rises, where residents live in proximity to hospitals, doctors' offices, and such cultural amenities as the Carnegie and Phipps Conservatory and Botanical Gardens. The Arts and Attractions chapters contain more in-depth information on the Carnegie and Phipps.

Although Oakland is only about 4 miles from downtown, it contains two shopping districts—student-oriented businesses along Forbes Avenue and more upscale galleries, shops, and restaurants near the Carnegie along South Craig Street.

In a word, Oakland will energize you. To learn more visit Oakland Planning and Development's Web site: www.oaklandplanning.org.

Oakmont

If you follow the professional golf tour, you've heard of Oakmont. It's the home of Oakmont Country Club, which has hosted a number of PGS and U.S. Open tournaments through the years and is considered one of America's premier country clubs. As you travel from the Allegheny River up steep Hulton Road toward the country club, you'll see many well-appointed homes with spacious grounds.

The commercial district is a charming slice of small-town Americana, featuring professional offices and artisans' shops. You won't find a mall anywhere near this business

district. Oakmont also offers a popular nature park for walking, a yacht club, and public golf courses near the private country club. To learn more about this area, visit the local chamber of commerce's Web site at www .oakmont-pa.com.

If you're traveling to Oakmont from downtown, it's best to stay on high-speed Route 28 on the other side of the Allegheny, then cross the Hulton Bridge to Oakmont. You can't miss the Hulton Bridge—it's lavender.

Penn Hills

Next to Pittsburgh, Penn Hills is the largest municipality in Allegheny County, some 46,800 residents strong. The community was formerly a cluster of independent local mining enclaves brought closer together by the completion of I-376 (the Parkway East).

Penn Hills spans 20 square miles as well as a variety of residential styles. You'll find single-family homes on quiet suburban streets as well as large multiunit residential buildings. The community boasts an appealing diversity of residents representing many races, income levels, and styles.

Shopping districts here are long and linear, stretching for miles along both Rodi and Frankstown Roads, and there are several smaller shopping clusters as well. Penn Hills is a few minutes' drive from the Pennsylvania Turnpike and about 25 minutes from downtown Pittsburgh. To learn more visit www .pennhills.org.

Shadyside

Shadyside often has been compared to Washington's Georgetown neighborhood, and there are similarities. In Shadyside you'll find

> **i** The hills are alive in Southwestern Pennsylvania. In the suburbs you'll find the North Hills, the East Hills, the South Hills, and the West Hills. In the city the hill bill includes Squirrel Hill, Troy Hill, Observatory Hill, Polish Hill, Spring Hill, Summer Hill, New Homestead Hill, the Hill District, and Perry Hilltop.

Close-up

Learning More about Pittsburgh Neighborhoods

Pittsburgh has much to offer, with numerous neighborhoods and suburbs full of character, a splendid variety of cultural and sports activities, great food and shopping, great health care, beautiful parks, and excellent schools. That's a start on life for those considering relocating here.

But how do you choose the neighborhood in which to live? With more than 88 neighborhoods in just the city alone, plus the surrounding small towns and cities, bedroom communities, and suburbs, the job can be a daunting one.

With the advent of the Web, more and more local governments are going online to provide helpful information regarding local services, community groups, events and issues. Here are several ways to find more "inside information" on each neighborhood's distinct character, people, and amenities. To learn more about a neighborhood's history, check out *Images of America*, published by Arcadia. Each of these brief, easy-to-read books focuses on one of Pittsburgh's neighborhoods (e.g., South Side, Squirrel Hill, Mt. Washington) and some areas around the city such as Ligonier and Greensburg.

For an up close and personal look, we suggest one of the many house tours offered. Here you can meet people who actually live and work in the area, see actual homes, and maybe even make a few friends along the way. To find out if the neighborhood that you are considering offers a house tour, contact the local government or community group. Some of the most popular tours are of the Mexican War Streets (September), Friendship (September), South Side (June), Mt. Washington (June), Mt. Lebanon (June), and Sewickley (May). For a different take on a neighborhood, you can go to the local community festivals. Two of our favorites are Little Italy Days in Bloomfield (September) and Art All Night in Lawrenceville (April). If you can't come here to research neighborhoods, you will find great articles about individual neighborhoods in the city through Pop City Media's free weekly e-magazine and Web site. With the objective of showcasing the positive and sustained transformation of the Pittsburgh region, Pop City features original stories and photography. To sign up, go to Pop City's Web site at www.popcitymedia.com.

some of the city's loveliest and largest homes, including stunning Victorian mansions. You'll also find one of the trendiest and nicest shopping districts along Walnut Street, home to a variety of restaurants and upscale boutiques. Exploring Walnut Street is a treat; you'll find many unusual and unheralded shops tucked around corners and up stairs. The neighborhood hosts two annual arts festivals, both on the same weekend.

Here you can find modest single-family homes, trendy condominiums, affordable apartment complexes, and even grand old mansions. The neighborhood is home to Chatham University and UPMC Shadyside Hospital, as well as a number of stately churches. Shadyside is an easy bus trip from downtown Pittsburgh, about 5 miles away. To learn more about the neighborhood, visit www.shadysideshops.com.

Squirrel Hill

Meet one of the most attractive and diverse neighborhoods in the city of Pittsburgh. Squirrel Hill is an especially large city neighborhood with nearly 25,000 residents. You'll find a broad variety of residential styles here, including many high-rise apartment buildings and sprawling brick mansions along Beechwood Boulevard and in the section of the neighborhood informally called "North of Forbes." One of the city's more expensive neighborhoods, it is still possible to find some modestly priced homes on side streets in Squirrel, especially in the area where the neighborhood borders on Greenfield.

Just as important as the attractive housing is the neighborhood's blend of residents. Squirrel Hill is an important center of Judaism, home to a dozen synagogues and temples as well as the Jewish Community Center. The defining characteristic of life here is ethnic diversity. Walk along the bustling Murray Avenue shopping district and you'll see delicatessens; pizza parlors; a Middle Eastern bakery; and Greek, Chinese, and sushi restaurants. At the hub of the neighborhood, the corner of Murray and Forbes Avenues, the Jewish Community Center stands alongside St. Edmund's Academy, which is a Diocese of Pittsburgh elementary school, and across the street from Sixth Presbyterian Church.

The shopping district lacks a major department store as anchor but is just about self-sufficient in every other way, with businesses ranging from convenience stores to movie theaters to couturiers. And you'll be only 10 minutes from the Waterfront— a shopping and entertainment mecca that boasts major anchor stores such as Macy's and discount stores such as Marshall's and Target, as well as restaurants and a huge movie theater. For recreation, Frick Park is an urban jewel, with miles of hiking and jogging trails, picnic areas, athletic fields, and a bird-

ing stand. For more on Frick Park, see our Parks chapter.

Squirrel Hill is about 5 miles from downtown Pittsburgh, easily accessible from I-376 (the Parkway East). When you visit the neighborhood, check out the former school where a portion of the film *Diabolique* was shot. The movie was bad; Squirrel Hill gets four stars. To learn more, visit the Squirrel Hill Urban Coalition at www.shuc.org.

Swisshelm Park

Ask Pittsburgh residents about Swisshelm Park and you'll probably evoke a lot of puzzled looks. That's because Swisshelm Park, though within the city of Pittsburgh, is cut off from the rest of the city by sprawling Frick Park. In fact, if you begin from any point in Pittsburgh, you can't drive to Swisshelm Park without first leaving the city.

That isolation has enabled Swisshelm Park to develop as a tight-knit, family-oriented neighborhood of about 1,400 residents. Residential style here is largely single family, with few rental properties available. You'll find primarily suburban-style ranch homes and two-story brick dwellings.

The center of recreational and civic life is the Sarah Jackson Black Community Center, with a wide range of outdoor activities offered in Frick Park. Swisshelm Park does not offer any businesses to speak of—a blessing or a curse, depending on your point of view. You'll find plenty of shopping opportunities, however, in adjacent Swissvale and the nearby Edgewood Towne Center.

For a great place to raise a family . . . and retain some mystery about your lifestyle . . . try the splendid isolation of Swisshelm Park.

South

Bethel Park

Some key statistics will give you a good feel for this attractive South Hills suburb of Pittsburgh. About 91 percent of the community's high school graduates go on to further education. Four of every five homes are owner-occupied.

If you're getting the sense of a family-oriented community of some means, welcome to Bethel Park. The community is less than 10 miles from downtown Pittsburgh, but many residents find all the amenities they need in local shopping malls, such as the massive South Hills Village. While the drive to Pittsburgh is easy, many commuters prefer to utilize park-and-ride lots and the "T" trolley-subway system. For more on this system see our Getting Here, Getting Around chapter.

Most homes in this community of nearly 34,000 were constructed after World War II. They tend to feature two to four bedrooms and well-maintained lawns. Bethel Park is adjacent to South Park, a 1,999-acre Allegheny County–run facility that glitters as one of the jewels of the municipal park system. For more on South Park, see our Parks chapter. For general information about the area, visit www.bethelpark.net.

Brookline

Brookline reflects many of the attractive qualities of Pittsburgh's South Hills. A large city neighborhood of nearly 15,000 people, Brookline is less than 4 miles from downtown, which is accessible by both bus and the trolley-subway system known as the "T." It's also on the doorstep of the region's heavily populated southern suburbs.

For many years, the near-exclusive residential style in Brookline was single family, with solid homes well spaced along tree-lined streets surrounding Brookline Boulevard. In recent years the neighborhood has entertained development of an apartment building, a town house development, and two senior citizen high-rises, diversifying residential life.

The neighborhood's business district, although without major anchors, will meet most of your shopping needs. Brookline also boasts two community swimming pools and Seton-LaSalle Catholic High School.

Mt. Lebanon

Mt. Lebanon is one of Pittsburgh's showcase communities; a home in this South Hills suburb represents the aspirations of many local residents. The typical Mt. Lebanon home is freestanding, made of brick, with three to four bedrooms and spacious grounds. Homes are set back from tree-lined streets that are part of Mt. Lebanon's rich history—the community was named for two Cedars of Lebanon trees planted on Bower Hill Road, a main thoroughfare.

Mt. Lebanon's many amenities provide another foundation for the community's reputation. The upscale Galleria Mall anchors the busy business district. For recreation the community offers 300 acres of parklands, a swimming pool, a tennis center, a nature reserve, an athletic field with artificial surface, an indoor ice-skating rink, and a nine-hole golf course.

For all that, it is Mt. Lebanon's education system that is perhaps its most admired feature. Excellent public and private school networks lead to the high school, from which 92 percent of graduates go on to post-secondary education. As you might expect, residents are aware and politically active. It's a great place for a debate . . . as you stroll along quiet, shady streets. Learn more by visiting www.mtlebanon.org.

Mt. Washington

Few urban areas can offer the visual excitement that Mt. Washington provides. Located at the top of Mt. Washington (naturally), the neighborhood offers breathtaking views of the city and its rivers below. Grandview Avenue, the neighborhood's main thoroughfare, provides several observation decks and souvenir shops, as most visitors to Pittsburgh include Mt. Washington on their itinerary. If you've enjoyed those sweeping views of Pittsburgh in films and advertisements, chances are they were shot from Mt. Washington.

Because of the view, homes in Mt. Washington can be quite dear. Newer condominiums—some of them actually cut into the mountain—can fetch more than $500,000.

Once past such conversation pieces, however, you'll find a community of more modestly priced homes. The grand view may be a

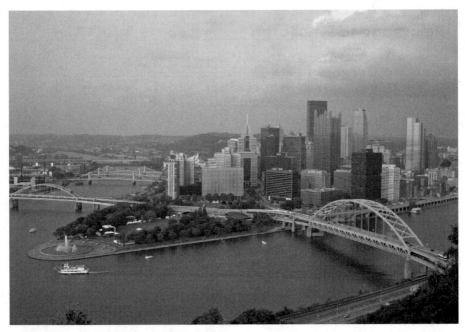

Downtown from Mt. Washington. ALAN AND BARBARA VENTO

block or two away, but you'll find an active business district along Shiloh Street and a stable population of about 10,000.

You'll also have an opportunity to utilize one of the most unusual means of transportation—that inclined plane, sort of a trolley car that shuttles passengers up and down the mountainside. The Duquesne and Monongahela inclines are tourist attractions, but residents who work downtown also ride the inclines; they're at work in a few minutes, and they avoid parking hassles. For more on the inclines see our Getting Here, Getting Around and Attractions chapters. And for more about Mt. Washington, visit the local community group's Web site at www.mwcdc.org.

Peters

Peters has been one of the strong growth areas in Western Pennsylvania. The township is strategically located just across the Allegheny County border in Washington County, thus able to attract residents from Pittsburgh's South

Hills as well as those in Washington County and points south and west.

Transformed from a semideveloped community, Peters is now home to almost 20,000 residents, who live in spacious homes with large, landscaped lots. Most homes—92 percent—are owner-occupied, and there is scant commercial development here. With its location along U.S. Route 19, residents have access to as many shopping malls as they would ever need. Peters residents value education—93 percent of the township's high school graduates continue their education. Learn more at www.peterstownship.com.

South Side

Frequently the phrase "neighborhood in transition" is a euphemism for a community on the downhill side. South Side is a city of Pittsburgh neighborhood that has been in transition, and the result is one of the most lively neighborhoods you'll find.

Relocating to Pittsburgh

So you've decided to relocate to Pittsburgh. There are several resources that can help in your move to the 'Burgh.

In 2008 VisitPittsburgh is set to launch a new section on its Web site (www.visitpittsburgh.com) dedicated to those interested in relocating to the area. Here you can find resources for moving companies, home builders, employment, and much more.

To find a real estate agent in the area, we suggest turning to one of the professional associations such as Realtors® Association of Metropolitan Pittsburgh (www.realtorspgh.com).

To find out more about local home sale prices, we suggest talking with a Realtor, using an online search of recent real estate data such as Trulia (www.trulia.com) or, if the properties are located in Allegheny County, searching the database for Allegheny County Real Estate at www.alleghenycounty.us.

If you need help with more than just home purchasing, we suggest contacting one of the local corporate relocation services—Getting to the Point (www.getting-to-the-point.com, 412-363-3363) or Presenting Pittsburgh (www.presentingpittsburgh.com, 412-481-5100). Traditionally, relocation services companies work exclusively with employers and the employer foots the bill. Employees and individuals negotiating their contracts can bargain to have relocation services included in the package. Presenting Pittsburgh offers detailed information, customized tours, and "settling in" assistance to individuals as well as employers.

Interested in renting rather than purchasing a home? For listings of apartments, townhomes, and other rental properties, you can search online at Apartment Finder (www.apartmentfinder.com) and Apartment Guide (www.apartmentguide.com). These sites also include maps of the area and lists of pet-friendly properties. This information is also available in free publications that can usually be found in local supermarkets.

South Side is actually two neighborhoods—the Flats, a long, linear community that stretches for about 30 blocks along the Monongahela River, and the Slopes, rows of homes nestled along the hills leading away from the river. In the past many residents worked at LTV's South Side Steel Mill, which would become a casualty of Big Steel's decline. The business district along East Carson Street was community serving but sedate.

In the 1980s young professionals discovered the South Side as a way to beat downtown rents and began renovating older structures for their offices. Trendy taverns, restaurants, galleries, and retail shops sprang up to serve this new younger crowd. South Side Local Development Company initiated a project, with the Urban Redevelopment Authority of Pittsburgh, to create 300 units of riverfront housing. The new South Side Works, the multiuse commercial redevelopment of the former LTV site, is lauded as one of the best examples of brownfield redevelopment in the region.

All this development has served to create an eclectic neighborhood, as renowned for its vibrant nightlife as it is for its strong family life. The price range and dwelling types for South Side homes is broad, reflecting the varying styles. You can still find many older, party wall–type homes, but now there are also older churches converted into lofts, new townhomes, and, on the Slopes, many renovated homes that feature some of the best views of the city. To learn more go to www.southsidepgh.com.

Upper St. Clair

When you see the initials "USC" in Western Pennsylvania, don't mistake the acronym for reference to the University of Southern California or the University of South Carolina. In these parts, USC means Upper St. Clair, an affluent community at the southwestern edge of Allegheny County near the Washington County border.

Why is USC so recognizable? Perhaps it's because of the quality of the township's homes. Most of the homes were built after World War II, and most—93 percent—are owner-occupied. You will find some modern apartment complexes, but large family-style homes remain the rule.

Perhaps USC is so prominent for its emphasis on education. An astonishing 98 percent of its high school graduates pursue post-secondary education, a figure that may be unequaled in the region.

Shoppers have access to a clutch of malls along US 19, the highway that connects Allegheny and Washington Counties, and Upper St. Clair is only a few minutes' drive from I-79. The township is about a 20-minute commute from downtown Pittsburgh. To learn more, visit the township's Web site: www.twpusc.org.

Washington

For years Pittsburgh area residents have referred to this city 25 miles southwest of Pittsburgh as "Little Washington." While that may seem a logical way to distinguish it from that city inside the Beltway, you can understand why residents of Pennsylvania's Washington could be a little miffed. This is a city with a colorful history and a strong modern identity.

Washington was the center of the Whiskey Rebellion, an 18th-century challenge to the federal government's taxing authority, as well as an important stop on the National Road and the Underground Railroad. Today the city is home to Washington & Jefferson College, where the Olin Fine Arts Center stages many cultural events, and 45 place of worship.

Washington is strategically positioned at the junction of two interstate highways—I-70 and I-79—providing easy access to West Virginia and Ohio. Once a center for manufacturing, Washington now relies on the service and professional sectors for employment opportunities. Learn more by visiting the city's Web site at www.washingtonpa.us.

West
Banksville

Just west of downtown is a neighborhood that combines many elements of city of Pittsburgh life. Banksville offers stately older homes as well as newer dwellings that seem more suburban, with sweeping, manicured lawns and colorful flower beds. While such homes are popular with families, the neighborhood is also home to Crane Village and Hiland Hills, two of Pittsburgh's largest garden apartment complexes, which typically cater to more transient residents. Homes in Banksville generally sell for between $60,000 and $90,000.

The heart of the shopping district is Banksville Road, a strip of shopping plazas that can satisfy most of your shopping needs. Banksville Road also functions as the main thoroughfare. Inbound it takes you to the Parkway West and downtown; outbound it leads on to the heavily populated South Hills. Banksville is a taste of the suburbs within the city.

Beaver

"Imagine a rolling English landscape, with the softest of blue skies, dotted at three-mile intervals with quiet little villages, or aggressive little manufacturing towns." That's how Rudyard Kipling described the Beaver Valley in a letter to a friend. Today the community of Beaver, the county seat of Beaver County about 30 miles southwest of Pittsburgh, retains much of the charm that so enamored Kipling.

With little or no industry in the town itself, Beaver offers broad, shaded streets; lush parks; and views of the nearby Beaver and Ohio Rivers. Most residents live in single-family homes and enjoy such amenities as the gazebo in the heart of town, which features live entertainment during warm-weather months.

Stability is the watchword in this community of about 5,500. The town's churches represent nine different denominations. Residents show such pride in their community—and such concern for their neighbors—that the police department and parent-teacher organizations sponsor an annual bicycle registration to discourage theft. To learn more visit the area's Web site at www.co.beaver.pa.us.

Beaver Falls

Among the notables who have called Beaver Falls home is Joe Willie Namath, one of the National Football League's legendary quarterbacks and partygoers. Sometimes it's hard to imagine Broadway Joe in this quiet, friendly town of about 10,500 located west of Pittsburgh along the Beaver River in Beaver County.

A center of social activities in Beaver Falls is 37th Street Park, where folks gather on park benches and kids enjoy the annual Easter egg hunt around the gazebo. The largest local employers include Republic Steel; Armstrong World Industries, a manufacturer of ceiling tiles; and Geneva College, situated in a popular residential area called College Hill. Residential style is eclectic, with single-family homes, duplexes, rental properties, and high-rise multiunit buildings all available.

Canonsburg

Is it possible that one small Southwestern Pennsylvania town produced both Perry Como and Bobby Vinton? Indeed it is, and that town is Canonsburg, off I-79 in Washington County, about 15 miles southwest of Pittsburgh. The community has changed a bit since the days when Mr. C. was crooning for the patrons of his barber shop.

Single-family homes still honeycomb the hillsides between I-79 and US 19, but the town also has seen a number of planned communities.

Most prominent among these is Southpointe, a complex that features industrial, office, residential, and recreational uses. You can admire Southpointe's townhomes and golf course from I-79; if you drive in for a closer look or inquire about residential opportunities, you won't be the first passerby to do so.

Many of the town's 9,500 residents work at local businesses, including Pennsylvania Transformer Technology, Sarris Candies, and the antiques shops that dot the main thoroughfare. One of the real attractions of Canonsburg is that location along I-79, about 35 minutes from the West Virginia and Ohio borders. For more information, visit the area's Web site at www.canonsburgboro.com.

Moon

Moon traces its history to 1788, when it was among Allegheny County's initial group of townships. The origin of its name remains something of a mystery, though some say it derives from the crescent-shaped bend in the Ohio River, which forms Moon's northern border.

In contemporary times, Moon has experienced significant residential and commercial growth, thanks in part to the expansion of Pittsburgh International Airport a few miles away. To meet the needs associated with the airport, Moon offers a variety of recently constructed housing, including both single-family dwellings and luxury multiunit buildings.

The township of about 23,000 residents is home to Allegheny County's Settler's Park as well as the township-operated Robin Hill Park, site of many recreational and cultural activities, and five golf courses. With its location near Interstate 279 (the Parkway West), Moon is within easy reach of both the airport and downtown Pittsburgh. For more information go to www.moontwp.com.

Sewickley

Once a summer retreat area for Pittsburgh's wealthiest families, Sewickley today is a charming residential community, one of a chain of such towns along the Ohio River in Allegheny County. In Sewickley and neighboring Sewickley Heights, you'll find some of the largest and most expensive homes in the region, but you'll also find lovely and more affordable housing as well.

The commercial district features a village atmosphere and quaint boutiques, art galleries, antiques shops, and restaurants. Sewickley's approximately 4,000 residents take great pride in the breadth and quality of the public services the community provides, including careful oversight of renovations to historic older homes.

Sewickley offers five recreational complexes. If you live in Sewickley you'll be well positioned for convenient travel. It's about 10 minutes from Pittsburgh International Airport, 20 minutes from downtown Pittsburgh, and right on the doorstep of Beaver County. To learn more visit the borough's Web site: www .sewickleyborough.org.

REAL ESTATE

Pittsburgh residents tend to stay put. Nevertheless, you'll find thousands of homes on the market at any given time, with activity peaking in the spring. The region's housing stock is a blend of older homes, many of them beautifully renovated, and recently constructed dwellings. Thus the price range for homes in the area is quite broad, beginning as low as around $20,000 for some "handyman's specials and soaring to $1 million and more at the high end.

Because neighborhoods in the region are numerous and diverse, you might find it helpful to work with a real estate agency to identify some options for you. The real estate sector here is large, active, and sophisticated. Their marketing thrusts include the traditional, such as printed materials, as well as the innovative, including television programs and comprehensive Web sites.

We've profiled a number of agencies to help point you in the right direction. The list is by no means exhaustive, but our profiles will introduce you to the largest agencies in the area as well as number of neighborhood specialists. Happy hunting!

Realtors

Albert Anthony Real Estate
4343 Murray Avenue
(412) 422-3430
http://albertanthonyrealestate.com/aare
Albert Anthony and his wife, Judie, handle the sale of homes in the East End and the South Hills. They also offer residential property management and commercial appraisals. While the median price range of homes they sell is $79,900 to $129,000, some homes—like large, stately places of residence in Squirrel Hill—may bring $500,000 or more. The Anthonys also are happy to sell marketable homes in their area in lower price ranges. Their son has also joined them in their business, and the Anthonys have added rental properties to their selections.

Barnes and Associates Real Estate
102 Lexington Avenue
(412) 784-1810
Barnes and Associates concentrates on homes in Fox Chapel and surrounding communities. They average about 50 sales per year, significant volume with such a small geographic concentration, so you know the agency is highly regarded in the community. The homes they handle range in price from about $50,000 to $250,000 and more, and each deal gets the personal attention of proprietor Maryanne Barnes.

Century 21
(800) 221-5737
www.century21.com
Century 21 offers 10 offices in Southwestern Pennsylvania, each independently owned and operated. The company offers an innovative program called Century 21 Communities, an America Online site that provides access to information about 700 neighborhoods across North America. Enter a zip code and you can

find what a community's residents like to drive, read, and watch on television.

Coldwell Banker Real Estate
(888) 308-6558
www.pittsburghmoves.com

With 17 offices and 800 agents in Southwestern Pennsylvania, Coldwell Banker tries to make buying and selling homes as convenient as possible for its clients. Dedicated divisions handle mortgages, relocations, and title services, while the company deploys a special unit for homes priced at $350,000 and above.

The company adheres to a 22-point guarantee for sellers and buyers. Among the company's service guarantees: If they don't convey a decision about your loan application the same day it's filed, they'll pay you $250; if they don't meet the scheduled closing date, they'll reduce your interest rate by ⅛ percent. (Certain restrictions apply; call for details.)

Coldwell Banker publishes the *Real Estate Buyers Guide,* featuring pictures and descriptions of every home in its inventory. It runs as an insert in a number of local newspapers, or you can subscribe for free by calling the agency.

Dunn Real Estate Services
512 Foreland Street
(412) 322-2000
www.dunnrealtor.com

Here's a small agency that specializes in city of Pittsburgh properties, with particular emphasis on 15 North Side neighborhoods that produce 85 percent of the company's business. You'll find an exhaustive knowledge of those 15 neighborhoods at Dunn, as well as familiarity with special financing programs—an important plus for first-time buyers. Because it's so well-known on its turf, the agency can reach special audiences, such as employees of North Side companies, that mass advertising might miss. Check out the agent's blog and a great list of resources and articles on the agency's Web site.

Equity Real Estate
2029 Murray Avenue
(412) 422-9200
www.equityrealestate.net

Locally owned and operated for 30 years, Equity is a midsize agency specializing in commercial sales and leasing in the city's eastern neighborhoods. The company has 40 agents with thorough knowledge of their territory. If you visit Equity, you'll find its ownership and senior management right there on the premises, every day. The agency maintains contacts with a wide variety of lenders to ensure that buyers have access to the best financing packages.

Howard Hanna Real Estate Services
(800) 656-7356
www.howardhanna.com

For more than 40 years, Howard Hanna Real Estate Services has been one of Western Pennsylvania's most prominent agencies. It's the largest, family-owned, full-service real estate company in the Pennsylvania, Ohio, West Virginia, and New York. It operates 120 offices in 55 counties. Among the services Howard Hanna provides are appraisals, financing, and relocation and closing services.

Lavelle Real Estate
2909 Central Avenue
(412) 621-2992

Many companies claim to be family businesses; Lavelle Real Estate walks the talk. Robert R. Lavelle received his broker's license in 1951 and still runs the business. His son and wife are Lavelle Real Estate brokers, while his daughter-in-law serves as office manager, coordinating the activities of the agents.

It's no coincidence that the agency is located in the Hill District, the hub of Pittsburgh's African-American community. "As a minority-owned institution," Robert Lavelle says, "we're trying to help black people own homes. We want to motivate people, to let them see a black business with the accoutrements of success." This is an agency with experience—and a mission.

Northwood Realty Services
4100 Route 8, Allison Park
(412) 487-3200, (800) 245-6172
www.northwood.com
Northwood is a full-service firm that operates 35 branch offices throughout Southwestern Pennsylvania. The agency has a number of special programs to serve customers. It offers a 30-minute television show each Sunday at 11:30 a.m. on WPXI-TV to showcase all homes on its current list. To learn the status of any home, you can call (412) 492-1100 around the clock, punch in the home's five-digit code, and hear a tape of an agent describing the unit and its status.

Prudential Preferred Realty
9401 McKnight Road
(800) 860-7653,
(800) 245-7356 (outside Pennsylvania)
www.prudentialpreferred.com
Although owned and operated locally, Prudential Preferred is a franchise of Prudential nationally, providing it with strong relocation services. With in-house capabilities for mortgages, insurance, and settlement services, Prudential Preferred can provide something approaching one-stop shopping for buyers. Prudential Preferred operates 21 offices with more than 600 sales associates, giving it broad reach throughout Southwestern Pennsylvania.

CHILD CARE

Few services are as important to families as quality, reliable child care. As the frequency of dual wage earners within families has increased, the quest for child-care services has become a key determinant in the availability of both parents to continue working, to meet their economic goals, and to provide a supportive and loving environment for their children. Fortunately the news on this front in Southwestern Pennsylvania is good. There is help as you embark on the search for reliable, safe, and educational care for your children.

For many local residents, child care goes by the decidedly unscientific names of Grandma and Grandpa. Family roots run deep in this region, with extended families often residing together or in the same neighborhood. For parents living in extended families, the need for professional child care may not be compelling. Yet that same emphasis on families and family values has helped inspire a broad network of professional child-care sources for those parents who live outside extended families.

Parents here have many choices. Not only will you find licensed day-care centers, but you'll also discover family-run child care in private homes. Hiring independent babysitters, signing up with a Mother's Day Out program, or enlisting the services of an au pair also may work well for your particular circumstances. In addition, there are agencies that can assist you if your child becomes ill and you're unable to take off work to be the primary caregiver.

With the exception of unique child-care arrangements, this chapter will not list, describe, or recommend individual day-care establishments. The purpose is to guide your decision-making, explore the standards for what most experts regard as quality care,

introduce community resources, and present alternatives. This chapter does contain a list of support groups and organizations that help both parents and other caregivers provide for healthy, happy nurturing.

UNDERSTANDING QUALITY CHILD CARE

The Pennsylvania Department of Public Welfare's Web site (www.dpw.state.pa.us/Services Programs/ChildCareEarlyEd) offers a child care checklist to guide parents in choosing quality child care. The list includes questions about the facility, staff, and safety procedures. The Pennsylvania Commission for Women also offers a printed checklist that includes questions to ask potential providers, such as "May I drop in any time?" and "Is there a parents' group or program?" To get your checklist, write the commission at Pennsylvania Commission for Women, 503 Finance Building, Harrisburg, PA 17120, or call (717) 787-8128.

In Pennsylvania the state Department of Public Welfare is the agency that regulates day-care facilities in the following categories:

- **Day Care Centers**—state-licensed facilities providing care for seven or more children
- **Group Day Care Homes**—state-licensed facilities providing care for no more than 12 children
- **Family Day Care Homes**—state-certified family residences that have one caregiver for four, five, or six children unrelated to the caregiver

In addition, the Pennsylvania Department of Education licenses nursery schools and part-time preschools in the area.

For more information about day-care facilities in the Commonwealth, call one of the state's regional toll-free hotlines. In Southwestern Pennsylvania that number is (800) 222-2149. Parents also may use this line, staffed by the Pennsylvania Department of Public Welfare, Office of Child Development, to investigate complaints, obtain day-care regulations, or ask other questions. An online directory of child care facilities can be found at www.dpw.state.pa.us/ServicesPrograms /ChildCareEarlyEd/003671396.aspx.

Additionally, Metlife Consumer Education Center has produced a useful pamphlet called "Choosing Childcare." While the booklet does not offer referrals for our region, it does an excellent job of explaining the differences in types of child care and presents points to cover when you inspect facilities and interview potential caregivers. For your free pamphlet, call (800) METLIFE. The material also is available online at www.marino.metlife.com /consumer_education.cfm under "Life Advice."

REFERRAL SERVICES

Child Care Information Serivces of Allegheny County (CCIS)
305 Wood Street
(412) 261-CARE (2273)
A program of the YWCA of Greater Pittsburgh, CCIS is committed to improving the quality of child care, providing referral services to parents at every economic level, providing subsidies to eligible parents, and enhancing the child-care system within the region.

If you're a parent searching for child care, CCIS's referral specialists will provide information on regulated (licensed or registered) child-care providers as reported by the Department of Public Welfare. CCIS staffs offices in downtown Pittsburgh, Allegheny Center, and East Pittsburgh.

Parents ultimately are responsible for screening and monitoring their child-care providers, but CCIS has valuable information to guide parents to the best choices.

Childcare Choices
1030 Eighth Avenue, Beaver Falls
(724) 847-0145, (800) 322-8504
Childcare Choices offers information to parents about the location, costs, and eligibility requirements of day-care programs in Beaver County. The office maintains a directory of available programs that offer both private and subsidized child care.

Pittsburgh Association for Education of Young Children (PAEYC)
5604 Solway Street
(412) 421-3889
www.pghaeyc.org
Serving the Southwestern Pennsylvania early learning community, PAEYC supports high quality early care and education for young children through professional development, collaboration with community resource, and advocacy for the needs and rights of children and their families. PAEYC offers a free list of accredited programs in the Pittsburgh area. These programs have met a stringent set of guidelines that promote the well-being of children. Child-care programs participate in the PAEYC assessment program on a voluntary basis.

SPECIAL CARE

The Get Well Room
327 Craft Avenue
(412) 641-1990
Located in the city's Oakland medical complex, the Get Well Room is a separate area of the Children's Center of Pittsburgh, comfortably equipped to care for children from 6 months through 12 years of age with mild respiratory or gastrointestinal illnesses. It's affiliated with Magee-Womens Hospital.

Supervised by a pediatric nurse, the staff provides a warm, caring atmosphere for children who cannot attend their regular child-care programs due to illness. The nurse decides how many children can be accepted on any given day.

Pennsylvania Pre-K Counts

For the 2007-2008 school year, the Pennsylvania Department of Public Education invested $75 million in Pennsylvania Pre-K Counts, a new early education program. The program provides high-quality pre-kindergarten services to 11,000 3 and 4 year olds in the Commonwealth of Pennsylvania so that they can enter school ready to learn and succeed in school and in life.

The education is free to families, with a focus on children at risk of academic failure, either because of income (300% of the federal poverty, or a family of four earning $61,950), language (English is not your first language), cultural or special needs issues.

Pennsylvania Pre-K is offered through established agencies and early learning programs.

Families enroll directly at each program. For a list, visit the Pennsylvania Department of Education's Web site at www.pde.state.pa.us and select "Pre K-12," then "Early Childhood," then "Pittsburgh Pre-K Counts."

on file at the Children's Center before your child can use the Get Well Room. The registration fee is $15 per family.

In addition, fees for services are due when those services are rendered. Fees are $65 a day for infants and toddlers (up to three years old) and $45 a day for children three to 12 years old. Some businesses offer their employees assistance in paying for this form of child care. All medications should be brought in their original, labeled containers. The Get Well Room is open from 7:00 a.m. to 5:30 p.m. Monday through Friday.

**The Therapeutic Parents'
and Children's Center
134 South Highland Avenue
(412) 363-1702
www.familyresourcesofpa.org**
The Therapeutic Parents' and Children's Center, a program of Family Resources, is a therapeutic preschool for children suffering developmental and emotional delays as a result of abuse or neglect. This service intervenes early in children's lives to help keep them on track developmentally and to aid their families in meeting their special needs. Call Family Resources for more information if you feel this type of care is appropriate for your child.

Other services of Family Resources are described under Support Organizations, below.

PART-DAY AND AFTER-SCHOOL PROGRAMS

In many communities in the region, you'll find part-time programs to help you meet your child-care needs. Churches and synagogues offer Mother's Day Out programs for infants to kindergarten-age children. After registering your child, you can arrange a schedule that gives you several hours of child care at nominal charges, similar in most cases to what you would pay a babysitter. To find such respite when you need it, contact churches and synagogues in your community.

Children may participate if they have mild fevers (103 degrees or less) or bronchitis, croup, asthma, diarrhea, occasional vomiting, or pain or fever from vaccinations. Children suffering from chicken pox, respiratory distress, continuous vomiting or diarrhea, and those with fevers higher than 103 degrees are not appropriate candidates for the Get Well Room.

If the service of the Get Well Room might help you, you'll need to complete a registration form and have your child's physician complete a health appraisal. Both forms must be

In addition, many school districts can direct parents to after-school programs. Check with your school district's administrative office to determine if it offers such a program (see the Education chapter for school district contact information).

A+ Schools, an independent community advocate for improvement in public education, offers a list of after-school providers on their Web site, www.aplusschools.org. Simply type in a subject (e.g., summer, tutoring, math, etc.) into the searchable database located on their home page, www.aplusschools.org.

Organizations such as the YMCA and YWCA offer after-school or latch-key programs, while some churches also provide midweek programs for children and youths. Since the Greater Pittsburgh community is so vast, the range of services offered varies considerably. Each YMCA or YWCA, for instance, reflects the social and economic needs of the individual community. Thus there could be subsidized child care available in some neighborhoods and latch-key programs in others.

Regardless of the type of program you consider, do ask a few basic questions, including:

- Are these programs for children of a particular age? Or are various ages combined within the same program?
- What kinds of activities are offered?
- Who supervises the children?
- Are the surroundings safe?
- Is there a fee to be involved, or is membership or residency required (in the case of the YWCA, a church, or a school district)?
- Does the program operate during summers, holidays or snow days, or solely on school days?

Armed with these questions, you should turn to your local telephone directory or Yellow Pages to begin your search for the care that's appropriate for your child.

SUPPORT ORGANIZATIONS

Alliance for Infants and Toddlers, Inc.
Hough Building, 2801 Custer Avenue
(412) 885-6000
www.afit.org
The alliance provides developmental screening and tracking for children from birth to 3 years of age throughout Allegheny County. Your child may participate if there is parental concern or a history of medical, environmental, or biological factors such as prematurity or a stay in a neonatal intensive care unit.

To be eligible for Infant/Toddler Early Intervention Services, children must be diagnosed with physical or mental conditions that place them at high risk for developmental delays. Services of the alliance are free and confidential. Call them to arrange an assessment to determine eligibility.

ARC of Greater Pittsburgh
711 Bingham Street
(412) 995-5000
www.achieve.info
The mission of ARC of Greater Pittsburgh (part of the ACHIEVA family of organizations) is to protect the rights of, and promote opportunities for, those with mental retardation and developmental disabilities, and to do so within a family context. The organization's diverse services include early intervention, assessments and therapy for infants and toddlers, family support networks, respite and sitter care, specially designed homes to meet the needs of older adults, employment initiatives, and recreational, vacation, and summer camp opportunities.

You'll find more on ARC of Greater Pittsburgh in the Health Care chapter. While ARC of Greater Pittsburgh serves Allegheny and Beaver Counties, you'll also find ARC organizations in three other counties within the primary service area. These are:

- ARC–Butler County, (724) 282-1500
- ARC–Washington County, (724) 745-3010
- ARC–Westmoreland County, (724) 837-8159

Allegheny Intermediate Unit
475 East Waterfront Drive, Homestead
(412) 394-5700
www.aiu3.net

The Allegheny Intermediate Unit (AIU) is the largest of Pennsylvania's 29 intermediate units, which provide curriculum-enhancement services to school districts. Working with school districts throughout Allegheny County, this nonprofit regional education agency administers such initiatives as Head Start, Project DART, and programs for gifted students.

Each school district in Pennsylvania is served by an intermediate unit. See the Education chapter for a description of intermediate units in our region.

Big Brothers and Big Sisters of Greater Pittsburgh
5989 Penn Circle South
(412) 363-6100
www.bbbspittsburgh.org

This agency matches caring adults with at-risk children from single-parent households in Allegheny and Washington Counties. These one-to-one mentoring relationships help children thrive. Volunteers are welcome, but the selection process is rather rigorous, including a thorough interview, background checks and clearances, and training.

You'll find a similar organization in each county in the primary service area. You can reach them at these numbers:

- Big Brothers Big Sisters of Armstrong County, (724) 763-4181
- Big Brothers Big Sisters of Beaver County, (724) 728-4300
- Big Brothers Big Sisters of Butler County, (724) 287-4733

i The United Way of Allegheny County hosts HelpConnections, a searchable database on their Web site. You can search this site for after school programs, extended day care, and other early childhood programs. Visit www.unitedwaypittsburgh.org for details.

- Big Brothers Big Sisters of Greater Pittsburgh, Greene County Office, (724) 883-2188
- Big Brothers Big Sisters of Greater Pittsburgh, Washington County Office, (724) 228-9191
- Big Brothers Big Sisters of Westmoreland County, (724) 837-6198

Family Communications, Inc.
4802 Fifth Avenue
(412) 687-2990
www.fci.org

The Mister Rogers' Neighborhood Childcare Partnership is a joint effort of Family Communications, public television stations, and others committed to the education and welfare of children. The partnership offers training and support materials for child-care providers as well as a quarterly newsletter. The Web site offers guidance and ideas to parents who are helping their children with issues such as resolving angry feelings, dealing with death or divorce, and overcoming fears.

Another project, *The Mister Rogers Plan & Play Book,* extends the popular television program to the child-care setting, with more than 400 richly illustrated pages of easy-to-do activities. For more about the late Mister Rogers and his pioneering work with children, see the Kidstuff chapter.

Family Resources
141 South Highland Avenue
(412) 363-1702
www.familyresourcesofpa.org

Family Resources is the largest child-abuse treatment and prevention agency in Allegheny County. It works to strengthen families and neighborhoods by providing training for professionals as well as crisis intervention for families where abuse has occurred. Licensed as an outpatient mental health facility and provider of enhanced mental health services, family resources is a United Way member agency.

The services offered by Family Resources are diverse. They include parent support serv-

To find a Parents Anonymous group in your county, call the state resource office of Parents Anonymous at (800) 448-4906, or got to www.parents anonymous.org.

ices such as Parents Anonymous groups, nurturing courses, The Therapeutic Parents' and Children's Center described above, and a 260-acre Family Retreat Center in Warrendale that is available year-round to community organizations, social and religious groups, schools, and businesses. Family resources can help connect parents with primary health care, substance abuse treatment, housing services, and job placement and recreational programs.

In addition, the agency operates the WARMLINE, a telephone service offering parenting information, referrals, and support. You can ask nonmedical questions regarding such topics as discipline, postpartum depression, children's bedwetting, and general parental stress. The WARMLINE is staffed by trained volunteers. It's free and confidential. You can reach it at (412) 641-4546, (800) 641-4546 if you're outside Allegheny County.

Family Links Parent & Child Guidance Center
250 Shady Avenue
(412) 661-1800
www.familylinks.org
This nonprofit organization provides a diversity of mental health, mental retardation, educational outreach, testing, and consultation services for children and families, as well as outpatient clinical treatment and a therapeutic school for children in preschool through grade 4 with severe social and emotional delays.

If you would like to learn about other organizations that provide mentoring in the area, contact The Mentoring Partnership of Southwestern Pennsylvania, (412) 281-2535, www.mentoring pittsburgh.org.

Parental Stress Center
5877 Commerce Street
(412) 361-4800
www.pscfamily.net
The mission of the Parental Stress Center is to prevent child abuse and neglect through education, counseling, and intensive services. They provide transportation and supervised visits for parents and their children when the children have been placed outside of the home. For families at risk of child abuse and/or neglect, they offer intensive family counseling. The center also offers an after-school program to youth ages 9 to 18 and they help families and older youth achieve economic independence through their Economic Empowerment Initiative.

Parents Anonymous
2001 North Front Street, Building 1
Suite 210, Harrisburg
(800) 448-4906
If you feel occasional anger and frustration associated with the challenges and pressures of raising children, Parents Anonymous support groups can help you develop coping and management strategies. When you contact the Parents Anonymous state resource office in Harrisburg at the number listed above, they'll put you in touch with support groups in your area. Parents Anonymous is run by various organizations throughout the state.

You also may contact Family Resources, (412) 363-1702, if you're in Allegheny County, or ParentWISE Inc. for Parents Anonymous of Westmoreland County, (800) 544-0227. In Beaver County, Family Enrichment runs the program; call (724) 774-0522. Family Services at Butler Memorial Hospital is the host agency in Butler County at (724) 284-4894.

Ronald McDonald House
500–512 Shady Avenue
(412) 362-3400
www.rmhcpgh.org
Opened in 1979, Ronald McDonald House is a home away from home for families who must travel hundreds, even thousands of miles

from their own communities for medical treatment for their children. Located near Children's Hospital, the house is designed to encourage interaction between guests and to help them cope during a trying period.

Safe Sitter
8604 Allisonville Road, Suite 248
Indianapolis, Indiana
(800) 255-4089
www.safesitter.org
Founded in 1980 by Indianapolis pediatrician Patricia A. Keener, M.D., Safe Sitter is a babysitter training program designed to reach young persons ages 11 to 13 before they begin actively babysitting. In one- or two-day courses, usually offered at local hospitals, Safe Sitter teaches youths what to expect when dealing with children, how to avoid difficult situations, and how to solve problems if they occur. Students learn such techniques as

i Children's Hospital of Pittsburgh provides dozens of educational classes for parents, many of them free. Call the Community Education line at (412) 692-7105 for class schedules and parenting information.

rescue breathing and accident management, and they're also grounded in the business aspects of babysitting.

The program helps young babysitting entrepreneurs, of course, but it also is a boon to parents, providing them with a pool of well-trained babysitters. Safe Sitter includes more than 550 participating hospitals and teaching sites in the United States and abroad. In fact, St. Clair Hospital in Pittsburgh's South Hills served as the pilot site for the rollout of Safe Sitter's one-day instructional program. For details, call (412) 344-6600, extension 1027.

EDUCATION

The diversity of local government in Southwestern Pennsylvania extends to the area of education. It's an arena that's always important, usually colorful, and sometimes frustrating. Sheer numbers tell a large part of the story here. Of the 501 school districts in the Commonwealth of Pennsylvania, 100 of them serve this guide's six-county principal coverage area. Since many aspects of public education are left to the discretion of local school districts, standardization in any area is rare.

Rather than provide you with profiles of 100 school districts, which would be numbing and counterproductive, a somewhat different approach is taken in this chapter. We've tried to explore the most important issues—most notably school choice and standards—and to provide some insight into how local school districts are dealing with these issues. This treatment is by no means exhaustive; it seems unlikely that any could be.

We've rounded out our look at the education scene with some background on diocesan schools and profiles of other private schools, or independent schools, as they sometimes prefer to be known. You'll find that when it comes to education in Southwestern Pennsylvania, you may have more options than you ever imagined.

PUBLIC SCHOOLS

Organization

Public education in Pennsylvania is provided by 501 school districts; our six-county coverage area boasts 100 of those school districts, making education here diverse and colorful. Many districts have been formed through consolidation so that most districts encompass several municipalities or more, though

this is not universally the case. Some districts have taken their names from the communities they serve. Carlynton School District in Pittsburgh's western suburbs, for example, spans the municipalities of Carnegie, Rosslyn Farms, and Crafton. On the other hand, on the heels of some mergers, district administrators couldn't find names that incorporated all their communities, so they threw up their hands and went in other directions. When schools in Dormont, Castle Shannon, and Green Tree merged into a single district, they opted for the name Keystone Oaks—a pleasant-sounding appellation with no syllabic echoes of any of the participating communities.

School districts are governed by nine-member elected boards that in turn name superintendents to lead district administration. Pittsburgh Public Schools, including the city of Pittsburgh and the borough of Mt. Oliver (a municipality surrounded by the city), is the region's largest, serving more than 29,447 students in kindergarten through grade 12 in 65 schools. Pittsburgh Public Schools Is the second largest district in Pennsylvania.

Outside of Pittsburgh, one of the largest districts in the region is the sprawling North Allegheny School District, which includes 12 schools and more than 8,038 students. One of the smallest districts in our region is Beaver County's Midland Borough School District, with 365 students and one school. In one of those regional quirks you'll come to love, Midland Borough high-school students actually attend East Liverpool High School across the border in Ohio because there aren't enough students to support a local high school.

Most districts have separate buildings for elementary, middle, and high schools, but you will find a number of junior-senior high schools. Several of the smallest districts teach all their students, irrespective of grade level, in the same building.

Grade Levels and Nomenclature

As with most facets of education in South-western Pennsylvania, grade levels and nomenclature are far from standard. Districts tend to group their students into three broad grade levels, but you'll find a great deal of variation in how the levels are defined and what they're called. A common structure is kindergarten through grade 5 for elementary school, grades 6 through 8 for middle school, and grades 9 through 12 for high school. A few school districts divide grades 9 through 12 into intermediate and senior high schools, while a few eliminate the middle level entirely. All school districts offer kindergarten, and some have preschool programs.

This may not be the most vital aspect of education in our region, but if you're used to a structure that includes middle schools, for example, you might want to seek out a district that offers such schools.

Standards

Academic standards are a matter of state policy—and an issue that generates more discussion locally than any education-related issue other than school choice. In fact, the Pennsylvania Legislature regularly considers revamping statewide standards.

Currently the state wants its students to achieve competence and understanding in the following areas: communications; arts and humanities; final form career education and work; civics and government; economics, environment and ecology; family and consumer sciences; geography; health; safety and physical education; history, mathematics; reading, writing, speaking, and listening; and science and technology.

To learn more about academic standards, visit the Pennsylvania Department of Education's Web site, www.pde.state.pa.us, and select "Academic Standards."

Curriculum

In a refrain you'll hear repeated throughout this chapter, curriculum is largely a district prerogative. Since all school districts must assure that their students meet state standards, the academic core at each curriculum is fairly standard. From there it's a wide-open affair. Electives vary widely. Driver's education, for example, is among the most popular electives but not universally offered. If you're considering locating in a local school district, one question you'll want to ask will be about electives offered.

Curriculum Enrichment

Enhancing and enriching the classroom experience is an area where Pennsylvania school districts shine. Some years ago the state realized that teachers and administrators would be too burdened with day-to-day matters to give much consideration to curriculum innovations, so they developed 29 new groups reaching every county of the state and charged them with the mission of innovation. The organizations, known as intermediate units, function in specific geographic areas. Our region boasts seven IUs: IU1, serving Washington, Greene, and Fayette Counties; IU2, for Pittsburgh and Mt. Oliver; IU3, the state's largest, covering Allegheny County, except Pittsburgh and Mt. Oliver; IU4, including Butler, Lawrence, and Mercer Counties; IU7, for Westmoreland County; IU27, covering the Beaver Valley; and IU28, serving Armstrong and Indiana Counties.

The impact of the IUs is varied and broad. Their services range from the Head Start program for preschoolers to programs for gifted students. They work with the Governor's Schools of Excellence, six residential summer programs held on college campuses. In Allegheny County the IU has worked with four schools to establish a distance learning network; at the same time, the Allegheny Intermediate Unit provides educational services to adjudicated students, such as those at the Shuman Center, the county's principal juvenile detention center. IU1, which works largely with rural school districts, has linked 45 schools in a fiber-optic network that provides teleconferencing capability.

The work of the IUs is challenging and exciting—the Allegheny Intermediate Unit applies 2,000 full- and part-time employees to the task. They're an essential element in Pennsylvania's education system. If there were no IUs, we'd have to invent them.

Textbooks

Since textbook selection is a school district prerogative, the region has no standard textbooks. Rather, there are many. While textbook selection has been a flashpoint in some parts of the country, it's generally been less than incendiary here. The only way you can get involved is to work with your school district.

Teachers

All public school teachers in the Commonwealth must be certified by the Pennsylvania Department of Education, which maintains different requirements for different teaching levels. Pennsylvania has reciprocal certification agreements with a number of other states, so if you're a teacher relocating to the Keystone State, you'll still have to apply for your certification, but you may not have to worry about any further requirements.

Hiring policies are pretty much the domain of school districts. A few, such as the Pittsburgh Public Schools, impose residency requirements, but most do not. Virtually all public school teachers in our six-county coverage area are represented by unions—the two most prominent are the Pennsylvania State Education Association, an affiliate of the National Education Association, and the Pennsylvania Federation of Teachers, an affiliate of the American Federation of Teachers.

One of the practical implications of the broad teacher unionization in Southwestern Pennsylvania is that as contracts expire, negotiations between unions and their school districts become quite public—and sometimes passionate. With 100 school district–teacher

union contracts in the region, bargaining is pretty much a constant. Counting down the days to a potential strike or lockout is something of an annual rite of summer here. Fortunately delays in the start of the school year are averted most of the time.

Special and Gifted Education

While all states require programs for students judged exceptional—often called special education—Pennsylvania is among the minority of states that also requires educational programs for those deemed gifted. The rules for both sets of programs are fairly similar. In each case, the designation "exceptional" or "gifted" is determined through a process called a multidisciplinary review, which may be requested by the school or a parent. In all cases, the schools prefer to consider parents part of the evaluation team and seek parental consent for, and participation in, the review. Where parental consent is withheld, the district may seek a court order for a review, but this is rare.

If the review panel determines that a student needs special programs, these may be provided through the district and specially assembled Individualized Educational Teams, or the students may be referred to one of 11 special services schools in our region, including the Western Pennsylvania School for the Blind and the Western Pennsylvania School for the Deaf. In a related program, preschoolers under the age of five may be eligible for a school-district's early intervention services following an evaluation; parents may request the evaluation.

That gives you some background on the rules, but it doesn't begin to describe the variety of programs for exceptional and gifted students. The state provides overall supervision but expects school districts to develop and fund their own programs. Pittsburgh Public Schools operates three centers that offer specially designed instruction for exceptional children; other districts offer their services on-site. Similarly, in the area of gifted education, the Pittsburgh Public Schools maintains special centers that elementary- and middle-school students attend one day per week; high-school students, on the other hand, typically receive their special programs on-site.

While there's no charge to parents for special or gifted education programs, there's no end to the variations in the ways area school districts provide these programs. If you're considering locating here, this is clearly an area you'll want to explore.

Alternative Education

Many districts provide alternative programming for suspended students and others who need support due to behavioral and academic difficulties. These may be site-based programs or schools dedicated to alternative education. Pittsburgh Public Schools, to cite one important example, offers both types of programming. Its alternative elementary-school programs are site-based, while middle-school and high-school students may be assigned to dedicated buildings. If you have the opportunity to choose your school district, you may want to inquire about its alternative education programs.

School Choice

This has been perhaps the hottest topic in the impassioned debates about education in Southwestern Pennsylvania, usually triggered by the busing plans that several districts employ to achieve racial balance in their schools. Groups rally round the "busing" and "neighborhood schools" flags with vigor and conviction. The issue, however, may be more symbolic than an actual concern, since even the few districts that bus students tend to keep it to a minimum. Thus the number of students affected by busing is relatively few.

A more far-reaching component of the school choice debate involves the possibility of public financial support for parents who opt to send their children to private schools. Advocates have proposed publicly supported tuition vouchers for students who attend private schools. While this proposal has failed to carry the Pennsylvania Legislature, look for

this debate to continue. For many students and their families, the debate about choice is theoretical, as students in most cases are required to attend the schools designated by the districts in which they reside. There are several opportunities for choice.

Under state law, students may opt to attend public schools outside their district, provided they pay tuition to the schools they attend. Tuition rates are established by the state, based on the cost of education in each district. You will find a catch here, however. No school district is required to accept students from other districts. So even if you're willing to pay the price for sending your child outside your district, you need the cooperation of the other school district.

Yet another element of choice is provided by the Pittsburgh Public Schools through its "magnet schools" program. Magnets are elementary and secondary schools that focus on particular areas of study. Since one of the goals of the magnet program is to achieve racial balance through voluntary choice, 50 percent of slots at each magnet are reserved for African-American students, 50 percent for students of other races. Some magnet options are sequential, beginning in kindergarten and continuing through middle school and high school. Some give preference to younger siblings of those enrolled in magnet programs, or to students who reside in particular neighborhoods.

At the high-school level, the district offers magnets in international studies, creative and performing arts, preengineering, computer science, and teaching. Law and public service, junior ROTC, public safety, high technology, and vocational-technical training, as well as one called a "Traditional Academy" in a highly structured and disciplined setting. Other magnets are available at the elementary and middle school levels.

Magnets are open to students throughout the city, so long as racial balances are preserved. When there are more applicants than a school can accommodate, slots are awarded by lottery.

Charter Schools

The sentiment for school choice has inspired a new type of educational option in the region—charter schools. In June 1997 Pennsylvania became the 27th state to enact legislation authorizing charter schools, which may be defined as independent public schools that are designed by individuals or groups to fulfill a specific educational mission. Each charter school must be approved and funded by the local school district in which the charter school is located. Any students can opt to attend charter schools in their districts, and no tuition charges are permitted.

In early 1998 school boards reviewed and approved a number of proposed charter schools. The first charter schools in Southwestern Pennsylvania opened their doors in September 1998. Among these were Manchester Academic Charter School, Urban League of Pittsburgh Charter School, and the Thurgood Marshall Academy. While the missions of charter schools differ, most plan longer school days and school years than found in traditional schools.

If a charter school sounds like an option you'd like to consider, you'll find several sources of information about them. A list of charter schools can be found at www.ed reform.com/charter_schoolsweb.

Transportation

The groundswell of support for school choice is manifest in the area of transportation as well. Under state law, school districts may provide transportation for their students, or they can elect not to. A number opt out of transportation, forcing students to find their own way to school. Why would they impose this requirement on their students? It might be because state law also mandates that districts providing transportation for their students must provide the same type of transportation for nonpublic school students within their districts. Moreover, students can attend nonpublic schools up to 10 miles

For more on the Pittsburgh Public Schools, see the district's home page, www.pps.k12.pa.us. If home schooling is more your bailiwick, check out www.pahomeschoolers.com. For information and guidance about charter public schools, visit the Pennsylvania Coalition of Charter Schools at www .edreform.com.

beyond a district's borders and still be eligible for free district-provided transportation.

Some public school districts have contested this requirement; the Pittsburgh Public Schools filed and lost court action against the requirement, pointing out that transportation for nonpublic students—by bus, van, and cab—accounts for about 28 percent of its annual transportation budget.

The purpose of the policy, of course, is to make it easier and less expensive for parents to choose private schools for their children. Whether or not you agree with the policy of public financing for certain aspects of private schools, there's no doubt that the state's transportation program has made private schools more accessible to more families.

Homeschooling

The increase in homeschooling throughout the Commonwealth is one final ramification of the thrust for school choice. Since 1986, parents, guardians, and legal custodians have been authorized to teach their children at home. Enrollment in home-schooling increased from 11,0227 in 1993 to 24,215 in 2002.

Those teaching their children at home must file an annual home education affidavit with their school districts. This notarized document must specify the name of the home education supervisor, an outline by subject area of proposed educational objectives, and evidence of each child's immunization and access to health services. The affidavit also must specify any curriculum materials—including textbooks—to be borrowed from the school district.

Public schools in our region are supported by the proceeds of wage taxes, real estate taxes, and a number of smaller taxes.

In many cases school districts welcome home-taught children to the fold, opening their extracurricular activities to such students. In other districts home-taught children will feel like beggars at the feast, with districts only grudgingly agreeing to their participation in school activities. If you plan to teach your children at home but want them to enjoy some of the socialization benefits of group schooling, the best approach may be to discuss your plans with district and school administration. At the very least you'll get a good idea where you stand.

Athletics

Interscholastic athletics in Pennsylvania is largely the domain of the Pennsylvania Interscholastic Athletic Agency (PIAA)—its administrative unit in our region is the Western Pennsylvania Interscholastic Athletic League (WPIAL). PIAA rules and regulations govern interscholastic sports for 1,450 schools in the Commonwealth—including 200 private schools—and 350,000 students. The PIAA operates and organizes championships in 11 boys' sports and 11 girls' sports.

The roster of interscholastic sports offered varies from district to district, but among the most popular are baseball, basketball, cross-country, football, soccer, swimming and diving, tennis, volleyball, and track and field. You'll also find interscholastic programs in bowling, golf, ice hockey, lacrosse, and rifle. Most districts also maintain active intramural programs.

To assure fair and fun competition, the PIAA classifies its member high schools by enrollment, with categories ranging from Class A for the smallest schools to Class AAAA—Quad A, as it's known—for the largest schools. Classifications may vary from sport to sport. For example, a high school with 175 boys in grades 9 through 12 would

play in Class A in baseball but in Class AA in basketball. The PIAA modifies its classification guidelines as enrollment fluctuations dictate. For the most current classification, playoff schedule, and other PIAA news, check out the agency's Web site: www.piaa.org.

Keep in mind that if your children want to participate in interscholastic sports, they must maintain certain academic standards. Generally the WPIAL requires a 1.5 grade point average for sports participation. School districts, however, have the option to impose more stringent standards. The Pittsburgh Public Schools has done that, requiring a 2.0 grade point average of its student-athletes.

Parent Involvement

The fragmentation of government in Southwestern Pennsylvania may be lamentable in some areas, but the great number and diversity of schools and school districts in the region provide unusually rich opportunities for parent involvement in their youngsters' education. Parent-teacher organizations are a traditional model for parent involvement, but there are others that afford a more hands-on approach. Consider the Pittsburgh Public Schools as an example. In the city, schools may have a Parent School Community Council (PSCC) that works with administrators on such operational areas as curriculum and other academic programs. They may also have a Parent Teacher Organization (PTO) that provides volunteers and funding support for social and educational programs. To learn more about parent engagement and involvement opportunities, contact A+ Schools (412) 258-2660 or visit www.aplusschools.org.

With 100 school districts in the region, voters must elect 900 school board members. You may never have considered public service as an elected official, but Southwestern Pennsylvania provides you with that chance. Many school board members have little prior political experience; they became involved because they wanted to help their children as the youngsters progressed through the system.

If you do consider a run for a school board seat, remember that this is full-fledged politics. The parties nominate their candidates in primary elections, with the winners determined in general elections. While some seats are uncontested, other elections are intense, involving media coverage and debate that may be less than genteel. Electoral politics is not for all tastes, but if you can endure the rough and tumble nature of elections, a school board seat may await you.

DIOCESAN SCHOOLS

Diocesan schools are a powerful and important force in our region. If you considered the Catholic schools of the Diocese of Pittsburgh a school district, they would constitute the fourth largest school district in the Commonwealth. The Diocese of Pittsburgh and the Diocese of Greensburg include all six counties in this guide's principal coverage area. Together they operate 114 schools, including 12 high schools.

Each diocese is divided into administrative units known as deaneries that include elementary and secondary schools, or elementary schools only. The two deaneries in Washington County, for example, offer elementary schools only, so graduates of those schools will have to travel a bit to continue their education at a diocesan secondary school. Teachers at most—but not all—diocesan high schools are represented by the Federation of Pittsburgh Diocesan Teachers.

The emphasis on academics at diocesan schools is tangible. Diocese of Pittsburgh secondary schools send 96 percent of their graduates on for further education, an impressive statistic. The high schools typically offer extensive honors and advanced-placement programs as well as innovative college-in-high school programs that inspire and prepare students for higher education.

Diocesan schools are private, so state mandates for gifted and special education don't apply to them in the same ways as they do to public schools. However, public school districts include students of diocesan schools in some of their programs for exceptional children. In two of its high schools, the Diocese of Pittsburgh also offers a noncollege-directed curriculum for developmentally challenged students, who take most courses in a resource room but share some regular courses with the general student body.

The range of extracurricular activities available to students is broad, including clubs for drama, instrumental and vocal music, and forensics, as well as school newspapers and yearbooks. In athletics the schools participate with public schools in the Western Pennsylvania Interscholastic Athletic League in such activities as baseball, basketball, bowling, crew, cross-country, field hockey, football, golf, ice hockey, lacrosse, soccer, softball, swimming, tennis, track, volleyball, and wrestling. Note that some schools offer a number of these sports as club or intramural activities, rather than as interscholastic sports, and that some diocesan high schools impose more stringent grade requirements than does the WPIAL.

Since diocesan schools are private, they maintain both admissions standards and tuition charges. While admission is generally open, the schools will review placement tests, academic records, and personal interviews. Many schools offer financial-aid programs, with need assessment performed by an independent outside agency, as well as work-study programs. In the Diocese of Pittsburgh, all students are eligible for support from the Bishop's Education Fund, which offers need-based grants.

The schools welcome parental involvement through such vehicles as school, parent advisory, and development boards, and activity booster organizations—these are particularly supportive of athletic and musical activities. If diocesan schools sound like an option you'd like to explore, you can contact the Diocese of Pittsburgh Education Secretariat at (412) 456-3090, www.diopitt.org/education.dcs.html, or the Diocese of Greensburg, (724) 837-0901, www.2.dioceseofgreens

burg.org, for information on schools. These sources may also be able to refer you to Catholic education contacts in other districts.

OTHER PRIVATE SCHOOLS

If you're shopping for a private school, you'll find a rich variety in Southwestern Pennsylvania. The region boasts a wide assortment of college-prep schools, religion-focused schools, and those targeted to students with special needs. Presented are profiles of schools that offer high-school education—private grade schools would be too numerous to cover effectively—but where such schools offer primary education as well, we've noted that. (Our one exception is the Waldorf School, which we felt was too noteworthy not to mention.) Unless otherwise noted, the schools charge tuition and are coeducational.

Keep in mind that private schools are just that—private. They operate largely outside the purview of the Pennsylvania Department of Education and so are free to establish their own guidelines and policies in most areas of operation. If you're researching private schools, ask as many questions as you can, as their programs and policies vary widely.

North

Shady Side Academy—Senior School
423 Fox Chapel Road, Fox Chapel
(412) 968-3182

Founded in 1883, Shady Side is the region's largest private school, with its junior, middle, and senior schools. The senior school (high school) offers a five-day boarding program, an attractive and unusual asset; 500 students are enrolled in the senior school alone. The campuses span 172 acres, 25 buildings, and 10 athletic fields. (If you're interested in the junior school, it's located in the East End of the City of Pittsburgh in a neighborhood called Park Place.)

Shady Side's emphasis on college preparation is strong; typically 100 percent of graduates attend four-year colleges or universities. Distinguished alumni include Pulitzer Prize–

winning author and historian David McCullough and former astronaut Jay Apt, who once served as director of Pittsburgh's Carnegie Museum of Natural History. The school boasts a student-teacher ratio of 9:1. Shady Side provides financial aid—most of it need-based—to more than 15 percent of its students.

Students participate in more than 50 clubs and are invited to become involved in the school's operations through membership on committees for curriculum, admissions, discipline, and independent study. For hands-on environmental study, Shady Side's Maine Coast Semester affords students the chance to live on a working farm for half a school year. Shady Side's varsity athletic teams compete in the Western Pennsylvania Interscholastic Athletic League as well as head to head with other independent schools.

If you're thinking about applying to the senior school, Shady Side requires both an interview and a campus tour.

Vincentian Academy—Duquesne University
Peebles and McKnight Roads
(412) 364-1616
www.vaduq.org

Vincentian Academy's relationship with Duquesne University is a strong attraction. The academy is linked to Duquesne's computer network, bringing its students access to that resource. Vincentian also is part of Duquesne's Campus Ministries Program to assist in its commitment to values and public service. Perhaps most importantly, Vincentian graduates who enroll at Duquesne University are eligible for both admission and 25 percent tuition scholarships. The academy emphasizes that it expects and encourages its students to enroll at prestigious colleges and universities across the country rather than at Duquesne exclusively.

Located in Pittsburgh's North Hills, Vincentian is a day school that participates in the International Baccalaureate, an academic program offered by more than 1,200 schools worldwide. The IB program strives for a balanced education that facilitates geographic and cultural mobility and promotes international understanding through shared academic experiences. The curriculum includes studies in language, individuals and societies, experimental sciences, mathematics, and a range of electives. One specific advantage of an IB diploma: A number of colleges and universities grant up to a year's academic credit for students who earn it.

The student-teacher ratio is an appealing 9:1. Vincentian offers financial aid but describes the program as "limited." Students participate in 12 sports and more than two dozen additional extracurricular activities. If someone in your family is interested in Vincentian, take advantage of the school's "shadowing" program, which invites prospective students to spend a day with current students.

East

The Ellis School
6425 Fifth Avenue
(412) 661-5992
www.theellisschool.org
Founded in 1916, Ellis is an independent school for girls in kindergarten through 12th grade. Its seven-acre campus lies in Pittsburgh's Shadyside neighborhood, just a quick bus trip from all the amenities of Oakland's university complex. Some statistics about Ellis will tell you much about the school. Its student-teacher ratio is 6:1, while its student-computer ratio is 4:1. Of the seniors among the 470 students, each typically is enrolled in at least one advanced-placement course.

The academic program at Ellis blends required courses with a diverse menu of electives. All ninth graders, for example, study the Concepts of Physics, which kicks off a three-year science sequence that also includes chemistry and biology. Ninth graders also write at least 10 papers for English class and a research paper in the social sciences. More than 90 percent of students opt for electives in the fine arts. In addition to their class work, students provide volunteer service for more than 50 organizations.

Ellis administers tests to all applicants for admission. These usually are scheduled in December and January, but the school will make special arrangements to accommodate your schedule. More than 20 percent of Ellis students receive financial aid.

The Kiski School
1888 Brett Lane, Saltsburg
(724) 639-3586, (877) 547-5448
www.kiski.org
In 1878 ambitious developers constructed a rambling Victorian hotel on the cliffs above the Kiskiminetas River in the Westmoreland County town of Saltsburg to serve pilgrims who flocked to the area for the alleged curative powers of its mineral springs. The "Magic Waters" soon dried up, leaving the hotel for purchase and conversion to the Kiskiminetas Springs School. It flourishes still on that site, but today, it's known more simply as the Kiski School.

It's a 350-acre residential, college preparatory school for 206 boys from grades 9 through 12. The academic schedule is demanding and Kiski doesn't apologize for it, claiming that a rigorous approach "is designed to allow a boy to enter a college equal to his ability and to succeed once he is there." Average student-teacher ratio is 7:1. Homework averages one hour per class meeting, and just to be sure underclassmen are completing that homework, Kiski conducts a two-hour supervised study period each evening. The school requires three years of language study and a Life Skills course, which includes instruction in computer literacy, health and wellness, and speech.

Kiski is serious about athletics as well. If you don't plan to participate in an interscholastic sport in each of the three athletic seasons, you may arrange an "alternate physical development activity" with the permission of the athletic director or headmaster. You'll find other extracurricular activities—including 30 special interest activities—that aren't quite so mandatory, as well as a summer program of classes and sports.

ℹ️ The Pennsylvania Association of Independent Schools, 37 East Germantown Pike, Suite 302, Plymouth Meeting, (610) 567-2960, offers an online directory of member schools. To view the directory, visit www.paispa.org.

Among Kiski's most distinguished alumni are actor David Conrad, John (Jack) B. Hanna, and U.S. Congressman John (Jack) Murtha.

The Oakland School
362 McKee Place
(412) 621-7878
www.theoaklandschool.org

If you're looking for individualized education for your children, you'll find it at the Oakland School, where the average class size is six. To maintain that class size, this day school limits its total enrollment to 55 students. The school is coeducational and situated in the heart of Oakland's university-medical complex, from which it draws both energy and resources.

The academic program includes studies in communications, mathematics, arts, humanities, science, social studies, and computer education, as well as programs in foreign languages like French and Spanish. Students may participate in a wide variety of extracurricular activities and are required to perform community service. A work-study program provides students with academic credit for field experience, while a mentor program pairs students with staff advisors. The Oakland School describes its financial aid opportunities as "limited."

Trinity Christian School
299 Ridge Avenue, Forest Hills
(412) 242-8886
www.trinitychristian.net

Since 1953 Trinity Christian School has been providing Christian education in the Pittsburgh area. The program is based on the Reformed tradition, but these days the school welcomes all denominations. Its 350 students in kindergarten through high school represent nearly 100 churches. More than 90 percent of Trinity Christian graduates seek higher education. The school enhances its curriculum with honors programs in physics, calculus, and advanced mathematics. Facilities include computer and photography labs, as well as an art room and soccer and softball fields.

The Waldorf School
201 South Winebiddle Street
(412) 441-5792
www.waldorfpittsburgh.org

Waldorf education was started in the early 1900s by a philosopher/scientist named Rudolf Steiner. The Waldorf School provides a classical education, with a firm grounding in language arts, math, history, and science. The school's distinction is the way children are encouraged to learn—through arts, music, and movement—and the emphasis that's placed throughout the different grades on children's self-awareness, self-trust, and confidence.

In the five-day, with three-day option, nursery program (8:30 a.m. to noon) and the five-day kindergarten program (8:15 a.m. to 3:00 p.m.), the focus is on imaginative play as the most important objective, with lots of artistic activities, singing, and movement games. As children are developmentally ready for learning academic subjects in larger blocks of time, for each subject, they create their own textbooks, using their neatly handwritten, original compositions and accompanying illustrations. Writing and reading are incorporated into all their subjects, in fact, and math is taught in a way that is imaginative, fun, and relevant for the students.

In addition, starting in first grade, children take two languages (Spanish and Russian), watercolor painting, beeswax modeling, and a handwork class, where they learn to knit, crochet, and do cross-stitch. They also learn to play the flute. Starting in third grade, there are stringed instrument, games, and music classes.

Attesting to the effectiveness of Waldorf education, as students graduate from the school and continue their studies elsewhere, they are confident among their peers and test higher in most subjects than other children. The school's current program is from its nursery through grade 6. The school also offers an Extended Care program for children ages 3 through 12.

The Winchester Thurston School
555 Morewood Avenue
(412) 578-7500
www.winchesterthurston.org

Winchester Thurston boasts two campuses— a campus in Pittsburgh's Shadyside neighborhood for students from pre-kindergarten through grade 12, and a campus in the northern suburb of Allison Park for students in pre-kindergarten through grade 5. In all, the school serves about 600 students with an attractive student-teacher ratio of 8:1, affording each student a great deal of individualized attention. Class size averages 16 students.

The school has undergone changes in recent years. From its founding in 1887 through 1991, Winchester Thurston admitted girls only. Beginning in 1991 boys were phased in, and the school is now fully coeducational. All receive strong preparation for college. Of graduates in one recent year, 98 percent went on to four-year colleges or universities, while the balance chose two-year colleges or vocational schools.

Areas of study include English, social studies, modern and classical languages, science, mathematics, health and physical education, computers, and visual and performing arts. Winchester Thurston encourages students to enhance their classroom instruction by taking advantage of the many cultural amenities of the nearby Oakland university-medical complex, and through participation in extracurricular activities. In addition to athletics, these include more than 30 clubs and activities that focus on interests as diverse as rocketry; poetry; math; world affairs; and the student newspaper, yearbook, and literary magazine. Students also may take advantage of opportunities for international travel, study, and exchanges.

Admission requirements include academic testing, which typically is scheduled in January and February. Financial aid takes the form of need-based grants.

Yeshiva Schools of Pittsburgh
2100 Wightman Street
(412) 422-7300
www.yeshivaschool.com

The goal of Yeshiva Schools, located in Pittsburgh's Squirrel Hill neighborhood, is to offer a traditional Jewish education that combines an emphasis on moral values and a comprehensive secular education. Classes range from Tiny Tots through high school, with boys and girls in separate classes and buildings once they reach high school. Total enrollment is 425.

For high-school students, the secular curriculum focuses on the development of analytical and communication skills, while the Jewish Studies curriculum includes coursework in Jewish Law and History, Jewish Philosophy, and Bible and Prophets with Commentaries. Students participate in a wide range of community projects, including a weekly hospital visitation program.

Yeshiva is such a magnet for Jewish youths that about 5 percent of its students come from out of town and board with local friends of the Yeshiva.

i Information on private schools can be hard to come by because the schools are, well, private. For a comprehensive listing, try the *Pennsylvania Education Directory*. This annual also lists every public school, by district and county, in the Commonwealth, as well as proprietary and trade schools. You can get yours from Applied Arts Publishers, 2100 State Road, Lancaster, PA 17601, (717) 272-9442. Cost is $16 plus tax.

West

Sewickley Academy
315 Academy Avenue, Sewickley
(412) 741-2230
www.sewickley.org

The facilities at Sewickley Academy are outstanding. Over its 30 acres about 12 miles northwest of downtown Pittsburgh, this day school boasts two libraries; six science labs; three computer labs; four athletic fields; two gyms; studios for music, dance, and art; a 635-seat auditorium; an art gallery; three playgrounds; and two tennis courts. That's enough to make a college jealous.

The academy offers an early childhood program as well as lower, middle, and senior schools; total enrollment is around 800 students, with an overall student-teacher ratio of 9:1. In the senior school, the academy supplements its core curriculum with a variety of electives and study-abroad options. These include programs in Paris, Munich, and Sydney. On the domestic front, students can opt for a Maine Coast Semester, which focuses on environmental studies.

The academy requires community service and gives seniors the option of undertaking a two-week field project to learn about career opportunities. Prospective students are evaluated on the basis of previous school records, teacher recommendations, an entrance examination, and an interview. Sewickley Academy provides financial aid to about 20 percent of its students.

HIGHER EDUCATION

It would be hard to imagine a richer selection of educational options than those offered by the colleges and universities of Southwestern Pennsylvania. In the six-county coverage area, there are many with a compelling diversity of academic programs, campus settings, and social and extracurricular opportunities.

You'll find private institutions, institutions owned by the state, and those that are somewhere in between; colleges with large enrollments spread over multiple campuses and colleges with fewer than 1,000 students; schools that focus on the liberal arts and those that emphasize technical disciplines; colleges that pulsate with the rhythm of urban Pittsburgh and those set in idyllic locales. Strong in their diversity, colleges and universities are a powerful force in the region.

Most of these institutions have proud histories that span many decades if not centuries. That's not to say, however, that higher education is static. In fact, few sectors have been more dynamic in recent years. As the market for traditional-age students has become more competitive, colleges and universities have changed accordingly. For many years the region had four institutions that admitted one gender only; three of those now are coed. Our liberal arts colleges have implemented career-related thrusts, and our technical institutes have introduced core curricula in the liberal arts.

A common denominator has been the expansion of services for nontraditional students. What this means for you is an unprecedented range of continuing education courses—both for credit and leisure learning—that the institutions often will deliver to your worksite or neighborhood.

It's an exciting scene, one you'll want to explore. Profiled here are the local institutions that offer associate, baccalaureate, or graduate degrees, capturing the highlights of their academic and continuing-education programs, campus life, and opportunities for social and education enrichment. Where institutions maintain multiple campuses, we've profiled each campus separately, in case you're targeting schools in specific geographic areas.

DOWNTOWN

Duquesne University
600 Forbes Avenue
(412) 396-6000
www.duq.edu
Duquesne University opened its doors in 1878 as the Pittsburgh Catholic College of the Holy Ghost, with an enrollment of 40 students. To say that the university has grown would be an understatement. Today Duquesne boasts an undergraduate student enrollment of more than 10,368, and it's one of the most important educational institutions in the region. Its 48-acre campus sits on "the Bluff," a hill overlooking both downtown Pittsburgh and the Monongahela River. The excitement of Downtown is only a few blocks away, but in the seclusion of the Bluff, Duquesne is very nearly a self-contained community.

Within the university, 10 schools of study offer baccalaureate, master's, and doctorate degree programs, many developed as partnerships with local corporations and philanthropists. These include the Bayer School of Natural and Environmental Sciences, developed with the support of the Bayer Corporation, and the A. J. Palumbo School of Business Administration. The Mylan School of Pharmacy features a six-year doctor of pharmacy program, while the Rangos School of Health ℹ️ In today's competitive market, local universities will go to great lengths to accommodate students. How far will they go? In 1997 Duquesne University staged a special commencement for one graduate, an Orthodox Jewish student who could not participate in the general commencement because it fell on the Jewish Sabbath.

Sciences offers programs in physical and occupational therapy, physician assistant, and perfusion technology. You'll also find schools of law, education, music, and nursing. The university offers a variety of study-abroad programs through affiliations with institutions in Spain, Colombia, France, and Belgium. In addition, Duquesne confers many graduate degrees (both master's and doctorate) in a multitude of disciplines. Eighty percent of students receive some form of financial aid.

Continuing education plays an important role at Duquesne. The university's Saturday College program leads to a bachelor's degree in professional studies and a master's degree in leadership and liberal studies. The university customizes leadership and liberal studies training programs for on-site delivery to local corporations, and it participates in the educational consortium that provides programs at the Harrisburg Dixon Center in the state capital. The University also offers online master level courses for nursing, music education, environmental sciences, and more.

Student activities take on a strong communications flavor, as students participate in the campus newspaper, *The Duke,* and two radio stations. WDSR is a campus-only station, while WDUQ-FM (90.5 on the dial) is a National Public Radio affiliate that broadcasts a full schedule of public affairs, jazz, and sports programming to the entire community.

Speaking of sports, Duquesne's varsity basketball teams participate in the NCAA Division I Atlantic 10 Conference, while its men's football program is a member of NCAA Division I-AA. For a more detailed look at Duquesne basketball, see the Spectator Sports chapter.

Duquesne is a Catholic university. When you study here, you'll find an emphasis on values. Duquesne has stressed that emphasis in a variety of advertising campaigns, perhaps an unusual pitch for a university in a highly competitive market. Duquesne's continued growth demonstrates how well that competitive market has responded.

Point Park University
201 Wood Street
(412) 391-4100, (800) 321-0129
www.pointpark.edu

If you're looking for a college in the heart of downtown Pittsburgh, look no further. Despite its name, Point Park University is not located exactly in Point State Park. It is, however, squarely in the center of Pittsburgh's business district, which provides it with energy and excitement.

The university offers its 3,200 full- and part-time students more than 50 academic programs leading to associate, baccalaureate, and master's degrees. Point Park is especially known for its programs in performing arts and communications, represented by majors in children's theater, dance, film and video production, journalism and communications, and theater arts. In addition, Point Park awards the master of arts in journalism and communications as well as the master of business administration. Classes at Point Park average 12 to 15 students.

The university's facilities also have the distinctive flavor of communications and performing arts. You'll find seven dance studios, a color television studio, a newsroom, a desktop publishing laboratory, and a radio station. Performing-arts students gain practical experience at the landmark Pittsburgh Playhouse of Point Park University, located in Pittsburgh's Oakland neighborhood, about 3 miles from the university. The Playhouse, which the university has owned and run since 1968, typically hosts 15 productions each year.

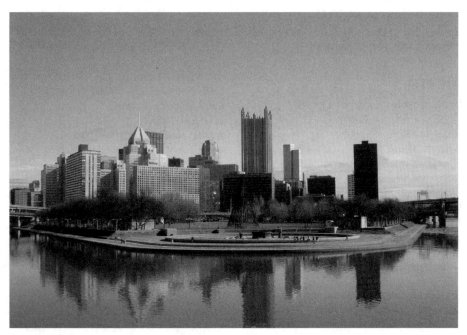

Point State Park. MICHAEL D. REED

If your schedule won't allow you to attend weekday classes, consider Point Park's "Saturday Fast" program, where you can earn your baccalaureate degree in business or applied corporate communications after two years of Saturday-only classes. The university offers the Saturday Fast program at its downtown campus, at Beaver County Community College, and at a satellite site in Cranberry, Butler County.

Point Park sponsors six varsity sports and competes in the Keystone-Empire Collegiate Conference of the National Association of Intercollegiate Athletics. Extracurricular activities include ad, television, environmental, health, and ski clubs, and the *Cavalcade* literary magazine. About 93 percent of Point Park students receive some form of financial aid.

Robert Morris University
Center for Adult and Continuing Education
600 Fifth Avenue
(412) 227-6857
www.rmu.edu

While we've profiled the main, Moon Township campus of Robert Morris University in the "West" section of this chapter, we'd be remiss if we didn't note RMU's Center for Adult and Continuing Education in downtown Pittsburgh. At the center, RMU provides an appealing roster of continuing-education programs, including programs for professional and career development; professional designation and certification; prelicensing and relicensing; certificates; supervisory and leadership development; and professional skills-building.

The center is only 2 blocks from Grant Street, the hub of Pittsburgh's political activity, and a quick walk from such major employment centers as USX Tower, One Oxford Center, and One Mellon Bank Center. Most courses are offered in the evening, and the college will customize courses for delivery at worksites.

In early 2008, RMU announced a $10 million renovation and expansion project at the center. For this project, the university will sell one building, purchase another, relocate the

Bayer Center for Nonprofit Management to the Regional Enterprise Tower, and expand its growing Media Arts department.

NORTH

Butler County Community College
107 College Drive, Butler
(724) 287-8711
www.bc3.edu

Chartered in 1966, BCCC was the region's first community college. It serves more than 3,500 enrolled students and a total of 14,000 people who take advantage of the college's many educational opportunities. BCCC awards three degrees—associate of arts, associate of science, and associate of applied science—but its reach extends far beyond degree programs.

The college offers for-credit courses at three community sites: Cranberry Community College Center in Butler County, Lawrence County Center in New Castle, and Mercer County Center at LindenPointe. In addition, BCCC provides an extensive schedule of leisure-learn courses in such areas as occupational advancement, public safety, literacy, and computers. Its Business and Industry Training Institute works with local business on training and productivity programs, while its Center for Economic Education provides workshops and instructional materials for elementary and secondary economics teachers.

The sprawling, 13-building campus is set on 323 acres of rolling hills with venerable oak trees. Among those buildings are the computer learning center, where students may access terminals, and the student union. The field house features a basketball court that converts to tennis courts, volleyball courts, a batting cage, racquetball courts, and weight-lifting apparatus, while outdoor facilities include golfing areas and jogging and walking trails—many available for community use.

BCCC maintains an open admissions policy—all high-school graduates and those with diploma equivalents are granted admission. Tuition is three-tiered. The tuition for Butler County residents is half that for residents of other Pennsylvania counties, which in turn is two-thirds of the charge for out-of-state residents. The college offers a diverse financial-aid program.

Community College of Allegheny County
800 Allegheny Avenue
(412) 237-4600
www.ccac.edu

The reach of the Community College of Allegheny County is hard to overestimate. It's the largest community college in Pennsylvania, with more than 29,799 enrolled students. Among the reasons for CCAC's popularity are its open admission policy and a tuition schedule that favors local residents. Tuition for Allegheny County residents is half that of tuition for residents of other Pennsylvania counties, and one-third of the charge for out-of-state residents. Nearly 50 percent of students receive financial aid.

It's more than attractive tuition that draws students to CCAC, as the college offers more than 170 academic programs leading to the associate of arts, the associate of science, and the associate of applied sciences degrees. In addition, students in CCAC's elementary education program can earn baccalaureate degrees from Indiana University of Pennsylvania while studying at CCAC. The average age of CCAC students is nearly 27, indicating that many are returning to studies after an extended absence.

While the college's academic programs defy easy summary, many are part of the following broad departments: business careers, health careers, social service careers, applied arts technologies, applied service and trade technologies, and engineering and science technologies. Through the information sciences program, students earn degrees and certificates in office technology and court reporting. Students in health programs may specialize in nuclear medicine, radiation therapy, or diagnostic medical sonography, while nursing students can participate in cooperative education programs with more than 200 area health-care agencies.

In a word, CCAC is accessible. It maintains four area campuses, in addition to its North Side administrative offices, for the convenience of students—you'll find profiles of these in the "North," "East," and "South" sections of this chapter. The average class size is 20, and students have access to more than 1,500 microcomputers linked across the campuses by local area network. The campuses together boast more than 1 million square feet of classroom space and more than 200,000 volumes in their libraries. CCAC offers child-care centers at each campus as well as intramural and varsity sports.

CCAC hosts intercollegiate National Junior College Athletic Association (NJCAA) men's and women's sports teams including bowling, basketball, cross country, baseball and golf. There are club teams, including hockey and softball. About the only thing you won't find at any of the sites is on-campus housing.

Among the most impressive and attractive aspects of CCAC is its broad program of continuing education. In addition to programs at its four campuses, the college maintains six off-campus continuing education centers—in Bethel Park, Braddock, Downtown, Homewood-Brushton, Washington County, and West Hills—where more than 40,000 people participate in continuing-education and community service programs. Even more impressive, CCAC delivers continuing-education programs, through its Workforce Development Team, to more than 70 companies in the region.

Community College of Allegheny County— Allegheny Campus
808 Ridge Avenue
(412) 237-2511
www.ccac.edu
Located on the North Side near CCAC's administrative offices, the Allegheny Campus is the largest of the college's four campuses, with more than 8,600 students. The campus is a blend of stately older buildings that trace their roots to the early-19th century and modern structures built in the 1970s. The 52,000-square-foot student services center features a theater-auditorium, classrooms, and a cafeteria.

The convenient locations mean you can walk from campus to Downtown or such North Side attractions as PNC Park and the National Aviary. Make sure you take a walking tour of the mansions near the campus. One was the home of industrialist Harry Thaw, who gained notoriety by gunning down architect Stanford White in a famous 19th-century love triangle.

Community College of Allegheny County— North Campus
8701 Perry Highway
(412) 369-3600
www.ccac.edu
The North Campus of CCAC serves students in Pittsburgh's northern and western suburbs. The campus serves more than 38,000 students enrolled in its community service classes and academic and continuing education programs. That's a far cry from the campus' more humble origins—a trailer in the parking lot in what was then North Hills Passavant Hospital.

Grove City College
100 Campus Drive, Grove City
(724) 458-2000
www.gcc.edu
Grove City College is dedicated to being "a Christian college of liberal arts and sciences," a mission infused in all aspects of study and life at this Butler County college. Though affiliated with the Presbyterian Church, the college is not narrowly denominational but expects attention to matters of faith from its students. Each student must attend a minimum of 16 chapel services per semester. If you need any other indications of Grove City's commitment to its vision, consider this: The college eschews all state and federal aid, the better to maintain its independent vision.

Grove City awards the bachelor of arts, the bachelor of science, the bachelor of music, the bachelor of science in electrical ℹ️ Most colleges and universities offer a full range of noncredit courses—sometimes tuition-free for senior citizens—so you can enjoy your favorite hobby or interest in a classroom near you.

engineering, and the bachelor of science in mechanical engineering degrees. The engineering programs are distinctive, offering dual emphases in science and technology and liberal arts. Core courses stress cultural literacy and communications skills, while nonengineering majors must study a language. Coursework is demanding but fulfilling—about 80 percent of entering freshmen graduate from Grove City.

One of the reasons that percentage is so high may be because of the value students receive. In 2007, Grove City was named No. 1 "Best Value" in its category by *U.S. News & World Report,* marking the fifth year in a row that Grove City was named in the top spot.

The lovely campus spans more than 150 acres and 27 buildings just a few minutes from Interstate 79, making it accessible from Pittsburgh some 60 miles to the south. Of the 2,450 students, more than 91 percent reside on campus. The Technological Learning Center includes 121 microcomputers and three big-screen projection systems. Grove City enhances those facilities by providing each freshman with a notebook-size computer and a color printer. For extracurricular activities, the college sponsors more than 120 organizations and special interest groups; for relaxation, students enjoy events at the J. Howard Few Fine Arts Center and bowling, handball, and racquetball at the student union. Grove City features an extensive intramural sports program and fields 19 intercollegiate teams for men and women.

Grove City is relatively affordable for a private school. Since the college maintains a sizable endowment, tuition is usually lower than similar schools. (Please call the college for details.) Admission to Grove City is quite competitive, which may be due to its popularity, price, and fine reputation. If you or a family member is thinking of applying, the college strongly recommends an interview with its staff. While visiting, check out the Prime Outlets (see Shopping) and the nearby towns (see Day Trips and Weekend Getaways).

Indiana University of Pennsylvania
1011 South Drive, Indiana
(724) 357-2100
www.iup.edu

Located about 50 miles northeast of Pittsburgh, Indiana is known as the "Christmas Tree Capital of the World" and the hometown of actor Jimmy Stewart. Founded in 1875 as Indiana Normal School, a small teacher-training institution, IUP has evolved into a major university with 14,200 students representing nearly every state and 60 countries. It's the largest university in the State System of Higher Education (which does not include Penn State University).

Academic offerings include more than 100 undergraduate majors with a variety of internship and study-abroad programs. At the graduate level, IUP offers more than 40 master's programs and nine doctoral programs. Extensive as those offerings are, the university further enhances them through a variety of creative partnerships. Through a joint initiative with the Western Pennsylvania Hospital in Pittsburgh, IUP provides a program of study in respiratory care that has achieved a 100 percent employment rate for its graduates. In cooperation with Allegheny General Hospital and MCP-Hanemann School of Medicine of Allegheny University of the Health Sciences, IUP offers a pre-professional program for students planning to serve as general practice physicians in the Pittsburgh area.

You'll find academic support services at IUP quite convenient and useful. Campus buildings are connected via a private fiber-optic link, which provides resident students with in-room Internet access and other computer capabilities. The university's Robert E. Cook Honors College is more than a mere designation, as members live together in the same residence hall and form a community.

IUP features a large resident student community—more than 3,900 strong—and about 220 student organizations including a newspaper and radio and television stations. The school sponsors an intramural sports program as well as 8 varsity sports for men and 11 for women, participating in the NCAA Division II Pennsylvania State Athletic Conference. Students living on campus enjoy IUP's unusual in-room video service. Rather than contract with the local cable television provider, IUP developed its own television programming service that blends the customary satellite-delivered fare with more education-oriented programming, such as foreign language channels.

IUP is a bit outside our principal coverage area, but as you can see, it's worthy of inclusion. IUP also runs the Monroeville Graduate and Professional Center in eastern Allegheny County. At the center, IP offers master's programs in adult and community education, business administration, criminology, elementary education, and industrial and labor relations.

La Roche College
9000 Babcock Boulevard
(412) 536-1048, (800) 838-4572
www.laroche.edu/
The Sisters of Divine Providence founded La Roche College in Pittsburgh's North Hills in 1963, when the northern suburbs began the great growth spurt that continues to this day. As a result this private, Catholic, liberal arts institution offers a beautiful suburban campus to a growing population base while still providing access to the business and social attractions of Pittsburgh. It's been a formula for success at La Roche.

La Roche awards the bachelor of arts, bachelor of science, and master of science in human resources degrees, as well as bachelor's and master's degrees in nursing. The college's 1,500 students select majors from 50 disciplines covering the humanities, including elementary education, language and literature, international studies, and sociology; the arts, including dance, professional writing, graphic design, and interior design; business, including

accounting, finance, and international management;·and science, including computer science, biology, chemistry, medical technology, and psychobiology. Students in virtually every major have the opportunity for internships— many with top Pittsburgh employers.

Residence life is one of the neatest aspects of the La Roche experience. The college's 350 resident students live in apartment-style suites that feature two or three bedrooms. Typically four to six students live in each suite. The Keer Fitness and Sports Center includes a gymnasium, an elevated track, a dance and karate studio, a weight room, and racquetball courts. Other activities include a student newspaper, a drama club, and men's and women's varsity and intramural sports. La Roche belongs to the NCAA Division III Allegheny Mountain Collegiate Conference.

One of the most interesting and satisfying opportunities for students is participation in the La Roche Challenge program, through which honor students teach pupils at 14 participating Catholic elementary schools. The younger students visit the La Roche campus for 20 classes each year, including instruction in such areas as computer graphics, desktop publishing, ballet, and Native American history. It's a great way to serve the community and get valuable practical experience in return.

Slippery Rock University
1 Morrow Way, Slippery Rock
(724) 738-9000, (800) 778-9111
www.sru.edu/
Founded as a teacher-education institution, Slippery Rock has grown into a multipurpose university with roughly 8,300 students and more than 100 degree programs in the four colleges and other departments and graduate studies. The university is in Butler County, about 75 minutes from Pittsburgh along I-79. It's one of 14 institutions in the State System of Higher Education.

If you study biology or geology at Slippery Rock, you'll have the opportunity to travel to the Marine Science Consortium at Wallops Island, Virginia. The consortium is a nonprofit corporation dedicated to research and instruction in the marine sciences, and Slippery Rock is a member of the consortium.

The university also offers a broad continuing-education program that features credit courses, workshops, and seminars. It offers classes at the Regional Learning Alliance in Cranberry. The community also takes advantage of Slippery Rock's conference facilities during the summer months, which include banquet halls that can accommodate up to 1,000 people and overnight facilities.

One of the most compelling aspects of the university is its campus, spread over more than 600 acres and dotted with woods, streams, and ponds. Moreover, it's near the McKeever Environmental Learning Center, a state-operated facility that provides general environmental education and instruction in environmental education for student-teachers. The college also boasts 11 residence halls, 9 auditoriums, 12 athletic fields, and tennis courts. If that's not enough, head to Morrow Field House, where you'll find a gymnasium, a swimming pool, handball courts, a dance studio, and a running track.

About 35 percent of students live on campus, and about 80 percent receive financial aid. Slippery Rock sponsors 18 varsity sports and competes in the NCAA Division II. Students take advantage of the setting and the facilities through such organizations as skiing and hiking clubs and the campus television and radio stations.

Westminster College
319 South Market Street, New Wilmington
(724) 946-8761, (800) 942-8033
www.westminster.edu

This Lawrence County liberal arts college is slightly north of our principal coverage area, but you ought to know about it—if only for its convenient location, excellent reputation, and nearby tourist attractions. It's about 60 miles from Pittsburgh, primarily via I-79, and only about 85 miles southeast of Cleveland, making it accessible from both major urban centers.

Westminster, however, is decidedly not urban. Its 300-acre campus in the rolling hills of Western Pennsylvania offers tranquility that you'll appreciate. Affiliated with the Presbyterian Church, Westminster was founded in 1852 and was among the first colleges to offer equal admissions to women seeking baccalaureate degrees. Today the college offers 39 academic majors—with internships available in each one—and 6 pre-professional programs. Among the most interesting majors is Sacred Music, a joint program with Duquesne University through which students take classes on both campuses. Class size typically is smaller than you'll find in many other colleges and universities.

Virtually all of Westminster's 1,650 students live on campus, where they take advantage of a broad computer network that provides them with Internet access and other functions from their dorm rooms. One of the most important volunteer activities on campus is service with Habitat for Humanity, which involves about 300 Westminster students in its programs of constructing homes for families in need. If you're looking for a less arduous leisure activity, try some stargazing at the observatory in the Hoyt Science Resource Center. Westminster sponsors an intramural sports program and 18 varsity sports at the NCAA Division II level. There's a proud tradition of sports excellence here. The football team has achieved six national titles and 11 undefeated seasons.

While Westminster is a college affiliated with the Presbyterian Church, it's known among students and graduates as being less strict in the areas of dorm room intervisitation and chapel attendance.

New Wilmington and the surrounding areas of Volant, Sharon, and Grove City (with the Prime Outlets) surely make this an attractive destination to visit while transporting kids to and from college, or merely checking out the campus. (See the Day Trips and Weekend Getaways and Shopping chapters.)

EAST

Carlow University
3333 Fifth Avenue
(412) 578-6000, (800) 333-CARLOW (2275)
www.carlow.edu

Carlow College was founded in 1929 by the Sisters of Mercy to help women realize their potential. Today a Catholic, liberal arts college primarily for women, Carlow is set on a hillside overlooking Pittsburgh's Oakland neighborhood; as you stroll through the quadrangle, you get a satisfying sense of community while knowing that the amenities of Oakland's university-medical complex are just down the hill below.

Carlow confers three baccalaureate degrees—bachelor of arts, bachelor of science, and bachelor of science in nursing—as well as three master's degrees. Undergraduates select from 50 academic programs. While these are rich in humanities programs, including creative writing, English, philosophy, history, social work, and sociology, they also feature such business programs as accounting, business management, and medical marketing and such science-based programs as chemistry and four biology tracks.

Carlow offers pre-professional programs in dentistry, medicine, optometry, osteopathy, pharmacy, physical therapy, podiatry, law, and veterinary medicine. Whatever your major, Carlow requires study in a core curriculum that represents the humanities, natural sciences, and social sciences.

Students participate in more than 20 organizations—when they're not too busy enjoying the many social and cultural opportunities of Oakland. While Carlow offers only one residence hall, students are guaranteed housing. The college sponsors five varsity sports; offers crew as a club sport; and provides a fitness center, swimming pool, and gymnasium. Approximately 92 percent of full-time students receive financial assistance. And an amazing 79 percent of graduates

Staying in State

If you're a Pennsylvania resident or thinking of relocating to the Commonwealth, you'll want to become familiar with the State System of Higher Education, the administrative agency for 14 universities in Pennsylvania. Profiled are the three member universities in our coverage area—California, Indiana, and Slippery Rock. You'll find the other 11 in Bloomsburg, Cheyney, Clarion, East Stroudsburg, Edinboro, Kutztown, Lock Haven, Mansfield, Millersville, Shippensburg, and West Chester.

It's a large system encompassing more than 110,000 students. One of the most important features of the system is the attractive tuition for state residents—generally, several thousand dollars lower than what out-of-state students and their families pay. It's no accident that 90 percent of system students are Pennsylvania residents.

obtain employment in their academic fields upon graduation.

One of Carlow's most appealing strengths is its extensive continuing-education programs. In addition to maintaining satellite sites in Beaver, Cranberry, and Greensburg, the college offers the Carlow Weekend College and the Carlow Accelerated Program. Both enable working students to develop class schedules that accommodate their professional schedules while working toward degrees. Through Carlow Hill College, a continuing-education program targeted to the primarily African-American residents of Pittsburgh's Hill District neighborhood, students develop leadership skills and enhanced career possibilities.

Carnegie Mellon University
5000 Forbes Avenue
(412) 268-2000
www.cmu.edu

Few degrees are as prestigious as those from Carnegie Mellon, a private university of about 10,400 students with a dual focus on education and research. It was founded in 1900 by industrialist and philanthropist Andrew Carnegie, whose vision was a vocational training school for the children of the city's working class. It was renamed Carnegie Institute of Technology in 1912 and merged with the Mellon Institute in 1967.

An important component of Oakland's university-medical complex, Carnegie Mellon includes four undergraduate colleges (in technology, fine arts, humanities and social sciences, and science) and three graduate schools—the Tepper School of Business, the School of Computer Science, and the H. John Heinz III School of Public Policy and Management.

The university is perhaps most prominent for its leadership in the arts and technology, an unusual combination but one that works well at Carnegie Mellon. The university introduced its undergraduate drama degree in 1917; since then, a number of young men and women who later would gain fame as actors, directors, and set and costume designers learned their art and craft at CMU. Among actors who have studied at the university are George Peppard, Holly Hunter, Ted Danson, and Jack Klugman.

In technology, Carnegie Mellon operates the National Robotics Engineering Center. Located in Pittsburgh's Lawrenceville neighborhood along the Allegheny River, the consortium develops robots to explore volcanoes

i The latest *U.S. News and World Report*'s rankings for the best colleges and universities in the United States place Carnegie Mellon in the top 25. The rankings are based on academic reputation, faculty resources, student selectivity, retention, graduation rate, financial resources, and alumni giving.

and other hazardous environments, and vehicles that can be driven without human operators on board. The work of Carnegie Mellon students and faculty in such fields as computer science, software development, and robotics has resulted in the creation of more than 200 Carnegie-Mellon affiliated companies.

Carnegie Mellon's strength in technology has important implications for the university's students. Through the university's computing network—called "Andrew" after benefactors Andrew Carnegie and Andrew Mellon—all students have access to personal computing workstations.

The campus spans 140 acres. Student activities vary from special-interest clubs and a newspaper and a radio station to fraternities and sororities. The university sponsors 17 varsity athletic teams—the men's football team participates in the University Athletic Association of NCAA Division III. Fitness and recreation facilities include tennis courts, gymnasiums, racquetball courts, swimming pools, and weight/fitness rooms. In an innovative arrangement, the university, through an affiliated corporation, operates the city of Pittsburgh's Schenley Park Golf Course, which is adjacent to campus. (For more on the course, see the Golf chapter.) About two-thirds of undergraduate students reside on campus, and about 58 percent receive some form of financial aid.

Chatham University
Woodland Road
(412) 365-1100, (800) 837-1290
www.chatham.edu

When you're enjoying the freshness and beauty of Chatham's 35-acre wooded campus, surrounded by the converted mansions that serve as the college's residence halls, you'll probably forget that Fifth Avenue, one of the city's busiest thoroughfares, is only a hillside away. That sense of splendid isolation within the bustling city is part of Chatham's charm.

Chatham is the last of the region's exclusively single-gender institutions of higher learning (men are admitted to graduate programs only)—it's been preparing women for

i The intersection of the campuses of Carnegie Mellon University and the University of Pittsburgh is one of the most engaging spots in the city. Along the informal border you'll find Carnegie Library of Pittsburgh, the Hillman Library, the Frick Fine Arts Building, Phipps Conservatory and Botanical Gardens, and Flagstaff Hill, a great site for lounging and people-watching. Look very carefully and you'll also pick out a brick wall that is the last surviving portion of Forbes Field, former home of the Pittsburgh Pirates.

personal and professional success since 1869. Its more than 30 baccalaureate degree programs feature small, seminar-style classes and a variety of hands-on learning experiences, including two guaranteed internships in a field related to your major as well as a mentoring relationship with a leading professional woman.

Chatham also offers master's level programs in physical therapy, occupational therapy, physician assistant studies, teaching, management, and counseling psychology. Chatham graduates receive preferred entry into these programs. Collaborative programs provide a bridge to medical school, engineering, and an environmental and occupational health master's program.

Providing broad and challenging experiences is one of Chatham's key goals, one the college achieves through several innovative programs. One is a senior tutorial, a yearlong independent research project on a topic of each student's choosing. Another is Chatham Abroad, an exciting opportunity for travel through which each student experiences a three-week trip with faculty and classmates to countries such as Egypt, France, Spain, England, Belize, Ireland, Morocco, and Italy. Chatham's Global Focus Program provides international events and activities, with a different area of the world highlighted each year.

Sixty-five percent of Chatham's 1,870 students, reside on campus or in college-owned apartments on Fifth Avenue. More than 98

percent of students receive some form of financial aid. A fiber-optic network connects everyone on campus and provides each student with Internet access. Chatham sponsors more than 50 student organizations, NCAA Division III teams in nine sports, and a variety of club and recreational sports. One of Chatham's most distinguished graduates is Rachel Carson, founder of the modern environmental movement. In her honor, Chatham maintains the Rachel Carson Institute, an advocate for the environment that also produces environmental awareness programs for high school students.

Community College of Allegheny County—Boyce Campus
595 Beatty Road, Monroeville
(724) 325-6614
www.ccac.edu
Nearly 13,000 students are enrolled in academic programs at Boyce Campus; sometimes it's hard to imagine how they concentrate on their studies. The campus serving Pittsburgh's eastern suburbs is adjacent to Allegheny County's Boyce Park, which offers the closest downhill skiing slopes to Pittsburgh. For students who can manage to stay off the slopes—we're only kidding here, as Boyce Campus students are as dedicated as any other students—the campus provides a multipurpose center that includes a gymnasium, a theater, and classrooms. If by some chance you are interested in Boyce Park, you'll find a profile in the Parks chapter.

Penn State Greater Allegheny
4000 University Drive, McKeesport
(412) 675-9000
www.ga.psu.edu
A regional campus of the Pennsylvania State University, Penn State Greater Allegheny offers the first two years of more than 160 baccalaureate degree programs. Those are far from the only academic options here, as students also pursue associate degrees in five programs and master's degrees in adult education and counselor education. Students in

the business administration and liberal arts associate degree programs have the opportunity to attend weekend and evening classes to better accommodate their schedules.

Founded in 1948, the college is about 10 miles southeast of Pittsburgh. Of the nearly 800 students, about 200 reside on campus. For those who commute, Penn State Greater Allegheny maintains plenty of free parking, an important perk. Students participate in such activities as theater production and the campus radio station. Through community outreach services such as the Penn State Educational Partnership Program and the Educational Opportunity Program, student tutors assist middle-school and high-school pupils in after-school study programs, a nice way of blending education and community service.

The student-faculty ratio is 16:1, while the student-computer ratio is 18:1, helping assure that students get the attention and support they need. Students participate in an intramural sports program as well as two varsity sports—men's basketball and women's volleyball. The teams compete in the Western Pennsylvania Collegiate Conference and the Penn State Commonwealth Campus Athletic Conference. More than 80 percent of students receive some form of financial aid.

Penn State New Kensington
3550 Seventh Street Road, New Kensington
(724) 334-5466
www.nk.psu.edu

Like the Penn State campuses in McKeesport and Beaver, Penn State New Kensington is part of the Pennsylvania State Commonwealth College and draws on its considerable resources. Students at the 72-acre Penn State New Kensington, founded in 1958 and located in Westmoreland County about 20 miles from Pittsburgh, can complete the first two years of almost any of Penn State's 160 baccalaureate degree programs.

Other options include four-year programs in nursing and electromechanical engineering technology that can be completed on-site. In addition, the college offers associate degree programs in business administration, allied health, engineering technology, liberal arts, and sciences. Class size is comfortable—the student-faculty ratio is 25:1. When they're not studying, students relax at the gymnasium, racquetball courts, and fitness center or broaden their experience through the Outdoor Adventure Club, the Multicultural Club, and such community projects as homebuilding with Habitat for Humanity.

Penn State New Kensington offers nine intramural sports as well as seven varsity teams—men's basketball and women's volleyball—that compete in the Western Pennsylvania Collegiate Conference and the Penn State Commonwealth Athletic Conference. You won't find on-campus housing; many students rent apartments in a building adjacent to campus. About 70 percent of students receive some form of financial aid.

Pittsburgh Institute of Aeronautics
5 Allegheny County Airport, West Mifflin
(412) 346-2100, (800) 444-1440
www.pia.edu

Pittsburgh Institute of Aeronautics was founded in 1927 by Glen Curtiss and Orville Wright—yes, that Orville Wright—so you know the history of the institute is solid. You may not be flying solo over Kitty Hawk, but you will have the chance to study for an associate degree in specialized technology in one of two programs. The Aviation Maintenance Technician Program leads to a test for the airframe and power plant license. The Avionics Technician (AVT) program will prepare you for the FCC General Radiotelephone license.

You can complete the programs in 21 months, making them especially attractive. For the first six weeks you'll study such basics as English, algebra, and physics. After that, it's all hands-on work with airplanes, jets, and helicopters, as well as work in the shop and the lab. You can begin your classes at one of four times during the year. Graduates interested in pursuing baccalaureate degrees can receive advanced standing credits at any of the 12 colleges and universities with which PIA maintains cooperative agreements. Two of those cooperating institutions are in Pittsburgh: Community College of Allegheny County and Point Park University.

PIA does not offer its 225 students housing or financial aid, though it gladly accepts grants, scholarships, and private funding you receive from other sources. PIA claims an outstanding placement record, indicating that its graduates typically receive from four to six job offers. Prepare for takeoff!

Pittsburgh Institute of Mortuary Science
5808 Baum Boulevard
(412) 362-8500
www.p-i-m-s.com
This is the region's only degree-granting institution for mortuary science, so it has a comparatively large enrollment—about 150 students. The institute welcomes about 50 new students each January, May, and September; the trimester approach means that most students can find a convenient time to launch their studies.

Located in Pittsburgh's Shadyside neighborhood, the institute awards the associate in specialized business degree, which usually leads to a career in funeral service management, and the associate in specialized technology degree, which focuses more on the technical aspects of mortuary science. In addition, the institute maintains cooperative programs with four colleges and universities—Point Park University, California University of Pennsylvania, Thiel College, and Gannon University—that enable its graduates to earn bachelor of science degrees at the campuses of the cooperating institutions.

In addition to the technological aspects of mortuary science, students learn about the human and historical components of the business through such courses as world religions, ethics, gerontology, communication skills, and the psychology of grief and counseling. The institute offers financial assistance but no on-campus housing.

Financial Aid for College

If you're considering college in the Commonwealth, it will be worth your while to become familiar with the Pennsylvania Higher Education Assistance Agency, the state's most important source of financial aid for college and university students. PHEAA offers more than financial aid, valuable though its dollars may be. Its Early Awareness Program, for example, introduces middle-school students and their families to the benefits of early planning for higher education.

You can reach PHEAA in a number of ways. For information the best number is (800) 692-7392. You can write PHEAA at P.O. Box 8141, Harrisburg, PA 17105-8141, or visit their Web site: www.pheaa.org.

Pittsburgh Theological Seminary
616 North Highland Avenue
(412) 362-5610
www.pts.edu
The seminary was founded in 1794 in a log cabin with six students and one teacher. For more than 200 years, it has pursued the same vision: nurturing men and women in their faith while preparing them for pastoral ministry and Christian lay leadership. The seminary is affiliated with the Presbyterian Church, but its community is ecumenical, with more than 20 denominations represented in the student body.

Located in Pittsburgh's East Liberty neighborhood and boasting 13 acres of green grounds, the seminary confers the master of divinity, master of arts, master of sacred theology, and doctor of ministry degrees. Joint degree programs with local colleges and universities allow students to earn a master of divinity degree from the seminary and a master's degree in law, social work, public health, business, or sacred music from the collaborating institution. Similarly a Ph.D. program from the University of Pittsburgh is available to seminary students. The seminary offers an evening program that enables master of divinity students to complete their work in six years.

Students can take advantage of a number of continuing-education programs as well as the Metro-Urban Institute, which provides field education experiences. The seminary provides both dorm rooms and unfurnished apartments (pets aren't permitted in either) as well as child-care services during regularly scheduled daytime class hours. The student association arranges recreation and athletic events, utilizing the seminary's tennis courts. Students also have limited access to the gym and swimming pool at Peabody High School, just across North Highland Avenue, and they enjoy a weekly volleyball game at a local church. Financial aid is available.

The purposes of the seminary clearly are serious, but you'll also appreciate the zest for life here as embodied in the warning signs along campus drives. The signs say THOU SHALT NOT PARK HERE.

Reformed Presbyterian Theological Seminary
7418 Penn Avenue
(412) 731-8690, (866) 778-7338
www.rpts.edu

If you drive along Penn Avenue in Pittsburgh's Point Breeze neighborhood, you might mistake this campus and its attractive grounds for the estate of a wealthy industrialist. It may look that way, but there's serious work going on here—the seminary's primary purpose is to train ministers of the gospel for church leadership. The student body is small, numbering about 100 students, yet those students represent more than 20 denominations.

The seminary was founded in 1810 and boasts a colorful history. In its early days the Synod of the Reformed Presbyterian Church elected a professor of theology; whenever he moved to a different congregation, his students moved with him. Thus the seminary had five different locations between 1810 and 1856.

Today the seminary awards the master of divinity degree with emphasis in biblical studies, systematic theology, church history, and pastoral theology. The institution stresses the importance of local churches, offering practical experience in different areas of ministry and requiring a local church recommendation for admission to seminary.

Technology plays an important role in scholarship at the seminary. A climatized rare book room houses more than 1,000 volumes, while computer terminals feature Hebrew and Greek characters for display and study of ancient texts.

Saint Vincent College
300 Fraser Purchase Road, Latrobe
(724) 532-6600
www.stvincent.edu

Saint Vincent is a Catholic, Benedictine liberal arts college in Westmoreland County, about 35 miles east of Pittsburgh. About 25 percent of the faculty are Benedictine monks, infusing the campus with a zest for life and learning. At Saint Vincent you'll find plenty of opportunity for both.

The college offers baccalaureate degrees in more than 50 disciplines, spanning a wide range of humanities, business, and science programs. You'll find a number of appealing concentrations in the arts, business administration, and family and consumer sciences tracks, as well as preparatory programs in law, medicine, dental medicine, engineering, health professions, chiropractic, optometry, podiatry, theology, and veterinary medicine. Through cooperative programs with Seton Hill College and Duquesne University, Saint Vincent students may pursue additional programs, including occupational therapy, pharmacy, and physical therapy, leading to graduate degrees at Duquesne. The college offers study abroad through its relationship with Fu Jen Catholic University of Taiwan.

Of Saint Vincent's 1,600 students, about 80% reside on the 400-acre campus. The campus features a number of neat structures. These include the central commons building,

i Financial aid at area colleges and universities can come from one or more sources—scholarships, grants, loans, or part-time employment.

which offers an amphitheater, a planetarium, and a robotics lab, and the Instructional Technology Resource Center, where students go online. You can participate in the campus radio and television stations, provide community service through the Campus Ministry Program, or participate in six men's varsity sports or five women's varsity sports. The college competes in the National Association of Intercollegiate Athletics. Saint Vincent provides financial assistance to more than 90 percent of the students who apply for it.

You'll come to appreciate the college's productive relationship with Seton Hill College, which is less than 10 miles west along U.S. Route 30. For most of their respective histories, when Saint Vincent admitted only men and Seton Hill only women, the two institutions developed a "brother-sister" relationship that featured cross registration for courses and joint social functions. Today both schools are coeducational, but their productive relationship remains. A free shuttle bus operates between the two campuses.

Seton Hill University
One Seton Hill Drive, Greensburg
(724) 834-2200, (800) 826-6234
www.setonhill.edu

The word "community" is used rather loosely these days, but when you visit Seton Hill University, you'll know at once that you've arrived at a community. Founded in 1918 by the Sisters of Charity, Seton Hill is a Catholic, liberal arts college with a lovely 200-acre campus high atop a Greensburg hill, about 35 miles east of Pittsburgh. For most of its years a women's college, Seton Hill now is fully coeducational with a faculty that features members of the Sisters of Charity and laypersons. The campus includes both retirement quarters and a cemetery for the sisters—both of them not far from tennis courts and an exercise course

for the college's roughly 2,000 students. The campus is dotted with intriguing pipe sculptures produced by Josefa Filkosky, a member of the Art Department faculty. You won't find many colleges with a stronger commitment to a mission and a community.

Undergrads choose from more than 40 areas of study, including physician assistant, biology, psychology, education, management, and visual and performing arts. Class size typically is comfortable, with a student-faculty ratio of 16:1. Honors programs, independent study, and seminar work are available to students, and study in most majors includes internships. At the graduate level, Seton Hill awards the master of arts degree in elementary education, special education, and art therapy. In addition, the college offers an innovative program in which students may earn a bachelor of arts degree, certification in elementary education, and a master's in elementary education in five years—all for the price of a bachelor's degree.

Seton Hill's Accelerated Saturday Degree Program is designed for students who wish to pursue degrees while continuing to work full time. Through the program, students can obtain their degrees in management, accounting, general studies, or human services within the traditional four years while taking classes on Saturday only.

Students participate in the campus newspaper and literary magazine as well as intramural and varsity sports. Seton Hill sponsors 21 varsity men's and women's programs including basketball, cross-country, equestrian, soccer, softball, tennis, and volleyball. For leisure you'll find a gymnasium, a swimming pool, volleyball and badminton courts, softball, and soccer fields, and a fitness trail that winds through the surrounding hills. The college also provides van transportation for trips to local and Pittsburgh shopping districts, while students plan regular excursions to New York City and Washington, D.C.

Seton Hill awards merit-based scholarships in theater, art, music, biology, chemistry, and mathematics. Through the Seton Hill

College Presidential Scholarship Program, students who graduate in the top 10, 20, and 30 percent of their high-school class are eligible for awards ranging from $7,000 to $11,000 annually. When you're checking out the facilities, make sure you stop in Reeves Memorial Library to enjoy the unusual sculpture of a student, head down on the table, weary or asleep from studying.

As befitting a college where community is so important, Seton Hill provides important services to the broader community. These include plays staged by the theater department in Reeves Theatre, exhibitions of student art in Harlan Gallery, and the Lynch Lecture Series, which brings nationally prominent speakers and performers to campus. The college is home to the National Catholic Center for Holocaust Education as well as the National Education Center for Women in Business, which serves as a nationwide clearinghouse for information and research on women's business ownership while offering consulting services and classes in entrepreneurship.

University of Pittsburgh
Fifth Avenue at Bigelow Boulevard
(412) 624-4141
www.pitt.edu

Located in Oakland, the University of Pittsburgh serves more than 27,000 undergraduate and graduate students. Despite its total population, Pitt boasts a 16:1 ratio with 60% of its classes having fewer than 30 students.

The school was founded in 1787 as the Pittsburgh Academy, and it has remained close to the community it serves. Its signature building, the 42-story Cathedral of Learning, was financed in the 1920s largely through the contributions of area residents, who "bought" bricks for a nickel apiece. The university has produced more than 200,000 graduates— many are among the region's business, professional, and civic leaders.

When you're speaking about the university, it's important to discuss both education and research, as Pitt is a leader in each. In education the university offers 367 distinct degree programs as well as other dual, joint, and cooperative degree programs. It offers graduate programs in arts and sciences, business, dental medicine, education, engineering, health and rehabilitation sciences, information sciences, law, medicine, nursing, pharmacy, public and international affairs, public health, and social work. The College of General Studies offers undergraduate programs on a part-time basis for students with full-time jobs or other commitments. The Honors College provides attractive seminar-style classes for high-achieving students. The university maintains regional campuses in Bradford, Greensburg, Johnstown, and Titusville.

In the area of research, Pitt is a member of the prestigious Association of American Universities, a consortium of the 62 leading research universities in North America. Its faculty has pioneered the way in such discoveries as silver-sheathed superconducting wire and development of a method to decontaminate chemical weapons. Among the university's most prominent research centers are the University Center for International Studies, the Center for Biotechnology and Bioengineering at the Pittsburgh Technology Center, the University Center for Social and Urban Research, the Thomas E. Starzl Transplantation Institute, and the University of Pittsburgh Cancer Institute. In addition, Pitt's six schools of the health sciences work closely with UPMC Health System, the region's largest network of hospitals, clinics, and research centers. For more on UPMC Health System, see the Health Care chapter.

You won't want for academic support here. Pitt's libraries house approximately 4 million volumes and subscribe to about 25,000 journals and periodicals. All dormitories are equipped with personal computing facilities, and you'll have access to portable laptop computers at Hillman Library, the university's principal library.

The split-level campus dominates the Oakland neighborhood, spanning 132 acres. On the lower level, on and around Fifth and

Forbes Avenues, you'll find the Cathedral of Learning and its Nationality Rooms, 26 authentically designed rooms depicting the ethnic art and culture of their respective lands. For more on the Nationality Rooms, see the Attractions chapter. Nearby, you'll see a trio of buildings both historic and functional. The Center for American Music is housed at the Stephen Foster Memorial, a tribute to the great Pittsburgh-born composer. Heinz Memorial Chapel, an interfaith chapel built in the French Gothic style, features magnificent stained glass windows that soar skyward and is a popular venue for weddings; better make your reservation before you pop the question, as the waiting list typically is lengthy. The William Pitt Union, the center of student life, opened in 1898 as the grand Hotel Schenley, a favorite stopping place for visiting dignitaries and actors.

On the upper campus you'll find such amenities as the brand-new sports arena— Petersen Events Center—the university's principal gymnasium, swimming pool, and other student and community athletic facilities, and the residences of campus fraternities and sororities.

Student life is as varied as you would expect. While many students are commuters, about 6,500 live on campus, and many others rent apartments off campus. Tuition for state residents is about half that for out-of-staters. About 70 percent of undergraduates receive financial aid. The university sponsors more than 350 student organizations, including a campus radio station (WPTS FM) and the *Pitt News,* a newspaper published five times each week. You'll want to scan the newspaper for coupons good at Oakland businesses and ads for sales and housing availabilities.

The university sponsors a full range of intramural sports and 19 varsity sports for men and women, who compete in the Big East Conference. For more on varsity football and basketball at Pitt, see the Spectator Sports chapter.

This is a vital urban campus, where social and cultural opportunities abound. Rare is the day when you can't find at least several appealing lectures or performances on campus. On the other hand, if you'd prefer to spend your noon hour sunning on the Cathedral lawn, that's part of the Pitt charm, too. And if you want to take classes in the Cathedral of Learning but not for degree status, investigate one of the many sources through Pitts' Informal Program (a noncredit division), with classes in everything from how to become a writer to learning more about Pittsburgh's history and architecture.

University of Pittsburgh at Greensburg
150 Finoli Drive, Greensburg
(724) 837-7040
www.upg.pitt.edu

This 219-acre regional campus of the University of Pittsburgh was built on the former private estate of Commander Charles McKenna Lynch. It's only 2 miles from downtown Greensburg, but it will give you an appealing sense of satisfaction and community. The university serves almost 1,800 students through 20 four-year programs leading to baccalaureate degrees and a number of pre-professional programs completed at the university's main campus in Pittsburgh. Approximately 67 percent of students receive financial assistance.

Majors include accounting, administration of justice, anthropology, biological sciences, environmental science, information science, management, and political science, and you also may design your own major. All students must complete general core requirements that include courses in communications, mathematics, and critical reasoning, as well as five courses each in humanities, social science, and natural sciences. If you can't attend class every day for personal or professional reasons, try the University External Studies Program. You'll attend three on-campus workshops per term and complete the balance of your studying at home.

About 650 of full-time students live on campus, where they enjoy the McKenna Computer Center; Chambers Hall, which features a gymnasium, a running track, and racquetball

i Hollywood producers Steven Bochco and Bud Yorkin studied at Carnegie Mellon University. Bochco studied drama, but Yorkin was an engineering student.

courts; and Millstein Library, which provides access to the Internet as well as the University of Pittsburgh Digital Library. A member of the NCAA Division III Allegheny Mountain Collegiate Conference, the university sponsors 12 varsity sports for men and women as well as intramural sports. The financial aid program is extensive and varied, with all awards based on need.

Westmoreland County Community College
145 Pavilion Lane, Youngwood
(724) 925-4000
www.wccc.edu
One of the most appealing aspects of WCCC is its reach. In addition to the main campus about 6 miles south of Greensburg and 35 miles east of Pittsburgh, the college maintains Westmoreland County campuses in Belle Vernon, Latrobe, New Kensington, Export, Waynesburg, and Indiana, to accommodate almost 6,000 full- and part-time students. In addition, WCCC uses distance-learning technology to teach certain courses simultaneously at several or all campuses, minimizing students' travel requirements, and it offers telecourses for students who can't make it to campus.

Academic programs prepare students for careers or transfer to baccalaureate degree programs at four-year institutions. The college awards the associate in arts degree and the associate in applied science degree, with nearly 55 majors available. Principal programs include accounting, allied health, business, computer information systems, engineering science and industrial technology, horticulture, hospitality management, human services, liberal arts, and science, media technology, and office administration. Study in certain specialties within those departments leads to a certificate or diploma.

The main campus in Youngwood spans 80 acres and four buildings. For relaxation the college provides a gymnasium, racquetball

courts, a health fitness center, and an indoor track. Area employees take advantage of the classrooms, laboratories, and offices in the Business and Industry Center at the Youngwood campus.

If you're a Westmoreland County resident, you'll like the tuition schedule—you'll pay half what nonresidents pay. WCCC offers a variety of financial aid programs, including many scholarships endowed by local businesses and foundations.

SOUTH

California University of Pennsylvania
250 University Avenue, California
(724) 938-4000
www.cup.edu
Nestled in a bend of the Monongahela River about 30 miles from Pittsburgh, California University is an important member of the State System of Higher Education and one of the key institutions of Washington County. The university awards associate, baccalaureate, and master's degrees in more than 100 academic programs offered through the College of Education and Human Services, the College of Liberal Arts, the Eberly College of Science and Technology and the School of Graduate Studies and Research. Continuing-education students will find a rich selection of courses in the Lifelong Learning program and at the university's satellite site at Southpointe Technology Park in Canonsburg.

California serves nearly 6,640 students on its 90-acre campus. There are six residence halls that house 1,500 students. One of the most inviting features on campus is the 93-acre Roadman Park, which includes athletic fields and courts, running facilities, and a stadium. You won't have to worry about academic support here, as the university boasts more than 1,800 computers—more than one-third of them available to students for e-mail and Internet access and other functions. The student-faculty ratio is 21:1.

Students participate in more than 130 organizations, including the *California Times* newspaper, the *Flipside* magazine, a radio station, and a television station. The university sponsors a program of intramural sports and 13 varsity sports, participating in the NCAA Division II Pennsylvania State Athletic Conference. In 1996–1997 the women's softball team captured the NCAA Division II national championship. If you're a Trekker, you'll get a kick out of the athletic team's nickname—the Vulcans. More than 75 percent of students receive some form of financial aid.

Community College of Allegheny County— South Campus
1750 Clairton Road, West Mifflin
(412) 469-4301
www.ccac.edu
The South Campus of CCAC serves Pittsburgh's southern suburbs on a 200-acre site near Century III Mall. Its six-story principal building features a learning assistance center, a community library, a theater, a student dining area, and classrooms. In addition, the campus boasts a learning resource center that offers computer labs and an allied health/nursing complex, and a gymnasium-fitness center. Nearly 20,000 students are enrolled. Classes are also offered at the Bethel Park Center and the Washington County Center.

Washington and Jefferson College
60 South Lincoln Street, Washington
(724) 222-4400, (888) 926-3529
www.washjeff.edu
"Two great presidents . . . one great college" is a tag line W&J frequently uses as a quick introduction to the institution. As you learn a little about W&J, you'll probably agree. It was founded in 1781, making it the oldest college west of the Allegheny Mountains, and has maintained its focus on liberal arts and small s student-faculty ratio of 12:1, W&J offers its 1,400 students plenty of individualized attention in its classes.

The college offers baccalaureate degrees in a broad variety of majors. The humanities— including programs in art, art education, education, French, German, Spanish, history, sociology, and political science—are well rep-

resented. You also can major in business-focused disciplines such as business administration and entrepreneurial studies and science-based areas including biology (the most popular major), biochemistry, chemistry, environmental science, and neuroscience. The college offers preparatory programs in law, medicine, dental medicine, optometry, physical therapy, podiatry, and veterinary medicine. Through exchange programs, W&J students may study abroad at the University of London and the College of Higher Studies in Colombia.

One of the highlights of the academic calendar is the break between terms, which W&J has formalized as "January Intersession," when students are encouraged to broaden their experiences. Many do just that. During one Intersession, students traveled to such destinations as Egypt, Greece, East Africa, and Australia for study trips led by W&J faculty. Other students contributed to the 4,200 hours of community service that the college's faculty, staff, and students log annually.

The 60-acre campus is located in the city of Washington, an easy 25-mile drive south from Pittsburgh along I-79. Ohio and West Virginia are about 30 minutes from the W&J campus via interstate highways. More than 80 percent of students live on campus. About 90 percent of students receive some sort of financial aid.

W&J belongs to the Presidents' Athletic Conference and the NCAA Division III, sponsoring 23 intercollegiate sports. More than 45 percent of students participate in intramurals, club teams, or intercollegiate sports. If you spend time on campus, you'll also get to know the Olin Fine Arts Center, which includes both an art gallery and a hall for performing arts.

i Washington and Jefferson College is the smallest school ever to play in the Rose Bowl. In the 1922 "Granddaddy of Them All," W&J played the University of California to a scoreless tie, using only 11 players in the process.

Waynesburg College
51 West College Street, Waynesburg
(724) 627-8191, (800) 225-7393
www.waynesburg.edu

While Waynesburg College is southwest of our principal coverage area, it's an important institution in our region that you should know about. Moreover, it's just off I-79 in Greene County, about 50 miles from Pittsburgh, so accessibility is no problem.

This private college, founded in 1849, is affiliated with the Presbyterian Church and serves more than 1,300 students on a campus just 2 blocks from the Waynesburg business district. Over 70 degree options are offered, including a master of business administration (offering a criminal justice track), bachelor of arts, bachelor of science, bachelor of science in business administration, bachelor of science in nursing, associate in business administration, and associate in general studies. Within those degree programs are several innovative initiatives.

Waynesburg offers a program in marine biology that features an academic year at Florida Institute of Technology in Melbourne, Florida. The college cooperates with several university schools of engineering to provide joint programs in chemical, electrical, and mechanical engineering, among other engineering-related disciplines, and offers similar joint programs in medical technology.

Community service is important here—the college requires 30 hours of such service from each student—and includes such activities as building homes with Habitat for Humanity and teaching computer skills aboard the college's mobile technology van. As further service to the community, Waynesburg maintains a center for education and technology to provide training and programming for local businesses as well as an adult continuing-education center in Pittsburgh's South Hills.

If you're studying communications, you'll enjoy the extracurricular opportunities at Waynesburg. They include a campus radio station, television studio, newspaper, year-book, and poetry magazine. The college is a member of the NCAA Division III and competes in 17 men's and women's varsity sports.

More than 80 percent of Waynesburg students receive financial aid in a typical year.

WEST

Community College of Beaver County
1 Campus Drive, Monaca
(724) 775-8561, (800) 335-0222
www.ccbc.edu

When CCBC moved from its temporary headquarters in 1971, the college's leadership was looking for a location that would be convenient for most Beaver County residents. They found it here, within 4 miles of the geographic center of the county. The distance from the 75-acre campus to the most remote point in the county is 17 miles, meaning that no Beaver County resident has more than a 30-minute drive to get here.

The college offers 39 programs of study leading to associate degrees. These include programs in allied health, nursing, and aviation sciences. The Aviation Sciences Center features a functioning air traffic control tower at Beaver County Airport, operated by students and college faculty who are professionals in the field. The program is so progressive that the Federal Aeronautics Administration has established an Aviation Education Resource Center on-site and has an agreement with CCBC for direct hire of the college's air traffic control graduates.

The college's open-admissions policy works particularly well for older students returning to classes after some time away; the average student age here is 26. You'll find three levels of tuition, with Beaver County residents offered the lowest tuition, followed by tuition for residents of other Pennsylvania counties and then for out-of-state residents. CCBC provides support to students with families through the Campus Child Care Center. The Library Resource Center offers multimedia retrieval capability among its research tools. All of the college's roughly 2,300 full-time students are commuters, as there are no on-campus housing facilities. 75 percent of all students receive some type of financial aid.

CCBC offers students three intercollegiate sports to choose from; including men's basketball and women's volleyball and softball. There are also a host of intramural activities offered. The campus also is home to the Beaver County Hall of Fame, where such sports legends as Joe Namath, Mike Ditka, and Tony Dorsett—all reared in Beaver County—are enshrined.

Geneva College
3200 College Avenue, Beaver Falls
(724) 846–5100, (800) 847-8255
www.geneva.edu

Set on 55 scenic acres overlooking the Beaver River, Geneva College is an institution with a mission: to educate students through biblically based programs anchored by the historic evangelical and reformed Christian faith. It's a mission that informs all of Geneva's programs.

Degrees offered by the college include bachelor of arts; bachelor of science in education, business administration, and engineering; and associate in business administration, engineering, and biblical studies. Geneva also provides pre-professional programs in cardiovascular technology, criminal justice, medical technology, and nursing.

While the college's mission is rooted in Christianity, that doesn't mean Geneva subordinates vocational preparation. A number of the college's most innovative programs include strong practical components. It offers a dual-degree program in aviation/business administration, in cooperation with the Community College of Beaver County, that leads to an associate degree in aerospace management, air traffic control, or professional piloting, as well as appropriate Federal Aviation Administration licenses and certification. Biology majors studying for a B.S. may spend one of their four years at Virginia's Fairfax Hospital. For study in other medical disciplines, Geneva maintains affiliations with the University Hospitals of Cleveland, St. Joseph's Hospital in Lancaster, and St. Vincent Health Center in Erie.

The college estimates that more than 95 percent of its students receive some form of financial aid. One of the more innovative methods of helping students is an honor scholarship presented—regardless of need—to each student in an academic program who meets certain academic standards.

The student center is the heart of campus life for the 1,900 Geneva students, more than half of whom are commuters. The student to faculty ratio is 14:1. Activities include a student newspaper, cable television and FM radio stations, a yearbook, a literary magazine, a marching band, and an a cappella choir. Geneva participates in a variety of intramural and varsity sports, the latter as a member of the National Association of Intercollegiate Athletics, The Presidents' Athletic Conference, and ECAC. Men's sports include football, basketball, baseball, track and field, cross country, and soccer. Women compete in basketball, volleyball, tennis, track, cross country, soccer, and softball.

Penn State Beaver
100 University Drive, Monaca
(724) 773-3800
www.br.psu.edu

State Commonwealth College, Penn State Beaver is a 100-acre campus set in the heart of Beaver County, about 30 miles northwest of Pittsburgh and 15 miles from Pittsburgh International Airport. For its 800 students, the college offers the first two years of more than 160 Penn State baccalaureate degree programs. In addition, the college offers four associate degree programs—liberal arts; science; electrical engineering technology; and hotel, restaurant, and institutional management. In one component of the hotel, restaurant, and institutions management program, students operate a dinner cafe one day a week as part of a field practicum. Penn State Beaver also offers professional certificate programs and a master's of education degree in teaching and curriculum.

Student life is full and varied, especially for those residing in the college's two residence halls. Among the most popular student activities is participation in the Masquers, which has brought live theatre to preschool and elementary school children since 1969. Students also participate in five intercollegiate sports, a variety of intramural sports, and the campus radio station, WBVR.

As the Masquers demonstrate, Penn State Beaver strives to be a force in the community, providing students with the opportunity to network and form useful contacts. Since 1976 the Broadhead Cultural Center on campus has staged free or low-cost concerts and theatrical productions in the 700-seat, open-air J.P. Giusti Amphitheater. The campus sponsors an annual celebration of the birthday of the Reverend Martin Luther King Jr. with a program and a guest speaker.

Penn State Beaver offers six varsity sports: men's baseball, basketball, and soccer and women's basketball, softball, and volleyball. There are also a dozen intramural and club sports and approximately 15 clubs and organizations active on campus.

The college's adult literacy program provides educationally disadvantaged adults with tutoring in reading, math, civic literacy, family support, and English as a foreign language, while its partnership with the Aliquipa School District enriches the lives of disadvantaged youths and their families by providing academic and life skills support.

Robert Morris University
6001 University Boulevard, Moon Township
(412) 262-8200, (800) 762-0097
www.rmu.edu

Robert Morris University is named for one of the key financiers of the Revolutionary War; most campus buildings bear the names of America's early heroes and patriots. The pleasant campus is spread over 230 sloping acres about 5 miles from Pittsburgh International Airport. It's a convenient location for visitors.

Once you start to talk about academics at RMU, you'll leave the 18th century pretty quickly, as this private university means business—literally. RMU focuses on business education at the undergraduate, graduate, and continuing education levels. Its productive relationships with many local businesses help graduates find jobs and advance in their careers. More than 18,000 RMU alumni live and work in the region. The university's Sewall Center for Leadership, a meeting, convocation, and athletic center, is a popular site for corporate training programs.

You can pick from more than 30 majors leading to the bachelor of arts, bachelor of science, and bachelor of science in business administration degrees. Among the undergraduate majors you won't find at many institutions are sport management, tourism management, and aviation management. The university awards associate degrees in business administration and computer and information systems; in a joint program with Allegheny General Hospital and Pittsburgh's Ohio Valley General Hospital, students may earn an associate in science degree from the college and a certificate in radiologic technology from one of the hospitals. At the graduate level, RMU offers 14 programs of study leading to the master of science, master of science in business administration, and master of business administration degrees. For students with busy professional schedules, the college offers the One-Day-a-Week Program, which enables students to take the bulk of their classes on Saturday. The program is available at both the Moon campus and the Center for Adult and Continuing Education in Pittsburgh.

For years, businesses have lamented the poor communications skills of their employees. RMU has come to the rescue with an innovative Communications Skills Core program for all students in bachelor's degree programs. The communications requirement includes five courses in the first several years of study and four courses during the upperclass years. The courses focus on five key areas: communication principles; skills and strategies; written, oral, and nonverbal language; collaborative, interpersonal, and inter-cultural skills; support technologies; and affective behaviors.

RMU's 5,000 full-time and part-time students enjoy access to the Academic Media Center, which features photography and audio production facilities as well as a crackerjack television production studio, one of the finest campus studios you'll find. TV production here is no academic exercise; RMU students program a channel for the local cable television operator, which provides in-room cable services to the college's 900 resident students. RMU competes in the 23 sports as part of the NCAA Division I Northeast Conference in all its varsity sports and offers seven intramural sports and nine club sports. (For a more detailed look at RMU basketball, see the Spectator Sports chapter.) More than 90 percent of RMU students receive financial aid.

RMU offers extensive continuing education programs through its Center for Adult and Continuing Education in downtown Pittsburgh. For a profile of the center, see the Downtown section of this chapter.

Trinity Episcopal School for Ministry
311 Eleventh Street, Ambridge
(724) 266-3838, (800) 874-8754
www.tesm.edu
"Serving Jesus Christ within the Episcopal Church, while welcoming committed Christians from all traditions." That's how Trinity Episcopal School for Ministry describes its mission, which it pursues in a variety of ways. Located in Beaver County, Trinity is a graduate school for religious study offering the doctor of ministry, master of divinity, master of divinity/master of arts in professional psychology, master of arts in religion, and master of arts in mission and evangelism degrees.

Trinity is set on a city block in the heart of Ambridge, symbolizing its role in the community. The school emphasizes field education opportunities, which include preaching, leading small groups, service as hospital chaplains, and work with missions for the homeless. Through the Trinity Episcopal

Checking Out Your School

For help coordinating your visit to check out colleges in Pittsburgh, view www.thecollegecity.com, which offers great travel tips and bona-fide deals, as well as information about schools and careers here. The site is associated with Campus Visit magazine, based in Wellesley, Massachusetts. Visit www.campusvisit.com.

Extension Ministries program, students may earn up to 24 credits prior to enrollment through home study supplemented by some time on campus. TEEM also is available to students in seven other cities.

While the school advises students to expect a demanding academic schedule, it provides plenty of support, including weekly meetings with advisee groups comprising both professionals and students and two quiet days each term, when students get a break from their studies to reflect and worship. Married couples are welcome here—consistent with the school's belief that husbands and wives should minister as partners—but school-provided housing is limited.

When you're here, check out the mural that covers the entire back wall of the library building. Painted by students, it blends biblical themes and representations of local settings.

PROPRIETARY SCHOOLS

In addition to degree-granting institutions, Southwestern Pennsylvania offers a large and eclectic group of for-profit trade schools, many of which award certificates in specialized trades. Business schools and beauty academies probably are the largest groups, but you'll also find schools for massage, pet grooming, gunsmithing, floral arrangement and care, truck driving and diesel technology, lethal weapons training . . . well, you get the idea.

These schools are so numerous—easily more than 70 in our principal coverage area—that they defy easy summary or description. For a statewide list of private licensed/registered schools, a good resource is the *Pennsylvania Education Directory,* an annual published by Applied Arts Publishers, 2100 State Road, Lebanon, PA 17601, (717) 272-9442. Cost is $16 plus tax. You'll get names, phone numbers, and addresses, but no descriptions.

HEALTH CARE

Southwestern Pennsylvania has many attractions, yet its health-care sector may be one of its most abiding strengths. The region is a center for medical treatment and research, bringing local residents high-quality health care and the promise that they will be the beneficiaries of cutting-edge developments. In addition, the region's reputation as a leader in health care serves as a magnet for medical professionals, who in turn contribute to the strength of the sector, creating a cycle of growth.

The center of the region's health-care sector is Oakland's medical complex, which derives much of its energy and personnel from the University of Pittsburgh Medical Center (UPMC). Community medicine is well represented in the region, too, both by independent hospitals throughout our six-county coverage area and by providers affiliated with Pittsburgh-based health systems.

One could chart the history of health care here through its pioneers and milestones, such as Dr. Jonas Salk's development of his polio vaccine; Dr. Thomas Starzl's trailblazing work in organ transplantation; even in the development of the Mr. Yuk poison-prevention program, an initiative that has saved an inestimable number of lives. Most recently, holistic medical alternatives have begun to be offered along with allopathic medicine at several UPMC hospitals, West Penn Allegheny Health System, and at doctors' offices throughout the area. You'll also find holistic practitioners, such as licensed acupuncturists and qualified practitioners of herbology and homeopathy, practicing in offices of their own. Just as Salk and Stazl were pioneers in saving lives, the holistic practitioners in the area are pioneers in saving the quality of lives.

No history of Pittsburgh health care would be complete without mentioning the contributions of Pittsburgh's workers and labor unions. When Pittsburgh was the industrial heart of America, it was laborers, unions, and their companies that advanced the notion of employer-provided health insurance. There may be no single person to credit for this, but it's an important contribution nonetheless.

In our look at the region's health-care system, you'll find profiles of holistic health practices, hospitals, rehabilitation centers, and health insurance providers. We've also provided descriptions of organizations that can serve as valuable resources—and sources of referrals—for you. Finally we've presented descriptions of some special services providers. You might not need them now, but it's sure comforting to know they're here.

WELLNESS

Unless you're experiencing a life-threatening emergency, you can call one of the referral sources listed in the Resources section to find the name of a physician, or confidently visit one of the practitioners listed below. In some cases, both acute and chronic, working with a holistic practitioner can heal your illness; in almost all others, you can improve your quality of life.

While the modalities holistic practitioners use vary widely, one thing you'll find in common among these trained professionals is that they all ask you questions about you and your life, not just questions about your symptoms of illness. They do this because they take into account the gestalt of who you are when they're treating you—that's the nature of the "holistic" approach. In addition, most holistic practitioners strive to create a comfortable and nurturing healing environment.

ℹ️ Choose a wellness provider with the same care you would any other medical professional. Natural medicine is a powerful tool.

Some of the most commonly used holistic modalities are acupuncture, chiropractic, massage, homeopathy, and herbology. Acupuncture—which involves the insertion of needles about the thickness of a strand of hair into particular, superficial points on the body—is useful in treating a range of symptoms, as well as the root causes of illness, including pain, headaches, hormonal imbalances, systemic weakness related to various diseases, addictions, and acute and chronic viral illnesses. In chiropractic, the spine is manipulated, with the goal of relieving pain and freeing the body's energy for health and well-being. While there are many types of massage, most are pleasant, pain-relieving, and relaxing; discuss your goals with the massage practitioner you contact to make sure the type of massage she or he does will help you achieve what you desire.

Homeopathy and herbology, often confused by new holistic health patients, are distinct sciences. Used widely in European countries, homeopathy works on the principle of "like produces like" and uses remedies containing only the "energy imprint" of the physical substances from which they were produced. These remedies address physical, mental, and emotional symptoms and can be used to bring the body back to balance during either acute or chronic illness—or simply to strengthen an individual's constitution. Herbology uses either Western or Chinese herbs in single or combination form to effect changes in the same way that pharmaceutical drugs do. Some traditional drugs are even made from herbs. For instance, the heart medication digitalis is made from foxglove, a plant originally found in the wild. In any case, many of the holistic modalities you may try have been used successfully for thousands of years—that's longer than any clinical trial we know of.

The list below is by no means exhaustive. Out of the many practitioners in the area, we've selected the people we or our trusted friends personally know are top notch. If you're looking for a type of practitioner we haven't described here, contact the Nuin Center at (412) 661-6108 or www.nuincenter.com or pick up a copy of *Point of Light* magazine at one of Pittsburgh's health-food stores. For a subscription, contact the publishers at (724) 863-4206 or www.pointoflight.com.

The Nuin Center is a Highland Park professional building and group-meeting location center once part of the Mellon estate. The majority of the tenants are healing-arts practitioners, as the intention of the center's founders was to create a space supportive of the healing arts. *Point of Light* is a free, quarterly magazine that covers healing arts and "New Age" happenings from a popular perspective. Many reputable practitioners advertise in the magazine.

Downtown

The Midwife Center for Birth and Women's Health
2825 Penn Avenue
(412) 321-6880
www.midwifecenter.org

Since 1982 the certified nurse-midwives at the Midwife Center for Birth and Women's Health have provided personalized health care to thousands of women and have assisted in the delivery of over 2,000 babies. It is the only freestanding, licensed birth center option in Northwestern Pennsylvania, and there is also the option of hospital birth facilitated by the center's physician.

The Midwife Center, located in the Strip District, strives to increase the health of women and their families by providing excellent woman-focused healthcare services and family-oriented birthing services. Many people think that midwives only help women have babies, but midwives also provide well-woman gynecological care and family planning to women during all stages of life, from puberty through to menopause. Services include pregnancy care and delivery; complete history and physical exams; pelvic exams and pap tests; referrals for mammography; natural family planning and fertility awareness; contraceptives; preconceptual counseling and testing; sexually transmitted disease screening and treatment; wellness promotion; menopausal care, including hormone replacement therapy or alternatives; and educational programs. All of the care is viewed within the context of reproductive and sexual health as part of normal life processes, and providers do not intervene without evidence of a problem, including during childbirth and menopause.

When care is called for, the midwives take the time to listen and talk with their clients about things that affect them, their family, work, and personal issues. The waiting area and exam rooms are cheerful and warm and are decorated in ways more typical of someone's living room than a "clinical environment." Reflecting the midwives' philosophy, it feels cozy and safe here.

During appointments the midwives take into account each woman's physical, emotional, and spiritual needs. The midwives believe that a woman should be in control of her own health care, including her birth experience. They are particularly knowledgeable and gentle in dealing with issues related to past sexual trauma, and overall the language they use and the way they interact with patients supports a positive sense of well-being, even during pelvic exams!

The Midwife Center is a private, nonprofit practice, supported in part by grants; patient fees; United Way Contributors Choice; and tax-deductible contributions from businesses, foundations, and individuals. They accept most insurance plans and are a member of Adagio Health, which enables them to provide gynecological care to women for free or on a sliding scale based on income and family size. For more information, inquire about "With Woman Fridays," a walk-in service held on Fridays for uninsured women who qualify.

North

The Integrated Medicine Program at Allegheny General Hospital
1307 Federal Street
(412) 359-8591
www.wpahs.com

Located on Pittsburgh's North Side, the Integrated Medicine Program at Allegheny General Hospital is dedicated to blending the science of allopathic medicine with the wisdom of natural healing practices to enhance the health and well-being of its patients, helping them learn to tap into their own self-healing capacity.

The Integrated Medicine Program offers "Mind/Body Medicine," such as biofeedback, yoga and meditation, breathwork, and prayer and nondenominational spiritual support; Traditional Chinese medicine, including acupuncture, Chinese herbology, and nutrition and lifestyle counseling; body and energy work, such as therapeutic massage, reflexology, and Reiki; the "R&R Program (Relaxation and Recovery)" that prepares patients for surgery and helps them recover afterward; the "Lifestyle Program," which combines customized medical and lifestyle changes for health management; and, perhaps most notably, the "Functional Bowel Program," one of only three programs in the country that offers a multidisciplinary approach to bowel disorders. Also quite notably, many of these therapies are available to inpatients as well as outpatients.

The Integrated Medicine Program was cofounded by Paul Lebovitz, M.D., and Kathleen Krebs, R.N. Lebovitz, who was nominated for the *Pittsburgh Business Times'* 2002 Healthcare Hero award, is a board-certified gastroenterologist and the program's medical director. He also leads the Functional Bowel team. Krebs, clinical director, was designated in 2002 by the *Pittsburgh Post-Gazette* as one of a "dozen making a difference in health care in Pittsburgh." She assesses patients' needs and their state of health and assists them in employing mind/body medicine techniques. Other staff include nationally board-certified

Close-up

The Proper Medicine: Community Drug Makes Filling Prescriptions an Exact Science

The sign that hangs beneath the pharmacy window at Community Drug reads: ASK YOUR PHYSICIAN IF COMPOUNDING IS RIGHT FOR YOU.

Eleven steps below in the basement of the Greenfield pharmacy is a brightly lit, 450-square-foot compounding lab. Here a handful of trained workers prepare specialized medications to help everybody from a two-week-old infant with seizures to a constipated cat.

"We are here to solve problems," said David Hairhoger, president of Community Drug Inc. and Community Drug Compounding Center. Both entities are licensed separately with the Pennsylvania Board of Pharmacy. Hairhoger bought Community Drug from the son of its original owner in 1980 and opened the compounding lab in 1996 because "we want to do the right thing," he said.

That right thing involves preparing medications to help solve challenging problems for patients and their pets, Hairhoger said. He explained that many medicines are available in limited strengths only and compounding pharmacists can custom-make prescriptions.

"I market to physicians, dentists, podiatrists, pediatricians, veterinarians, physical therapists, and other pharmacies," said Hairhoger. He spends about 15 to 20 hours a week in marketing and making office visits on behalf of Community Drug Compounding.

"When I call on physicians, I stress that we're here to solve medication problems," Hairhoger said. He added that he typically receives favorable feedback from physicians. "The one thing they say is that, 'I've never seen a pharmacist stop by and talk to me,'" Hairhoger reported.

And every physician can find the need for a compounding pharmacist, according to Hairhoger. "Even if it's as simple as customized doses," he said.

---

acupuncturist Don Thompson, L.Ac., and Dr. Jorge Vazquez, who is board-certified in both internal medicine and nutrition.

In addition, the Integrated Medicine Program operates a volunteer component that trains mature adults in Reiki, Healing Touch, and hand massage so they can offer these therapies free of charge to the inpatient and outpatient population. The program also serves as clinical site for the Community College of Allegheny County's massage therapy program.

East

Acupuncture Energetics and the Wellspring Valley
183 Donegal Lake Road, Stahlstown
(724) 593-6237
www.wellspringvalley.com
Acupuncture Energetics forms the cornerstone of the Wellspring Valley Center, which was founded by Christine Simmons, R.ac. Christine holds a master's degree in acupuncture and Chinese medicine from the Traditional Acupuncture Institute in Columbia, Maryland.

Dr. Wynne Browne, an obstetrician/gynecologist who retired from conventional medicine after 17 years, said she began working with compounding pharmacies about four years ago because she—and her patients—weren't happy with conventional hormone prescriptions.

"I wasn't satisfied with conventional hormone prescriptions because the 'one-dose-fits-all' just doesn't work," said Dr. Browne, who now practices alternative medicine and has offices in Highland Park and White Oak. "Women are all very different."

She said that compounding pharmacies are helping to bring back relationships among physicians, patients, and pharmacists. "It's the relationship we've heard about from years ago. We've re-created that," said Dr. Browne.

Dr. Browne holds informational seminars with Susan Merenstein, a pharmacist at Community Drug Compounding, to educate women on natural alternatives to conventional hormone replacement therapies that can be used during menopause. Merenstein said this area is expected to grow for the compounding center. "It's easy to count and put some pills in a bottle, but it's a whole different ball game when interfacing [with patients] like this," said Merenstein.

All told, the Community Drug Compounding Center works with at least 100 different physicians, filling on average 30 to 35 compounded prescriptions daily. Upstairs, the traditional pharmacy fills about 200 prescriptions a day.

"It takes time," said Hairhoger of compounding. Turnaround on compounded prescriptions usually takes about two days. While Hairhoger declined to reveal sales figures, he said the compounding pharmacy is operating in the black.

By Lynne Glover, reprinted with permission
from the *Pittsburgh Business Times*

To assist her clients in achieving greater health, along with acupuncture Christine often uses Chinese and Western herbs, Jin shin acupressure process, polarity therapy, movement therapy, and the Feldenkrais and Alexander techniques. One of Christine's specialties is helping clients access and recognize their emotions, with the goal of transforming emotional blocks that contribute to reduced mental and physical health. She treats clients of all ages with both acute and chronic illnesses, as well as those who are seeking preventative medical treatment, and describes the purpose of her work as being "to help people help themselves as they travel their personal journey to wholeness and self-knowledge."

Although it will take you at least 45 minutes to travel from Pittsburgh to see Christine, it's worth it. She's an experienced and talented practitioner, and you'll enjoy the lush country setting across from Donegal Lake, where Christine lives and works.

Wynne Browne, M.D.
5841 Forward Avenue
(412) 521-2236

Wynne Browne is a board-certified OB-GYN and a licensed acupuncturist, as well as a practitioner of "energy medicine." She retired from "conventional medicine" after 17 years and now offers a nontraditional practice with numerous areas of specialty. Her office environment today offers comfortable chairs, soft music, and is decorated with objects reflecting her Native American heritage.

Dr. Browne says she's "never really believed that people have to suffer," and she "holds the space" for her patients to experience "physical, mental, emotional, and spiritual healing." She views a major part of her role as a doctor as being able to "help people take responsibility for their health and health care." Her philosophy that "medical care is a process that happens with a patient, not to them" goes hand in hand with that.

Dr. Browne is well known in the Pittsburgh area for her work with natural hormone replacement therapy for women and men (men, she explains, go through an "andropause"). She provides traditional acupuncture sessions, and in particular, has seen this modality be effective for many patients with fertility issues.

She also offers energy work sessions using Flow Alignment and Connection and Cellular Expansion, and often combines Flow Alignment and Connection with acupuncture. She has seen dramatic shifts within patients experiencing both severe physical and mental illnesses while they committed themselves to the Cellular Expansion modality, and she's especially excited about this pioneering form of energy practice, which works on the somatic level.

Her other areas of specialty include nutrition and weight management; anger management; and medical hypnosis, in which her training is quite extensive. Dr. Browne received her medical training at the University of Pittsburgh Medical School and did her residency at Magee-Womens Hospital.

Julie Ann Caryl, D.C. and Pamela Huston, D.C.
2020 Ardmore Boulevard, Forest Hills
(412) 273-3600

Julie and Pam are graduates of the Palmer College of Chiropractic and are certified in applied kinesiology and the Nambudripad Allergy Elimination Technique (NAET). Applied kinesiology is a system that evaluates structural, chemical, and mental aspects. It employs muscle testing and other standard methods of diagnosis. Nutrition, chiropractic adjustments, acupressure, exercise, and education are used therapeutically to help restore wellness.

In addition to the standard applications of chiropractic, Julie and Pam help clients with problems with environmental sensitivities, allergies, and myriad acute and chronic health problems. NAET is one of the means they use to do this. NAET diagnosis and treatment of allergies integrates methods from the disciplines of kinesiology, chiropractic acupressure, and nutritional science. It's likely your insurance will reimburse you for treatment with the doctors, who offer comprehensive 30-minute and 1-hour sessions.

The doctors are members of the Pennsylvania Chiropractic Association, the Human Ecology Action League, the Center for Science in the Public Interest, and the Physicians Committee for Responsible Medicine. You'll start feeling more relaxed as soon as you sit down next to the burbling meditation fountain in their waiting room and have a cup of tea.

Pittsburgh School of Massage Therapy
3600 Laketown Road
(412) 241-5155, (800) 860-1114
www.pghschmass.com

When the Pittsburgh School of Massage Therapy opened its doors in 1986, the school was the first in Western Pennsylvania to offer professional massage therapy training, and today it remains the only school devoted exclusively to massage and related subjects in Southwestern Pennsylvania. The school continues to train professionals, provide professional continuing education courses, and offer weekend introductory courses, such as "Massage for Friends and Family," that are popular among community members at large.

The school offers a "massage therapist locator" service to individuals who call the school looking for referrals. A receptionist can search a database during the call or send a directory of graduates who've agreed to be listed. Qualified graduates of the school have offices throughout Pittsburgh and the surrounding area. All have core training in Swedish and sports massage, and some practitioners go on to do advanced or specialized training in such techniques as neuromuscular work, trigger-point myotherapy, myofascial release, shiatsu, pregnancy massage, and reflexology, among others.

At the school there's also a professional clinic, where it's possible to make appointments with a professional who is either a graduate of the school or an instructor there. Visitors to the school will also find a retail store on-site, stocked with massage and bodywork supplies, aromatherapy and spa items, and books and videos related to wellness and massage.

Squirrel Hill Family Wellness Center
5801 Beacon Street, Squirrel Hill
(412) 422-5433
www.drberez.com

Franne Berez, M.D., N.D., founded the Squirrel Hill Family Wellness Center in 1988. She is a board-certified family practitioner with a special interest in holistic medicine for women and children, although she treats patients of all ages and genders. Complete evaluation includes a standard Western medical interview, lab evaluation, hospital testing with referral to appropriate medical specialists if needed, and psycho-social evaluation. These conventional medical practices are combined with time-honored methods of naturopathic, homeopathic, and traditional Chinese diagnosis; in fact, most patients coming to see Franne seek her expertise in homeopathy.

And don't worry if doctors' offices usually set your teeth on edge. You won't even see

the exam room until the last few minutes of your interview with the doctor, and forget the paper gown. You'll tell Franne about what ails you while you sit in a rocking chair in her casually decorated office. You might even still be sipping the last bit of that tea you made for yourself in the waiting room.

Franne shares space with several practitioners at the center who work closely with her. For more information about her colleagues, visit the Web site.

UPMC Shadyside
The Center for Integrative Medicine
5230 Centre Avenue
(412) 623-2121
http://integrativemedicine.upmc.com

Interestingly enough, when it originally opened its doors in the early-19th century, Shadyside was an independent, homeopathic hospital. While that ceased to be its identity a long time ago, Shadyside was one of the first hospitals in the country to offer such programs as medical hypnosis, pain management utilizing therapeutic touch and biofeedback, and therapeutic touch for inpatients. When national demand pushed doctors and hospitals to consider how complementary medicine could interface with conventional, allopathic medicine, the hospital was a natural site for innovation.

UPMC Shadyside's Center for Integrative Medicine was chosen by New Age magazine as one of the top six complementary medicine centers in the country. The center's mission is to work in cooperation with physicians treating patients with all kinds of health conditions and to individually tailor programs for patients that suit not only their presenting conditions, but that also take into consideration what suits their personality types and spiritual and emotional needs.

The center offers acupuncture, traditional Chinese medicine, botanical medicine, biofeedback, polarity therapy, chiropractic manipulative therapy, naturopathic counseling, EMDR, medical hypnosis relaxation therapy and guided imagery, body-centered psychotherapy, reflexology, shiatsu, therapeutic massage and touch, and comprehensive holistic evaluations by physicians.

Whole Health Resources
Kenmawr Building, Suite 201C
401 Shady Avenue
(412) 361-8600
www.wholehealthresources.com

Whole Health Resources is synonymous with the work of Deborah Barr, who founded this center for holistic counseling in 1985. Deborah—who has many years of training in meditation, yoga, whole-foods nutrition, and spiritual development—provides counseling sessions relating to holistic health, macrobiotics and other forms of nutrition, natural weight loss, and attitudinal healing. She frequently gives personal development workshops and provides corporate and personal wellness coaching and teleseminars. She also offers shiatsu massage, foot reflexology, acupressure facial massage, and whole-foods cooking instruction. Deborah's clients, all of whom participate in a wellness program they've designed with her, regularly report improvements in their health, such as stable blood sugar levels, better sleep quality, and more balanced energy. We find Deborah's positive attitude rubs off—a nice bonus.

Classes in tai chi, yoga, aromatherapy, and other forms of personal and professional development are held at Whole Health Resources on a regular basis. One-on-one yoga therapy sessions are available by appointment.

South

The Birch Center
1931 East Carson Street, 2nd Floor
(412) 381-0116
www.birchcenter.com

Operated by Pennsylvania licensed acupuncturists, The Birch Center offers quality acupuncture, therapeutic massage, including tui na, acu-massage—a combination of acupuncture, massage, and herbal medicine.

Traditional Chinese Medicine (TCM) is a complete system of medicine that searches for the causes of illnesses and treats the patient as a whole. According to the World Health Organization, acupuncture can treat colds and flus, deafness and earaches, sinus infections, hay fever, high blood pressure, and diabetes.

The Birch Center also offers energy healing, weight loss consultations, classes and lectures, and wild edible and medicinal plant walks. To learn more, check out The Birch Center's Web site or the blog written by owners Melissa and Dave Sokulski.

The Center for Pain Treatment
1312 East Carson Street
(412) 431-9180
www.centerforpaintreatment.com

The Center for Pain Treatment comprises a chiropractor, Dr. Michael G. Savko, and four board-certified trigger-point myotherapists, Tassos Spanos, Mark Spanos, Nancy Shapiro, and Richard Finn. In addition to their certification, all the myotherapists have personally studied with Dr. Janet Travell, the originator of trigger-point myotherapy and White House physician to Presidents Kennedy and Johnson.

To understand how trigger-point myotherapy works, it's useful to know that a trigger point is a self-sustaining irritable spot on a muscle. This irritable spot gradually causes the affected muscle to become tighter and shorter, limiting the function and motion of the muscle and causing weakness and/or pain. Most of the time the trigger point, which is at the site of a trauma to a muscle, refers pain to another area of the body, just like a hole in a roof may cause a leak in a distant area of the ceiling. Using various massagelike techniques, a trigger-point myotherapist stretches the muscle, unwinding the trigger point and thus easing the patient's pain.

Trigger-point myotherapy is useful in treating a wide variety of pain syndromes, including carpal tunnel, TMJ, migraines, sciatic, tendonitis, arthritis, and both fibromyalgia and myofascial pain syndrome (which is often misdiagnosed as fibromyalgia). The therapy is also useful in improving the performance of athletes and musicians, and in cases where muscle weakness or distortion, rather than pain, is present. (Cases like the latter might include people recovering from strokes, for instance.) There's a good chance your insurance carrier will reimburse you for your sessions, as long as treatment is supervised by the chiropractor on staff.

HOSPITALS

Southwestern Pennsylvania is justifiably renowned for its leadership in medical research and treatment. Its many teaching, community, general, and specialized hospitals form the core of the health sector. In recent years, however, the region's medical group has experienced considerable volatility, as hospitals have in some cases merged to form networks and absorb physicians' practice groups, restructured to create for-profit arms in other cases, and downsized in still other cases. The result has been a new look for the health sector here; while many of the players remain the same, the names and services may have changed.

The two largest networks are UPMC Health Center, which encompasses 20 hospitals and a number of other units, and the West Penn Allegheny System, which includes two tertiary and four community hospitals. Smaller networks include Excela Health and Heritage Valley Health System.

In the description of area hospitals, we've noted where facilities are part of a network. Where a network or system operates multiple hospitals we've listed each hospital in its proper geographic section, while noting its affiliation with the network. If a network or system provides services apart from its hospitals, we've described those under the system or network header. Keep in mind that the sector continues to be volatile, experiencing at least several consolidations each year.

Downtown

Pittsburgh Mercy Health System
1400 Locust Street
(412) 232-8111

Mercy Health System boasts one of the richest traditions in the region's health-care sector, tracing its roots to the 1847 founding of its predecessor hospital by seven Sisters of Mercy from Carlow, Ireland. System executives describe the organization as a "Catholic system of health care."

The system operates Mercy Behavioral Health, a network of community-based mental health, mental retardation, drug and alcohol services, and an outpatient physical rehabilitation facility.

UPMC Mercy
1400 Locust Street
(412) 232-8111
www.upmcmercy.com

In January 2008, The Mercy Hospital of Pittsburgh—the first hospital in Pittsburgh and the first Mercy Hospital in the world—merged with UPMC and was renamed UPMC Mercy. Today, UPMC continues to provide compassionate care in the Catholic tradition.

UPMC Mercy, a 500-bed facility, specializes in providing neurology, neurosurgery, and treatments for strokes; cardiology, cardiovascular, and thoracic surgery services; trauma and burn care; orthopedics, hip resurfacing, and joint replacement surgery; physical medicine and rehabilitation services; and obstetric and gynecology treatment. Other services include medical and surgical care, emergency care, oncology, pediatrics, diabetes, occupational health, and palliative care.

The hospital sponsors nine graduate medical education programs and a diploma school of nursing.

North

ACMH Hospital
One Nolte Drive, Kittanning
(724) 543-8500
As a community hospital, ACMH emphasizes outreach and education programs, featuring classes on 10 different topics including breast-feeding, CPR, babysitters emergency care, osteoporosis education, and a safe-driving course for seniors. The hospital operates primary care centers in the communities of Elderton, Leechburg, and South Bethlehem.

At its main campus, the 215-bed hospital offers magnetic resonance imaging, psychiatric care, home health services, the Richard G. Laube Cancer Center, physical and occupational therapy, and programs in rehabilitation therapy and aquatic therapy. You'll find programs in cardiac rehabilitation, organ and tissue donation, sentinel node biopsy, Stereo TacTic, breast biopsy, bracytherapy (prostate seeding program), and pre- and post-natal care, as well as a sleep disorders lab and a wound care clinic. You can get your annual flu shots at ACMH and attend the annual health fair that the hospital sponsors.

Butler Health System—Butler Memorial Hospital
911 East Brady Street, Butler
(724) 283-6666
www.butlerhealthsystem.org
Butler Health System describes itself as a community-based system of health-care services that provides multiple facets of health care, including prevention, treatment, and expanded outpatient services. What that means for you is a variety of useful and timely programs and services. The system centers around Butler Memorial Hospital, a 234-bed facility with more than a century of experience. An acute care hospital, Butler Memorial offers inpatient and outpatient services, as well as skilled-nursing beds.

Among the services the hospital offers are a heart center, including open-heart surgery; a center for sleep disorders; a women's health center; a round-the-clock emergency department; CAT scanning and magnetic resonance imaging; and pain management programs. The hospital also offers prenatal care and delivery services, postpartum care, pediatric assessment, and home visits. Its birthing suites allow for labor, delivery, and recovery—all in the same room. The hospital also sponsors the Butler Regional Recovery Program for drug and alcohol abuse treatment, with community centers in Butler, Cranberry, and Natrona Heights.

Butler Health System provides outpatient lab and X-ray services at several community locations, including the Butler Mall and locations in the East Brady, Slippery Rock, Zelienople, and Saxonburg communities. As part of its education program, the hospital offers classes in babysitting, diabetes care, personal stress management, and smoking cessation.

UPMC Passavant, Cranberry
One St. Francis Way, Cranberry
(724) 772-5300
http://www.upmc.com/HospitalsFacilities/UPMCPassavant/default.htm
UPMC Passavant, Cranberry, is only 0.5 mile from Interstate 79, providing easy access for residents of Butler and Beaver Counties and the North Hills of Allegheny County. It offers round-the-clock emergency care, enhanced by an on-site helicopter to transport critically ill patients, as well as other state-of-the-art care.

AGH Suburban Campus
100 South Jackson Avenue, Bellevue
(412) 734-6000
www.wpahs.org/sgh/index.html
Part of the West Penn Allegheny Health System, the AGH Suburban Campus provides important services to residents of the Pittsburgh suburbs known as the North Boroughs. The 195-bed community hospital offers care in more than 30 medical surgical services, outpatient services, critical care, physical rehabilitation, kidney dialysis, cosmetic surgery, and occupational medicine. In addition, the hospital features an emergency department and a physical rehabilitation unit.

The Suburban Campus provides a free health education club for those older than 55 years of age. It's called the Senior Advantage Club, and it holds monthly health education programs and provides free flu shots, blood pressure readings, and a variety of health screenings. The hospital also sponsors a wide range of health education programs and support groups.

UPMC Passavant - McCandless
9100 Babcock Boulevard
(412) 367-6700
www.upmc.com/HospitalsFacilities/UPMCPassavant/default.htm
Located 12 miles north of Pittsburgh, UPMC Passavant—McCandless is a 260-bed facility serving northern Allegheny County and southwestern Butler County. Founded in 1849, Passavant offers medical specialties in cancer and cardiac care, emergency medicine, obstetrics and gynecology, and orthopedics. The hospital features a chest pain center; subacute care units; surgical services; physical and occupational therapy departments; and centers for sleep, pain management, and speech, voice, and swallowing disorders.

UPMC St. Margaret
815 Freeport Road
(412) 784-4000
http://stmargaret.upmc.com/
UPMC St. Margaret provides 250 acute care beds and has more than 500 physicians on staff offering medical specialties in arthritis, rehabilitation, orthopedics, family practice, gerontology, and occupational health. The hospital was founded in 1898, merged with UPMC in 1997, and serves as a valuable resource for more than 250,000 residents of Pittsburgh's northern and eastern suburbs. St. Margaret reaches into the community through such programs as paramedic response teams to assist local volunteer units, athletic training services for schools, and a variety of health screening programs.

One quirk about the hospital's location: While it's surrounded by suburban municipalities, it is part of the city of Pittsburgh.

VA Medical Center
325 New Castle Road, Butler
(724) 287-4781, (800) 362-8262
www.butler.va.gov
Approximately 35 miles north of Pittsburgh, this U.S. Department of Veterans Affairs center provides a wide range of primary medical services, including outpatient care, preventive services, and acute hospitalization. Special programs include geriatric/extended care, physical rehabilitation, substance abuse treatment, and mental health care. The center offers home-based primary care, a program for homeless veterans, and an outpatient facility in the Butler County community of West Middlesex. While affiliated with the VA Pittsburgh Healthcare System, the Butler facility is administered separately.

VA Pittsburgh Healthcare System
1010 Delafield Road, Aspinwall
(412) 688-6000,
24-hour phone: (866) 482-7488

7180 Highland Drive
(412) 365-4900,
24-hour phone: (866) 482-7488

University Drive
(412) 688-6000,
24-hour phone: (866) 482-7488
www.va.gov/pittsburgh
While the U.S. Department of Veterans Affairs VA Pittsburgh Healthcare System operates three facilities in the Pittsburgh area, we'll address them as a single unit, since that's the way system administrators regard it. Together the three divisions make up a major medical/surgical tertiary care facility with

The University of Pittsburgh Medical Center includes 40 buildings in a "superblock" in Oakland bounded by Fifth Avenue and DeSoto, Terrace, and Darragh Streets. It's one of the world's most concentrated medical complexes.

programs in orthopedics, same-day surgery, rehabilitation, radiation therapy, mental health, and substance abuse. The system features a liver transplant center, a regional cardiac surgery center, and an oncology network center. For your initial contact with the system, try the Aspinwall Division at the number listed above.

East

Children's Hospital of Pittsburgh
3705 Fifth Avenue
(412) 692-5325
www.chp.edu

Children's Hospital has a legendary history. Dr. Jonas Salk developed and introduced his polio vaccine here. Children's personnel developed the "Mr. Yuk" poison-prevention campaign in 1971—a program still saving lives today. More recently, Children's developed one of the world's largest pediatric transplantation centers in association with the University of Pittsburgh and Dr. Thomas Starzl.

Part of Oakland's Medical Complex, Children's is the only freestanding hospital in the region dedicated solely to the care of infants, children, and young adults. This facility and its approximately 600 physicians pursue a three-part mission that encompasses patient care, biomedical research, and education. Children's offers services in cardiology, cardiothoracic surgery, diabetes, hematology/oncology, neurosurgery, organ and tissue transplantation, orthopedics, otolaryngology, and pediatric surgery. The hospital maintains centers for pediatric trauma and pediatric emergency care, treating more than 150 children each day in these units.

With its $35.7 million annual research budget, Children's focuses on such conditions as juvenile diabetes and the causes and treatment of otitis media (inner ear disease) in infants and children. Special services include a child abuse investigation unit, summer campaign programs that focus on quality of life after transplantation and heart disease, and community education classes in positive parenting and injury prevention.

The hospital functions as a regional referral center, caring for infants, children, and adolescents who pay more than 500,000 visits to this hospital and its neighborhood locations each year. It also operates three regional facilities: Children's South in Bethel Park, Children's North in Sewickley, and Children's East in Monroeville. The regional facilities offer a wide variety of outpatient services as well as same-day surgical services. For directions to any of the Children's current facilities, call the Direction Hot Line, (412) 692-8088.

Citizens General Hospital
651 Fourth Avenue, New Kensington
(724) 337-5000

Since 1912, Citizens General has been serving residents of the Allegheny and Kiski Valleys. Its medical staff numbers nearly 200 physicians operating in more than 35 specialties. Among the hospital's most important services are a Radiology Department that assists in the early detection of breast cancer, a Heart Station with advanced diagnostic capabilities, and a Rehabilitation Services Department that offers a far-reaching sports medicine program. In addition, Citizens offers a senior behavioral health center geared specifically toward seniors experiencing mental illness.

The Citizens General Health Place program offers screenings and seminars, including sessions on diabetes management, relaxation and massage techniques, urinary incontinence, hypertension, breast cancer awareness, and insurance counseling. The hospital provides rehabilitation at a community-based site in Plum.

Latrobe Hospital
121 West Second Avenue, Latrobe
(724) 537-1000
www.lah.com

Located in the eastern section of Westmoreland County, Latrobe Hospital offers a complete array of acute, surgical, and specialized services. A 196-bed hospital, Latrobe features gynecological services for women of all ages and obstetrical care including 10 labor-

New Home for Children's Hospital

As a result of outgrowing its location in Oakland, Children's Hospital is currently constructing a new $620 million hospital campus to serve its patients and families.

In the spring of 2009, Children's Hospital will open the 10-acre campus in Pittsburgh's Lawrenceville neighborhood.

The new hospital, housed in 1.5 million square feet of usable space, was designed with patients, families and staff in mind. Its design is grounded in five principles: family-centered care, technological sophistication, environmental sustainability, quiet building, and patient safety and quality.

The campus buildings will include 296 licensed beds of which 41 will be located in the Emergency Room and Trauma Center. Thirteen operating suites, a critical care unit, and a 20,000-square-foot family resource and activity center will also reside in the nine-floor hospital building.

The John G. Rangos Sr. Research Center, a 10-story, 300,000-square-foot research facility will be dedicated to medical research activities. A child care center, fitness center, and family housing will be included in the Plaza Building. Two additional buildings, the 130,000-square-foot Faculty Pavilion and the 75,000-square-foot Administrative Office Building are also being constructed.

delivery-recovery-postpartum (LDRP) suites and traditional delivery rooms for more complicated and Cesarean section births, and a Special Care Nursery, as well as mammography and bone density services, breast clinic and childbirth/outreach education. Extensive cardiac diagnostic testing and treatment abound with a cardiac rehabilitation program, available for post-surgery patients. The hospital also features a 20-bed transitional living unit; sleep disorders services; diabetes care and endocrine clinic; outpatient surgery and short procedure suites; emergency services; critical care units, wellness programs and more. Home to Excela Health's child and adolescent inpatient unit, Latrobe Hospital also offers adult, child and adolescent outpatient services as part of a comprehensive behavioral health services program. A Family Medicine Residency Program at Latrobe Hospital allows medical residents hands-on experience flexible enough to prepare them for rural, suburban, or urban medical practice. The program, begun in 1974, is affiliated with the Jefferson Medical College of Thomas Jefferson University.

LifeCare Hospitals of Pittsburgh
225 Penn Street, Wilkinsburg
(412) 247-2363
www.lifecare-hospitals.com/hospitals_pittsburgh.htm
This 196-bed facility, part of the Allegheny University Hospitals system, is located just across the city of Pittsburgh border and specializes in extended acute care, a specialized treatment program targeted to acutely ill patients who face a prolonged hospital stay due to complex medical problems. The emphasis is on intensive nursing attention and frequent physician care as part of a multidisciplinary approach. The hospital estimates that it can provide such care for 60 to 75 percent of the cost of a traditional hospital stay.

The program includes a high-observation unit as well as a therapeutic apartment used by patients prior to discharge to help them adjust to life at home.

Magee-Womens Hospital of UPMC
300 Halket Street
(412) 641-1000, (866) 696-2433
www.magee.edu
Since the opening of Magee-Womens Hospital in 1911, women have been at the center of the institution's mission: providing excellence and innovation in clinical care, education, research, and the health of women and infants. The hospital's impact on the region has been, and continues to be, far reaching. Rare is the Pittsburgh-area family that hasn't selected Magee for a birth or some aspect of neonatal care.

The hospital calls its philosophy "Womancare," and a review of Magee's services leaves no doubt that the name is appropriate. Highlights of Magee's services include the latest in infertility treatment; a maternal-fetal medicine program for high-risk mothers and infants; a comprehensive array of educational programs to prepare parents and siblings; and an obstetrics program that boasts the region's newest labor, delivery, and recovery suites, plus private postpartum rooms in a totally family-centered environment.

Magee is a nationally designated Center of Excellence in Women's Health and one of the top recipients for National Institutes of Health funding for women's and infants' health research. In addition, Magee believes in empowering women with education and resources to give them the confidence they need to take an active role in their health-care decisions. Testifying to Magee's excellence in this area, the Magee/University of Pittsburgh Cancer Institute Breast Program was rated as one of the top 10 breast programs in the country by *SELF* magazine and encompasses the most up-to-date, research-driven care for the prevention and treatment of breast cancer. Magee also makes itself a part of the Greater Pittsburgh Community. Five Womancare Centers located throughout Allegheny County act as sites for Magee's educational programs and offer mammography, ultrasound, bone density screenings,

i Among its many medical firsts, Pittsburgh was the site of the first hospital-based helicopter in the Northeast—Life Flight.

specialty physician services, and ob/gyn practices. In addition, Magee has seven Neighborhood Health Centers that provide prenatal and primary care to patients.

UPMC Braddock
400 Holland Avenue, Braddock
(412) 636-5000
http://braddock.upmc.com
This 217-bed hospital serves the Turtle Creek and Mon Valleys with 225 respected community-based physicians. Medical specialties include chemical dependency/detoxification, emergency medicine, orthopedics, coronary and medical/surgical intensive care, and same-day surgery. The hospital features three units dedicated to the needs of patients coping with mental illness, as well as a 30-bed progressive care center that functions as a long-term care facility.

UPMC Health System
200 Lothrop Street
(412) 647-8762, (800) 533-8762
www.upmc.com
UPMC Health System, affiliated with the University of Pittsburgh Schools of the Health Sciences, strives to be an integrated system for health care in Western Pennsylvania, offering a full range of health-care services. At its Oakland campus, UPMC operates UPMC Presbyterian, UPMC Montefiore, Eye and Ear Hospital, Western Psychiatric Institute and Clinic, and the University of Pittsburgh Cancer Institute. With a team of about 48,000 employee and 4,000 licensed beds in 20 hospitals, UPMC serves the health needs of more than 4 million people each year.

UPMC operates its hospitals in its coverage area of 29 western Pennsylvania counties. The UPMC Reham Network includes more than 50 hospitals and outpatient facilities for physical, occupational, speech, and specialty therapies.

At the hospitals on UPMC's Oakland campus, medical specialties include cardiology, human genetics, sports medicine and orthopedics, geriatrics, occupational and environmental medicine, AIDS treatment and immunology, trauma and emergency medicine, ophthalmology and otolaryngology, neurosurgery, cardiothoracic surgery, psychiatry (including inpatient care), and critical care medicine. The complex also includes the renowned Thomas E. Starzl Transplantation Institute, named for Pittsburgh's pioneering organ transplant surgeon.

UPMC's Physician Division manages practices encompassing more than 3,000 primary care physicians and physician specialists, while its Insurance Division offers managed care products. Through this Diversified Service Division, UPMC provides rehabilitation and in-home services, a mail-order pharmacy, durable medical services, technology transfer ventures, international health care initiatives, and retirement living options.

UPMC Shadyside
5230 Centre Avenue
(412) 623-2121
http://shadyside.upmc.com

This 486-bed hospital in Pittsburgh's Shadyside neighborhood traces its roots to 1866 and merged with UPMC Health System in 1997. Its specialty areas include primary care, cardiology, cardiovascular surgery, oncology, women's health services, neuroscience, orthopedics, geriatric services, endocrinology, gastroenterology, sinus surgery, diagnostic imaging, rehabilitation, and obstetrics and gynecology services. The medical staff includes more than 600 primary care physicians and specialists. Getting back to its roots as a homeopathic hospital, Shadyside opened the Center for Integrative Medicine several years ago. For more information on the center and the modalities it offers, refer to the "Wellness" section in this chapter.

Western Pennsylvania Hospital
4800 Friendship Avenue
(412) 578-5000
www.wpahs.org

One of the flagship hospitals of the Western Penn Allegheny Health System, West Penn is a 512-bed tertiary care medical center, founded in 1848 and set in Pittsburgh's Bloomfield neighborhood. Services provided by the 900-member medical staff include sophisticated treatments for cancer, cardiovascular disease, high-risk pregnancies, and diabetes, as well as an innovative, aggressive approach to burn care. The hospital's bone marrow transplantation program is one of the top 20 in the nation, and its burn trauma center was the first in the region to successfully pass the rigorous verification procedures of the American Burn Association and the American College of Surgeons Committee on Trauma. West Penn also has a breast diagnostic imaging center, an infant apnea center, and an outpatient rehabilitation center.

The hospital was one of the first in the region to have a dedicated patient-focused care unit, and in July 1995 the hospital opened the nine-story Patient Care Tower, specially designed around the patient-focused care concept.

The Western Pennsylvania Hospital - Forbes Regional Campus
2570 Haymaker Road, Monroeville
(412) 858-2000
http://www.wpahs.org/frh/

Part of the West Penn Allegheny Health System, this 318-bed hospital serves Pittsburgh's eastern suburbs with a broad variety of specialties. These include obstetrics and gynecology; pediatrics; mental health; oncology; emergency medicine; and cardiology and diagnostic imaging, including magnetic resonance imaging and cardiac catheterization. The hospital's campus also includes the Forbes Family Health Center and the InterCommunity Cancer Center, which provides outpatient radiation therapy and chemotherapy as part of the hospital's cancer care services.

The facility's extensive obstetrics services include classes in Lamaze, prenatal care, breastfeeding, infant/child CPR, and understanding puberty and sibling relationships. At the Forbes LifeStyle Center, you'll find programs in wellness, weight loss, diabetes management, and cardiac rehabilitation.

Westmoreland Regional Hospital
532 West Pittsburgh Street, Greensburg
(724) 832-4000

A part of the Excela Health System, Westmoreland Hospital, located in central Westmoreland County, is a full-service, acute care hospital and regional referral center with 301 licensed beds (plus 25 skilled care beds). Among the hospital's specialty areas are cardiovascular services featuring a chest pain emergency center, three cardiac catheterization laboratories, open heart surgery, and a cardiac rehabilitation program. Westmoreland offers services for women planning or considering pregnancy and gynecological services. A home-like atmosphere for delivery exists in the labor-delivery-recovery suites (LDRs) with operating suites for Cesarean or high-risk births, and a Special Care Nursery. Other services include the behavioral health services, featuring an adult inpatient unit as well as outpatient services for children, adolescents, and adults; a breast health center; outpatient services, including the SurgiCenter at Westmoreland and the Short Stay Surgery unit; sleep disorders services; diabetes care and endocrine clinic; digestive disorders center; a pain and spine center; fixed-site and open MRI units; a large critical care unit with an intensivist program (offering 24-hour-a-day, in-house physician specialist coverage in the critical care areas), and emergency care.

South

Canonsburg General Hospital
100 Medical Boulevard, Canonsburg
(724) 745-6100
www.wpahs.org/cgh

If you're scheduled for surgery at this Washington County facility, you have the option of enrolling in the hospital's Custom Care Program, an initiative that prepares patients for surgery and rehabilitation through education and one-on-one relationships with staff. Nurses will visit your home to explain the surgery process and help you fill out the necessary paperwork, and you'll also get a visit from a physical therapist, who will discuss medication and rehabilitation and possibly conduct a home safety evaluation.

The 120-bed hospital, part of the West Penn Allegheny Health System, features a subacute skilled-care unit (for patients no longer in need of acute care but not quite ready to return home), an emergency department, rehabilitation and laboratory services, medical imaging, and a mammography center.

Canonsburg General offers a number of innovative community programs. Project Healthy Children, an early detection and prevention initiative, offers health fairs, babysitting training, and shadowing/mentoring programs. Lifeline provides nearly 200 chronically ill senior citizens with the ability to communicate from their homes directly with the hospital's emergency department. Through the Watchful Shepherd program, children at risk for abuse—those referred to the hospital by county authorities or court order—are equipped with push-button devices that activate alarm signals to the hospital's emergency department. Nurses answering the alarms speak directly to the children to assess the situation and can dispatch police to the home.

Jefferson Regional Medical Center
Coal Valley Road, Jefferson
(412) 469-5000
www.jeffersonhospital.com

The largest component of the Jefferson Regional Medical Center is a 392-bed facility that boasts a medical staff of more than 400 physicians in 37 specialties. Jefferson offers a wide variety of emergency, inpatient, diagnostic, rehabilitative, and therapeutic services. Among its special initiatives are an occupational medicine program, a sleep lab, drug and alcohol detoxification, speech pathology, and a sports medicine program. One of the most consumer-friendly aspects of the hospital is its spacious parking lot, which features nominal rates and security guards.

Monongahela Valley Hospital
1163 County Club Road, Monongahela
(724) 258-1000
www.monvalleyhospital.com

Mon Valley Hospital was formed in 1972 through the merger of Charleroi-Monessen Hospital and Memorial Hospital in Mononga-hela, both of which traced their roots to the turn of the 20th century. This facility has an outstanding track record of service to Mon Valley residents.

The 277-bed facility boasts a 180-member medical staff representing more than 40 spe-cialties. Among the services offered are obstetrics/gynecology, psychiatric, critical and cardiac care, rehabilitation, emergency medi-cine, occupational health, and drug and addictive disease treatment. Mon Valley pro-vides comprehensives oncology services, including a regional Cancer Treatment Center, and it features a Same Day Surgery Center. The campus also includes an education con-ference center complex.

St. Clair Hospital
1000 Bower Hill Road, Mt. Lebanon
(412) 942-4000
www.stclair.org

St. Clair Hospital is a 308-bed, general acute care community hospital that principally serves 13 communities in the South Hills. Medical services include family practice, obstetrics/gynecology, pediatrics, psychiatry, surgery, anesthesiology, emergency medi-cine, medical imaging, and laboratory func-tions. The hospital operates a fertility center and a heart center that offers patients the convenience of testing, treatment, recovery, and rehabilitation, all at the same hospital.

St. Clair reaches out to the community through a variety of educational and support programs, many at no cost. These include Feminine Focus, the Cancer Support Group, Maternity Education, and Changes and Choices for Older Adults and Their Caregivers. You can get a complete guide to the hospital's community programs through its Public Rela-tions Department (412) 962-6280.

Uniontown Hospital
500 West Berkeley Street, Uniontown
(724) 430-5000
www.uniontownhospital.com

Since opening its doors in 1903, Uniontown Hospital has been the primary health-care provider for Fayette County. In the late 1980s the hospital underwent a major expansion, adding a four-story ancillary service wing. Today this 195-bed community hospital employs more than 150 staff physicians, who practice more than 30 medical specialties. Services offered include cardiac care, a com-prehensive cancer program, diagnosis and treatment of gastrointestinal disorders, reha-bilitation, same-day surgery, a comprehensive obstetrical program, and a variety of home-care services.

UPMC South Side
2000 Mary Street
(412) 488-5550

Part of the UPMC Network since 1996, this hospital was founded in 1889 and today boasts 216 beds and a variety of medical spe-cialties. These include acute medical/surgical services; rehabilitation; physical, occupa-tional, and speech therapy; geriatric services; emergency and occupational medicine; and subacute care. The facility on Pittsburgh's South Side also offers an inpatient psychiatric unit, a cardiac catheterization laboratory, a sleep laboratory, and a peripheral vascular lab.

The Washington Hospital
155 Wilson Avenue, Washington
(724) 225-7000
www.washingtonhospital.org

The Washington Hospital and its School of Nursing have provided valuable services to

Washington and Greene County residents since 1897. The 258-bed facility, the largest employer in Washington County, offers cardiac care; obstetrics and women's services; occupational medicine; rehabilitation, home health and hospice services; emergency care; mental health treatment; sleep disorder care; and a wellness center.

In addition, you'll find a children's therapy center, a cancer care center, and a reentry program that helps patients return to everyday living. Washington Hospital operates 20 satellite facilities in the region.

West

Aliquippa Community Hospital
2500 Hospital Drive, Aliquippa
(724) 857-1212

Part of the UPMC Health System between 1996 and 2001, ACH became an independent facility in 2001. The hospital features 104 beds and numerous medical specialties including home health and hospice care, skilled nursing, emergency medicine, psychiatry, cardiac catheterization, and occupational medicine. The hospital provides extensive community health education programs and works with other community organizations in providing primary care in medically underserved areas.

Heritage Valley Beaver
1000 Dutch Ridge Road, Beaver
(724) 773-4636

Part of Heritage Valley Health System, the Beaver facility is a 358-bed facility that traces its roots to 1894. The hospital offers emergency treatment and maternity and child-care services, as well as cancer and cardiology treatment, including open-heart surgery. Other services include home care, occupational medicine, plastic and reconstructive surgery, psychiatry, rehabilitation, and rheumatology care.

Heritage Valley Sewickley
720 Blackburn Road, Sewickley
(412) 741-6600

Sewickley Valley Hospital, a component of Heritage Valley Health System, offers 191 beds and a variety of services that include cardiology, diagnostic radiology, orthopedic surgery, rehabilitation, peripheral vascular surgery, ophthalmology, oncology, psychiatry, and transitional care.

Pittsburgh's Ohio Valley General Hospital
25 Heckel Road, Kennedy Township
(412) 777-6161
www.ohiovalleyhospital.org

This 103-bed hospital was founded in 1906 as McKees Rocks General Hospital, so its record of service to the community spans more than a century. Ohio Valley's services include emergency and primary care, specialty medicine, cancer care, cardiology, cardiac rehabilitation, critical care, general and specialty surgery, respiratory therapy, rehabilitation, obstetrics and gynecology, home care, lithotripsy, and such diagnostic services as magnetic resonance imaging and SPECT imaging.

The hospital also offers a number of special services, including the Wound Care Center, for treatment of chronic, nonhealing wounds; the Cataract & Eye Surgery Center; the Sleep Evaluation Center; and a health and wellness program for those age 50 and older. Ohio Valley operates a school of nursing, which offers a 22-month diploma program with 36 credits from Carlow College, and a school of radiology, leading to a certificate and an associate degree from Robert Morris College.

To fulfill its mission of service to the community, Ohio Valley maintains a speakers' bureau and community education programs.

REHABILITATION CENTERS

While a number of area hospitals offer rehabilitation services, Southwestern Pennsylvania also boasts facilities that focus on rehabilitation. The organizations described below span the full range of services, including physical rehabilitation and rehabilitation from alcohol, drug, and chemical dependency.

Eagle Physical Therapy
201 Smith Drive, Suite B, Cranberry
(724) 772-4700

Eagle provides a full range of outpatient physical rehabilitation services at almost a dozen locations north and west of Pittsburgh, including Allison Park, Moon, Robinson, Murrysville, Westview, Bridgeville, and Wexford in Allegheny County; Butler, Mars, and Zelienople in Butler County; Baden in Beaver County; and Uniontown in Fayette County. Treatment covers such conditions as athletic joint and spinal injuries, hand therapy, arthritis, pediatric rehabilitation, osteoporosis, TMJ, headaches, foot and ankle sprains, women's health, and neurological disorders. Eagle also offers occupational and speech-language therapy.

You'll need a doctor's prescription before utilizing any of the services of this for-profit company. Insurance plans typically cover—in full or in part—many of Eagle's services.

Gateway Rehabilitation Center
100 Moffett Run Road, Aliquippa
(724) 378-4461, (800) 472-1177
www.gatewayrehab.org

A nonprofit agency, Gateway offers both inpatient and outpatient chemical dependency treatment programs—for adults and adolescents—at multiple locations in Southwestern Pennsylvania. Gateway provides specialized programs for women, youths, and young adults; residents of public-housing communities; and referrals from the Pennsylvania Department of Corrections. Gateway has opened a dual disorders treatment program at its Aliquippa facility for adults with concurrent chemical dependency and mental health problems.

Gateway offers comprehensive community and school-based prevention services through its VISION Prevention Program. The center also provides employee assistance program services, training, and professional conferences.

A special touch: When clients have achieved six months' sobriety, they're invited to participate as Gateway volunteers.

The Watson Institute
301 Camp Meeting Road, Sewickley
(412) 741-1800, (866) 893-4751
www.thewatsoninstitute.org

The Watson Institute provides comprehensive special education programs for children ages 3 to 12 who have developmental disabilities, including autism (the Watson Institute's specialty), cerebral palsy, muscular dystrophy, neurological impairments, and pervasive developmental disorders.

HEALTH MAINTENANCE ORGANIZATIONS

HMOs have become a vital aspect of daily life. Many Southwestern Pennsylvanians—whether self-employed or employed by firms large or small—now have the option to receive medical insurance from HMOs. They've become so important, if not downright omnipresent, that a local nonprofit organization, the Pittsburgh Business Group on Health, has begun publishing regular statistical reports on certain aspects of HMOs. Those reports are described in the "Resources & Referrals" section below. In the following section, we'll introduce you to the primary players. The category "commercial enrollees" includes enrollees not receiving Medicare or Medicaid assistance.

Aetna US HealthCare
5313 Campbell's Run Road, Robinson
(412) 788-0500, (800) 233-3105

A total of 52 hospitals, 1,500 primary care physicians, and 2,600 physician specialists in the region participate in Aetna US HealthCare plans. The plan boasts 120,000 commercial enrollees and 30,000 Medicare enrollees in the Western Pennsylvania region.

Keystone Health Plan West
120 Fifth Avenue
(412) 544-7000

Keystone Health Plan West is operated by Highmark Blue Cross Blue Shield, the region's largest health insurer. The plan operates in 29 counties and has 2.5 million members in Western Pennsylvania alone.

HealthAmerica Pennsylvania
11 Stanwix Street, Suite 2300
(412) 553-7300, (800) 735-4404
www.healthamerica.cvty.com
HealthAmerica and HealthAssurance, head-quartered in Pittsburgh and Harrisburg, Pennsylvania, provide managed health care products and services including HMO, POS, PPO, and Medicare + Choice to 6,300 employers and more than 500,000 members in Pennsylvania and Ohio. HealthAmerica earned Excellent Accreditation by the National Committee for Quality Assurance (NCQA).

Med Plus Three Rivers Health Plans
300 Oxford Drive, Monroeville
(800) 400-4003
Nearly 100 hospitals and close to 5,000 doctors participate in the company's programs, which serve Medicaid and CHIP program recipients only. (CHIP is a health plan for uninsured children and youth ages 18 and younger.)

UPMC Health Plan
112 Washington Place
(800) 644-1046
Owned by UPMC Health System, UPMC Health Plan serves nearly 350,000 members. In our principal coverage area, the plan features dozens of participating hospitals and over 6,000 participating doctors. One notable feature of UPMC Health Plan is that if your doctor orders something, you've got it. There are no administrators policing doctor's decisions in this plan.

UPMC For You
One Chatham Center
112 Washington Place
(800) 286-4242
This program, which operates in 10 counties, serves many of Pennsylvania's Medicaid recipients.

RESOURCES & REFERRALS

Western Pennsylvania presents a rich variety of health-care opportunities—so rich, in fact, that determining the best opportunity for you and your family can be challenging. A number of organizations are dedicated to helping you navigate the health-care system. Consider these organizations valuable resources for referrals and pertinent information.

Allegheny County Medical Society
713 Ridge Avenue
(412) 321-5030
www.acms.org
When you're looking for a physician, the Allegheny County Medical Society can provide you with information that will help in your selection. The society will not make specific recommendations, of course, but it will provide information on office location; hospital privileges; specialties and subspecialties; and board certification and education, including undergraduate, medical school, and residency credentials.

There's no charge for the information, but the service has limitations. You can request information for up to three physicians per call. The society does not provide information on specific procedures performed or disciplinary actions. Finally, while the society includes more than 3,000 member physicians, it has no information to offer you about nonmember physicians.

Consumer Health Coalition
650 Smithfield Street, Suite 2130
(412) 456-1877
www.consumerhealthcoalition.org
The coalition focuses on educating the public about children's health and managed care issues—and on important policy changes in these areas. The group holds information meetings, distributes a free quarterly newsletter, and works with policy makers to convey public input. When you call them, they'll be happy to provide information and referrals.

Contact HelpLine
P.O. Box 111294, Pittsburgh, PA 15238
(412) 578-2450, (412) 255-1155

Imagine a friend you could call around the clock, seven days a week, for advice on any medical or emotional problem that was troubling you. You don't have to imagine it, because you have just that friend in HelpLine. Operating with Contact Pittsburgh, HelpLine is an information and referral center staffed all day, every day, by phone counselors who will listen as you describe your situation, then refer you to community resources.

HelpLine is affiliated with a number of self-help and support networks. While their service area generally is Allegheny County, they won't let you down if you call them from another county. If they can't offer immediate assistance, they'll refer you to a sister information and referral center that operates with a nationwide scope.

HelpLine also publishes *Where To Turn,* a directory of health and human services in Allegheny County, a guide that first appeared in 1908. While HelpLine's phone counseling and referrals are free of charge, there is a cost for the directory. HelpLine is a partnership of Contact Pittsburgh and United Way of Allegheny County.

Pittsburgh Business Group on Health
507 Virginia Avenue, Ambridge
(724) 251-0230
www.pbghpa.com

The Pittsburgh Business Group on Health (PBGH) is a nonprofit organization promoting the delivery of quality, cost-effective, value-based health care in Southwestern Pennsylvania. Members include large and mid-size employers who combined provide health-care benefits to more than 400,000 employees, retirees, and dependents in the region.

While many PBGH services are targeted to its members, the organization performs several important functions of considerable interest and value to consumers. Perhaps the most significant of these is an annual report called the *Western Pennsylvania HMO Performance*

Scorecard that provides information about local HMOs in many key categories. For example, the Scorecard will tell you the percentage of participants in each HMO who benefited from such services as mammography screening, pap smears, prenatal care, immunizations, retinal screening, and a number of other procedures. This information can help you determine which HMO might work best for you. There is a charge for the Scorecard. You can get yours by contacting PBGH at the address or phone number above.

Special Kids Network
5320 North Pioneer Road, Gibsonia
(800) 986-4550

If you have a child with a chronic or disabling health condition, Special Kids Network can help you find the services you need. A service of the Pennsylvania Department of Health, it's a statewide network with six regional offices throughout the Commonwealth. Trained telephone counselors will provide referrals from a statewide database grouped into six broad categories: education/training, health-care products/services, recreation/leisure, social service/counseling, support/advocacy, and therapy. The database includes more than 5,300 agencies.

SPECIAL SERVICES

With its active and multifaceted health-care field, Southwestern Pennsylvania is blessed with a broad variety of special services providers. For example, you'll find support groups for most ailments and many hospital-based community outreach programs. While it would be impossible to profile all of the region's special services providers, described below are some that stand out because of the broad applicability of their services.

The Alliance for Infants & Toddlers
Hough Building, 2801 Custer Avenue
(412) 885-6000

Do you have questions about the way your child plays, learns, moves, or talks? The

Alliance for Infants & Toddlers coordinates early intervention services for the children from birth to their third birthday. The various early intervention supports and services are designed to build and enhance the natural learning that occurs in a child's life. Services include developmental screening and assessment, family support, and resources coordination. All services are provided in the home, day care, or other community setting identified by the family. Services are provided at no cost to the family.

ARC of Greater Pittsburgh
711 Bingham Street
(412) 995-5000

The mission of ARC of Greater Pittsburgh is to promote opportunities for, and protect the rights of, people with retardation and developmental disabilities. In ARC's Children's Division, 600 infants and toddlers each year receive assessment and therapy through early intervention. The agency's Senior Project includes three homes specially designed for older adults.

Other programs include Parent to Parent, which links families whose children may have similar circumstances or needs; integrated camping and recreational opportunities for children and adults; ESPRIT, which offers families raising at-risk children instruction in housekeeping skills; medical appointment scheduling; toy selection; and Time-Out, which provides respite care for families. ARC's Parc-Way Supported Employment program employs 238 workers at four facilities and has placed more than 100 adults with retardation on the payrolls of local businesses.

Burger King Cancer Caring Center
4117 Liberty Avenue
(412) 622-1212
www.cancercaring.org

The center is a nonprofit organization dedicated to helping people diagnosed with cancer—as well as their families and friends—cope with the emotional impact of the disease. This is not a medical treatment facility; its services help those undergoing treatment cope with the emotional impact of cancer.

Services—all free of charge—include a telephone helpline; professional guidance from social workers; and support groups targeted to children, young adults, women with breast cancer, families of those with cancer, and survivors of those claimed by the disease. The center provides a newsletter, a resource library, and community resource referrals, as well as workshops in nutrition, exercise, music therapy, and journaling. The center is funded by Southwestern Pennsylvania Burger King franchisees and their corporate partners, Heinz USA and Coca-Cola Foundation.

Child's Way
5324 Penn Avenue
(412) 365-6065

A joint program of the Children's Home of Pittsburgh and the Rehabilitation Institute, Child's Way is an outpatient day facility that supports the prescribed care needs of medically complex children. When children are here, they enjoy socialization and interaction with other youngsters while receiving care from pediatric nurses, therapists, development specialists, and caregivers. In addition, Child's Way pioneered the first pediatric extended-care center in Pennsylvania.

The two sponsoring organizations founded Child's Way after watching families struggle to meet the needs of medically fragile children. In such situations, one parent often is forced to sacrifice employment to care for their child, aggravating the financial strain. One of the goals of Child's Way is to enable parents to return to work or school, knowing that their children are well cared for.

Donated Dental Services
907 West Street
(412) 243-4866

DDS provides complimentary dental service to people who are disabled, elderly, or what the program calls "medically compromised." That includes those who have a permanent disability and can neither afford dental care nor receive it through other programs. Services also may be provided for those who are Medicaid eligible but with dental needs not covered by any current provider. The condition must be severe enough to prohibit or significantly limit gainful employment. Due to the overwhelming need, no one may receive program services more than once.

DDS is a program of the Foundation of Dentistry for the Handicapped, with funding from the Mellon Foundation and support from the Pennsylvania Dental Association and Eastern Area Adult Services. More than 350 Western Pennsylvania dentists, as well as many specialists and laboratories, contribute their services to DDS.

**Family House and the Inn
at Montefiore Hospital
242 McKee Place
(412) 578-5811**

**514 North Neville Street
(412) 578-3640**

**5245 Centre Avenue
(412) 802-8200, (412) 647-8777**
While Pittsburgh was growing as a medical center—and particularly prominent for its treatment of children—it became apparent that something was lacking in services offered. Families who journeyed to town for medical care for their relations often could not locate affordable lodgings that also were convenient to Oakland's medical complex. Family House was one of several local organizations that stepped into that breach.

Family House maintains the three facilities listed here for minor and adult patients and their families who travel to Pittsburgh for evaluation or treatment of serious illnesses. Patients and their families may stay at the inn or at either Family House location—they're both within walking distance of Oakland's medical center, but UPMC also provides courtesy shuttle service.

The facilities feature both single and double rooms as well as suites for four to six peo-

ple. All rooms have private telephone lines. You'll find communal kitchens, private bathrooms, television lounges, and laundry facilities. Guests at Family House residences are responsible for fees, but these are well below the market rate for commercial lodgings.

**Forbes Hospice
115 South Neville Street
(412) 325-7200**
Forbes Hospice opened in 1979 as the first of its kind in the state, offering both inpatient and home-care services. The hospice provides for the physical, emotional, and spiritual needs of patients with terminal illnesses and their families. Through its extensive homecare program, and bereavement counseling services, the hospice supports death with dignity, removing the stigma and isolation that often accompanies a terminal illness. Part of the West Penn Allegheny Health System, Forbes Hospice has been a model for both its innovative care protocols and for reimbursement reform.

**Jewish Association on Aging
200 JHF Drive
(412) 420-4000
www.jaapgh.org/**
Among the many valuable services provided by the association is the Sivitz Jewish hospice, which is staffed by professionals and volunteers who are specially trained to understand Jewish values and traditions. Other services include adult day services; kosher meals for delivery to homebound adults; and personal care, assisted-living, and nursing/rehabilitation centers.

**John J. Kane Regional Centers
955 Rivermont Drive
(412) 422-6800**

**100 Ninth Street, McKeesport
(412) 675-8600**

**110 McIntyre Road, Ross Township
(412) 369-2000**

**300 Kane Boulevard, Scott Township
(412) 429-3000**

The Kane Regional Centers are skilled-nursing facilities offering 360 beds per facility. While the region boasts other providers of skilled nursing services, the Kanes have a distinguished and unusual history. Formerly operated by Allegheny County as a broad health-care provider for the indigent elderly, the Kanes were turned over to a private operator in the 1990s and have broadened their mission. They offer a variety of rehabilitation services including physical, occupational, and speech therapy, as well as dietary services for those with special needs. Physicians and other medical specialists are brought to the centers to care for patients' needs.

The Kane environment offers large activity rooms, intimate sitting areas, outdoor barbecue courts, acres of landscaped grounds, nonsectarian chapels, and on-site barber-beauty shops. Accepted methods of payment include medical assistance, medical assistance pending, third-party insurance, private payment, and contracts with HMOs on a case-by-case basis. Evening and weekend admissions are common to help families manage their busy schedules.

Parental Stress Center
5877 Commerce Street
(412) 361-4800

Parental Stress Center provides solution-focused family education, counseling, and support in Southwestern Pennsylvania and beyond. Locally, intensive in-home service is combined with neighborhood-based parenting education and support to provide the necessary assistance to families. The agency operates seven days a week.

Specific populations are served, including families, foster and adoptive families, grandparents and other caregivers, noncustodial parents (especially fathers), and teens. Special programs include Family Unification Services, Community Visitation Network, Critical Differences (support, information, referral), Father's Resource Center, Parenting Education, Training and Support, and Grandparents as Parents.

No family is denied service due to difficulty with payment. Private donations cover these costs. Also, anyone may make a referral, and self-referral is acceptable as well.

If you're interested in furthering the work of this nonprofit agency, they'll welcome you as a volunteer.

The Pittsburgh Poison Center at Children's Hospital of Pittsburgh
3705 Fifth Avenue
(412) 390-3300, 24-hour emergency line: (800) 222-1222

If you have kids, chances are you're pretty familiar with Mr. Yuk, that nasty-looking green-faced guy whose face you've slapped on dozens of potentially dangerous household products. Mr. Yuk—and the accompanying Poison Prevention Program—were developed here in 1971 and now constitute the largest poison-prevention program in the nation, spanning 22 states and the United Kingdom.

Beyond its prevention program, the center is staffed by registered nurses—available around the clock—who also are clinical toxicologists and certified specialists in poison information. When you need advice about a substance or treatment, call the hotline at (412) 681-6669. They'll tap a database that provides instant access to treatment protocols on thousands of chemicals, medicines, plants, and everyday household products. The center is funded by government monies and private contributions.

Pittsburgh Specialty Hospital
215 South Negley Avenue
(412) 661-0814

Located in Pittsburgh's East End, Pittsburgh Specialty Hospital (formerly the Podiatry Hospital) has expanded its services to now include podiatry, pain management, and plastic and reconstructive surgery. For the past 26 years, Pittsburgh Specialty Hospital has provided comprehensive foot and ankle care. Of its services, 90 percent are performed on an outpatient basis in a well-staffed, comfortable environment. Within the hospital, the outpatient department provides quality non-surgical evaluation and treatment of ankle and foot problems.

The Pain Management program offers a multidisciplinary approach to the evaluation and treatment of chronic neck and back pain, fibromyalgia, reflex sympathetic dystrophy, and migraines. Patients are evaluated by a board certified anesthesiologist, chiropractor, and physical therapist working as a team to provide the maximum pain relief and return to a normal lifestyle.

To maximize your comfort, the hospital invites you to spend the night before and after any scheduled surgery as its guest, at no charge to you.

Ronald McDonald House Charities of Pittsburgh
500 Shady Avenue
(412) 362-3400
www.rmhcpgh.org/

Ronald McDonald House Charities of Pittsburgh meets the lodging needs of people traveling to Pittsburgh for medical treatment of family members. This organization, however, specializes in the needs of parents, and it achieves this goal through three important services.

First the organization developed and maintains the Ronald McDonald House of Pittsburgh, a short-term facility for the families of children being treated in the city. The facility offers each resident family a room of their own, a kitchen, laundry facilities, and toys for their children. The group living arrangements help families interact and cope.

In 1994 the Ronald McDonald House expanded its services by opening a second house to provide long-term housing. Finally the organization established a grants program that awards funds to other nonprofit groups. The organization is funded by individual and corporate donations, as well as fund-raisers. Guests at the organization's house pay a small fee, but the organization pledges to help all, regardless of anyone's ability to pay.

Transitional Infant Care Hospital
5618 Kentucky Avenue
(412) 441-4884

Operated by the Children's Home of Pittsburgh, Transitional Infant (TIC) Hospital is a pioneer in providing medical and nursing care for infants who have progressed from natal intensive care units but may not be ready for home just yet. TIC patients, all of whom must be medically stable, typically are premature infants, at-risk babies with congenital anomalies, and babies under the care of hospices. Your physicians may refer you to TIC, but you're also welcome to contact the hospital yourself.

Families benefit from TIC's care by developing hands-on ability to deal with complicated treatment regimens,and by learning to recognize potential problems at their earliest stages. In addition, TIC will work with you to create a care schedule that is feasible for you to manage. The hospital develops a care team for each infant that includes a physician, a primary care nurse, a medical social worker, and an infant development specialist. TIC offers transitional ventilator services and an infant massage program; they're happy to teach parents massage techniques.

If you or your physician is considering TIC, they ask that you take a preadmission tour. You'll find softly playing music, a nursery, nesting rooms where families can care for their infants privately, a rocking chair beside each crib, cameras so that you may take pictures of your child, and handmade baby quilts in each room—a gift from TIC's volunteers when you're ready to take your baby home.

William and Mildred Orr Compassionate Care Center
250 North Highland Avenue
(412) 361-5549
www.eecm.org/orr.htm

With hospitals discharging patients more quickly than ever, elderly patients and those at risk of homelessness can be placed in a precarious position upon their discharge, sometimes lacking residences and caregivers to help them through their recuperation.

The Orr Compassionate Care Center has stepped into that breach by providing post-hospitalization respite care for the elderly, the frail, and the homeless.

The Facility is a Christian ministry that not only provides three meals a day, laundry service, case management, and pastoral care to residents, but it also helps them work toward self-sufficiency for their eventual release from the center. Physicians, social workers, and clergy typically refer prospective residents to the center. Because the facility is not a medical center, residents must provide and administer their own medication, make arrangements for any nursing care or therapy, and provide detailed information about their medical histories. Most stays at the center range from a few days to three weeks.

MEDIA

As we've indicated in other chapters, Pittsburgh is a city of divergent cultures, many different interests, and great loyalty. Thus it's no surprise that the media serving its populace is just as varied in its commitment to disseminating news, information, and entertainment.

Pittsburgh used to be a two-newspaper town, with the *Pittsburgh Post-Gazette* and the *Pittsburgh Press* both publishing from downtown offices. Following a lengthy strike in the early 1990s by nonreporting staff of both papers, the *Press* fell by the wayside, leaving the city with only the *Pittsburgh Post-Gazette*. But others saw the void and quickly filled it. So when you read the following listings you'll see that, once again, Pittsburgh is a two-paper place.

Because we're so neighborhood oriented, you'll find a plethora of weekly community newspapers. And rest assured, we're wired. Many of the newspaper, radio, and television listings offer Web sites where you can find out plenty of information online.

As of this writing, Greater Pittsburgh ranks 21st in terms of national television market size, as measured by Nielsen. Arbitron puts our radio market ranking at 23rd nationwide. Regarding radio, there are so many choices on the dial that we don't give individual write-ups to the stations but have provided a thorough list to guide your listening choices. Note that if you're a fan of National Public Radio, you can tune into WDUQ, a radio station broadcast from Duquesne University at 90.5 on the FM dial.

Also worth mentioning is that we have local affiliate television stations for all major networks, not to mention the first public educational station in the nation (WQED). You may be surprised to learn that a young Fred Rogers left a promising career at NBC in New York City to pioneer educational television in Pittsburgh at WQED.

We believe you'll enjoy perusing the list, and most likely you'll find a media outlet to bring you the news, commentary, listings, or entertainment you need to fill your disposable time. We'll start with a rundown of metro and community daily newspapers. Next we'll turn our attention to magazines and specialty publications in our region, followed by television and radio outlets. For sure, you won't be without information!

METROPOLITAN NEWSPAPERS

Pittsburgh Post-Gazette
34 Boulevard of the Allies
(412) 263-1100
www.post-gazette.com

William and John Block serve as the publishers of this daily newspaper, founded in 1786. A decade ago Pittsburgh was a two-newspaper town with the *Pittsburgh Post-Gazette* published in the morning and the *Pittsburgh Press* published every afternoon. As odd as it may sound, both papers were housed in the same building and shared some combined services and support staffs under a joint operating agreement. Editorial functions, however, were always kept on separate floors, and indeed the two papers were competitors.

In May 1992 a strike by nonreporting staff effectively halted operations for both papers. The *Pittsburgh Post-Gazette* introduced a town crier who stood on particular downtown street corners to essentially shout the news to passersby. A fax service was also popular for those who simply needed their daily fix of headlines and top stories in print.

The strike lasted eight months and culminated in the disbanding of the *Pittsburgh Press,* which was a Scripps-Howard paper. The *Pittsburgh Post-Gazette* bought the *Press,* and incorporated numerous reporters and support personnel into its staff. Today the paper is considered by many to be more liberal in its editorial views than its main rival, the *Tribune-Review.* Well-known syndicated columnists as well as a few local favorites are found within the pages of the *Pittsburgh Post-Gazette,* sometimes known as "the PG" for short.

Readers will come to look for particular sections they may deem their favorites each week, such as Health on Wednesday or Homes and Gardens on Saturday. If you want to know who was "seen" around town, read Monday's magazine section. Other *Post-Gazette* columnists include Tony Norman, Bryan O'Neill, and Sally Kalson for general commentary, and others covering television, radio, and restaurant beats. The *Post-Gazette* on Sunday features the "Parade" magazine supplement.

Pittsburgh Tribune-Review
503 Martindale Street, Third Floor
(412) 321-6460
www.pittsburghlive.com/x/pittsburghtrib
This daily paper, once known more commonly as the *Greensburg Tribune-Review,* gained great ground during the newspaper strike in 1992. With both Pittsburgh dailies out of commission, Richard Scaife, conservative owner of the paper, began publishing more Pittsburgh news that year. The new paper was known as the *Pittsburgh Tribune-Review,* and it continued after the strike ended. Thus, if you hear someone speak of "the Trib," you'll know they mean the *Tribune-Review* and some of the history associated with this paper. Scaife bought several smaller newspapers in 1997, incorporating them into his publishing umbrella. Among them were the *Valley News Dispatch* and the *Leader Times* in Kittanning.

Founded in 1889 the *Tribune-Review* is known to have a more conservative slant than

the more liberal *Post-Gazette.* Each Thursday the *Trib* publishes "the Ticket," filled with the weekend entertainment offerings. Sports writers Mike Prisuta, Scott Brown and John Harris cover the hometown teams. Ed Blank writes about entertainment, and John Orovitz keeps an eye on the business scene. Jean Horne covers high society and charitable events. Other local columns are written by Dimitry Vassilaraos, Eric Heyl, and Mike Seate, and you can find them on the paper's Web site as well.

OTHER DAILY NEWSPAPERS

Beaver County Times
400 Fair Avenue, Beaver
(412) 761-7441
www.timesonline.com
A daily paper serving all areas in Beaver County and the western suburbs of Allegheny County, the *Beaver County Times* was founded in 1946, making it a younger paper than many of its peers. Beaver Newspapers, Inc. publishes the newspaper.

Butler Eagle
114 West Diamond Street
(724) 282-8000
www.butlereagle.com
A daily newspaper founded in 1869, this newspaper serves Butler County readers, including the areas of Cranberry Township and Slippery Rock. Vernon Wise Jr. is the current publisher.

Latrobe Bulletin
1211 Ligonier Street, Latrobe
(724) 537-3351
Published Monday through Saturday, this newspaper was founded in 1902 to serve eastern Westmoreland County communities. Gary Siegel serves as publisher.

Observer-Reporter
122 South Main Street, Washington
(724) 222-2200
www.observer-reporter.com
Founded in 1808, this daily paper serves all of

Washington and Greene Counties and some parts of Pittsburgh's South Hills, including Canonsburg, Waynesburg, Peters Township, Monessen, McMurray, and parts of Greene County. Thomas Northrop is the current publisher.

The Daily News
409 Walnut Street, McKeesport
(412) 664-9161
www.dailynewsmckeesport.com
Published Monday through Saturday, this paper is also known as the *McKeesport Daily News*. It primarily covers this town as well as the surrounding communities of Clairton, Duquesne, Homestead, Munhall, West Mifflin, and White Oak. Richard Scaife serves as the publisher. The paper was founded in 1884.

Valley News Dispatch
210 Fourth Avenue, Tarentum
(724) 224-4321
www.valleynewsdispatch.com
Founded in 1891, this daily newspaper serves the areas of Armstrong and Allegheny Counties as well as parts of Butler and Westmoreland Counties. Richard Scaife, publisher of the *Tribune-Review,* purchased the paper in 1997 along with several other newspapers in outlying communities.

ALTERNATIVE WEEKLY/ MONTHLY NEWSPAPERS

City Paper
650 Smithfield Street
(412) 316-3342
www.pghcitypaper.com
Billed as a locally owned news and entertainment weekly, the *City Paper* is managed by Steel City Media and was founded by Brad Witherell. Since its start in 1991, it has covered a wide range of off-beat news from local vocals to the current buzz on the street, newly released movies, the arts scene, dining, and nightlife. Each issue features an in-depth cover story. While you can subscribe to the paper for a fee, why bother? It's given away,

free of charge, at many locations and outdoor boxes, especially at music and bookstores as well as some movie theaters.

New Pittsburgh Courier
315 East Carson Street
(412) 481-8302
www.newpittsburghcourieronline.com
Founded in 1910, this newspaper is published every Wednesday for the African-American community, with relevant issues and prominent Pittsburghers. Rod Doss serves as the current editor and publisher. The paper's editorial offices are on the city's South Side.

Pittsburgh's Out
Out Publishing Co. Inc.
801 Bingham Street, Suite 100
(412) 381-3350
www.outpub.com
One of the oldest gay publications in the country, *Out* began in 1973 as a single-page newsletter produced by Gay Alternatives Pittsburgh. As it grew, it tried various formats until 1980, when it slipped into its current garb as a monthly tabloid serving the GLBT (gay, lesbian, bisexual, transgendered) community in Allegheny and surrounding counties, eastern Ohio, and West Virginia. Its current publishers, Tony Molnar-Strejcek and Ed Molnar-Strejcek, purchased the company in November 1994 and have added color, more pages, and more advertising.

Out offers the GLBT community a wide range of information not readily available in any other single source: local and national news, health information, commentary, arts and entertainment features and reviews, a complete guide to the month's local events ("Out and About" and "Nightlife" sections), announcements and a "What's Happening" calendar of events and local resources.

A few years ago, *Out* became a national star when it began to be prominently featured on Showtime's *Queer as Folk* as an important source of news—which many consider the only realistic detail in the fictionalized Pittsburgh.

MAJOR WEEKLY NEWSPAPERS

Gateway Publications
610 Beatty Road, Monroeville
(412) 856-7400 (800) 704-9232 (Circulation)
www.gatewaynewspapers.com
Several community newspapers are published
by Gateway Publications, part of Trib Total
Media. The company is headquartered in Monroeville, but there are local offices for many of
the papers outside the eastern suburbs.

Gateway Publications include the *Times
Express, Penn Hills Progress, Woodland
Progress, Oakmont Verona Advance Leader,
Plum Boro Advance Leader, Murrysville Star,
Norwin Star, Penn-Trafford Star, Signal Item,
Bridgeville News, South Hills Record,
Coraopolis-Moon Record, Sewickley Herald,
Pine Creek Journal, North Journal, McKnight
Journal,* and *The Herald.*

Pittsburgh Business Times
2313 East Carson Street
(412) 481-6397
www.bizjounrals.com/pittsburgh/
Published weekly for the business community,
the *Pittsburgh Business Times* covers regional
issues of interest to executives and industry
leaders as well as Pittsburgh business headlines. The paper often profiles business trends
and prominent people, and it offers a diet of
popular columnists. The publisher is Alan
Robertson. Offices are on the city's South
Side. The paper is affiliated with American City
Business Journals Inc. The *Business Times,* as
it's frequently referred to, also publishes the
Employment Paper, distributed through the
mail, at libraries, and various other locations
with information for job seekers.

The Jewish Chronicle of Pittsburgh
5600 Baum Boulevard, #1
(412) 687-1000
www.pittchron.com
Published on Thursday by the Pittsburgh
Jewish Publication and Education Foundation,
this weekly paper is printed in tabloid form.
Founded in 1962, it provides local, national,
and global news of Jewish interest.

The Mount Pleasant Journal
23 South Church Street, Mount Pleasant
(724) 547-5722
www.laurelgrouponline.com
This weekly newspaper covers the Westmoreland County community of Mount Pleasant
and surrounding neighborhoods. The paper
was founded in 1873, and its current publisher is Joseph Soforic.

The Pittsburgh Catholic
135 First Avenue
(412) 471-1252
www.pittsburghcatholic.org
Founded in 1844, this paper relates news of
importance to the Catholic community.
Parishioners usually obtain a copy of the
paper at church each Sunday, so the paper is
published at the end of each week. Or, you
can subscribe for $19 a year, plus delivery.

Suburban Gazette
421 Locust Street, McKees Rocks
(412) 331-2645
Founded in 1892, this community newspaper
covers the areas of Robinson and Kennedy
Townships and nearby Ingram—all of which
make up the Montour School District. Virginia
Schramm is the current publisher of this
paper that comes out in tabloid format on
Wednesday.

MAGAZINES

Monroeville Matters
2700 Monroeville Boulevard, Monroeville
(412) 856-1000
This glossy magazine is published three times
a year by the Municipality of Monroeville. It
includes full-length and short features of local
interest, as well as the Recreation and Parks
activities guide for each season. The magazine is mailed free of charge to local residents
and businesses.

Two large communities have their own magazines that are distributed to residents. *Mt. Lebanon Magazine* is distributed in the South Hills, while *Monroeville Matters* features news of Monroeville and Pitcairn.

Pittsburgh Magazine
4802 Fifth Avenue
(412) 622-1360
www.wqed.org

Pittsburgh Magazine is a division of WQED Pittsburgh, home to the city's public television and radio stations. Those who become members of WQED during pledge drives or mail solicitations automatically receive a subscription to *Pittsburgh Magazine*. This monthly magazine features all things Pittsburgh, including dining listings and a schedule of upcoming programming on both WQED-TV and WQED-FM. Look for the magazine to name its Pittsburgher of the Year each December. Past recipients have included Fred Rogers and Mario Lemieux. Each summer the magazine publishes its annual City Guide edition. *Pittsburgh Magazine* is distributed by mail and is also available for sale on newsstands.

Pittsburgh Parent
P.O. Box 374, Bakerstown, PA 15007
(724) 443-1891
www.pittsburghparent.com

If you're a parent or soon will be one, this is the resource for you. In fact, since *Pittsburgh Parent* is distributed free of charge to more than 500 locations in Allegheny, Beaver, Butler, and Westmoreland Counties, teachers and many other professionals read it as well. Each issue features an in-depth cover story, while the rest of the editorial matter comes largely from wire services or public relations material. Look for the annual "Around & About Pittsburgh Guide," and each issue be sure to peruse the calendar of events and fun activities for families.

Whirl Magazine
1731 Grandview Avenue
(412) 431-7888
www.whirlmagazine.com

Look out Vogue, you've got a rival in Pittsburgh. Actually, *Whirl*'s focus is the social scene here, but you'll see plenty of fashion in the photos on every page and in *Whirl*'s advertisements, which, says publisher Jack Tumpson, are so eye-catching its consumers read them like the rest of the magazine. *Whirl*'s mission is to present successful Pittsburgh, and it does that very well. It's readership, by the way, has the highest per capita income population in the region. *Whirl* is available by subscription and on newsracks with other fine magazines.

TELEVISION STATIONS

FSN Pittsburgh
323 North Shore Drive, Suite 200
(412) 316-3800
www.foxsports.com

The channel you receive Fox Sports broadcasts on will vary according to the cable or satellite system you use, but for all things sports-related, you'll want to tune in here.

KDKA-TV
One Gateway Center
(412) 575-2200
www.kdka.com

Airing on Channel 2, KDKA-TV is the Pittsburgh CBS affiliate, with offices and studios in downtown Pittsburgh. With newscasts in the morning, at noon, at 5:00 and 6:00 p.m., and wrapping up the day with the 11:00 p.m. news, KDKA's coverage is comprehensive in all areas, including sports, weather, and consumer and investigative reporting.

The station plays up its "Hometown Advantage," stemming from the fact that many reporters and anchors hailed from Pittsburgh. Locally produced programs include the *Lynn Hayes-Freeland Show,* focusing on

African-American issues each Sunday morning, and Jon Delano's *Sunday Business Page.* Community initiatives have included raising funds for Pittsburgh's Children's Hospital and the KD Turkey Fund each Thanksgiving.

WTAE-TV
400 Ardmore Boulevard
(412) 242-4300
www.thepittsburghchannel.com

This television station is the local ABC affiliate, with offices and studios just off the Parkway East in Wilkinsburg. "DeNardo Weather" is short for the forecasts brought to viewers by WTAE's chief meteorologist Joe DeNardo. Two hours of local news each morning leads into *Good Morning America.* WTAE-TV also offers noon, 5:00, and 6:00 p.m. broadcasts, and a wrap-up of the day's events at 11:00 p.m. It offers a full range of quality reporting on consumer and investigative issues, as well as sports.

For many years the station has been involved with a program called Project Bundle-Up, which provides coats and warm clothing for needy families. The station hosts an auction to raise funds. In addition, WTAE-TV has been aligned with the Race for the Cure, a charity run-walk to raise awareness and funds for breast cancer research. The station has been the media partner for this event since its inception in 1993.

WPXI-TV & PCNC
11 Television Hill
(412) 237-1100
www.realpittsburgh.com/partners/wpxi/

This NBC affiliate has its offices and studios high atop a hill on the city's North Side. Known for its reports aboard Chopper 11, this station also gives you Carnegie Science weather—there is a weather station set up in the Carnegie Science Center, also on the North Side. On Channel 11 watch for health tips and the medical beat covered by Dr. Mike Rosen, a medical doctor now on the station's reporting staff.

Channel 11 also works closely with its cable channel, PCNC (the Pittsburgh Cable News Channel). WPXI-TV news is rebroadcast on PCNC throughout the day, but also look for original television talk shows on the cable channel each morning.

WQED-TV
4802 Fifth Avenue
(412) 622-1300
www.wqed.org

WQED-TV is Pittsburgh's affiliate for the Public Broadcasting System (PBS). It airs locally on Channel 13 (though this will vary on each cable system).

The best-known program produced here at WQED is undoubtedly *Mister Rogers' Neighborhood,* still being seen around the country. There's also *On Q, which* made its debut as a televised magazine show five nights each week at 7:30 p.m. beginning in January 2000. The half-hour program covers area business, politics, and current happenings with guests and special reporters appearing alongside the hosts.

WPCB-TV
One Signal Hill Drive, Wall
(412) 824-3930
www.ctvn.org

Founded by the late Rev R. Russell Bixler in the 1970s, WPCB-TV is a Christian-based broadcasting station owned by Bixler's company, Cornerstone Television. This station and Bixler's mission survived during a time period when many televangelists fell to scandals. Yet Bixler and his wife built the station into a small network with four broadcast facilities—WPCB in Wall, WKBS in Altoona, and low-powered stations in Hermitage and Brookville, as well as a 24-hour satellite channel and 163 affiliate stations.

WPGH-TV
750 Ivory Avenue
(412) 931-5300
www.wpgh53.com

WPGH-TV is a Fox affiliate that also produces 10:00 p.m. local news each evening on

Channel 53 (that number, of course, varies according to your cable system).

WPCW
1 Gateway Center
(412) 575-2200
www.wpcw.tv.com
WPCW-TV Channel 19 airs CW programming as well as syndicated shows such as *Everybody Loves Raymond* and *The People's Court*.

RADIO STATIONS

There are numerous radio stations throughout our six-county coverage area. Here we present the major stations, classified by the type of programming offered: -

News, Talk, and Sports

ESPN 1250 AM, http://sports.espn.go.com/stations/espnradio1250
KDKA 1020 AM, www.kdkaradio.com
KQV 1410 AM, www.kqv.com
WPTT 1360 AM, www.1360wptt.com

Alternative

WYEP 91.3 FM, www.wyep.org

Rock

KISS 91.6 FM, www.kissfm961.com
WBZZ 93.7 FM, www.b94fm.com
WDVE 102.5 FM, www.dve.com
WRRK 96.9 FM, www.rrk.com
WXDX 105.9 FM, www.wxdx.com

Hip-Hop and R&B

WAMO 106.7 FM/860 AM, www.wamo.com

Contemporary/Soft Rock

Q92.9 FM, http://q929fm.com
WSHH 99.7 FM, www.wshh.com

Oldies

WJPA 95.3 FM/1450 AM, www.wjpa.com
WWSW 94.5 FM/970 AM, www.3wsradio.com

Country

WDSY 107.9 FM, www.y108.com

Classical

WQED 89.3 FM, www.wqed.org/fm

Jazz

WDUQ 90.5 FM, www.wduq.org

Christian

WGBN 1150 AM
WORD 101.5 FM, www.wordfm.com
WPIT 730 AM, http://wpitam.com
WPGR 1510 AM, www.wpgram.com/
WWNL 1080 AM

Music/News/Sports/Talk

WISR 680 AM, www.wisr680.com

SENIOR SCENE

If you're looking for a town with a vital senior citizens community, with diverse programs and services for older residents, wonderful and meaningful volunteer opportunities, and government and nonprofit organizations that understand the needs of seniors, then you've come to the right place in Pittsburgh. You may not consider Pittsburgh an ideal retirement community just yet, but we'll give you plenty of reasons to change your mind.

The fact is that family and neighborhoods are so important to most local residents that many not only live and work their entire careers here, but they also choose to retire close to their roots. Statistics tell a key part of the story. For example, of the more than 1.2 million people in Allegheny County, better than 21 percent are age 60 or older, giving Allegheny the second highest percentage of seniors among America's counties.

With seniors composing such an important part of the population, both the private and public sectors are attuned to their contributions and particular needs and concerns. You'll find a wide variety of senior recreational centers, residential communities, support organizations—even opportunities to use your experience and expertise to contribute to the region's businesses. The senior scene is vigorous in Pittsburgh.

Government in Pittsburgh, at both the municipal and county levels, is active in sponsorship of programs tailored to seniors. Some government-offered services may be restricted to residents of the offering municipality or county. Even where such services are open to all, you're probably more likely to take advantage of opportunities close to your home.

Therefore, to help you best utilize Senior Scene, material has been organized in two ways. The first section is a county-by-county look at programs, services, and opportunities for seniors; in this section, the city of Pittsburgh is grouped with Allegheny County, as the two entities share administrative responsibility for many services.

Following that, the second section features unrestricted services and opportunities, as well as those where some travel might be expected.

Have fun exploring Pittsburgh's Senior Scene. You'll find it a rewarding journey.

PITTSBURGH & ALLEGHENY COUNTY

The extensive services and programs for seniors in Pittsburgh and Allegheny County are coordinated by two agencies: the Allegheny County Department of Human Services, Area Agency on Aging (ACAAA), (412) 350-5460, and the Pittsburgh Parks & Recreation, (412) 422-6405, popularly known as Senior Interests.

Nineteen other agencies, including nonprofit groups and church-related organizations, assist in the administration of programs in the city and county, with services distributed geographically to every community in the county. Want to know the location of the senior center nearest you or the most active support group in your neighborhood? The best way is to call the county's Agency on Aging for its annual directory of services. It's free of charge, and it will give you all the information you need to make those first phone calls.

Seventy-seven senior centers are located throughout Allegheny County, including some twenty-three centers within the city of Pittsburgh. The centers offer hot meals each weekday—most of them once per day—as well as recreation and socialization opportunities. And don't expect that recreation to be sedentary only. In addition to such standards as bingo, cards, and movies, the centers offer dancing, exercise, crafts, and classes in languages, music, and art appreciation. Up for something a little wilder? The South Side center in Pittsburgh offers basketball—on a regulation court—as one of its senior activities.

Transportation opportunities in Pittsburgh and Allegheny County are far reaching. Older Persons Transportation (OPT) will deliver you to medical appointments, grocery shopping, and senior centers, weekdays from 6:00 a.m. to 6:00 p.m. Service is door to door, and the cost is nominal.

Even broader is the service provided by ACCESS, a shared-ride service that will take you anywhere in the county. Call ACCESS at (412) 562-5353 to set up an account with them; about two weeks thereafter, Access will put you in touch with your local carrier, which is likely to be a local taxi service. ACCESS operates from 6:00 a.m. through midnight, seven days a week, with advance reservations required. You'll pay for your rides with tickets purchased form ACCESS, but if you're age 65 or older, you'll pay only 15 percent of the regular charge.

ARMSTRONG COUNTY

In Armstrong County, adjacent to Allegheny County about 25 miles north of Pittsburgh, the Armstrong County Agency on Aging is the principal provider of services and programs for seniors. To qualify for some services, you must be formally assessed by the agency. Give them a call, toll free, at (800) 368-1066, or (724) 548-3290, if you don't mind paying for the call. They'll help you determine which services fit your needs.

The county operates 11 seniors centers in all its major population points—Apollo, Brady's Bend, Dayton, Elderton, Ford City, Freeport, Kittanning, Leechburg, Parker, Rural Valley, and Worthington. General hours are from 8:00 a.m. to 4:00 p.m. Monday through Friday, with hot meals served at noon. Reser-

i Want to know what you're entitled to in Pennsylvania now that you've reached retirement age? Feel you've been done wrong? Check out the Pennsylvania Department of Aging's *Benefits and Rights for Older Pennsylvanians.*

vations for lunch must be made one day in advance. If you're unable to cook for yourself, the county will deliver meals to you, once your eligibility for the program has been certified.

In addition to providing opportunities to socialize, the centers offer valuable services, including blood pressure and general health checks under the supervision of registered nurses. For fun, try the craft outlets located at the Ford City and Kittanning centers. And if you'd like to visit more than one center, don't worry about transportation. The centers provide complimentary rides between all facilities for center programs and activities.

From time to time we all encounter household chores that we just can't handle. The county is ready to help with those chores, as well as light housekeeping, errands, and laundry. If you have legal questions, the county also will provide legal counseling and representation in such areas as wills and power of attorney.

BEAVER COUNTY

The Beaver County Office on Aging, (724) 728-7707, provides services and programs for senior citizens in Beaver County, a picturesque 20-minute drive from Pittsburgh along the Ohio River through attractive riverfront communities. The office operates five senior centers, in Aliquippa, Baden, Beaver Falls, Midland, and Monaca. The centers serve hot lunches and welcome spouses to join in. To participate, make your meal reservations one week in advance. Once approved by a caseworker, you also may order home-delivered meals Monday through Friday and take advantage of county-provided assistance with household chores.

Independently Monroeville

The Monroeville Senior Citizens' Center, 6000 Gateway Campus Boulevard, Monroeville, (412) 856-7825, is a particularly active hub for adults 50+. Regular activities at the center include aerobics, yoga, shuffleboard, computer classes, numerous types of card games, woodcarving, Brazilian embroidery, quilting, crocheting, creative scrapbooking, and bingo. Anyone 50 or older, from any geographical area, may participate in the center's activities, attend the informative lecture series held by ThirdAge Forum, or attend the two special meals held monthly. In addition, Monroeville and Pitcairn residents may join one of the four membership clubs, which regularly feature meetings, programs of interest, luncheons, dinners, and trips and tours. The center is especially notable in that it's not part of Allegheny County's network of senior centers. Funding for the Monroeville Senior Citizen's Center, built in 1980 for its present purpose, is generated by participants' fundraising efforts, state grants, and the Municipality of Monroeville. Two annual fundraisers of special interest are the center's flea market and the large golf tournament, both of which, of course, may be attended by people of any age.

If you're age 65 or older, transportation is a snap in Beaver County, as you may ride Beaver County Transit Authority buses free from 9:00 a.m. to 3:30 p.m. If you're more than a quarter mile from public transportation, you may arrange door-to-door, shared-ride transportation with Demand and Response Transit (DART) buses.

The county also sponsors varied activities for seniors; many of these are important, but others are just plain fun. To make sure seniors are aware of all appropriate events, the county produces an insert in the monthly Beaver County Senior News newsletter called *Kenn-Age News* featuring articles of interest to seniors, as well as a weekly radio show, *Spotlight on Senior Citizens,* which airs Sunday on WBVP-AM, 1230 on the dial.

For fun, join other seniors at the Beaver Valley Mall the second Wednesday of every month. Beginning at 10:00 a.m., "Day at the Mall" features refreshments, prizes, entertainment, blood pressure screening, and store discounts.

And if gardening is your thing, you'll love the county's "Mini Gardens" program, operated in conjunction with the Pennsylvania State University, which reserves gardening lots for senior citizens each spring.

BUTLER COUNTY

If you're a senior citizen in Butler County, about 25 miles north of Pittsburgh, you'll have every opportunity to tune in to county happenings. The Butler County Area Agency on Aging, (724) 282-3008, provides a number of useful communications vehicles to ensure that you're aware of local happenings.

The *Senior Voice* radio show airs every Sunday at 7:10 a.m. on WISR-AM, 680 on the dial, while subscribers of Armstrong Cable can catch *Seniors Today* on Channel 10 for a look at events and timely features.

The agency also produces and distributes a monthly newsletter called *Senior Express.*

The agency maintains 10 senior centers—in Bruin, the city of Butler, Chicora, Cranberry, Evans City, Mars, Mt. Chestnut, Saxonburg, Slippery Rock, and Zelienople—which serve hot meals daily. Don't forget to make your meal reservations at least one day in advance.

The agency also offers home delivery of meals to those who qualify, as well as a referral service for caretaking and home chores. Perhaps the most comprehensive of agency services is transportation, provided by the Butler Area & Rural Transit (724) 282-6060. Known locally as B.A.R.T., the shared-ride service will transport those age 60 and older from their homes to senior centers, medical appointments, shopping malls, and grocery stores. You can ride anywhere in the county at no charge.

WASHINGTON COUNTY

The hub for senior services and programs in Washington County, which lies about 20 miles southwest of Pittsburgh, is the Southwestern Pennsylvania Area Agency on Aging, which serves Washington, Greene, and Fayette Counties, (724) 489-8080 or (888) 300-2704. The agency has more than three decades' experience in helping seniors and serves more than 5,000 residents each month.

You can choose from nine Senior Community Centers that feature recreation, socialization, and educational programs. Each center provides a free hot lunch each weekday and will deliver meals Monday through Friday for those unable to cook for themselves. The centers are located in Avella, Bentleyville, Burgettstown, Canonsburg, Claysville, McDonald, and Vestaburg, with two centers in the city of Washington.

Seniors in need of home support services, including laundry, shopping, and cleaning, will find agency workers ready and willing to help.

WESTMORELAND COUNTY

The Westmoreland County Area Agency on Aging, (724) 830-4444 or (800) 442-8000 , likes to describe life as an orienteering event, in which contestants navigate unfamiliar terrain using a map and a compass. The agency thinks of itself as the compass, helping senior citizens reach their destination.

The nerve center for the agency's services to senior citizens is the network of senior centers it operates. A total of 13 such centers dot this county to the east of Pittsburgh. They're located in Avonmore, East Vandergrift, Greensburg, Herminie, Jeannette, Latrobe, Laughlintown, Laurel Valley, Monnessen, New Alexandria, New Kensington, New Florence, and West Newton.

As do senior centers throughout the Pittsburgh area, Westmoreland's centers offer hot meals as well as the opportunity for home delivery of those meals. Centers in Westmoreland also emphasize health and wellness through a variety of neat and unusual classes, exercise, tai chi, and aqua aerobics among them.

For transportation to key activities, you'll find two types of subsidized services available. If you're age 60 or older, you're eligible to use Priority Transportation, funded through the county, for rides to medical appointments, senior centers, senior center–based shopping, adult day care, and the county's vision center only. You'll receive a 95 percent discount on the cost of your taxi or van trip. If you're age 60 or older, you'll receive the same discount and be able to travel to many more destinations in your area, using a shared-ride service funded through the state. You may also ride Westmoreland county buses for free. Now you're all set for life's orienteering!

SERVICES & OPPORTUNITIES
Publications

With senior citizens such an important force in Pittsburgh, it could be difficult to keep up with all the services, programs, and opportunities available. Fortunately the private and public sectors have teamed to produce a number of publications to help you identify just the right opportunities for you.

Particularly useful is *Pittsburgh Senior News*, (412) 367-2522, a tabloid that can keep you current with activities because of its monthly publication schedule. The newspaper blends information about activities and services with cultural and entertainment news, as well as feature stories by and about senior citizens. Pay close attention to the advertisements, which often bring news of discounts and bargains for seniors.

The newspaper also offers up-to-date information about current activity schedules for local chapters of the American Association of Retired Persons (AARP)—a valuable tool, as

Because You Drive Safely...

Here's a great way to save money on your auto insurance. If you're age 55 or older, have a Pennsylvania driver's license, and take a driver refresher course, your insurance company must offer you a discount of 5 percent or more for three years. Three organizations in the state offer refresher courses:

AARP
(717) 238-2277, (888) 227-7669

AAA Western Pennsylvania–West Virginia
(412) 365-7211

National Safety Council
(412) 856-5400

Pittsburgh offers more than 100 AARP chapters. You can pick it up for free at scores of distribution points, many of them located at newspaper honor boxes.

The *Resource Guide for Older Adults and Their Families* takes a somewhat different, but equally effective, approach. This publication comes out every two years and focuses on well-detailed listings of services and programs. The guide cannot deal with current events, of course, but it provides a broad look at opportunities for seniors that are unlikely to change.

Categories covered include community outreach and referral services; crisis, mental health, and caregiver services; Medicare, Medicaid, and medical insurance; medical and health-care services; and housing options. The outreach section, in particular, is as good as any you're likely to find, offering both familiar and more obscure service providers.

The guide is published under the auspices of Older Adult Service and Information System (OASIS), a public-private partnership headquartered in Macy's department store in downtown Pittsburgh. You can order your free copy from OASIS, (412) 232-9583 or (800) 921-9443.

A second helpful publication is the *Senior Citizens Guide to Pittsburgh,* which is produced by Spindle Publications, headquartered in suburban Pittsburgh. As an annual, this guide, too, is limited in the current information it can convey. Instead the publication focuses on interesting travel features and "how-to" pieces, as well as service directories.

Two of the best directories offered are the listing of senior citizens centers and the guide to volunteer organizations. If one of your goals is to remain active in the community, you'll find plenty of opportunities in this publication. The publication, begun in 1987, is available free at any of the area agencies on aging described in this chapter. You also may contact Spindle Publishing, (412) 278-4900; they'll be happy to mail you one copy for free, but if you require multiple copies you're responsible for postage.

VOLUNTEER PROGRAMS

Volunteerism is alive and well in Pittsburgh, at least in part because of the leadership of senior citizens. Seniors provide valuable assistance to both nonprofit and for-profit organizations, which are happy to rely on the experience and expertise that would otherwise be hard to acquire. When seniors volunteer, they—and the organizations they assist—are sharper for it.

One of the most fertile and rewarding volunteer opportunities is helping fellow senior

i The State of Pennsylvania offers "ombudsman" services to answer your questions and provide information about your rights as a consumer. To reach the ombudsman's office, call (717) 783-7247, or contact any county area agency on aging. Also, see the Web site www.aging.state.pa.us.

Statewide Senior Discount

With more than 2.4 million of its citizens age 60 or over, the Commonwealth of Pennsylvania has a significant stake in the well-being of senior citizens. The state reaches out to seniors in a variety of ways—by providing funding for 52 area agencies on aging across the Commonwealth, by dedicating proceeds from the Pennsylvania Lottery exclusively to programs for seniors, and by operating a number of major programs on a statewide basis. In all, the state funds or administers more than 50 programs or benefits for seniors.

Among the most far-reaching programs are Pharmaceutical Assistant Contract for the Elderly (PACE), which helps to pay for prescribed medicines, and rent and property tax rebates, which can amount to as much as $500 per year. Both programs are targeted to those age 65 and older who meet income eligibility guidelines.

To enroll in PACE or for rent and property tax rebates, pick up your application at any area agency on aging, pharmacy, senior community center, or legislator's office, or contact the Pennsylvania Department of Aging in Harrisburg. The toll-free number for PACE is (800) 225-7223.

citizens in need. Allegheny County Area Agency on Aging needs volunteers at least 60 years old for its Senior Companionship Program, (412) 350-5460 or (800) 344-4319. Volunteers are asked to volunteer 20 hours per week. Meals on Wheels, operated by the Lutheran Service Society, (412) 734-9330, needs volunteers to serve as drivers, deliverers, kitchen helpers, and bakers. Meals on Wheels delivers food to elderly in the area.

More comprehensive still are the check-in services offered by Interfaith Volunteer Caregivers of Southwestern Pennsylvania, (412) 345-7420. Volunteers call on seniors in need and help out with shopping, transportation, and completion of Social Security and Medicare forms. Interfaith Volunteer Caregivers also offer errand, "friendly visiting," and "telephone reassurance" services.

Hospice Preferred Choice, (412) 271-2273, works with home-care patients. Volunteers provide companionship as well as respite for caregivers.

Perhaps working with children would give you the most satisfaction. If so, try the Foster Grandparents Program, (412) 263-3163, which operates in Allegheny, Beaver, Butler, and Washington Counties. Through the program,

low-income volunteers age 60 and older spend 20 hours each week with disabled or special-needs children. You'll receive a tax-exempt stipend—and immeasurable satisfaction—for your efforts.

At the University of Pittsburgh, in the Generations Together program, (412) 648-7155, senior volunteers mentor and tutor youths. A special Generations Together feature matches seniors who have been professional artists with kids eager to learn artistic skills. A similar program in Westmoreland County, also called Generations Together, (800) 442-8000, utilizes senior volunteers to counsel abused and neglected children. There's an added benefit—volunteers are paid at minimum wage rates for their valuable efforts.

If using your experience to help consumers is your primary concern, try the Better Business Bureau of Southwestern Pennsylvania at (412) 456-2700 and ask for the volunteer coordinator. BBB is well known for helping consumers answer questions about, and resolve complaints against, local businesses. Senior volunteers perform many of these key functions. You'll play an important role in telephone answering, complaint handling, mediation and arbitration, data

Close-up

Miles to Go

When Horace Miles retired from his multifaceted career, he expected to enjoy a leisurely retirement. Some retirement. Today Miles is a very active member of the Pittsburgh chapter of the Service Corps of Retired Executives (SCORE), a volunteer agency that mentors young companies across the entire business spectrum. The Pittsburgh chapter of SCORE, formed in 1964, was among the nation's first. Its membership numbers 60 strong, all of them retired and all on the prowl for young companies they can counsel in such key areas as personnel, financing, marketing, and other operational challenges. SCORE is sponsored by the Small Business Administration, which propelled Miles into his leadership role.

"The former district director of SBA suggested that I consider this as a way to keep my skills up," Miles recalled. "I found it appealing because to me, the most interesting thing is doing something new, learning something new, I'm working harder now than I ever did."

Miles's varied career helped prepare him for his "retirement," providing him with diverse expertise in all facets of management and business development. With undergraduate degrees in math and physics, he entered the computer field in the late 1950s. In the infant computer industry, Miles's expertise was in demand. He worked for a bank and later founded an international consulting company that coordinated computer services for clients in Canada, Italy, and France.

"The thing that always interested me is business," Miles said. "It's the toughest thing you'll ever do, and it's becoming more of a challenge. But in a sense, business problems are business problems are business problems. It's formulaic in that sense. From that standpoint, when you work with young companies, you can find out what's needed. They can feed back, and you find out where the cracks are."

The companies that Miles has mentored reflect the breadth of his career:

- A pet-sitting business that was expanding and considering new hires. Miles's advice: Use contractors rather than full-time employees, to avoid the expense of benefits packages and the like.
- A plasma physicist in the business of producing robots for semiconductor manufacturing. "He had some technical problems in making his product,

entry, and public speaking. Check out the BBB's Web site, www.pittsburgh.bbb.org, to learn more about these opportunities.

For broader volunteer opportunities, several agencies will do the job. Since 1972 the Southwestern Pennsylvania Chapter of the American Red Cross has sponsored the Retired and Senior Volunteer Program (RSVP) of Allegheny County, (412) 263-3179, a program that matches volunteers with such nonprofit but what he really needed was an inventory system, and to make sure he was ordering his parts in an economical manner."

- A singer-songwriter who wanted to reach a broader, more lucrative market. "I don't feel qualified to comment on whether his songs are good or bad, but I do have some friends who have listened to his work and essentially blessed it. My role is to see how he might market his work while retaining control over it."

Success stories are not uncommon for SCORE. Perhaps its most amazing rags-to-riches tale is that of Riverside Design Group, a producer of high-design giftware, including private-label products for corporate clients. Aided by a SCORE counseling team, Riverside Design streamlined its planned product lines and now sells to more than 400 museums, giftware retailers, restaurants, and catalogs.

Miles does not commit all his hard-earned leisure time to SCORE. In his idle moments he produces videos with musical themes, tinkers with magic, fences, and serves on the boards of two nonprofit organizations. But even his recreational activities benefit SCORE. In the workshop staged for all potential SCORE clients, for example, Miles works in several of his magic tricks.

While the organization includes women and minority volunteers, one of the chapter's goals for the future is to further diversify its membership. Because there are comparatively few minorities who are both retired and former executives, this one may take more than sleight of hand.

If you're looking for a way to contribute your years of expertise to young businesses, call SCORE at (412) 395-6560, or visit them at their headquarters in the Federal Building, 1000 Liberty Avenue, in downtown Pittsburgh, or at their McKeesport or Beaver outreach centers. If you volunteer with SCORE, you'll get your transportation costs reimbursed . . . and a large measure of satisfaction.

"Business is a blood sport," Horace Miles said, "It's difficult to create and sustain a business. The satisfaction in this work is helping a company grow and seeing it progress over a number of years. The frustration is that a lot of companies we see either don't have the wherewithal or they don't really understand what needs to be done. So you don't see them again.

"It doesn't mean they aren't good entrepreneurs, it's just that 'this' isn't a good idea. If you save people from going down that road, that's satisfying, too."

His broad experience has given him firm ideas about what separates successful businesses from mere wannabes.

organizations as arts and cultural groups, hospitals and schools, and consumer agencies.

The program is large and diverse. More than 1,000 volunteers participate in at least 117 organizations, contributing meaningful volunteer service and enriching their own lives as well. RSVP also hosts an annual awards dinner to recognize outstanding volunteers. If you're age 55 or older, respond to RSVP. It may kick-start you on a new career.

Pittsburgh Cares, (412) 471-2114, offers a similar broad range of opportunities for its 1,450 volunteers, which continue to increase in number. The agency schedules more than two dozen monthly events, ranging from delivering holiday meals to the homebound to craftmaking with mentally challenged people. Pittsburgh Cares works with more than 80 community service agencies, an indication of how deeply the roots of volunteerism grow in Pittsburgh. Yet another Pittsburgh trademark, the agency encourages families to volunteer together. Check out this organization on the Web at www.pittsburghcares.org.

RETIREMENT COMMUNITIES

We're living longer, we're enjoying our mature years more, and we're looking for more residential options that are tailored for our needs and desires. In Pittsburgh, with its sizable population of seniors, you'll find just those options in an appealing variety of retirement communities.

The number of such communities has mushroomed in Pittsburgh in recent years, although not quite as fast as the number of people who want to live in them. This has resulted in waiting lists at a number of the most popular communities. Nevertheless, such a rich variety is available today that you'll want to carefully consider your preferences before making a selection. Do you prefer communities away from the city center, tucked into the rolling hills of Western Pennsylvania? Or would you be most happy in an urban setting, close to all the city's opportunities? You'll find both types in Pittsburgh and environs.

You'll also want to carefully consider the services, amenities, and pricing options. At some communities residents pay a monthly rental fee. In other communities you can own your home by making a sizable up-front payment, which in some cases is partially refundable when the unit is turned over. Condominiums also can be an option.

Make sure that you inquire about the common or community fee, which typically is assessed monthly. Services and amenities that come with such fees can vary widely. These can range from the most basic, such as meals and laundry, to the most lavish, such as use of a nearby golf course.

If you're selecting a retirement community, probably the best initial advice anyone can give you is this: Take your time. Do your homework. Make a day out of visiting a prospective new home, taking the tour that each will gladly offer you and asking a lot of questions to make sure the community fits your needs. Your patient research will result in the best match for you.

i Looking for a home? Get on the Web and check out www.senior housing.net. This site, a link of www.rent .net, allows you to search for retirement community listings in any geographic area within the United States, with regional and city searches as options. A search for "Pittsburgh and surrounding communities" yielded 213 listings when we tried it. The site also lists great explanations of the terms used to describe senior residence options.

Stay in Contact

Questions about programs and services for seniors? Often the best places to look for answers are the area agencies on aging, which administer state programs and supplement them with local initiatives. You'll find them at these numbers:

Allegheny County Department of Human Services,
Area Agency on Aging (ACAAA)
(412) 350-5460, (800) 344-4319

SeniorInterests
(412) 422-6405

Armstrong County Agency on Aging
(724) 548-3290, (800) 368–1066

Beaver County Office on Aging
(724) 728-7707

Butler County Area Agency on Aging
(724) 282-3008, (888) 367-2434

Southwestern Pennsylvania Area Agency on Aging
(724) 489-8080, (800) 300-2704

Westmoreland County Area Agency on Aging
(724) 830–4444, (800) 442-8000

Other frequently called numbers include:
Contact Helpline
(412) 578-2450

Eldercare Locator
(800) 677-1116

Elderlink
(412) 422-0400

South Hills Health System Senior Services
(412) 469-7099

WORSHIP

Immigrants who settled in Southwestern Pennsylvania for the purpose of prosperity brought with them riches of another kind—adherence to their spiritual past. As a result, our region is as diverse in its religious makeup as it is in its ethnicity.

Many of the churches and synagogues in which Pittsburghers worship tell their stories better than any words could. For instance, the stained-glass windows inside St. John the Baptist, a Ukrainian Catholic church on the South Side, chronicle immigrant life, including the life of the church. The Strip District's St. Patrick—St. Stanislaus Parish, more commonly referred to as Old St. Patrick's, was founded by Irish immigrants in 1808. Here you'll find a set of 28 marble stairs, a replica of the holy stairs that Jesus had to climb to reach the court of Pontius Pilate. To comply with local custom, you may ascend these stairs only on your knees.

Perhaps the most spectacular religious building in Pittsburgh is Rodef Shalom synagogue, the fountainhead of Reformed Judaism in Western Pennsylvania and one of only five synagogues in the nation designated as a national landmark. The building, 4905 Fifth Avenue, Oakland (www.rodefshalom.org), was designed by Henry Hornbostel, the same architect Andrew Carnegie commissioned to produce blueprints for Carnegie Mellon University (then Carnegie Tech). The building's exterior was modeled after the Church of Hagia Sophia, now a mosque, in Istanbul, Turkey. Built of bricks made from local clay, Rodef Shalom is also notable for its double dome ceiling 90 feet in diameter. The breathtaking "Eye of God" stained-glass window on top of the dome, made by the famous Willet Studio, dramatically filters light down into the large sanctuary. Outside, a one-third acre biblical botanical garden displays more than 150 plant varieties, each with a biblical name or reference. The garden setting is reminiscent of ancient Israel, with a stream representing the River Jordan flowing through it. The garden is open from June 1 through September 15, Sunday through Thursday 10:00 a.m. to 2:00 p.m., Wednesday 7:00 to 9:00 p.m., and Saturday noon to 1:00 p.m. Admission is free, and tours of both the garden and temple can be arranged by calling (412) 621-6566.

Family heritage is largely responsible for the strength and continuity of religion in Greater Pittsburgh. Because many extended families remain in the region, it's not uncommon for them to remain in their religious institutions of origin as well. Some congregations boast three or four generations of Pittsburgh families in their membership, a sturdy and natural conveyor belt for traditions and beliefs. Whether it's making pierogies (potato dumplings) in the church kitchen, teaching children the art of *pysanky* (hand-painted Easter eggs), or simply preserving historic houses of worship, such cherished rituals make churches, synagogues, and other congregations pivotal players in their respective communities.

Most smaller communities have newspapers that may list worship services as well as social and educational events sponsored by local houses of worship. Sampling these

i If you're looking for listings of worship opportunities, check out the Saturday editions of the daily newspapers, or your own community weekly paper.

opportunities is a great way to get to know people, and ultimately, find a religious home.

Christian Associates of Southwest Pennsylvania, (412) 688-9070 offers information about churches and denominations in nine regional counties. The nonprofit organization encompasses 24 Christian faith traditions.

Likewise, the United Jewish Federation of Pittsburgh (412-681-8000, www.ujf.net) is a wonderful resource for locating a synagogue in the area, where many branches of Judaism flourish. The site also posts community news and an extensive list of resources related to living a Jewish lifestyle.

STRENGTH IN DIVERSITY

Of the many religions represented in Southwestern Pennsylvania, Catholicism has the most adherents. Second in number are the Presbyterian denominations. In fact, there are more Presbyterian churches here than anywhere else in the country, perhaps due to the influence of the Scotch-Irish immigrants who brought their religious fervor with them. Lutherans, Methodists, Episcopalians, Baptists, Charismatics, and Unitarians also thrive here, as do Christian and Missionary Alliance, Church of the Brethren, United Church of Christ, Assembly of God, and Greek and Russian Orthodox congregations.

Pittsburgh's Squirrel Hill neighborhood is the hub of the Jewish community, and the hub of the hub is the Jewish Community Center; (412) 521-8010. Several major branches of Judaism are well-represented within Pittsburgh. In addition to the Reformed congregation at Rodef Shalom, you will find a strong Orthodox congregation at Poale Zedeck in Squirrel Hill (412-421-9786); two conservative congregations, also in Squirrel Hill, Beth Shalom (412-421-2288) and Tree of Life (412-521-6788); and Dor Hadash, a Reconstructionist congregation (412-422-5158), which varies its meeting place. You'll also find synagogues throughout the suburbs and outlying counties.

African Methodist Episcopal churches dot the Hill District, the heart of the region's

i St. Anthony's Chapel in the Troy Hill area of Pittsburgh houses the largest collection of Catholic relics outside Rome. Tours are given on Tuesday, Thursday, Saturday, and Sunday afternoons. Call ahead at (412) 323-9504 or (412) 231-2994.

African-American community, as well as suburban communities just beyond the city. While they make up a small percentage of the religious population on this side of the state, the Amish also are represented in Western Pennsylvania, particularly in Lawrence and Mercer Counties somewhat north of our principal coverage area. (See our Day Trips and Weekend Getaways chapter for more information on the Amish.)

In Pittsburgh's eastern suburbs of Monroeville and Penn Hills, many more congregations make their home. There are followers of the Baha'i, Hindu, Sikh, Zen, and Islamic traditions. Indeed, the SV Temple, just off Interstate 376 (the Parkway East) in Penn Hills, is said to be the first authentic Hindu structure in America. The Muslim Community Center of Greater Pittsburgh, in Monroeville, offers both a mosque and a social hall. The center conducts services five times daily and offers special services during holy periods. All are welcome at the center, as it maintains no membership as such.

The region also boasts a healthy number of independent congregations and churches that attract residents and visitors with their unique missions and spiritual focus. The Western Pennsylvania division of the Salvation Army, to name only one, comprises many corps where worshippers can participate.

Finally, you may be seeking a setting for that once-in-a-lifetime service, such as a wed-

i Quaker services are held at the Friends Meeting House, in Oakland (412-683-2669). A variety of classes and group meetings, such as yoga, tai chi, and women's groups, are also held here.

ding. For these events, nondenominational churches are available, including Heinz Chapel on the University of Pittsburgh campus, as well as the Old Stone Church in Monroeville (maintained by the Monroeville Historical Society). Contact campus personnel—or municipal officials where appropriate—to determine how you may use historic or prominent churches for your special event.

WHERE TWO OR THREE ARE GATHERED . . .

As diverse as worship is here, it's reassuring to note that organized religious bodies regularly collaborate on worthy causes. Examples of this include interfaith efforts to combat racism, religious institutions joining together to raise funds for the hungry, and multidenominational support for the erection of domestic violence shelters.

Interfaith consortiums, such as the Monroeville Interfaith Ministerium, bring religious leaders together to promote unity and work for the good of the community. Congregations within such groups wholeheartedly support each others' efforts. While one organization might sponsor a food pantry, another might provide a clothing ministry; religious leaders routinely encourage their members to support the efforts of other congregations.

UNIQUE MINISTRIES

If you look through any local newspaper's worship listings, you'll discover services that are taped for radio broadcast or televised for homebound viewers. Some of these services are signed for the hearing-impaired. Cornerstone Television, incorporated in the 1970s as a nonprofit organization, is a television ministry that provides religious and inspirational programming throughout much of Pennsylvania. From its headquarters midway between Greensburg and Pittsburgh, its signal reaches such distant points as Altoona and Jefferson, Perry, Lawrence, and Mercer Counties. To

enhance Cornerstone's programming, volunteers staff telephone prayer lines as a form of outreach. You'll find more about Cornerstone in our Media chapter.

Another unusual ministry is that of Fred Rogers, highly acclaimed host of public television's *Mister Rogers' Neighborhood,* which was produced in Pittsburgh at WQED-TV and broadcast nationally. Although Rogers passed away in 2003, his ministry continues through archives of his program over the years. Some may find it surprising to learn that he was an ordained Presbyterian pastor. Indeed, Mister Rogers attended the Pittsburgh Theological Seminary, took graduate courses in child development at the University of Pittsburgh, and worked with Pittsburgh's Arsenal Family and Children's Center. When he was ordained in 1963, he was given the special charge of ministering to children through television. He accomplished it by creating a sanctuary of truth and honesty where his young viewers are accepted just as they are—a founding principle of many faiths. (See our Kidstuff chapter for a profile of Fred Rogers and his work with children.)

Sharing the story of God through the drama and arts, Hot Metal Bridge Faith Community (www.hotmetalbridge.com or 412-481-4010) recently renovated a bar in Pittsburgh's South Side into its worship space. Here, you'll find young and old, from all walks of life, watching original dramas based on stories from the Bible, usually with a modern twist.

Featured in the *Wall Street Journal* and on the *Today Show,* Hot Metal is a United Methodist/Presbyterian Federated Church that features ministries such as Bible Fight Club (debates about social issues held at a local tattoo shop), and The Table (a weekly dinner open to all in the community).

VALUES AND SPIRITUALITY

To describe the region's stately churches, diversity of faiths and unusual ministries, useful though that may be, does not quite get to the heart of religion in Southwestern Pennsylvania. Just as the immigrants who settled here built houses of worship to resemble those they had left behind, they also constructed a system of values based on those of the Old World. Those values remain as the foundation of modern Pittsburgh.

The strength of religious beliefs in Southwestern Pennsylvania infuses our region with spirituality that is an important component of our personal and professional lives. Religion and commerce here are intertwined. Clergy have served as elected officials, labor leaders, chiefs of important civic organizations. Their impact goes well beyond their immediate roles. Our clergy often serves as directors for nonprofit organizations and public corporations, bringing a set of values and a spiritual outlook to the world of commerce and public service.

Of the degree-granting institutions and hospitals that we profile in our Health Care and Higher Education chapters, many are administered by, or affiliated with, religious orders. The Catholic Diocese of Pittsburgh

i Numerous opportunities exist for GLBT-friendly worship in the Pittsburgh area. There's the Metropolitan Community Church, which holds services at the Friends Meeting House in Oakland (412-683-2669) as well as other organizations that are affiliated with mainstream religious organizations. For example, Dignity serves GLBT Catholics and their friends and families (412-362-4334) and Beth Tikvah addresses the spiritual and social needs of its growing Jewish Community (412-362-7025, www.bethtikvah .org).

operates an elementary and secondary school network that, were it a public school district, would be the fourth largest in the state. Is it any wonder, then, that our hospitals play a key role in providing services to the homeless and other populations in need?

Usually the interrelationship of religion and commerce works to the benefit of each. Some years ago during the death throes of Big Steel, when bitter disputes between labor and management were common and costly, the warring sides in one impasse were encouraged to meet over breakfast and prayers. The results were so successful for the relationship that prayer breakfasts became commonplace.

Community spirit is something you'll find not only among the religious institutions here, but also among many different kinds of organizations and groups of people. Volunteerism is popular here, and networking among business people is usually done with a spirit of openness and trust. You'll also find many a good neighbor in the 'Burgh. Overall, you might say, Pittsburgh is a city with a good soul.

INDEX

A

ABOUT THE AUTHORS

JENN PHILLIPS

Jenn Phillips is a writer, editor, and consultant who works internationally from her office in Pittsburgh. She regularly works in the areas of magazine writing and editing, branding and marketing, grant writing, and editing for books and journals, offering a particular specialty in medical and wellness topics. She has recently begun expanding her business, Writing Well Communications, to include corporate training in writing and editing.

She holds a bachelor's degree in professional and creative writing from Carnegie Mellon University. She's now completing a master of fine arts degree in creative writing at the University of Pittsburgh, where she formerly taught as an adjunct faculty member.

She loves Pittsburgh.

LORIANN HOFF OBERLIN

Loriann Hoff Oberlin was born and raised in Pittsburgh. She is the author of several other books, including *Surviving Separation & Divorce: A Women's Guide to Making It Through the First Year* and *The Angry Child,* written with Timothy F. Murphy, Ph.D. Loriann has also written *Writing for Money* and *Working at Home While the Kids Are There, Too.* Loriann has been a guest on numerous talk shows and news programs, including the CNN Morning News, and she has spoken at writers' conferences throughout the country.

EVAN M. PATTAK

Evan M. Pattak, a Pittsburgh native, is a writer, editor, publicist, and teacher, among other pursuits. His magazine writing has won Golden Quill and Women in Communications Matrix Awards and was anthologized in *Our Roots Grow Deeper Than We Know,* a collection featuring Pennsylvania writers. He began his career as a reporter for the Associated Press after graduating from the University of Pittsburgh.

He is an official scorer for Major League Baseball's National League and serves as part-time host and handicapper for the Ladbroke Racing Network.

MICHELE MARGITTAI

Michele Margittai is a writer and marketing and communications consultant who lives in Pittsburgh. Working with private and not-for-profit organizations, Michele helps her clients to tell their stories through articles, newsletters, Web sites, and speeches. She particularly enjoys using written words to convince people to take action—commit to a cause, donate money to a project, support a resolution, or relocate to Pittsburgh. With a writing degree from the University of Pittsburgh, Michele has also published 30 software manuals and edited the workbook, *Understanding Self-Injury.* Michele lives with her husband Peter and two children, Sophia and Nico, in Pittsburgh's South Side.